White-Collar Crime

Second Edition

SAGE was founded in 1965 by Sara Miller McCune to support the dissemination of usable knowledge by publishing innovative and high-quality research and teaching content. Today, we publish over 900 journals, including those of more than 400 learned societies, more than 800 new books per year, and a growing range of library products including archives, data, case studies, reports, and video. SAGE remains majority-owned by our founder, and after Sara's lifetime will become owned by a charitable trust that secures our continued independence.

Los Angeles | London | New Delhi | Singapore | Washington DC | Melbourne

White-Collar Crime

The Essentials

Second Edition

Brian K. Payne
Old Dominion University

Los Angeles | London | New Delhi
Singapore | Washington DC | Melbourne

FOR INFORMATION:

SAGE Publications, Inc.
2455 Teller Road
Thousand Oaks, California 91320
E-mail: order@sagepub.com

SAGE Publications Ltd.
1 Oliver's Yard
55 City Road
London EC1Y 1SP
United Kingdom

SAGE Publications India Pvt. Ltd.
B 1/I 1 Mohan Cooperative Industrial Area
Mathura Road, New Delhi 110 044
India

SAGE Publications Asia-Pacific Pte. Ltd.
3 Church Street
#10-04 Samsung Hub
Singapore 049483

Copyright © 2017 by SAGE Publications, Inc.

Printed in the United States of America

Library of Congress Cataloging-in-Publication Data

Names: Payne, Brian K., author.

Title: White-collar crime : the essentials / Brian K. Payne, Old Dominion University, Georgia State University.

Description: Second Edition. | Thousand Oaks : SAGE Publications, Inc., 2016.| ©2017 | Revised edition of the author's White-collar crime, 2013. | Includes bibliographical references and index.

Identifiers: LCCN 2016000433 | ISBN 978-1-5063-4477-5 (pbk. : alk. paper)

Subjects: LCSH: White collar crimes.

Classification: LCC HV6768 .P396 2016 | DDC 364.16/8—dc23
LC record available at http://lccn.loc.gov/2016000433

Publisher: Jerry Westby
eLearning Editor: Nicole Mangona
Editorial Assistant: Laura Kirkhuff
Production Editor: David C. Felts
Copy Editor: Elizabeth Swearngin
Typesetter: C&M Digitals (P) Ltd.
Proofreader: Caryne Brown
Indexer: Wendy Allex
Cover Designer: Scott Van Atta
Marketing Manager: Amy Lammers

This book is printed on acid-free paper.

SUSTAINABLE FORESTRY INITIATIVE
Certified Chain of Custody
Promoting Sustainable Forestry
www.sfiprogram.org
SFI-01268
SFI label applies to text stock

16 17 18 19 20 10 9 8 7 6 5 4 3

Brief Contents

Preface   xiii

  What's New in the Second Edition   xv
  Acknowledgments for the First Edition   xv
  Acknowledgments for the Second Edition   xvi

**Chapter I. Introduction and Overview
  of White-Collar Crime: A Systems Perspective**   1

**Chapter II. Understanding White-Collar Crime:
  Definitions, Extent, and Consequences**   23

Chapter III. Crimes in Sales-Related Occupations: A Systems Perspective   45

Chapter IV. Crimes in the Health Care System   61

**Chapter V. Crime in Systems of Social Control:
  White-Collar Crime in Criminal Justice,
  Political, and Religious Systems**   84

Chapter VI. Crimes in the Educational System   116

Chapter VII. Crime in the Economic System   139

Chapter VIII. Crime in the Cyber System   163

Chapter IX. Crimes in the Housing System   194

Chapter X. Crimes by the Corporate System   217

Chapter XI. Environmental Crime   253

Chapter XII. Explaining White-Collar Crime   281

Chapter XIII. Policing White-Collar Crime   315

Chapter XIV. Judicial Proceedings and White-Collar Crime   352

Chapter XV. The Corrections Subsystem and White-Collar Crime   385

Appendix. Executive Order—Improving Critical Infrastructure Cybersecurity   418

Glossary   422

References   429

Index   458

About the Author   485

Detailed Contents

Preface   xiii

What's New in the Second Edition   xv
Acknowledgments for the First Edition   xv
Acknowledgments for the
   Second Edition   xvi

**Chapter I. Introduction and
Overview of White-Collar
Crime: A Systems Perspective**   **1**

Why Study White-Collar Crime?   2
Researching White-Collar Crime   4
   *Survey Research and
     White-Collar Crime*   4
   *Archival Research and
     White-Collar Crime*   6
   Field Research   8
   Experiments   9
   Case Studies   10
Studying White-Collar Crime
   From a Scientific Perspective   10
   Objectivity and White-Collar Crime   11
   Parsimony and White-Collar Crime   13
   *Determinism and White-Collar
     Crime*   13
   Skepticism and White-Collar Crime   14
   Relativism and White-Collar Crime   14
The Student Role in White-Collar Crime   17
Plan for the Book   20
Summary   20
Key Terms   21
Discussion Questions   21
Web Resources   22

**Chapter II. Understanding
White-Collar Crime: Definitions,
Extent, and Consequences**   **23**

White-Collar Crime: An Evolving Concept   24
Modern Conceptualizations
   of White-Collar Crime   26
Extent of White-Collar Crime   32
Consequences of White-Collar Crime   36
Public Attitudes Toward
   White-Collar Crime   40
Characteristics of White-Collar Offenders   42
Summary   43
Key Terms   44
Discussion Questions   44
Web Resources   44

**Chapter III. Crimes in
Sales-Related Occupations:
A Systems Perspective**   **45**

Employee Theft in the Retail System   46
Crimes in the Entertainment
   Services System   49
Fraud in the Sales/Service System   52
   Home Repair Fraud   52
   Auto Repair/Sales Fraud   54
Crimes in the Insurance System   56
   *Types of Insurance Crimes
     by Professionals*   56
   *Consequences of Insurance
     Crimes*   58
   Insurance Crime Patterns   58
Summary   59

Key Terms 60
Discussion Questions 60
Web Resources 60

Chapter IV. Crimes in the Health Care System 61

Fraud by Doctors 64
Unnecessary Surgery 69
Medication Errors 71
General Offending by Doctors 71
Fraud by Pharmacists 72
Drug Use by Pharmacists 73
Sexual Abuse 74
Elder Abuse by Health Care Workers 75
Home Health Care Fraud 78
Durable Medical Equipment Fraud 78
Medical Malpractice 80
Summary 81
Key Terms 82
Discussion Questions 83
Web Resources 83

Chapter V. Crime in Systems of Social Control: White-Collar Crime in Criminal Justice, Political, and Religious Systems 84

Crimes in the Criminal Justice System 85
Police Corruption 85
Attorney Misconduct 88
Judicial Misconduct 89
Prosecutorial Misconduct 92
Correctional Officer Misconduct 96
Crimes in the Political System 98
Election Law Violations 99
Campaign Finance Violations 100
Political Corruption Related to Extortion, Bribery, and Illegal Gratuities 100
Apolitical White-Collar Crime 101
Crimes in the Military 101
State-Corporate Crime 104
Crimes by Officials in the Religious System 105
Financial Offenses in the Religious System 105

Deception in the Religious System 106
Catholic Church Sexual Abuse Scandal 106
Summary 112
Key Terms 114
Discussion Questions 115
Web Resources 115

Chapter VI. Crimes in the Educational System 116

Crimes by Professionals in the Educational System 117
Research Misconduct by Professors 118
Ghostwriting 123
Pecuniary-Oriented Offenses 125
Embezzlement 125
Textbook Fraud 125
Double Billing 126
Engaging in Unapproved Outside Work 127
Sexual Harassment 128
Disciplining Professors 131
Crimes in the Educational System by Students 134
Summary 136
Key Terms 137
Discussion Questions 137
Web Resources 138

Chapter VII. Crime in the Economic System 139

Crime in the Economic System 141
Investment Fraud 141
Market Manipulation 143
Broker Fraud and Embezzlement 144
Hedge Fund Fraud 144
Insider Trading 145
Futures Trading Fraud 147
Foreign Exchange Fraud, High-Yield Investment Schemes, and Advanced-Fee Fraud 147
Ponzi and Pyramid Schemes 148
Bernie Madoff's Ponzi Scheme: From Armani Suits to a Bulletproof Vest 149

Patterns Surrounding Investment Fraud ... 151
Student Loan Fraud ... 157
Summary ... 160
Key Terms ... 161
Discussion Questions ... 161
Web Resources ... 162

Chapter VIII. Crime in the Cyber System ... **163**

Conceptualizing Crime
  in the Cyber System ... 165
Types of Cybercrime ... 166
  Theft as a Computer Crime ... 169
  Unauthorized Access
    as a Computer Crime ... 169
  Virus Introduction
    as a Computer Crime ... 171
  Software Crime as a
    Computer Crime ... 172
  Internet Crimes ... 173
Characteristics of Cybercriminals ... 173
Costs of Cybercrime ... 176
  Explaining Computer Crime ... 178
  Problems Responding to
    Computer Crimes ... 180
  The Interdisciplinary
    Response to Cybercrime ... 182
  Colleges and Cybercrime ... 183
Responding to Cybercrime ... 186
  Police Strategies ... 186
  Legislative Strategies ... 189
  Retributive Strategies ... 189
  General Prevention Strategies ... 189
Summary ... 192
Key Terms ... 193
Discussion Questions ... 193
Web Resources ... 193

Chapter IX. Crimes in the Housing System ... **194**

Mortgage Fraud ... 196
  Straw Buyer Fraud ... 197
  Short Sale Fraud ... 199
  Appraisal Fraud ... 199
  Equity Skimming/Equity Fraud ... 201

  Reverse Mortgage Fraud ... 201
  Fraud During Closing/Settlement ... 203
  Foreclosure Rescue Scams ... 203
  Builder-Initiated Fraud ... 204
  Flipping ... 205
  Qualifications Fraud ... 206
  Real Estate Agent/Investor Fraud ... 206
Consequences of Mortgage Fraud ... 206
Patterns Surrounding Mortgage Fraud ... 207
Slumlords as White-Collar Criminals ... 210
  Consequences of Slumlord
    Behaviors ... 211
  Responding to Slumlords ... 214
Summary ... 215
Key Terms ... 216
Discussion Questions ... 216
Web Resources ... 216

Chapter X. Crimes by the Corporate System ... **217**

Conceptualizing Corporate Crime ... 218
Types of Corporate Crime ... 220
  Antitrust Offenses ... 220
  False Advertising ... 225
  Deceptive Sales ... 227
  Unfair Labor Practices ... 230
  Unsafe Work Environments ... 234
  Harmful Consumer Products ... 240
  Harmful Treatment of Consumers ... 247
Dynamics of Corporate Offending ... 248
Public Concern About
  Crimes by the Corporate System ... 250
Summary ... 251
Key Terms ... 252
Discussion Questions ... 252
Web Resources ... 252

Chapter XI. Environmental Crime ... **253**

Conceptualizing Environmental Crime ... 255
Varieties of Environmental
  White-Collar Crime ... 257
  Illegal Emissions ... 258
  Illegal Disposal of
    Hazardous Wastes ... 259
  Illegal Dumping ... 261

Harmful Destruction of
  Property/Wildlife   261
Environmental Threats   262
Environmental State Crime   263
International Environmental Crimes   263
Consequences of
  Environmental Crime   264
The U.S. Environmental
  Protection Agency (EPA)   266
EPA as an Enforcer of
  Criminal and Civil Laws   266
EPA as a Protector of Public Health   267
EPA as a Deterrent   269
EPA as a Fund Generator
  and Cost-Saving Entity   272
Criticisms of EPA   275
Problems Addressing
  Environmental Crimes   276
Media Portrayals of
  Environmental Crime   276
Evidentiary Issues
  and Environmental Crime   276
Empirical Issues and
  Environmental Crime   277
Summary   279
Key Terms   280
Discussion Questions   280
Web Resources   280

Chapter XII. Explaining White-Collar Crime   281

Culture and White-Collar Crime   283
Deterrence Theory/Rational Choice
  Theory and White-Collar Crime   284
Strain Theory and White-Collar Crime   285
Classical Strain Theory   286
Institutional Anomie Theory   287
General Strain Theory   288
Learning Theory and White-Collar Crime   289
Neutralizing and Justifying
  White-Collar Crime   291
Neutralizations and
  White-Collar Offending   291
Accounts and White-Collar Crime   294
Purposes of Rationalizations
  and Accounts   296

Control Theory and White-Collar
  Crime   296
Self-Control Theory and
  White-Collar Crime   297
Routine Activities Theory
  and White-Collar Crime   299
Conflict Theory and White-Collar
  Crime   302
Explaining Corporate Crime   304
Organizational Structure
  and Corporate Crime   304
Organizational Processes
  and Corporate Crime   304
Dynamic Organizational
  Explanations and
  Corporate Crime   305
Theories Ignored in the
  White-Collar Crime Literature   306
Life Course Theories
  and White-Collar Crime   306
Social Disorganization Theory
  and White-Collar Crime   307
Gender Theories and
  White-Collar Crime   308
Labeling Theory and
  White-Collar Crime   308
Biological Theories   309
Integrated Efforts to
  Explain White-Collar Crime   310
Systems Theory   311
Summary   312
Key Terms   313
Discussion Questions   313
Web Resources   314

Chapter XIII. Policing White-Collar Crime   315

Agencies Involved in Responding
  to White-Collar Crime   317
The FBI and White-Collar
  Crime   317
Law Enforcement Strategies
  and White-Collar Crime   323
Stages of the White-Collar
  Crime Investigation   324
Evidence Gathering Strategies   325

Problems Addressing
White-Collar Crime Through
a Law Enforcement Response   331
Suggestions for Improving
the Law Enforcement Response
to White-Collar Crime   337
Self-Policing and White-Collar Crime   338
Loss Prevention Strategies   338
Compliance Strategies   340
Audits   341
Forensic Accounting   341
Regulatory Policing and
White-Collar Crime   342
*Conceptualizing Regulatory
Policing*   342
*Regulatory Officials
as Police Officers*   344
Regulatory Policing Styles   345
*Criticisms of Regulatory
Policing*   348
The Global Police and
White-Collar Crime   348
Summary   349
Key Terms   350
Discussion Questions   351
Web Resources   351

Chapter XIV. Judicial Proceedings and White-Collar Crime   352

Types of Judicial Proceedings
Responding to White-Collar
Misconduct   354
The Role of Judges in Addressing
White-Collar Crime   356
*The Role of Prosecutors in
Addressing White-Collar Crime*   358
*Deciding Whether to
Prosecute a White-Collar
Crime Case*   358
Deciding Charges   361
Deciding About Plea Bargains   364
*Deciding Whether to
Charge Corporations*   364
*Deciding Whether to
Defer Prosecution*   367

The Role of Defense Attorneys
in White-Collar Crime Cases   368
Other Actors Involved in
White-Collar Judicial Proceedings   372
Jurors   373
Witnesses   374
*The Role of White-Collar
Defendants*   375
*The Role of Victims in White-
Collar Judicial Proceedings*   377
Civil Lawsuits and White-Collar
Crime   377
Issues in White-Collar Judicial
Networking and the Judicial Process   380
*Networking and the Judicial
Process*   380
Class Bias   380
The Use of Parallel Proceedings   381
*Conceptual Ambiguity
Surrounding Corporate
Crime Prosecutions*   382
Summary   382
Key Terms   383
Discussion Questions   384
Web Resources   384

Chapter XV. The Corrections Subsystem and White-Collar Crime   385

Sentencing Dynamics and
White-Collar Offenders   388
*Sentencing Practices and
White-Collar Offenders*   388
*Sentencing Policies and
White-Collar Offenders*   389
Sentencing Patterns   389
The Prison Experience for
White-Collar Offenders   395
*Depression and the
White-Collar Offender*   395
*Danger and the
White-Collar Offender*   396
*Deprivations and the
White-Collar Offender*   397
*Prison Deviance and the
White-Collar Offender*   398

Doldrums 398
Adjusting to Prison Life 399
The Probation and Parole Experience
for White-Collar Offenders 400
Monetary Fines and
White-Collar Offenders 401
Alternative Sanctions and
White-Collar Offenders 404
House Arrest and
White-Collar Offenders 404
Community Service 408
Shaming 409
Loss of Job 411
Punishing Corporations
for White-Collar Crime 411
Fining Corporate Offenders 412
Probation and Corporate Offenders 412
Issues Surrounding
Corporate Sanctions 413
Reasons for Punishing
White-Collar Offenders 413
Retribution and
White-Collar Offenders 413

Specific Deterrence and
White-Collar Offenders 413
General Deterrence and
White-Collar Offenders 414
Rehabilitation and
White-Collar Offenders 414
Just Deserts and
White-Collar Offenders 415
Summary 415
Key Terms 416
Discussion Questions 417
Web Resources 417

**Appendix. Executive
Order—Improving Critical
Infrastructure Cybersecurity** 418

Glossary 422

References 429

Index 458

About the Author 485

STUDENT RESOURCES

Prepare for class and exams with the open-access Student Study Site at study.sagepub.com/paynewccess2e
Review and apply what you've learned in class and access helpful study tools and resources—all in one place!

- Exclusive SAGE journal articles
- Carefully selected multimedia resources

Preface

Compared to other subjects in the social sciences, relatively few white-collar crime texts are available for use in criminal justice, criminology, and sociology courses. Those that are available have done a great job introducing students to the topic. One thing I found missing among available texts, however, was a book that approached the topic as a crime problem, a criminal justice problem, and a social problem. In effect, my intent has been to create a work that examines the many facets of white-collar crime by focusing on different crimes committed during the course of work as well as the various systems that are given the task of responding to white-collar misconduct.

In addition, I have addressed white-collar crime by balancing consensus and conflict perspectives. The need to objectively understand white-collar offending and the most appropriate response to white-collar offending is central to my approach in this text. All too often, white-collar crimes and white-collar criminals are vilified with little thought given to the intricacies surrounding the event or the system's response to the event. This vilification limits our understanding of the topic.

To demonstrate why it is important to address white-collar crime objectively, consider a book we can call *Introduction to Criminal Justice* as an example. If the author presented crime and criminals as inherently evil, readers would not be given an accurate picture of criminal justice (or crime, for that matter). The same can be said of a white-collar crime book—if authors discuss white-collar crime or white-collar criminals as inherently evil, an inaccurate foundation from which readers can understand the criminal justice response to white-collar crime is created.

Of course, I am not saying that white-collar crime is not bad or that white-collar criminals do not harm society. Instead, I am suggesting that we need to go beyond these emotions and perceptions in order to fully understand white-collar crime. Indeed, throughout *White-Collar Crime: The Essentials*, readers will learn about the various consequences stemming from white-collar misconduct. Readers will also be exposed to the different systems involved in both perpetrating and responding to white-collar crime.

Following the format of the SAGE Criminology and Criminal Justice *The Essentials* series, this book summarizes each relevant topic and creates a foundation from which readers will be able to understand various issues related to white-collar crime. The book is intended as either a stand-alone or a supplemental book for undergraduate and graduate classes focusing on white-collar crime.

The book will be of value to criminal justice, criminology, and sociology courses focusing on white-collar crime. Criminal justice and criminological topics related to white-collar crime are integrated throughout the text. Because many white-collar crime texts fail to address either criminal justice or criminological themes, integrating these topics together should make the text more appealing to a wider audience.

This book is divided into 15 chapters that represent the topics covered in most white-collar crime courses. They include the following:

- Introduction and Overview of White-Collar Crime
- Understanding White-Collar Crime
- Crimes in Sales-Oriented Occupations
- Crimes in the Health Care System
- Crimes in the Systems of Social Control
- Crimes in the Educational System
- Crime in the Economic System
- Crime in the Cyber System
- Crimes in the Housing System
- Crimes by the Corporate System
- Environmental Crime
- Explaining White-Collar Crime
- Policing White-Collar Crime
- Judicial Proceedings and White-Collar Crime
- The Corrections Subsystem and White-Collar Crime

Several features have been included to make the book more user friendly for students and professors. These features include these elements:

1. Each chapter concludes with a bulleted summary statement.

2. A list of 5 to 10 critical thinking questions is included after the summary statements.

3. Each chapter includes between two and four photographs that are appropriate to the topic.

4. A list of key terms is included at the end of each chapter and defined in the glossary.

5. Recent examples, particularly those that are interesting to college students, are integrated throughout the work.

6. Inserts called "In Focus" are included in Chapters III through XV to further describe real examples of white-collar crimes and issues related to each specific chapter.

7. Each chapter includes a feature called "Careers Responding to White-Collar Crime." These inserts include a description of the duties performed in a job related to the topic discussed in the chapter.

8. Each chapter includes a feature called "White-Collar Crime in the News." These features include recent press releases describing white-collar crime cases "plucked from the media."

A number of different ancillaries are available for students and professors using *White-Collar Crime: The Essentials*. Visit http://study.sagepub.com/paynewccess2e to access these valuable instructor and student resources:

- The password-protected Instructor Teaching Site includes a test bank, PowerPoint slides, class activities, tables and figures from the book, SAGE journal articles, and multimedia resources.
- The free, open-access Student Study Site provides SAGE journal articles and multimedia resources.

It is my hope that this text and the accompanying ancillaries will help readers to fully appreciate and understand white-collar crime and the justice system's response to this misconduct.

● ● ● What's New in the Second Edition

- A chapter on cybercrime was added (Chapter 8). Material that was previously in Chapter 7 was expanded so that this topic received the amount of attention it warrants given the current concerns about cybersecurity.
- A section on fraud in the student loan industry was added in Chapter 7.
- New research and cases are included throughout. This included more than 250 new references. Some of the new research added builds on prior studies, while other additions provide new directions for white-collar crime research. For example, in Chapter 12, a discussion about biological factors related to white-collar crime is included.
- New photos were added throughout the text.
- New figures and tables were added throughout the text where appropriate.
- An appendix including a recent presidential executive order on cybersecurity and the critical infrastructure is now included.
- Box features called "Careers Responding to White-Collar Crime" were added to each chapter. These boxes highlight the duties performed in a job discussed in the chapter.
- Box features called "White-Collar Crime in the News" were added in each chapter. These features include press releases from government agencies responding to a white-collar crime.

● ● ● Acknowledgments for the First Edition

This work would not have been completed without the guidance, direction, and support of many different individuals. I am indebted to Craig Hemmens (Boise State University) for calling me one Thursday afternoon and asking if I would be interested in authoring the work. Also, SAGE Executive Editor Jerry Westby had a way of making it seem like deadlines really meant something, and his excitement about this project helped me to move along. I very much appreciate the efforts of Jerry's development editors, Erim Sarbuland and Leah Mori, in helping to move the project along as smoothly as possible. In addition, I am indebted to production editors Karen Wiley and Libby Larson, and to Patrice Sutton for her detailed skills as a copy editor. Thanks also to Erica Deluca for her careful attention given to marketing this work. As well, the rest of the SAGE team has been a pleasure to work with.

I am also indebted to a small army of graduate assistants who helped with different parts of the project. Tatum Asante, Andrea Barber, Erin Marsh, Susannah Tapp, and Johnnie Cain spent countless hours locating references for me. Danielle Gentile and Katie Taber created the Glossary and performed numerous other tasks that I often assigned at the last minute. A white-collar crime professor could not ask for a better group of graduate assistants!

Several friends and colleagues also helped in different ways. Randy Gainey and Ruth Triplett (both at Old Dominion University) read different parts of the book and provided valuable feedback. Leah Daigle (Georgia State University) was an invaluable sounding board for those moments when I felt like whining about workload. It was particularly enjoyable to write the book at the same time that Randy and Leah were working on their own separate projects for SAGE. Just as I would not want to be stranded in the desert by myself, it was refreshing to have friends plowing through this sort of project at the same time.

I cannot say enough about the invaluable feedback provided by reviewers throughout this process. The final product looks nothing like the original proposal. The feedback from the reviewers helped me to shape a book that best meets the needs of the discipline. Those who reviewed different parts of drafts of the book included the following:

George Burrus, Southern Illinois University Carbondale

William Calathes, New Jersey City University

John Casten, Old Dominion University

William Cleveland, Sam Houston State University

Heith Copes, University of Alabama at Birmingham

Dean Dabney, Georgia State University

Lisa Eargle, Francis Marion University

Robert Handy, Arizona State University

Patrick Hegarty, Stonehill College

Roy Janisch Pittsburg State University

Shayne Jones, University of South Florida

Kent Kerly, University of Alabama at Birmingham

Jiletta Kubena, Sam Houston State University

Tom O'Connor, Austin Peay University

Paul Leighton, Eastern Michigan University

Nicole Leeper Piquero, Florida State University

Jerome Randall, University of Central Florida

Dawn Rothe, Old Dominion University

Rashi Shukla, University of Central Oklahoma

Christopher Warburton, John Jay College

Bruce Zucker, California State University, Northridge.

● ● ● **Acknowledgments for the Second Edition**

Obviously, a second edition never comes to fruition without a successful first edition. I would be remiss, then, not to repeat my appreciation to everyone (described above) who helped get this first edition to the finish line. For the second edition, I again relied on many individuals for help and support. Susannah Tapp (Georgia State University) updated tables, figures, and statistics throughout the book and updated the new reference list. Lora Hadzhidimova (Old Dominion University) helped locate many of the new studies included in this edition. The SAGE team (led by Jerry Westby) continued to offer a level of support and professionalism that I seriously doubt others could match. I am especially grateful to David Felts for guiding this book through production and Elizabeth Swearngin for her copy-editing skills.

I also very much appreciate the feedback that students and professors have provided about the first edition. I have listened to their feedback and shaped this edition in a way that makes the work even more responsive to the world we now live in. My appreciation is also extended to the cadre of white-collar crime researchers who continue to bring scholarly attention to this problem. I hope that we can bring other scholars into this fold (new scholars and seasoned scholars alike) so that this problem receives the attention it deserves. All of the researchers whose work is cited in this edition deserve a note of personal gratitude for helping me to better understand white-collar crime. As well, some suggest that the criminal justice system does very little to respond to this behavior. While we most certainly need a stronger response to these crimes, I am certain that there are many criminal justice officials who do, in fact, respond appropriately and aggressively to the misdeeds committed by white-collar professionals. A special thanks to those working in this understaffed and under resourced area.

Finally, I am grateful to the following reviewers for their input on developing the second edition:

Cindy A. Boyles, University of Tennessee at Martin

Bob Jeffery, Sheffield Hallam University

Michael S. Proctor, Texas A&M University–San Antonio

Gary Feinberg, St. Thomas University

Christopher Salvatore, Montclair State University

Andrea Schoepfer, California State University, San Bernardino

Zahra Shekarkhar, Fayetteville State University

Rashi Shukla, University of Central Oklahoma

I am indebted to my family—Kathleen, Chloe, Charles, and Claire. Now nine years old, Claire was born with a traumatic brain injury. Her mother and I suspect, but may never be able to prove, that the injury was the result of a medical error. She is severely intellectually disabled, unable to talk, and in need of near constant attention. Her injury has changed our family. We love her—not in spite of her injury nor because of it—but because that's what families do: they love one another. Our love for one another holds us together and reminds us what really matters. This book is dedicated to all other Claires and their family members. May they find the same love and comfort that we have.

—bkp

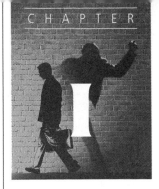

Introduction and Overview of White-Collar Crime

A Systems Perspective

CHAPTER HIGHLIGHTS

- Why Study White-Collar Crime?
- Researching White-Collar Crime
- Studying White-Collar Crime From a Scientific Perspective
- The Student Role in White-Collar Crime
- Plan for the Book

Rule breaking in the workplace is common. Not long ago, an animal sciences professor was indicted for theft, fraud, computer tampering, and forgery after an investigation alleged that the professor misappropriated funds from a student-run meat store he supervised at his university. The professor had worked at the university for nearly 50 years. The investigation was the result of a tip from someone who said that funds from the store were being used for private purposes (Alaimo, 2015). Around the same time, the chief executive officer of a peanut butter company was sentenced to 28 years in prison after being convicted of knowingly selling peanuts tainted with salmonella. The tainted peanut butter resulted in the deaths of nine individuals and harmed an additional 700 consumers. That same year, a doctor lost his medical license after improperly distributing painkillers.

Three similarities exist across each of these examples: (1) In terms of time, they were committed during the course of work; (2) in terms of location, they occurred in a work setting; (3) in terms of offender role, the offender served as a worker. At the most general level, one might be tempted to refer to these behaviors as workplace offenses. On another level, one could argue that each of these examples helps us understand what is meant by the concept of white-collar crime.

Edwin Sutherland first introduced the concept of *white-collar crime* in 1939 during a presentation to the American Sociological Association. A decade later, in his now classic book, *White Collar Crime*, he defined the concept as "crime committed by a person of respectability and high social status in the course of his occupation" (Sutherland, 1949, p. 9). Sutherland was calling attention to the fact that criminal acts were committed by individuals from all social and economic classes. He used the phrase *white-collar* to emphasize the occupational status assigned to individuals.

In Chapter II, more attention will be given to how white-collar crime is conceptualized. As a brief introduction to the concept, three factors are typically used to distinguish white-collar crimes from other crimes. First, white-collar crimes are committed during the course of one's job. Second, the offender's occupational role plays a central feature in the perpetration of the crime. Third, the offender's occupation is viewed as a legitimate occupation by society (e.g., a drug dealer's occupation is illegitimate, but a pharmacist's occupation is legitimate).

Perhaps an example can help to clarify what is meant by crime committed as a part of one's employment. Believe it or not, some professors have committed crimes. Consider a case in which a psychology professor was charged with scientific fraud for hiring actors to pretend that they had participated in his research study. The actors were interviewed by investigators, but they did not realize that the interviews were official because the professor had told them the interviews were part of a mock trial he was conducting for his research study (Office of New York State Attorney General, 2010). This would be a white-collar crime—the offender's employment role was central to the act. Alternatively, consider a case where a criminal justice professor was charged with sexually assaulting students (Elofson, 2010). Or, consider a case where a professor was convicted of drug smuggling after he flew to Argentina to meet a bikini model but instead ended up carrying a suitcase with two kilos of cocaine in it for scam artists (Greenblatt, 2015). The latter two cases would not typically be considered white-collar crimes because the offender's employment role was not central to the commission of the act.

Distinguishing between white-collar crime and traditional crimes is not meant to suggest that one form of crime is worse than the other. Instead, the intent is to note that different forms of crime exist and that full understandings of crime, explanations of crime, and responses to crime will not occur unless the differences between these forms of crime are understood.

▲ **Photo 1.1** White-collar crime is distinguished by the location of the offense, the status of the offender, and the nature of the behavior. These offenses occur in the workplace and are committed by workers.

US Government Work

● ● ● Why Study White-Collar Crime?

Six reasons support the need to study white-collar crime. First, and perhaps foremost, white-collar crime is a serious problem in our society. Estimates provided by the Federal Bureau of Investigation (FBI) routinely suggest that far more is lost to white-collar crimes than to traditional property crimes, such as larceny, robbery, and burglary. Beyond these economic costs, and as will be shown later in this text, white-collar offenses have the potential to cause serious physical and emotional damage to victims.

Second, it is important to recognize that, unlike some offense types, white-collar offenses affect everyone. While a specific street offense might have just one or two victims, white-collar offenses tend to have a large number of victims, and on a certain level, some white-collar offenses are so traumatic that they actually may influence all members of society. For instance, Bernie Madoff's transgressions duped thousands of individuals and organizations out of billions of dollars. It was not just these individuals, however, who were victims. Members of society who then felt distrust for financial institutions and their employees were also affected by Madoff's behavior. Members of society may also experience what one social scientist calls demoralization costs (Coffee, 1980). In this context, demoralization means that individuals have less faith in societal values, and this reduction in faith may actually create a situation where individuals justify their own future misdeeds based on the illicit behaviors of those white-collar and corporate organizations we have been socialized to trust. As one author team wrote, "Because most white-collar offenses violate trust, they breed distrust" (Moore & Mills, 1990, p. 413).

A third reason it is important to study white-collar offending is that by studying white-collar offending we can learn more about all types of crime. Just as medical researchers might learn more about all forms of diseases by studying one form of disease, so the study of white-collar crime allows criminologists, students, members of the public, and policy makers greater insight into all variations of criminal behavior and types of criminal offenders.

Fourth, it is important to study white-collar crime so that effective prevention and intervention systems and policies can be developed. It cannot be assumed that prevention and intervention policies and strategies developed for, and used for, traditional forms of crime are appropriate for responding to offenses committed during the course of one's occupation. The underlying dynamics of different forms of white-collar crime need to be understood so that response strategies and policies based on those dynamics can be developed.

Fifth, and as will be discussed in more detail below, studying white-collar crime provides important information about potential careers related to white-collar crime. This is not meant to suggest that you can learn how to be a white-collar criminal by studying white-collar crime; rather, a number of occupations exist that are designed to help the criminal and civil justice systems respond to white-collar crimes. These occupations typically require college degrees, and many are more lucrative than traditional criminal justice occupations. To actually enter one of those careers, one would need a keen understanding of white-collar crime. Thus, we study white-collar crime in order to develop the critical thinking skills and base of awareness needed to understand white-collar crime.

Finally, studying white-collar crime allows additional insight into a particular culture and various subcultures. On the one hand, the study of white-collar crime provides an insider's view of the American workforce and the cultural underpinnings that are the foundation of values driving the activities of the workforce. On the other hand, the study of white-collar crime provides all of us additional insight into specific occupational subcultures with which we have some degree of familiarity—whether accurate or inaccurate. Many individuals assume that a trip to the auto mechanic has the potential to result in unnecessary repairs and outrageous bills. Few, however, assume that trips to the doctor or pharmacist might result in similar outcomes. As will be shown later in this text, however, white-collar crime research shows that misconduct occurs in all occupations. By understanding misconduct in these occupations, we better understand the occupational subcultures where the misconduct occurs.

▲ **Photo 1.2**   Many careers exist that target white-collar offending. In this photo, FDA officials examine food to make sure it is safe for consumption.

FDA photo by Michael J. Ermarth

● ● ●   Researching White-Collar Crime

Several different research strategies are used to study white-collar crime and white-collar criminals. For the most part, these research strategies are similar to those used to study other social problems. The way that these strategies apply to white-collar crime, however, is somewhat different from how they might be applied to research studies of other topics. Strategies that can be used to research white-collar crime include but are not limited to the following:

- Surveys
- Archival research
- Field research
- Experiments
- Case studies

Survey Research and White-Collar Crime

Surveys are perhaps among the more common research strategies used to study white-collar crime. Survey methods include on-site administration surveys, face-to-face interviews, telephone interviews, and mail surveys. Strengths and weaknesses exist for each of these strategies (see Table 1.1). The aim of surveys is to gather information from a group of individuals and use that information to paint a picture of the topic under consideration.

Groups who are surveyed in white-collar crime research studies include criminal justice officials, members of the public, victims of white-collar crime, and white-collar offenders. Each of these groups has the potential to provide important information about various issues related to white-collar crime.

Surveys of criminal justice officials in the white-collar crime literature tend to focus on the strategies used to identify and respond to white-collar offenses, the kinds of offenses encountered by the officials, and the barriers that must be overcome to successfully respond to the cases. One author interviewed probation officers to determine how white-collar offenders were supervised by community corrections officials (Mason, 2007). Another author described a survey of 1,142 fraud examiners conducted by the Association of Certified Fraud Examiners (Holtfreter, 2005). As will be demonstrated later in this text, this research provided important insight about the types of offenders, offenses, and organizations involved in occupational fraud cases.

White-collar crime researchers have also surveyed members of the public to assess attitudes about, and experiences with, white-collar crime. Such research is useful for at least five reasons. First, determining what members of the public think about white-collar crime provides a baseline that helps to paint a picture about a culture at a given moment of time. For example, if surveys of the public show that the public is tolerant of white-collar offending, this would tell us something about the culture at that moment in time. Second, focusing on citizens' attitudes about white-collar crime provides an indication of the likelihood that individuals might engage in white-collar criminal activity. Third, surveying members of the public potentially allows researchers access to a larger group of white-collar offenders than they might otherwise get, particularly in self-report studies. Fourth, and in a similar way, surveys of members of the public could provide researchers access to a large group of **white-collar crime victims**. A survey of 400 residents of Tennessee, for example, found that 227 (58%) reported being victimized by fraud in the prior 5 years (Mason & Benson, 1996). Fifth, surveys of the public could provide policymakers with information they can use to develop policies and laws designed to prevent white-collar crime.

Researchers have also surveyed white-collar crime victims to increase our understanding about the victimization experiences of this group. In this context, victims could be (1) individuals, (2) businesses and nongovernmental institutions, or (3) "government as a buyer, giver, and protector-gatekeeper" (Edelhertz, 1983, p. 117). One of the issues that arise in such studies is the ability to identify a sample of white-collar crime victims. An early study on appliance "repairman" fraud used a sample of 88 victims of one offender, "Frank Hanks" (not his real name) (Vaughan & Carlo, 1975). Victims were identified through press reports, prosecutors' files, and public files. Incidentally, the researchers identified 133 victims who had complained about the repairman to various consumer agencies. Through this survey, the researchers were

Table 1.1	Strengths and Weaknesses of Different Survey Methods	
Survey Method	**Strengths**	**Weaknesses**
On-site administration	• Surveys occur in one setting • Large sample is possible • Does not take long to gather • Convenient	• Difficult to give surveys on site to both offenders and victims • No database of white-collar offenders • Educational differences make it hard to use the same surveys for everyone • Hard for some to recall incidents • Gaining entrance and trust of victims hard
Face-to-face interviews	• Can watch respondent's reactions • Probing is an option • Rapport is easier to develop	• More time consuming • More expensive • Difficulty in finding participants and place to conduct interviews • Trust and rapport are important • Must gain access and permission of businesses
Telephone interviews	• Most comprehensive studies have been conducted using telephone interviews. • Respondents seem more open to answering questions over the phone.	• People without home phones are excluded from the study. • Some do not answer their phones due to increase in telemarketing.
Mail surveys	• Less costly • Able to survey a large number of respondents	• May not fully understand the questions • No opportunity to develop rapport • Takes time to develop a comprehensive list of residents • Certain subjects are excluded from mailing list

Source: Adapted from Payne, Brian K. (2005) *Crime and elder abuse: An integrated perspective.* 2nd ed. Springfield, IL: Charles C Thomas.

able to identify complaint patterns, provide insight into the victims' interactions with Hanks, and delineate the experience of victimization. The authors also drew attention to the plight of victims trying to formally resolve the cases. They noted that "pursuing justice became more expensive than being a victim and they [often] dropped the matter" (p. 158).

Another issue that arises in surveys of white-collar crime victims is that victims may be reluctant to discuss their experiences. Survey respondents may not trust researchers who ask about fraud victimization, perhaps partly because they are on guard about having been scammed in the first place (Mason & Benson, 1996). Despite these issues, the need to study white-collar crime victims continues because they have been ignored historically in victimization studies and the victims' movement (Moore & Mills, 1990).

Surveys of white-collar offenders are equally difficult to conduct. Sutherland (1941) recognized this as a barrier in white-collar crime research shortly after introducing the concept. White-collar offenders simply do not want to participate in research studies. As noted above, general self-report surveys of members of the public might help to develop samples of white-collar offenders. Other times, researchers have surveyed members of a specific occupational group with the aim of identifying attitudes about white-collar offending among members of that occupational group. Criminologist Dean Dabney, for example, interviewed nurses (1995) and pharmacists (2001) to shed light on the types of crimes occurring in those fields. After he built up rapport over time, participants in his study were willing to open up about crimes in their occupations, particularly crimes committed by their coworkers.

▲ **Photo 1.3** Telephone interviews are an effective way to do some types of white-collar crime interviews.

Other researchers have confronted barriers in their efforts to interview convicted white-collar offenders. This group of offenders experiences a significant amount of stigma, and that stigma may keep them from wanting to talk about their experiences with researchers. One journalist tried contacting 30 different convicted white-collar offenders who had been released from prison in an effort to try to get them to contribute to a story she was writing. She described their resistance to talking with her the following way: "Understandably, most of them told me to get lost. They had done their time and that part of their life was a closed chapter. They had made new lives and did not want to remind anyone of their pasts" (Loane, 2000).

Across each of these survey types, a number of problems potentially call into question the validity and reliability of white-collar crime surveys. First, as one research team has noted, the field of criminology has not yet developed "comprehensive measures . . . that tap into the concepts of white-collar and street crime" (Holtfreter, Van Slyke, Bratton, & Gertz, 2008, p. 57). The lack of comprehensive measures makes it difficult to compare results across studies and generalize findings to various occupational settings. Second, difficulties developing representative samples are inherent within white-collar crime studies. It is particularly difficult to develop a random sample of white-collar crime victims or offenders. Third, questions about white-collar crime on surveys are potentially influenced by other items on the survey, meaning the findings might actually reflect methodological influences as opposed to actual patterns. Fourth, the scarcity of certain types of white-collar crime surveys (like those focusing on offenders) has made it even more difficult to develop and conduct these sorts of studies—if more researchers were able to do these surveys, then others would learn how to follow in their path. Despite these potential problems, surveys are useful tools for empirically assessing various issues related to white-collar offending.

Archival Research and White-Collar Crime

Archival research is also relatively common in the white-collar crime literature. In this context, archival research refers to studies that use some form of record (or archive) as a database in the study (Berg, 2009). Archives commonly used in white-collar crime studies include official case records, presentence reports, media reports, and case descriptions of specific white-collar offenses.

Case records are official records that are housed in an agency that has formal social control duties. One problem that arises with using case records is locating a sample that would include the types of offenders that criminologists would label as white-collar offenders (Wheeler, Weisburd, & Bode, 1988). Still, with a concerted effort, researchers have been able to use case records to develop databases from which a great deal of valuable information about white-collar crime will flow. Crofts (2003), for example, reviewed 182 case files of larcenies by employees. Of those 182 cases, she found that gambling was a direct cause of the larceny in 36 cases. Of those 36 cases, Crofts found that 27 offenders were responsible for 1,616 charges of larceny by employees. Note that there is absolutely no other way Crofts could have found these findings other than by reviewing case records.

Researchers have also used presentence reports to study different topics related to white-collar crime. **Presentence reports** are developed by probation officers and include a wealth of information about offenders, their life histories, their criminal careers, and the sentences they received. In one of the most cited white-collar crime studies, criminologist Stanton Wheeler and his colleagues (Wheeler, Weisburg, & Bode, 1988) used the presentence reports of convicted white-collar offenders from seven federal judicial circuits to gain insight into the dynamics of offenders, offenses, and sentencing practices. The authors focused on eight offenses: securities fraud, antitrust violations, bribery, tax offenses, bank embezzlement, post and wire fraud, false claims and statements, and credit and lending institution fraud. Their research provided groundbreaking information about how white-collar offenders compared to traditional offenders, as well as information about the way offenders are sentenced in federal court. The findings are discussed in more detail in later chapters of this text.

Researchers have also used **media reports** to study white-collar crime. Using news articles, press reports, and television depictions of white-collar crimes helps researchers (a) demonstrate what kind of information members of the public are likely to receive about white-collar crime and (b) uncover possible patterns guiding white-collar offenses that may not be studied through other means. With regard to studies focusing on what information the public receives about white-collar offenders, criminologist Michael Levi (2006) focused on how financial white-collar crimes were reported in various media outlets. His results suggested that these offenses were portrayed as "infotainment" rather than serious crimes, suggesting that the cases were sensationalized to provide somewhat inaccurate portrayals of the offenses. Another researcher who used newspaper articles to study the portrayal of white-collar crime found that the cases tended to be reported in business or law sections rather than the crime sections of newspapers, suggesting that the behaviors are not real crimes (Stephenson-Burton, 1995).

With regard to the use of press reports to describe patterns surrounding specific forms of white-collar crimes, a dissertation by Philip Stinson (2009) focused on 2,119 cases of police misconduct committed by 1,746 police officers that were reported in the national media between 2005 and 2007. In using media reports, Stinson was able to access a larger number of police misconduct cases than he would have been able to access through other methods. His findings provide useful fodder for those interested in generating awareness about police misconduct.

Another archive that may be of use to white-collar crime researchers involves case descriptions of specific white-collar offenses that may be provided by some agencies. In some states, for example, the state bar association publishes misdeeds committed by attorneys. Researchers have used these case descriptions to examine how lawyers are sanctioned in Alabama (Payne & Stevens, 1999) and Virginia (Payne, Time, & Raper, 2005). Some national agencies provide reports of white-collar crimes committed by occupations they are charged with regulating. The National Association of Medicaid Fraud Control Units, for instance, describes cases prosecuted by Medicaid Fraud Control Units in a publication titled *Medicaid Fraud Reports.* This publication has served as a database for studies on crimes by doctors (Payne, 1995), crimes in nursing homes (Payne & Cikovic, 1995), crimes in the home health care field (Payne & Gray, 2001), and theft by employees (Payne & Strasser, 2010). Table 1.2 shows the kinds of information available in the fraud reports for these offense types.

With each of these types of archival research, researchers often develop a coding scheme and use that scheme much as they would use a survey instrument. Instead of interviewing an individual, the researcher "asks" the archive a set of questions. Several advantages exist with the use of case records for white-collar crime research (see Payne, 2005). For example, such strategies provide white-collar crime researchers access to a large group of subjects that they would not be able to otherwise access. It would have been impossible, for example, for Stinson to locate and interview more than 1,700 police officers who had been arrested for misconduct. Another benefit is that these strategies enable white-collar crime researchers to explore changes over long periods of time, particularly if the researchers have access to case records that cover an extended period of time. A third benefit is that the research subject, in this case the white-collar offender or victim described in the case record, will not react to being studied simply because there are no interactions between the researcher and the subject.

As with any research strategy, a number of limitations arise when researchers use archives to study white-collar crime. The saying, "you get what you get," comes to mind. The case files are inflexible, and white-collar crime researchers will not be able to probe as they would with interview strategies. Also, the way that records are coded or saved over time may change, which will create problems when researchers try to study white-collar crimes over longer periods of time. Perhaps the most significant problem that arises is that these cases typically represent only those that have come to the attention of the authorities. In effect, unreported white-collar crimes would not be included in most types of archival research. Common reasons that victims will not report white-collar crimes include (a) a belief that there is not enough

Table 1.2	Types of Information Available in Fraud Reports
Type of Crime	**Case Description Example**
Financial abuse by workers against patients	Attorney General Abbott announced on June 19 that ****** was indicted by a state grand jury for misapplication of fiduciary [duty]. ***** was the former business office manager at ***** Nursing Facility. He allegedly misappropriated money from the patient trust fund accounts. (*Medicaid Fraud Report May/June*, 2013, p. 21).
Physical abuse against patients	Attorney General Abbott announced on April 30 that registered nurse (RN) ***** was sentenced by a jury in state court to four years of incarceration for injury to the elderly and one year (concurrent) for assault and was fined $14,000. ***** allegedly hung plastic bags filled with fecal matter around clients' necks as punishment for soiling themselves (*Medicaid Fraud Report March/April*, 2013, p. 19).
Fraud by doctors	Attorney General Abbott announced on August 15, that ****, MD, and ***** were indicted by a federal grand jury for conspiracy and health care fraud. ***** allegedly billed for vestibular testing that was not needed or provided. **** allegedly provided ***** with the recipient information for the billing in return for a percentage of the reimbursement (*Medicaid Fraud Report November/December*, 2013, p. 17).
Fraud by pharmacists	Attorney General Eric T. Schneiderman announced on March 8 that **** pleaded guilty to larceny and stealing more than $93,000 from the Medicaid program after submitting phony Medicaid billings for pharmaceutical drugs, treatments, and supplies that were never dispensed (*Medicaid Fraud Report March/April*, 2013, p. 17).
Home health care fraud	Attorney General Martha Coakley announced on October 30 that *******, the owner of an in-home care company for elderly and disabled individuals, pleaded guilty and was sentenced to two-and-a-half years in jail in connection with billing the state's Medicaid program for services that were not provided (*Medicaid Fraud Report September/October*, 2013, p 1).
Drug theft by nurses	Attorney General Abbott announced on May 14 that licensed vocational nurses ******* and ******* were indicted by a state grand jury for obtaining a controlled substance by fraud, a third-degree felony. The two allegedly diverted patient narcotics on February 27, 2008, from Woolridge Nursing Home, where they were employed as LVNs. Both admitted to taking the narcotics (*Medicaid Fraud Report May/June*, 2009, p. 15).

evidence; (b) the offense is not seen as that serious; (c) concerns that reporting would be futile; (d) concerns that reporting the victimization could be costly, particularly for businesses that are victims of white-collar crimes; (e) shame; (f) businesses may want to handle it on their own; and (g) realization that it may take more time than it seems worth taking to respond to the case (Crofts, 2003). If nobody reports the white-collar crime, it will not be a part of an official record.

Indeed, Sutherland (1940) recognized decades ago that official statistics (and records) typically exclude many white-collar crimes.

Field Research

Field research involves strategies where researchers enter a particular setting and gather data through their observations in those settings (Berg, 2009). In some instances, researchers will share their identity as a researcher with those in the setting, while in other instances, researchers may choose to be anonymous. These strategies can be quite time consuming and are conducted much less frequently than other white-collar crime studies, but they have the potential to offer valuable information about behavior in the workplace. For example, Stannard (1973) entered a nursing home as a janitor and worked there for several months. While the staff knew that he was a researcher, they seemed to forget this over time, and their actions included various types of misconduct (ranging from minor offenses to more serious ones that could have resulted in one resident's death).

In many white-collar crime studies, field research methods are combined with other research strategies. As an illustration, Croall (1989) conducted court observations as part of a broader study focusing on crimes against consumers. She observed 50 cases and used the time she spent doing those observations to develop rapport with the justice officials involved in handling the cases. Over time, the officials later granted Croall access to their case files. Had she not "put in her time," so to speak, she probably would have been denied access to the case files.

Experiments

Experiments are studies where researchers examine how the presence of one variable (the causal or independent variable) produces an outcome (the effect or dependent variable). The classic experimental design entails using two groups—an experimental group and a control group. Subjects are randomly selected and assigned to one of the groups. Members of the **experimental group** receive the independent variable (or the treatment) and members of the control group do not. The researcher conducts observations before and after the independent variable is introduced to the experimental group to determine whether the presence of the independent variable produced observable or significant changes.

Consider a situation where we are interested in whether a certain treatment program would be useful for reintegrating white-collar offenders into the community. The researcher would develop a measurement for assessing white-collar offenders' reintegration values. As well, a sample of white-collar offenders would be randomly assigned to two groups—an experimental group and a control group. The researcher would ask members of both groups to complete the reintegration values survey. Then the experimental group would be exposed to the treatment program, and the control group would receive traditional responses. At some point after the treatment has been completed, the researcher would ask members of both groups to complete a similar (or even the same) reintegration values survey. Any differences between the two groups of offenders could then potentially be attributed to the treatment (or independent variable) received by the experimental group.

A recent experiment in the Netherlands compared the way that car mechanics sell goods to consumers (students) in different scenarios. The experiment found that mechanics frequently provided more services than were necessary, presumably because "experts often face strong incentives for providing 'safe solutions'" (Beck et al., 2011). This study demonstrates that experiments can, in fact, be done on topics related to white-collar crime. Of course, the use of students as consumers limited the generalizability of the findings.

Because of difficulties in recruiting white-collar individuals to participate in these studies, very few white-collar crime studies have actually used a classic experimental design. Some, however, have used what are called **quasi-experimental designs**. Quasi-experiments are studies that mimic experimental designs but lack certain elements of the classic experimental design. One author team, for example, compared two similar businesses (health care offices) to determine whether an "ethical work climate" contributed to employee theft (Weber, Kurke, & Pentico, 2003). The two organizations included one in which an internal audit revealed that workers were stealing and one in which an audit did not reveal theft. The authors surveyed workers from both businesses and found that an ethical work climate appeared to influence theft. In this case, the authors did not randomly select the comparison groups, and they did not manipulate the independent variable (ethical work climate). Still, their design mimicked what would be found in an experimental design.

While some criminologists have used quasi-experiments to study white-collar crime issues, the use of experiments in the broader body of white-collar crime research remains rare. This may change in the future, however, as experimental research is becoming much more common in criminology and criminal justice. In 1998, for example, a group of criminologists created the Academy of Experimental Criminology (AEC) to recognize those criminologists who conduct experimental research. Part of AEC's current mission is to support the *Journal of Experimental Criminology*, which was created in 2005 as an outlet for promoting experimental research on crime and criminal justice issues. According to the journal's website, the *Journal of Experimental Criminology* "focuses on high quality experimental and quasi-experimental research in the development of evidence based crime and justice policy. The journal is committed to the advancement of the science of systematic reviews and experimental methods in criminology and criminal justice" (http://www.springer .com/social+sciences/criminology/journal/11292, "About This Journal"). Incidentally, the founding editor of the journal (David Weisburd) has a long history of conducting prominent white-collar crime research studies.

Case Studies

Case studies entail researchers selecting a particular crime, criminal, event, or other phenomena and studying features surrounding the causes and consequences of those phenomena. Typically, the sample size is "one" in case studies. Researchers might use a variety of other research strategies (such as field research, archival research, and interviews) in conducting their case studies. Case studies are relatively frequent in the white-collar crime literature. An early case study was conducted by Frank Cullen and his colleagues (Cullen, Maakestad, & Cavender, 1987), who focused on what is now known as the *Ford Pinto Case*. In the mid- to late 1970s, Ford Motor Company had come under intense scrutiny over a series of high profile crashes. Eventually, prosecutor Michael Cosentino filed criminal charges against Ford Motor Company after three teenage girls—Judy, Lin, and Donna Ulrich—driving a Ford Pinto, were killed in an August 1978 collision. The authors chronicled the situational and structural factors that led to Cosentino's decision to pursue criminal penalties against the large automaker. While the details of this case will be described in more detail later, as Cullen and his coauthors note, this case "signified the social and legal changes that had placed corporations under attack and made them vulnerable to criminal intervention in an unprecedented way" (p. 147).

Different criminologists and social scientists have also studied the role of white-collar and corporate crime in the U.S. savings and loan crisis, which occurred in the 1980s and 1990s. Perhaps the most comprehensive case study of this crisis was conducted by criminologists Kitty Calavita, Henry Pontell, and Robert Tillmann (1997). The research team, through a grant funded by the National Institute of Justice, explored those criminogenic factors contributing to the collapse of the savings and loan institutions in the late 1980s and 1990s. The authors relied on public records, congressional testimony, media reports, and interviews with key informants to demonstrate how white-collar offending contributed to a significant proportion of the bank failures. While Calavita and her colleagues focused on the crisis from a national perspective, other researchers used a more specific case study approach to consider specific instances where a bank failed. One author team, for example, conducted a case study on the Columbia Savings and Loan Association of Beverly Hills (Glasberg & Skidmore, 1998b). Using congressional testimony, interviews, and media reports, their research drew attention to the way that structural changes in the economic policies (deregulation and federal deposit insurance policies) promoted individual greed.

Case studies are advantageous in that they allow criminologists an insider's view of specific white-collar and corporate crimes. As well, these studies have provided a great deal of insight into the dynamics, causes, and consequences of various types of white-collar crimes. In many ways, because case studies use multiple strategies to gather data, the potential strengths of those strategies (e.g., nonreactivity for archival research, etc.) exist with case studies. At the same time, though, the same disadvantages that arise with these other strategies also manifest themselves in case studies. In addition, it is important to note that case studies can take an enormous amount of time to complete.

● ● ● Studying White-Collar Crime From a Scientific Perspective

Almost everyone has heard about crimes committed by individuals in the workplace or by white-collar offenders. In recent times, a great deal of media attention has focused on infamous white-collar offenders, such as Bernie Madoff, Martha Stewart, and Ken Lay. The reality is, however, that these media depictions—while providing a glimpse into the lives and experiences of a select few high profile white-collar offenders—provide a superficial, and somewhat confusing, introduction to white-collar crime. To fully understand white-collar crime, it is best to approach the topic from a scientific perspective.

Studying white-collar crime from a scientific perspective requires that students understand how the principles of science relate to white-collar crime. In 1970, Robert Bierstedt described how various principles of science were related to the study of human behavior. Fitzgerald and Cox (1994) used these same principles to demonstrate how social research methods adhered to traditional principles of science. Taking this a step further, one can use these principles as a framework for understanding why, and how, the principles of science relate to the study of white-collar crime. The principles include these qualities:

- Objectivity
- Parsimony
- Determinism
- Skepticism
- Relativism

Objectivity and White-Collar Crime

Objectivity as a principle of science suggests that researchers must be value-free in doing their research. The importance of objectivity is tied to the research findings. Researchers who allow their values to influence the research process will be more apt to have findings that are value laden rather than objective. Researchers who violate this principle may create significant damage to the scientific endeavor. (See White-Collar Crime in the News: Researcher Barred From Federal Programs After Federal Conviction.)

With regard to white-collar crime, the challenge is to approach the behaviors and the offenders objectively. In many cases, white-collar offenders are vilified and portrayed as evil actors who have done great harm to society. While the harm they create is clearly significant, demonizing white-collar offenders and white-collar offenses runs the risk of (a) ignoring actual causes of white-collar crime, (b) relying on ineffective intervention strategies, (c) failing to develop appropriate prevention strategies, and (d) making it virtually impossible for convicted white-collar offenders to reintegrate into society.

Consider that many individuals attribute the causes of white-collar crime to greed on the part of the offender. Intuitively, it makes sense that individuals who already seem to be making a good living are greedy if they commit crime in order to further their economic interests. However, as Benson and Moore (1992) note, "self-reports from white-collar offenders suggest that they often are motivated not so much by greed as by a desire to merely hang on to what they already had" (p. 267). Inadequately identifying the causes of behavior will make it more difficult to respond appropriately to these cases.

Furthermore, in promoting understanding about the criminal justice system's response to white-collar offenders, it cannot be automatically assumed that the justice system is doing a bad job or treating these offenders more leniently than other offenders. An objective approach requires an open mind in assessing the ties between white-collar crime and the criminal justice system. As will be seen later, for example, several studies show that convicted white-collar offenders are more likely than other convicted offenders to be sentenced to jail, albeit for shorter periods of time (Payne, 2003b). The lack of an objective approach might force some to automatically assume that white-collar offenders are treated more leniently than conventional offenders. This is problematic because a lack of objectivity may create faulty assumptions about the criminal justice system's handling of white-collar crime cases, which in turn could reduce the actual deterrent power of the efforts of criminal justice practices.

On another level, some criminologists have argued that a lack of objectivity among criminologists has resulted in some researchers overextending the concept of white-collar crime. According to V. Ruggiero (2007),

> given the increasing variety of white-collar criminal offenses being committed, and the avalanche of crime committed by states and other powerful actors, scholars are faced with a fuzzy analytical framework, with the result that some may be tempted to describe as crime everything they, understandably, find disturbing. . . . The word nasty is not synonymous with criminal, and the concept of crime may be useless if it is indiscriminately applied to anything objectionable by whoever uses the term. (p. 174)

WHITE-COLLAR CRIME IN THE NEWS

Researcher Barred From Federal Programs After Federal Conviction

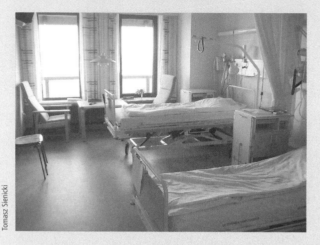

Tomasz Sienicki

Scientific research can be a matter of life and death.

SUMMARY: Notice is hereby given that the Deputy Assistant Secretary for the Office of Acquisition Management and Policy of the Department of Health and Human Services (HHS) has taken final agency action in the following case:

Paul H. Kornak, Stratton VA Medical Center, Albany, New York [was convicted of homicide, fraud, and false statements]. As part of his guilty plea, Mr. Kornak admitted to the following facts:

In August 2000, Mr. Kornak applied for employment to the VA, submitting a false "Declaration for Federal Employment" form. Mr. Kornak denied that he had been convicted or on probation in the preceding 10 years, whereas in fact, he had been convicted of mail fraud in 1992 and placed on probation for 3 years.

By October of 2000, Mr. Kornak was responsible for organizing, coordinating, implementing, and directing all research elements in the Stratton VA Medical Center oncology research program. Specifically, Mr. Kornak was the site coordinator at the Stratton VA Medical Center for the "Iron (Fe) and Atherosclerosis

Study" (FeAST), cancer studies known as Tax 325 and Tax 327, and a bladder cancer study. The FeAST study was a clinical trial that tested a novel procedure for controlling atherosclerosis, also known as hardening of the arteries, by reducing the iron in the body through blood drawing. The Tax 325 cancer treatment study involved the administration of pharmaceutical products to patients with metastatic or locally recurrent gastric cancer previously untreated with chemotherapy for advanced disease. The Tax 327 study involved the administration of pharmaceutical products to patients with metastatic hormone refractory prostate cancer. The purpose of the bladder cancer study, which was co-sponsored by the National Cancer Institute, National Institutes of Health, was to compare the use of difluoromethylornithine (DFMO) to the use of a placebo in patients with low grade superficial bladder cancer according to time to first recurrence of the tumor and toxicities.

From May 14, 1999, to July 10, 2002, in connection with the above protocols, Mr. Kornak participated in a scheme to defraud the sponsors of the clinical studies in that "he would and repeatedly did submit false documentation regarding patients and study subjects and enroll and cause to be enrolled persons as study subjects who did not qualify under the particular study protocol."

Mr. Kornak caused the death of a study subject when he "failed to perceive a substantial and unjustifiable risk that death would occur when he knowingly and willfully made and used documents falsely stating and representing the results of [the study subject's] blood chemistry analysis, which false documents purported that [the study subject] met the inclusion and exclusion criteria for participation in Tax 325 when the actual results did not meet the inclusion and exclusion criteria and showed impaired kidney and liver function, and [the study subject] thus was administered the chemotherapeutic drugs docetaxel, cisplatin, and 5-FU in connection with Tax 325 on or about May 31, 2001, and died as a result thereof on or about June 11, 2001."

Source: Reprinted from NIH (2006). Findings of Research Misconduct. https://grants.nih.gov/grants/guide/notice-files/NOT-OD-06-042.html

In terms of objectivity and the study of white-collar crime, researchers should not define white-collar crimes simply as those things that are "nasty" or as behaviors that offend them. Instead, white-collar crime must be objectively defined, measured, researched, and explained.

Parsimony and White-Collar Crime

The principle of **parsimony** suggests that researchers and scientists keep their levels of explanation as simple as possible. For explanations and theories to be of use to scientists, practitioners, and the public, it is imperative that the explanations be reduced to as few variables as possible and explained in simple terms. In explaining white-collar crime, for instance, explanations must be described as simply as possible. One issue that arises, however, is that many white-collar crimes are, in fact, very complex in nature and design. As will be shown later in this text, this complexity often creates obstacles for criminal justice officials responding to these cases.

While many types of white-collar crimes may be complex and it may be difficult to explain the causes of these offenses in simple terms, this does not mean that the offenses cannot be understood through relatively simple explanations. Consider fraud by physicians, misconduct by lawyers, or misdeeds by stockbrokers. One does not need to be a doctor, attorney, or financial advisor to understand the nature of these offenses, ways to respond to these offenses, or the underlying dynamics contributing to these behaviors. By understanding relatively simple descriptions of these behaviors, readers will be able to recognize parallels between the offenses and will develop a foundation from which they can begin to expand their understanding of white-collar crime.

Determinism and White-Collar Crime

Determinism means that behavior is caused or influenced by preceding events or factors. With regard to crimes in the workplace, a great deal of research has focused on trying to explain (or "determine") why these offenses occur. Understanding the causes of white-collar crime is important because such information would help in developing both prevention and intervention strategies. In terms of prevention, if researchers are able to isolate certain factors that seem to contribute to white-collar misconduct, then policymakers and practitioners can use that information to develop policies and implement practices that would reduce the amount of crime in the workplace. Consider a study on student cheating that finds that the cheating is the result of the nature of the assignments given. With this information, professors could redo the assignment so that cheating is more difficult and less likely.

Understanding the causes of white-collar crime also helps to develop appropriate intervention strategies. If, for example, a study shows that certain types of white-collar offenses are caused by a lack of formal oversight, then strategies could be developed that provide for such oversight. One study, for example, found that patient abuse in nursing homes was at least partially attributed to the fact that workers were often alone with nursing home residents (Payne & Cikovic, 1995). To address this, the authors recommended that workers be required to work in teams with more vulnerable patients and video cameras be added where feasible.

To some, the principle of determinism is in contrast to the idea of free will, or rational decision making. However, it is not necessary, at least in this context, to separate the two phenomena. Whether individuals support deterministic ideals or free-will ideals, with white-collar offenses it seems safe to suggest that understanding why these offenses occur is informative and useful. For those adhering to deterministic ideals, explaining the source of workplace misconduct helps to develop appropriate response systems. For those adhering to free-will ideals, the same can be said: Figuring out what makes individuals "choose" to commit white-collar offenses means that strategies can be developed that would influence the offender's decision making. In other words, choices are caused by, and can be controlled by, external factors. Put another way, by understanding *why* individuals commit crime in the workplace, officials are in a better position to know *how* to respond to those crimes.

Skepticism and White-Collar Crime

Skepticism simply means that social scientists must question and re-question their findings. We must never accept our conclusions as facts! Applying this notion to the study of white-collar crime is fairly straightforward and simple. On the one hand, it is imperative that we continue to question past research on white-collar crime in an effort to develop and conduct future white-collar crime studies. On the other hand, in following this principle, some may find it difficult to think differently about the occupations covered in this book. Put simply, crime and deviance occur in all occupations.

Sociologist Emile Durkheim noted that deviance occurs in all cultures and subcultures. He used the example of a "society of saints" to illustrate this point. Even a group of nuns or priests would have someone committing deviant behavior. So, as readers, when we think of any occupation, we must question and re-question how and why crime is committed in that occupation. We cannot assume that because the occupation is "trustworthy" crime does not occur in that occupation. Doing so would provide an inaccurate and incomplete picture of white-collar crime.

Relativism and White-Collar Crime

Relativism means that all things are related. If all things are related, then, this principle implies that changes in one area will lead to changes in other areas. A simple example helps to highlight this principle. Think of a time when you are driving your car, listening to your favorite Lady Gaga, Eminem, or Taylor Swift song with the music turned up loudly, and you suddenly smell something that makes you think that your engine is failing. What's the first thing you do? For many of us, the first thing we do is turn the music down so we smell better. Think about that—we do not smell with our ears; we smell with our noses. But we turn the music down because it helps us to smell. Changes in one area (smelling) lead to changes in other areas (hearing).

White-collar crime is related to the ideal of relativism in three ways: (1) how white-collar crime is defined, (2) the nature of white-collar crime, and (3) how the criminal justice system responds to white-collar crime. First, the notion of *white-collar* is a relative concept in and of itself. What makes someone a white-collar worker? Is it the clothes worn to work? Are your professors "white-collar" workers? Do they all wear "white collars" to work? Are you a white-collar worker? Will you ever be a white-collar worker? In using the concept of white-collar to describe these offense types, Sutherland was highlighting the importance of status. However, the very concept of status is relative in nature. What is high status to one individual might actually be low status to another person. What one group defines as a white-collar occupation may be different from what another group defines as white-collar. A basic understanding of white-collar crime requires an appreciation for the relative nature of status and occupations.

Second, the principle of relativism highlights the need to recognize how changes in society have resulted in changes in white-collar offending. Throughout history, as society changed and workplace structures changed, the nature of, and types of, workplace offenses changed. Describing this pattern from a historical review of the 1800s, one author team commented:

> During this time period, large scale changes within the business environment brought new opportunities for acts of workplace taking, particularly those associated with "respectable" echelons of staff hierarchies. Such acts were labeled as illegitimate and criminalized. . . . The representation of fraud and embezzlement as activities that were criminal was bolstered through a reconceptualization of the nature of property rights and, in particular, the relationship between staff and the property worked with. (Locker & Godfrey, 2006, p. 977)

In effect, changes in the occupational arena create new opportunities for, and strategies for, white-collar crime. In our modern society, note that globalization has created worldwide opportunities for white-collar offending (Johnstone, 1999). As an example of the way that changes in society result in changes in misbehavior that may hit home with some students, "studies by the Center for Academic Integrity show a decline in traditional peeking over someone's shoulder cheating, but a steady increase in Internet plagiarism" (Zernike, 2003). Changes in society resulted in changes in the way some students cheat.

Third, the notion of relativism relates to white-collar crime in considering how the criminal justice system responds to white-collar crimes and the interactions between the criminal justice system and other societal systems. John Van Gigch's (1978) **applied general systems theory** helps to illustrate this point. Van Gigch noted that society is made up of a number of different types of systems and that these systems operate independently, and in conjunction with, other systems (see Figure 1.1). At a minimum, systems that are related to white-collar crime include those shown in Figure 1.1.

At the most basic level, the **political system** is involved in defining laws and regulations relating to all forms of crime, including white-collar crimes. Three levels of the political system include local, state, and federal systems of government. Each of these levels plays a role in defining various white-collar offenses, detecting offenders, adjudicating cases, and punishing offenders. On a separate level, one chapter of this book will focus on crimes committed in the political system. Note also that the political system plays a central role in developing and implementing policies designed to prevent and respond to white-collar crime. Throughout this text, significant attention is given to the inter-

▲ **Photo 1.4** Crime occurs in all societal systems, even the educational system. You will read more about offenses in colleges and universities in Chapter 6.

play among white-collar crime policies, the occurrence of white-collar crimes, and the actions of various systems assigned the tasks of preventing and responding to white-collar crime.

The **educational system** relates to white-collar crime inasmuch as white-collar careers typically come out of this system. From preschool through higher education, one can see that the educational system prepares individuals for their future careers and lives. Some research has focused on how the educational system might promote certain forms of white-collar offending, with students potentially learning why committing crimes is part of their training (Keenan, Brown, Pontell, & Geis, 1985). At the same time, the educational system provides opportunities to increase understanding about white-collar crime through college coursework and advanced training for criminal justice professionals. As with the political system, white-collar crimes occur in the educational system.

The **religious system** relates to white-collar crime (and other crimes) in that this system has been seen as providing institutions that have the potential to prevent misconduct. Many studies have focused on the ties between religion and crime, and while few have focused on how religion relates to white-collar crime, the underlying assumption is that religion has the potential to prevent these behaviors or, at least, provide a setting where definitions of appropriate and inappropriate misconduct can be developed. Interestingly, white-collar crime pioneer Edwin Sutherland's father "was a religious fundamentalist who believed in strict adherence to the Baptist faith" (Martin, Mutchnick, & Austin, 1990, p. 140). While Sutherland eventually parted ways with his father's church, it has been noted that "a prominent and overt expression of his moralistic side appears in *White Collar Crime* (1949) where Sutherland calls for something other than a strict legal definition of acceptable behavior" (Martin et al., 1990, p. 141). As an aside, just as crime is found in the political and educational systems, so do white-collar offenses occur in the religious system.

The **technological or cyber system** has evolved greatly over the past few decades. This system is related to white-collar crime in at least two distinct ways. First, and as was noted earlier, changes in the technological system have led to changes in the way that some white-collar offenders commit their crimes. Second, the technological system has provided additional tools that government officials can use in their pursuit of identifying and responding to white-collar crimes.

The **social system** represents a setting where individuals have various needs fulfilled and learn how to do certain things, as well as reasons for doing those behaviors. In terms of white-collar crime, some individuals may learn how to commit white-collar offenses, and why to commit those offenses, as part of the social systems in which they exist. Research, for example, shows that nurses learn from their peers how to rationalize their workplace misdeeds (Dabney, 1995).

The **social services system** includes numerous agencies involved in providing services to members of the public. In some cases, the services they provide might be in direct response to white-collar crime victimization. For example, individuals who lose their life savings to fraudulent investors may need to seek assistance from the social service system to deal with their victimization. As with the other systems, white-collar crimes could be committed by workers in the social services system.

The **occupational system** is, for the purposes of this discussion, that system where the bulk of professions are found. This system is composed of other systems, which at the broadest level can be characterized as lower-class and upper-class occupational systems. Within the lower-class and upper-class occupational systems, specific subsystems exist. White-collar offenses are found in each of these subsystems. As outlined in this text, these subsystems include the legal system, the health care system, the higher education system, the religious system, the technological system, the housing system, the insurance system, and the **economic system.**

The **economic system** represents the system that drives our economy. This system is influenced by, and has an influence on, each of the other types of systems. In recent times, problems in the economic system have had far-reaching and serious effects on countries across the world. Many of the white-collar crimes discussed in this text originate in the economic system.

The **corporate system** includes the businesses and corporations that carry out business activity as part of our capitalist system. These corporations strive to make profits and grow in strength and numbers. Various types of white-collar crimes have been uncovered in the corporate system. As well, the corporate system is sometimes given the power to regulate itself.

The **regulatory system** describes those local, state, and federal agencies that have been charged with regulating various businesses. This system is different from the criminal and civil justice systems in many different ways. For example, the formal source of rules comes from administrative regulations in the regulatory system. As well, the rights of offenders, corporations, and victims are different in the three types of systems (e.g., offenders have one set of rights in the criminal justice system, another set of rights in the civil justice system, and another set of rights in the regulatory system). Procedures and guidelines used to process the cases also vary in the three types of systems.

The **civil justice system** represents that system of justice where individuals (plaintiffs) seek recourse for offenses by way of a civil lawsuit. The accused (defendant) could be an individual or a company. In cases of white-collar crime, for example, it is common for lawsuits to be filed by victims in order to recover their losses. Note that the victim, in many cases, may actually be an individual, company, or governmental agency.

The **criminal justice system** is that system of justice where violations of the criminal law are handled. The criminal law is the branch of law dealing with crimes against the state. Like each of these systems, our criminal justice system is composed of various subsystems: the police, courts, and corrections. On one level, the criminal justice system operates independently from other agencies when white-collar offenses are investigated, prosecuted, and sentenced. On another level, it is imperative to note that the system's responses to white-collar crimes, and behaviors of actors in the criminal justice system, are influenced by changes in other societal systems. Changes in the technological system (brought about by advances in the educational system) led to the development of the Internet. The Internet, in turn, created new ways for criminals to offend. These new strategies, then, meant that the criminal justice system had to alter its practices. As society changes, criminal justice and other systems of formal control are forced to change how they respond to white-collar offenses (Edelhertz, 1983). As one author put it several years ago, "an emerging area of difficulty is the challenge of devising powers of investigation that are responsive to the needs of enforcement in a modern corporate society" (Fisse, 1991, p. 7). Two decades later, this same challenge remains "an emerging area of difficulty."

A full understanding of white-collar crime requires an understanding of (a) the changing nature of crime occurring in various systems; (b) how the criminal justice, civil justice, and regulatory systems respond to white-collar crimes; and (c) how interactions between the systems influence criminal behavior as well as response systems. To promote broad insight into white-collar crime, this text relies on the systems perspective to guide the discussion about white-collar crime. In doing so, it argues that students (a part of the educational system) have a significant role in white-collar crime.

Figure 1.1   The Systems Perspective

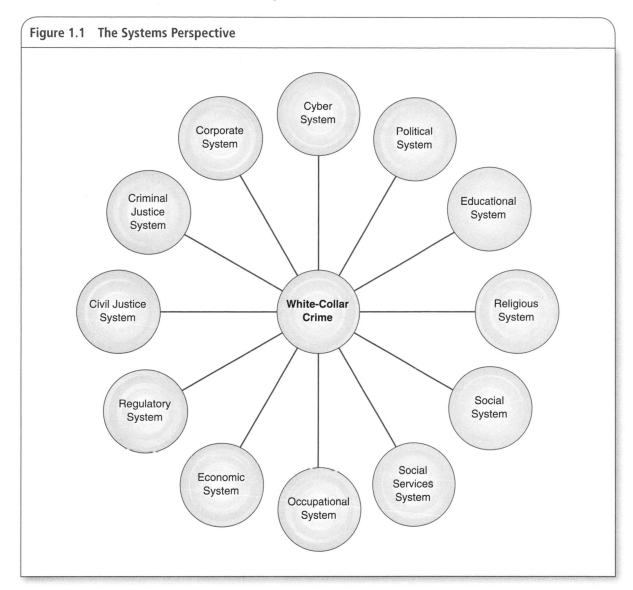

● ● ●   The Student Role in White-Collar Crime

Some readers may have given very little thought to their role in white-collar crime. In reading this text, students are encouraged to think about how white-collar crime relates to their lives—their past, their current lives, and their future. In effect, students have at least 10 potential roles in white-collar crime. These roles include (1) past victims, (2) past offenders, (3) current offenders, (4) current victims, (5) future offenders, (6) future victims, (7) future crime fighters, (8) future policymakers, (9) current research subjects, and (10) future white-collar crime researchers.

First, most students have been victimized by white-collar crimes in the past, though many likely may not have realized they were victimized at the time. From being overcharged for services to being a victim of corporate misconduct, students—like the rest of society—are not immune from victimization by white-collar or corporate offenders.

Second, some students may have actually been past offenders, particularly if broader definitions of occupational offending are used. These definitions will be addressed in Chapter II. For now, several questions could be asked to determine whether students have broken the rules in their past jobs. Did they take breaks for too long? Did they give away company food or merchandise? Did they skip work and lie to their boss about the reason? One of the exercises I use in my white-collar crime classes is to have students write about occupational offenses they have committed in past jobs. Very few of my students ever had a problem identifying past misdeeds. Some even described actions that would have resulted in felony convictions had they been caught for their transgressions!

Third, another role that students may have in white-collar crime is that some may be current victims of white-collar crime. In Chapter X, attention will be given to the way that colleges and universities sometimes break rules in recruiting students and providing financial aid. (Some have even argued that ineffective instruction by college professors victimizes students, but that can be saved for another text.) Students might also be victims of white-collar and corporate misconduct in their roles as consumers of various goods and services that extend beyond the college boundaries.

Fourth, some students can also be seen as current occupational offenders if they are violating the rules of their jobs or the rules set by their educational institution. This will be discussed in more detail in Chapter VI. At this point, it is sufficient to suggest that college students can be seen as "pre-white-collar" professionals. In this context, then, some misdeeds that college students commit could technically be seen as versions of white-collar offending.

Fifth, some college students may have the role of future white-collar offenders. Note that most white-collar offenders have at least some college education. While most readers of this text will not (it is hoped) go on to careers of white-collar offending, the fact remains that some college graduates eventually graduate into these criminal careers.

Sixth, all college students will be future victims of white-collar and corporate misconduct at least on some level. There is no reason to expect that these offenses will end. Because the consequences of white-collar offenses are so far reaching, none of us will be completely immune from future misdeeds—though we may not always know when we have been victimized.

Seventh, some college students will also have a future role as white-collar crime fighters or white-collar criminal defense lawyers. At first blush, a career battling white-collar offenders may not seem as exhilarating as other law enforcement careers. However, nothing could be further from the truth. A major focus of this text will be on how the criminal justice system and criminal justice professionals respond to white-collar offenses. In addressing the mechanics of the response to these offenses, it is hoped that readers will see just how important, and exciting, these careers are. From going undercover in a doctor's office to sifting through complex computer programs, the search for misconduct and clues of wrongdoing can far outweigh more mundane or routine criminal justice practices. To help you become acquainted with these careers, each chapter includes a box feature titled "Careers Responding to White-Collar-Crime." The feature describes a career related to the topic under consideration in the chapter. These careers often go far beyond what one might think of as a typical criminal justice career. Careers in White-Collar Crime: Investigator in Department of Agriculture provides one such example.

Eighth, some college students will go on to employment positions where they will play a role in developing and implementing various crime policies. As future policymakers, college students will be better prepared to develop policies addressing white-collar crime if they have a full understanding of the dynamics of white-collar crime, the causes of the behavior, and the most effective response systems. Without an understanding of these issues, future (and current) policymakers run the risk of relying on crime prevention policies and strategies that might work for traditional forms of crime but not necessarily for white-collar crimes. A recent study found that less than seven percent of all studies published in fifteen top criminal justice journals between 2001 and 2010 were focused on white-collar crime (McGurrin et al., 2013). The discipline is counting on you to change this!

Ninth, some college students will also assume the role of research subjects. It is particularly useful to study students as white-collar crime subjects because, presumably, many will be entering white-collar careers after graduating (Watt, 2012). Many researchers have used college student samples to generate understanding about white-collar offending.

CAREERS RESPONDING TO WHITE-COLLAR CRIME

Investigator in Department of Agriculture

Duties:

- Researches, selects, plans and independently conducts investigations relating to alleged, fraudulent violations of SNAP rules, committed either by authorized retailers and/or store personnel.
- Conducts those investigations that are of an extremely complex or sensitive nature or those involving highly technical problems relating to legal or evidentiary issues, matters or questions.
- Evaluates all alternatives to develop the proper investigative approach, by examining files, records and data of the firm's program participation and redemption history; complaints and rumors; observed fraudulent violations, and/or past investigation records to detect clues or links in a chain of evidence or information which are most likely to result in successful investigations
- Prepares accurate, detailed, and complete reports on investigations conducted. Provides documentation of information obtained on fraudulent violations committed by firms, including benefits used, evidence obtained, and proper disposal of evidence when no longer required.
- Analyzes automated reports of recipient benefit transactions and retailer redemptions to identify possible widespread program abuse of participating firms in the assigned area. Generates investigations based on report information.
- Maintains liaison with other units within USDA and FNS, including serving as a technical point of contact for FNS's field offices, and with other agencies at the Federal, State and local levels within given geographic area.
- Cooperates with USDA's Offices of General Counsel and US Attorneys' Offices, and negotiates on False Claims Act cases.
- Independently contacts State and local investigative agencies (e.g., Alcoholic Beverage Control Boards and welfare fraud investigators), and law enforcement, regulatory and licensing agencies.

Source: Reprinted from USAJobs.Gov

One researcher used a sample of college students to learn about the kinds of crimes committed in fast-food restaurants (O'Connor, 1991). Another research team surveyed students to learn about digital piracy and illegal downloading (Higgins, et al., 2006). The same research team surveyed college students to test the ability of criminological theories to explain different forms of occupational misconduct. Another study of 784 undergraduate students found that the way items are sequenced in questionnaires influences attitudes about white-collar crime (Evans & Scott, 1984). The simple fact of the matter is that criminology and criminal justice scholars have a great deal to learn from students, just as students have a great deal to learn from their professors! Indeed, many of the studies cited in this book will come from studies involving college students on some level.

Tenth, as you read about the studies discussed in this text, one thing to bear in mind is that the authors of these studies and articles were students themselves in the not-so-distant past (well, maybe the more distant past for some of us). Edwin Sutherland, once a college student at Grand Island College, went on to create the study of white-collar crime. His students, his students' students, and their students have created a field of study that has significantly evolved over the past 70 years. Thus, the tenth role that students have in white-collar crime is that the discipline of criminology and criminal justice is counting on some of you to take the torch and become future white-collar crime researchers. This text provides a foundation for understanding white-collar crime. It is hoped that this foundation will spark your interest so that you will want to learn more about this important criminological issue and one day go on to help generate future empirical and scientific awareness about white-collar crime.

▲ **Photo 1.5** While many careers exist to respond to white-collar crime, most of those careers require employees to have a college degree. It is equally important that college students have an understanding of white-collar crime so they are better able to enter those careers.

● ● ● Plan for the Book

This text uses the systems perspective as a guide for understanding white-collar crime. Each chapter provides readers an introduction to topics related to white-collar crime. The text is divided into the following chapters:

- Understanding White-Collar Crime
- Crimes by Workers in Sales-Oriented Occupations
- Crimes in the Health Care System
- Crimes in Social Control Systems
- Crimes in the Educational System
- Crime in the Economic System
- Crime in the Cyber System
- Crimes in the Housing System
- Corporate Crime: Crimes Against Workers and Consumers by Private Corporations
- Crimes Against the Environmental System
- Explaining White-Collar Crime
- The Police Response to White-Collar Crime
- Judicial Proceedings and White-Collar Crime
- Corrections and White-Collar Crime

Throughout each chapter, both criminological and criminal justice themes are covered. White-collar crime has been addressed with little or no attention given to white-collar criminal justice. Pulling together criminological and theoretically driven issues with criminal justice-oriented discussions will help to provide a full picture of white-collar crime and the responses to white-collar crime.

SUMMARY

- According to Edwin Sutherland, white-collar crime is "crime committed by a person of respectability and high social status in the course of his occupation" (1949, p. 9). The distinguishing features of white-collar crime are that the crime was committed (a) during work, (b) when the offender was in the role of worker, and (c) as part of the employment duties of the offender.
- We study white-collar crime (a) because it is an enormous problem, (b) because it affects everyone, (c) to learn more about all forms of crime, (d) to develop prevention and intervention systems, (e) to learn about careers, and (f) to learn about subcultures.
- Survey research with white-collar offenders tends to include surveys of offenders, victims, criminal justice officials, and members of the public.
- Archival research on white-collar offenders includes reviews of case records, presentence reports, media reports, and case descriptions of specific white-collar offenses.
- Field research involves situations where researchers enter a particular setting to study phenomena. While relatively rare in the white-collar crime literature, these studies provide direct insight into issues related to the behaviors of offenders, criminal justice officials, and other members of society.
- Experiments involve studies where researchers assess the influence of a particular variable on an experimental group (which receives the "treatment" or the variable) and a control group (which does not receive the treatment or the variable). It is expected that white-collar crime experiments will increase in the future as experimental criminology grows as a research strategy.

- Case studies entail researchers selecting a particular crime, criminal, event, or other phenomenon and studying features surrounding the causes and consequences of those phenomena.
- It is important that those studying white-collar crime be objective in conducting research on the topic. As well, readers are encouraged to keep an open mind about the topic to help as they critically assess issues related to white-collar crime and the study of the topic.
- Researchers are encouraged to keep their explanations as simple as possible. For white-collar crime researchers, this means that one does not need to understand everything about a career in order to understand issues related to crime in that career.
- The aim of many white-collar crime studies is to explain why white-collar crime occurs. Determinism suggests that behavior can be explained. Explaining why white-collar crimes occur enables development of appropriate prevention and intervention remedies.
- Skepticism as a principle of science means that scientists question and re-question everything. For students of white-collar crime, this means that we must question and re-question all of our assumptions about various careers and recognize that crime occurs in all careers.
- Relativism means that all things are related. From a systems perspective, this means that all societal systems are influenced by and have an influence on white-collar crime. Those systems considered in this chapter included the (1) political-governmental system, (2) educational system, (3) religious system, (4) technological system, (5) social system, (6) social services system, (7) occupational systems, (8) economic system, (9) corporate systems, (10) regulatory system, (11) civil justice system, and (12) criminal justice system.
- Students have at least eight potential roles in white-collar crime. These roles include (1) past victims, (2) past offenders, (3) current offenders, (4) current victims, (5) future offenders, (6) future victims, (7) future crime fighters, (8) current research subjects, and (9) future white-collar crime researchers.

KEY TERMS

Applied general systems theory	Educational system	Presentence reports
Archival research	Experimental group	Quasi-experimental designs
Case records	Experiments	Regulatory system
Case studies	Field research	Relativism
Civil justice system	Media reports	Skepticism
Corporate system	Objectivity	Social services system
Criminal justice system	Occupational system	Social system
Determinism	Parsimony	Technological System
Economic system	Political system	White-collar crime victims

DISCUSSION QUESTIONS

1. Below are examples of misdeeds committed by celebrities. Read each of them and classify them according to whether the acts are crimes or, to borrow Ruggiero's concept, just "nasty." Also, identify those actions that you think are white-collar crimes and those that would be traditional crimes.

   a. Former boy-band manager Lou Pearlman (former manager of 'N Sync and Backstreet Boys) was convicted of defrauding more than $300 million from investors as part of a Ponzi scheme.

   b. In November 2015, rapper DMX was arrested for allegedly failing to pay child support.

c. Former New England Patriots tight end Aaron Hernandez was convicted of murder.

d. "Real Housewife" Teresa Giudice was sentenced to prison after being convicted of bankruptcy and mortgage fraud along with her husband.

e. Kanye West interrupted the MTV music awards while Taylor Swift was giving an acceptance speech.

f. In January 2009, Dane Cook's manager was charged with embezzling $10 million from Cook. The manager, Darryl J. McCauley, was Cook's half brother.

g. Actor Zac Efron told a reporter that he has stolen costumes from movie sets after the filming was completed. He said: "I think I stole some of the stuff. Always, on the last day, they try and get it out of your trailer really quick. Always steal some of your wardrobe. You never know what you're going to need" (Hasegawa, 2010).

h. Actor Bill Cosby was accused of sexually assaulting numerous women by using a sedative and taking advantage of them.

i. Hugh Grant was arrested for having sexual relations with a prostitute.

j. Martha Stewart was convicted of perjury after it was found that she lied to investigators about some of her stock purchases.

2. Why does it matter how you classify these behaviors?

3. How are the behaviors you labeled *white-collar crime* different from those you labeled as *traditional crimes*?

4. Why do we study white-collar crime?

5. What is your role in white-collar crime?

WEB RESOURCES

Federal Trade Commission, Bureau of Consumer Protection: https://www.ftc.gov/about-ftc/bureaus-offices/bureau-consumer-protection

National White Collar Crime Center: White Collar Crime Research Consortium (WCCRC): http://www.nw3c.org/research/white_collar_crime_consortium.cfm

U.S. Department of the Treasury: http://www.treasury.gov/Pages/default.aspx

STUDENT RESOURCES

The open-access Student Study Site, available at study.sagepub.com/paynewccess2e, includes useful study materials including SAGE journal articles and multimedia resources.

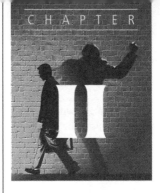

CHAPTER

II

Understanding White-Collar Crime

Definitions, Extent, and Consequences

CHAPTER HIGHLIGHTS

- White-Collar Crime: An Evolving Concept
- Modern Conceptualizations of White-Collar Crime
- Extent of White-Collar Crime
- Consequences of White-Collar Crime
- Public Attitudes Toward White-Collar Crime
- Characteristics of White-Collar Offenders

A s noted in the introduction, Edwin Sutherland created the concept of **white-collar crime** more than 70 years ago to draw attention to the fact that crimes are committed by individuals in all social classes. As will be seen in this chapter, one of the largest difficulties in understanding white-collar crime has centered on an ongoing debate about how to define white-collar crime. After discussing various ways that white-collar crime can be defined, attention will be given to the extent of white-collar crime, the consequences of this illicit behavior, public attitudes about white-collar crime, and patterns describing the characteristics of white-collar offenders.

As a backdrop to this discussion, consider the following recent white-collar crimes quoted from the media:

- [The CPA] admitted she falsified hundreds of tax returns and refund amounts on IRS forms without her clients' knowledge. She diverted money to her own accounts and to her spouse, who told the judge he never suspected her criminality until she was arrested in May. (McMahon, 2015)
- A former Tulsa police officer who was sentenced to 33 months in prison for embezzling from the state and local Fraternal Orders of Police has paid more than $306,000 in restitution and fines. . . . ******, former treasurer for the Fraternal Order of Police Oklahoma State Lodge and the Tulsa Fraternal Order of Police, had been charged with embezzling $419,092 from the organizations. (Harkins, 2015)
- A former assistant manager for State Bank was sentenced Wednesday in the theft of $263,700 between 2010 and 2014 . . . [the assistant manager] pleaded guilty in federal court to fraudulently transferring $15,000 from a customer's account to an account she set up in her brother's name without his knowledge. (Fabian, 2015)
- The man who was in charge of maintenance at Our Lady of Mount Carmel in Niles pleaded guilty to stealing nearly $100,000 from the parish. (wfmj.com, 2015)
- A former City of Douglas employee has been sentenced to 30 days in jail, three years of supervised probation, and ordered to pay back over $42,000 following his conviction for attempting to commit forgery. (Whetten, 2015)

In reviewing these cases, five questions come to mind. First, are each of these cases white-collar crimes? Second, how often do these kinds of crimes occur? Third, what are the consequences of these crimes? Fourth, how serious do you think these crimes are? Finally, who are the offenders in these cases? While the questions are simple in nature, as will be shown in this chapter, the answers to these questions are not necessarily quite so simple.

● ● ● White-Collar Crime: An Evolving Concept

While Edwin Sutherland is the pioneer of the study of white-collar crime, the development of the field and the introduction of the concept of white-collar crime did not occur in a vacuum. Indeed, prior academic work and societal changes influenced Sutherland's scholarship, and his scholarship, in turn, has had an enormous influence on criminology and criminal justice. Tracing the source of the concept of white-collar crime and describing its subsequent variations help demonstrate the importance of conceptualizing various forms of white-collar misconduct.

Sutherland was not the first social scientist to write about crimes by those in the upper class. In his 1934 *Criminology* text, Sutherland used the term *white-collar criminaloid* in reference to the **"criminaloid concept"** initially used by E. A. Ross (1907) in *Sin and Society.* Focusing on businessmen who engaged in harmful acts under the mask of respectability, Ross further wrote that the criminaloid is "society's most dangerous foe, more redoubtable by far than the plain criminal, because he sports the livery of virtue and operates on a titanic scale" (p. 48). Building on these ideas, Sutherland called attention to the fact that crimes were not committed only by members of the lower class. As noted in the introduction, Sutherland (1949) defined white-collar crime as "crime committed by a person of respectability and high social status in the course of his occupation" (p. 9).

Sutherland's appeal to social scientists to expand their focus to include crimes by upper-class offenders was both applauded and criticized. On the one hand, Sutherland was lauded for expanding the focus of the social sciences. On the other hand, the way that Sutherland defined and studied white-collar crime was widely criticized by a host of social scientists and legal experts. Much of the criticism centered on five concerns that scholars had about Sutherland's use of the white-collar crime concept. These concerns included (1) conceptual ambiguity, (2) empirical ambiguity, (3) methodological ambiguity, (4) legal ambiguity, and (5) policy ambiguity.

In terms of conceptual ambiguity, critics have noted that white-collar crime was vaguely and loosely defined by Sutherland (Robin, 1974). Robin further argued that the vagueness surrounding the definition fostered ambiguous use of the term and vague interpretations by scholars and practitioners alike. Focusing on the link between scholarship and practice, one author suggested that the concept was "totally inadequate" to characterize the kinds of behavior that are at the root of the phenomenon (Edelhertz, 1983). Further describing the reactions to this conceptual ambiguity, white-collar crime scholar David Friedrichs (2002) wrote, "perhaps no other area of criminological theory has been more plagued by conceptual confusion than that of white-collar crime" (p. 243).

Criticism about Sutherland's work also focused on the empirical ambiguity surrounding the concept. In effect, some argued that the concept only minimally reflected reality. For example, one author said that Sutherland's definition underestimated the influence of poverty on other forms of crime (Mannheim, 1949). Another author argued that by focusing on the offender (in terms of status) and the location (the workplace) rather than the offense, the concept did not accurately reflect the behaviors that needed to be addressed (Edelhertz, 1983). Edelhertz went as far as to suggest that this vague empirical conceptualization created barriers with practitioners and resulted in a lack of research on white-collar crime between the 1950s and 1970s. Shapiro (1990) also recognized the problems that the conceptualization of white-collar crime created for future researchers. She wrote:

> The concept has done its own cognitive mischief. It . . . is founded on a spurious correlation that causes sociologists to misunderstand the structural impetus for these offenses, the problems the offenses create for systems of social control, and the sources and consequences of class bias in the legal system. (p. 346)

> Describing the tendency to treat lower-class workers as white-collar offenders has been described as "improper and misleading" (Dobovsek & Slak, 2015, p. 310).

The consequences of this empirical ambiguity are such that findings from white-collar crime studies sometimes call into question the nature of white-collar offenders. One study of white-collar offenders convicted in seven federal districts between 1976 and 1978, for example, found that most offenses described as white-collar were actually "committed by those who fall in the middle classes of our society" (Weisburd, Chayet, & Waring, 1990, p. 353).

Sutherland was also criticized for methodological ambiguity. He defined white-collar crime as behaviors committed by members of the upper class, but his research focused on all sorts of offenses, including workplace theft, fraud by mechanics, deception by shoe salespersons, and crimes by corporations (see Robin, 1974). One might say that Sutherland committed a "bait and switch" in defining one type of crime, but actually researching another variety.

A fourth criticism of Sutherland's white-collar crime scholarship can be coined "legal ambiguity." Some legal scholars contended that the concept was too sociological at the expense of legal definitions of white-collar offending (Tappan, 1947). To some, white-collar crimes should be narrowly defined to include those behaviors that are criminally illegal. Some even take it a step further and suggest that white-collar criminals are those individuals convicted of white-collar crimes (suggesting that if one were not caught for a white-collar crime one actually committed, then one would not be a white-collar criminal). Sutherland, and others, have countered this argument by suggesting that conviction is irrelevant in determining whether behaviors constitute white-collar crimes (Geis, 1978). Still, the criticism that the term is too general persists.

A final criticism of the white-collar crime concept is related to the policy ambiguity surrounding the concept. In particular, some have argued that the vagueness of the definition and its purely academic focus created a disconnect between those developing policies and practices responding to white-collar crime and those studying white-collar crime (Edelhertz, 1983). Over the past decade or so, criminologists have become more vocal about the need for evidence-based practices to guide criminal justice policies and activities. In terms of white-collar crime, an issue that has been cited is that unclear definitions about white-collar crime make it extremely difficult for policymakers and practitioners to use criminological information to guide policy development and criminal justice practices. In effect, how can criminologists call for evidence-based practices for certain types of crime when they have not adequately provided the evidence needed to develop subsequent practices?

Sutherland was aware of the concerns about the concept potentially being vague. He noted that his point was not precision but to note how white-collar crime is "identical in its general characteristics with other crime rather than different from it" (Sutherland, 1941, p. 112). He wrote:

> The purpose of the concept of white-collar crime is to call attention to a vast area of criminal behavior which is generally overlooked as criminal behavior, which is seldom brought within the score of the theories of criminal behavior, and which, when included, call for modifications in the usual theories of criminal behavior. (p. 112)

Thus, Sutherland conceded that the concept was vague in nature, but it was necessarily vague in order to promote further discussion about the concept.

Sutherland was successful in promoting further discussion about the phenomenon, though the topic received very little attention in the 1950s and 1960s. This began to change in the early 1970s when criminologists Marshall Clinard and Richard Quinney published *Criminal Behavior Systems.* Building on Sutherland's work, Clinard and Quinney (1973) argued that white-collar crime can be divided into two types: corporate crime and occupational crime. They focused their definition of **corporate crime** on illegal behaviors that are committed by employees of a corporation to benefit the corporation, company, or business. In contrast, they described **occupational crime** as law violations committed at work with the aim of benefiting the employee-offender. By distinguishing between crimes by corporations and crimes against corporations, Clinard and Quinney took an important step in addressing some of the ambiguity surrounding the white-collar crime concept. Indeed, corporate crime and occupational crime are viewed as "the two principal or 'pure' forms of white-collar crime" (Friedrichs, 2002, p. 245).

After Clinard and Quinney's work, white-collar crime research by criminologists escalated in the 1970s and 1980s. Much of this research focused on ways to conceptualize and define the phenomenon in ways that addressed the criticisms surrounding Sutherland's definition. Table 2.1 shows eight different concepts and definitions that criminologists have used to describe these behaviors. Just as Sutherland's definition was criticized, each of the concepts provided in Table 2.1 is imperfect. Still, they illustrate the impact that Sutherland's white-collar crime scholarship has had on criminology and criminal justice.

A definition of white-collar crime acceptable to all groups is yet to be developed. This is troublesome for at least five reasons. First, the lack of a sound definition of white-collar crime has hindered detection efforts. Second, without a concrete definition of white-collar crime, the most effective responses to the problem cannot be gauged. Third, varying definitions among researchers have made it difficult to draw comparisons between different white-collar crime studies. Fourth, vague conceptualizations have made it more difficult to identify the causes of the behavior. Finally, varied definitions of white-collar crime have made it difficult to determine with great accuracy the true extent of white-collar crime.

● ● ● Modern Conceptualizations of White-Collar Crime

Today, criminologists and social scientists offer various ways to define white-collar crime (see Table 2.1). These variations tend to overlap with one another and include the varieties shown in Figure 2.1.

Defining *white-collar crime as moral or ethical violations* follows ideals inherent within principles of what is known as natural law. **Natural law** focuses on behaviors or activities that are defined as wrong because they violate the ethical principles of a particular culture, subculture, or group. The immoral nature of the activities is seen as the foundation for defining certain types of white-collar activities as criminal. Some individuals, for example, define any business activities that destroy animal life or plant life as immoral and unethical. To those individuals, the behaviors of individuals and businesses participating in those activities would be defined as white-collar crimes.

Some prefer to define *white-collar crime as violations of criminal law.* From this framework, white-collar crimes are criminally illegal behaviors committed by upper-class individuals during the course of their occupation. From a systems perspective, those working in the criminal justice system would likely define white-collar crime as criminally illegal behaviors. Crime, in this context, is defined as "an intentional act or omission committed in violation of the criminal law without defense or justification and sanctioned by the state as a felony or misdemeanor" (Tappan, 1960, p. 10). Applying a criminal-law definition to white-collar crime, white-collar crimes are those criminally illegal acts committed during the course of one's job. Here are a few examples:

- An accountant embezzles funds from his employer.
- Two nurses steal drugs from their workplace and sell them to addicts.
- A financial investor steals investors' money.

- A prosecutor accepts a bribe to drop criminal charges.
- Two investors share inside information that allows them to redirect their stock purchases.
- A disgruntled employee destroys the computer records of a firm upon her resignation.

These acts are instances where the criminal law has been violated during the course of employment. Accordingly, members of the criminal justice system could be called on to address those misdeeds.

Certainly, some rule breaking during the course of employment does not rise to the level of criminal behavior, but it may violate civil laws. Consequently, some may define *white-collar crime as **violations of civil law**.* Consider cases of corporate wrongdoing against consumers. In those situations, it is rare that the criminal law would be used to respond to

Table 2.1	Evolution of the White-Collar Crime Concept	
Concept	Definition	Reference
Criminaloid	The immunity enjoyed by the perpetrator of new sins has brought into being a class for which we may coin the term *criminaloid*. By this we designate such as prosper by flagitious practices that have not yet come under the effective ban of public opinion. Often, indeed, they are guilty in the eyes of the law; but since they are not culpable in the eyes of the public and in their own eyes, their spiritual attitude is not that of the criminal. The lawmaker may make their misdeeds crimes, but, so long as morality stands stock-still in the old tracks, they escape both punishment and ignominy.	E. A. Ross (*Sin and Society*, 1907, p. 48)
White-collar crime	Crime committed by a person of respectability and high social status in the course of his occupation.	Sutherland (1949, p. 9)
Corporate crime	Offenses committed by corporate officials for their corporation and the offenses of the corporation itself.	Clinard and Yeager (1980, p. 189)
Occupational crime	Offenses committed by individuals in the course of their occupations and the offenses of employees against their employers.	Clinard and Yeager (1980, p. 189).
Organizational deviance	Actions contrary to norms maintained by others outside the organization . . . [but] supported by the internal operating norms of the organization.	Ermann and Lundman (1978, p. 7)
Elite deviance	Acts committed by persons from the highest strata of society . . . some of the acts are crimes . . . may be criminal or noncriminal in nature.	Simon (2006, p. 12)
Organizational crime	Illegal acts of omission or commission of an individual or a group of individuals in a formal organization in accordance with the operative goals of the organization, which have serious physical or economic impact on employees, consumers, or the general public.	Schrager and Short, (1978, p. 408)
Occupational crime	Any act punishable by law which is committed through opportunity created in the course of an occupation that is legitimate.	Green (1990)

the offending corporation. More often, cases are brought into the civil justice system. When the *Exxon Valdez* ran aground in Prince William Sound, Alaska, and caused untold damage to the environment, for example, the case was brought into the civil justice system. Eventually, it was learned that the cause of the crash could be attributed to the ship's overworked crew. To date, Exxon has paid $2 billion in cleanup efforts and another $1 billion in fines. Ongoing legal battles are focusing on whether Exxon should pay even more in damages.

Individuals have also defined *white-collar crime as violations of regulatory laws.* Some workplace misdeeds might not violate criminal or civil laws, but may violate a particular occupation's regulatory laws. Most occupations and businesses have standards, procedures, and regulations that are designed to administratively guide and direct workplace activities. The nursing home industry provides a good example. The government has developed a set of standards that nursing home administrators are expected to follow in providing care to nursing home residents. At different times during the year, government officials inspect nursing homes to see if they are abiding by the regulations. In most instances, some form of wrongdoing is uncovered. These instances of wrongdoing, however, are not violations of criminal law or civil law; rather, they are violations of regulatory law. Hence, some authors focus on white-collar crimes as violations of regulatory laws.

Sometimes, behaviors performed as part of an occupational routine might be wrong but not necessarily illegal by criminal, civil, or regulatory definitions. As a result, some prefer to follow definitions of *white-collar crime* as *workplace deviance*. This is a broader way to define white-collar crime, and such an approach would include all of those workplace acts that violate the norms or standards of the workplace, regardless of whether they are formally defined as illegal or not. Violations of criminal, civil, and regulatory laws would be included, as would those violations that are set by the workplace itself. Beyond those formal violations of the law, consider the following situations as examples of workplace deviance:

- Professors cancel class simply because they don't feel like going to class.
- A worker takes a 30-minute break when she was only supposed to take a 15-minute break.
- A worker calls his boss and says he is too sick to come to work when in fact he is not actually sick (but he uses that "fake sick voice" as part of his ploy).
- A wedding photographer gets drunk at a client's wedding, takes horrible pictures, and hits on the groom.
- An author uses silly examples to try to get his point across.

In each of these cases, no laws have necessarily been broken; however, one could argue that workplace or occupational norms may have been violated.

Somewhat related, one can also define *white-collar crime* as *definitions socially constructed by businesses*. What this means is that a particular company or business might define behaviors that it believes to be improper. What is wrong in one company might not necessarily be wrong in another company. Some businesses might have formal dress codes while others might have casual Fridays. Some companies might tolerate workers taking small quantities of the goods it produces home each night, while other companies might define that behavior as inappropriate and criminal. The expectations for workplace behavior, then, are defined by the workplace. Incidentally, some experts have suggested that expectations be defined in such a way as to accept at least minor forms of wrongdoing (see Mars, 1983, for a description of the rewards individuals perceive from workplace misconduct). The basis for this suggestion is that individuals are more satisfied with their jobs if they are able to break the rules of their job at least every now and then. As a simple example, where would you rather work: (1) in a workplace that lets you get away with longer breaks every now and then or (2) in a workplace where you are docked double pay for every minute you take over the allotted break?

In some cases, workplace behaviors might not be illegal or deviant, but they might actually create forms of harm for various individuals. As a result, some prefer to define *white-collar crime* as *social harm*. Those defining white-collar crime from this perspective are more concerned with the harm done by occupational activities than whether behavior is defined either formally or informally as illegal or deviant. According to one author, "by concentrating on what is defined as illegal or criminal, a more serious threat to society is left out" (Passas, 2005, p. 771). Galbraith (2005, p. 731) offers the following examples: "The common practices of tobacco companies, hog farmers, gun makers and merchants are legal. But this is only because of the political nature of the perpetrators; in a democracy free of their money and influence, they would be crimes." Additional examples of white-collar crimes that are examples of this social harm perspective have been noted by

Passas (2005), who highlighted the following "crimes" that occur without lawbreaking occurring: cross-border malpractices, asymmetrical environmental regulations, corrupt practices, child labor in impoverished communities, and pharmaceutical practices such as those allowing testing of drugs in third world countries. Passas emphasized that lawbreaking does not occur when these actions are performed but argues the actions are, in fact, criminal.

Another way to define these behaviors is to consider *white-collar crime* as **research definitions**. When researchers study and gather data about white-collar crime, they must operationalize or define white-collar crime in a way that allows them to reliably and validly measure the behavior. As an example, in 2005, the National White-Collar Crime Center conducted its second national survey on white-collar crime. The results of this survey will be discussed later. For now, the way that the researchers defined white-collar crime illustrates what is meant by research-generated white-collar crime definitions. The researchers defined white-collar crime as "illegal or unethical acts that violate fiduciary responsibility or public trust for personal or organizational gain" (Kane & Wall, 2006, p. 1). Using this definition as their foundation, the researchers were able to conduct a study that measured the characteristics of white-collar crime, its consequences, and contributing factors. Note that had they chosen a different definition, their results might have been different. The way that we define phenomena will influence the observations we make about those phenomena.

Another way to define these behaviors is to consider *white-collar crime* as **official government definitions**. Government agencies and employees of those agencies will have definitions of white-collar crime that may or may not parallel the way others define white-collar crime. The Federal Bureau of Investigation (FBI), for example, has used an offense-based perspective to define white-collar crime as part of its Uniform Crime Reporting Program. The FBI defines white-collar crime as

> those illegal acts which are characterized by deceit, concealment, or violation of trust and which are not dependent upon the application or threat of physical force or violence. Individuals and organizations commit these acts to obtain money, property, or services to avoid payment or loss of money or services; or to secure personal or business advantage. (U.S. Department of Justice, 1989, p. 3, as cited in Barnett, n.d.)

In following this definition, the FBI tends to take a broader definition of white-collar crime than many white-collar crime scholars and researchers do. *Identity theft* offers a case in point. The FBI includes identity theft as a white-collar crime type. Some academics, however, believe that such a classification is inappropriate. One research team conducted interviews with 59 convicted identity thieves and found that offenses and offenders did not meet the traditional characteristics of white-collar crimes or white-collar offenders. Many offenders were unemployed and working independently, meaning their offenses were not committed as part of a legitimate occupation or in the course of their occupation (Copes & Vieraitis, 2009).

Another way to define white-collar crime is to focus on *white-collar crime* as **violations of trust** that occur during the course of legitimate employment. To some authors, offenders use their positions of trust to promote the misconduct (Reiss & Biderman, 1980). Criminologist Susan Shapiro (1990) has argued for the need to view white-collar crime as abuses of trust, and she suggests that researchers should focus on the *act* rather than the *actor*. She wrote:

> Offenders clothed in very different wardrobes lie, steal, falsify, fabricate, exaggerate, omit, deceive, dissemble, shirk, embezzle, misappropriate, self-deal, and engage in corruption or incompliance by misusing their positions of trust. It turns out most of them are not upper class. (p. 358)

In effect, Shapiro was calling for a broader definition of white-collar crime that was not limited to the collars of the offenders' shirts.

Others have also called for broader conceptualizations that are not limited to wardrobes or occupational statuses. Following Clinard and Quinney's 1973 conceptualization, some have suggested that these behaviors be classified as *white-collar crimes* as occupational crimes. One author defines occupational crimes as "violations that occur during the course of occupational activity and are related to employment" (Robin, 1974). Robin argued vehemently for the broader conceptualization of white-collar crime. He noted that various forms of lower-class workplace offenses "are more similar to white-collar crime methodologically than behaviorally," suggesting that many occupational offenders tend to use

Figure 2.1   Defining White-Collar Crime

the same methods to commit their transgressions. He further stated that the failure of scholars to broadly conceive white-collar crime "results in underestimating the amount of crime, distorts relative frequencies of the typology of crimes, produces a biased profile of the personal and social characteristics of the violators, and thus affects our theory of criminality" (p. 261).

Criminologist Gary Green (1990) has been a strong advocate of focusing on occupational crime rather than a limited conceptualization of white-collar crime. He defined occupational crime as "any act punishable by law which is committed through opportunity created in the course of an occupation that is legal" (p. 13). Green described four varieties of occupational crime: (1) organizational occupational crimes, which include crimes by corporations; (2) state authority occupational crimes, which include crimes by governments; (3) professional occupational crimes, which

Table 2.2	Arrests Reported in *UCR* for Three "White-Collar" Offenses, 1990–2014		
Year	Forgery/Counterfeiting	Embezzlement	Fraud
1990	50,403	7,708	182,752
1991	53,853	7,458	188,100
1992	66,608	8,860	279,682
1993	69,063	8,886	246,127
1994	71,322	9,155	233,234
1995	84,068	10,832	295,584
1996	81,319	11,763	248,370
1997	77,773	10,935	298,713
1998	70,678	10,585	220,262
1999	56,813	9,692	166,413
2000	58,493	10,730	155,231
2001	77,692	13,836	211,177
2002	83,111	13,416	233,087
2003	79,188	11,986	208,469
2004	73,082	9,164	235,412
2005	87,346	14,097	231,721
2006	79,477	14,769	197,722
2007	78,005	17,015	185,229
2008	68,976	16,458	174,598
2009	85,844	17,920	210,255
2010	78,101	16,616	187,887
2011	70,211	16,190	168,217
2012	60,969	15,730	143,528
2013	67,046	16,023	153,535
2014	56,783	16,227	141,293

Source: Reprinted from FBI

include those crimes by individuals in upper-class jobs; and (4) individual occupational crimes, which include those crimes committed by individuals in lower-class jobs. The strength of his conceptualization is that it expands white-collar crime to consider all forms of misdeeds committed by employees and businesses during the course of employment.

Using each of the above definitions as a framework, white-collar crime can also be defined as *violations occurring in occupational systems*. This text uses such a framework to provide a broad systems perspective about white-collar crime. White-collar crime can therefore be defined as "any violation of criminal, civil, or regulatory laws—or deviant, harmful, or unethical actions—committed during the course of employment in various occupational systems." This definition allows us to consider numerous types of workplace misconduct and the interactions between these behaviors and broader systems involved in preventing and responding to white-collar crimes. As will be shown in the following paragraphs, the extent of these crimes is enormous.

● ● ● Extent of White-Collar Crime

Determining the extent of white-collar crime is no simple task. Two factors make it particularly difficult to accurately determine how often white-collar crimes occur. First, many white-collar crimes are not reported to formal response agencies. One study found that just one third of white-collar crime victims notify the authorities about their victimization (Kane & Wall, 2006). When individuals are victims of white-collar crimes, they may not report the victimization because of shame, concerns that reporting will be futile, or a general denial that the victimization was actually criminal. When businesses or companies are victims, they may refrain from reporting out of concern about the negative publicity that comes along with "being duped" by an employee. If victims are not willing to report their victimization, their victimization experiences will not be included in official statistics. The bottom line is that a lack of data has made it hard to determine the extent of white-collar crime (Simpson, 2013).

A second factor that makes it difficult to determine the extent of white-collar crime has to do with the conceptual ambiguity surrounding the concept (and discussed above). Depending on how one defines white-collar crime, one would find different estimates about the extent of white-collar crime. The federal government and other government agencies offer different definitions of white-collar crime than many scholars and researchers might use. The result is that white-collar crime researchers typically caution against relying on official statistics or **victimization surveys** to determine the extent of white-collar crime victimization. Despite this caution, the three main ways that we learn about the extent of white-collar crime are from official statistics provided by government agencies, victimization surveys, and research studies focusing on specific types of white-collar crime.

With regard to official statistics and white-collar crime, the FBI's *Uniform Crime Reports (UCR)* and National Incident Based Reporting System (NIBRS) provide at least a starting point from which we can begin to question how often certain forms of white-collar crime occur. These data reflect crimes known to the police. The *UCRs* include eight Part I, or index, offenses (homicide, robbery, rape, aggravated assault, motor vehicle theft, larceny, arson, and burglary) and 29 Part II offenses, which are typically defined as *less serious* crimes. With regard to white-collar crime, Part II offenses have been regarded as possible white-collar crimes. Table 2.2 shows the number of times these crimes occurred between 1990 and 2014. As shown in the table, the number of forgery or counterfeiting and embezzlement cases increased somewhat dramatically between 1990 and 2009, but each type has declined some since 2009. The number of forgery and embezzlement cases was still higher in 2014 than in 1990.

A word of caution is needed in reviewing these estimates. Not all criminologists agree that these offenses are appropriate indicators of white-collar crimes. Many of these offenses may have occurred outside the scope of employment. Also, because the UCR Program does not capture information about offender status, it is not possible to classify the crimes according to the occupational systems where the offenses occurred.

Limitations in the UCR Program prompted the federal government to expand its efforts in reporting crime data through the National Incident Based Reporting System (NIBRS). NIBRS data provide more contextual information surrounding the crimes reported to the police. For example, this reporting system provides information about where the crime occurred, the victim-offender relationship, victim characteristics, and so on. While more contextual information is provided from NIBRS data, the same limitations that plague the UCR data with regard to the measurement of white-collar crime surface: (1) Not everyone would agree these are white-collar crimes, (2) the database was created for law enforcement and not for researchers, (3) many cases are reported to regulatory agencies rather than law enforcement, (4) some white-collar crime victims are unaware of their victimization, and (5) shame may keep some victims from reporting their victimization (Barnett, n.d.). Also, the NIBRS data are not as "user friendly" as UCR data at this point.

Simpson and Yeager (2015) proposed a data series that would publish information about white-collar crimes handled by various federal agencies. The primary purpose of such a series would be to assist in policy development and research on the topic. The types of data included in the series should include information about criminal and civil offenses, offenders, and case outcomes from those agencies addressing the cases. After piloting their ideas through a grant from the National Institute of Justice, the authors recommended developing a working group that would be assigned the task of creating the processes needed for a white-collar crime database, developing a memorandum of understanding between those agencies currently holding the data on the offenses, and initiating an incremental approach to develop the database. Such an approach is needed because relying on official government data currently produces a limited view of white-collar crime. Said one author, "Reproducing FBI property crime rates from the 1990s to the present without noting the Savings and Loan looting, Enron era scams and the latest episode of barely contained looting is tantamount to propaganda" (Leighton, 2013, p. 45).

Victimization surveys offer an opportunity to overcome some of these problems. These surveys sample residents and estimate the extent of victimization from the survey findings. The 2010 National White-Collar Crime Center (NW3C) victimization survey is the most recent, and most comprehensive, white-collar crime victimization survey available. The results of this survey, a phone interview with 2,503 adults in the United States, show that 24 percent of households and 17 percent of individuals reported experiencing forms of white-collar crime in the prior year (Huff et al., 2010).

Table 2.3 shows the types of victimization reported by respondents in the NW3C victimization survey (Huff et al., 2010). As shown in the table, nearly 40 percent of the respondents experienced credit card fraud, and more than a fourth indicated that they had been lied to about prices in the prior year, and one-fourth reported being victims of credit card fraud. Also, about one-fifth reported being victimized by unnecessary object repairs and corporate scandals.

The NW3C interviewers also asked victims about their decisions to report their victimization to various agencies. Table 2.4 shows the formal agencies that respondents reported their victimization to (among those who did report the victimization). As shown in the table, respondents tended to report their victimization to either their credit card company or the entity involved. Perhaps most interesting is how infrequently respondents reported their victimization to formal governmental agencies of social control. Less than one-fifth of respondents reported their victimization to the police.

Researchers have also used specific studies to gauge the extent of various forms of white-collar crime. One author, for example, cites a study by the Government Accountability Office that found fraud in "every single case" of the savings and loan institutions included in the study (Galbraith, 2005). Another study found that one in 30 employees (out of 2.1 million employees) was caught stealing from his or her employer in 2007 ("Record Number of Shoplifters," 2008). A Federal Trade Commission (FTC) survey of 3,638 adults in the United States found that consumer fraud was rampant (Anderson, 2013). Based on the survey findings, Anderson estimates that "an estimated 10.8 percent of U.S. adults—25.6 million people—were victims of one or more of the frauds included in the 2011 FTC Consumer Fraud Survey"" (p. ES-1). The most popular form of victimization that year was purchasing fraudulent weight loss products. It was estimated that 5 million individuals experienced this victimization. Anderson further estimated that nearly 38 million cases of consumer fraud occurred in 2011.

Figure 2.2 shows the extent of the types of consumer fraud considered in the most recent FTC survey. As shown in the figure, the most common frauds were paying for items never received and purchasing

▲ **Photo 2.1**   The FDA monitors dietary supplements in an effort to limit the distribution of unsafe or ineffective products. Here an FDA scientist is showing products seized after being illegally imported into the U.S. Millions of victims report purchasing ineffective weight loss products.

FDA photo by Michael J. Ermarth

WHITE-COLLAR CRIME IN THE NEWS

FTC Announces Consumer Protection Week

Wikimedia Commons.

Consumer advocates such as Ralph Nader (pictured) engage in various efforts to increase awareness about consumer protection. In recent times, the FTC has joined others to celebrate National Consumer Protection Week.

The Federal Trade Commission, in collaboration with 74 federal, state and local agencies, consumer groups, and national organizations, celebrates National Consumer Protection Week, beginning Sunday, March 2, and running until Saturday, March 8.

Now in its 16th year, NCPW encourages American consumers to learn about their rights in the marketplace and to recognize and report scams, identity theft, and unfair business practices. Visitors to NCPW.gov can find information about a range of consumer topics, including managing credit and debt, staying safe online, stopping telemarketing calls, and the latest scam alerts.

"As our NCPW partnerships and outreach continue to grow, we encourage consumers to participate in their communities too," said Jessica Rich, director, FTC's Bureau of Consumer Protection. "Consumers can help by checking out our toolkit from the NCPW site, and sharing the materials with family and friends to help people be more informed."

NCPW partners and hundreds of community groups across the country host events to promote general consumer education or highlight a specific issue, such as a shred-a-thon to reduce the risk of identity theft.

Source: Reprinted from FTC

credit card insurance. Note that these are only estimates about the extent of victimization. Accurately determining the extent of white-collar crime remains a difficult task. In an effort to generate more consumer awareness about these offenses, the Federal Trade Commission recognizes National Consumer Protection Week each year. The White-Collar Crime in the News: FTC Announces Consumer Protection Week box above shows a recent press release describing the event.

Thus far, the extent of white-collar crime in the United States has been considered. To be sure, white-collar crime occurs across the globe. The 2014 PricewaterhouseCoopers Global Economic Crime Survey surveyed 5,128 business representatives from 95 countries across the world. Asking about whether their business experienced fraud, the survey found that 37 percent of the businesses reported experiencing fraud. Nearly one-fifth of the businesses experiencing fraud reported losses between $1,000,000 and $100,000,000. Two percent of the victimized businesses reported losses in excess of $100,000,000. There is some indication that the amount of fraud occurring (or at least reported) varied across the globe. The amount of fraud reported in various regions was the following:

- Africa—50 percent
- North America—41 percent
- Eastern Europe—39 percent
- Latin America—35 percent
- Western Europe—35 percent

- Asia Pacific—32 percent
- Middle East—21 percent (PricewaterhouseCoopers, 2015).

While it is difficult to gauge the extent of white-collar crime, all indications are that these offenses occur with great regularity. The regularity of these offenses exacerbates their consequences.

Table 2.3 Household Victimization Trends (12 months)	
False stockbroker info	7.6%
Fraudulent business venture	9.7%
Mortgage fraud	4.3%
Unnecessary repair	22.3%
Monetary loss (Internet)	15.8%
Affected by national corporate scandal	21.4%
Credit card fraud	39.6%
Price misrepresentation	28.1%

Source: Adapted from Huff, R., Desilets, C., & Kane, J. (2010). *The national public survey on white collar crime.* Fairmont, WV: National White Collar Crime Center. Retrieved from http://www.fraudaid.com/library/2010-national-public-survey-on-white-collar-crime.pdf

Table 2.4 Agencies Receiving Victimization Complaints from Victims	
Internet crime complaint center	.4%
Consumer protection agency	.8%
Personal lawyer	.6%
District attorney or state attorney general	1.3%
Better Business Bureau	5.1%
Police or law enforcement	18.8%
Perpetrating business or person	14.8%
Other	11%
Credit card company	30.9%
Banks	15.6%
Credit bureau	.6%

Source: Adapted from Huff, R., Desilets, C., & Kane, J. (2010). *The national public survey on white collar crime.* Fairmont, WV: National White Collar Crime Center. Retrieved from http://www.fraudaid.com/library/2010-national-public-survey-on-white-collar-crime.pdf

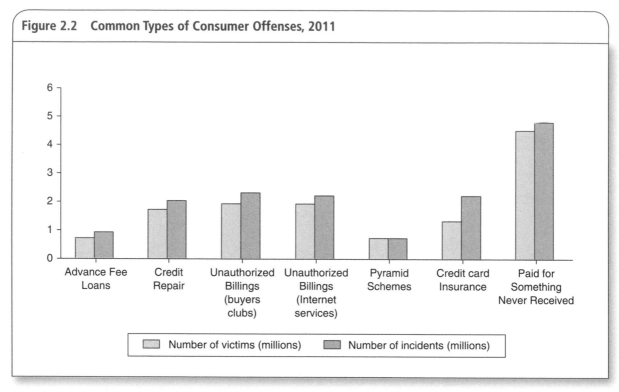

Figure 2.2   Common Types of Consumer Offenses, 2011

Legend: Number of victims (millions) ■ Number of incidents (millions)

Source: Anderson, K. B. (2013, April). *Consumer fraud in the United States: The third FTC survey.* Washington, DC: Government Printing Office. Retrieved from https://www.ftc.gov/sites/default/files/documents/reports/consumer-fraud-united-states-2011-third-ftc-survey/130419fraudsurvey_0.pdf

● ● ● Consequences of White-Collar Crime

Crime, by its very nature, has consequences for individuals and communities. White-collar crime, in particular, has a set of consequences that may be significantly different from the kinds of consequences that arise from street crimes. In particular, the consequences can be characterized as (1) individual economic losses, (2) societal economic losses, (3) emotional consequences, (4) physical harm, and (5) "positive" consequences.

Individual economic losses refer to the losses that individual victims or business experience due to white-collar crimes. One way that criminologists have captured these losses is to compare them to losses experienced by victims of conventional crimes. A study of 554 major embezzlement cases active in 2013 found that the average loss was approximately $1.1 million per case (Marquet, 2014).

By comparison, consider the following:

- The average street or highway robbery entails losses of $871
- The average gas station robbery entails losses of $1,026
- The average convenience store robbery entails losses of $699 (Federal Bureau of Investigation, 2015b)

It is important to note that a small group of offenders can create large dollar losses. One study found that 27 white-collar offenders were responsible for dollar losses in the amount of $2,494,309 (Crofts, 2003). Each offender stole an average of $95,935. Other studies have also found large dollar losses as a central feature of white-collar crimes (Wheeler et al., 1988). In fact, Sutherland (1949) argued that white-collar crimes cost several times more than street crimes in terms of financial losses. While his estimate may be a little dated, the fact remains that a white-collar crime will likely cause larger dollar losses to victims than a street crime would.

Societal economic losses entail the total amount of losses incurred by society from white-collar crime. Kane and Wall (2006) cite estimates suggesting that white-collar crime costs the United States between 300 and 600 billion dollars a year in financial losses. These costs are increased when considering the secondary societal economic costs such as business failures and recovery costs. In terms of business failures, one estimate suggests that one third to one half of business failures are attributed to employee theft (National White Collar Crime Center, 2009). With regard to recovery costs, taxpayers pay billions of dollars to support the efforts of the criminal, civil, and regulatory justice systems. As an illustration of how these costs can quickly add up, one white-collar criminal involved in a $7 million Ponzi scheme eventually lost everything and was unable to

▲ **Photo 2.2**   In the aftermath of the *Exxon Valdez* grounding, workers worked tirelessly to eradicate harmful effects of the white-collar offense. Researchers have not yet been able to identify the full extent of the consequences of this disaster.

afford his own attorney. In this case, the federal public defender's office was assigned the task of representing the accused (Henning, 2010). Attorney costs in white-collar crime cases are believed to be particularly exorbitant.

Emotional consequences are also experienced by victims of white-collar crime and by all members of society exposed to this misconduct. These emotional consequences include stress from victimization, violation of trust, and damage to public morale. With regard to stress, any experience of victimization is stressful, but the experience of white-collar crime victimization is believed to be particularly stressful. Much of the stress stems from the violation of trust that comes along with white-collar crimes.

According to Sutherland (1941), the violation of trust can be defined as the "most general" characteristic of white-collar crime. Victims of a street robbery didn't trust the stranger who robbed them in the first place. Victims of a white-collar crime, in addition to the other losses incurred from the victimization, have their trust violated by the offender. There is reason to believe that the level of trust may be tied to the specific level of trust given to different types of white-collar offenders (e.g., we trust doctors and pharmacists at a certain level but auto mechanics on another level).

Researchers have used various strategies to consider how these trust violations manifest in white-collar crimes. Spalek (2001) interviewed 25 individuals who lost some of their pension funds to a fraudulent scheme by Robert Maxwell. She focused on the degree to which victimization bred distrust. She found that many of the victims already distrusted their offender before the victimization came to light. The victims said that they felt forced or coerced into trusting the offender as part of his investment scheme. In terms of trust, they placed their trust in outside agencies to protect them from the offender. The following comments from Spalek's (2001) participants highlight this pattern:

- I've always mistrusted Maxwell. But I felt that because pensioners were, to a large extent, the province of the state . . . that there was very little Maxwell could do to make off with the money.
- I suppose at the time I actually thought that the law would actually safeguard against anything that was mine so I wasn't too worried about it, although I thought that Maxwell would do his best to get his hands on the money.

With regard to public alienation, violations of trust potentially do damage to the economy and social relationships. According to Frankel (2006), "with few exceptions, trust is essential to economic prosperity" (p. 49). If individuals do not trust financial institutions, they are not likely to invest their funds in the economy. Sutherland (1941) recognized this relationship between trust, the economy, and social relationships. He wrote:

The financial loss from white-collar crime, great as it is, is less important than the damage to social relations. White-collar crime violates trust and therefore creates distrust; this lowers social morale and produces disorganization. Many white-collar crimes attack the fundamental principles of the American institutions. Ordinary crimes, on the other hand, produce little effect on social institutions or social organization. (p. 13)

Building on Sutherland's ideas, Moore and Mills (1990) described the following consequences of white-collar crime:

- Diminished faith in a free economy and in business leaders
- Erosion of public morality
- Loss of confidence in political institutions, processes, and leaders (p. 414)

Criminologist Michael Lynch (2013) provided an impassioned plea for recognizing these serious consequences. He wrote the following:

Societies do not collapse because of the behavior of street offenders, but rather in many cases because the power elite and the capitalist system of exploitation in which they are enmeshed, lead us in the wrong direction. The financial crimes of the power elite and the inability of other segments of the power elite to control those crimes presents a serious example of how it becomes possible for the power elite to undermine the very basis of social organization, and, indeed, even undermine the social organization on which their system depends. (p. 58)

Physical harm may also result from white-collar crime victimization. In the words of one author, "white-collar crime can easily lead to violent results" (Verstein, 2014, np). Sometimes, physical harm may be a direct result of the white-collar offense. For example, cases of physical or sexual patient abuse will result in physical harm for victims. Other times, experiencing financial harm can lead to physical problems. The loss of one's entire retirement savings, for example, has been found to contribute to health problems for white-collar crime victims (Payne, 2005).

Death or serious physical injury is also a possible consequence of white-collar crimes. In one case, for instance, seven people died after a doctor "used lemon juice instead of antiseptic on patients' operation wounds" (Ninemsn Staff, 2010). In another case, Reinaldo Silvestre was running a medical clinic in Miami Beach when it was discovered that he was practicing without a license, using animal tranquilizers as sedatives for humans, and performing botched surgeries. In a widely publicized case, a male body builder was given female C-cup breast implants—he had requested pectoral implants to make his chest look bigger ("Fugitive Phony Doctor Nabbed," 2004).

US Government Work

▲ **Photo 2.3**   The FDA warned consumers not to use certain types of skin cream after mercury was found in various types of ointments in seven different states.

It is possible to more generally highlight the physical harm stemming from white-collar crime. Consider the following estimates:

- According to the Consumer Product Safety Commission, more than 37,000 deaths were related to consumer products between October 2009 and September 2010. There were an additional 38.3 million injuries requiring medical care from unsafe products (U.S. Consumer Product Safety Commission, 2013).
- It has been estimated that between 12,000 and 15,000 individuals died each year in the U.S. between 1999 and 2013 from asbestos exposure (Lunder, 2015).

- Approximately 7.5 million unnecessary surgeries result in 12,000 deaths each year (Black, 2005).
- Estimates from the World Health Organization suggest that more than 7,000,000 individuals die each year from air pollution (Kuehn, 2014).
- Consumer advocate Ralph Nader (2013) cites estimates suggesting that 60,000 Americans die each year from unsafe working conditions.

In line with the objective approach presented in Chapter I, it is important to stress that not all consequences of white-collar crime are necessarily bad. Sociologist Emile Durkheim has highlighted four functions of crime that illustrate how crime in some ways has positive influences on individuals and communities (see Martin et al., 2009). These four functions can also be applied to white-collar crime. They include warning light syndrome, boundary maintenance, social change, and community integration.

The **warning light syndrome** refers to the fact that outbreaks of white-collar crime could potentially send a message to individuals, businesses, or communities that something is wrong in a particular workplace system. If an outbreak of employee theft occurs in a hospital, for example, then the administrators would be warned that they need to address those aspects of the occupational routines that allowed the misconduct to occur.

In terms of **boundary maintenance**, it is plausible to suggest that individuals learn the rules of the workplace when some individuals are caught breaking those rules. In effect, they learn the boundaries of appropriate and acceptable behaviors by seeing some individuals step over those boundaries. Some even recommend that white-collar offenders, when caught, be arrested at times when the vast majority of workers would be able to see the arrests (Payne & Gray, 2001). What this is suggesting is a strategy for promoting boundary maintenance.

US Government Work

▲ **Photo 2.4** "Unsafe products cause millions of injuries each year. Dolls and other children's toys are among those products most often implicated in these injuries."

With regard to **social change**, our society has changed significantly because of white-collar misdeeds. Some people have talked about how survivors of violent crime actually become stronger because of their experience with violence. Following this same line of thinking, those who survive white-collar crime victimization might actually become stronger. As well, when cultures and societies survive corporate victimization, they too may actually grow stronger.

Community integration is a fourth function of white-collar crime. In particular, groups of individuals who otherwise would not have become acquainted with one another may come together in their response to white-collar crime. When there is a crime outbreak in a neighborhood, those neighbors come together to share their experiences and make their neighborhood stronger (Martin et al., 2009). A crime outbreak in a business could have the same result. Coworkers who never talked with one another might suddenly become lunch buddies simply because they want to get together to talk about the crimes that occurred in their workplace. As well, at the societal level, new groups have been formed to prevent and respond to white-collar crime.

Consider the National White-Collar Crime Center (NW3C). Formed in 1992, the center includes professionals, academics, and researchers interested in addressing white-collar crime on different levels. The NW3C's mission is "to provide training, investigative support, and research to agencies and entities involved in the prevention, investigation, and prosecution of economic and high tech crime" (National White Collar Crime Center, 2009). Without the problem of white-collar crime, this center would never have been created and its members would never have been brought together (or integrated as a community).

Other possible positive consequences of white-collar crime can be cited. For example, some criminologists have noted that occasional forms of deviance might be enjoyable or pleasurable to commit. The 2010 Conan O'Brien–Jay Leno debacle comes to mind. It was announced in January 2010 that O'Brien was to be replaced by Leno after he had been promised a long-term contract to host *The Tonight Show*. In the last several episodes of his National Broadcasting Company (NBC) show, O'Brien spent much of his show trashing his bosses at NBC. He even had skits suggesting that he was blowing NBC's money on pointless props for his show. The studio and home audiences raved about these skits. Who wouldn't want to go on national television every now and then and blow their company's money while trashing their bosses? (For the record, the thought never entered my mind.) In a similar way, some cases of workplace deviance might have the positive benefit of making the worker a more satisfied worker (see Mars, 1983). Authors have talked about "the joy of violence" (Kerbs & Jolley, 2007). In some ways, there might also be "the joy of white-collar deviance."

For some students, the numerous careers available to respond to white-collar crime might also be seen as a positive. Most large businesses have human resource specialists who deal with workplace misconduct (see Careers Responding to White-Collar Crime: Human Resource Specialist). Whenever I teach my criminal justice classes, I always ask my students if they would make crime go away if they could. Seldom do any students indicate that they would make crime disappear. In their minds, if they made crime disappear, they'd have to change their majors! So, in some ways, white-collar crime helps keep some criminal justice officials employed. A few of these careers can be particularly lucrative—one defense attorney was paid $50,000 simply for providing counsel to a white-collar worker who had to testify in a grand jury proceeding (Nelson, 2010).

Of course, this brief overview of the "functions of white-collar crime" should not be interpreted as an endorsement of white-collar criminal behavior. In fact, the seriousness of many white-collar crimes means that the offenses cannot be taken lightly. The question that arises is whether members of the public view the offenses seriously.

CAREERS RESPONDING TO WHITE-COLLAR CRIME

Human Resource Specialist

The duties of the position include:

- Provide HR management advisory and technical services on complex and wide-ranging management/employee relations functions and work practices.
- Advise managers appropriate disciplinary and other corrective techniques responsive to a range of conduct and performance issues.
- Resolve disputed actions and interpret facts, events, and/or identifying aggravating or mitigating factors relevant to the case.

- Explain rules and procedures to employees and help them understand their rights and obligations.
- Maintain and encourage objectivity in situations that may be charged with emotion and involve assumptions.
- Conduct extensive probing and analysis to identify obscure or underlying causes of misconduct or poor performance.

Source: Reprinted from USAJobs.Gov

● ● ● Public Attitudes Toward White-Collar Crime

A large body of criminological research has focused on public attitudes about crime and different crime policies. Unfortunately, of the hundreds of criminological studies focusing on attitudes about crime, only a handful have focused on what the public thinks about white-collar crime. Yet research on white-collar crime attitudes is important for empirical, cultural, and policy-driven reasons (Piquero, Carmichael, & Piquero, 2008). In terms of empirical reasons, because so few studies have considered what the public thinks about white-collar crime, research on this topic will shed some light on how members of the public actually perceive this offense type. As well, such research will provide interesting and important insight into a particular culture or subculture. Perhaps most important, such research provides policymakers information they can use to implement prevention, response, and sentencing strategies.

In one of the first studies on public attitudes toward white-collar crime, Cullen and his colleagues (Cullen, Clark, Mathers, & Cullen, 1983) surveyed a sample of 240 adults and assessed various perceptions of this behavior. The researchers found that the sample (1) supported criminal sanctions for white-collar offenders, (2) viewed white-collar crimes as having greater moral and economic costs than street crimes, and (3) did not define the offenses as violent. In a separate study, Cullen, Link, and Polanzi (1982) found that perceptions of the seriousness of white-collar crime increased more than any other offense type in the 1970s and that physically harmful offenses were viewed as the most serious forms of white-collar crime (see Cullen et al., 1982).

Other studies have shown similar results. A study of 268 students found that perceptions of the seriousness of white-collar crime have increased over time and that these perceptions were tied to wrongfulness and harmfulness (Rosenmerkel, 2001). The NW3C national victimization survey also included items assessing perceptions of seriousness. The researchers found that the sample of 1,605 adults viewed (1) white-collar crime as serious as conventional crime, (2) physically harmful white-collar offenses as more serious than other white-collar crimes, (3) organizational offenses as more serious than individual offenses, and (4) offenses by higher-status offenders as more serious than offenses by lower-status offenders (Kane & Wall, 2006).

More recent research has built on these findings. A telephone survey of 402 residents of the United States focused on perceptions about white-collar crime and the punishment of white-collar offenders (Holtfreter, Van Slyke, Bratton, & Gertz, 2008). The authors found that one-third of the respondents said that white-collar offenders should be punished more severely than street criminals. They also found that two-thirds of the respondents believed that the government should "devote equal or more resources towards white-collar crime control" (p. 56).

Around the same time, telephone interviews with 1,169 respondents found that the majority of respondents defined white-collar crime equally serious as, if not more serious than, street crime (Piquero, Carmichael et al., 2008). They also found that the presence of a college education impacted perceptions of seriousness. Those with a college education were more likely to define street crime and white-collar crime as equally serious. Another study using the same data set found that respondents believed that street criminals were more likely than other white-collar offenders to be caught and to receive stiffer sentences (Schoepfer, Carmichael, & Piquero, 2007). Respondents also believed that robbery and fraud should be treated similarly. Another way to suggest this is that the respondents believed that robbers and occupational offenders committing fraud should be handled the same way. A more recent study found that respondents perceived Ponzi schemes and embezzlement as more serious than street crimes, such as burglary and prostitution (Dodge, Bosick, & Van Antwerp, 2013). Describing these findings, the authors suggested that the "general public might be willing to support devoting greater resources to fighting white-collar crime" (p. 412).

It is believed that the media play a strong role in shaping our attitudes about white-collar crime. More so than in the past, social media is likely beginning to play an important role in generating understanding about white-collar offending, and all types

▲ **Photo 2.5**   After his dispute with NBC, Conan O'Brien mocked his employer, joking about ways he could waste the company's money.

Table 2.5   Tweeting About Significant White-Collar Crimes Over Time

Incident	What Happened	Podgor's Tweet
Sutherland's definition	Critics complained that the definition was too sociological.	"Focus on the offense—not the offender" (p. 542).
New York Central and Hudson River Railroad Company v. U.S.	Supreme Court case from 1909 that found that corporations could be held criminally liable for misdeeds.	Defense attorneys might tweet, "At last (sigh) paying clients" (p. 538).
Bernie Madoff's Ponzi Scheme	Bernie Madoff orchestrated the largest and most brazen Ponzi scheme in U.S. history, stealing billions of dollars.	"Bernie Madoff did what!!!" (p. 548)
Lengthy prison sentences given to prominent offenders	Following the development of sentencing guidelines, WorldCom CEO Bernard Ebbers was sentenced to 25 years in prison, and Enron CEO Jeffrey Skilling was sentenced to 24 years following their convictions.	"Ebbers to Skilling—must be tough being runner up" (p. 556).
Martha Stewart's case	Martha wore a poncho during her incarceration and served the end of her sentence on electronic monitoring with house arrest.	"Nice Poncho and Bracelet, Martha" (p. 554).

Source: Adapted from Podgor, E. (2011). 100 years of white-collar crime in Twitter. *The Review of Litigation*, 30(3), 535–58.

of crime for that matter. White-collar crime scholar Ellen Podgor has discussed how some of the past "highlights" from white-collar crime research and incidents might have been tweeted about if Twitter had existed several decades earlier. Table 2.5 provides a synopsis of Podgor's "tweets."

● ● ●   **Characteristics of White-Collar Offenders**

Because white-collar offenses are viewed as equally serious as street crimes, there may be a tendency among some to view white-collar criminals as similar to street criminals (Payne, 2003b). Such an assumption, however, is misguided and represents an inaccurate portrait of "the white-collar criminal." As well, focusing narrowly on white-collar offenders may result in individuals failing to recognize the interactions between the offenders' background characteristics and their offensive behaviors (Wheeler et al., 1988).

Criminologists have devoted significant attention to describing the characteristics of various types of white-collar offenders. Comparing records of street offenders and white-collar offenders, Benson and Moore (1992) concluded: "Those who commit even run-of-the-mill garden variety white-collar offenses can, as a group, be clearly distinguished from those who commit ordinary street offenses" (p. 252). In one of the most comprehensive white-collar crime studies, Wheeler and his colleagues (1988) found that white-collar offenders were more likely than conventional offenders to (1) have a college education, (2) be white males, (3) be older, (4) have a job, (5) commit fewer offenses and (6) start their criminal careers later in life. Focusing on the interactions between offender characteristics and offense characteristics, the same research demonstrated that white-collar crime was more likely than street crime to involve the following:

- National or international scope
- Involve a large number of victims
- Have organizations as victims
- Follow demonstrated patterns

- Be committed for more than a year
- Be committed in groups

Recognizing the differences between white-collar crime and white-collar offenders and between street crimes and street offenders is significant for theoretical and policy reasons. In terms of theory, as will be demonstrated later in this text, if one of the criminological theories can explain both types of crimes, then that theory would be seen as having strong explanatory power. In terms of policy, it is important to recognize that different criminal justice strategies may be needed for the two types of offenses and that street offenders and white-collar offenders may respond differently to the criminal justice process.

Consider efforts to prevent crime. Strategies for preventing street crimes might focus on community building and poverty reduction; preventing white-collar crime is much "more complex" (Johnstone, 1999, p. 116). The impact of convictions and incarceration is also different between street offenders and white-collar offenders (Payne, 2003b). While such events may actually allow street offenders to gain "peer group status," the white-collar offender would not experience the same increase in status as the result of a conviction (Johnstone, 1999; Payne, 2003b). At the most basic level, recognizing the differences between street offenders and white-collar offenders helps to promote more useful prevention and intervention strategies. On a more complex level, recognizing these differences fosters a more objective and accurate understanding of the dynamics, causes, and consequences of the two types of behavior.

SUMMARY

- Sutherland (1949) defined white-collar crime as "crime committed by a person of respectability and high social status in the course of his occupation" (p. 9).
- Criticism of the concept centered on (1) conceptual ambiguity, (2) empirical ambiguity, (3) methodological ambiguity, (4) legal ambiguity, and (5) policy ambiguity.
- Corporate crime and occupational crime are viewed as "the two principal or 'pure' forms of white-collar crime" (Friedrichs, 2002, p. 245).
- Criminologists and social scientists offer various ways to define white-collar crime. These variations tend to overlap with one another and include the following: (1) white-collar crime as moral or ethical violations, (2) white-collar crime as social harm, (3) white-collar crime as violations of criminal law, (4) white-collar crime as violations of civil law, (5) white-collar crime as violations of regulatory laws, (6) white-collar crime as workplace deviance, (7) white-collar crime as definitions socially constructed by businesses, (8) white-collar crime as research definitions, (9) white-collar crime as official government definitions, (10) white-collar crime as violations of trust, (11) white-collar crime as occupational crimes, and (12) white-collar crime as violations occurring in occupational systems.
- Determining the extent of white-collar crime is no simple task. Two factors make it particularly difficult to accurately determine how often white-collar crimes occur: unreported crimes and conceptual ambiguity.
- With regard to official statistics and white-collar crime, the FBI's *Uniform Crime Reports (UCR)* and National Incident Based Reporting System (NIBRS) provide at least a starting point from which we can begin to question how often certain forms of white-collar crime occur.
- The consequences of white-collar crime can be characterized as (1) individual economic losses, (2) societal economic losses, (3) emotional consequences, (4) physical harm, and (5) "positive" consequences.
- Research on white-collar crime attitudes, however, is important for empirical, cultural, and policy-driven reasons (Piquero, Carmichael et al., 2008).
- Because white-collar offenses are viewed as equally serious as street crimes, there may be a tendency among some to view white-collar criminals as similar to street criminals (Payne, 2003b). Such an assumption is misguided and represents an inaccurate portrait of "the white-collar criminal."
- Wheeler and his colleagues (1988) found that white-collar offenders were more likely than conventional offenders to (1) have a college education, (2) be white males, (3) be older, (4) have a job, (5) commit fewer offenses, (6) start their criminal careers later in life, and (7) be Jewish.

KEY TERMS

Boundary maintenance

Community integration

Conceptual ambiguity

Corporate crime

Criminaloid concept

Definitions socially constructed by businesses

Emotional consequences

Empirical ambiguity

Government definitions

Individual economic losses

Natural law

Occupational crime

Physical harm

Research definitions

Social change

Social harm

Societal economic losses

Victimization surveys

Violations of criminal law

Violations of regulatory law

Violations of trust

Warning light syndrome

White-collar crime

Workplace deviance

DISCUSSION QUESTIONS

1. Review the five white-collar crimes described in the beginning of this chapter. Answer the following questions for each offense description:

   a. Is it a white-collar crime?

   b. How often do these crimes occur?

   c. What would the consequences of this crime be?

   d. How serious do you think this crime is?

   e. Who is the offender in each case?

   f. How does that offender differ from street offenders?

2. Why does it matter how we define white-collar crime?

3. How serious is white-collar crime in comparison to street crimes?

4. What are the negative and positive consequences of white-collar crime?

WEB RESOURCES

FBI White-Collar Crime: http://www.fbi.gov/about-us/investigate/white_collar/whitecollarcrime

Protect yourself online: http://stlouis.jobing.com/protectagainstfraud.asp

10 Biggest White-Collar Crimes in History: http://www.businesspundit.com/white-collar-crimes-history-and-how-they-were-unravelled/

STUDENT RESOURCES

The open-access Student Study Site, available at study.sagepub.com/paynewccess2e, includes useful study materials including SAGE journal articles and multimedia resources.

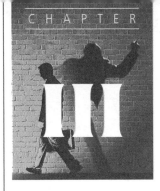

CHAPTER

III

Crimes in Sales-Related Occupations

A Systems Perspective

CHAPTER HIGHLIGHTS

- Employee Theft in the Retail System
- Crimes in the Entertainment/Services System
- Fraud in the Sales/Service System
- Crimes in the Insurance System

Nearly a decade ago, three student workers were caught stealing textbooks from their university bookstore. One of the culprits was actually hired to sit at the front of the store and watch the entrance of the store in an effort to keep shoppers from stealing books. Instead, conspiring with two coworkers, he stole textbooks and sold them to fellow students at reduced prices. The bookstore manager told a reporter, "It's always shocking when someone you trust steals from you" (DeJesus, 2007).

While shocking to victims of employee theft, to those who study workplace crimes it is not surprising when workers are caught stealing from their workplace or committing other types of crime in the workplace. In sales-oriented occupations, in particular, the likelihood of theft is high. In retail settings, for example, employees are often younger, part-time workers who do not feel attached to the business, and many workplace environments have an assortment of items (including goods and money) that can be targeted for theft. In other sales-oriented occupations, the aim of making profits through the provision of different services may foster misconduct. There is a long-standing perception that salespersons cannot be trusted as they are seen as simply trying to sell goods or services that may not be worth the asking price. From this perspective, it should not be shocking when sales-oriented officials engage in wrongdoing.

As an illustration of the breadth of offenses occurring in sales-oriented occupations, consider the following examples as they were described verbatim in various press reports:

- A former Sears employee at the Staten Island Mall is accused of stealing $600 from the register while he was working there, according to authorities. [The employee] dipped into the store's register on six separate occasions between November and December, taking $100 each time, prosecutors allege. The suspect was caught on the store's video surveillance removing the money from the register, according to court documents. (Lavis, 2015)
- A couple's attempt to improve their home resulted in disastrous consequences. Now the bad renovation could mean the loss of their home of nearly 40 years . . . Linda and Truman Crigger said the contractor walked out before finishing anything, taking their money with him. (Sweetman, 2015)
- The Missouri Attorney General Chris Koster announced Thursday that he sued a Clay County auto-repair shop for not doing the repairs customers were paying for. In the case, Koster accuses . . . the operators of *****, of charging at least 14 customers for repair work that was never completed. According to the lawsuit, the two have allegedly scammed customers out of more than $9,000 since December 2010. (Graflage, 2015)
- A 52-year-old Springfield woman has been indicted by a federal grand jury on eight counts of mail fraud in connection with an alleged scheme to embezzle money from a Springfield auto repair business. The federal indictment . . . alleges that *** embezzled more than $500,000 from Kim's Auto Body from 2009 to 2014. (Nevel, 2015)

Melissa Collie purchased a 2005 Nissan Maxima with 120,000 miles. But when she went to register the black sedan she was surprised to learn it actually had over 220,000 miles on it. It turns out Collie is not alone. Many newer vehicles have gadgets and digital odometers. Experts say the technology makes it easier for thieves to fool you by rolling back mileage (Terry, 2015). As with all white-collar crimes, these offenses have four things in common: (1) They occurred during the course of the offender's work; (2) the offender was engaged in the role of a worker; (3) in terms of setting, the offenses occurred in a workplace setting; and (4) on one level or another, each of them involved occupations where employees were selling goods or services. Literally hundreds of different types of sales-oriented occupations exist. It would be impossible to address the way crime occurs in each of those occupations, but I attempt here to introduce students to the nature of crime in these sales-oriented occupations. In this chapter, attention will be given to the crimes occurring in the following systems: employee theft in the retail system, crimes in the entertainment and service systems, fraud in sales and service systems, and crimes in the insurance system.

These systems were selected because they capture the kinds of occupational systems of which students likely already have some awareness and a degree of interest. Some of these areas are possibly fields where students have already worked, others are fields they may one day work in, and others are service occupations that students have encountered or will encounter in the future. It is important to stress that other sales-oriented occupations, while not covered here, are not immune from crime.

● ● ● Employee Theft in the Retail System

The **retail system** is the setting where consumers purchase various types of products. As shown in recent times, the success of our economic system is tied to the success of the retail system. When individuals buy more in the retail system, our economic system is stronger. While consumers drive the success of the retail system, employees steer the direction of the retail system. The key to success for retail stores lies in having employees able to perform assigned tasks. One problem that retail outlets face is employee theft. Indeed, internal theft has been "linked to 30% of U.S. business failures" (Mullen, 1999, p. 12).

Experts use the concept of shrinkage to refer to the theft of goods in the retail industry. Estimates from the National Retail Security Survey suggested that $44 billion was lost to theft. Just over one-third of the theft was attributed to employee/internal theft (K. G. Allen, 2015). Theft is believed to increase the amount Americans spend shopping by $403 per household

(Fisher, 2015). According to the National Federation of Independent Businesses, "An employee is 15 times more likely than a non-employee to steal from an employer" (J. Anderson, 2015). Employee theft did increase, though, at the end of the 2000s. In line with the idea that changes in one system lead to changes in other systems, some have attributed this increase to the economic changes, such that changes in the economic system resulted in changes in the extent of employee theft in retail settings ("Record Number of Shoplifters," 2008; Rosenbaum, 2009). Explaining this increase in employee theft, loss prevention expert Richard Hollinger has suggested that more workers being alone in stores (because so many workers have been fired or laid off) means that workers will have more opportunities to steal (Goodchild, 2008).

It is difficult to determine with any degree of precision how often employees steal in retail settings. Surveys in these settings would probably underestimate the extent of employee theft (Oliphant & Oliphant, 2001). One study found that 1 in 30 employees (out of 2.1 million) was caught stealing from an employer in 2008 ("Record Number of Shoplifters," 2008). Regardless of the number of employees who steal and the fact that most employees in retail settings do not steal, Daniel Butler, the former vice president of the National Retail Federation, notes, "a habitual internal thief can cost a lot of dollars" (Pratt, 2001, p. 37).

Several different varieties of employee theft in retail settings occur. Here are some examples.

- **Overcharging:** Employees charge customers more than they should have.
- **Shortchanging:** Employees do not give customers all of their change and pocket the difference.
- **Coupon stuffing:** Employees steal coupons and use them later.
- **Credits for nonexistent returns:** Employees give credit for returns to collaborators.
- **Theft of production supplies and raw materials:** Employees steal items used to produce goods in retail settings.
- **Embezzlement:** Employees steal money from an account to which they have access.
- **Over-ordering supplies:** Employees order more supplies than are needed and keep the supplies that were not needed.
- **Theft of credit card information:** Employees steal customers' credit card information.
- **Theft of goods:** Employees steal the items the retail setting is trying to sell.
- **Theft of money from the cash register:** Employees take money out of the register.
- **Sweetheart deals:** Employees give friends and family members unauthorized discounts (Albright, 2007; Belser, 2008; Mishra & Prasad, 2006).

Explaining why these offenses occur is no simple task. Some have attributed certain types of employee theft to organized crime on the notion that organized crime families have conspired with employees to develop widespread and lucrative employee theft schemes (Albright, 2007). Others have focused on individual motivations among employees and have highlighted the employees' perceived needs, drug problems, and sense of entitlement as causes of employee theft (Leap, 2007). Still others contend that some instances of employee theft (such as stealing from the cash register) are not planned events but impulsive ones that offenders commit when the opportunity presents itself (Anderson, 2007). Some have suggested that retail settings with more turnover will have more employee theft (Belser, 2008). Still others have noted that organizational culture contributes to employee theft (Leap, 2007). Much more attention will be given to explaining all forms of white-collar crime in a later chapter in this text. For now, it is sufficient to suggest that these offenses are caused by multiple factors.

Because so many different factors potentially contribute to employee theft in the retail system, it

▲ **Photo 3.1** Overcharging is one type of employee theft. Consumers may not realize they have been overcharged unless they look closely at their receipts on a regular basis.

should not be surprising that many different types of prevention strategies have been cited as ways to limit the extent of employee theft. These prevention strategies include (a) importation strategies, (b) internal strategies, (c) technological strategies, (d) organizational culture strategies, and (e) awareness strategies. **Importation strategies** are those strategies that aim to import only the best types of employees, who are less likely to engage in employee theft. Strategies would include background checks, drug tests, employee screening instruments, and credit checks (Friedman, 2009).

Internal strategies include policies and practices performed within the retail setting in an effort to prevent employee theft. Random inspections, audits, developing rules that guide returns, and developing internal control policies are examples (Mishra & Prasad, 2006). Random inspections include checking cash registers, employee lockers, and other locations for evidence of wrongdoing. Audits are strategies in which supervisors review cash distribution patterns of employees. Rules guiding returns focus on ways to limit the possibility that employees misuse return policies. Internal control policies refer to a "set of policies and procedures that provide reasonable assurance that an organization's assets and information are protected" (Mishra & Prasad, 2006, p. 819). Some companies employ security specialists whose sole purpose is to protect the assets and workers. The Careers Responding to White-Collar Crime: Industrial Security Specialists box below describes the types of duties performed by these employees.

CAREERS RESPONDING TO WHITE-COLLAR CRIME

Industrial Security Specialists

Industrial security specialists review the nature of classified contracts to identify the level and kind of secure work to be performed in the facility and the kind and extent of security protection required for the programs involved. They work with subject-matter specialists in developing statements of need, descriptions of work, and other considerations relating to the security requirements under a contractual arrangement. They assure that security is considered in the earliest stages of procurement planning and that all requirements are fulfilled. They work with contracting officers to assure that bidders can meet security requirements of the contract. They attend preaward and pricing conferences to assure that security costs are not excessive and assist the contracting office in carrying out security responsibilities.

Industrial security specialists develop security plans involving access to grounds by employees, vendors, government personnel, and others; badge and pass systems; clearance records and controls; fences; alarms; intrusion detection and other electronic devices; guard force levels and their duties, responsibilities, and response times; special room construction including vaulting, shielded cable, and wiring requirements; and other means of limiting entry (locks, vaults and safes) or technical penetration (electronic emanations, eavesdropping, or others). The specialist resolves issues with industry officials involving security plans and makes adjustments based on costs, alternative methods available, other security programs in place, and similar considerations.

Industrial security specialists conduct continuing inspections of facilities possessing sensitive information to assure adherence to security requirements. They perform periodic reviews of facilities and their personnel to assess protection against espionage; investigate suspected security violations; and recommend or take appropriate measures to correct security deficiencies, up to and including removal of classified material from the organization's possession or stopping work operations when a significant breach of security is probable. They plan, organize, and conduct training programs to make facility personnel aware of security matters and procedures and to alert them to dangers of espionage and sabotage. Industrial security specialists are responsible also for periodic inspections of private organizations to determine whether the organizations still have need for active facility clearances, and to keep at a minimum the number of authorized personnel clearances by restricting as much as possible the need to know.

Source: Reprinted from: Position Classification Standard For Security Administration Series, GS-0080.

Technological strategies entail the use of various forms of technology to prevent employee theft in retail settings. The use of video cameras, for example, can be preventive in nature, assuming employees know that they are being "watched." If the cameras don't prevent an employee from stealing, the video will provide direct evidence of the employee "in action" (Holtz, 2009). With color and digital cameras now available, the pictures provided by the videos are even clearer, and security officials can store the video longer than they were able to in the past (Pratt, 2001). Closed-circuit television, in particular, has been hailed as the most effective deterrent in retail settings (Anderson, 2007).

Organizational culture strategies aim to promote a sense of organizational culture that would inhibit theft. Most business and management experts agree that the way bosses treat their employees will influence the workers' behavior (Kresevich, 2007). The task at hand is for supervisors and managers to promote an organizational culture that values honesty and loyalty. One expert advises, "From the start, employees should know company values and feel a part of a team committed to eliminating theft" (Mullen, 1999, p. 12). Along this line, Kent Davies (2003) recommends that supervisors (a) get advice to from experts about security incidents, (b) build loyalty between the employee and the employer, (c) establish a trusting relationship between workers, and (d) eliminate temptations. Echoing these themes, Mazur (2001) calls for the building of a "strong integrity program" as a strategy for preventing retail theft. Such a program would entail four elements. First, managers would be held accountable for employees' behavior and provided incentives as part of this accountability. Second, managers would ensure that all employees be aware of the rules of conduct in the retail setting. Third, an effort would be made to give employees a "sense of authority." Fourth, managers would provide employees an outlet for reporting misconduct (Mazur, 2001). Anonymous reporting systems have been found to be particularly useful in detecting wrongdoing (Holtfreter, 2005).

Awareness strategies focus on increasing awareness among employees about various issues related to employee theft. In particular, it is recommended that employees be told about or exposed to the following:

- Anonymous tip lines
- New hire orientation
- Formal codes of conduct
- Bulletin board posters related to theft prevention
- Periodic lectures on theft and the consequences of theft
- Loss prevention compensation programs (Korolishin, 2003)

A loss prevention compensation program would provide employees monetary rewards for reporting and substantiating employee theft by their coworkers.

● ● ● Crimes in the Entertainment Services System

While the retail system encompasses the setting where retail goods are sold to consumers, the **entertainment services system** describes settings where consumers consume or purchase various forms of services designed at least partially for entertainment or pleasure. Many different occupations exist in the entertainment service system. The White-Collar Crime in the News: Bad Hair Day box on the next page shows one recent press release for a crime occurring in the beauty services industry. For purposes of simplicity, in this text, attention will be given to just two types of industries in this system: the restaurant industry and the hotel industry.

In considering crimes in the restaurant industry, two broad categories of crime can be highlighted: crimes by the restaurant against consumers and crimes by workers against the restaurant. In her review of crimes by businesses, Hazel Croall (1989) identified four types of crimes committed by restaurants against consumers: (1) adulterating food, (2) failing to keep the restaurant as clean as required by standards, (3) using false advertising to describe goods and prices, and (4) selling food at a smaller amount than advertised (short weighting). Restaurants appeared to be over-represented in "hygiene" offenses in her study. Croall studied 118 businesses and uncovered 37 hygiene offenses; restaurants accounted for 29 of the 37 offenses. In all, restaurants accounted for 29 of the 37 hygiene offenses. Croall also calls attention to instances where

WHITE-COLLAR CRIME IN THE NEWS

Bad Hair Day or Bad Hair Show?
Woman Convicted for Hair Scam

Tamira Fonville's job might be described as "recruiter." For a time, she profited substantially by enlisting college-age women to participate in a hair show. The problem was, there never was any show, and everything about Fonville's line of work was a fraud.

Anytime money exchanges hands for services, the opportunity for fraud is present – even when we are having our hair done.

She and her partner—both of whom are now in prison—regularly traveled the Interstate 95 corridor from New York to Washington, D.C., visiting shopping malls and other places where young women were known to spend time.

Using a series of phony names, Fonville would interest the women in the hair show, offering to pay for their services. But to pay them, she said, she needed their debit card numbers and access to their accounts.

With that access, she would not simply clean out their accounts. Instead, her partner and mastermind of the scam, Ricardo Falana, would deposit bogus checks into the legitimate accounts, and then immediately begin withdrawing funds before the bank realized the fraud.

"It was a crazy, hit or miss scheme," said Special Agent Sean Norman, who investigated the case from the FBI's Philadelphia Division. "But they did it at such a high volume that they made a lot of money for several years. There was approximately $600,000 in actual losses to banks and other financial institutions."

For a time, the money rolled in, and Fonville "got addicted to the lifestyle," Special Agent Sean Norman said. According to court documents, between 2008 and 2013, Fonville personally benefited from the scheme to the tune of more than $230,000. She used some of the proceeds to pay for plastic surgery, the car loan on her $30,000 Chevrolet Camaro, and the $2,100 monthly rent on her New York apartment.

Eventually, some of the women whose accounts had been used came forward and told the truth. Norman was able to trace withdrawn funds to Fonville and Falana, and Falana was identified on surveillance video depositing what turned out to be bogus checks. Norman also used E-ZPass toll receipts to link the pair's recruiting trips to account holders and subsequent fraudulent transactions on their accounts.

"After the pieces all fit together," said Norman, who is a certified public account and specializes in financial fraud investigations, "their actions were highly predictable." Fonville was arrested in August 2014. She pled guilty the following month to conspiracy to commit bank fraud and three counts of bank fraud and was sentenced in April to 15 months in prison. Falana pled guilty to similar bank fraud charges in October 2014 and in February received an 80-month sentence.

In the end, Norman said, "they blew all the money and had nothing to show for it."

Source: Reprinted from FBI.

restaurants short-measure items. She writes, "Fiddles, including the sale of short-measure drinks, are so institutionalized that they represent part of an 'informal reward structure'" (p. 160). As Croall notes, while one person being ripped off over a drink may not be significant, when one adds up the number of short-measures, the total sum can be especially significant.

In terms of crimes by workers against the restaurant, patterns similar to those of employee theft in retail settings are found. Surveys of 103 restaurant employees found that their most common offenses included eating the restaurant's food without paying for it, giving food and/or beverages away, selling food at a lower price than it was supposed to be sold for, and taking items for personal use (Ghiselli & Ismail, 1998). In this same study, three fourths of respondents admitted committing some type of employee deviance. Stealing from the cash register is an additional type of crime that can occur in restaurants. In one case, a waitress-manager stole $60,000 from her restaurant's cash register over a 2-year time span (Schaefer, 2003).

A combination of factors is believed to foster theft by workers in restaurants. Restaurants tend to hire younger workers, and younger people in general have been found to be more prone toward deviance than older people. The low wages paid to workers may create settings where workers feel they are underpaid and underappreciated. The nature of the work is part-time, meaning that workers will be less invested in their employer. Also, the erratic hours of restaurant work may contribute to various opportunities for misconduct (Ghiselli & Ismail, 1998). To address these offenses, Ghiselli and Ismail cite the following policies as strategies for reducing theft in restaurants: (a) inventory control, (b) controlled exits so managers know when workers are leaving, (c) inspections of employees' belongings, (d) video cameras, (e) locks on goods and items, and (f) restricted access to the cash register.

White-collar crime also occurs in the hotel industry. Crime types include theft of hotel food, theft of items owned by the hotel, and theft of hotel guests' items. These crimes are particularly difficult to detect (Bloomquist, 2006). When offenders are caught, it is usually because they did something that made the case truly easy to solve. Consider, for example, a case in which two security guards were arrested for stealing three cellular phones and two wallets from a hotel room. They were caught because they used one of the cell phones (Nammour, 2009). Certainly, some of the crimes committed in

Hagerty Ryan, U.S. Fish and Wildlife Service

▲ **Photo 3.2** A study by Ghiselli and Ismail (1998) found that three fourths of restaurant employees reported committing some variety of employee deviance. Consumers would rarely notice these violations.

the hotel industry might be committed by hotel guests. However, there is reason to believe that most hotel crimes are committed by workers. One early estimate suggested that 90 percent of all crimes committed in hotels were due to employee theft (Worcester, 1998). According to Worcester, employee theft in hotels is believed to be particularly problematic during summer months when temporary employees are hired.

Few studies have focused specifically on white-collar crimes in the hotel industry. Nonetheless, anecdotal evidence suggests that these crimes are somewhat pervasive. Recall that I mentioned that I have students enrolled in my white-collar crime classes write about crimes they committed on their jobs. One of my students worked in a hotel and described his typical workday as beginning when his manager told him the going rates for that evening. The manager would say something like, "The rate tonight is $90.00 a night. If customers ask for the rate, tell them it is $100.00 a night. If they don't like the rate, tell them you will lower it to $90.00 to get them to stay." The student then shared that he would tell customers that the rate was $120 a night. If customers paid that rate in cash, he would pocket $30 each night and tell his boss that the customer paid $90.00. If the customer said the price was too high, he would offer to reduce it a little and still keep the difference if it was higher than $90.00. Just to be clear, this was not a student at my current university. One can't help but wonder, though, where this student is now working. One hopes he's not working anywhere that we will be vacationing!

● ● ●   **Fraud in the Sales/Service System**

Whereas the entertainment service system sells goods and services that are designed to provide some form of entertainment to consumers, the **sales/service system** entails businesses that sell basic goods and services to consumers. These "basic" goods and services are those that most individuals need in order to function in their communities. The home and the automobile are two examples of basic goods many individuals need in order to carry out their daily routines. When considering fraud in this system, one can draw attention to automotive repair/sales fraud and home repair fraud. While few studies have empirically demonstrated how often these types of fraud occur, they are believed to be particularly pervasive. In Focus 3.1 shows the top 10 consumer complaints made to state and local authorities in 2014. As shown in the box, complaints about auto sales/repairs, home improvement, and retail services ranked among the top four complaints. In the following paragraphs, more attention is given to the dynamics surrounding home repair fraud and auto repair/sales fraud.

IN FOCUS   **3.1**

Top 10 Consumer Complaints Made to State and Local Authorities in 2014

1. Auto sales

2. Home Improvement/Construction

3. Credit/Debt

4. (Tie) Retail Sales

5. Services

6. Landlord/Tenant

7. Home Solicitations

8. (Tie) Health Products/Services

9. Fraudulent scams

10. Household Goods

Source: Reprinted From Consumer Federation of America. (2015). Top 10 consumer complaints.

Home Repair Fraud

Home repair fraud occurs when contractors and repair persons rip off individuals for various types of repairs. One police department cites the following offenses as the most common types of home repair fraud: roof repair, asphalt paving or driveway sealing fraud, house painting fraud, termite and pest control fraud, and tree pruning and landscaping fraud (St. Louis Police Department, 2006). In most of these cases, the fraud begins as part of a door-to-door scam initiated by the offender. Experts believe that the door-to-door scams target older persons more often, partly because they are more likely to be home during the day (Coffey, 2000) and partly because they are seen as more vulnerable (Davila, Marquart, & Mullings, 2005).

Scammers are able to profit significantly from their offenses. Estimates suggest, for example, that those involved in driveway paving scams make $10,000 a day from their schemes. Typically, they underestimate the repair costs and then try to charge more once they are done (Sambides, 2009).

To be sure, while some of the frauds result from aggressive door-to-door targeting by offenders, others occur as a result of consumers seeking repairs. Consumers are particularly vulnerable to repair frauds when considering the underlying dynamics of repair seeking. When individuals seek repairs, they are already admitting to the repairer—at least indirectly—that they do not know how to fix the item themselves. If the contractor commits fraud, the consumer may not even know it. Even when consumers are aware of the fraud, they are often unsure whom they should report the offense to (Vaughan & Carlo, 1975).

The consequences of home repair fraud can be particularly problematic. If items are not fixed appropriately, further damage to the home can result. Additional expenses will be incurred by homeowners seeking to repair their homes. Such an experience can cause significant stress to those dealing with the fraud. Family relationships can also be negatively influenced for those living in homes in need of repair as a result of contractor fraud (Burnstein, 2008a, 2008b). Perhaps recognizing the seriousness of these consequences, one police officer made the following comments to a

Photo by Tina Shaw/USFWS. Creative Commons Attribution 2.0 Generic. https://creativecommons.org/licenses/by/2.0/

▲ **Photo 3.3** Fraud by contractors may be particularly difficult to identify. Consumers may lack the knowledge to know what services are actually warranted.

reporter: "Some of the contractors that we arrest, I think of them as worse than armed robbers. At least when it's an armed robbery, you know you're being robbed" (Lee, 2009).

Allegations of home repair frauds appear to increase after natural disasters, likely because many homeowners are in need of labor to fix their damaged homes. In the wake of Hurricane Katrina, authorities investigated more than 400 cases of contractor fraud. Said one official, "There's not enough skilled labor out there, and it's causing chaos" (Konigsmark, 2006, p. 3A). In Mississippi, 87 contractors were arrested after Katrina, and 60 additional contractors were in mediation with homeowners for allegations that they committed fraud against residents of Mississippi whose homes were damaged in the hurricane (Lee, 2009).

In the wake of home repair fraud scandals, many states have passed criminal laws specifically targeting home repair fraud. In Maine, for example, the **home repair fraud** law is stated under the following section:

§908. Home repair fraud

1. A home repair seller is guilty of home repair fraud if the seller knowingly enters into an agreement or contract, written or oral, with any person for home repair services and the seller, at the time of entering into that agreement or contract:

   A. Intentionally misrepresents a material fact relating to the terms of the agreement or contract or misrepresents a preexisting or existing condition of any portion of the property that is the subject of the home repair services. Violation of this paragraph is a Class D crime; [2001, c. 383, §110 (AMD); 2001, c. 383, §156 (AFF).]

   B. Intentionally creates or reinforces an impression relating to the terms of the agreement or contract that is false and that the seller does not believe to be true or fails to correct such an impression that the seller had previously created or reinforced. Violation of this paragraph is a Class D crime; [2001, c. 383, §110 (AMD); 2001, c. 383, §156 (AFF).]

   C. Intentionally promises performance under the terms of the agreement or contract that the seller does not intend to perform or that the seller knows will not be performed. Violation of this paragraph is a Class D crime; [2001, c. 383, §110 (AMD); 2001, c. 383, §156 (AFF).]

   D. Intentionally uses or employs deception, false pretense or false promise in securing the agreement or contract (Maine Law §908. Home Repair Fraud).

The advantage of criminal laws (and policies) directed toward home repair fraud is that officials have clear guidance on how these cases should be processed. Whereas these wrongs would have been handled as civil wrongdoings in the past, if they were handled at all, the criminal laws create additional formal policies that can be used to respond to this group of offenders.

In addition to formal policies to respond to home repair fraud, experts urge homeowners to use various prevention strategies to try to avoid fraud in the first place. Common suggestions for preventing home repair fraud include the following practices: obtaining references, relying on local businesses, verifying licensure, obtaining multiple estimates, and using written contracts (Riggs, 2007).

Auto Repair/Sales Fraud

At the broadest level, one can distinguish between auto repair fraud and auto sales fraud. In the early 1990s, auto repair rip-offs were "the most frequently reported consumer complaint" (Munroe, 1992, p. C3). An early estimate suggested that "consumers lose $20 billion annually on faulty auto repairs" (Brown, 1995, p. 21). Automotive industry insiders counter that "faulty" repairs are not the same as "fraudulent" repairs. Recall the discussion in Chapter I about white-collar crime being defined differently by various groups. To those in the automotive repair industry, faulty repairs would not be a white-collar crime. To those following a broader approach to defining white-collar crime, such repairs can be conceptualized as white-collar crime.

Auto repair fraud includes *billing for services not provided, unnecessary repairs, airbag fraud*, and *insurance fraud*. **Billing for services not provided** occurs when auto mechanics bill consumers (or insurance companies) for services not provided. Consider a study by the California Department of Consumer Affairs/Bureau of Automotive Repair (BAR) that found "42% of collision repair work done in California to be fraudulent" (Sramcik, 2004, p. 16). In this study, the Bureau inspected 1,315 vehicles that received collision repairs and found that on 551 of the vehicles, "parts or labor listed on the invoice . . . were not actually supplied or performed" (Thrall, 2003, p. 6). Industry insiders critiqued the BAR study for being methodologically flawed and for using vague definitions of fraud, which included billing mistakes (Grady, 2003). Again, the importance of how one defines white-collar crime surfaces. Critics also suggested that the BAR study was politically driven as a strategy to suggest that the Bureau's existence was justified in a time of tough budgets in order to protect consumers from fraud (Thrall, 2003).

Unnecessary auto repairs occur when mechanics perform mechanical services that are not necessary and bill the consumer for those services. Such practices are believed to be well planned by those who perform them. These actions are particularly difficult for consumers to detect. Said one assistant attorney general to a reporter, "Most consumers are not knowledgeable enough about auto repairs to know if their cars have been subjected to unneeded repairs" (Munroe, 1992, p. C3). Presumably, an automotive repair shop will advertise cheap specials as a way to get consumers into the shop and then convince consumers that they need certain repairs. One owner of 22 repair shops agreed to pay $1.8 million in fines in response to allegations that he engaged in this type of scam (Olivarez-Giles, 2010, p. 7).

Airbag fraud occurs when mechanics fraudulently repair airbags. In general, two types of airbag fraud exist (Adams & Guyette, 2009). The first type involves outright fraud in which mechanics clearly intend not to fix the airbag appropriately. Adams and Guyette (2009) provide the example of situations where "old rags or foam are shoved into dashboard cavities" (p. 56). The second type of airbag fraud is inaccurate repair. This entails situations in which mechanics simply fail to repair the airbag correctly. Unfortunately, these fraudulent or inept repairs may not be noticed until an accident occurs.

Auto insurance fraud occurs when mechanics dupe the insurance company into paying for unnecessary or nonexistent repairs. Types of auto insurance fraud include enhancing damages, substituting parts, and creating damage. Enhancing damages involves situations where mechanics cause further damage to a damaged car in order to collect more from the insurance company. Substituting parts includes situations where mechanics put used parts in the repaired car but bill the insurance company for new parts (Seibel, 2009). Creating damage occurs when mechanics work with car owners to damage a car so that the owner can file a claim with the insurance company (Bertrand, 2003). This would include stripping and vandalizing cars so that they will be paid to repair the damage they created.

One strategy that has been shown to be effective in limiting auto insurance fraud involves the use of direct repair programs and aftermarket auto parts (Cole, Maroney, McCullough, & Powell, 2015). Presumably, when auto repair shops are working directly with the insurer, the opportunity and motivation for fraud decreases. Also, using after-market auto parts (or used parts) is much cheaper than using new parts.

In some cases, professionals may collaborate with a wide range of individuals to perpetrate their fraudulent acts. Some health care businesses have been labeled as "auto insurance treatment mills" in reference to the overrepresentation of certain health care businesses in auto insurance claims (Schram, 2013, p. 33). Lawyers are frequently blamed for being ambulance chasers, but it turns out that some ambulances may consistently be going to the same health care facility!

Very few academic studies have focused on auto repair fraud. In one of the first studies done on the subject, Paul Jesilow and his colleagues (Jesilow, Geis, & O'Brien, 1985) conducted a field experiment in which they sought battery testing services from 313 auto shops in California. The researchers found that honesty was related to the size of the shop, with smaller shops exhibiting more honesty than larger shops. How workers were paid (commission vs. hourly rate) was not related to honesty. Commissioned workers tended to be just as honest as hourly workers.

Building on this study, the authors (Jesilow, Geis, & O'Brien, 1986) studied a publicity campaign to see if publicity and awareness would influence mechanics' honesty. The public awareness campaign included letters from a formal regulatory agency, a major lawsuit, and press announcements. After the campaign, the research assistants revisited the shops for battery testing. They found that honesty rates were similar among the shops exposed to the public awareness campaigns and the shops that were not exposed to the campaign. In other words, the campaign had no effect.

Automotive sales fraud is another type of fraud in the automotive industry. Varieties of auto sales fraud include turning odometers back, selling unsafe cars, and selling stolen cars (Smith, 1997). Odometer fraud, also known as clocking (see Croall, 1989), is sometimes part of a broader scheme. In those situations, mechanics work in collaboration with dealers in an effort to maximize a particular car sale. One estimate suggested that 452,000 cases of odometer fraud occur each year in the United States, costing consumers more than a billion dollars annually (National Highway Traffic Safety Association [NHTSA], 2002). The National Highway Traffic Safety Association advises consumers to engage in certain steps in order to avoid falling victim to odometer fraud. In Focus 3.2 shows these preventive actions.

IN FOCUS 3.2

NHTSA's Recommendations for Avoiding Odometer Fraud

- ASK to see the title and compare the mileage on it with the vehicle's odometer. Be sure to examine the title closely if the mileage notation seems obscured or is not easy to read.
- COMPARE the mileage on the odometer with the mileage indicated on the vehicle's maintenance or inspection records. Also, search for oil change and maintenance stickers on windows or door frames, in the glove box or under the hood.
- CHECK that the numbers on the odometer gauge are aligned correctly. If they're crooked, contain gaps or jiggle when you bang on the dash with your hand, walk away from the purchase.

- EXAMINE the tires. If the odometer on your car shows 20,000 or less, it should have the original tires.
- LOOK at the wear and tear on the vehicle—especially the gas, brake and clutch pedals—to be sure it seems consistent with and appropriate for the number of miles displayed on the odometer.
- REQUEST a CARFAX Vehicle History Report to check for odometer discrepancies in the vehicle's history. If the seller does not have a vehicle history report, use the car's VIN to order a CARFAX vehicle history report online. (NHTSA, 2010)

Source: Reprinted From Fact Sheet from http://www.nhtsa.gov/Odometer-Fraud

Flickr Commons project, 2008.

▲ **Photo 3.4**   Concerns about auto sales and auto repair fraud are nothing new.

In addition to these types of auto repair fraud, one author team also identifies overtreatment, overcharging, and undertreatment (Beck, Kerschbamer, Qui, & Sutter, 2013). **Overtreatment** refers to instances when mechanics do more work than is needed, either to rip the customer off or because they want to make sure the customer is safe. *Overcharging* refers to instances when mechanics do the repairs, but charge for more expensive repairs. **Undertreatment** involves doing shoddy or ineffective work on the automobile. A recent automobile repair field experiment using undercover researchers found that "under and overtreatment are widespread and that reputation via a repeat business mechanism does not improve outcomes significantly" (Schneider, 2012, p. 406).

● ● ● Crimes in the Insurance System

The insurance system includes the wide range of agencies and institutions responsible for providing insurance to consumers. Many different types of insurance exist, including homeowners insurance, rental insurance, auto insurance, property insurance, and more. The topic is rarely studied for two reasons: (1) It is hard to understand, and (2) people don't typically know when they have been victimized by insurance crimes (Ericson & Doyle, 2006). Of the research that has been done, much has focused on crimes by consumers against insurance companies, including overstating losses, arson for profit, bogus insurance claims, and understating property value to get lower insurance rates (Litton, 1998). Crimes by consumers, however, encompass just one portion of the types of crimes committed against in the insurance system. As with other occupations, a wide range of offenses are committed by those working in the insurance system. In the following paragraphs, attention is given to the types of crimes in this system, the consequences of insurance crimes, and the patterns surrounding these offenses.

Types of Insurance Crimes by Professionals

Four different categories of insurance crimes by workers in the insurance system exist: (1) crimes by agents against the insurance company, (2) investment-focused crimes, (3) theft crimes against consumers, and (4) sales-directed crimes against consumers. With regard to crimes by agents against the insurance company, some agents or brokers engage in activities that ultimately defraud the insurance company. Examples include lying about a potential client's income and unauthorized entity fraud (lying about assets). By lying about these items to the company, the agent is able to provide benefits to the consumer and thereby get the consumer to purchase the insurance.

Investment-focused crimes occur when insurance agents commit crimes that are designed to get consumers to invest in various insurance products. These include viatical settlement fraud, promissory note fraud, and annuities fraud. **Viatical settlement fraud** occurs when agents conceal information on viatical settlement policies, which allow individuals to invest in other people's life insurance policies (meaning they collect money when the other person dies). Fraud occurs when agents lie about the income, health of the insured individual, or other matters the investors should know about (Brasner, 2010; Federal Bureau of Investigation [FBI], 2010b).

Promissory note fraud refers to situations where agents get clients to invest in promissory notes that ultimately are scams. A promissory note is basically an IOU. Consumers are told that if they invest in a particular business, then after a certain amount of time, they will get their entire investment back plus interest. While promissory notes are legitimate investment strategies, here is how investment strategy fraud schemes work:

> A life insurance agent . . . calls with an intriguing investment opportunity. A company is looking to expand its business and needs to raise capital. But instead of borrowing money from a traditional lender such as a bank, it is offering investors an opportunity to purchase "promissory notes," typically with a maturity of nine months and an annual interest rate between 12 percent and 18 percent. Investors are sometimes told the promissory notes, which are like IOUs, are "guaranteed" by a bond from an offshore bonding company. Investors lose money either because fake promissory notes that look authentic are issued on behalf of fraudulent companies, or the crooks abscond with people's money before the notes mature. (Singletary, 2000, p. H01)

In some cases, insurance agents are not aware that they are selling fraudulent promissory notes because they too have fallen for the scam. In other cases, they are knowing conspirators who profit from the crimes. A series of investigations in the late 1990s found 800 incidents of promissory note fraud costing investors $500 million (Knox, 2000).

Annuities fraud occurs when insurance agents misrepresent the types of returns that their clients would get from investing in annuities. Annuities are "insurance contracts that offer a guaranteed series of payments over time" (Jenkins, 2008). Insurance agents get a 3 percent to 8 percent commission for selling annuities, giving them incentive to get clients to invest in annuities (Haiken, 2011). However, annuities can sometimes be quite risky investments, and agents have been known to persuade investors, particularly older individuals, to take their investments out of safe investment portfolios and place them in annuities that could eventually result in the investors' losing their savings. One victim described his experiences with annuities fraud in this way:

> The first scam started when the agent showed up and did not tell us he was from Salt Lake City, Utah. . . . His sales pitch convinced me I could use the immediate monthly income from an annuity, it was not disclosed he was selling "life insurance" or that Mr. Smiley was actually an insurance salesman. I was misled into thinking I was investing into a . . . mutual fund program. The instructions he gave me about the contract details such as "single life contract," "no guarantee," "no beneficiary," "no joint annuitant," and "no IRA disclosure statement was presented," these details were all misleading and coordinated in favor of [the insurance company]. Now I understand, the more I was defrauded, the bigger the commission for the insurance agent, they are trained to deceive. I have now ultimately lost the entire $57,779.00 IRA savings and I have nothing for my years of work and no retirement nest egg. (Adam, 2008)

Theft crimes against consumers occur when agents steal directly from insurance clients. Examples include broker embezzlement, forgery, and falsifying account information (FBI, 2010b). In broker embezzlement cases, agents steal funds from a client's account that the agents have access to. In forgery cases agents sign clients' names on documents and forms and benefit financially from the deception. **Falsifying account information** refers to instances when agents or brokers change account information without the client's knowledge. In these crimes, no actual sale, or even effort to make a sale, occurs, and agents are not trying to get clients to invest in anything—they are simply stealing from consumers.

Sales-directed crimes against consumers occur when agents or brokers steal from consumers by using fraudulent sales tactics. Premium diversion theft is the most common form of sales-directed insurance crime (FBI, 2010b). In these situations, brokers or agents persuade clients to purchase insurance, but they never actually forward the payment from the client to the insurance company; instead, they pocket the payment. This means that clients don't actually have insurance when they think they do.

Other forms of sales-directed insurance crimes are more institutionalized in the insurance sales process. For instance, **churning** refers to situations where agents and brokers introduce new products and services simply to get policyholders to change their policies so the agents and brokers can collect commissions (Ericson & Doyle, 2006). Such practices are often called "good business" among officials in the insurance agency; the practice certainly is distinguished from cases of direct theft, which are not institutionalized as part of sales strategies. Other sales-directed insurance crimes include the following:

- **Stacking:** persuading persons to buy more policies than are needed
- **Rolling over:** persuading customers to cancel an old policy and replace it with a more expensive "better" policy
- **Misrepresentation:** deliberately misinforming the customer about the coverage of the insurance policy
- **Switching:** where the sales person switches the consumer's policy so that the coverage and the premiums are different from what the victim was told
- **Sliding:** when agents include insurance coverage that was not requested by customers (Payne, 2005)

Beyond the deception that is tied to these offenses, consumers and the rest of society experience a number of different consequences from crimes committed in the insurance system.

Consequences of Insurance Crimes

Estimates suggest that insurance fraud collectively "raises the yearly cost of premiums by $300 for the average household" (FBI, 2009c). For individuals victimized by these offenses, the consequences of insurance crimes can be particularly devastating. Consider cases of premium diversion thefts—where individuals pay for insurance they don't actually receive. One woman didn't realize she didn't have insurance until after an automobile accident. Her garage called and told her that the insurance company had no policy in her name. She had thought for more than 2 years that she had insurance. The investigation revealed that the agent did the same thing with 80 other clients. In another scheme, an agent who sold fake policies "left dozens of customers without coverage during hurricane seasons [in Florida] in 2003, 2004, and 2005 during which eight hurricanes struck the neighborhood" ("Insurance Agent Accused," 2007, p. 1).

Many of the insurance crimes target elderly persons, making the consequences of lost income particularly significant. One Florida insurance agent defrauded 60 victims, but only 37 of them participated in the trial. Many of the others "died before the trial took place" (Varian, 2000, p. 1). The agent had asked them "to invest in expansions of his insurance business or for short-term loans to book entertainers from the former Lawrence Welk program." In another case, 75-year-old Martha Cunningham "owned a $417,000 home in Prince George's County and held $61,000 in annuities before she met Edward Hanson [an insurance agent]. . . . Today the widow is essentially broke and inundated with debt" (Wiggins, 2009, p. B02). Hanson stole everything the elderly woman owned. The breadth of these schemes is but one pattern surrounding insurance crimes.

U.S. Navy Photo by Photographer's Mate 3rd Class Todd Frantom (http://www.navy.mil/view_single.asp?id=14885)

▲ **Photo 3.5**   Researchers suggest that fraudulent insurance agents try to paint the worst scenario possible to get clients to purchase as much insurance as possible. Is this sales tactic a good business practice, or is it criminal? What do you think?

Insurance Crime Patterns

In addressing the dynamics of crimes in the insurance system, industry insiders either attribute the offenses to rotten apple explanations or engage in victim blaming (Ericson & Doyle, 2006). The rotten apple explanations suggest that a few rogue agents and brokers commit the vast majority of insurance crimes, while the victim blaming explanations suggest that failures on the part of victims (and greed) make them potential targets for the few rogue insurance employees that exist. Ericson and Doyle point out that these explanations are shortsighted and argue that insurance crimes are institutionalized in the industry by the practices and strategies encouraged among insurance employees. Aspects of the insurance industry that they discuss as evidence of the way that these crimes are institutionalized in the insurance system include the following:

- The complex products sold by insurance companies
- The construction of risk as calculable
- The commission structure
- A revolving door of agents
- Mixed messages about an aggressive sales culture
- Limited regulation of market misconduct

A related pattern that surfaces is that these are offenses that seem to occur in various cultures. What this suggests is that the insurance market and practices at the core of this industry might promote fraud. The phrase "opportunistic fraud" has been used to describe those times when fraudulent insurance providers use a disaster or other misfortune to commit their offenses (Pao, Tzeng, & Wang, 2014). As will be discussed later, sometimes white-collar crimes are rationalized by offenders as "sharp business practices." This is particularly the case in insurance crime cases. One former life insurance agent is quoted as saying, "you have to understand, everything is crooked" (Ericson & Doyle, 2006, p. 993). Ericson and Doyle provide an example that describes how "deceptive sales are rife and institutionalized in the life insurance industry" and point to the scare tactics used by agents and brokers that are euphemistically called "backing the hearse up to the door" by insurance insiders. Good business practices, or crime? You can decide for yourself.

SUMMARY

- To introduce students to the nature of crime in lower-class occupations, in this chapter, attention was given to the crimes occurring in the following systems: (1) employee theft in the retail system, (2) crimes in the entertainment service system, (3) fraud in the sales/service system, and (4) insurance system.
- Several different varieties of employee theft in retail settings occur. Here are some examples: overcharging, shortchanging, coupon stuffing, credits for nonexistent returns, theft of production supplies and raw materials, embezzlement, over-ordering supplies, theft of credit card information, theft of goods, theft of money from the cash register, and sweetheart deals.
- Employee theft prevention strategies include (a) importation strategies, (b) internal strategies, (c) technological strategies, (d) organizational culture strategies, and (e) awareness strategies.
- In considering crimes in the restaurant industry, two broad categories can be highlighted: crimes by the restaurant against consumers and crimes by workers against the restaurant.
- The most common types of home repair fraud are believed to be roof repair, asphalt paving or driveway sealing fraud, house painting fraud, termite and pest control fraud, and tree pruning and landscaping fraud.
- Auto repair fraud includes billing for services not provided, unnecessary repairs, airbag fraud, and insurance fraud.
- Insurance crimes are rarely studied for two reasons: (1) They are hard to understand, and (2) people don't typically know when they have been victimized by insurance crimes (Ericson & Doyle, 2006).
- Four different categories of insurance crimes by workers in the insurance system exist: (1) crimes by agents against the insurance company, (2) investment-focused crimes, (3) theft crimes against consumers, and (4) sales-directed crimes against consumers.
- Estimates suggest that insurance fraud collectively "raises the yearly cost of premiums by $300 for the average household" (FBI, 2010b).

- For individuals victimized by these offenses, the consequences of insurance crimes can be particularly devastating.
- Industry insiders either attribute the insurance offenses to rotten apple explanations or engage in victim blaming (Ericson & Doyle, 2006).
- Ericson and Doyle (2006) point out that insurance crimes are institutionalized in the industry by the practices and strategies encouraged among insurance employees.

KEY TERMS

Airbag fraud	Internal strategies	Sweetheart deals
Annuities fraud	Misrepresentation	Switching
Auto insurance fraud	Promissory note fraud	Technological strategies
Automotive sales fraud	Organizational culture strategies	Theft crimes against consumers
Auto repair fraud	Over-ordering supplies	Theft of credit card information
Awareness strategies	Overcharging	Theft of goods
Billing for services not provided	Overtreatment	Theft of money from the cash register
Churning	Retail system	Theft of production supplies and raw materials
Coupon stuffing	Rolling over	
Credits for nonexistent returns	Sales-directed crimes	Undertreatment
Embezzlement	Sales/service system	Unnecessary auto repairs
Entertainment services system	Shortchanging	Viatical settlement fraud
Falsifying account information	Sliding	
Home repair fraud	Stacking	

DISCUSSION QUESTIONS

1. What types of employee theft do you think are most serious? Why?
2. Should employees always be fired if they are caught engaging in crime in a restaurant? Explain.
3. How are home repair frauds and auto repair frauds similar to one another?
4. Why do you think insurance crimes occur?
5. Do you think you have ever been overcharged by an auto mechanic? If so, why do you think the offense occurred?
6. Do you know anyone who has committed retail theft? Why do you think that person committed the offense?

WEB RESOURCES

Avoid Student Insurance Scams: http://www.studentfinancedomain.com/budgets/avoid_student_insurance_scams.aspx

Coalition Against Insurance Fraud: http://www.insurancefraud.org/scam_alerts.htm

Prevent Home Repair Fraud: http://hbaa.org/wp/remodeling/prevent

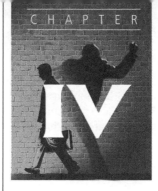

Crimes in the Health Care System

CHAPTER HIGHLIGHTS

- Fraud by Doctors
- Unnecessary Surgery
- Medication Errors
- General Offending by Doctors
- Fraud by Pharmacists
- Drug Use by Pharmacists
- Sexual Abuse
- Elder Abuse by Health Care Workers
- Home Health Care Fraud
- Durable Medical Equipment Fraud
- Medical Malpractice

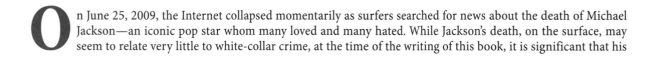

O n June 25, 2009, the Internet collapsed momentarily as surfers searched for news about the death of Michael Jackson—an iconic pop star whom many loved and many hated. While Jackson's death, on the surface, may seem to relate very little to white-collar crime, at the time of the writing of this book, it is significant that his doctor, Conrad Murray, was charged with involuntary manslaughter for giving Jackson a lethal dose of propofol. Murray administered the drug to Jackson to help him sleep. Instead, investigators believed that the drug killed the pop star. Two years later he was convicted of involuntary manslaughter for the pop star's death. Murray spent two years in prison before being released. As will be shown later in this chapter, hundreds of thousands of others have died from medication errors.

It is not just Michael Jackson's doctor, however, who has been accused of misconduct in performing health care services. Consider the following cases as they were described verbatim from their original sources:

- Jeffrey H. Sloman, Acting United States Attorney for the Southern District of Florida, and Bill McCollum, Florida Attorney General, announced that two Miami doctors have been convicted of Medicare and Medicaid fraud. . . . [The defendants] were convicted for their involvement in a scheme with Diagnostic Medical Choice, a Southwest Miami clinic that billed the Medicaid and Medicare programs for expensive infusion medications intended to treat a rare illness suffered by a small portion of those inflicted with HIV/AIDS. The physicians wrote prescriptions for large quantities of these medications and sought federal and state reimbursement, but the clinic had little if any of the medications in stock and rarely if ever provided infusions to patients. ("Two Miami Doctors," 2009)

- The Tennessee Bureau of Investigation announced on May 20 that . . . a health care aide, pleaded guilty in district criminal court to one count of TennCare Fraud. Austin was given a two year suspended sentence and four years probation. Additionally, [the defendant] was ordered to pay restitution in the amount of $3,075 to the Bureau of TennCare. . . . [The defendant], a personal assistant employed by United Cerebral Palsy, billed TennCare for services not rendered between June 2006 and June 2007. [She] submitted to her employer contact notes for services and upon investigation, it was discovered that the majority of these contacts never occurred. (*Medicaid Fraud Report May/June*, 2009, p. 9)

- An indictment was filed charging ***** with Medicaid fraud and theft. **** was a home health care aide. Video surveillance was reviewed and found that **** was billing for services not provided. Of the 48 units billed during the surveillance period, **** only worked 11 units. (*Medicaid Fraud Report January/February*, 2015, p. 3).

- Attorney General DeWine announced on January 13 that **** entered a no contest plea to attempted unauthorized use of property. . . . **** was using one of his patient's cellphone without the patient's consent. An investigation revealed that **** used the cellphone to text his girlfriend and to take inappropriate pictures of himself to send to his girlfriend. ***** was interviewed and admitted to using the cellphone without the patient's consent. (*Medicaid Fraud Report January/February*, 2015, p. 9)

- [The] licensed vocational nurse was sentenced to two years of deferred adjudication community supervision, ordered to complete 200 hours of community service, and to pay a $500 fine after she pleaded guilty in state court to possession of a controlled substance by fraud. ***** allegedly stole Norco from residents of Wellington Care Center for her own use. (*Medicaid Fraud Report November/December*, 2014, p. 6)

- Attorney General Abbott announced on December 18 that [the doctor] was sentenced in federal court to 15 months in prison followed by three years of supervised release, and was ordered to pay $328,238.41 in restitution. **** pleaded guilty to conspiracy to commit health care fraud for his role in the operation of his facility, Beaumont Medical Clinic. **** allegedly allowed unlicensed staff to operate his opiate detox program, including seeing patients and prescribing schedule II narcotics to substance abuse patients, and then billed as if he had treated the patients. (*Medicaid Fraud Report November/December*, 2014, p. 16)

As this brief synopsis shows, health care employees from a range of health care occupations have been accused of wrongdoing. To shed some light on white-collar crime among these employees, in this chapter, attention is given to crimes committed by offenders working in the health care system. Five points about the health care system help to create a foundation from which insight about health care crimes will evolve:

- Most offenders in the health care system have specific training related to their occupations, and some have advanced degrees.
- Individuals seek services from those in the health care system when they are in need of some form of medical care. This may create vulnerability for those seeking services.
- The health care system interacts with other systems. For example, changes in the educational and technological systems influence the type of health care provided. These broader changes also impact the types of crimes committed in the health care system.
- For the most part, citizens place a great deal of trust in health care providers, with significant respect given to upper-class members of both groups.
- The health care profession tends to self-regulate itself in an effort to promote appropriate conduct.

When we go to see our doctors, dentists, pharmacists, or other health care provider, most of us likely give little thought to the possibility that these professionals would engage in criminal actions. In fact, most of us likely assume that our health care providers would never even consider breaking their ethical code or the criminal law. For the most part, we are correct in this assumption because most health care providers do not commit occupational crimes. Some, however, do.

Drew H. Cohen. Creative Commons Attribution 3.0 Unported license. https://creativecommons.org/licenses/by3.0/deed.en

▲ **Photo 4.1** Do you think Michael Jackson's death was caused by a white-collar crime?

IN FOCUS 4.1

When Physicians Go Bad

Physicians: District of Columbia

The District of Columbia Medicaid Fraud Control Unit announced on December 18 that Dr. *****, a medical doctor licensed in the District of Columbia, who practiced medicine under the name of *****, was found guilty on December 17 by a federal jury of one count of Health Care Fraud and sixteen counts of False Statements in Health Care Matters. ***** was already ordered to forfeit $133,418 of proceeds derived from the health care fraud conviction.

According to the government's evidence at trial, during the period between December 2002 and May 2005, *****

repeatedly submitted false claims to Amerigroup Corporation (Amerigroup), which contracted with the District of Columbia Medicaid Program to provide health care services to low income DC residents. *****, who prepared and submitted his own billing to Amerigroup, repeatedly submitted false claims in which he purported to have performed invasive surgical procedures on DC Medicaid patients that were never performed, billed for "ghost office" visits that never occurred, and continued to bill for a period of time after a minor or major procedure during which no additional bills could be submitted, in violation of global billing rules. To substantiate

(Continued)

(Continued)

the false billing, ***** created false progress notes indicating the dates, times, and surgical procedures that he claimed to have performed, and inserted the false progress notes into his patients' medical files.

During the trial, the defense claimed that a now deceased individual was responsible for preparing and submitting the false claims to Amerigroup. The defense called two individuals currently employed by *****, who testified that the deceased individual was responsible for the false billing. In rebuttal, the government was able to establish that neither the deceased individual nor the defense witnesses worked for the defendant during the relevant time.

For further information contact Special Assistant U.S. Attorney Jacqueline Schesnol (202) 727-8008.

Source: Reprinted From National Association of Attorneys Generals. (2009). Medicaid Fraud Reports. November/December 2009, p. 14. Available from http://www.namfcu.net/resources/medicaid-fraud-reports-newsletters/2009-publications/09NovDec.pdf

● ● ● Fraud by Doctors

As Paul Jesilow and his colleagues (Jesilow, Pontell, & Geis, 1985) note, few criminal justice and criminology textbooks give a great deal of attention to crimes by doctors, "probably because of the respect, power, and trust that the profession engenders" (p. 151). Even Sutherland implied that doctors were unlikely to engage in white-collar crime, and as a result, Sutherland gave "only scant attention to doctors [and] maintained that physicians were probably more honest than other professionals" (Wilson, Lincoln, Chappell, & Fraser, 1986, p. 129).

The level of trust that individuals place in doctors cannot be **overstated**. Illustrating the trust that we have in the profession, one author team quoted a Federal Bureau of Investigation (FBI) agent who said to them, "What other stranger would you go in and take your clothes off in front of? It's that kind of trust." (Pontell, Jesilow, & Geis, 1984, p. 406). While readers might be able to think of at least one other profession where "clients" remove all of their clothes in front of strangers, the other profession is an illegal profession in most places in the United States (except parts of Nevada). The medical profession is a legal profession that is plagued by illegal acts.

The most pervasive form of fraud committed by doctors entails the commission of Medicare and Medicaid fraud and abuse. Both medical programs were created in the mid-1960s. **Medicare** was created as a federal program to serve elderly citizens, while **Medicaid** operates at the state level to serve the poor. When Medicare and Medicaid were first created, there was no concern about fraud; instead, the concern was whether doctors would actually participate in the programs because Medicare and Medicaid faced opposition from the American Medical Association (Pontell et al., 1984).

In time, doctors increasingly participated in the insurance programs, and by the mid-1970s, authorities recognized that fraud was pervasive in Medicare and Medicaid. This pervasiveness continues today. It is estimated that between 3 percent and 10 percent of health care spending is lost to fraud. This means that in the United States between 68 and 226 billion dollars is lost to fraud each year (National Health Care Anti-Fraud Association [NHCAA], 2010). The NHCAA points out that the lower limit of these estimates is still "more than the gross domestic product of 120 different countries including Iceland, Ecuador, and Kenya" (2010). Incidentally, it is expected that, by 2019, one-fifth of the gross domestic product in the United States will entail health care spending (Center for Medicare and Medicaid Services, 2011).

Several varieties of misconduct are committed by doctors. At the broadest level, legal experts make a distinction between fraud and abuse. **Fraud** refers to intentionally criminal behaviors by physicians, whereas abuse focuses on unintentional misuse of program funds. If a doctor intentionally steals from Medicaid, this would be fraud. Alternatively, if a doctor accidentally overuses Medicaid services, this would be abuse. Note that authorities will respond to abuse cases as well in an effort to recoup lost funds. The distinction is significant because it predicts the types of justice systems that are likely to respond to the cases. In fraud cases, the criminal justice system will be involved, and criminal penalties, such as incarceration, probation, and fines, will be applied. In abuse cases, the civil justice system or other regulatory system will respond, and penalties will be monetary in nature. See In Focus 4.1, When Physicians Go Bad, for an overview of the way that a justice system got involved in a case involving a doctor who clearly and intentionally committed fraud, though he tried to blame his actions on others.

Within these broader categories, several specific forms of fraud and abuse exist (FBI, 2010b; Payne, 1995; Pontell, Jesilow, & Geis, 1982). **Phantom treatment** occurs when providers bill Medicare, Medicaid, or other insurance agencies for services they never actually provided. This is also known as fee-for-service reimbursement. **Substitute providers** occur when the medical services were performed by an employee who was not authorized to perform the services. **Upcoding** (or upgrading) refers to situations where providers bill for services that are more expensive than the services that were actually provided. The **provision of unnecessary services** occurs when health care providers perform and bill for tests or procedures that were not needed (just as auto mechanics might perform unnecessary repairs to our cars). **Misrepresenting services** occurs when providers describe the service differently on medical forms in an effort to gain payment for the services (e.g., elective surgeries might be defined as medically necessary). **Falsifying records** occurs when providers change medical forms in an effort to be reimbursed by the insurance provider. **Overcharging patients** refers to situations where providers charge patients more than regulations permit. **Unbundling** refers to instances when the provider bills separately for tests and procedures that are supposed to be billed as one procedure (imagine that you ordered a package meal and the restaurant tried to bill you for each type of food separately). **Pingponging** occurs when patients are unnecessarily referred to other providers and "bounced around" various medical providers. **Ganging** refers to situations where providers bill for multiple family members, though they treated only one of them. **Kickbacks** occur when providers direct patients to other providers in exchange for a pecuniary response for the other provider. **Co-pay waivers** occur when providers waive the patient's co-pay but still bill the insurance company. **Medical snowballing** occurs when providers bill for several related services, though only one service was provided.

These types of fraud occur with different degrees of regularity. Figure 4.1 shows the relative frequency of various types of Medicaid fraud by health care providers that were criminally prosecuted in a study of 572 cases of fraud by health care professionals. As shown in the figure, fee-for-service reimbursement cases were prosecuted most often, followed by upgrading. Unnecessary surgery cases were rarely prosecuted.

Several studies have considered different aspects of fraud by physicians. One consistent finding from these studies is that psychiatrists and psychologists are accused of fraud more often than other providers (Geis, Jesilow, Pontell, & O'Brien, 1985; Payne, 1995). Figure 4.2 shows the types of providers accused of fraud in the Payne (1995) study. It is striking that so many of the cases involved psychiatrists and psychologists—as compared to the number of psychiatrists and psychologists in the medical profession. Another study found that 12.8 percent of 584 physician disciplines over a 30-month period in California were psychiatrists (Morrison & Morrison, 2001). This was nearly twice as many psychiatrists than would be expected if the percentages were equivalent to the total number of psychiatrists in the professions.

Before assuming that their overrepresentation stems from levels of honesty, it is important to consider the nature of billing practices for psychiatrists and psychologists as compared to other health care professionals (Geis et al., 1985). Briefly, mental health professionals often bill for time, whereas other professionals bill for more complicated medical procedures. For investigators, it is much easier to prove "time violations" than "treatment violations." Investigators can ask patients how long they spent with their provider and compare the patient's statement with the providers' bill submitted to the insurance company. If investigators ask about the treatment they received from physicians, it is unlikely that the patient would be able to identify the services with the same degree of precision. As an illustration of the way that time violations are easy to identify, see In Focus 4.2, When Psychologists Go Bad: Billing for Time.

Other patterns characterizing health care fraud have also been identified in prior research. For example, research shows that when females are accused of health care fraud, they tend to be accused along with other providers more than male offenders are (Payne, 1995). It is plausible that females are prosecuted along with more powerful providers in an effort to get female providers to testify against their colleagues, or in some cases, their bosses.

Another pattern surrounding health care fraud is related to the systems approach—changes in the broader system have influenced the distribution and characteristics of health care fraud (Payne, 2005). For example, just as the nature of health care changes, so too does the nature of health care fraud. As the technological system changed, opportunities for health care fraud changed. As the number of doctors changed in the 1970s and 1980s (a period in which the number of doctors increased by 66 percent), allegations of fraud and convictions for health care fraud also increased (Bucy, 1989). In fact, "convictions of health care providers increased almost 234 percent between 1979 and 1986" (Bucy, 1989, p. 870).

Explanations for fraud have focused on structural explanations, socialization factors, cultural factors, and enforcement dynamics. In terms of structural explanations, some have argued that the structure of the Medicare and Medicaid systems is believed to "invite fraud and abuse" (Pontell et al., 1982, p.119). Low reimbursement rates, complex red tape, and bureaucratic confusion make participation in the programs difficult for health care providers. To get paid the same amount that they get paid for treating patients with private insurance, some physicians and other health care providers have fraudulently billed Medicare and Medicaid.

Socialization explanations focus on how medical students perceive Medicaid and Medicare. In general, research shows that students have less than favorable attitudes toward the programs (Byars & Payne, 2000; Keenan, Brown, Pontell, & Geis, 1985). Surveys of 144 medical students found that the students supported tougher penalties for fraudulent providers, but they also believed that structural changes in Medicare and Medicaid were warranted (Keenan et al., 1985). In effect, there is a possibility that medical students are learning to perceive the insurance programs negatively during their medical training.

Cultural factors explore how health care fraud occurs in various cultures. Across the globe, it has been estimated that "any health care organization will lose between 3 and 10 percent to fraud and abuse" (Brooks, Button, & Gee, 2012). The amount lost is tied to specific features of the health care system. In Sweden, for example, the country shifted its health care system toward privatization. According to Jesilow (2012), the move "will likely increase fraud" (p. 32). His suggestion is traced to the fee-for-service payment system that, in his view, incentivizes fraud. In essence, cultures with public health care would, theoretically, have less fraud than those that have payment systems encouraging fraud.

Enforcement explanations suggest that the pervasiveness of fraud is attributed to the historical lack of criminal justice enforcement activities against health care providers. This changed in the 1990s when state and federal enforcement efforts in this area increased. Legislative changes also occurred. For example, the **Health Insurance Portability Act of 1996** was passed to make health care fraud a federal offense, with penalties ranging from 10 years to life (if the fraud leads to a death).

CAREERS RESPONDING TO WHITE-COLLAR CRIME

Investigative Analyst

Candidates must possess knowledge of, and skill in applying, a wide range of concepts, principles, and practices involving

- criminological theories and research methodologies;
- the use of investigative and intelligence gathering systems;
- information search and retrieval techniques and procedures; and
- automated intelligence systems

sufficient to:

- conduct analysis of investigative cases (e.g., financial crimes, access device fraud, telecommunications fraud, electronic crimes, counterfeit U.S. currency and obligations);

- access, collect, examine, and analyze data, evidence, and other information from a variety of sources, including public access and law enforcement databases;
- conduct independent research, reconstruct complicated events, establish possible criminal associations, detect trends, and develop case-specific subject profiles;
- prepare link analysis in highly complex criminal investigations; and
- prepare reports of findings to use as evidence in prosecuting cases.

Source: Reprinted from Job Family Position Classification Standard for Administrative Work in the Inspection, Investigation, Enforcement, and Compliance Group, 1800. Available online at https://www.opm.gov/policy-data-oversight/classification-qualifications/classifying-general-schedule-positions/standards/1800/1800a.pdf

Note that while physicians are held in high regard, when they violate their codes of conduct, the public reaction is more severe than when someone of lower status breaks the rules. Rosoff (1989) refers to this dynamic as status liability.

Data mining by investigative analysts has proved to be an effective tool in identifying possible cases of health care fraud (See Box 4.1 for the duties associated with this career). This process includes gathering (extracting) the data, cleaning the data (making sure it is accurate), developing a data profile, transforming the data so it is consistent, and examining the data for trends and patterns that might suggest fraud (Margret & Sreenivasan, 2013). In a similar way, data can be used to predict the extent of fraud. One such effort reviewed claims from Medicare beneficiaries and estimated that fraud and abuse payment technology could save $20.70 for the benefit system (Margret & Sreenivasan, 2013). Preventing health care fraud will reduce the costs of health care. Ironically, though, when health care cost saving efforts are considered, efforts to limit costs in health care fraud are rarely considered (Brooks et al., 2012).

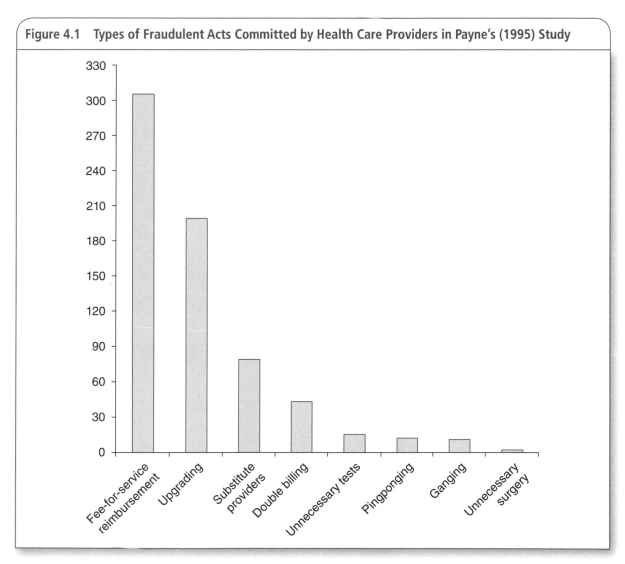

Figure 4.1   Types of Fraudulent Acts Committed by Health Care Providers in Payne's (1995) Study

Source: Adapted from Payne, B. K. (1995). Medicaid fraud. *Criminal Justice Policy Review, 7,* 61–74.

Figure 4.2   Types of Providers Accused of Fraud and Abuse in Payne's (1995) Study

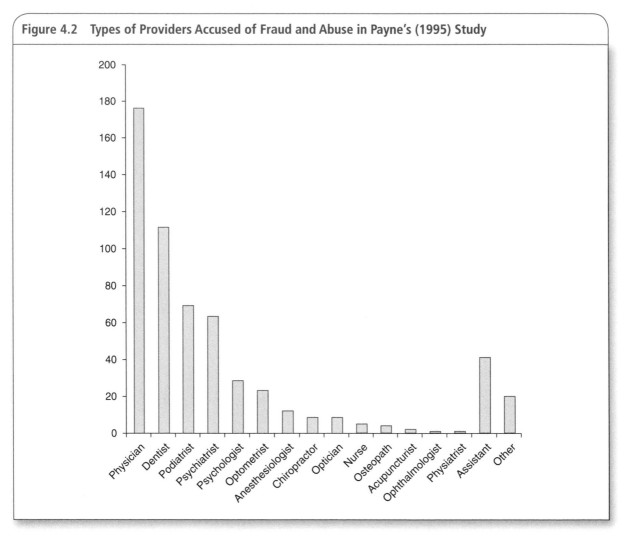

Source: Adapted from Payne, B. K. (1995). Medicaid fraud. *Criminal Justice Policy Review, 7*, 61–74.

IN FOCUS   4.2

When Psychologists Go Bad: Billing for Time

The Tennessee Bureau of Investigation announced on April 20 that *****, a clinical psychologist, pleaded guilty in United States District Court of Middle Tennessee to one count of health care fraud. ***** was sentenced to serve 18 months in the custody of the United States Bureau of Prisons, to be followed by three years probation upon his release. Additionally, ***** was ordered to pay restitution in the amounts of $44,825.95 to the Centers for Medicare and Medicaid Services and $32,264.75

to the Bureau of TennCare. This case was opened on September 29, 2005 based upon a referral from the Department of Health and Human Services, Office of Inspector General. It was alleged that Dr. *****, a provider of psychological services for nursing homes and rehabilitation facilities, billed for services not rendered and overbilled for individual psychotherapy services. *An initial review of the data indicated that ****** billed 139 days in which the total time spent with the beneficiaries exceeded 24 hours per day.* Further investigation showed that over a 90 day period in 2005, ***** billed for 14 days on which he did not travel to a facility or perform psychotherapy services. ***** did travel to facilities on 28 of those days, however in many cases the amount of time billed exceeded the actual amount of time he was present at the facility. On January 27, 2007, Dr. ***** was charged with one count of health care fraud. (emphasis added)

For more information contact Special Agent Ramona Smith (615) 744-4229.

Source: Reprinted From National Association of Attorneys General. (2009). *Medicaid Fraud Reports.* May/June 2009, p. 18. Available from http://www.namfcu.net/resources/medicaid-fraud-reports-newsletters/2009-publications/09MayJune.pdf

● ● ● Unnecessary Surgery

As noted in the introduction of this text when the consequences of white-collar crime were addressed, it is estimated that 7.5 million unnecessary surgeries and medical procedures occur annually and 12,000 Americans are killed each year by these unnecessary surgeries (Black, 2005). This estimate, if accurate, means that these unnecessary medical surgeries and procedures occur once every 4 seconds or so. Put another way, by the time you finish this paragraph, someone has had an unnecessary surgery or procedure. Describing the overuse of screening methods and treatments for prostate cancer, Otis Brawley (2009), chief medical officer for the American Cancer Society, commented, "Every treatment looks good, when *more than* 90% of men getting it *do not* need it" (p. 1295).

At least six overlapping reasons help explain the pervasiveness of unnecessary surgeries. First, differing opinions among medical providers will likely

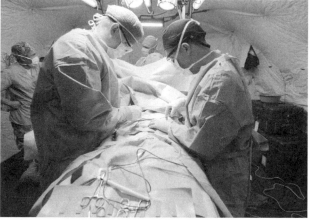

▲ **Photo 4.2**   Unnecessary surgeries are one type of white-collar offense in the health care field. The vast majority of these cases, though, are undetected.

Jim Eryant/NW Guardian. Creative Commons Attribution 2.0 Generic. https://creativecommons.org/licenses/by/2.0/

result in some providers recommending surgery and other providers recommending a different course of action. Medicine is not an exact science, and those providing unnecessary services would likely justify the services on various medical grounds.

Second, the stigma of various forms of disease is such that patients are willing to expose themselves to procedures in order to battle and overcome the disease. Consider prostate cancer. While Brawley notes that many prostate cancer treatments are not needed, he recognizes that the very concept creates fear in individuals who have long assumed that all forms of cancers must be eradicated to live a full life. Most of us would never assume that we can live with cancer or that it would go away on its own. Brawley suggests that we are misinformed in that sense.

Third, the degree of trust that individuals have for their health care providers is such that patients tend to assume that procedures ordered by doctors are necessary. Assuming otherwise opens us up to the risk of the consequences of whatever ailment we are battling. The adage "better safe than sorry" comes to mind. In general, we trust our doctors and will follow their surgical and procedural advice as a matter of protecting ourselves from harm. The irony is that unnecessary procedures may create harm.

Fourth, while we are socialized to trust our health care providers, we have at the same time been socialized not to trust insurance companies. Regularly, we hear of situations where insurance companies deny coverage on the grounds that procedures are not needed. The typical reaction is to assume that the medical provider's recommendation is correct and any suggestion otherwise, particularly those offered by representatives of the insurance industry, are cast aside.

Fifth, and somewhat related to the above explanations, one can draw attention to what can be coined the "medicalized socialization" that we experience in our lives. In effect, we are socialized to turn to the health care system to fix our illnesses, diseases, and ailments. Although more attention has recently been given to preventing diseases in the first place, as consumers we have an expectation that our health care needs will be met by health care providers. In effect, we have long played a passive role in receiving health care rather than administering our own health care. As a result, we pass our health care decisions off to our providers.

Finally, one can point to conflict explanations to address the persistence of unnecessary surgeries. Conflict explanations point to the economic gains of health care for those with power. Consider that the United States spends 53 percent more on health care per person than other countries spend (Anderson, Hussey, Frogner, & Waters, 2005). Anderson and his coauthors argue that it is not overuse that is causing these high expenditures but high prices in the first place. From a conflict perspective, those with power control the pricing of health care. Moreover, by pricing surgeries and procedures at a high price, an even stronger incentive may exist to commit unnecessary surgeries. It's one thing to perform an unnecessary wart removal, which would be a low-cost surgery; it's quite another to perform unnecessary coronary bypass, which is the most common unnecessary surgery in the United States (Black, 2005). As another example, consider that women in the United States have four times more hysterectomies than women in Sweden (Parker, 2009). According to Black (2005), "the only people who seem to really benefit from these unnecessary medical procedures are the medical professionals who stand to make exorbitant amounts of money from performing them."

Many severe consequences may arise from unnecessary surgeries. A case described by Jesilow and his colleagues (1985) suggests that unnecessary surgeries are analogous to assaults. They cite a case where an ophthalmologist performed several unnecessary eye surgeries that left patients with either impaired vision or blindness. The doctor performed the procedures simply so he could bill Medicaid for them. Also, note that unnecessary surgeries deprive poor individuals of the health care they need (Pontell et al., 1982). Another irony arises—when practitioners dole out health care procedures to people who don't need them, those who need the health care services are deprived of the care they do need.

Other consequences also surface. For example, the element of time is relevant. Think about how long a visit to the doctor takes. Individuals need to take off from work, drive to the office or clinic, wait in the waiting room, get moved back to the exam room only to wait some more, and then experience the procedure or surgery. Then, they are sent to the pharmacist where they will have to spend more time to complete that particular transaction. In the end, if the procedure or surgery was unnecessary, all of this time was wasted (Payne & Berg, 1997). Somewhat related is being told that one needs surgery or a procedure that is sure to create some sort of mental anguish or stress for some individuals. That the surgeries or procedures are unnecessary suggests that providers are basically bullying patients mentally.

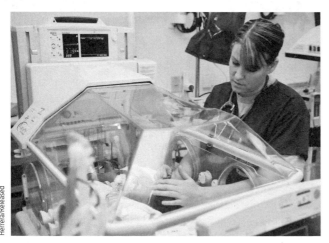

U.S. Navy photo by Mass Communication Specialist 2nd Class John O'Neill Herrera/Released

▲ **Photo 4.3**   Health care providers hold the lives of their patients in their hands. Most are ethical and law abiding. A few, however, are not.

● ● ● Medication Errors

Medication errors occur when health care providers deliver or prescribe the wrong medications to patients. These errors can be harmful in two ways: (1) The patient is given a drug he or she does not need, and this drug could cause harm; or (2) the patient could experience harm from not getting the drug that is actually needed. Cox (2010) notes that doctors have long said, "Do not let your friends and family schedule hospital visits in July." The basis for this "warning" is the increase in medication errors that seem to occur each July. Cox describes a study by sociologists David Phillips and Gwendolyn Parker that addressed why this spike in errors seems to occur.

Phillips and Parker, sociologists from the University of San Diego, examined 244,388 deaths occurring from medication errors between 1979 and 2006. They found that deaths at a high number of teaching hospitals increased by 10 percent in July each year. This finding supported previous speculation that the "July effect" could be attributed to the fact that new doctors and residents begin practicing in July. Thus, their lack of experience is believed to contribute to medication errors.

Phillips shared an interesting exchange with another reporter: "One physician—not knowing I was studying this issue—referred to the issue and said to me: 'It's possible, you should probably avoid going in [being hospitalized] during July'" (Raloff, 2010). As noted in the beginning of this chapter, it is believed that medication errors led to the death of Michael Jackson. Incidentally, his death occurred 5 days before the beginning of July, and his doctor had several years of experience practicing medicine.

● ● ● General Offending by Doctors

A number of other types of misconduct are committed by malfeasant doctors during the course of their occupational routines. These other types can be characterized as general offending by doctors. The nonprofit group Public Citizen collects data on physicians involved in misconduct and has published a report and database called **Questionable Doctors.** The report includes information about doctors, their violations, and sanctions given to doctors (Lim, 2002). According to Public Citizen, the types of physician misconduct are wide ranging. From most serious to least serious, the general types of offending by doctors include the following:

- Conviction of a crime
- Practicing without a license or issuing and writing prescriptions without a license
- Losing hospital privileges
- Failing to comply with an order from a medical board
- Deceiving a medical board
- Proving substandard or incompetent care
- Sexually abusing a patient
- Drug or alcohol abuse
- Overprescribing drugs
- Practicing medicine with a mental illness that inhibits service delivery
- Committing insurance fraud
- Falsifying patient records
- Overcharging
- Professional misconduct (e.g., unprofessional behavior)
- Failure to comply with a professional rule (e.g., child abuse reporting) (Lim, 2002, pp. 154–155)

Lim (2002) used the Questionable Doctors database to review the types of violations and crimes committed by women doctors in California between 1990 and 1994. Of the 425 violations she reviewed, just 30 were committed by female physicians. Most frequently, female physicians were sanctioned for being convicted of a crime, providing substandard care, and failing to comply with a professional rule. Lim noted that the violations committed by women doctors were usually "self-inflicted" (p. 163).

Public Citizen also collects data on the rates of sanctions against physicians by state medical boards for "serious violations" (Wolfe, Kahn, & Resnevic, 2010). Between 2009 and 2011, the states with the lowest rates of violations and violation rates per 1,000 physicians were

- South Carolina (1.33)
- Washington, DC (1.47)
- Minnesota (1.49)
- Connecticut (1.82)
- Wisconsin (1.90)
- Rhode Island (2.02)
- Nevada (2.07)
- New Jersey (2.26)
- Florida (2.28) (Wolfe, Williams, and Zaslow, 2012)

In reviewing these states, some might assume that lower rates means a lower rate of offending by physicians. While this might be the case, Public Citizen points to another possibility—these may be states where medical boards are allowing physicians to get away with more violations than other states. This is likely a more plausible suggestion as there is nothing to suggest why certain states would have a higher number of malfeasant physicians. It is plausible, though, to suggest that sanctioning behaviors are a product of state medical boards.

● ● ● Fraud by Pharmacists

Doctors are not the only upper-class members of the health care profession to engage in fraudulent activities. Pharmacists have also been implicated in numerous frauds and abuses against the insurance system. Interestingly, pharmacists have long been rated among the top most trusted professions on trust surveys of the public. That some of them commit fraud is not a reason to lower the profession's trust ratings, but one must be careful not to assume that all pharmacists are playing by the rules that guide their occupational activities.

Because pharmacists have long been viewed as so trustworthy, few criminologists have focused on deviant action in this profession. One researcher, Dean Dabney, conducted several studies examining illicit drug use by pharmacists. Interviewing dozens of pharmacists, Dabney's research suggests that proximity to drugs that are readily available and belief that they know enough about the drugs to self-medicate contribute to their decisions to use and subsequently abuse drugs.

In one of his pharmacist studies, Payne and Dabney (1997) (that's me, by the way) examined 292 cases of **prescription fraud** prosecuted by fraud control units across the United States. Our research uncovered eight types of fraud among the prosecuted cases. **Generic drug substitution** involved cases where the pharmacist gave the consumer a generic drug but billed the insurance company for a more expensive drug (imagine if you bought a box of your favorite cereal made by one of the top cereal makers and generic cereal was in the box, but the box was branded with the more expensive cereal). **Short counting** occurs when pharmacists dispense fewer pills than prescribed, but they bill the insurance company as if they had dispensed all of the pills (do you count the pills to make sure you got them all?). Like fraud by doctors, **double billing** occurs when pharmacists bill more than two parties for the same prescription. **Billing for nonexistent prescriptions** occurs when pharmacists bill for prescriptions that never actually existed. **Forgery** occurs when pharmacists forge the signature of the doctor or the consumer or forge the name of a more expensive drug on the prescription. **Mislabeling of drugs** occurs when pharmacists label drugs incorrectly in an effort to hide the fact that the pharmacist did not provide the prescribed drug to the patient. **Delivery of a controlled substance** is more of a legal term and a reference to instances when the pharmacist wrongfully, perhaps without a prescription, provides controlled substances to consumers. Finally, **illegally buying prescriptions** involves situations where pharmacists buy prescriptions from patients and then bill the insurance company without filling the prescription.

This last variety of prescription fraud typically involves schemes whereby pharmacists work with drug addicts to carry out the offense. The pharmacist instructs the addict to go to different doctors and get prescriptions filled. The addict is instructed to fake an illness (one that the pharmacist suggests) so that the doctor writes an expensive prescription for the addict. The addict gives the pharmacist the prescription. The pharmacist gives the addict some drugs (usually something addictive like painkillers); then, the pharmacist bills the insurance agency for the prescription that was never actually filled. As will be shown in the policing chapter, to respond to these cases, undercover law enforcement officers sometimes pose as drug addicts to establish a case against the pharmacist.

Past research has demonstrated difficulty convicting pharmacists. Excluding those schemes where pharmacists illegally buy prescriptions, a common defense used by pharmacists is that they must have misread the doctor's handwriting. If you have ever tried to read a prescription, you will likely be inclined to accept this claim. After all, the handwriting of doctors does, in fact, seem to be very difficult to read. However, pharmacists are trained to read their shorthand, and if they are unable to read it, regulations stipulate that they are supposed to call the doctor's office for clarification.

My research with Dabney identified six patterns of prescription fraud by pharmacists. First, offenders tended to be male. Second, the cases rarely resulted in incarceration, except for egregious cases. Third, in some cases, assistants were convicted, presumably in an effort to sustain a conviction against the pharmacist. Fourth, the vast majority of convictions were obtained through guilty pleas, with 95 percent of the convicted pharmacists entering guilty pleas. Fifth, the cases of misconduct were hard to detect, with forgery being the hardest to detect. Finally, when cases were identified, convicted pharmacists tended to have committed several cases of misconduct. Consider the following case:

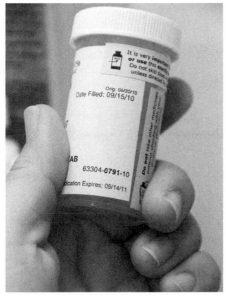

▲ **Photo 4.4** Pharmacists accused of prescription fraud often tried to blame their misconduct on an error or by stating they could not read the doctor's handwriting. Such defenses may have occasionally worked, but with automated prescription orders they are no longer an option.

> [Defendant] submitted false claims for 9,042 prescriptions for 43 patients whose physician never issued the prescriptions and for patients who never received the prescriptions. On some occasions, it is alleged that [the defendant] billed for as many as 37 fraudulent prescriptions for a single patient on the same day. . . . [The defendant] was paid a total of $220,588 to which he was not entitled by the Medicaid program for these fraudulent claims. (*Medicaid Fraud Report March,* 1991, p. 18)

Certainly, the case demonstrates how some instances of prescription fraud can be particularly egregious.

● ● ● Drug Use by Pharmacists

Illicit drug use by pharmacists is another area of concern in the pharmacy industry. Estimates suggest that up to 65 percent of practicing pharmacists have engaged in "some form of illicit drug use at least once during their career" and approximately one-fifth "used drugs regularly enough that they experienced negative life outcomes" (Dabney & Hollinger, 2002, p. 182). It appears that, compared to other professionals, pharmacists have higher rates of substance abuse problems.

To determine how pharmacists initiated their drug use, Dabney and Hollinger (2002) interviewed 50 drug-addicted pharmacists who were in recovery. They identified two distinct pathways to drug use among addicted pharmacists.

Twenty-three of the pharmacists followed a **"recreational path"** to their addiction. These pharmacists began by using illegal street drugs, and then, after entering pharmacy training, they expanded their drug use to include prescription drugs. Experimentation and social acceptability themes (by fellow pharmacy students) were common patterns found in the pharmacists' recreational drug use.

The second type of pharmacist addict was labeled **"therapeutic self-medicators"** by Dabney and Hollinger (2002). These pharmacists had little exposure to recreational drug use in their pre-employment lives. Their involvement in drug use typically "focused on specific therapeutic goals" (p. 196) and was often the result of health problems (such as insomnia, arthritis, etc.) or trauma (from car accidents, broken bones, or other traumatic incidents). The authors suggested that in the early stages of use, these pharmacists appeared to be "model pharmacists." They defined their drug use in noble terms, suggesting, for example, that they did not want to miss work as a result of their ailment and the drug use allowed them to go to work and help consumers who needed their own prescriptions filled. Eventually, these pharmacists began to create illnesses in order to convince themselves that they needed more drugs. Calling these pharmacists "drug-thirsty pharmacists," the research team quoted one pharmacist who said, "I had a symptom for everything I took" (p. 199).

Elsewhere, the same research team focused on how opportunity, awareness about drugs, and technical knowledge interacted to promote drug use by pharmacists (Dabney & Hollinger, 1999). They wrote, "In the absence of proper appreciation of the risks of substance abuse, [technical knowledge and opportunity] can delude pharmacists into believing that they are immune to prescription drug use" (p. 77). The authors characterized 40 of the 50 pharmacists as *poly-drug* users, meaning that the pharmacists used more than one type of drug. Thirty of the pharmacists were referred to as "garbage heads," alluding to a drug treatment term that describes those who use whatever drug they can get their hands on. The authors also highlighted the process of "titrating," where pharmacists used "their pharmaceutical knowledge to manage their personal drug use, enhancing or neutralizing specific drug effects by ingesting counteractive drugs" (p. 90).

Dabney and Hollinger (1999) described the "paradox of familiarity" that characterized pharmacists' drug using patterns. Pharmacists were exposed to positive aspects of the substances through aggressive marketing campaigns by pharmaceutical representatives, and their routine exposure to prescription drugs was such that drugs were defined as positive substances designed to help consumers. As the authors wrote, "they believed that these drugs could only improve lives; and therefore, they dismissed or minimized the dangers. Self-medication became a viable and attractive form of medicating every problem" (p. 95). In other words, pharmacists believed they knew enough about drugs that they would not succumb to the dangers of drug use.

Note that drug use by pharmacists is not in and of itself a white-collar crime. One of two conditions must be present for the substance abusing behavior to be considered a white-collar crime. First, if drugs are stolen from the workplace in order to feed the pharmacist's habit, then a white-collar crime has been committed. Second, if the pharmacist is under the influence of illicit substances while at work, one can argue that a white-collar crime has occurred.

● ● ● Sexual Abuse

In this context, **sexual abuse** refers to situations where health care providers (doctors, dentists, psychologists, psychiatrists, etc.) engage in sexual relationships with their patients. Four types of health care provider-patient sexual relationships exist: (1) power and prestige relationships, (2) mental health controlling relationships, (3) drug-induced relationships, and (4) sexual assault. First, in terms of power and prestige relationships, in some situations, patients may become enamored of their health care providers and open themselves up to the relationships based on the prestige and power that the providers have over the patients. Such relationships run counter to the provider's ethical codes and can do a great deal of emotional harm to patients.

Second, mental health controlling relationships occur in situations where individuals have sexual relationships with the mental health providers (psychiatrist, psychologist, counselor, etc.). It is impossible to know how often these relationships occur, but note that those who seek mental health counseling are in vulnerable states. Surveys of 30 adult incest survivors found that the survivors sought professional therapy from 113 different professionals. Seven of those 30 survivors had a sexual relationship with their helping professional (Armsworth, 1989). Research suggests that psychiatrists are overrepresented in accusations of sexual misconduct with patients (Morrison & Morrison, 2001). Factors that contribute to this include the following dynamics:

- Working in isolation
- An increased amount of direct contact with patients
- Longer appointments
- More personal discussions with patients.
- Vulnerability of patients (Morrison & Morrison, 2001)

Third, drug-induced relationships occur when health care providers get their patients addicted to drugs so they can have sex with the patients in exchange for access to drugs. These actions are clearly illegal on several different levels. In addition, besides feeding a chemical addiction and harming the victim physically, the health care provider is harming the victim emotionally. In one recent case, a doctor had his license suspended after it was alleged that the he had provided a "pain-killer addicted woman drugs in exchange for sex" (Pulkkinen, 2010). In another case, it was alleged that Dr. Michael Rusling, a doctor in Britain, "threatened to withhold drugs from a depressed patient if she refused to have sexual intercourse with him" ("Doctor 'Threatened to Withhold,'" 2009). Three patients said they had sexual relationships with Rusling, with one of them having sex with him at her home so often that one of her neighbors thought she had a serious health condition.

Fourth, sexual assault occurs when the provider sexually abuses (e.g., rapes) a patient during the course of providing care. One dentist, for example, was convicted of "feeling up" women as part of their dental treatment. In all, 27 women claimed that dentist Mark Anderson groped their breasts during dental examinations. Anderson defended his actions on the grounds that he was providing medical therapy in an effort to treat temporo-mandibular joint disorder, better known as TMJ ("Accused Dentist," 2007). The dentist was eventually convicted and sentenced to 6 years in prison.

Some of these cases can be quite brazen. One case that stands out in my mind involved a psychiatrist I read about during my dissertation work several years ago. In this case, the psychiatrist had sex with his patient; then, he billed Medicaid for the time he spent having sex with the patient. In fact, not only did he bill Medicaid for having sex with his patient, but he also billed Medicaid for more time than he actually took having sex with her!

● ● ● Elder Abuse by Health Care Workers

Elder abuse can be defined as "any criminal, physical, or emotional harm or unethical taking advantage that negatively affects the physical, financial, or general well being of an elderly person" (Payne, Berg, & Byars, 1999, p. 81). In terms of crimes by workers in the health care field, the following types of elder abuse are relevant: (1) elder physical abuse, (2) elder financial abuse, (3) elder neglect, (4) elder sexual abuse, and (5) failure to report crimes.

In this context, **elder physical abuse** entails instances where workers hit, slap, kick, or otherwise physically harm an older person for whom they are being paid to provide care. **Pacification** (or overmedicating) and restraining are also included as forms of elder physical abuse. In one of the earliest studies on physical patient abuse, Pillemer and Moore (1990) conducted phone interviews with 577 nurses' aides and nurses working in nursing homes in Massachusetts. In all, more than a third of the workers said they had seen instances where a resident was abused in the previous year, and one-tenth of the respondents indicated they had been abusive themselves in the prior year. In another study, researchers suggested that 8 out of 10 nurses and aides saw elder abuse cases in the prior year (Crumb & Jennings, 1998).

Payne and Cikovic (1995) examined 488 cases of patient abuse prosecuted by Medicaid Fraud Control Units across the United States. They found that the offenses typically occurred in isolation, and aides seemed to be overrepresented in allegations of abuse. They also found that the victim-offender relationship followed gender patterns: Males were more likely to abuse males, and females were more likely to abuse females. More recently, a study of 801 cases of patient abuse identified three types of offenders: (1) stressed offenders who committed the offense as a result of a stressful interaction with the patient, (2) serial abusers who committed multiple offenses at work, and (3) pathological tormentors who committed heinous offenses designed to humiliate or control victims (Payne & Gainey, 2006).

Elder financial abuse is a second type of elder abuse committed by care providers. The National Center on Elder Abuse offers the following definition of elder financial abuse:

Financial or material exploitation is defined as the illegal or improper use of an elder's funds, property, or assets. Examples include, but are not limited to, cashing an elderly person's checks without authorization or permission; forging an older person's signature; misusing or stealing an older person's money or possessions; coercing or deceiving an older person into signing any document (e.g., contracts or will); and the improper use of conservatorship, guardianship, or power of attorney. (National Center on Elder Abuse, 2008)

Researchers have suggested that elder financial abuse can be distinguished from elder physical abuse in the following ways: Financial abuse occurs more often, it has different causes, different response systems are used to address the crimes, and it has different consequences from other forms of elder abuse (Payne & Strasser, 2012).

In one of the largest studies on theft in nursing homes, criminologists Diane Harris and Michael Benson (1999) surveyed 1,116 nursing home employees and 517 family members of nursing home residents. Their results showed that one-fifth of the workers suspected that their colleagues had stolen something from residents, and one-fifth of the family members believed that a staff member had stolen something from their relative.

In another study, Harris and Benson (1996) interviewed employees, relatives, and nursing home residents to gain insight into the patterns surrounding theft in nursing homes. They found that the items stolen most often tended to be items of value that could be easily concealed, such as jewelry and money. They also found that theft increased around the holidays and that new workers and dissatisfied workers were more apt to engage in theft. Other research suggests that theft in nursing homes is related to aggressive behaviors by nursing home residents—workers who experienced abuse at the hands of residents were suggested to be more likely to steal from residents (Van Wyk, Benson, & Harris, 2000). Harris and Benson (1999) argue that theft is even less socially acceptable than physical patient abuse on the grounds that the behaviors are intentional and not simply a reaction to a stressful working situation.

In another study, Payne and Strasser (2012) compared cases of elder physical abuse ($n = 314$) and elder financial abuse ($n = 242$) provided in the *Medicaid Fraud Reports* (described in the Introduction). Financial abusers were more likely to be directors or employees in another category, while physical abusers tended to be aides. The authors (2012) also found that "physical abusers were more likely to be sentenced to jail than financial abusers were, but financial abusers were more likely to be sentenced to prison" (n.p.). A comparison of sentence lengths indicated that financial abusers received longer probation sentences, shorter prison sanctions, and higher fines than physical abusers did.

The authors identified four patterns that characterized the financial exploitation cases: (1) Victims often had serious health issues, (2) multiple victims were frequently targeted by specific offenders, (3) offenses occurred on multiple occasions, and (4) a lack of witnesses made it difficult to investigate the cases.

Elder neglect is a third type of elder abuse. Elder neglect occurs when workers fail to provide the appropriate level of care required by the patient. Experts distinguish between active (intentional) and passive (unintentional) neglect. In cases of active neglect, offenders know the type of care that an individual requires—they simply choose not to provide that care. In cases of passive neglect, offenders are not aware of the most appropriate care—their neglect stems from ignorance. In terms of workplace offenses, neglect is more likely to be active than passive in nature. Workers typically know the type of care the patient needs. In some situations, workplace demands may foster neglect inasmuch as administrators expect workers to provide care to a higher number of patients than is actually possible.

Elder sexual abuse is another variety of elder abuse. One expert cites three types of elder sexual abuse: (1) hands-on offenses where the offender inappropriately touches victims, (2) hands-off offenses such as voyeurism and exhibitionism, and (3) harmful genital practices where genital contact is made between the offender and the victim (Ramsey-Klawsnik, 1999). Sexual abuse is believed to be particularly common against disabled residents of long-term care institutions.

A study of 126 elder sexual abuse cases and 314 elder physical abuse cases committed as part of the offender's workplace activities and prosecuted by criminal justice officials found that elder sexual abuse cases were more likely to involve (1) male offenders, (2) cognitively impaired victims, and (3) instances without witnesses (Payne, 2010). Payne highlighted the element of control involved in elder sexual abuse cases. He described the following three case scenarios as illustrations of this control:

- The sexual assault involved inserting a banana into the rectum of a patient who suffered from left side paralysis and mental confusion. [They] put the soiled banana into another patient's mouth. Not only did the defendants commit these acts while laughing with amusement, but they bragged and laughed about the assault to their friends. (*Medicaid Fraud Report March*, 1994, p. 1)
- [He] is accused of hitting a 78-year-old patient in the face with a diaper and pretending to kiss and simulate sexual intercourse with a 92-year-old resident. (*Medicaid Fraud Report September*, 1995)
- [The defendant] agitated an 83-year-old dementia patient at least nine times by telling the man that he was having sex with his own daughter. (*Medicaid Fraud Report September*, 1995)

A final type of elder abuse by workers in the health care field is the **failure to report** suspected cases of elder abuse. The vast majority of states have laws stipulating that certain types of workers are mandated to report elder abuse cases to the authorities if they suspect an elder abuse incident has occurred. These laws are known as mandatory reporting laws. Several criticisms surround the use of mandatory reporting laws. These criticisms include the following:

- A lack of empirical basis supporting the need for the laws
- Questions about the effectiveness of the laws
- Concerns that the laws are based on ageist assumptions
- Concerns about patient–health care worker confidentiality
- The likelihood that revictimization will occur from reporting
- A belief that discretion results in inconsistent reporting (Payne, 2013)

In a study focusing on mandatory reporting laws, three patterns were found. First, mandatory reporting violations tend to involve multiple collaborators who work together to cover up a case of elder abuse. Second, mandatory reporting violators come from a wider range of health care occupations than is found in other types of elder abuse. Third, fines were commonly used as a sentencing tool in these cases (Payne, 2013). Based on these patterns, my research suggests policy implications that center on broadening investigations to capture multiple offenders and increasing awareness about the laws.

Health care administrators use a number of different practices and follow various policies in an effort to prevent elder abuse in the workplace. Surveys of 76 nursing home directors identified four broad types of measures commonly used to prevent crimes against nursing home residents (Payne & Burke-Fletcher, 2005). First, facility-based measures are those strategies that directors choose to implement that are driven by facility policies, such as background checks, drug tests, and safety committees. Second, educational strategies focus on increasing awareness among workers and residents about strategies for preventing abuse. Third, community outreach efforts entail strategies where crime prevention officials from outside the nursing home are called on to provide information and resources to protect residents. Finally, building security strategies includes measures that are designed to make the actual physical structure safer (e.g., locked doors, security alarms, and video cameras). The results of this survey showed that the conceptual ambiguity surrounding elder abuse laws made it more difficult to prevent elder abuse. Also, the results showed that the lack of clear and consistent elder abuse response policies created an obstacle to identifying and responding to cases of elder abuse occurring in nursing homes.

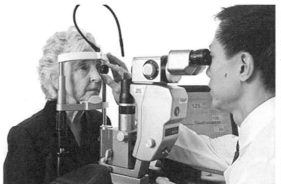

▲ **Photo 4.5** Because older people are, in general, more likely to need health care, they are more likely to be victims in these offenses.

● ● ● Home Health Care Fraud

Home health care entails the provision of health care services at home. In recent years, there has been an increase in the use of home health care due to demographic changes, changes in patient preferences, technological advancements, legislative changes, and cost containment strategies (Payne, 2003a). Along with these changes, there has been evidence of an increase of crimes committed by home health care workers. In *Crime in the Home Health Care Field* (2003a), I describe the way that the following crimes occur in the home health industry: (a) murder, (b) physical abuse, (c) sexual abuse, (d) neglect, (e) drug-related offenses, (f) emotional abuse, (g) theft from patients, and (h) theft from Medicare and/or Medicaid.

I argue that fraud against the Medicare and Medicaid systems is particularly pervasive. I describe eight different types of fraud that home health care workers have committed:

1. Providing unnecessary services to clients and billing the system for those services

2. Billing the system for services that were not provided to the client

3. Overcharging either the system or client for services

4. Forging signatures on medical documents

5. Negative charting (changing the clients' medical records so clients seem sicker than they are, thereby convincing the insurance provider to pay for services that may not have been necessary)

6. Having unlicensed (or substitute) workers provide medical care and billing the insurance company as if the services were provided by a licensed professional

7. Double billing the client and one or more insurance companies

8. Providing kickbacks to other service providers in exchange for client referrals

Reviewing hundreds of home health care fraud cases, I identified three patterns that were common in the cases. First, I noted that many of the cases involved offenders who had past criminal histories. Second, the offenses were described as occurring over time. Whereas a robbery occurs in one moment in time, fraudulent acts may be more spread out over time. Third, I called attention to the fact that many home health care frauds were committed in groups, and the groups sometimes included workers and clients conspiring together to defraud the system. Based on these patterns, the following three policy implications were suggested: (1) the need for background checks in hiring home health care workers, (2) the need to conduct lengthy investigations to substantiate cases, and (3) the practice of investigating multiple offenders simultaneously in an effort to build a case against a specific offender (Payne, 2003a).

● ● ● Durable Medical Equipment Fraud

Another variety of fraud in the health care system can be coined durable medical equipment fraud. In this context, durable medical equipment fraud refers to criminal behaviors that involve the rental or sale of health equipment. Durable medical equipment includes items such as prosthetics, orthotics, wheelchairs, oxygen equipment, walkers, and other items that are supposed to be used over the long-term. In the Medicaid system alone, it is estimated that a billion dollars a year is spent on this equipment (Policastro & Payne, 2013). Two aspects of the industry—(1) the types of services provided and (2) the types of employees involved—distinguish this field from other health care fields. In terms of types of services, the durable medical equipment industry sells items rather than providing a specific form of health care. The employees would not necessarily be licensed health care professionals, but act more as sales persons (Policastro & Payne, 2013).

WHITE-COLLAR CRIME IN THE NEWS

When Health Care Providers Go Bad: 243 Arrested in Strike Force Operation

Reprinted from FBI

Attorney General Loretta Lynch announces the largest health care fraud crackdown.

More than 240 individuals—including doctors, nurses, and other licensed professionals—were arrested this week for their alleged participation in Medicare fraud schemes involving approximately $712 million in false billings.

The arrests . . . were part of a coordinated operation in 17 cities by Medicare Fraud Strike Force teams, which include personnel from the FBI, the Department of Health and Human Services (HHS), the Department of Justice (DOJ), and local law enforcement. The Strike Force's mission is to combat health care fraud, waste, and abuse.

At a press conference . . . at DOJ Headquarters in Washington, D.C., officials said the arrests constituted the largest-ever health care fraud takedown in terms of both loss amount and arrests.

"These are extraordinary figures," said Attorney General Loretta Lynch. "They billed for equipment that wasn't provided, for care that wasn't needed, and for services that weren't rendered."

The charges are based on a variety of alleged fraud schemes involving medical treatments and services. According to court documents, the schemes included submitting claims to Medicare for treatments that were medically unnecessary and often not provided. In many of the cases, Medicare beneficiaries and other co-conspirators were allegedly paid cash kickbacks for supplying beneficiary information so providers could submit fraudulent bills to Medicare. Forty-four of the defendants were charged in schemes related to Medicare Part D, the prescription drug benefit program, which is the fastest growing component of Medicare and a growing target for criminals.

"There is a lot of money there, so there are a lot of criminals," said FBI Director James B. Comey. He described how investigations leveraged technology to collect and analyze data, and rapid response teams to surge where the data showed the schemes were operating. "In these cases, we followed the money and found criminals who were attracted to doctors offices, clinics, hospitals, and nursing homes in search of what they viewed as an ATM."

Since their inception in 2007, Strike Force teams in the nine cites where they operate have charged more than 2,300 defendants who collectively falsely billed Medicare more than $7 billion.

Here's a look at some of the cases:

In Miami, 73 were charged in schemes involving about $263 million in false billings for pharmacy, home health care, and mental health services.

In Houston and McAllen, 22 were charged in cases involving more than $38 million. In one case, the defendant coached beneficiaries on what to tell doctors to make them appear eligible for Medicare services and then received payment for those who qualified. The defendant was paid more than $4 million in fraudulent claims.

In New Orleans, 11 people were charged in connection with home health care and psychotherapy schemes. In one case, four defendants from two companies sent talking glucose monitors across the country to Medicare beneficiaries regardless of whether they were needed or requested. The companies billed Medicare $38 million and were paid $22 million.

Source: Reprinted from FBI (2015, June 18). Health care fraud takedown. Reprinted from https://www.fbi.gov/news/stories/2015/june/health-care-fraud-takedown/health-care-fraud-takedown

As with other health care fields, initially there was little concern about fraud in the durable medical equipment field when the industry first began to provide equipment to Medicaid recipients. As in other health care occupations, however, fraud does occur in this field. Below are two recent examples of fraud in this industry:

- Attorney General Abbott announced on November 10 that ****, *****, and **** were indicted by a state grand jury for engaging in organized criminal activity. ****** owners of Steadfast Healthcare, allegedly billed for power wheelchairs and provided scooters, billed for dead clients, and billed for power wheelchairs that were not prescribed by physicians. The identified overpayment is approximately $266,000. (*Medicaid Fraud Reports November/ December*, 2014, p. 3)
- Attorney General Abbott announced on December 17 that *****, owner and operator of Unity Medical Equipment & Supply was indicted by a state grand jury for theft. ***** allegedly billed Medicaid for incontinence supplies, namely adult diapers, not provided to recipients or recipients received a different product or diapers in quantities less than billed Medicaid. (*Medicaid Fraud Reports November/December*, 2014, p. 4)

In one of the few studies on fraud in the durable medical field, Policastro and Payne (2013) examined the characteristics, causes, and patterns surrounding durable medical equipment fraud against Medicaid. Among other things, their study of 258 equipment fraud cases revealed:

- Roughly six in ten cases involved male offenders.
- Owners were implicated in three-fourths of the cases.
- False claims were the most common offense.
- In nearly two-thirds of the cases, offenders committed their offense along with another offender.
- Wheelchairs and incontinence supplies were the types of equipment most often involved in fraudulent cases.
- When sanctions were given, fines were given in 90 percent of the cases.
- For every offender involved in an incident, the odds of incarceration increased 1.3 times.

One aspect of their findings is that the types of fraud committed in the durable medical field were different from those fraudulent acts committed in other health care fields. Using past research as a guide, the authors attribute the differences to the structural organization of various occupations rather than class status. In effect, it's not class that predicts offending, but the types of opportunities that may surface based on the way that various fields are organized and structured.

Another point worth stressing is that although these offense types have been discussed separately according to the health care occupation, in many cases offenders collaborate with various types of professionals. Doctors, nurses, aides, pharmacists, and other professionals—depending on the nature of the offense type—might in fact commit crimes together. The White-Collar Crime in the News: When Health Care Providers Go Bad box on the previous page includes a recent press release detailing the arrest of many different health care professionals after a covert law enforcement operation.

● ● ● Medical Malpractice

Medical malpractice refers to situations where health care providers "accidentally" injure patients while delivering health care. These cases will almost never be treated as crimes. As a result, they do not enter the criminal justice system. Strategies for recourse for victims of medical malpractice include (1) filing a lawsuit against the health care provider and (2) filing an insurance claim with the provider's insurance company.

With regard to filing an insurance claim with the provider's insurance company, it may be useful to compare medical malpractice with automobile "accidents." If driver A runs into driver B and is clearly responsible for an accident, then driver B's insurance company will file a claim with driver A's insurance company. In the end, driver A's insurance company will be responsible for paying the claim. In medical malpractice insurance cases, a similar process is followed: The "accident" victim or his or her representative files a claim with the provider's insurance company.

IN FOCUS   4.3

What Is a Medical Malpractice Insurance Claim?

A medical malpractice insurance claim arises when a person (the claimant) alleges that negligent medical treatment resulted in an injury. The treatment may have been provided by a physician, surgeon, or other health care professional or an organization, such as a hospital, clinic, or nursing home.

In a typical medical malpractice claim, the person claiming an injury or a related family member retains an attorney to file a claim with the medical provider's insurance carrier requesting compensation for the injury. After a claim is filed, the insurance carrier may settle, negotiate with the claimant over the amount of compensation, or refuse to compensate the claimant. If the parties do not come to an agreement, the claimant's attorney may file a lawsuit in the appropriate court or abandon the claim.

Some states require review of medical malpractice claims before a panel of experts prior to a lawsuit, while other states mandate arbitration or alternative dispute resolution as a means of resolving medical malpractice claims. The filing of a lawsuit may produce several outcomes. These include the settlement of the case prior to or during trial, a trial decision in favor of the claimant or the defendant, or the dismissal of the case by the court. Claims may also be abandoned or withdrawn after a lawsuit.

Source: Reprinted From Cohen, T., & Hughes, K. (2007). Medical malpractice claims in seven states, 2000–2004. Bureau of Justice Statistics, Washington, DC: U.S. Department of Justice.

A review of 43,000 medical malpractice insurance claims in seven states between 2000 and 2004 found that "most medical malpractice claims were closed without any compensation provided to those claiming a medical injury" (Cohen & Hughes, 2007, p. 1). Payouts were higher for those who suffered "lifelong major or grave permanent injuries" and lower in cases with temporary or emotional injuries. Other patterns found in the medical malpractice insurance claims included the following:

- Claims were typically filed 15 to 18 months after the injuries.
- It generally took about 2 to 2.5 years to close the claims.
- In some states, less than 10 percent of the claims resulted in payouts. In other states, payouts were given in about a third of the cases.
- When injuries occurred, they were more likely to occur in hospitals.
- Females were claimants in 54 percent to 56 percent of the cases.
- Approximately 95 percent of the claims were settled without going to trial.
- The amount of payouts to claimants increased as the case progressed through the justice system.
- Medical malpractice insurance payouts increased from 1990 to 2004.

SUMMARY

- In general, categories of crimes committed by health care providers include fraud by doctors, fraud by pharmacists, drug use, unnecessary surgery, medication errors, sexual abuse, elder abuse, home health care fraud, and medical malpractice.
- Sutherland implied that doctors were unlikely to engage in white-collar crime, and as a result, Sutherland gave "only scant attention to doctors [and] maintained that physicians were probably more honest than other professionals" (Wilson et al., 1986).

- The most pervasive form of fraud committed by doctors entails the commission of Medicare and Medicaid fraud and abuse.
- *Fraud* refers to intentionally criminal behaviors by physicians, whereas *abuse* focuses on unintentional misuse of program funds.
- Several specific forms of fraud and abuse exist, including phantom treatment, substitute providers, upcoding, provision of unnecessary services, misrepresenting services, falsifying records, overcharging patients, unbundling, pingponging, ganging, kickbacks, co-pay waivers, and medical snowballing.
- Briefly, mental health professionals often bill for time, whereas other professionals bill for more complicated medical procedures. For investigators, it is much easier to prove "time violations" than "treatment violations."
- Research shows that when females are accused of health care fraud, they tend to be accused along with other providers more than male offenders are (Payne, 1995). Explanations for fraud have focused on structural explanations, socialization factors, and enforcement dynamics.
- It is estimated that 7.5 million unnecessary surgeries and medical procedures occur annually, and 12,000 Americans are killed each year from these unnecessary surgeries (Black, 2005).
- At least six overlapping reasons help explain the pervasiveness of unnecessary surgeries: differing opinions, stigma, trust of health care, lack of trust of insurance companies, medicalized socialization, and conflict explanations.
- Many severe consequences may arise from unnecessary surgeries.
- Medication errors occur when health care providers deliver or prescribe the wrong medications to patients.
- Public Citizen has identified 16 varieties of misconduct by physicians. The group believes that variations in sanctions for violations across states can be attributed to differences in the way state medical boards sanction offenders.
- Eight types of prescription fraud are generic drug substitution, overbilling, double billing, billing for nonexistent prescriptions, short counting, mislabeling, delivery of a controlled substance, and illegally buying prescriptions.
- The following types of elder abuse can be seen as white-collar crimes: (1) elder physical abuse, (2) elder financial abuse, (3) elder neglect, (4) elder sexual abuse, and (5) failure to report crimes.
- Types of home health care fraud include providing unnecessary services, billing the system for services that were not provided to the client, overcharging, forgery, negative charting, substitute workers, double billing, and kickbacks.
- Durable medical equipment fraud involves the fraudulent sale or rental of medical supplies, such as wheelchairs, walkers, scooters, and so on.
- Medical malpractice refers to situations where health care providers perform negligent care and/or injure patients. Patients can seek recourse by filing medical malpractice insurance claims against the provider's insurance company or by filing a lawsuit against the provider.

KEY TERMS

Billing for nonexistent prescriptions

Co-pay waivers

Delivery of a controlled substance

Double billing

Elder abuse

Elder financial abuse

Elder neglect

Elder physical abuse

Elder sexual abuse

Failure to report

Falsifying records

Fraud

Ganging

Generic drug substitution

Health Insurance Portability Act of 1996

Home health care

Illegally buying prescriptions

Kickbacks

Medicaid

Medical malpractice

Medical snowballing

Medicare

Medication errors

Mislabeling of drugs

Overcharging

Pacification

Phantom treatment

Pingponging

Prescription fraud

Provision of unnecessary services

Questionable Doctors

Recreational path

Sexual abuse

Short counting

Substitute providers

Unbundling

DISCUSSION QUESTIONS

1. What's worse—retail theft or health care fraud? Explain.

2. What can be done to limit crimes by health care professionals?

3. Why do doctors engage in inappropriate conduct?

4. What are the similarities between misconduct by pharmacists and crimes by doctors? What about the differences?

5. Why do unnecessary surgeries occur? Do you know anyone who has had a potentially unnecessary surgery? What can be done to prevent them?

6. How do television shows portray misconduct by doctors?

7. How is drug use a white-collar crime? What can be done to prevent drug use by health care providers?

WEB RESOURCES

Federal Bureau of Investigation (FBI) Health Care Fraud: http://www.fbi.gov/news/stories/2010/june/health-care-fraud/health-care-trends

Medicare Fraud: https://www.medicare.gov/forms-help-and-resources/report-fraud-and-abuse/fraud-and-abuse.html

Pharmacist Drug Abuse: http://www.ashp.org/menu/News/PharmacyNews/NewsArticle.aspx?id=1446

Prescription Fraud: http://www.popcenter.org/problems/prescription_fraud/

Public Citizen: http://www.citizen.org

Stop Medicare Fraud: http://www.stopmedicarefraud.gov/

STUDENT RESOURCES

The open-access Student Study Site, available at study.sagepub.com/paynewccess2e, includes useful study materials including SAGE journal articles and multimedia resources.

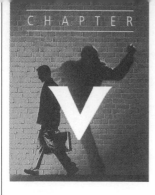

Crime in Systems of Social Control

White-Collar Crime in Criminal Justice, Political, and Religious Systems

CHAPTER HIGHLIGHTS

- Crimes in the Criminal Justice System
- Crimes in the Political System
- Crimes by Officials in the Religious System

It sounds like a bad joke—a police officer, lawyer, judge, correctional officer, politician, military officer, and priest walk into a bar together. What do you think they could discuss that they have in common? Several answers come to mind. For example, they could talk about the fact that they each are public servants. Their occupations exist to serve members of the public. They could also talk about the fact that their salaries are not the highest one would find among various occupations. Or they could talk about their colleagues who have been caught committing white-collar crimes. After all, no profession is immune from white-collar misconduct. As well, they could talk about the main thing their professions have in common across all of their professions: They each work in *systems of social control*.

As examples of the crimes committed by professionals in these systems of social control, consider the following examples quoted from their original sources:

- In June of 2013, after a five-week trial, former United States Congressman Richard G. Renzi was convicted of 17 felony offenses, including conspiracy, honest services wire fraud, extortion under color of official right, racketeering, money laundering, and making false statements to insurance regulators. His co-defendant, James Sandlin, was convicted of 13 felony offenses, including conspiracy, honest services wire fraud, extortion under color of official right, and money laundering. (U.S. Department of Justice, 2014a, p. 11)
- In May 2013, Mitchell Potts, the former Traffic Office Supervisor for the Defense Logistics Agency (DLA), and Jeffrey Philpot, the former Lead Transportation Assistant in the Traffic Office, pleaded guilty to receiving bribes related to a scheme to funnel freight hauling business to a local transportation company resulting in the loss of millions of dollars to the United States government. (U.S. Department of Justice, 2014b, p. 13)
- On May 29, 2013, former Puerto Rico police officer Abimael Arroyo-Cruz was convicted by a jury of bribery, extortion, and conspiracy for his role in a scheme to obtain $50,000 in exchange for arranging the dismissal of a local firearm and drug prosecution. Midway through trial, co-defendant Josue Becerril-Ramos, also a former police officer, pleaded guilty for his role in the bribery and extortion scheme. On November 18, 2013, Arroyo was sentenced to 63 months in prison, and Becerril was sentenced to 60 months in prison. (U.S. Department of Justice, 2014c, p. 15)
- On September 12, 2013, the former Mayor of South Pittsburg, Tennessee, James Michael Killian, and co-conspirator Robert Cole pleaded guilty to operating an illegal gambling business out of a convenience store owned by Killian. Killian and Cole also admitted running an illegal sports betting ring (U.S. Department of Justice, 2014, p. 15).
- [The pastor] was charged in 2012 with fraudulently obtaining state Child Care Assistance Program subsidy payments by submitting false documents for a succession of three Chicago-area child care centers that he operated through his church. [The pastor] used the money to fuel a lavish lifestyle that included a leased Bentley, trips and stays at fancy hotels, according to prosecutors. (Meisner, 2015)
- A Roman Catholic pastor of two city parishes, including one that counted Vice President Joe Biden as a past congregant, is being accused of embezzling more than $350,000 from his parishes. (O'Sullivan, 2011)

One irony arises when considering crimes by officials in social control systems: Their occupations exist in order to reduce or prevent wrongful behaviors, but in some cases, those given the duty to stop misconduct actually engage in misconduct themselves.

● ● ● Crimes in the Criminal Justice System

Entrusted to enforce the law, criminal justice officials have duties that are not given to any other occupational group. Unfortunately, as with other professions, crime occurs in the criminal justice professions. The types of white-collar crime occurring in the criminal justice system include the following:

- Police corruption
- Attorney misconduct
- Judicial misconduct
- Prosecutorial misconduct
- Correctional officer misconduct

Police Corruption

Police corruption occurs when police officers violate the trust they have been given and abuse their law enforcement authority (Punch, 2009). Different typologies have been presented to characterize the numerous types of police corruption known to occur. One of the clearest (and earliest) typologies was set forth by Barker and Roebuck (1973), who identified the following types of police corruption:

▲ **Photo 5.1** Police are expected to maintain the integrity of crime scenes. In a few instances, behavior of police at crime scenes may, in fact, be crimes in and of themselves.

Corruption of authority (e.g., using the law enforcement role to gain favors such as gratuities)

Kickbacks (e.g., sending victims or offenders to certain service providers—such as tow truck drivers—in exchange for a fee from the service provider)

Opportunistic theft (e.g., stealing from crime scenes when the opportunity arises)

Shakedowns (e.g., taking or soliciting bribes from offenders in exchange for not enforcing the law)

Protection of illegal activities (e.g., protecting gangs, organized crime units, or others in exchange for payment)

Fixing cases (e.g., fixing traffic tickets or changing testimony)

Direct criminal activities (e.g., engaging in crime while on the job)

Internal payoffs (e.g., engaging in schemes where other criminal justice officials are paid off for their illicit participation in the scheme)

Criminologist Phil Stinson (2015) offered another useful typology captured under the heading of "police deviance." His conceptualization focuses on all types of deviance by police officers—including those committed on the job and off the job. The categories of deviance identified by Stinson include (1) drug-related police crimes, (2) profit-motivated police crimes, (3) violence-related police crimes, (4) alcohol-related offenses (such as being drunk in public or driving under the influence), and (5) sex-related deviance. This final category includes harassment, intimidation, and sexual misconduct. Maher (2003) offers the following definition of **police sexual misconduct:**

Any behavior by a police officer, whereby an officer takes advantage of his or her unique position in law enforcement to misuse his or her authority and power to commit a sexually violent act or to initiate or respond to some sexually motivated cue for the purpose of personal gratification. This behavior must include physical contact, verbal communication, or a sexually implicit or explicit gesture directed toward another person. (p. 357)

Examples of sexual misconduct exist on a continuum, ranging from situations where no contact occurs between the officer and the citizen to situations where forced contact occurs. Surveys of 40 police officers by Maher (2003) showed evidence of police behaviors dictated by sexual interests. Officers reported routinely stopping motorists to "check out" those that they found attractive. A study of 501 cases of police sexual violence found that many of the offenders committed multiple acts of sexual violence (McGurrin & Kappeler, 2002). The authors suggested that the badge and gun were substitutes for physical force, particularly in situations where police officers solicited sexual favors in exchange for police decisions that would benefit the victim.

The consequences of police corruption can be far reaching. As Hunter (1999) notes, "one incident of police misbehavior in a distant locality can have adverse effects on police community relationships in police agencies across the country" (p. 156). For departments where corruption occurs, the corruption diminishes police effectiveness, creates demoralization in the department, and creates barriers between the department and the community (Hunter, 1999).

Police corruption cuts across all countries. Even countries that have low rates of other forms of workplace offending have some police corruption. Describing this phenomenon in Australia, one author team wrote, "There will always be at least a small group of corrupt police officers, even though Australians are culturally averse to corruption" (Lauchs, Keast, & Yousefpour, 2011, p. 110).

Various perspectives have been offered in an effort to explain police corruption. The phrase *bad apples* has frequently been used to suggest that corruption is limited to a few rogue officers in a department. More recently, it has been suggested that the phrase *bad orchards* would more aptly describe how the broader police culture and dynamics of policing contribute to police misconduct (Punch, 2009). Others have suggested that overreaching cultural and community factors are potential causes of police misconduct (Kane, 2002).

Some researchers have explored social psychological factors that might contribute to corruption. The phrase **noble cause corruption** describes situations where officers engage in corruption in order to assure what they see as justice (Cooper, 2012). In these situations, "getting the bad guys off the street to protect the innocent" (p. 171) is viewed as the noble cause. Cooper asserts that some officers experience role conflict in these cases. Officers who are more protector-oriented are believed to experience more role conflict than those who focus more on community policing.

In an effort to identify the individual officer characteristics that contribute to police misconduct, one study compared all 1,543 police officers dismissed from the New York Police Department between 1975 and 1996 with a sample of police recruits who had never been disciplined. This study found that those who were dismissed for misconduct were more likely to have past arrests, traffic violations, and problems with previous jobs. Those who had college degrees were less likely to be dismissed (Fyfe & Kane, 2005).

Others have attributed police misconduct to a lack of policies to prevent misconduct, faulty control mechanisms, and a lack of appropriate training (Kinnaird, 2007). **Organizational justice** explanations consider the way that organizational features might lead to corruption. Research shows that police supervisors' attitudes about corruption will influence how officers in their chain of command view corruption. Not surprisingly, those who have lax attitudes toward corruption will be more prone to employ officers who hold less serious views about corruption (Lee, Lim, Moore, & Kim, 2013).

A survey of 208 police managers found that for some types of police misconduct, the police manager would not be likely to report the behavior (Vito, Wolfe, Higgins, & Walsh, 2011). Out of 109 sergeants surveyed, nearly 86 percent reported that they would not report officers working off-duty in a security business. Just under half indicated that they would not report instances when officers receive free meals. Middle managers offered similar results, though they were slightly more likely to indicate they would report misconduct (Vito et al., 2011). One author team concludes, "Police departments themselves play an important role in shaping the patterns and timing of officer misconduct" (White & Kane, 2013, p. 1301).

Another recent study also found that perceptions of organizational justice in a police department are tied to misconduct (Wolfe & Piquero, 2011). Officers perceiving their department as adhering to ideals of organizational justice tend to engage in lower amount of misconduct. Based on this, the researchers suggest that treating officers in a fair and transparent way will increase the likelihood that officers will do the same in their interactions with citizens. Strategies suggested for demonstrating fairness included the following:

- Ensuring that promotions are distributed and awarded fairly
- Communicating clearly about the purpose of discipline
- Conducting internal investigations in a fair manner
- Reviewing policies to make sure they are consistent with ideals of fairness
- Demonstrating that police leaders value the contributions of officers (Wolfe & Piquero, 2011)

Other suggestions for preventing police misconduct have centered on addressing these potential causal factors. One author stresses that police agencies must have policies that clearly define police misconduct so officers are aware of the rules and sanctions (Martinelli, 2007). Other strategies that have been suggested include screening backgrounds (White & Kane, 2013), promoting external accountability (Barker, 2002), improving police supervision strategies (Hunter, 1999; Martinelli, 2007), focusing on early warning signs (Walker & Alpert, 2002), and promoting ethics (Hunter, 1999).

Hunter (1999) surveyed 65 police officers to determine which strategies the officers most supported for dealing with police misconduct. Strategies that officers supported the most included strict and fair discipline, clear policies, professional standards, promoting capable supervisors, and having administrators serve as examples or role models. The need for adequate policies aimed at preventing and responding to police corruption is in line with the systems theme guiding the discussion in this text—systems policymakers must develop policies to address misconduct in occupations that are a part of the system, clearly define misconduct, identify ways to detect the misconduct, describe ways to respond to the misconduct, and clearly communicate the sanctions that will be imposed for misconduct.

Researchers have also considered off-duty police crimes (or crimes committed when they were not working). Technically, these would not be white-collar crimes, but because of the media attention these cases receive and the nature of the offense, they certainly warrant attention. These off-duty offenses might include domestic violence, drug offenses, theft, or other offenses that having nothing to do with the officer's job (Stinson, Liederbach, & Freiburger, 2012). One issues that arises, according to Phil Stinson and his colleagues, is that these offenses may, in some cases, open up the locality or the department to liability or lawsuits if the offense is somehow tied to the officer's official capacity. Alcohol crimes were the most common offenses uncovered in past research (Stinson et al., 2012).

Attorney Misconduct

It is likely that many readers, criminal justice majors in particular, have at one point considered a career as an attorney. After all, the media—in television, movies, and books—have glorified the careers of attorneys. From *Perry Mason* to *L.A. Law* to *Law & Order,* attorneys enter our homes on a regular basis through our televisions. While criminal justice majors might tend to have favorable attitudes toward attorneys, members of the public tend to view attorneys in a less favorable light. One author notes that lawyers are viewed as "simply a plague on society" (Hazard, 1991, p. 1240).

This negative view of attorneys likely contributes to formal complaints about attorney conduct (or misconduct). Over the past several decades, the number of accusations against attorneys has increased to the point that a heightened concern about being accused of misconduct has arisen (Payne & Stevens, 1999). The reason for their concern is that complaints to a state bar association have the potential to result in drastic consequences to an attorney's career.

States have different expectations and definitions for what is viewed to be appropriate conduct for attorneys. In Alabama, for example, the state bar identifies the following behaviors as warranting discipline toward attorneys:

- Failing to respond to charges brought forth by the state bar
- Violating disciplinary rules
- Neglecting a legal matter
- Felony conviction
- Misdemeanor conviction
- Keeping a client's money that should have been returned
- Keeping a client's money after failing to provide services
- Keeping fraudulently obtained money
- False statements to authorities
- False statements to clients
- Misuse of the client's funds
- Failure to provide competent representation
- Disciplined for a violation in another state
- Failure to comply with an order from a disciplinary authority
- Excessive, unfair, or unclear fees
- Failure to meet legal education requirements
- Financial conflict of interest with a client
- Behavior unbecoming a court official (Payne & Stevens, 1999, pp. 42–43)

In the few studies that have been done on attorney misconduct, the focus tends to be on types of sanctions levied against attorneys. Morgan (1995) identified three reasons that such research is important, both for society and the field of criminal justice. First, understanding how and why attorneys are sanctioned helps clarify "what the substantive law really is" (p. 343). Second, such research helps formulate degrees of misconduct by understanding how severity of sanction is tied to misconduct type. Third, such research helps dispel misguided beliefs that "professional standards are largely unenforced and unenforceable" (p. 343). In fact, research shows that offenders are routinely disciplined, and this discipline may result in loss of prestige, destruction of self-worth, embarrassment, social and professional ostracism, loss of professional affiliation, and strain in personal relationships.

If attorneys violate criminal or civil laws, they can be subjected to penalties stemming from those bodies of law (e.g., incarceration, probation, fines, restitution, etc.). Research shows that allegations of misconduct against solo, inexperienced attorneys are more likely to be prosecuted, particularly during economic recessions (Arnold & Hagan, 1992). This relationship is attributed to (a) the powerlessness of solo professionals and (b) conceptions about the legal profession that suggest that inexperienced attorneys are more likely to engage in deviance, which then results in more surveillance of these attorneys. As an analogy, if law enforcement targets particular neighborhoods prone to crime, they will arrest more offenders from those neighborhoods. If controlling authorities target inexperienced attorneys more, they will catch more inexperienced attorneys engaging in misconduct.

Various sanctions can be given to attorneys by their professional associations. Such sanctions usually include warning letters, private reprimands, public reprimands, suspensions, and disbarment. With the exception of the private reprimands, all of the sanctions are public knowledge, and many states identify sanctioned attorneys on the state bar website. Note that simply participating in the disciplinary complaint process can be an informal sanction for attorneys accused of misconduct.

Researchers have also considered factors that contribute to sanctioning decision making. Authors have examined how attorneys are sanctioned in Alabama (Payne & Stevens, 1999) and Virginia (Payne, Time, & Raper, 2005). The Alabama study found gender patterns: Female attorneys were more likely to be publicly reprimanded, and they were slightly more likely to be accused of failing to provide competent representation. One-third of female attorneys were accused of this, as compared to one-fifth of male attorneys.

These patterns can be at least partially understood through an application of the systems approach or patriarchal theory. Broader societal changes resulted in more females in the legal field in the 1980s. Because female attorneys, in general, have fewer years of experience than male attorneys, the lack of experience may contribute to the accusation of failing to provide competent representation. Indeed, research shows that years of experience are tied to allegations of misconduct. Conversely, it could be that a male-dominated profession uses its sanctioning body to control females. Such a possibility is in line with patriarchal theory.

Figure 5.1 compares the ways attorneys are sanctioned in Alabama and Virginia. A few interesting patterns are evident in the figure. For example, suspensions were used more often in Virginia, with one-third of the disciplined attorneys suspended in Virginia, as compared to one-fourth of Alabama attorneys. Also, private reprimands were routinely used in Alabama but rarely used in Virginia. In addition, license revocation occurred frequently in Virginia but infrequently in Alabama.

On the surface, these differences point to the varied response systems between states. Also, the difference in the way misconduct is defined between states is in line with a social construction definition of white-collar misconduct, or attorney misconduct, in this case. Though these differences exist, the bottom line is that all states define appropriate behavior for attorneys and all states have formal structures, for responding to and controlling attorney misconduct. A similar pattern is evident with regard to judicial misconduct.

Judicial Misconduct

Just as lawyers are depicted in certain ways in television shows and movies, judges are a regular part of the "cast of characters" portrayed in crime-related media. These portrayals often show cantankerous judges controlling their courtrooms by humiliating attorneys and other courtroom participants. Such a portrayal is not an accurate depiction of judicial conduct. In fact, in many situations if judges actually behaved the way they are portrayed on television shows and in the

Figure 5.1   Sanctions Against Attorneys in Virginia and Alabama

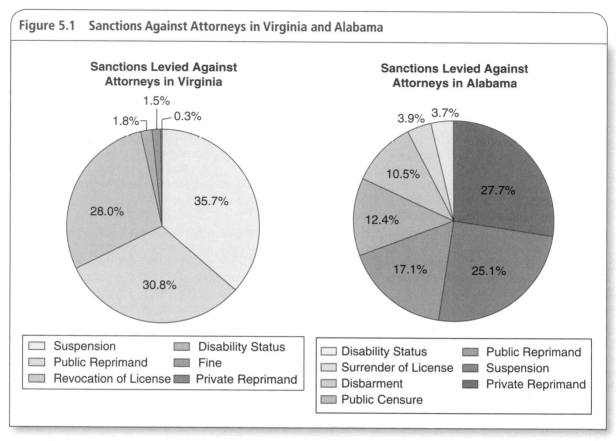

Source: Adapted from Payne, B. K., Time, V., & Raper, S. (2005). Regulating legal misconduct by lawyers in the Commonwealth of Virginia: The gender influence. *Women and Criminal Justice, 15,* 81–96; and Payne, B. K., & Stevens, E. H. (1999). An examination of recent professional sanctions imposed on Alabama lawyers. *The Justice Professional, 12,* 17–43.

media, they would face disciplinary behaviors for conduct unbecoming a judge. Consider the following description of the popular *Judge Judy* show:

> Visually, Judge Judy's courtroom looks very much like one might imagine a New York State courtroom to appear if they had never actually been inside one. . . . However, there is one very significant difference between what is seen in Judge Judy's courtroom and what occurs in a real courtroom: the behavior of the judge. Judges have several checks on how they do their job. . . . In addition to laws that prescribe how the judiciary will function, the personal reputation of judges is a major incentive to do their job in an appropriate manner. . . . Because the behavior of a syndic-court judge has Nielsen ratings as a standard, they are allowed to engage in acts that would generally not be appropriate in court. The more "straight-talking" that a judge appears, which often means being as mean as possible to unlikable litigants, the better ratings he or she receives. (Kimball, 2005, p. 150)

The Model Code of Judicial Conduct outlines various rules that prescribe appropriate behavior by judges. The rules cover judicial behavior throughout the entire justice process, which means that misconduct can occur at different phases of judicial proceedings. During jury deliberations, for example, two kinds of misconduct are known to occur: (1) pressuring the jury for a verdict and (2) communicating with jurors in private. Instances where misconduct occurs during jury deliberation may result in an appeal, but appellate courts will not automatically overturn the jury's decision. The cases of judicial error are reviewed on a case-by-case basis (Gershman, 1999).

Similar to the way that states define attorney misconduct differently, states offer different typologies for judicial misconduct. Kentucky, for example, identifies three general types of judicial misconduct: (1) improper influence, (2) improper courtroom decorum, and (3) improper illegal activities on or off the bench (Judicial Conduct Commission, 2011). Within each of these general categories, specific types of misconduct are identified. In California, a more exhaustive list of types of judicial misconduct is provided by the state's judicial commission. The acts identified as misconduct in California include the following:

- Abuse of contempt/sanctions
- Administrative malfeasance, improper comments, treatment of colleagues
- Alcohol or drug related criminal conduct
- Bias or appearance of bias toward particular groups
- Bias or appearance of bias but not toward particular groups
- Comment on pending case
- Decisional delay
- Demeanor or decorum
- Disqualification, disclosure, or post-disqualification conduct
- Ex parte communications
- Failure to cooperate with regulatory authority
- Failure to ensure rights
- Gifts, loans, favors, or ticket fixing
- Improper business, financial, or fiduciary activities
- Improper political activities
- Inability to perform judicial duties
- Miscellaneous off-bench conduct
- Misuse of court resources
- Nonperformance of judicial functions, attendance, or sleeping
- Nonsubstance abuse criminal conviction
- Off-bench abuse of authority
- On-bench abuse of authority
- Pre-bench misconduct
- Sexual harassment or inappropriate comments
- Substance abuse (State of California Commission on Judicial Performance, 2010)

Stacey Ilyse Photography

▲ **Photo 5.2** Judges have an incredible amount of power in the courtroom. Most judges do not abuse that power. A few, however, do.

Just as allegations of attorney misconduct increased in the past few decades, allegations of judicial misconduct increased significantly in the early 1990s (Coyle, 1995). Part of this increase was likely caused by the development of formal commissions in different states that provided citizens with a mechanism they could use to file judicial complaints. In California, voters approved Proposition 190 around this same time. Proposition 190 created the Commission on Judicial Performance and authorized the commission to review judicial misconduct cases and impose sanctions, which would be reviewed by the state Supreme Court.

The way the complaint process is designed in California mirrors the complaint process followed in other states. Anyone can file a written complaint to the commission. If the complaint describes an allegation of misconduct, the judge is asked to provide information in response to the allegation. Members of the commission will interview witnesses and review court transcripts and case files. The judge will be given 20 days to respond to the complaint. After the information has been reviewed, the commission meets to review cases. On average, the commission meets every 7 weeks or so (State of California Commission on Judicial Performance, 2010). In recent years, the number of judicial complaints filed has been relatively stable (see Figure 5.2).

In Focus 5.1 provides an overview of one of the cases reviewed by the California Commission on Judicial Performance. Note that the judge was ultimately removed from the bench for these actions. In most cases, judges are not removed from the bench because this sanction is reserved for the most obvious and most severe types of misconduct. Advisory letters are commonly used, as are private admonishments, and public sanctions are used less frequently. Also, as others have noted, in some cases involving judicial misconduct, judges resign before they are sanctioned in order to keep their pensions intact (Lewis, 1983).

It is estimated that 90 percent of complaints filed against judges are dismissed (Gray, 2004). Many of the complaints are dismissed because the allegations do not rise to levels of misconduct outlined in judicial regulations. By the very nature of their jobs, judges will, at the end of the day, make decisions that disappoint or even anger several of the individuals participating in the judicial process. The result is that a number of egregious allegations are made. Gray describes a case where a prison inmate filed a complaint against the judge—described as his former wife in the complaint. The inmate said that the judge was biased against him because of their prior marriage. Upon reviewing the case, it was learned that the judge and the inmate did not, in fact, have a prior marital relationship.

It is also important to note that a difference exists between "making a mistake" and committing judicial misconduct. Said Gray (2004), "It is not unethical to be imperfect, and it would be unfair to sanction a judge for not being infallible while making hundreds of decisions under pressure" (p. 1247). Somewhat related is that if a judge makes an error, then that error will not automatically result in the judicial decision being overturned. Instead, the case would be reviewed, and the relevance of the mistake would be considered in determining whether the case should be overturned. It is important to stress that judicial misconduct commissions cannot overturn judicial decisions made in courts of law. Only appellate courts have the authority to reverse judicial decisions. The White-Collar Crime in the News: Convicted Judge Sits on the Other Side of the Bench box shows a case where the misconduct was much more than a mistake.

In some countries, judicial corruption is addressed by allowing violators to bring civil actions (or sue) the judge accused of corruption. It is hard to prove corruption, but it is believed that such actions might have a punitive value (Mariani, 2013). If damages are awarded, another question that arises centers on who should pay the damages (the judge or the government).

An entire chapter of this text will discuss why white-collar misconduct occurs. In terms of judicial misconduct, some have argued that a combination of three factors contributes to misdeeds by judges. These factors include (1) office authority, (2) heavy case loads, and (3) interactions with others in the judicial process (Coyle, 1995). Briefly, judges have a great deal of power, but they are expected to express that power under the demands of large caseloads, and their interactions with others in the judicial network may provide opportunities for misconduct. One group they interact with is prosecutors—a group that also is not immune from misconduct.

Prosecutorial Misconduct

The prosecutor position has been described as "the most powerful position in the criminal justice system" (Schoenfeld, 2005, p. 250). In addition to deciding whether charges should be filed against individuals, prosecutors have a strong voice in deciding what sanction should be given to defendants. While the judge ultimately assigns the sanction, it is the prosecutor who decides what types of charges to file against defendants, and these charges will help determine the sentence given by the judge. For instance, it is the prosecutor who decides whether a defendant should be tried for capital murder—a crime that may ultimately result in the death penalty.

WHITE-COLLAR CRIME IN THE NEWS

Convicted Judge Sits on the Other Side of the Bench

While crimes are adjudicated in the courtroom, in rare circumstances they might actually occur in the courtroom.

In a case that exposed widespread corruption in a South Texas county's judicial system—reaching all the way to the district attorney's office—a former state judge was recently sentenced to six years in prison for taking bribes and kickbacks in return for favorable rulings from his bench.

Abel Limas, 59, a lifelong resident of Brownsville, Texas, served as a police officer and practiced law before becoming a state judge in Cameron County in 2001. He served eight years on the bench, during which time he turned his courtroom into a criminal enterprise to line his own pockets.

"The depth of the corruption was shocking," said Mark Gripka, a special agent in our San Antonio Division who was part of the team that investigated the case. "What was more shocking was how cheaply Judge Limas sold his courtroom—$300 here, $500 there—in return for a favorable ruling."

Evidence also showed that Limas made a deal with the attorneys in the helicopter crash case to become an "of counsel" attorney with the firm. He was promised an advance of $100,000 and 10 percent of the settlement—all while the case was still pending in his court.

Over a 14-month period beginning in November 2007, investigators used court-authorized wiretaps to listen to the judge's phone calls. "That's when we really learned the scope of what he was doing," Gripka explained. The judge's nearly $100,000 annual salary was not enough to support his lifestyle, which included regular gambling trips to Las Vegas.

In 2010, when Limas was faced with the cooperate in a wider public corruption investigation—and our agents learned that the Cameron County district attorney at the time, Armando Villalobos, was also corrupt. The investigation showed, among other criminal activities, that Villalobos accepted $80,000 in cash in exchange for taking actions that allowed a convicted murderer to be released for 60 days without bond prior to reporting to prison. The murderer failed to report to prison and remains a fugitive.

Limas pled guilty to racketeering in 2011. By that time, he had helped authorities uncover wide-ranging corruption in the Cameron County judicial system. To date, 10 other defendants have been convicted by a jury or pled guilty as part of the FBI's six-year investigation, including a former Texas state representative, three attorneys, a former investigator for the district attorney's office, and Villalobos, who is scheduled to be sentenced next month on racketeering, extortion, and bribery charges.

Source: Reprinted from FBI (2013). Public Corruption: Courtroom for Sale (press release) Available online at https://www.fbi.gov/news/stories/2013/september/public-corruption-courtroom-for-sale/public-corruption-courtroom-for-sale.

Criminologist Jocelyn Pollock (2004) has identified several different types of prosecutorial misconduct. First, instances where prosecutors have improper communications with defendants (e.g., without their attorney present if one was requested, personal communications) are examples of misconduct. Second, if prosecutors have ex parte communications (without the other party present) with the judge, then the prosecutor has developed an unfair advantage over the defense.

IN FOCUS   5.1

Case Study: Judicial Misconduct Leads to Removal

The following is a rendered press release from the California Commission on Judicial Performance.

JUDICIAL PERFORMANCE COMMISSION ISSUES DECISION AND ORDER REMOVING JUDGE ******* FROM OFFICE

The Commission on Judicial Performance has issued a decision and order removing Judge *****, of the Tulare County Superior Court, from office. The commission's determination becomes final in 30 days, subject to discretionary review by the California Supreme Court.

The commission ordered Judge ******* removed from office for a course of conduct toward his courtroom clerk that included manufacturing an anonymous letter that accused her in crude terms of having an affair with a court bailiff, using the letter and numerous gifts worth thousands of dollars in an attempt to pressure the clerk into a close, personal relationship, and providing legal advice to her son. After the clerk informed the judge that she was going to request a transfer from his department, he deposited $8,000 into her bank account. Later that day, during a court proceeding, the judge gave a note to the clerk, accusing her of extortion, in an attempt to intimidate the clerk and ensure her silence. Judge ******* denied writing the anonymous letter and the other essential facts of the case, blaming the clerk for his misconduct, and claiming he was only "mentoring" her. The

commission found that significant portions of the judge's testimony lacked credibility.

The commission stated that "[t]he deceitful, calculated and unseemly nature of the judge's misconduct, compounded by his lack of candor in response to the commission's investigation and untruthful testimony under oath before the masters" compelled his removal from office. The commission found that the judge's highly improper course of conduct violated numerous canons of the Code of Judicial Ethics and was committed in bad faith. The commission found that some of the judge's conduct was undertaken in a judicial capacity and therefore constituted willful misconduct, the most serious constitutional basis for censure or removal of a judge. However, the commission stated that, even if the judge had not been acting in a judicial capacity, "the entirety of his misconduct warrants removal." While recognizing and appreciating the judge's many contributions to his community and the legal profession, the commission concluded, "Certain misconduct is so completely at odds with the core qualities and role of a judge that no amount of mitigation can redeem the seriousness of the wrongdoing or obviate the need for removal in order to fulfill our mandate to protect the public, enforce high standards of judicial conduct, and maintain public confidence in the integrity of the judiciary. This is such a case."

Source: Reprinted From State of California Commission on Judicial Performance

Third, if prosecutors fail to disclose evidence, which they are required to do by law, then misconduct has occurred. Fourth, if a prosecutor knows that a witness has provided false testimony and fails to correct the testimony, the prosecutor has committed misconduct just as the perjurer did.

Legal expert Alschuler (1972) discussed a different set of prosecutorial misconduct examples. Examples of misconduct he discussed include the following:

- Commenting on the defendant's lack of testimony
- Asserting facts that are not supported by the evidence
- Expressing personal beliefs about the defendant's guilt
- Verbal abuse of the defense attorney
- Verbal or mental abuse of the defendant

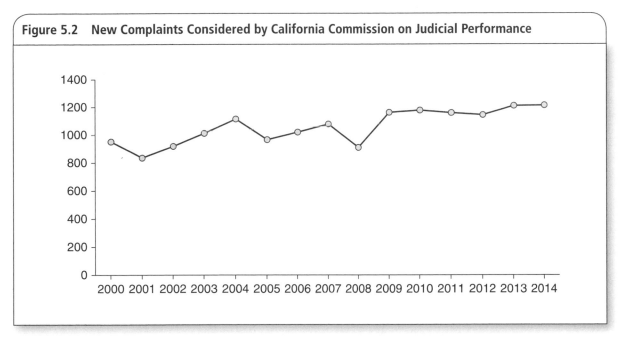

Figure 5.2   **New Complaints Considered by California Commission on Judicial Performance**

Source: Adapted from State of California Commission

More recently, Cramm (2009) discussed additional forms of prosecutorial misconduct, including (a) "withholding, destroying, or changing evidence"; (b) "failing to preserve evidence"; (c) "making prejudicial comments about the defendant during opening or closing remarks"; (d) "coercing guilty pleas from defendants"; (e) "intimidating defense witnesses"; and (f) "obstructing defense attorney access to prosecution witnesses."

Although it is difficult to identify precisely how often prosecutorial misconduct occurs, estimates suggest that these behaviors are particularly common. One author notes that prosecutorial misconduct is "a factor in 42 percent of DNA exonerations" according to Barry Scheck and Peter Neufeld's Innocence Project (Roberts, 2007). Roberts also quotes a report from the Center for Public Integrity, which includes a group of journalists who analyzed 11,000 appellate opinions where prosecutor misconduct appeared to occur. The Center found that "since 1970, individual judge and court panels cited prosecutorial misconduct as a factor when dismissing charges, reversing convictions, or reducing sentences in over 2,000 cases" (Roberts, 2007).

A number of direct and indirect negative consequences arise from prosecutorial misconduct. Beyond limiting the defendant's right to a fair trial, influencing the jury, and creating public resentment (Alschuler, 1972), prosecutorial misconduct has the potential to breed crime. If the most powerful representatives of the justice system break the rules, others might use the "official misbehavior" to justify their own transgressions. Also, and perhaps more significant, prosecutorial misconduct has the potential to wrongfully sentence individuals to life in prison or, even worse, death. Schoenfeld (2005) cites a *Chicago Tribune* study that found "since 1963, 381 people have had their convictions for homicide overturned because of prosecutorial misconduct. Sixty-seven of those defendants were sentenced to death" (p. 266).

Students should not think that they are insulated from cases of prosecutorial misconduct. Consider the case of the Duke Lacrosse players accused of raping Crystal Gail Magnum. Overzealous in his efforts to prosecute the students from the moment the allegations surfaced, former prosecutor Mike Nifong was initially praised by advocates, university faculty, and feminists because he was demonstrating a willingness to prosecute seemingly elite students accused of raping an

African American woman. His zeal for the case did not dissipate, even after evidence surfaced that seemed to refute the woman's claim. Eventually, the case was dismissed.

A state bar examination of Nifong's actions in the case found that he had (a) refused to hear exculpatory evidence, (b) made false statements to the media to "[heighten] public condemnation of the accused," (c) failed to provide evidence to the defendants, (d) failed to provide the results of tests to the defendants, and (e) denied knowing about the results of a rape kit exam that potentially exonerated the defendants. Nifong was disbarred but not before sending some rather interesting letters to the state bar. In one letter, for instance, Nifong claimed that the license he was surrendering to the state bar was damaged because his puppy had chewed on it. According to *News and Observer,* the falsely accused students incurred legal expenses in excess of $3 million in their efforts to respond to Nifong's misconduct.

Few studies have empirically assessed prosecutorial misconduct, or any of the types of misconduct by upper-class criminal justice professionals, for that matter. Describing the need to broaden research past conceptual divides, McBarnet (1991) writes, "We need to explore how economic elites actively use the institutions, ideologies, and methods of law to secure immunity from legal control" (p. 324). Taking this a step further, much more research needs to focus on how power elites within the justice system misuse their legal authority to protect their own interests.

Correctional Officer Misconduct

Much more research has focused on police corruption, judicial misconduct, and attorney misconduct than on corruption by correctional officers. One of the first studies done on corruption by correctional officers was a doctoral dissertation by Bernard McCarthy (1981). McCarthy's dissertation was a case study of misconduct in one state's prison system. He classified the offenses into theft (from inmates, from the institution, and from civilians), trafficking (bringing contraband into the prison), abuse of authority, and embezzlement (from prison accounts, non-prison accounts and so on).Various patterns were tied to misconduct in the prison system. First, the degree of discretion given to low-level workers in an isolated work environment appeared to promote the opportunity for corruption. Second, the nature of the prison as an institution was such that inmate demand for contraband was high. Third, low morale (with workers' individual goals being different from the collective goals of the criminal justice system) was viewed as a predictor of correctional misconduct.

As with the law enforcement profession, sexual misconduct has been cited as a variety of misconduct occurring in the corrections profession. Varieties of sexual misconduct in the corrections field have been categorized as sexual contact offenses, sexual assault, and sexual gratification between officer and supervisee (Smith & Yarussi, 2007). Another author team classifies sexual misconduct by corrections officials into the following four categories: (1) verbal harassment, (2) improper visual surveillance, (3) improper touching, and (4) consensual sex (Burton, Erdman, Hamilton, & Muse, 1999). It is believed that "consensual relations" are the most common forms of sexual misconduct between correctional officers and inmates, with rape believed to be infrequent (Layman, McCampbell, & Moss, 2000).

The notion of consensual, however, is somewhat ambiguous. Consider that sexual relations between probation or parole officers and their supervisees are prohibited by the criminal law in many states. While little research has been done in this area, experts warn against assuming that probationers and parolees (or inmates, for that matter) are able to fully consent to such relationships (Buell, Layman, McCampbell, & Smith, 2003).

A General Accounting Office study focused on sexual misconduct allegations in women's prisons in the Federal Bureau of Prisons as well as the Texas, California, and District of Columbia's corrections departments between 1995 and 1998. The study uncovered 506 complaints of sexual misconduct by staff. Criminal prosecutions were rare, and less than one-fifth of the complaints were substantiated. When complaints were substantiated, termination from employment was the most common response (Burton et al., 1999).

The consequences of sexual misconduct for sexual assault victims are likely no different from the consequences that other sexual assault victims experience. It is important to note, however, that sexual misconduct by corrections officials will lead to consequences that also impact the correctional system. Potential consequences of correctional sexual misconduct include the following:

- Jeopardizing staff safety if inmates react against nonoffending staff members
- The risk of legal action for staff members, supervisors, and the agency
- Health risks for inmates and staff exposed to sexually transmitted diseases
- Family problems for offenders, victims, and staff responding to the allegations
- Negative perceptions of the corrections department among community members
- Reduced trust between inmates and staff (Smith & Yarussi, 2007)

Concern about an increase in sexual misconduct by community corrections officers led the National Institute of Corrections to develop a 36-hour training program to assist officials in their efforts to prevent and intervene in cases of sexual misconduct. The training focused on defining misconduct, policy development, legal issues, ethical issues, investigatory strategies, and other related topics (Buell & McCampbell, 2003). General strategies that have been suggested for preventing sexual misconduct include (a) developing clear policies that are enforced as needed, (b) improving the quality of workers, (c) enhancing supervisory practices, (d) implementing various social control mechanisms, and (e) providing ethics training to officers and staff (Souryal, 2009).

Table 5.1 **Federal Convictions: Federal, State, and Local Public Corruption Cases, 1990–2013**

Year	Federal	State	Local
1990	583	79	225
1991	665	77	180
1992	532	92	211
1993	595	133	272
1994	488	97	202
1995	438	61	191
1996	459	83	190
1997	392	49	169
1998	414	58	264
1999	460	80	219
2000	422	91	183
2001	414	61	184
2002	429	132	262
2003	421	87	119
2004	381	81	252
2005	390	94	232

(Continued)

Table 5.1   (Continued)

Year	Federal	State	Local
2006	407	116	241
2007	405	85	275
2008	458	123	246
2009	426	102	257
2010	397	108	280
2011	392	143	276
2012	369	78	295
2013	315	119	303

Source: U.S. Department of Justice. (2014). *Report to Congress on the activities and operations of the public integrity chapter for 2013.* Washington, DC: U.S. Department of Justice.

● ● ●   Crimes in the Political System

Readers are likely not surprised by the suggestion that crimes also occur in the political system. Unlike professionals working in some of the other systems, professionals in the political system routinely confront suspicion and distrust from citizens. This distrust stems at least partly from several high-profile political and government scandals that have occurred over the years. Table 5.1 shows the number of public corruption convictions prosecuted by U.S. attorneys since 1990. As shown in the table, the number of prosecuted federal public corruption cases has decreased some since 1990, but the number of local and state officials prosecuted increased slightly over this time frame. Figures 5.5 through 5.9 show the various types of individuals involved in these cases over time and whether convictions were obtained. Across all types of corruption, there has been an increase in the number of officials convicted for public corruption. To be sure, these cases continue to occur, and they tend to receive a great deal of public scrutiny.

Indeed, it seems every decade has been marked by national political scandals. In the 1970s, Watergate served as an introduction to political corruption on the grandest scale. In June 1972, burglars connected to the Committee to Re-elect the President broke into the Democratic National Committee's offices in the Watergate Office Complex. After the investigation began, President Nixon insisted that he knew nothing about the burglary. During the course of the investigation, recordings were uncovered showing that the president participated in covering up the break-in. The investigation also revealed other abuses, including warrantless wiretaps to listen in on the conversations of reporters. Watergate has been described as "the touchstone, the definitive point of

US Government Work

▲ **Photo 5.3**   Political officials take an oath to uphold the law and engage in ethical behavior. Some politicians have violated their oaths.

reference for subsequent political scandals in the United States" (Schudson, 2004, p. 1231). Another author noted that political corruption is not new but that efforts to control corruption through public law enforcement efforts can be traced to the 1970s in the aftermath of Watergate (Mass, 1986).

Abscam was the next major national political scandal following Watergate. In the late 1970s and early 1980s, Abscam was an FBI investigation in which undercover agents used the fictional identity of Abdul Enterprises, Ltd., to offer bribes to various officials in exchange for help making it easier for two sheiks "to emigrate to the U.S." (Gershman, 1982, p. 1572). At least a handful of congressmen immediately accepted bribes. A few offered assistance after being groomed by undercover agents. The same "scam" was repeated in Philadelphia where local officials agreed to the bribe. Once the case became public, media attention uncovered wide-ranging instances of corruption. Gershman (1982) wrote:

> Seen as public theatre, Abscam cast the three branches of government in a morality play whose plot called for the portrayal of disguised heroes and hidden villains, intricate charades with racial overtones, and lavish scenery against invitations to corruption set the characters in motion. (p. 1565)

The **Iran-Contra affair** was the next major national political scandal. In the mid-1980s, political officials authorized the sale of weapons to Iran, despite the presence of an arms embargo, as part of a secret effort to trade arms for hostages. Proceeds from the weapons sales were then sent to the Contras in Nicaragua although Congress had prohibited Contra funding. While evidence suggested that Reagan was involved in the cover-up, he escaped negative fallout from the scandal, prompting one reporter to call the Iran-Contra affair "the cover up that worked" (Brinkley, 1994) to distinguish the scandal from Watergate.

The 1990s and 2000s saw a series of ongoing political scandals. From the Clintons being tied up in allegations of real estate fraud in Whitewater to President Clinton's sexual contact with Monica Lewinsky to President George W. Bush's failure to uncover weapons of mass destruction in Iraq, it seemed that at any given moment in time, a political scandal was brewing over these two decades. To provide a framework for understanding these crimes in the political system, attention can be given to the following types of crimes occurring in the political system:

- Election law violations
- Campaign finance violations
- Political corruption related to extortion and bribery
- Apolitical white-collar crime
- Crimes in the military
- State-corporate crime

These varieties of crimes are discussed below.

Election Law Violations

Election law violations are situations where political officials violate rules guiding the way that elections are supposed to be conducted. Election fraud laws exist in order to guard against crimes such as voter registration fraud, vote counting fraud, and balloting fraud (Aycock & Hutton, 2010). More specifically, election fraud involves situations where individuals try to corrupt "the process by which ballots are obtained, marked, or tabulated; the process by which election results are canvassed or certified; or the process by which voters are registered" (Donsanto & Simmons, 2007, p. 25). Schemes are characterized as either public or private, depending on who initiated the fraud. The Federal Election Commission can levy civil fines against those who violate provisions of the Federal Election Campaign Act. Criminal prosecutions would be initiated by the U.S. Department of Justice (Aycock & Hutton, 2010).

The extent of voter fraud is particularly hard to assess. Traditional empirical strategies are not useful in studying voter fraud. One author team has suggested data mining strategies as a tool to study voter fraud (Hood & Gillespie, 2012). Using this technique, the author found no evidence of voter fraud (as measured by voting by deceased individuals) in the 2006 Georgia election.

Voter identification laws have been adopted as a way to curb some of these offenses. Under some of these laws, voters must prove that they are able to vote by showing a license or other official identification card. Some have argued that the laws discriminate against minorities. One study found that while the public favors voter ID laws, a majority prefer voter access over fraud prevention (Atkeson, Alvarez, Hall, & Sinclair, 2014).

Campaign Finance Violations

Campaign finance laws place restrictions on the way political campaigns are financed, with specific attention given to contributions and expenditures. Expenditures are limited only if candidates "elect to participate in a public funding program" (Aycock & Hutton, 2010, p. 358). Contributions from certain groups are prohibited (e.g., current or former government contractors, foreign nationals, contributions in the name of another). Tom DeLay, former house majority leader, was convicted in November 2010 of violations of Texas campaign finance laws after he funneled corporate donations made to the Republican National Committee to candidates in Texas. Texas law prohibits corporate contributions to candidates. In February 2011, DeLay's attorneys appealed the case on the grounds that the Texas law was unconstitutional (Epstein, 2011). An appellate court overturned the conviction in September 2013. A year later, in September 2014, the Texas Court of Criminal Appeals affirmed the lower appellate court's decision, effectively dismissing the conviction.

Campaign finance laws also stipulate that contributions cannot be used for personal use. At the time of the writing of this text, former vice presidential candidate and North Carolina Senator John Edwards was indicted after a grand jury investigation that focused on how his campaign used funds to pay his mistress for work she did for his campaign. In particular, she produced three videos for the campaign at a cost of $250,000. Prosecutors alleged that the funds were actually a payment to get his mistress to keep quiet about her affair with the former senator (Smith, 2011). After a mistrial and acquittal on one count, charges were eventually dropped against the former political heavy weight. His political career, however, appears to be over.

Political Corruption Related to Extortion, Bribery, and Illegal Gratuities

In this context, **political extortion, bribery, and illegal gratuities** refers to situations where political officials use their political power to shape outcomes of various processes, including lawmaking, awarding of contracts, policy development, and so on. The line between bribery and illegal gratuities has to do with intent. In bribery cases, authorities must prove that the official intended to provide political favors in exchange for some item, good, or service. In illegal gratuity cases, the official simply received something that they were not supposed to receive (Jarcho & Schecter, 2012).

Operation Bid Rig was a political corruption investigation case by the FBI. One sting as part of this investigation resulted in the arrests of 44 suspects, including three mayors, a city council president, two state legislators, and five rabbis. In this sting, hundreds of hours of audio and video recordings were collected. In one of the recordings, a newly elected mayor, Peter Cammarano from Hoboken, New Jersey, bragged that he would have won his election even if he had been indicted because he had votes of certain groups "locked down" (Richburg, 2009). The newly minted mayor had been mayor for less than a month when he was arrested. He allegedly took a bribe of $25,000 in exchange for his support of a building project (McShane, 2009).

Various sources of public corruption have been identified. Some researchers note that corruption is tied to bureaucratic forces, political forces, and historical/cultural factors (Meier & Holbrook, 1992). One study found that political corruption is lower in political systems that have "closely contested elections and high voter turnouts" (Meier & Holbrook, 1992, p. 151). The underlying premise is that politicians will be on their guard more if more voters are voting and the politicians have a higher likelihood of losing an election. If no one is voting and elections are shoo-ins, the message given to the politician is that constituents really don't care about politics.

Public corruption has also been tied to factors such as a country's stage of development (Batabyal & Chowdhury, 2015), how government workers are paid (Mendez, 2014), and fiscal decentralization (Goel & Nelson, 2011). Access to information has also been attributed to public corruption (Candeub, 2013; Ionescu, 2013a; 2013b). One common thread is woven through these factors: technology. Technology is related to a country's stage of development, level of bureaucracy, the ability to decentralize fiscal matters, efforts to promote voter turnout, strategies to strengthen campaigns and create more closely contested elections, and access to information.

Few researchers have explored how technology is related to public corruption, though the theoretical foundation for a relationship between the two can be found in the literature. Consider a study that found that "greater Internet awareness through news reports, blog posts and legal opinions, tends to embolden potential whistleblowers to expose corruption" (Goel & Nelson, 2011, p. 4). Internet awareness was found to be stronger than the laws themselves. A similar conclusion has been offered by others: "Internet diffusion has a significant effect on transparency and corruption . . . having a strong positive effect on levels of transparency and a strong negative effect on levels of corruption. Access to the Internet leads to significant decreases in corruption" (Ionescu, 2013b).

The consequences of such political corruption can be significant. In particular, individuals lose faith in their government as a result of public corruption. Criminology professor Alan Block (1996) said, "there is a loss of faith in the U.S.A. today in public institutions because of the sense that they do not work . . . for they either have been corrupted or are run by nincompoops" (p. 18). As well, political scandals have made it more difficult for honest politicians to lead and govern. According to Ginsberg and Shefter (1995), "efforts to link members of the opposition party to ethical lapses have become important weapons in American political warfare" (p. 497). Government officials must spend at least part of the time— that could be spent governing—in warding off ethics attacks from their opponents.

Apolitical White-Collar Crime

Apolitical white-collar crime refers to situations where politicians get into trouble for doing things that are outside of the scope of politics but are violations of the public trust. Mark Sanford, former governor of South Carolina, came under fire after he told his staff that he was "hiking on the Appalachian Trail" when, in fact, he was in Argentina with his mistress. His wife later divorced him, and his ability to govern in South Carolina took a significant hit. Once a presidential hopeful, he was subsequently censured by his state government for misusing travel funds to support his "hiking." Sanford was able to resuscitate his political career, however. He was later elected as a South Carolina representative to the U.S. House of Representatives.

The violations of trust in apolitical white-collar crimes often seem far out of character for the politicians caught in the scandals. In May 2010, U.S. Representative Mark Souder resigned from office "after admitting to an affair with a female staffer" ("Congressman Resigns Over Affair," 2010). One news outlet found that Souder had actually filmed a public service video with the staffer he had an affair with. The topic of the video was abstinence.

Conviction of former mayor of Washington, DC, Marion Barry, for using crack cocaine in 1990 showed a similar irony. Only a few hours before his arrest, Barry "preached an antidrug sermon to high school students" ("Hours Before Arrest," 1990). More recently, Eliot Spitzer resigned as governor of New York after he was caught in a prostitution sting. As attorney general, Spitzer had orchestrated several prostitution busts himself.

A well-publicized case of apolitical white-collar offending involved Larry Craig, a former U.S. Republican senator. In September 2007, Craig was caught in an undercover sex sting and accused of trying to initiate sex in an airport bathroom with an undercover officer. He tapped his foot in a bathroom stall in a way that signaled his interest in "sharing some time" with the individual in the next stall. Craig pleaded guilty, though he later tried to recant his guilty plea. That he was caught in such a scandal was somewhat ironic given his history of voting for legislation restricting the rights of homosexuals. One fellow Republican senator, John Ensign from Nevada, called Craig's actions embarrassing. Less than 2 years later, Ensign admitted having an "affair with a former campaign staffer who is married to one of the lawmaker's former legislative aides" (Kane & Cillizza, 2009, p. A01).

Crimes in the Military

As a system of social control, the military system includes several branches of the military that are charged with various duties related to wartime efforts and the promotion of peace. Clifford Bryant (1979) used the phrase *khaki-collar crime* for situations where individuals in the military break rules guiding their workplace activities. According to Bryant, khaki-collar crime occurs in five contexts:

- **Intra-occupational crimes** are crimes committed against the American military system. These crimes include property crimes (e.g., theft of military property, misuse of property, and destruction of property), crimes against persons (e.g., cruelty to subordinates and assaults against superiors), and crimes against performance (e.g., mutiny, faking illness, and conduct unbecoming an officer).

- **Extra-occupational crimes** are committed against the American civilian social system. These crimes include property crimes (e.g., theft, forgery, and vandalism), personal crimes (e.g., rape, robbery, assault, and murder), and performance crimes (e.g., fighting and disturbing the peace).
- **Foreign friendly civilian crimes** are committed against citizens of another country. The same types of crimes found under extra-occupational crimes but committed against foreigners, are examples.
- **Enemy civilian social system crimes** are crimes against residents of countries in which the U.S. military is fighting. Examples of such crimes include property crimes (e.g., looting and pillaging), personal crimes (e.g., committing atrocities and massacres), and performance crimes (e.g., colluding with citizens to harm the U.S. military).
- **Inter-occupational crimes** are crimes committed against the enemy military system. These include property crimes (e.g., misappropriation of captured supplies), personal crimes (e.g., torture and mistreatment of prisoners of war), and performance crimes (e.g., helping the enemy).

Bryant notes that the source of law for military crimes, and the application of laws, is different from what would be found with other white-collar crimes. Depending on where the crime was committed and which crime was committed, sources of law in khaki-collar crime cases include the U.S. *Uniform Code of Military Justice*, international treaties, the *Law of Land Warfare*, and the laws of the government of the country where the crime was committed.

It is safe to suggest that the military has more rules than other occupations guiding workplace behavior. Consider the following examples:

- If my colleagues in my department (that I chair) don't do as I ask them to do, it will make me sad. If members of the military do not do as their bosses tell them, they can be charged with insubordination.
- If I get tired of my job as department chair and quit going to work, I will be fired. If a member of the military leaves his or her military assignment, this will be called desertion.
- If my colleagues try to overthrow my department and run me off as chair, again I will be sad. If members of the military try to overtake their commanding officer, mutiny is occurring.
- If I fake being sick and try to get out of going to a meeting, this will be a minor form of occupational deviance. If members of the military feign illness to get out of their assignments, this will be called malingering and can be met with a court martial.
- If I quit my job and go work for another university, I will miss my current colleagues tremendously. If I leave the military and go work for another military, this will be called foreign enlistment.
- Up until recently, if a gay or lesbian soldier told people about his or her sexual orientation, he or she could have been disciplined by the military (Bryant, 1979).

The list could go on and on. The simple point is that there are more rules to break in the military than there are in other occupations. One Navy scandal involved the former commanding officer of the USS *Enterprise*. The commander was relieved of his command in January 2011 after videos he produced while at sea were shown on the *Virginian-Pilot*'s website as part of a news article the newspaper published about his activities. Allegedly, in an effort to promote morale among those on the ship, the commander produced videos starring himself as the emcee. In the videos, he used patriarchal types of humor—making fun of women, gays, and his superiors. In one of the videos, for example, he said, "Over the years, I've gotten several complaints about inappropriate material during these videos— never to me personally, but gutlessly through other channels. . . . This evening, all of you bleeding hearts—and you fag SWO [Surface Warfare Officer] boy—why don't you go ahead and hug yourself for the next 20 minutes or so, because there's a good chance you're going to be offended tonight" (Reilly, 2011). After the videos surfaced publicly (more than 3 years after he had made them), the commander was sanctioned by the military. Two of his superiors were also sanctioned by the military.

One current controversy regarding crimes in the military centers on the use of private contractors, such as Xie, Dyncorp International, and Triple Canopy, to provide military security functions. Regulations stipulate that private contractors should use only defensive types of violence; however, evidence points to several horrific situations where private military contractors initiated violence (Welch, 2009). The case of Blackwater (since renamed Xie), a security firm created in 1997 by a former Navy Seal, is particularly illustrative. By all accounts, Blackwater has been overrepresented in allegations of offensive force by private military contractors. Welch (2009) wrote that Blackwater has a "shooting rate" two times higher than similar private military security businesses. He added that the

> company has gained a reputation as one that flaunts a quick-draw image, thereby enticing its guards to take excessively violent actions. Some suggest that its aggressive posture in guarding diplomats reflects the wishes of its principle client, the State Department's Bureau of Diplomatic Security. (p. 356)

Another current controversy has to do with the way members of the military treat prisoners of war. The tortures occurring at Abu Ghraib made international headlines when photos surfaced showing military officials sexually degrading prisoners. Hamm (2007) noted that three explanations had been offered to explain abuses at Abu Ghraib. First, the government promoted a bad apples explanation, suggesting that just a few bad members of the military were involved in the abusive activities. Second, some suggested that Zimbardo's *automatic brutality* theory applied (suggesting that all individuals have the capacity to torture if they are placed in a situation where it is possible). Third, historian Alfred McCoy argued that the practices had a long history in the Central Intelligence Agency. Hamm concluded that McCoy's theory made the most sense. He said that evidence suggests "that the torturing of detainees at Abu Ghraib followed directly from decisions made by top government officials, from President George W. Bush on down" (p. 259). Hamm stated that the Bush administration "took off the gloves in prisoner interrogation" (p. 259).

The military hires individuals whose sole purpose is to identify and respond to crimes committed by military professionals. The Careers Responding to White-Collar Crime: Air Force Criminal Investigator box below shows the job duties of one such position.

CAREERS RESPONDING TO WHITE-COLLAR CRIME

Air Force Criminal Investigator

Duties:

- Assists senior agents or performs on-the-job training in criminal investigative activities involving violations of the Uniform Code of Military Justice (UCMJ) and Titles 10 and 18 of the U.S. Code
- Knowledge of criminal laws, precedent court decisions, and federal rules of procedures that apply to cases involving crimes against the United States and possesses general knowledge of investigative techniques, principles and methods
- Ability to detect and recognize evidence of a crime, personally conduct less complex investigations accurately, thoroughly, and objectively; and report facts in a logical, concise, and understandable matter
- Ability to learn the basic knowledge required in the conduct of select specialized investigations such as narcotics operations, undercover operations, and development cases
- Ability to analyze problems, identify significant factors, gather pertinent data, and recognize solutions
- Ability to deal effectively with others to gain their confidence and cooperation and [performs] duties satisfactorily under stress
- Ability to communicate effectively both orally and in writing
- Presents criminal investigative findings and reports both orally and in writing
- Manages human sources of information to aid in the development and resolution of investigative, counterintelligence, and special security matters
- Assists with liaison with local, state, and federal law enforcement agencies and host nation counterparts (where applicable)

Source: Reprinted from USAJobs.Gov

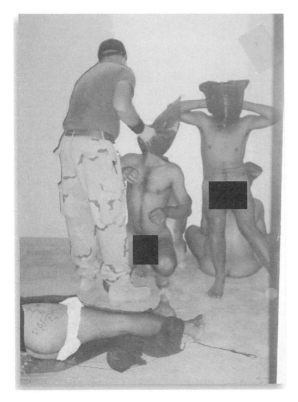

▲ **Photo 5.4** Evidence of war crimes and torture surfaced when photos of prisoners at Abu Ghraib showing the prisoners in various shameful poses were released to the press.

▲ **Photo 5.5** Members of the military tend to be a tight-knit group. This camaraderie may protect them against accusations of misconduct toward one another.

State-Corporate Crime

The phrase **state-corporate crime** draws attention to the fact that governmental agencies are employers (or "corporations") and that these agencies and their employees sometimes commit various types of misconduct—either independently or in conjunction with other corporations. The concept of state-corporate crime was first introduced by Ronald Kramer in a series of presentations he made at the Southern Sociological Association, the Edwin Sutherland Conference on White-Collar Crime, and the Society for the Study of Social Problems (Kramer, Michalowski, & Kauzlarich, 2002, p. 263). Kramer notes that the term came from a "spontaneous comment" he made at a restaurant while discussing his research with colleagues. Although Kramer developed the concept, he credits Richard Quinney's work with serving as its "intellectual origins." Quinney's early work drew attention to the need to categorize white-collar crime into corporate crime and occupational crime, and another body of his research focused on the sociology of law, with an emphasis on the way that the powerful shape the law to protect their interests. Combining Quinney's white-collar crime research with his sociology of law research lends credence to Kramer's call for a focus on "state-corporate crime." The concept of state-corporate crime is useful in (a) demonstrating how the consequences of behaviors are tied to interrelationships between social institutions and (b) highlighting the power of formal (e.g., political and economic) institutions to harm members of society (Kramer et al., 2002).

Scholars also use the phrase **state crime** to describe situations where governments or their representatives commit crime on behalf of the government. Again, bear in mind that a government can be seen as a corporation. International law is seen as the "foundation for defining state crime as this includes standards such as human rights, social and economic harms, as well as the judicable offenses" (Rothe, 2009, p. 51). From this perspective, state crime has been defined as

> any action that violates international public law and/or a state's own domestic law when these actions are committed by individual actors acting on behalf of, or in the name of the state, even when such acts are motivated by their own personal, economical, political, and ideological interests. (Mullins & Rothe, 2007, p. 137)

Not surprisingly, it is extremely unlikely that formal governmental institutions will self-police or impose sanctions on themselves for the commission of state crimes. As a result, efforts to control state crime often stem from the actions of advocates, including individuals and organizations, seeking to expose the wrongdoing of particular government officials. According to Ross and Rothe (2008), those who expose state crime offenders run the risk of experiencing the following responses from the state:

1. **Censure:** Officials may withdraw support or withhold information.

2. **Scapegoating:** Officials may blame lower-level employees for the misconduct.

3. **Retaliation:** Officials may target the advocates exposing the wrongdoing.

4. **Defiance or resistance:** Officials may block any efforts toward change.

5. **Plausible deniability:** Officials may conceal actions to make behavior seem appropriate.

6. **Relying on self-righteousness:** Officials minimize allegations.

7. **Redirection/misdirection:** Officials feign interest but change the subject.

8. **Fear mongering:** Officials create fear to "overshadow" real issues.

State crime scholars have addressed a number of different topics, including President Reagan's war on Nicaragua (Rothe, 2009); the state of Senegal's role in the sinking of a ferry, killing more than 1,800 citizens (Rothe, Muzzatti, & Mullins, 2006); the violent deaths of more than 400,000 civilians in the Darfur region of Sudan (Mullins & Rothe, 2007); and the torture of prisoners in Abu Ghraib (Rothe & Ross, 2008).

Although research on state crime has grown significantly over the last decade, in general, criminological attention to the concept is seemingly rare (Rothe & Ross, 2008). Critical criminologists Dawn Rothe and Jeffrey Ross reviewed leading criminology texts to determine how much attention was given to state crime. They found that authors typically provided only a description of incidents by government officials when discussing crimes by state officials, thereby "failing to provide the contextual, theoretical, and historical factors associated with this subject" (p. 744). The authors attribute this lack of attention to "the perceived potential of the market" (p. 750). Despite this lack of attention, state crime experts have come a long way in advancing understanding about this phenomenon, and it is entirely likely that an entire field of study will develop in the next several decades, just as the field of study focusing on white collar crime has grown since the 1940s (Rothe & Friedrichs, 2006).

● ● ● Crimes by Officials in the Religious System

In the past, many individuals probably gave little thought to the possibility that crime occurs in the religious system. However, like other occupational settings, churches and religious institutions are not immune from misconduct. To provide a general introduction to crimes in the religious system, attention can be given to financial offenses in the religious system, deception in the religious system, and the Catholic Church sexual abuse scandal.

Financial Offenses in the Religious System

One type of white-collar crime occurring in the religious system involves financial offenses, where church leaders embezzle funds from church proceeds. Such acts are relatively simple to commit because church funds are easy to target, and there is often little oversight of the church's bank accounts (Smietana, 2005). One pastor, for example, who was accused of stealing more than a million dollars from his church over a 10-year time frame, alleged that he had the authority to use the church funds as he saw fit because he was the "pastor and overseer" of the church ("Ex-Pastor Testifies in Embezzlement Trial," 2010).

One of the most famous instances of embezzlement by a religious leader involves the case of Rev. Jim Bakker, a former televangelist who co-hosted the TV show *The PTL Club* with his wife Tammy Faye. Bakker's television show, which had an acronym standing for "praise the Lord," brought in millions of dollars. Eventually, Bakker and his wife created their own network and organization called the PTL Television Network. In 1989, Bakker was convicted of stealing $3.7 million from the PTL organization. At his sentencing hearing, prosecutor Jerry Miller focused on the vulnerable groups that had given money to Bakker's organization so Bakker could divert funds to support his lavish lifestyle. The judge, nicknamed "Maximum Bob" in reference to the long sentences he had given offenders, sentenced Bakker to 45 years in prison, with parole eligibility after 10 years (Harris, 1989). An appeals court ruled that a new sentencing hearing should be held, and Bakker was subsequently sentenced to 8 years and paroled in 1994. He is now the host of the *Jim Bakker Show,* which appears on various networks.

Financial offenses by church leaders are often stumbled on only by accident. In one case, for example, it was not until a pastor left his church and "collections went up dramatically" that officials had any suspicion of wrongdoing. The subsequent investigations revealed that the pastor had stolen about $1 million from his church over a 5-year time frame (Smietana, 2005). Other times, offenses are uncovered as a result of routine audits (O'Sullivan, 2011). Regardless of how the financial offenses are detected, their consequences can be devastating to the church that was victimized. Said one pastor about these consequences, "It's not about the money so much. It's about the trust" (Smietana, 2005).

Deception in the Religious System

Religious system deception refers to situations in which church leaders lie to their congregants in an effort to promote an appearance of "holier than thou." Lying in and of itself is not illegal. However, the violation of trust that arises in these situations warrants that these cases be classified as white-collar crime. Consider, for instance, the case of Jimmy Swaggart, who was banned from preaching for 3 months by national leaders of the Assemblies of God Church after he confessed to liaisons with a prostitute. Ironically, Swaggart was implicated by a pastor he had exposed for adultery 2 years before (Kaufman, 1988). In a more recent case, in the fall of 2006, Rev. Ted Haggard's affairs with a former male escort came to light. At the time, Haggard was the president of the National Association of Evangelicals and the founding pastor of the Colorado Springs–based New Life Church—a megachurch with 14,000 members. After his adultery became public, he resigned from his presidential position, and the board of his church dismissed him from pastoral duties (Banerjee & Goodstein, 2006). Haggard and his wife now travel around the United States, appearing in different churches to talk about forgiveness (Jacobson, 2009).

Catholic Church Sexual Abuse Scandal

Historically, the Catholic Church has been viewed as a safe haven where individuals can retreat for protection. Over the past 15 years, however, the image of the Catholic Church became more and more tarnished as cases of child sexual abuse by priests began to be reported in the media with increasing frequency. After a while, it was clear that the number of allegations was not indicative of a few events but of a problem that appeared to be structurally situated within the Catholic Church. To address the sexual abuse scandal, the U.S. Catholic bishops approved the Charter for the Protection of Children and Young People. Among other things, the Charter developed a National Review Board that was charged with commissioning a study on sexual abuse in the Catholic Church. All dioceses were required to participate in the study. The board hired John Jay College of Criminal Justice of the City University of New York to conduct the study. The resulting study provided the most comprehensive picture of the issue of sexual abuse in the Catholic Church (U.S. Conference of Catholic Bishops, 2004).

Using a variety of research methodologies, including interviews, reviews of case files, mail surveys, and so on, the John Jay study provided the following highlights:

- Four percent of active priests "between 1950 and 2002 had allegations of abuse" (p. 4).
- In all, 10,677 individuals accused priests of sexually abusing them as children. Approximately one-sixth of them "had siblings who also were allegedly abused" (p. 4).
- Two-thirds of allegations were made since 1993, though most incidents occurred in the 1970s and 1980s.

Figure 5.3 Priest's Primary Function at Time of Alleged Incident in Cases From John Jay Study

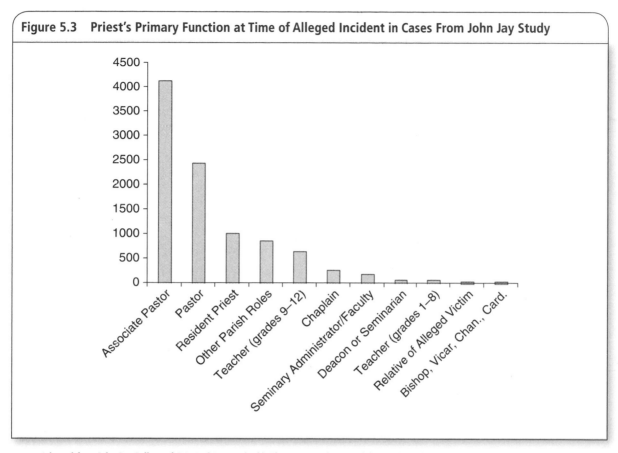

Source: Adapted from John Jay College of Criminal Justice. (n.d.). The nature and scope of the problem of sexual abuse of minors by catholic priests and deacons in the United States. In *A Research Study Conducted by the John Jay College of Criminal Justice.* Available from http://www.nccbuscc.org/nrb/johnjaystudy/

- It was estimated that the Catholic Church had already spent $650 million in settlements and on treatment programs for priests.
- One-fifth of the priests were believed to have substance abuse problems that may have been related to the misconduct.
- About half of the victims were between the ages of 11 and 17.

Figure 5.3 shows the priest's role in the Catholic Church when the allegations occurred. As shown in the figure, the vast majority of the suspects were serving as some form of a pastor or priest, though a variety of different roles were represented among the accused. Figure 5.4 shows the location where the abuse occurred. As shown in the figure, most of the incidents occurred in the priest's home, the church, or the victim's home.

Researchers have used the John Jay data to examine similarities between sexual abuse in the Catholic Church and victimization or offending patterns among other offender groups. For example, Smith, Rengifo, and Vollman (2008) examined disclosure patterns and found that disclosure of child sexual abuse by clergy in the Catholic Church did not mimic disclosure patterns found in other child sexual abuse cases. In 2002, nearly 3,000 incidents of child sexual abuse by priests were reported. Of those, 90 percent had occurred more than 20 years earlier.

Figure 5.4   Location Where Abuse Occurred in Sexual Assault Cases Examined in John Jay Study

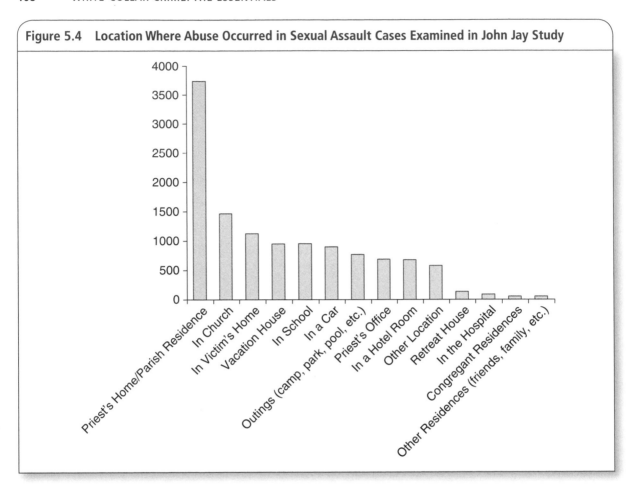

Source: Adapted from John Jay College of Criminal Justice. (n.d.). The nature and scope of the problem of sexual abuse of minors by Catholic priests and deacons in the United States. In *A research study conducted by the John Jay College of Criminal Justice.* Available from http://www.nccbuscc.org/nrb/johnjaystudy/

Alex Piquero and his colleagues (Piquero, Piquero, Terry, Youstin, & Nobles, 2008) used the John Jay data to examine the criminal careers of the clerics and compare their careers to the careers of traditional criminals. The research team found similarities and differences between the two types of offenders. In terms of similarities, both clerics and traditional career criminals exhibited relatively similar rates of prevalence and recidivism. Differences between the two groups were attributed to "a function of the unique position in which the clerics find themselves" (p. 596). Their age of criminal onset, for example, is older, likely because they enter their careers at a later age. The researchers also found higher rates of recidivism among married clerics. Marriage typically reduces the likelihood of re-offending, but this did not appear to be the cases among the clerics assessed in the John Jay data.

Michael White and Karen Terry (2008) used the John Jay data to apply the rotten apples explanation to the sex abuse scandal. In doing so, they demonstrated that this explanation does not provide an adequate explanation for the cases of child sexual abuse perpetrated by the clerics. The authors draw out parallels between the police profession and the clergy (e.g., both are unique subcultures that are isolated, where individual members have a significant amount of

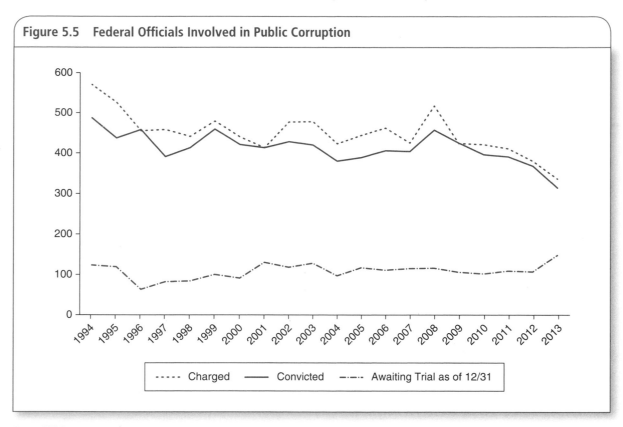

Figure 5.5   Federal Officials Involved in Public Corruption

····· Charged   ——— Convicted   —·—·· Awaiting Trial as of 12/31

Source: U.S. Department of Justice

authority and little oversight) to bring attention to the subcultural factors that may have contributed to the existence of sexual abuse in the Catholic Church. The authors also addressed police deviance prevention strategies that could have been used to limit the abuse. These included (a) careful selection of personnel and training, (b) supervision and accountability, (c) guidelines, (d) internal affairs units, (e) early warning systems, (f) changing the subculture, (g) criminal cases, (h) civil liability, and (i) citizen oversight. The authors conclude that "church leaders would be well-advised to follow the lead of professional police departments who institute rigorous internal and external accountability controls" (p. 676).

Mercado, Tallon, and Terry (2008) used the John Jay data to examine factors that increased the likelihood that priests would victimize more than one victim. Their analyses identified the following three factors as increasing the likelihood that priests would target multiple victims:

- Having victims older or younger than typical victims
- Age of cleric when abuse began (the younger at onset, the more likely to abuse multiple victims)
- Targeting male victims

Also using the John Jay data to increase understanding about the causes of child sexual abuse, Marcotte (2008) examined the structural factors associated with Catholicism and changes in the American culture that may have contributed to the high rates of child sexual abuse in the Catholic Church. He notes that the offending priests tended to be socialized in

Figure 5.6   State Officials Involved in Public Corruption

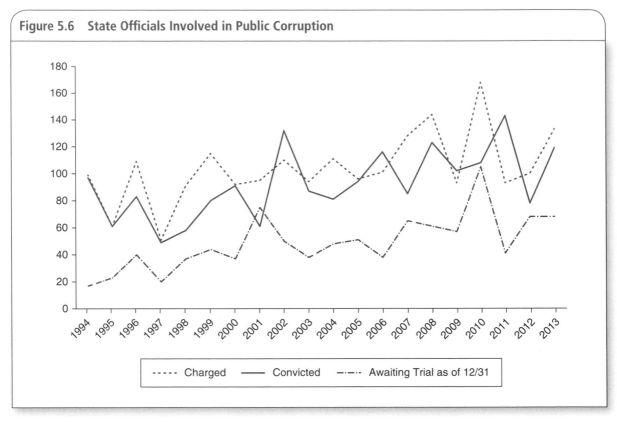

Source: U.S. Department of Justice

the Catholic Church in the 1950s and 1960s, and this socialization process potentially explained the high number of incidents occurring in the 1960s and 1970s.

Other researchers have focused on the Catholic Church scandal, collecting original data. Many of these other studies have examined the consequences of the child sexual abuse for individuals, parishes, the Catholic Church, and society. Research shows that, like other child sexual assault victims, those assaulted by priests are more likely than those who never experienced any sexual abuse to experience social isolation and require extensive therapy (Isely, Isely, Freiburger, & McMackin, 2008). Some researchers have identified consequences that may be unique to victims of clergy. Surveys of 1,810 Catholics found that those who had been abused by priests were more distrustful of religion than those who were sexually abused by someone other than a priest. All sexual assault victims were more likely to experience various forms of "spiritual damage" (Rossetti, 1995). Other studies have found no difference between those abused by priests and victims abused by someone else (Shea, 2008). The long-term consequences are particularly salient for both groups.

Kline, McMackin, and Lezotte (2008) conducted three focus groups with Catholics whose church had been involved in one of the sex abuse scandals. The author team focused on the consequences of the scandal for the parish community. Themes they uncovered included (a) a reflection on past Catholic Church wrongdoings, (b) hurt over betrayal by their church leaders, (c) recognizing that one's relationship with God is separate from one's relationship to a parish, and (d) interest in children and spiritual needs.

Figure 5.7   Local Officials Involved in Public Corruption

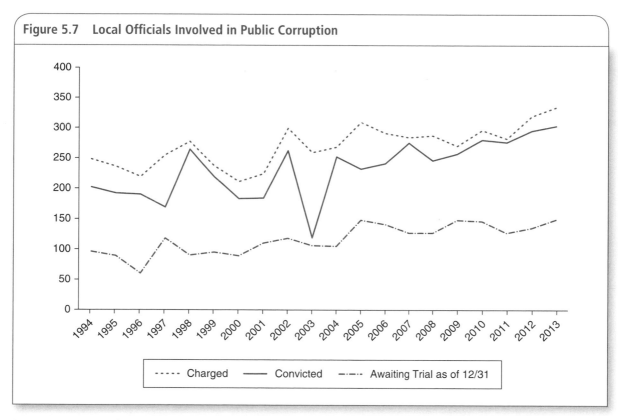

Source: U.S. Department of Justice

The impact of the scandal on the Catholic Church cannot be overstated. Beyond the economic toll that has come along with paying for settlements and treatment programs, raising funds was likely more difficult for their church leaders during these times. Also, the child sexual abuse scandal received widespread coverage in the press, far more coverage than other forms of child sexual abuse have received (Cheit & Davis, 2010). There are no simple answers to what can be done to help victims or the Catholic Church recover. Still, lawsuits, therapy, and punishing offenders are all seen as elements that can help victims recover (Dreese, 1998).

As far as what the Catholic Church can do is concerned, experts have noted that it must take measures to prevent these actions in the future. Some experts have suggested that situational crime prevention ideals be applied to prevention strategies developed by the Catholic Church. This would entail limiting access to potential victims, increasing awareness about prevention strategies among potential victims, strengthening surveillance, and reducing risk factors (Terry & Ackerman, 2008).

Some will question whether sexual abuse by priests is actually a form of white-collar crime. After all, the offense of child sexual abuse seems more like a violent street crime than a white-collar crime. A. R. Piquero and his colleagues (2008) do an outstanding job making an argument that these offenses can be characterized as white-collar crimes. The offenses are committed (a) by a trusted professional (b) who is respected by members of society (c) during the course of work. Also, recall Rosoff's (1989) concept of status liability: By the very nature of their status, when priests "fall from grace," the response from the public will be far more severe than that associated with other offenders.

Figure 5.8   Private Citizens Involved in Public Corruption

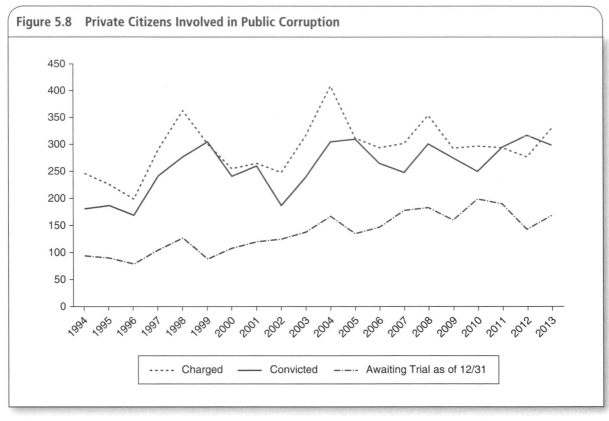

Source: U.S. Department of Justice

SUMMARY

- Varieties of police misconduct include corruption of authority, kickbacks, opportunistic theft, shakedowns, protection of illegal activities, fixing cases, direct criminal activities, internal payoffs (Barker & Roebucks, 1973), and sexual misconduct.
- McCarthy (1981) identified four varieties of corruption in corrections: embezzlement (stealing from the institution), drug smuggling into the institution, coercion, and transporting contraband into the prison system.
- The public's negative view of attorneys likely contributes to formal complaints about attorney conduct (or misconduct).
- States have different expectations and definitions for what is viewed to be appropriate conduct for attorneys.
- Of the few studies that have been done on attorney misconduct, the focus tends to be on types of sanctions levied against attorneys.
- If attorneys violate the criminal or civil laws, they can be subjected to penalties stemming from those bodies of law (e.g., incarceration, probation, fines, restitution). A variety of different sanctions can be given to attorneys by their professional associations. Most commonly, these sanctions include warning letters, private reprimands, public reprimands, suspensions, and disbarment.

Figure 5.9   Total Number of Public Corruption Cases

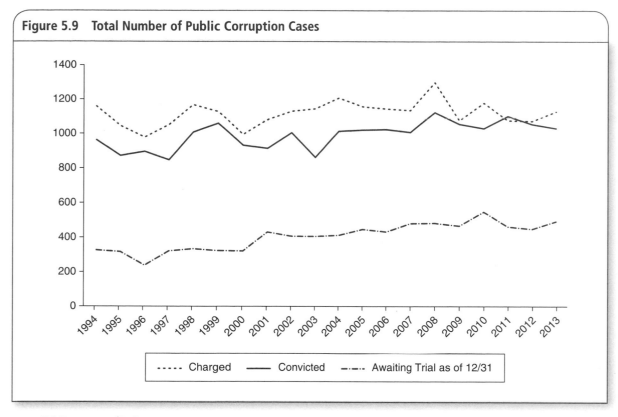

Source: U.S. Department of Justice

- Just as lawyers are depicted in certain ways on television shows and movies, judges are also a regular part of the "cast of characters" portrayed in crime-related media.
- Kentucky identifies three general types of judicial misconduct: (1) improper influence, (2) improper courtroom decorum, and (3) improper illegal activities on or off the bench.
- Allegations of judicial misconduct increased significantly in the early 1990s (Coyle, 1995).
- It is estimated that 90% of complaints filed against judges are dismissed (Gray, 2004).
- Some have argued that a combination of three factors contributes to misdeeds by judges. These factors include (1) office authority, (2) heavy caseloads, and (3) interactions with others in the judicial process (Coyle, 1995).
- Criminologist Jocelyn Pollock (2004) has identified five different types of prosecutorial misconduct. Legal expert Alschuler (1972) discussed a different set of prosecutorial misconduct examples.
- While it is difficult to identify precisely how often prosecutorial misconduct occurs, estimates suggest that these behaviors are particularly common.
- A number of direct and indirect negative consequences arise from prosecutorial misconduct.
- Unlike professionals working in some of the other systems, professionals in the political system routinely confront suspicion and distrust from citizens.
- Types of crimes occurring in the political system include election law violations, campaign finance violations, political corruption related to extortion and bribery, apolitical white-collar crime, crimes in the military, and state-corporate crime.

- Election law violations refer to situations in which political officials violate rules guiding the way that elections are supposed to be conducted.
- Campaign finance laws place restrictions on the way political campaigns are financed, with specific attention given to contributions and expenditures.
- In this context, political corruption related to extortion or bribery refers to situations in which political officials use their political power to shape outcomes of various processes, including lawmaking, awarding of contracts, policy development, and so on.
- Apolitical white-collar crime refers to situations in which politicians get into trouble for doing things that are outside of the scope of politics but are violations of the public trust.
- Clifford Bryant (1979) used the phrase *khaki-collar crime* to describe situations where individuals in the military break rules guiding their workplace activities.
- The phrase *state-corporate crime* draws attention to the fact that government agencies are employers (or "corporations"), and these agencies and their employees sometimes commit various types of misconduct—either independently or in conjunction with other corporations.
- Historically, the Catholic Church has been viewed as a safe haven where individuals can retreat for protection.
- Using a variety of research methodologies, including interviews, reviews of case files, mail surveys, and so on, the John Jay study found that 4% of active priests "between 1950 and 2002 had allegations of abuse" (United States Conference of Catholic Bishops, 2004, p. 4).
- Researchers have used the John Jay data to examine similarities between sexual abuse in the Catholic Church and victimization or offending patterns among other offender groups.
- Alex Piquero and his colleagues (Piquero, Piquero, et al., 2008) used the John Jay data to examine the criminal careers of the clerics and compare their careers to the careers of traditional criminals.
- Michael White and Karen Terry (2008) used the John Jay data to apply the rotten apples explanation to the sex abuse scandal.
- Other researchers have focused on the Catholic Church scandal, collecting original data. Many of these other studies have focused on the consequences of the child sexual abuse for individuals, parishes, the Catholic Church, and society.
- The impact of the scandal on the Catholic Church cannot be overstated.
- As far as what the Catholic Church can do, experts have noted that the church must take measures to prevent these actions in the future.
- Some will question whether sexual abuse by priests is actually a form of white-collar crime. A. R. Piquero and his colleagues (2008) do an outstanding job of arguing that these offenses can be characterized as white-collar crimes.

KEY TERMS

Apolitical white-collar crime	Foreign friendly civilian crimes	Political extortion/bribery
Campaign finance laws	Inter-occupational crimes	Redirection
Censure	Intra-occupational crimes	Religious system deception
Defiance	Iran-Contra affair	Relying on self-righteousness
Election law violations	Misdirection	Retaliation
Enemy civilian social system crimes	Plausible deniability	Scapegoating
Extra-occupational crimes	Police corruption	State-corporate crime
Fear mongering	Police sexual misconduct	State crime

DISCUSSION QUESTIONS

1. Discuss the similarities and differences between the types of crimes discussed in this chapter.

2. All white-collar crimes involve violations of trust. Review the crimes discussed in this chapter and rank them from the highest trust violation to the lowest trust violation.

3. Compare and contrast the terms *white-collar crime* and *khaki-collar crime.*

4. Should police officers lose their jobs if they commit workplace misconduct? Explain.

5. Why do you think judges commit white-collar crime?

6. Explain how a college education might reduce corruption in the criminal justice system.

7. Review the case study included in In Focus 5.1. What do you think should be done to this judge?

8. What is state-corporate crime? How is it different from khaki-collar crime?

WEB RESOURCES

Bishop Accountability: http://www.bishop-accountability.org/

Commission to Combat Police Corruption: http://www.nyc.gov/html/ccpc/html/home/home.shtml

Public Corruption, FBI. https://www.fbi.gov/about-us/investigate/corruption

Report Public Corruption: http://www.reportpubliccorruption.org/

Scambusters Church Scams: http://www.scambusters.org/churchscam.html

STUDENT RESOURCES

The open-access Student Study Site, available at study.sagepub.com/paynewccess2e, includes useful study materials including SAGE journal articles and multimedia resources.

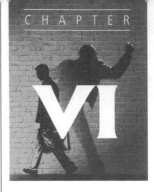

CHAPTER

VI

Crimes in the Educational System

CHAPTER HIGHLIGHTS

- Crimes by Professionals in the Educational System
- Pecuniary-Oriented Offenses
- Sexual Harassment
- Disciplining "Bad" Professors
- Crimes in the Educational System by Students

About fifteen years ago, a College of William and Mary adjunct English professor penned an article titled "The Professor of Desire" in *GQ* magazine. In the article, he wrote firsthand about a sexual relationship he had with a married student at the small liberal arts college located in Williamsburg, Virginia. The article made local, state, and national headlines. One story repeated over and over in the news focused on how the affair led to the husband's suicide. It was not long after the *GQ* article that William and Mary passed a policy restricting student-professor sexual relationships.

The case was particularly problematic because of the honesty underlying the professor's open confession. The stories read almost as if they should have been shared in a locker room, if they should have been shared at all. College professors are supposed to educate students about topics that will help them in their future careers; they are not supposed to have sex with their students— and then promote their career by writing about it. College professors are supposed to help students learn to think and write critically about their world, so they can better understand the worlds in which they live.

In a more recent case receiving national headlines, a Northwestern University philosophy professor was accused of sexual harassment after a student claimed that the professor "assaulted her after an evening out together at an art exhibit and several bars" (Flaherty, 2015). While the university did not find the professor guilty of assault, he was found guilty of sexual harassment and was sanctioned by the university. After information about the incident became public, a second student (this time a doctoral student) came forward and accused the same professor of nonconsensual sex. The professor's defense was that the behavior was consensual. Not long after the second allegation surfaced, the university initiated termination proceedings. During the proceedings and shortly before the professor was set to testify, he resigned from the university (Flaherty, 2015). Mixed into the termination hearing were allegations by the students that their Title IX rights were violated because the university allegedly failed to address their complaints appropriately.

To be sure, a variety of different types of misconduct occur in the educational system. Consider the following examples as they were described verbatim from their original sources:

▲ **Photo 6.1** We learn early on as students to respect and grant power to our teachers. This socialization translates into our respecting and giving power to professors. Some professors, unfortunately, abuse this power.

- [The professor and his wife] appeared to be talented researchers dedicated to advancing science, jurors in their federal fraud trial said. But the [professor] . . . failed to tell the space agency that Zotova's role in the project had ended. The jury Friday found [the professor and his wife] guilty of six out of 10 counts of wire fraud for sending NASA fake invoices from the research company [the professor] owned. (Hall, 2015)
- Two former University of Houston physics professors were sentenced to federal prison on Monday for their roles in a $1.4 million research grant scheme. . . . Investigators determined ***** and their business received nearly $1.4 million in government grants and contracts from 2007 to 2013 with the assistance of a doctored recommendation letter. (George, 2015)
- *****, a former biomedical scientist at Iowa State University in Ames, was sentenced to 57 months for fabricating and falsifying data in HIV vaccine trials. *** has also been fined US$7.2 million and will be subject to three years of supervised release after he leaves prison. (Reardon, 2015)
- [The graduate came] forward to tell the story of how a professor offered to give her an 'A' grade in exchange for oral sex. The recent graduate, who has remained unidentified . . . shared the email she received from [the professor] reportedly asking "will you blow me for an A?" (Collman, 2014)

In this chapter, attention is given to crimes committed in the educational system. Students fulfill one of three roles in these cases: (1) they are witnesses, (2) they are victims, or (3) they are offenders. In one recent case, a graduate student testified that he never met his professor's wife, even though the professor was billing a grant agency for the wife who was purportedly supervising the laboratory team the student was a part of (Hall, 2015). In another recent case, a professor was convicted after, among other things, he falsely told students they had to return parts of their stipends to him (Wells, 2014). The majority of the discussion in this chapter will focus on crimes by professors and researchers working in the educational system. After discussing how professionals have committed misconduct in this system, attention will be given to the way that students have committed workplace crimes in the educational system.

● ● ● Crimes by Professionals in the Educational System

It's probably not something we go around bragging about, but as professors, we work in an occupation that is not immune from white-collar crime. Not only do we study white-collar crime, but we are also a part of an occupational subculture that experiences various forms of white-collar crime. Four types of misconduct that appear to be among the more common types of academic misconduct include the following:

- Research misconduct by professors
- Ghostwriting
- Pecuniary-oriented offenses
- Sexual harassment

After discussing these varieties of crimes in higher education, attention will be given to crimes by students as types of occupational crimes.

Research Misconduct by Professors

Research misconduct refers to a range of behaviors that center on researchers (many of whom are faculty members) engaging in various forms of wrongdoing during the course of their research. These forms of wrongdoing include, but are not limited to, fabricating data, masking findings, plagiarism, and treating research subjects unethically. Over the past two decades or so, increased efforts have been directed toward identifying research misconduct. Such activities have always been known to occur, but they are now perceived and responded to differently. Describing this shift in philosophy, one author writes:

> Sadly, history includes many egregious examples of fraudulent scientists, but they were, until recently, regarded as isolated oddballs who did little to damage science, a self-correcting enterprise. But, in the past twenty years, country after country has recognized increasing examples of fraud and has come to think that it cannot be ignored, but needs to be recognized and managed. (R. Smith, 2006, p. 232)

In the United States, efforts to recognize and manage research misconduct are typically led by the funding agencies providing financial support for the research. The Office of Research Integrity (ORI), part of the Office of Public Health and Sciences within the U.S. Department of Health and Human Services, oversees research supported by the Public Health Services (PHS). The mission of ORI focuses on

> (1) oversight of institutional handling of research misconduct allegations involving research, research training, or related research activities support by the PHS; (2) education in the responsible conduct of research; (3) prevention of research misconduct, and (4) compliance with the PHS Policies on Research Misconduct. (Office of Research Integrity, 2010)

Careers exist to help identify and respond to cases of research misconduct. The Careers Responding to White-Collar Crime: Investigative Scientist box describes the duties performed in one such career.

The increased federal oversight and efforts to respond to research misconduct have not gone unnoticed. Some researchers have tried to explain why the federal government has become so intense in its efforts to weed out research misconduct. Hackett (1993) identified several factors that contributed to the increased oversight. First, the federal government has been investing more and more money in scientific endeavors, and science has become more visible to members of society as a result of this increased funding. Second, science is viewed as a "resource for power," and those who control science would potentially become more powerful through that control. Third, to some, science is like a religion and enforcement efforts toward misconduct are defined as ways to protect the "religion" of science. Fourth, Hackett noted that opposition to the "intellectual elite" may have contributed to political officials' decisions to increase efforts toward controlling research misconduct. Finally, science has become increasingly important to universities, businesses, and the government. The growing importance of science potentially increased the need of the government to expand its ability to control science.

CAREERS RESPONDING TO WHITE-COLLAR CRIME

Investigative Scientist

The Investigative Scientist's principal responsibility is handling allegations of misconduct in science and engineering as defined at 45 CFR 689. This includes recommending deferral of necessary inquires and/or investigations as well as conducting any required inquires and/or investigations.

- Plans, completes, and submits written reports on special studies, assignments and projects that frequently cut across disciplinary and organizational lines.
- Contributes written materials to the IG's Semiannual Report to the Congress. This requires some knowledge of NSF policies; activities, and procedures as adapted to the entire range of NSF programs.

- Assists the Head of Administrative Investigations (HAI) by handling allegations of misconduct in science and engineering as well as charges of improper actions by NSF staff in the conduct of other OIG reviews, and in outreach activities.
- Coordinates his or her activities as appropriate with NSF program officers, with those outside NSF as well as outside the federal government.
- Engages in relevant training activities and attends and participates in professional scientific or engineering meetings as appropriate.

Source: Reprinted from USAJobs.Gov

As with other forms of white-collar crime, it is difficult to estimate how often research misconduct occurs. It may, however, be even more difficult to estimate for the simple reason that few researchers have actually empirically assessed research misconduct. Experts have noted that research misconduct is "real and persistent" (Herman, Sunshine, Fisher, Zwolenik, & Herz, 1994). Anecdotally, the former editor of the *British Medical Journal* indicated that he "dealt with about 20 cases [of research misconduct] a year" (R. Smith, 2006, p. 232).

One of the more infamous cases of research misconduct involved Ward Churchill, a professor of ethnic studies at the University of Colorado at Boulder. Prior to the allegations of misconduct, Churchill had come under fire for making disparaging comments about the victims of the 9/11 attacks. His notoriety grew and greater attention was given to his work, and accusations surfaced surrounding the authenticity of some of Churchill's writings. An investigation followed and the university's investigative committee found that Churchill engaged in "serious research misconduct" (University of Colorado Investigative Committee Report, 2006, p. 31). In July 2007, the university's regents fired Churchill. He appealed the decision, and, though a jury found in his favor—awarding him one dollar—the judge overturned the verdict and upheld the university's actions.

One of the charges against Churchill was that he plagiarized some of his writings. Interestingly, researchers have suggested that plagiarism by professors is more likely to occur in the humanities and social sciences than in the hard sciences due to the nature of the disciplines. In particular, the level of creativity required in the humanities and social sciences is higher, and the need for creativity may create situations where professors are more apt so borrow someone else's creativity (Fox, 1994). In the hard sciences, where several authors typically appear on published manuscripts, loose authorship—where some authors are included on the manuscript who should not be—is believed to be more problematic.

Today, plagiarism is often uncovered when computer-based text searching tools are used to search for it (Huckabee, 2009). Plagiarism is discovered in at least four other ways:

- Researchers accidentally stumble upon it.
- Reviewers identify it during the peer review process.
- A disgruntled colleague or subordinate searches for it and finds it.
- The plagiarized author finds it.

In what would seem to be a plagiarism case, but technically is not, one professor published parts of one of his student's dissertation in an article he wrote. Jeannette Colman was a graduate student working on her dissertation under the supervision of her professor. After she successfully completed her dissertation, the professor used parts of Colman's dissertation in a work he published in the *Journal of Sports Sciences* in 2007. The professor listed Colman as third author of the article. Because she was listed as a coauthor, he didn't technically plagiarize her work, even though she never gave him permission to use her work. The university panel reviewing the case found that Colman (the student) "did not own copyright to her dissertation" (Newman, 2010). As a result, the professor was found not guilty of research misconduct.

Other varieties of research misconduct exist that do not receive as much attention. Consider image manipulation as an example. Image manipulation refers to "undocumented alterations to research images" (Jordan, 2014, p. 441). It is also known as "photo-fiction." It is believed that researchers do this in order to paint a picture that does not necessarily exist. This picture, then, is misleading and inaccurate in terms of the image's portrayal of the phenomena being studied. Jordan (2014) recommends that images be treated as research data and held to strict ethical standards.

Research misconduct has severe consequences on several different levels. These include (1) consequences for the individual faculty member, (2) financial consequences for the college or university, (3) morale consequences for the college or university, (4) image consequences for science, (5) consequences for members of society, and (6) consequences for various cultures. In terms of individual consequences, when research misconduct is exposed, the status of the offender takes a significant hit. While some may be able to overcome allegations—the president of the Southern Illinois University system was accused of plagiarizing both his master's thesis and 1984 dissertation in 2007, but he remained as president for several years after he told the board of trustees that his faculty committees never told him he had to use quotation marks—others are not able to overcome allegations. For example, the former president of University of Texas–Pan American resigned after it was alleged that she had plagiarized parts of her dissertation 35 years ago (Montell, 2009).

Colleges and universities will also suffer financial consequences from research misconduct. On one level, federal funding agencies may withhold funding if it is determined that the college or university was complacent in its efforts to limit research misconduct. Such a loss could amount to millions of dollars for the higher education institution. On another level, donors may be less likely to give to institutions if they believe that research misconduct has occurred. As with the losses in federal support, such economic losses can prove significant.

Higher education institutions will also experience morale consequences from the negative exposure that comes with the allegations of research misconduct. Instances where professors are caught engaging in research misconduct and fraud are sure to make the news. Consider the following headlines from several different news sources:

- "Professor Whose Article Was Retracted Resigns From Harvard Medical School" (Huckabee, 2009)
- "UAB Animal Transplant Studies by Two Researchers Found Falsified" (Sims, 2009)
- "Two CMU Math Faculty Members Violate Integrity Policy: University Returns $619,489 in Grant Money" (Bolitho, 2009)
- "Lehigh University Professor and Wife Convicted of Cheating NASA" (Hall, 2015)
- "Morgan State University Professor Convicted of Fraud Scheme" (Wells, 2014)
- "Ex-UH Professors Sentenced in Research Grant Scheme" (George, 2015)
- "Former Penn State Professor Accused of $3M Fraud" (CBSNews.com, 2012)
- "Patients, Researchers Demand Further Prosecution in Duke Case" (Hinkes-Jones, 2015)
- "UA Professor Receives Tenure After Plagiarizing Student's Work" (Vukelic, 2015)
- "ASU Professor . . . Accused of Plagiarism Withdrawing From $268,000 Contract With City" (Bartels, 2015)

Two interesting patterns appear in these headlines. First, the headlines rarely identify the professor's name. Second, and on the other hand, note that all but one of the headlines lists the name of the college or university where the misconduct occurred. In many ways, research misconduct may damage the higher-education institution's image as much as it damages the actual professor who engaged in the misconduct.

Colleges and universities will experience significant time losses in responding to cases of research misconduct. Investigations can take a great deal of time and resources. For example, a University of Washington investigation took 7 years to conclude that an assistant professor should be fired. The investigation concluded that the researcher "had falsified seven figures and tables in two research papers" (Doughman, 2010). Time that administrators and faculty could have spent in productive activities had to be directed toward addressing misconduct by the assistant professor.

Research misconduct also has consequences for the image of science. In particular, these sorts of activities ultimately paint the scientific enterprise in a negative light. Consider the case of one anesthesiologist who fabricated his findings in 21 studies. Consequently, "the reliability of dozens more articles he wrote is uncertain, and the common practice supported by his studies—of giving patients aspirin-like drugs and neuropathic pain medicines after surgery instead of narcotics is now questioned" (Harris, 2009).

In a similar way, research misconduct has ramifications for members of society who are exposed to new practices and policies as a result of research. While a goal of research is to provide information that can be used to improve the human condition, if new practices and policies are based on data obtained through flawed research, then individuals exposed to those new practices and policies are put at risk. Giving patients aspirin instead of narcotics after surgery, for example, may have been a risk for patients. Also, the results of another fabricated research study (described below) led doctors to prescribe hormones to treat menopause for years. In effect, treatments were being determined by "fake" research. Once the research was exposed as fabricated, one couldn't help but wonder whether prescribing hormones was actually helpful or harmful.

Research misconduct can also have negative consequences for an entire culture. In China, a university professor was heralded as a top scholar until it was revealed that his prize invention—a mobile phone chip—was simply a Motorola phone chip that had been sanded down with sandpaper. The "revelation . . . shocked China, where the 'home-grown' invention had become a source of national pride" (Burns, 2006). Just as Olympic athletes who cheat embarrass their countries when they are caught, so internationally recognized researchers caught cheating have a similar effect.

Two patterns are common in research misconduct cases—one that is common in other white-collar crime cases and one that is not. First, as in other white-collar crime cases, many of those who commit research misconduct commit various forms of misconduct on multiple occasions. If researchers engage in one type of misconduct, like fudging data—it is likely that they have engaged in others, like fudging accounting data on funded research (see Schmidt, 2003). Consider the case of a former staff research associate for UCLA's Semel Institute for Neuroscience and Human Behavior. Working on a study focusing on the long-term experience of female opiate addicts who visited methadone clinics three decades ago, the associate "knowingly and intentionally falsified and fabricated interviews, urine samples, and urine sample records" (Chong, 2007). The investigation showed that Lieber had not interviewed the subjects he was supposed to have interviewed and had altered their urine samples. It was also revealed that he stole travel funds. Hence, he committed multiple types of violations.

A second pattern in these cases—and one that distinguishes it from many other white-collar crimes—is that in most cases the offenders acted alone. This is part of the process of committing research misconduct. Whereas certain types of health care fraud, for example, might require multiple participants to carry out the fraud, for research misconduct, a rogue professor aiming to achieve a certain end is able to accomplish this task without the help of others. Working alone insulates the professor from detection and allows the academic to continue to use his or her research to gain power and prestige.

Some have pointed to the pressure to publish and get grants as being the source of research misconduct. Fox (1994) notes that economic incentives may play more of a role and points out that "the economic stakes of science have heightened" (p. 307). Top professors—with strong research portfolios—can earn hundreds of thousands of dollars in annual salary from their college or university, and some will earn far more providing consulting services. While most of these scientists conduct their research legitimately, it is plausible that those who commit misconduct are doing so, at least partly, for economic reasons.

Another possible reason that faculty engage in these activities is that their mentors did not supervise them appropriately (Brainard, 2008). Brainard cites a study that found that in three-fourths of misconduct cases, the supervisors did not give the supervisee appropriate training in reviewing lab results. Recall the university president who indicated that his allegations of plagiarism could be explained by the fact that his faculty committees never told him he was supposed to put quotation marks around quotes.

Because of the potential role that mentors have in contributing to misconduct, some have argued that mentors should play an active role in training their students how to conduct research appropriately. One author team suggests that mentors should train students how to (a) review source data, (b) understand research standards, and (c) deal with stressful work situations (Wright, Titus, & Cornelison, 2008). In a similar way, mentors should teach their students how to protect the rights of their research subjects, the consequences of research misconduct, and the importance of research integrity. Another author called for a "[shift] to an exploration of the moral issues involved in conducting research" (Gordon, 2014, p. 89).

One author team suggests the following as an effort to reduce research misconduct:

- Educate employees of research institutions about the signs of research misconduct
- Reassure workers that there are no repercussions from reporting misconduct
- Encourage article reviewers to watch for it (Stroebe, Postmes, & Spears, 2012)

Typically, accusations of misconduct begin with information from someone involved in the research on at least some level. Rarely are local or state criminal investigations undertaken against researchers, and federal investigations are conducted only when direct evidence of wrongdoing exists. In a rather controversial move, Virginia Attorney General Ken Cuccinnelli launched an investigation into the work of meteorology researcher Michael Mann (McNeill, 2010; Walker, 2010). The case is controversial for at least four reasons:

- The attorney general issued a subpoena for data from the University of Virginia, where Mann *used to* work.
- It is alleged by some that the attorney general was using the case to gain "cool points" from the political Right for "going after" a researcher whose findings showed support for the evidence of global warming.
- State agencies don't typically address these types of issues.
- The professor had already been cleared of misconduct by a Penn State University review panel (McNeill, 2010; Walker, 2010).

▲ **Photo 6.2**   White-collar crimes occur in laboratories when scientists fabricate data or violate rules guiding their profession. This scientist, like most scientists, did not break any workplace rules. The few who do, however, create enormous problems for the field of science.

Sanctions for all types of misconduct in the educational arena will be discussed below. One particular sanction that may be given specifically for research misconduct is retraction of a published research article. *Retraction* means that the journal publisher has "removed" the article from the scientific literature. Of course, the article still remains in print, but the "retraction" label is meant to suggest that the article should not be viewed as a scientific contribution. Journal articles can be retracted for error or fraud. A recent study found that one-fourth of retracted articles were due to fraud, while most were retracted because of error (Steen, 2011).

Steen (2010) studied the dynamics of retracted papers due to fraud. One variable examined was the country where the first author worked (see Figure 6.1). As shown in Figure 6.1, the majority of first authors worked in the United States. Additional findings Steen uncovered from the review of 788 retracted articles:

- Papers retracted for fraud targeted journals with higher impact factors
- Fraudulent papers were more likely to be written by a repeat offender (e.g., an author who had prior retractions)
- In the United States, more papers were retracted due to fraud than for error in comparison to other countries

Retractions demonstrate that publishers will not tolerate research misconduct. Sage Publications, the very fine publisher of this book, uncovered research misconduct involving authors who managed to

Figure 6.1 Country Affiliations for First Authors of Papers Retracted Due to Fraud, 2000–2010, for Articles in PubMed

US	84
China	20
Japan	18
India	17
South Korea	8
UK	7
Italy	6
Germany	3
Australia	3
Canada	2
Turkey	2

Source: Steen, 2010, p. 3.

create false identities to review their own work. A leader in scientific publishing, the company took immediate and stern measures in responding to the misconduct. The White-Collar Crime in the News: SAGE Retracts Articles After Fake Peer Review Scam box on the next page shows a press release the company released in the aftermath of the misconduct.

Ghostwriting

Ghostwriting refers to situations in which professors or researchers have their work written by someone else, but the professor's name appears on the work. Typically, "papers are produced by companies or other parties whose names do not appear as authors" (Lederman, 2009). Situations where university professors allow their names to be put on papers written by ghost authors hired by pharmaceutical companies have been described as "distressingly common in top medical journals" (Basken, 2009). In some cases, the real author's name appears on the article along with a top scientist who did not actually contribute to the article. In these cases, the top scientists can be labeled "honorary" authors, though in print it appears that they were actually contributing authors.

A study of ghostwriting and honorary authorship published in the *Journal of the American Medical Association* found the following rates of ghost authorship and use of honorary authors among six top medical journals in articles published in 2008: 26 percent of the articles had honorary authors, 8 percent had ghostwriters, and 2 percent had both honorary and ghostwriters (Wislar, Flanagin, Fontanarosa, & Dangelis, 2010). This means that more than one third of the articles published in the top medical journals listed authors who actually should not have been listed! Figure 6.2 provides a visual portrayal of the degree of ghostwriting and honorary authorship in these journals.

WHITE-COLLAR CRIME IN THE NEWS

SAGE Retracts Articles After Fake Peer Review Scam

In a recent case of research misconduct, the *Journal of Vibration and Control* uncovered a peer-review scheme where authors appeared to submit fake reviews.

London, UK - SAGE announces the retraction of 60 articles implicated in a peer review and citation ring at the *Journal of Vibration and Control* (JVC). The full extent of the peer review ring has been uncovered following a 14 month SAGE-led investigation, and centres on the strongly suspected misconduct of Peter Chen, formerly of National Pingtung University of Education, Taiwan (NPUE) and possibly other authors at this institution.

In 2013 the then Editor-in-Chief of JVC, Professor Ali H. Nayfeh, and SAGE became aware of a potential peer review ring involving assumed and fabricated identities used to manipulate the online submission system SAGE Track powered by ScholarOne Manuscripts™. Immediate action was taken to prevent JVC from being exploited further, and a complex investigation throughout 2013 and 2014 was undertaken with the full cooperation of Professor Nayfeh and subsequently NPUE.

In total 60 articles have been retracted from JVC after evidence led to at least one author or reviewer being implicated in the peer review ring. Now that the investigation is complete, and the authors have been notified of the findings, we are in a position to make this statement.

While investigating the JVC papers submitted and reviewed by Peter Chen, it was discovered that the author had created various aliases on SAGE Track, providing different email addresses to set up more than one account. Consequently, SAGE scrutinised further the co-authors of and reviewers selected for Peter Chen's papers; these names appeared to form part of a peer review ring. The investigation also revealed that on at least one occasion, the author Peter Chen reviewed his own paper under one of the aliases he had created.

Following Committee of Publication Ethics (COPE) guidelines, SAGE and Professor Nayfeh contacted Peter Chen with an opportunity to address the accusations of misconduct. After a series of unsatisfactory responses from Peter Chen, in September 2013 NPUE were notified and have since been working closely alongside SAGE and JVC to uncover the full extent of the peer review and subsequent citation ring. SAGE has notified Thomson Reuters about the citation ring and both parties have worked together to index the retractions in full.

SAGE is committed to maintaining a rigorous peer-review process to maintain the high quality of our journals. We regret that individual authors have perverted the JVC peer review process, misled readers and compromised the academic record of this journal.

Although attempts to mislead the academic community with fake or inaccurate results are extremely rare, there will occasionally be fraudulent and unethical individuals seeking to abuse the system. Both SAGE and JVC are committed to upholding the true spirit of peer review while continuing to introduce new measures to reinforce the peer review process.

Source: Sage Statement of Journal of Vibration and Control. (2014, July 8). Available online at https://us.sagepub.com/en-us/nam/press/sage-statement-on-journal-of-vibration-and-control

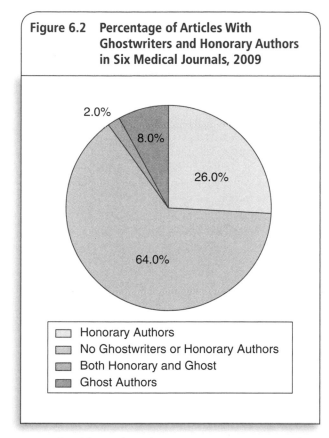

Figure 6.2 Percentage of Articles With Ghostwriters and Honorary Authors in Six Medical Journals, 2009

2.0%

8.0%

26.0%

64.0%

Honorary Authors
No Ghostwriters or Honorary Authors
Both Honorary and Ghost
Ghost Authors

Source: Adapted from Wislar, J., Flanagin A., Fontanarosa, P., & DeAngelis, C. (2009). Prevalence of honorary and ghost authorship in 6 general medical journals, 2009. Peer Review Congress. Available from http://www.ama-assn.org/public/peer/abstracts-0910.pdf

Research shows that ghostwriting occurs more in research articles than in reviews and editorials (Wislar, Flanagin, Fontanarosa, & DeAngelis, 2010). In an effort to limit the extent of ghostwriting, many journals now ask authors to sign a form indicating that they are the only authors of the manuscript and that all of the authors listed did, in fact, contribute to the manuscript. Penalties imposed by journals on ghost writers might include a ban on submitting future articles, retraction of article, and/or notifying the author's institution (Stern & Lemmens, 2011). For the record, the author of this book is no ghost, and he certainly isn't an honorary author.

● ● ● Pecuniary-Oriented Offenses

In this context, **pecuniary-based offenses** include misbehaviors that are committed by professors for the economic gain that comes along with the commission of the offenses. Four varieties of pecuniary-oriented offenses exist, as follows:

- Embezzlement
- Textbook fraud
- Double billing
- Engaging in unapproved outside work

Embezzlement

Faculty embezzlement occurs when faculty members or college and university staff steal funds from an account to which they have access. Consider the case of a former dean of the School of Education at the University of Louisville who was convicted of misappropriating $2.3 million from contracts with three schools and a federal grant he was supervising. The dean was sentenced to more than 5 years in federal prison (Glen, 2010).

Not all cases of **embezzlement by college professors** are necessarily million-dollar scams. One scholar, a former professor of anthropology at John Jay College, was accused of stealing $5,000 in grant funds to fund personal trips, purchase heroin, and buy ABBA CDs, an allegation that one author called "the most heinous accusation—a crime against humanity" (Morris, 1999). Incidentally, the charges against him were eventually dropped, but not before he lost his job.

Textbook Fraud

Textbook fraud, in this context, refers to instances where faculty sell the complimentary textbooks they receive from publishers to book dealers who resell the books. Some faculty may see nothing wrong with these activities. As a new faculty member, I recall my then-dean's take on this issue. He explained that our college at the time viewed it as unethical and inappropriate to sell textbooks that we had requested from publishers; however, it was legitimate in his view to resell textbooks that we did not actually request from the publisher but received as part of an unsolicited marketing campaign. Not surprisingly, research shows that faculty members view it as more ethical to sell unsolicited books than to sell solicited books (Robie, Kidwell, & King, 2003).

Many colleges and universities have express, written policies forbidding the selling of complimentary textbooks under any circumstances. Some of these policies even state that book dealers are not permitted on campus. Here is how my university, Georgia State University, spells out its policy on selling textbooks:

313.05 Ethical Behavior with Regard to Complimentary Textbooks

The University Senate passed the following resolution on February 2, 1989:

The distribution of complimentary textbooks is an important part of the process whereby professors review the full range of instructional materials available for their courses. However, the integrity of this process must be respected.

Selling complimentary copies of textbooks adversely affects the entire academic community.

Professor-authors are deprived of economic return in royalties, and incentives to write textbooks are diminished.

Students generally do not benefit from the sale of complimentary copies, as these books are sold at or only slightly below the new book price.

Selling complimentary textbooks inflates the cost of all textbooks, as publishers must compensate for revenue lost from the sale of new books.

Selling complimentary copies violates the tradition of respect by professors for the intellectual work of their colleagues and for the textbook publishers.

The future of availability of complimentary textbooks may be seriously jeopardized by the reluctance of publishers to risk further financial loss.

Faculty members receive complimentary textbooks as a result of their position at the University. These textbooks should not be viewed as a source of faculty income. We recommend the following:

1. Complimentary textbooks are not to be resold for faculty profit. The books may be maintained for faculty reference or contributed to a library for student reference.

2. Solicitors for complimentary copies are forbidden from campus.

3. The campus bookstore may not sell copies which are identifiable as complimentary copies whatever their source may be. (Georgia State University Faculty Handbook, 2010)

More than 20 years ago, it was estimated that publishers lost $60 million a year to these activities (Sipes, 1988). The practice appears to remain widespread, and likely costs publishers far more today. A survey of 236 faculty from 13 community colleges and universities found that 30 percent of the sample had resold complimentary books in the prior year, and they made $80 per sale on average (Robie et al., 2003).

To address this, some publishers stamp the word "complimentary" or "not for resale" on many of the textbooks' pages, others put the professor's name on the book, and some even tell professors that if they do not plan on using the book, they can return it to the publisher, which will make a donation to charity for each returned complimentary book received (Hamermesh, 2009).

For the record, if faculty try to sell their complimentary copies of this book to book dealers, an invisible ink will explode all over both the faculty member and the book dealer.

Double Billing

Faculty double billing occurs when professors bill more than one source for the same effort of work or reimbursement. Examples of double billing include (a) instances where professors bill two sources for the same travel reimbursements and (b) instances where faculty bill multiple universities for the same instructional effort. In one case involving double billing for travel reimbursements, one professor resigned after being placed on unpaid leave after being allegedly caught double billing travel expenses for $150,000. What makes his case particularly interesting is that he was—at the time—the head of Yale's International Institute for Corporate Governance (Sherman, 2005). Sherman quotes the *Wall Street Journal* as describing the professor as "a strong advocate of prompt disclosure of financial misdeeds" (2005).

Engaging in Unapproved Outside Work

Faculty working full-time for a college or university also commit workplace offenses by engaging in outside work that is not approved by the institutions. Three overlapping types of conflicts arise with unapproved outside work: (1) research-based conflicts of interest, (2) teaching and service-based conflicts of interest, and (3) time-based conflicts of interest. With regard to research-based conflicts of interest, colleges and universities have policies restricting outside work to ensure that the institution's research agenda does not seem to be influenced by specific companies. For example, medical schools would not want their research to appear to be partial to certain pharmaceutical companies. As a result, these schools limit the amount of consulting and outside work that professors can do with such companies.

The case of Charles Nemeroff, former chair of the Emory University's Department of Psychiatry, is illustrative. His bosses suspected that Nemeroff was doing too much consulting for GlaxoSmithKline, so they ordered him to limit his outside income from the drug company to less than $10,000 a year. The very same day that he signed this agreement, he reportedly was paid $3,000 in consulting fees from the company and the following year, it was reported that he received $170,000 from the company. In all, it was estimated that Nemeroff was paid $500,000 in payments he never reported to his university (Goldstein, 2008). Nemeroff's misdeeds came to light when U.S. Senator Charles Grassley "released documents indicating that Nemeroff earned millions of dollars in fees from drug companies, but reported little of that money to Emory" (White & Schneider, 2008, p. A1). The subsequent investigation revealed that the professor made more than $2.8 million between 2000 and 2007 from consulting with drug companies (Harris, 2008). As a result of his actions, the National Institutes of Health suspended a $9.3 million grant that had been awarded to the university, and Emory's entire federal funding portfolio was in jeopardy.

In terms of teaching and service-based conflicts of interest that arise from unapproved outside work, when full-time faculty are hired by colleges and universities, the institution in effect "owns" that person's efforts for the duration of the contract. Institutions gain notoriety when certain professors are on their payrolls. Also, having the best professors at a college or university allows institutions to promote their educational mission by suggesting that students will be exposed to some of the greatest minds in higher education. By forbidding outside work, administrators are able to maintain their competitive edge and keep professors from working for their competitors.

In terms of time conflict and unapproved outside work, the expectation is that full-time faculty will work 40 hours a week in performing teaching, research, and service activities. The reality is that most faculty likely work in excess of 55 hours a week on these activities. A handful, however, may actually work fewer hours in teaching, conducting research, and engaging in service activities.

Those who have unapproved outside jobs, for example, might be unable to meet the hourly obligations of a full-time job in higher education. Rarely would these behaviors be treated as illegal criminally, but professors could face formal or informal repercussions from their supervisors or university administrators for these behaviors. If your white-collar crime professor, for instance, routinely canceled class because of outside work (or other unapproved reasons, for that matter), your professor could be subject to a range of potential disciplinary actions. In some instances, canceling even one class could be problematic, and I suspect that readers are grossly disappointed when their professor cancels a class. Typically, colleges and universities will permit occasional cancellations as long as students are given an assignment that corresponds to the topic that students would have covered in class and the topic at hand.

The advent of online classes poses different issues in that classes would never be canceled. Most faculty who teach online actually spend more time engaging with their students than faculty spend in traditional courses. For full-time faculty, issues arise when faculty fail to correspond with students and instruct them in ways that are necessary in order to teach students adequately about the topic (in this case, white-collar crime). Again, faculty won't be criminally prosecuted for failing to meet the time demands of the class. Imagine if they were, and if they were actually sent to jail for abusing class time. The following conversation would occur in jail:

Street offender to professor:	Why are you in the pokey?
Professor to street offender:	I canceled a few too many of my classes.
Street offender to professor:	You know you're going to get beat up in here, right?

● ● ● Sexual Harassment

Sexual harassment refers to a range of behaviors where employees perform sexually inappropriate actions against their colleagues or students. Legal definitions of sexual harassment suggest that sexual harassment is "any unwelcome or unwanted sexual attention [that affects] an individual's job, raise, or promotion" (Andsager, Bailey, & Nagy, 1997, p. 33). Fitzgerald (1990) identified four categories of sexual harassment:

- **Gender harassment:** sexist remarks and behavior
- **Seductive behavior:** inappropriate sexual advances
- **Sexual bribery:** offering rewards for sex
- **Sexual coercion:** threatening punishment to get sex

For purposes of this book, sexual harassment offenses committed by college professors include (a) sexualized comments, (b) sexualized behaviors, (c) academic incest, (d) sexual relationships with students taking their classes, (e) grades for sex, and (f) rape.

With regard to **sexualized comments**, harassment occurs when professors make comments to students that are of a sexual nature. One criminal justice professor, for example, told a researcher that one of her former professors would "make comments about my breasts" (Stanko, 1992, p. 334). Note that simply using foul language is not in and of itself sexual harassment. Typically, the language would need to be of a sexual nature to be considered harassment. I recall one of my sociology professors who began the semester asking the class if anyone minded if he used the "f-word." He didn't use the phrase *f-word* when he asked—he actually said the word. And this really was the very first thing he said to our class that semester. Then, he even wrote the four letters making up the word in huge letters on the chalkboard (this was back when professors used the chalkboard to communicate course notes). The professor explained that by itself, the word is just a word. Depending on the context in which the word is used, the word will have different meanings, consequences, and ramifications. We knew that we would not be taking notes that day—other than writing one word in our notebook.

Sexualized behaviors go beyond comments and include actual activities of a sexual nature committed by the offending party. This could include staring, touching, groping, hugging, and a range of other behaviors. In some cases, such behavior may be unintentional, while in others it may be intentional.

Academic sexual relationships refers to consensual "student faculty relationships in which both participants are from the same department but not necessarily in a student-teacher relationship" (Skinner et al., 1995, p. 139). Surveys of 583 university students and 229 community college students by Skinner and her research team found that students tend to define such relationships as ethically inappropriate. Surveys of 986 students uncovered gender patterns regarding stereotypes about sexual harassment (Hippensteele, Adams, & Chesney, 1992). Perhaps not surprisingly, males were found to have more stereotypical attitudes. They were more likely than females to agree with statements such as, "it is only natural for a man to make sexual advances to a woman he finds attractive."

Sexual contact with students refers to instances where the professor has some form of direct contact of a sexual nature with students in his or her classes or under his or her supervision. Questions are sure to arise about whether sexual relationships are consensual or not between students and faculty. The types of policies that colleges have to address student-faculty relationships exist on a continuum. On one end of the continuum, some colleges and universities have either no policy or permissive policies that allow such relationships so long as they are consensual. At the other end of the continuum, other colleges and universities have more restrictive policies, with some even forbidding consensual relationships altogether. Not only do the policies exist on a continuum, but perceptions of harassment also exist on a continuum. Consider the following comments from a university dean:

A couple of weeks ago, a troubled member of staff came to see me for a confidential meeting. He had started a relationship with an undergraduate and thought he'd better confess. "She's a third year," he blurted, hoping this might mitigate the offense. "Oh, well, that certainly helps," I mused . . . wondering where I filed the number of the university attorney.

"Is she in your course?" [I asked]. She wasn't. She wasn't even in his department. I breathed a sigh of relief. At least he wasn't teaching her. (Feldman, 2009, p. 29)

Another type of sexual harassment in college settings involves professors awarding **grades for sex**. Euphemistically called "an A for a lay" (Fearn, 2008, p. 30), these situations use the power of grading in order to solicit sexual favors from students. Some experts contend that exchanging grades for sex "is accepted without question or noticeable comment by most members of the university community" (Reilly, Lott, & Gallogly, 1986, p. 341).

Rape is sometimes classified with sexual harassment, although it is actually a violent, felonious assault. It is the most rarely reported type of sexual assault or harassment. In one case, a 62-year-old criminal justice professor was indicted in January 2010 on grounds that he sexually assaulted a 21-year-old student ("Troy Criminal Justice Professor Indicted on Rape Charge," 2010). According to court records, the sexual assault allegedly occurred in the fall 2009 semester at a polygraph business that the professor ran. Incidentally, the same professor was charged with misdemeanor harassment on the grounds that he had inappropriately touched a woman 4 years earlier. He was found not guilty on the earlier charge (Elofson, 2010). Although cases of rape are clearly violations of the criminal law, many instances of sexual harassment are not generally treated as crime violations but as either civil wrongs or administrative violations.

Recall from the introduction that different cultures define workplace misconduct in varying ways. Cross-cultural definitions of sexual harassment demonstrate this pattern. As an illustration of the cultural variations in defining sexual harassment, note that other countries—such as Britain—are more accepting of faculty-student romantic relationships (Fearn, 2008). Part of their openness to these relationships is based on the differences in the way that colleges function in Britain, as compared to the United States. In Britain, students tend to be slightly older, and faculty begin teaching at a younger age—making the age difference between faculty member and student less pronounced. Also, in the United States, the system of grading creates more power than what is found in grading systems used in Britain (Fearn, 2008). To put this in perspective, Fearn cites a British study that found that one-fifth of "academics reported having sexual relations with a student" (2008).

Fearn is quick to note that an increasing trend in Britain is to be less tolerant of these sorts of relationships. Describing this trend firsthand, one British professor commented on her experiences as a student:

I have been chased around offices, leapt on in a lift, groped under . . . tables and been the recipient of unpleasantly explicit anonymous notes, and I do not think I am any different from any other woman of my generation. . . . I welcome the fact that today young women are sufficiently empowered to know that they have a right to complain about it. (Bassnett, 2006, p. 54)

It is difficult to know how often sexual assaults occur—as students, though they are empowered to report them, often decide not to report their harassment experiences to authorities or to researchers studying the topic. One author team cites estimates that suggest that one-fourth to one-half of female university students are sexually harassed as students, with 5 percent to 10 percent of them experiencing serious forms of harassment (Skinner et al., 1995). A survey of 597 students found that 15.2 percent of the respondents reported being "hit on" by one their professors (Andsager et al., 1997). Fourteen of the students said they had sexual relationships with a professor. Another study focused on the sexual harassment experiences of female college students ($n = 319$) and employees ($n = 446$) (Kelley & Parsons, 2000). This study found that 42 percent of the sample had experienced at least one incident of sexual harassment and that different patterns of harassment exist between students and employees. For example, undergraduate students were sometimes harassed by graduate teaching assistants, graduate students were harassed by male faculty, and employees were more likely to experience gender harassment than students were.

Sexual harassment occurs in all academic disciplines, including criminal justice. A survey of 65 criminologists found that 59 percent of them experienced some form of sexual harassment during graduate school (Stanko, 1992). One-third of the respondents said they were harassed in their field research by criminal justice professionals or by the subjects they were studying. The criminal justice professors described a range of harassment experiences, including the following:

- An ongoing problem occurred when I was a graduate assistant and actually ended up with the professor trying to kiss me. Most of the time, though, he simply managed to direct the conversation . . . to sex.
- My research professor would make comments about my physical attractiveness and invite me to dinner. I declined.
- Faculty told me as a graduate student that my demeanor was not feminine enough.
- At the interview for the RA position which led to my main fellowship in grad school, he grabbed me out of the blue and started kissing me. I did not know what to do, so I pulled away and continued as if nothing happened. He kissed me several more times, my response was the same. . . . On several occasions, he pulled up my shirt and fondled my breast. I started wearing fondle-proof clothes. (Stanko, 1992, p. 334)

The consequences of sexual harassment can be quite devastating for students—both in the short term and the long term. In the short term, being exposed to harassing experiences will make it more difficult for students to learn, which will affect their grades, mental health, and attachment to school. Students might change majors, transfer, or even drop out of college. Each of these decisions will have long-term consequences for victims of sexual harassment. As well, the experience of sexual harassment may impact the victim's own personal relationships with loved ones.

Describing her experience of being sexually harassed by her counseling professor, one former student wrote the following:

> My anxiety was of such concern that I began seeing a therapist. She helped me understand that I had certain personality traits that had made me a likely target for Professor X. I had always idealized teachers and had done so particularly with him. I had trusted him implicitly during a busy, stressful time. . . . My experience of being sexually harassed by my counseling professor has changed my life forever. I know that although the trauma has lessened considerably, it will never disappear. (Anonymous, 1991, p. 506)

As noted above, students who are harassed by their professors tend not to report their victimization to anyone. In fact, as compared to university employees, students are more likely to ignore the behavior, whereas employees are more likely to tell their supervisor or file a complaint (Kelley & Parsons, 2000). One study identified the following as reasons that students, in this case medical students, chose not to report their harassment experience: (a) loyalty to the "team," (b) seen as not serious enough, (c) reporting defined as a weakness, (d) reporting defined as futile, and (e) concern about repercussions on future evaluations (Wear, Aultman, & Borges, 2007).

▲ **Photo 6.3**   President Barack Obama met his future wife, Michelle Robinson, when she was assigned as his mentor in the Sidley Austin law firm. Obama, a first-year law student at Harvard, was serving as a summer associate there. Because of their professional relationship, she put him off because she felt "self-conscious" being his mentor (Mundy, 2008). Eventually, she agreed to go out with him.

Of course, colleges are not the only workplace where sexual harassment occurs. The topic was discussed in the context of colleges and universities for two reasons. First, as students, readers will likely better understand the topic by seeing it through the lens of students. Second, colleges and universities "are institutions that reflect reality in the greater society" (McCormack, 1985, p. 23). What is going on in colleges and universities simply reflects activities that occur in other institutions. Unfortunately, what this means is that you won't escape the risk of sexual harassment when you graduate from college. Instead, when you enter your careers, you will be confronted with the potential for different types of sexual harassment.

● ● ● Disciplining Professors

Some professors actually ended up in prison for their wrongdoing, but these cases are typically ones where quite serious wrongdoing occurred. Even more rarely are criminal sanctions applied to researchers who fabricate research findings. Eric Poehlman, a former tenured professor at the University of Vermont, became the first scientist jailed for research misconduct in the United States after he "pleaded guilty to lying on a federal grant application and admitted to fabricating more than a decade's worth of scientific data on obesity, menopause, and aging" (Interlandi, 2006).

Incidentally, the fraud came to light when Walter DeNino, one of his former students who had become a lab worker for Poehlman, noticed some discrepancies in the lab reports. DeNino viewed his professor as a mentor but still notified university administrators about his concerns—which eventually panned out after an investigation. His former student was in the courtroom when Poehlman pleaded guilty. The disgraced professor apologized to his former student (Interlandi, 2006). Poehlman was sentenced to 366 days in federal prison. His case has been described as the "most extensive case of scientific misconduct in the history of the National Institutes of Health" (Kintisch, 2006). One can only imagine what DeNino went through as he mulled over the decision to report his former professor to administrators. Think about it— would you report your professor for misconduct? See In Focus 6.1, When Professors Go Bad, to read the press release issued by the U.S. Department of Justice describing the case and its outcome.

As one journalist points out, "Rare is the scientist who goes to prison on research misconduct charges." (Reardon, 2015). But with increased congressional oversight from political leaders, including Iowa Senator Charles Grassley, we are beginning to hear of more prosecutions for these cases. In a recent prosecution, an Iowa State University biomedical scientist was sent to prison for nearly five years after pleading guilty for lying to the NIH in his grant submissions and grant reports. The researcher falsified results of his research by spiking blood samples so that it appeared a vaccine made the blood immune to HIV (Reardon, 2015). Obviously, lying about such a vaccine has enormous implications for the safety of individuals who might have eventually used the vaccine.

Very few professors end up prosecuted in the criminal justice system for their misdeeds; more often, administrative sanctions are applied by the university. Common types of discipline against professors include (a) oral reprimands; (b) written reprimands; (c) recorded reprimands; (d) loss of benefits for a period of time, such as forgoing a raise; (5) restitution; (6) fines; (7) salary reductions; (8) suspensions with or without leave; (9) dismissals; (10) tenure revocations; and (11) departmental reassignments (Euben & Lee, 2005). A number of court cases have focused on the appropriateness of these sanctions after professors sued for being disciplined. Table 6.1 provides an overview of some of these cases. One thing that stands out in these cases is that the courts have tended to uphold the sanctions unless it was clear that the professor's rights were violated. For example, the courts have said that professors cannot be placed on unpaid leave until after a hearing has occurred (Euben & Lee, 2005).

Also, note that the types of discipline will vary according to the type of misconduct. Faculty who "blow off" class a little too often would be subjected to one form of discipline, whereas those who fabricate data would be subjected to another form of discipline. Also, even within specific types of misconduct, different forms of discipline are necessary. For example, "no single punishment is appropriate for all sexual harassment cases, but it is the faculty member's misconduct, not his ideas, that should be punished" (Knight, 1995, as cited in Euben & Lee, 2005). The key is that behaviors are disciplined, not beliefs or ideas.

IN FOCUS   6.1

When Professors Go Bad: A Case of Research Misconduct

Press Release—Dr. Eric T. Poehlman

U.S. Department of Justice

United States Attorney

District of Vermont

United States Courthouse and Federal Building

Post Office Box 570

Burlington, Vermont 05402-0570

(802) 951-6725

Fax: (802) 951-6540

Burlington, Vermont—March 17, 2005

The United States Attorney's Office for the District of Vermont, the U.S. Department of Health and Human Services (HHS), Office of Inspector General (OIG), and Office of Research Integrity (ORI) announced today that Dr. Eric T. Poehlman, 49, a former tenured research professor at the University of Vermont (UVM) College of Medicine in Burlington, Vermont, has agreed to a comprehensive criminal, civil, and administrative settlement related to his scientific misconduct in falsifying and fabricating research data in numerous federal grant applications and in academic articles from 1992 to 2002.

According to court documents filed today, Dr. Poehlman has agreed to plead guilty to making material false statements in a research grant application in April 1999, upon which the National Institutes of Health (NIH) paid $542,000 for Dr. Poehlman's research activities. In addition, Dr. Poehlman has agreed to pay $180,000 to settle a civil complaint related to numerous false grant applications he filed while at UVM. In addition, Dr. Poehlman will pay $16,000 in attorney's fees to counsel for Walter F. DeNino, a research assistant whose complaint of scientific misconduct spurred an investigation by UVM. Also, Dr. Poehlman has agreed to be barred for life from seeking or receiving funding from any federal agency in the future, including all components of the Public Health Service, and to

submit numerous letters of retraction and correction to scientific journals related to his scientific misconduct. Dr. Poehlman also agreed to be permanently excluded from participation in all Federal health care programs. In these agreements, Dr. Poehlman has admitted that he acted alone in falsifying and fabricating research data and filing false grant applications.

"Preserving the integrity of the grant process administered by the Public Health Service is a priority for the Department of Justice," said United States Attorney David V. Kirby. "This prosecution demonstrates that academic researchers will be held fully accountable for fraud and scientific misconduct. Dr. Poehlman fraudulently diverted millions of dollars from the Public Health Service to support his research projects. This in turn siphoned millions of dollars from the pool of resources available for valid scientific research proposals. As this prosecution proves, such conduct will not be tolerated."

Acting Assistant Secretary for Health, Cristina V. Beato, M.D., acknowledges the "invaluable assistance of the Department of Justice in bringing this case to a conclusion and upholding the high standards for research integrity in research supported by the Public Health Service." HHS actions against Dr. Poehlman include a life time debarment from receiving Public Health Service research funds and an agreement to retract or correct ten scientific articles due to research misconduct. Dr. Beato added that "while criminal charges against research scientists are rare, the egregiousness of Dr. Poehlman's conduct in this case fully supports the actions of the U.S. Attorney's Office and the administrative actions taken by HHS." Through ORI, HHS is authorized to investigate and oversee institutional investigations of allegations of research misconduct in order to protect the integrity of Public Health Service funded research.

Dr. Poehlman will appear for arraignment and to plead guilty to the criminal charge filed today at a date to be determined by the Court. Dr. Poehlman faces up to five years imprisonment on the criminal charge, but the United States has agreed to take no position on a request by Dr. Poehlman to receive a more lenient sentence based upon his cooperation with authorities and his acceptance of responsibility. The civil settlement agreement will become effective after approval by the Court. The administrative settlement will be effective immediately.

From 1987 to 2001, Dr. Poehlman held various research positions as an assistant, associate, and full professor of medicine at the UVM College of Medicine in Burlington, Vermont (1987–1993; 1996–2001), and the University of Maryland in Baltimore, Maryland (1993–1996). In these academic positions, Dr. Poehlman conducted research on human subjects related to exercise physiology and other topics that was funded primarily by grants from federal public health agencies and departments, including the NIH, the U.S. Department of Agriculture ("USDA"), and the Department of Defense.

From in or about 1992 to 2000, Dr. Poehlman submitted seventeen (17) research grant applications to federal agencies or departments that included false and fabricated research data. In these grant applications, Dr. Poehlman requested approximately $11.6 million in federal research funding. In most cases, Dr. Poehlman falsified and fabricated research data in the "preliminary studies" sections of grant applications in order to support the scientific basis for and his expertise in conducting the proposed research. Reviewers of these grant applications relied on the accuracy of the "preliminary studies" to determine if a grant should be recommended for award. While many of the grant applications were not awarded, NIH and USDA expended approximately $2.9 million in research funding based on grant applications with false and fabricated research data.

Dr. Poehlman falsified and fabricated research data in grant applications and research papers related to several topics including his study of the impact of the menopause transition on women's metabolism ("the Longitudinal Menopause Study"), his study of the impact of aging in older men and women on a wide range of physical and metabolic measures ("the Longitudinal Study of Aging"), and his proposal to study the impact of hormone replacement therapy ("HRT") on obesity in post-menopausal women ("the Prospective HRT Study"). Dr. Poehlman also presented falsified and fabricated data in grant applications and academic papers related to his study of metabolism in Alzheimer's patients and the effect of endurance training on metabolism.

Source: Reprinted From Office of Research Integrity. (2011). Washington, DC: U.S. Department of Justice. Available from http://ori.dhhs.gov/misconduct/cases/press_release_poehlman.shtml

Table 6.1 Legal Decisions Regarding Faculty Discipline

Case	Sanction	Action	Judicial Decision
Hall v. Board of Trustees of State Institutions of Higher Learning	Warning/reprimand	Faculty member touched a student's breasts after she asked a question about mammograms	Sanction did not violate the faculty member's rights
Newman v. Burgin	Public censure	Plagiarism	Sanction was upheld
Wirsing v. Board of Regents of Univ. of Colorado	One-time denial of salary increase	Professor refused to use departmental evaluation forms	Sanction upheld
Williams v. Texas Tech University Health Sciences Center	Permanent salary reduction	University told him to bring in more grants, but he didn't	The university could do this, particularly because the faculty member was given 6 months to do so.
Edwards v. California Univ. of Pennsylvania	Paid suspension	Bad language in classroom	No violation of the professor's rights

(Continued)

Table 6.1	(Continued)		
Bonnell v. Lorenzo	Unpaid suspension	Suspended without pay pending hearing on sexual harassment charges	University must pay salary before hearings
Klinge v. Ithaca College	Demotion in rank	Professor plagiarized and was demoted from professor to associate professor	No violation of rights
McClellan v. Board of Regents of the State Univ.	Modified teaching assignments	Made sexual comments to students, was told he couldn't teach specific class for years	No violation of rights
Bauer v. Sampson	Mandatory counseling	Alleged to have anger management issues because of temperament	Violated free expression rights

Source: Adapted from Euben, D. & Lee, B. (2005). Faculty misconduct and discipline. In Presentation to National Conference on Law and Higher Education, February 22, 2005. Available from http://www.aaup.org/AAUP/programs/legal/topics/misconduct-discp.html

● ● ● Crimes in the Educational System by Students

Some may question whether crimes by students are actually white-collar crimes. In this context, it is argued that a broad conceptualization of white-collar crime that views white-collar crime as offenses committed in various occupational systems allows one to consider student offenses as white-collar misconduct. Three types of behavior by students, in particular, can be seen as white-collar crimes: (1) offenses students commit on their jobs, (2) academic dishonesty, and (3) Internet or digital piracy by college and university students.

With regard to offenses committed on their jobs, note that many of the occupational offenses discussed in earlier chapters of the book might actually entail crimes committed by students employed in those professions. Restaurants and other service industries, for instance, routinely hire students as employees. In addition to students as occupational offenders in jobs outside of the college or university setting, students have opportunities to commit white-collar crimes in their positions as student workers or students affiliated with university workers. Consider the following cases as examples:

- A student worker at one university "was caught changing 75 Fs to As for 8 students" (Dyer, 2004).
- A university student in California was arrested after being charged with stealing two professors' identities and using those stolen IDs to change her grades and several other students' grades (La, 2005).
- Students in Louisiana collaborated in a scheme with an assistant registrar to have their grades changed. The worker also "manufactured entire academic transcripts for people who never enrolled on . . . the campus." It was estimated that grades were changed for 541 students in the scheme, at prices ranging from $200 to $500 (Dyer, 2004).

Academic dishonesty can also be seen as a variety of white-collar crime. On one level, students are "pre-professionals" seeking an education that will, everyone hopes, prepare them for their future professional careers. On another level, students assume the role of a "worker" in their efforts to pursue an education. They perform "work-like" activities as part of their coursework. Just as some workers in legitimate occupations break occupational rules and criminal laws while performing their jobs, some students break college and university rules (and various laws) while performing as students.

In this context, academic dishonesty can be defined as "intellectual theft" (Petress, 2003). One author cites estimates suggesting that between 63 percent and 75 percent of students self-report cheating (Iyer & Eastman, 2006). Interviews with 31 undergraduates found that the "students did not seem to have any deep moral dilemmas about plagiarism" (Power, 2009, p. 643). Plagiarism using information copied from the Internet has been described as a "monumental problem" (Strom & Strom, 2007, p. 108), with researchers noting that of the 30,000 papers reviewed in one popular plagiarism detection tool each day, "more than 30 percent of [the] documents include plagiarism" (Strom & Strom, 2007, p. 112).

Research on academic dishonesty has focused on the characteristics of dishonest students, the connections between academic dishonesty and white-collar crime, the causes of academic dishonesty, the role of instructors in academic dishonesty, and the appropriate response strategies and policies for limiting academic dishonesty. To gain insight into the characteristics of students who engage in academic dishonesty, Iyer and Eastman (2006) compared 124 business students with 177 nonbusiness students and found that business students were more honest than nonbusiness students. They also found that males, undergraduates, and members of fraternities and sororities were more likely be dishonest than females, graduate students, and students who are not members of fraternities and sororities. Focusing specifically on types of business students, one research team surveyed 1,255 business students and found that accounting majors were more honest than management majors (Rakovski & Levy, 2007). This study also found that males and students with lower grade point averages were less honest than females and students with higher grade point averages.

▲ **Photo 6.4**   Misconduct also occasionally occurs in college classrooms.

Examining the connection between academic dishonesty and crime at work, R. L. Sims (1993) surveyed 60 MBA students, asking about various forms of academic dishonesty and workplace misconduct. Sims found that respondents "who engaged in behaviors considered severely dishonest in college also engaged in behaviors considered severely dishonest at work" (p. 207).

Researchers have identified a number of potential predictors of academic dishonesty. Reviewing prior studies on academic dishonesty, one author team cited the following causes: (1) low self-control, (2) alienation, (3) situational factors, and (4) perceptions that cheating is justified (Aluede, Omoregie, & Osa-Edoh, 2006). A survey of 345 students found that the more television they watched, the more likely it was that they would engage in academic dishonesty (Pino & Smith, 2003). Some have argued that academic dishonesty is part of a developmental process "in which students learn to behave professionally and morally by making choices, abiding by consequences, and (paradoxically) behave immorally" (Austin, Simpson, & Reynen, 2005, p. 143).

In a rather interesting study that may raise some critical-thinking questions among readers, one professor focused on the ties between opportunity and self-control (T. R. Smith, 2004). The professor had his students complete a self-control survey at the beginning of the semester. Later in the semester, the professor returned exams to the students and told them that he did not have time to grade the exams. Students were told they would have to grade their own exams and were given a copy of an answer key to complete this task. In reality, the professor had made copies of all students' exams before returning them ungraded to the students. This allowed the professor to grade the students' exams and compare their "earned" grade with the grades the students gave themselves. Of the 64 students in the class, 30 scored their exams higher than they should have. The author found that opportunity seemed to play a role in fostering the academic misconduct and that low self-control was related to academic dishonesty. Incidentally, the students received the "earned" grade on their exams, and the professor waited until the end of the semester to tell them about his experiment.

Some researchers have focused on the college professor's role in promoting (and preventing) academic dishonesty. Surveys of 583 students found that an instructor's perceived credibility influenced academic dishonesty (Anderman, Cupp, & Lane, 2010). If students perceived a professor as credible, they were less likely to commit academic dishonesty in that professor's course. Somewhat referring to this possibility, one author commented, "the value of individual and collective honesty has to be taught, role modeled, and rewarded in schools; to neglect or refuse to do so is malfeasance" (Petress, 2003, p. 624). Also highlighting the professor's role in preventing academic dishonesty, D. E. Lee (2009) advises professors to practice role modeling:

- Demonstrate to students why academic dishonesty is wrong
- Develop assignments and class activities that make it virtually impossible for students to engage in academic dishonesty
- Promote and foster values of respect and honesty between students and faculty

Some authors have noted that professors can prevent (or at least detect) these offenses by implementing aggressive academic dishonesty policies and using available tools to identify cases of academic dishonesty. For example, computer software is available that detects cheating on multiple choice exams that use scantrons to score the exams. The software detects similar wrong answer patterns and alerts professors to possible academic dishonesty (Nath & Lovaglia, 2008). A popular company, Turnitin, provides software that reviews papers submitted in classes and identifies plagiarized papers. Turnitin has been hailed as a "potent weapon against academic dishonesty" (Minkel, 2002, p. 25). Students filed a lawsuit against Turnitin, arguing that the collection tool violated students' copyright ownership rights over the papers they wrote because the tool stored their papers in order to compare them with past and future submissions to Turnitin, and the company made money off of the students' papers. In 2008, a federal judge ruled that the software program does not violate copyright laws (Young, 2008).

Internet and digital piracy is another type of white-collar crime believed to be particularly popular on college campuses across the United States. This topic will be addressed in detail in the chapter focusing on computer crime. At this point, it is prudent to warn you that the authorities take digital piracy by college students seriously. Not long ago, Michel Crippen, a student at California State University, Fullerton, was arrested by Homeland Security officers after he modified "Xbox video game consoles to play copied games" (Sci Tech Blog, 2009). So, if you are sitting in your dorm room or at home near your computer, make sure that you haven't illegally downloaded materials from the Internet or stored illegally copied software on your computer. The next knock on your door could be Homeland Security officers coming to take you away. The irony is that the Homeland Security officers were once college students themselves. One can't help but wonder if they broke any rules when they were college students.

SUMMARY

- In this chapter, attention was given to crimes committed by professionals and students in the educational system.
- Four types of misconduct that appear to be among the more common types of academic misconduct are research misconduct, ghostwriting, pecuniary-oriented offenses, and sexual harassment.
- Research misconduct refers to a range of behaviors that center on researchers (many of whom are faculty members) engaging in various forms of wrongdoing during the course of their research. These forms of wrongdoing include, but are not limited to, fabricating data, masking findings, plagiarism, and treating research subjects unethically. Experts have noted that research misconduct is "real and persistent" (Herman et al., 1994).
- Researchers have suggested that plagiarism by professors is more likely to occur in the humanities and social sciences than in the hard sciences due to the nature of the disciplines.
- Research misconduct has severe consequences on several different levels. These consequences include (1) consequences for the individual faculty member, (2) financial consequences for the college or university, (3) morale consequences for the college or university, (4) image consequences for science, (5) consequences for members of society, and (6) consequences for various cultures.

- Because of the potential role that mentors have in contributing to misconduct, some have argued that mentors should play an active role in training their students how to conduct research appropriately.
- Ghostwriting refers to situations in which professors or researchers have their work written by someone else, but the professor's name appears on the work.
- Pecuniary-based offenses include misbehaviors that are ultimately committed by professors for the economic gain that comes along with the commission of the offenses. Four varieties of pecuniary-oriented offenses are embezzlement, textbook fraud, double billing, and engaging in unapproved outside work.
- Embezzlement occurs when faculty members or university staff steal funds from an account to which they have access.
- Textbook fraud refers to instances where faculty members sell complimentary textbooks that they receive from publishers to book dealers who resell the books.
- Double billing occurs when professors bill more than one source for the same effort of work or reimbursement.
- Faculty members working full-time for a college or university also commit workplace offenses by engaging in outside work that is not approved by the institutions. Three overlapping types of conflicts arise with unapproved outside work: (1) research-based conflicts of interest, (2) teaching and service-based conflicts of interest, and (3) time-based conflicts of interest.
- Sexual harassment refers to a range of behaviors whereby employees perform sexually inappropriate actions against their colleagues or students.
- Sexual harassment offenses committed by college professors include (1) sexualized comments, (2) sexualized behaviors, (3) academic incest, (4) sexual relationships with students in class, and (5) grades for sex.
- Eric Poehlman, a former tenured professor at the University of Vermont, became the first scientist jailed for research misconduct in the United States after he "pleaded guilty to lying on a federal grant application and admitted to fabricating more than a decade's worth of scientific data on obesity, menopause, and aging" (Interlandi, 2006).
- Common types of discipline against professors include (1) oral reprimands; (2) written reprimands; (3) recorded reprimands; (4) loss of benefits for a period of time, for example, no raise; (5) restitution; (6) fines; (7) salary reductions; (8) suspensions with or without leave; (9) dismissals; (10) tenure revocations; and (11) departmental reassignments.
- Three types of behavior by college students can be seen as white-collar crimes: (1) offenses students commit on their jobs, (2) academic dishonesty, and (3) Internet piracy by college and university students.

KEY TERMS

Academic dishonesty	Grades for sex	Sexual contact with students
Academic incest	Pecuniary-based offenses	Sexual harassment
Faculty double billing	Research misconduct	Sexualized behavior
Faculty embezzlement	Seductive behavior	Sexualized comments
Gender harassment	Sexual bribery	Textbook fraud
Ghostwriting	Sexual coercion	

DISCUSSION QUESTIONS

1. Which is worse—sexual assault by a fellow student or sexual assault by a professor? Explain.

2. What are some similarities and differences between crime in the educational system and crime in the health care system?

3. Should professors be fired for plagiarism? Explain.

4. If professors have their names listed on articles they didn't actually write, would this violate the honor code established for students? Explain.

5. Who is responsible for preventing research misconduct?

6. If you found out that one of your professors committed research misconduct, would it change the way you evaluated him or her on the teaching evaluations? Explain.

7. What are appropriate penalties for academic dishonesty by students?

8. How can academic dishonesty be categorized as white-collar crime? Explain.

WEB RESOURCES

Office of Research Integrity: http://ori.dhhs.gov/

Online Plagiarism Checker: http://plagiarisma.net/

Sexual Harassment at School: http://www.equalrights.org/publications/kyr/shschool.asp

STUDENT RESOURCES

The open-access Student Study Site, available at study.sagepub.com/paynewccess2e, includes useful study materials including SAGE journal articles and multimedia resources.

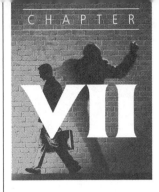
Crime in the Economic System

CHAPTER HIGHLIGHTS

- Crime in the Economic System
- Investment Fraud
- Ponzi and Pyramid Schemes
- Patterns Surrounding Investment Fraud
- Fraud in the Student Loan and Financial Aid Process

Many readers likely have Facebook pages. When visiting your friends' pages, tagging their photos, making cute comments on their posts, and posting information yourself, you likely have given very little thought to how Facebook relates to white-collar crime. Believe it or not, the social networking site relates to white-collar crime in four ways. First, some people (when they are supposed to be working) spend time lurking through their friends' Facebook pages. Second, some workers have actually lost their jobs over information they posted on Facebook pages. Third, the computer technology that makes Facebook possible is the same technology that provides the opportunity for computer crimes by white-collar offenders. Fourth, Mark Zuckerberg—the founder of Facebook—has been accused of various white-collar crimes related to his creation of the website and the administration of it.

As an undergraduate student at Harvard, Zuckerberg worked for Divya Narenda and Cameron and Tyler Winklevoss on a social network called ConnectU. After his experiences at ConnectU, Zuckerberg created Facebook but was sued by his former bosses on the grounds that he stole ConnectU's source code to create Facebook. So, his first accusation of white-collar crime was for copyright infringement (or theft of computer codes). Eventually, the parties reached an out-of-court settlement where ConnectU was sold to Facebook and the owners were given $65 million, with much of the payment being in the form of shares in Facebook. Later, however, it was learned that the stocks included in the settlement agreement were actually worth much less than what the ConnectU creators were led to believe.

It was eventually determined that the settlement was paid in cheaper shares (known as common shares) rather than the more expensive shares (known as preferred shares). The result—the original owners appealed the out-of-court settlement and accused Zuckerberg of securities fraud (O. Thomas, 2010). So, his second accusation of white-collar crime arose. The court subsequently found in favor of Zuckerberg. Interestingly, while these allegations were being reviewed, some unwelcome information about Zuckerberg surfaced. While a 19-year-old Harvard student, Zuckerberg, instant messaging a college friend, reportedly wrote the following comments about the information social networkers sent in to be posted on ConnectU: "People just submitted it. I don't know why. They 'trust' me. Dumb fu**s" (N. Carlson, 2010). The instant message he had allegedly sent years ago came to light while Facebook users were criticizing the site for its lax privacy policies. Thus, a third possible allegation of white-collar crime surfaced—misuse of computer information.

Incidentally, Divya Narenda—the one who sued Zuckerberg after he created Facebook—joined Facebook in 2008 (D. Carlson, 2009). Perhaps with too much time on my hands, I checked to see if Narenda had "friended" Zuckerberg. At the time of the writing of this book, he had not.

The accusations against Zuckerberg are examples of the kinds of white-collar crimes occurring in the economic and technological systems. In this chapter attention is given to crime in the economic system. In the following chapter, attention will be given to crime in the technological system.

Zuckerberg is not alone in being accused of misconduct occurring in the economic system. Consider the following examples quoted verbatim from their original sources:

- The Securities and Exchange Commission today charged a former Citigroup investment banker for repeatedly tipping his brother about upcoming merger deals in an insider trading scheme that involved friends and family throughout Northern California and the Midwest and reaped more than $6 million in illicit profits. The SEC alleges that *****, a former director in Citigroup Global Markets' investment banking division in New York, repeatedly told his brother about upcoming deals involving Citigroup's health care industry clients. The SEC further alleges that *****, in addition to buying stock and options in target companies that were the subject of the Citigroup deals, leaked the information to a network of friends and family who also traded in advance of the deals. The SEC has charged the ***** brothers and six others in the case. (Securities and Exchange Commission [SEC], 2009b)
- The Securities and Exchange Commission today filed securities fraud charges against a Scottish trader whose false tweets caused sharp drops in the stock prices of two companies and triggered a trading halt in one of them . . . According to the SEC's complaint filed in federal court in the Northern District of California, *****, tweeted multiple false statements about the two companies on Twitter accounts that he deceptively created to look like the real Twitter accounts of well-known securities research firms . . . The SEC's complaint alleges that *****'s first false tweets caused one company's share price to fall 28 percent before Nasdaq temporarily halted trading. The next day, ****'s false tweets about a different company caused a 16 percent decline in that company's share price. On each occasion, **** bought and sold shares of the target companies in a largely unsuccessful effort to profit from the sharp price swings. (SEC, 2015)
- ******* operated a fraudulent investment scheme, through which he obtained more than $44 million from over 200 investors in Charlotte and elsewhere, causing nearly $18 million in losses to more than 100 investors by the time the scheme collapsed. Court records show that ****** lied to his victims, promising their money would be invested in wireless Internet equipment, Internet towers, and other facilities and companies. According to court records, rather than investing the victims' money as promised, **** used the majority of the funds to run a Ponzi-style scheme and used a portion to fund his personal lifestyle. Court records show that over the course of the fraud, **** invested only $7.7 million of the victims' money and used approximately $32 million to pay some of his victims' supposed "profits" on their investments and to cover personal expenses. (FBI, 2015, October 28)
- A Canton couple was sentenced to prison for defrauding the United States Department of Education out of more than $2.3 million by obtaining fake high school diplomas for prospective students, fraudulently applying for financial aid on their behalf by representing that the students had the necessary educational credentials, and then

enrolling them in the college that the couple operated, law enforcement officials said.

The [Couple] recruited students who had not
earned high school diplomas or G.E.D. certificates, and
thus were not eligible for SFA funds, and submitted
fraudulent financial aid documents to the Department
of Education. They used online high schools, including
Australia-based Adison High School, to purchase
fake high school diplomas and coursework transcripts for students who were not required to attend
any classes or complete any coursework, according to
court documents. (FBI, 2015, March 11)

These examples demonstrate the breadth of offenses that are
committed in the economic system. When the term *white-
collar offender* comes to mind, it is often images of offenders
from the economic or technological systems that come to
mind. Prominent white-collar offenders who committed
crimes against at least one of these systems include Bernie Madoff, Ken Lay, Martha Stewart, and Michael Milken. While
many people recognize these names, the actual behaviors that got them into trouble are less understood.

▲ **Photo 7.1** From student to creator of Facebook, Mark
Zuckerberg has faced his share of accusations of white-collar
misconduct.

Official White House Photo by Pete Souza

● ● ● Crime in the Economic System

The economic system includes banks; investment companies; stock markets across the world; commodities markets; and
other exchanges and markets where individuals are able to make investments, purchase raw materials, and secure goods.
Generally speaking, crimes in the economic system can be classified as investment frauds. In describing these behaviors,
real examples are discussed in order to better illustrate each offense type.

● ● ● Investment Fraud

Investment fraud occurs when investments made by consumers are managed or influenced fraudulently by stockbrokers
or other officials in the economic system. *Securities and commodities fraud* is a broad concept capturing a range of behaviors designed to rip off investors. At the broadest level, securities fraud refers to fraudulent activities related to stocks,
bonds, and mutual funds. Consider a case where Andrew McKelvey, the former head of the employment recruitment firm
Monster Nationwide Inc., was charged with fraud and conspiracy after he backdated several employees' stock options. In
doing so, he fraudulently changed the value of their stock options. In another case, four executives were convicted after
backdating contracts and filing false SEC documents, lying in press releases, and being dishonest with the company's own
auditors (Taub, 2006). Again, these actions were done to increase the value of the company's stocks. In Focus 7.1 provides
an overview of how one investment advisor "went bad."

Commodities fraud is defined as the "fraudulent sale of commodities investments" (FBI, 2009b). **Commodities** are
raw materials such as natural gas, oil, gold, agricultural products, and other tangible products that are sold in bulk form.
Consider a case where one offender was convicted after he persuaded 1,000 victims to invest in commodities such as oil,
gold, and silver. The problem was that the commodities did not exist ("Kingpin of Commodities Fraud," 2006).

Commodities fraud is believed to be particularly prevalent in Florida. In 2006, one-fourth of advisories of enforcement activities by the Commodity Futures Trading Commission were tied to companies in Florida. It is believed that the
weather, proximity to other countries, and established telemarketing firms contributed to the high rate of commodities
fraud in that state (Katz, 2007).

While "securities and commodities" fraud is a general label given to fraud in the economic system, several specific varieties of these frauds exist, including these:

- Market manipulation
- Broker embezzlement
- Hedge fund fraud
- Insider trading
- Futures trading fraud
- Foreign exchange fraud, high-yield investment schemes, and advanced-fee fraud
- Ponzi and pyramid schemes

Each of these is discussed below. Because most white-collar crime students have likely had little exposure to the workings of the stock market and other financial institutions, where appropriate, analogies to the experiences of college students are made in an effort to better demonstrate the context surrounding the offenses. After discussing these fraud types, attention will be given to Bernie Madoff's historic scheme and patterns surrounding these offenses, with a specific focus on the consequences of these frauds for individuals, community members, and society at large.

IN FOCUS   7.1

When Investment Advisors Go Bad

The sole owner and president of Magnolia Capital Advisors, a registered investment adviser [was convicted of securities fraud].

This Decision bars ***** from association with any broker or dealer or investment adviser. He was previously enjoined from violating the antifraud provisions of the federal securities laws, based on his wrongdoing while associated with a registered investment adviser and a registered broker-dealer in trading collateralized mortgage obligations. Additionally, he was convicted of several federal crimes involving dishonest conduct. . . .

His May 13, 2009, Plea Agreement includes a Factual Basis for Plea that describes *****'s conduct that violated each of the above provisions. ***** was sentenced to fifty-one months of imprisonment and ordered to pay restitution of $667,890.28 and a special assessment of $700.

As set forth in the Factual Basis for Plea, ***** committed numerous dishonest acts. For example, in order to obtain a $223,245 boat loan in 2003 to fund a $265,394 purchase of a boat, ***** submitted financial documents to a bank that included a copy of his purported income tax return that grossly inflated his income as compared with the income stated on

the return that he actually filed. In 2006, he filed a voluntary petition for bankruptcy and failed to disclose numerous significant assets, such as the boat, other objects, and investment accounts. Additionally, ***** falsely represented that he had made no gifts of $200 or more during the preceding year, when in fact he had paid $20,240 for plastic surgery for his girlfriend, paid off $7,554 of her car loan, and paid $11,200 into her bank account during that time frame. While the bankruptcy proceeding was pending, he transferred unreported assets, and deposited most of the approximately $40,000 in proceeds in his girlfriend's bank account. Additionally, he filed materially false tax returns for 2001, 2002, and 2005, that included false representations including overstating expenses and understating income. The amount of intended loss involved in the bank, bankruptcy, and tax fraud was approximately $995,874. . . .

***** will be barred from association with a broker-dealer or an investment adviser. His criminal conduct was egregious, involved a high degree of scienter, and was recurrent, extending over a period of three years. His occupation, if he were allowed to continue it, would present opportunities for future violations of the securities laws. The degree of harm to investors and the marketplace from the conduct underlying *****s antifraud injunction is quantified in his ill-gotten gains of $5,857,241.09 plus prejudgment interest of $2,258,940.58 that the court ordered disgorged.... Even disregarding the injunction entered by default or assuming *arguendo* that Reinhard was the victim, not the perpetrator, of conduct referenced in the injunctive complaint, as he has suggested in this proceeding, his criminal conduct shows a lack of honesty and indicates that he is unsuited to functioning in the securities industry. The degree of harm to the public from the conduct underlying his criminal conviction was approximately $995,874. Bars are also necessary for the purpose of deterrence.

Source: Reprinted From Initial decision release no. 396 administrative proceeding file no. 3–13280 United States of America before the Securities and Exchange Commission Washington, DC 20549 In the Matter of Don Warner Reinhard Supplemental Initial Decision June 1, 2010 Available online at http://www.sec.gov/litigation/aljdec/2010/id396cff.pdf

Market Manipulation

Market manipulation refers to situations where executives or other officials do things to artificially inflate trading volume and subsequently affect the price of the commodity or security. This is sometimes called *pump and dump* because participants will "pump" up the price of the stocks by sharing false information in chat rooms, e-mail messages, or other forums before "dumping" (or selling) the stocks that have been artificially inflated (FBI, 2009b).

A scene from the classic 1986 Rodney Dangerfield film *Back to School* comes to mind. Thornton Melon (the likable nouveau riche character Dangerfield was playing) was standing in a long line with his son and two of his son's friends, waiting to register for classes, when he thought of a way to make the line shorter. He had his chauffer stand in front of his limousine with a sign that read Bruce Springsteen on it. Eventually, word spread through the registration area that "The Boss" was in the limo, and all of the students stampeded out of the registration hall to get to the limo. Melon and the other three were immediately at the front of the line and able to register for their courses. In effect, Melon's lie had manipulated others to behave differently. In terms of market manipulation, officials share false information to get others to invest differently, and by dumping their own stocks after prices increase, they profit from their lies.

Market manipulation is believed to be pervasive in the natural energy industry, particularly in the gas and electricity markets. In fact, according to some, market manipulation is partly to blame for the unprecedented energy crisis in California in the early 2000s, a crisis that threatened to make the state go bankrupt (Oppel, 2003). Not surprisingly, market manipulation has been described as a "contentious topic" in energy markets (Pirrong, 2010). Energy industry leaders make a distinction between "market power" manipulation and "fraud-based" manipulation. Market power manipulation strategies manipulate the market through aggressive buying and selling strategies. Fraud-based manipulation strategies manipulate the market by distorting information (Pirrong, 2010).

The Enron scandal included fraud-based market manipulations. Among other things, the energy giant's operatives "used names such as 'Fat Boy,' 'Death Star,' 'Get Shorty,' and 'Ricochet' for programs to transfer energy out of California to evade price caps and to create phony transmission congestion" (Bredemeier, 2002, p. A04). The strategies allowed the company to charge a higher price for the energy it was supplying than what the energy was worth. Enron executives unjustly profited more than $1.1 billion from these efforts.

Three federal statutes exist to "prohibit manipulation of various energy commodities and empower federal agencies to impose penalties" (Pirrong, 2010, p. 1). These laws include the Commodity Exchange Act, the Energy Policy Act of 2005, and the Energy Independence and Security Act of 2007. The latter act, in particular, calls on the Federal Trade Commission to treat market manipulations by petroleum and oil company insiders as false and deceptive business practices that could be subject to fines of up to $1 million.

US Government Work

▲ **Photo 7.2**   Believe it or not, this is the crime scene for some market manipulation cases involving situations where offenders manipulate the cost of energy.

Broker Fraud and Embezzlement

Broker fraud occurs when stockbrokers fail to meet their legal obligations to investors. It is believed that "one of the most common frauds is brokers omitting important types of information that investors need to make intelligent decisions about where to put their money" (Knox, 1997, p. 56). Imagine your professor failed to tell you about the due date for a paper and then held you accountable for not turning the paper in on time. Omitting useful information can create negative consequences for investors.

Broker embezzlement occurs when brokers take money that is supposed to be in an investment account and use it for their own personal use (Ackerman, 2001). Trust is an important element of these offenses. Investor-broker relationships are built on trust. It is not uncommon to hear of situations in which fraudulent brokers developed that trust through forming relationships at various institutions that have historically been seen as trustworthy. Consider the case of Gregory Loles, a broker accused of stealing more than $2 million from three parishioners of St. Barbara's Greek Orthodox Church in Easton, Connecticut. Loles "allegedly used the funds to support his private businesses" (McCready & Tinley, 2009).

Hedge Fund Fraud

Somewhat similar to broker embezzlement, **hedge fund fraud** refers to fraudulent acts perpetrated in **hedge fund systems**. A hedge fund is a "private investment partnership . . . [with] high net worth clients" (FBI, 2009b). Problems that arise include situations where the hedge fund managers overstate the assets in a fund in an effort to lie to the investors about their investments. In one case, a hedge fund manager mailed investors false statements making it appear as if the investors' accounts were doing well, when in fact the accounts had lost money. While hedge fund managers have many motives for lying, in this particular case the manager did it so he could continue to receive the 2 percent fee for managing the account. One client was led to believe he had $6.3 million, when all he had was $173,000. Think about the 2 percent commission—2 percent of $6.3 million is $126,000. By continuing to make the investor think he had more than $6 million, the hedge fund manager was able to collect $126,000 in commission—just on this client alone!

As an analogy, consider a situation where a college or university fraternity has a tight-knit group of members who all contribute their membership fees to the treasurer. The treasurer is supposed to transfer the fees to the national membership but steals the funds instead. While not exactly hedge fund fraud, such a situation would be similar in that the deception integrates the dynamics of (a) a privatized and elite partnership and (b) deceit by the trusted manager of the funds.

Various strategies have been suggested for curbing hedge fund fraud. These include hiring external agencies to do internal compliance, developing a hedge fund information depository, and conducting routine assessments of compliance officers with the aim of evaluating their effectiveness (U.S. Government Accountability Office, 2005). Insider trading is a type of fraud that occurs regularly in hedge funds.

Insider Trading

Insider trading occurs when individuals share or steal information that "is material in nature" for future investments. The notion of "material in nature" means that the information "must be significant enough to have affected the company's stock price had the information been available to the public" (Leap, 2007, p. 67). Media mogul Martha Stewart was accused of insider trading after it was learned that she sold some ImClone stocks upon hearing that one of the company's drugs was not going to be approved. Ultimately, Stewart was convicted of perjury and not insider trading.

In testimony before the U.S. Senate Judiciary Committee, Linda Chatman Thomsen (2006), who at the time was the Director of the Division of Enforcement for the U.S. Securities and Exchange Commission (SEC), provided this historical overview of insider trading:

- In the mid-1980s, information that was illegally traded focused on information about pending takeovers and mergers.
- In the late 1980s and early 1990s, due to the recession, illegally traded information tended to be "bad news" information about upcoming company closings or downsizings.
- In the mid-2000s, illegally traded information tended to involve illegally obtained or distributed information about technology, globalization, mergers, and hedge funds.

Somewhat reflecting Thomsen's assertions, in 2007, *Wall Street Journal* reporter Kara Scannell (2007) penned an article titled "Insider Trading: It's Back With a Vengeance." Not coincidentally, Thomsen described insider trading as "an enforcement priority" at the time.

To put into perspective why insider trading is so unfair, imagine the student sitting next to you in your white-collar crime class is dating a student worker from the criminal justice department, and your classmate accesses copies of the exam ahead of time. In the end, the student would have an unfair advantage over the rest of the students in your class. In a similar way, those who receive material information about stocks and other investments have an unfair advantage over the rest of us. Of course, simply receiving the information is not in and of itself criminal; the action becomes illegal when the investor acts on the inside information.

By their very nature, these cases typically involve more than one offender, and in some cases, insider trading schemes may involve several offenders. In November 2009, Preet Bharara, a Manhattan U.S. Attorney, charged nine defendants for their intricate scheme of receiving, selling, and buying inside information. As evidence of the breadth of this case, here is how the SEC summarized this scheme:

The Securities and Exchange Commission today announced insider trading charges against nine defendants in a case involving serial insider trading by a ring of Wall Street traders and hedge funds who made over $20 million trading ahead of corporate acquisition announcements using inside information tipped by an attorney at the international law firm of Ropes & Gray LLP, in exchange for kickbacks. The SEC alleges that Arthur J. Cutillo, an attorney in the New York office of Ropes & Gray, misappropriated from his law firm material, nonpublic information concerning at least four corporate acquisitions or bids involving Ropes & Gray clients. . . . The complaint alleges that Cutillo, through his friend and fellow attorney Jason Goldfarb, tipped inside information concerning these acquisitions to Zvi Goffer, a proprietary trader at the broker-dealer Schottenfeld Group, LLC ("Schottenfeld"). The complaint further alleges that Zvi traded on this information for Schottenfeld, and had numerous downstream tippees who also traded on the information, including other professional traders and portfolio managers at two hedge fund advisers. (SEC, 2009c)

In another case demonstrating the "group" nature of insider trading, Yonni Sebbag was arrested along with his girlfriend, Disney employee Bonnie Hoxie, in May 2010. Hoxie, an administrative assistant at the resort, reportedly acquired insider information on Disney's quarterly earnings and shared that information with her boyfriend. He apparently anonymously contacted 33 different investment companies offering to sell the insider information. Several of the investment companies he called notified the authorities about Sebbag's offers (H. Johnson, 2010). The White-Collar Crime in the News:

Insider Trading Leads to Bankers Seeing the Inside of Prisons box includes a recent press release describing another insider case involving multiple offenders.

WHITE-COLLAR CRIME IN THE NEWS

Insider Trading in Banks
Leads to Seeing the Inside of Prisons

Insider trading can occur in virtually any setting, including banks.

ATLANTA – Douglas Ballard, Guy Mitchell and Joseph Todd Foster have been sentenced for their roles in a conspiracy to commit bribery and bank fraud, insider trading and tax evasion that occurred at the now-failed Integrity Bank.

"Our nation's financial crisis was fueled in part by bank insiders and major borrowers whose greed led them to break the law," said United States Attorney Sally Quillian Yates. "The conduct of these defendants, two of whom once held prominent positions in banking, helped pave a path to the shocking number of bank failures Georgia has experienced in the last ten years."

Mark F. Giuliano, Special Agent in Charge, FBI Atlanta Field Office, stated: "The magnitude and impact of this financial institution based fraud case clearly illustrates why these types of criminal investigations are a priority matter at the FBI. We will continue to work with our various investigative partners to identify, investigate, and present for prosecution those individuals who betray their positions of trust within these institutions for the sake of personal greed."

"The sentence today does not replace the losses that were incurred due to this scheme," stated Veronica F. Hyman-Pillot, Special Agent in Charge with IRS Criminal Investigation. "However, today's sentence is a message to others that regardless of who you are, there are consequences for committing these types of crimes."

"The FDIC OIG is pleased to join the U.S. Attorney's Office and our law enforcement colleagues in announcing the sentencing of individuals whose criminal actions caused serious harm to Integrity Bank," said Fred W. Gibson, Jr., Acting Inspector General, Federal Deposit Insurance Corporation. "It is particularly troubling to the FDIC OIG when a bank insider like Mr. Ballard, who is entrusted with operating the bank in a safe and sound manner, violates that trust and engages in activities that contribute to losses to the Deposit Insurance Fund. Mr. Mitchell's sentencing should deter others who face similar opportunities to conspire with bank insiders in such criminal behavior. Today's sentencing confirms that those who undermine the integrity of the financial system will be brought to justice and held accountable for their crimes."

According to United States Attorney Yates, the charges and other information presented in court: Ballard, a former Executive Vice-President at the now-failed Integrity Bank, formerly headquartered in Alpharetta, Ga., received more than $200,000 in cash bribes from Mitchell, the bank's largest borrower. At the same time in 2006, when Ballard was being bribed, he allowed Mitchell to draw more than $7 million from a loan that was supposed to be used for renovation and construction at the Casa Madrona Hotel in Sausalito, Calif., despite the fact that no renovation or construction work was done. Instead, Mitchell used the money to buy an island in the Bahamas, travel by private jet, purchase Miami Heat basketball tickets, buy fancy jewelry and expensive cars, and a mansion in Coconut Grove, Fla.

Mitchell received $20 million in additional business loans from Integrity Bank after the Casa Madrona loan proceeds were exhausted, and he continued to use some of that money for impermissible, personal expenses. Mitchell defaulted on the loans and Integrity Bank eventually failed.

Source: Reprinted from: U.S. Department of Justice. (2013, November 6). Three sentenced for conspiracy, insider trading, and tax evasion. Available online at from https://www.fdicig.gov/press/pr-11-06-13a.html.

Insider trading is attributed to a number of factors, including an increase in the number of mergers, lightly regulated hedge funds, and more complex funding strategies (Scannell, 2007). Scannell also notes that the "rapid trading style" of hedge funds makes it "harder to pin trades on non-public information" (p. B1).

Futures Trading Fraud

Futures trading fraud refers to fraud occurring in the trading of futures contracts and options on the futures trading market. **Futures contracts** are "agreement[s] to buy or sell a given unit of a commodity at some future date" (Schlegel, 1993, p. 60). Brokers "in the pits" buy and sell commodities based on a contract between the investor and the broker. The sale could be contingent on a specific date or a specific value of the commodity.

Schlegel (1993) describes several types of futures trading fraud, including prearranged trading, front running, and bucketing. Here is how he describes these schemes:

▲ **Photo 7.3** Insider trading is essentially telling secrets that give one person profits and another person losses.

- **Prearranged trading:** "Brokers, or brokers and local brokers, first agree on a price and then act out the trade as a piece of fiction in the pit, thereby excluding other potential bidders from the offering. The prearranged deal ensures a given profit for the colluding traders while denying their customers the best possible price." (p. 63)
- **Front running:** "Broker takes advantage of the special knowledge about a pending custom order and trades on his or her own account before executing that order." (p. 63)
- **Bucketing:** "A floor trader will take a position opposite that of a customer's position, either directly or by using another floor trader, again in collusion." (p. 63)

In each of these actions, the broker unjustly profits from the fraudulent actions. To limit the extent of fraud in the futures markets, in 1974 the Commodity Futures Trading Commission (CFTC) was created.

Foreign Exchange Fraud, High-Yield Investment Schemes, and Advanced-Fee Fraud

Other types of securities and commodities fraud include foreign exchange fraud, high-yield investment schemes, and advance-fee fraud. **Foreign exchange fraud** occurs when brokers or other officials induce "victims to invest in the foreign currency exchange market" through illegitimate and fraudulent practices (FBI, 2009b). Typically, the frauds involve situations where offenders either don't provide the investor what was promised or simply take the funds and fail to perform the promised financial transaction.

High-yield investment schemes promise investors low-risk or even no-risk investment strategies, when in fact the funds are not actually invested (FBI, 2009b). Sometimes offenders claim to the investor that the investment schemes are backed by the Federal Reserve or the World Bank, when they have no backing whatsoever (Behrmann, 2005). Investors are also told that they are being given access to a "prime" bank, thereby making investors falsely believe that they are a part of an exclusive group of investors in a "private club" (Welch, 2008). The offender fakes the investment and moves it through several international bank accounts, making "the chase futile for the original investors" (Behrmann, 2005).

Ed Yourdon. Creative Commons Attribution 2.0 Generic. https://creativecommons.org/licenses/by/2.0/

Advance-fee fraud occurs when investors are promised certain actions in exchange for an up-front fee. Investors are pressured to invest and pay the broker, and never receive any services. This is the top online scam reported to the SEC (Welch, 2008). Imagine your professor charging an advance fee for a study session—then, the professor doesn't show up for the event. Not only would you be ripped off, but you'd probably also be a bit angry at the professor.

● ● ● Ponzi and Pyramid Schemes

Ponzi and pyramid schemes scam investors by paying them from future investors' payments into the offender's scheme. Table 7.1 shows the differences between Ponzi and pyramid schemes. Pyramid schemes recruit individuals by promising them profits from getting others to invest, whereas Ponzi schemes do not require participants to recruit investors. In pyramid schemes, the participants' interactions are generally limited to interactions with the investor who got them to join the scheme; in Ponzi schemes, interactions are often with the individual who created the scheme. The source of payments in both schemes is from new participants—those in pyramid schemes know this, but those in Ponzi schemes do not. Pyramids collapse quickly, but Ponzi schemes may not (SEC, 2009a). A recent study suggested that Ponzi and pyramid schemes are perpetrated through deliberate information delivered in trusting relationships, with the offender socially embedded in a high status group, and technological changes and promises of high returns have increased the "lure" of these offenses (Nolasco, Vaughn, & del Carmen, 2013).

To illustrate how these schemes are developed, consider the basic definitions of the schemes. Here is how the SEC defines **Ponzi schemes:**

> A Ponzi scheme is an investment fraud that involves the payment of purported returns to existing investors from funds contributed by new investors. Ponzi scheme organizers often solicit new investors by promising to invest funds in opportunities claimed to generate high returns with little or no risk. In many Ponzi schemes, the fraudsters focus on attracting new money to make promised payments to earlier-stage investors and to use for personal expenses, instead of engaging in any legitimate investment activity. (SEC, 2009a)

Table 7.1 Differences Between Pyramid and Ponzi Schemes		
	Pyramid Scheme	**Ponzi Scheme**
Typical "hook"	Earn high profits by making one payment and finding a set number of others to become distributors of a product. The scheme typically does not involve a genuine product. The purported product may not exist, or it may be "sold" only within the pyramid scheme.	Earn high investment returns with little or no risk by simply handing over your money; the investment typically does not exist.
Payments/profits	Must recruit new distributors to receive payments.	No recruiting necessary to receive payments.
Interaction with original promoter	Sometimes none. New participants may enter scheme at a different level.	Promoter generally acts directly with all participants.
Source of payments	From new participants—always disclosed.	From new participants—never disclosed.
Collapse	Fast. An exponential increase in the number of participants is required at each level.	May be relatively slow if existing participants reinvest money.

Source: U.S. Securities and Exchange Commission

Ponzi schemes have received a great deal of scrutiny in recent times. To understand the increase in these schemes in the United States, it is helpful to understand the history of the schemes. Charles Ponzi was the mastermind behind the first Ponzi scheme. He developed a scheme in 1919 in which he persuaded investors to invest in an international postage stamp program. He paid off early investors with funds contributed by new investors. His scheme was uncovered when *The Post* asked Clarence Barron, who published the *Barron's Financial Report* at the time, to review Ponzi's company. Barron learned that Ponzi's investors were making significant profits without Ponzi actually investing any money. A federal investigation followed, and Ponzi eventually pleaded guilty and served just under four years in federal prison. After his federal prison stay, he was convicted in state court and sentenced for seven to nine years as a "common and notorious thief" (Zuckoff, 2005, p. 305). Today, his legacy is not as a common offender, but as a notorious white-collar criminal.

Today, Ponzi schemes seem to be so common in the United States that some have referred to the country as "a Ponzi nation" ("A Ponzi Nation," 2009). One author labeled 2009 as the "Year of the Ponzi" (C. Anderson, 2010). In 2009, 150 Ponzi schemes collapsed, as compared to 40 in 2008. Also, in 2009, one-fifth of the SEC's workload was directed toward responding to Ponzi schemes. By comparison, in 2005, just one-tenth of their workload was for Ponzi schemes. C. Anderson notes that the financial crisis brought the scams to light more quickly. Investors, in need of funds to respond to the economic downturn, tried to withdraw from their investments, only to learn that their investor was actually operating a Ponzi scheme. The most famous of these Ponzi schemes was orchestrated by Bernie Madoff.

Bernie Madoff's Ponzi Scheme: From Armani Suits to a Bulletproof Vest

Bernie Madoff was the mastermind behind what has come to be called the largest Ponzi scheme in the history of the United States. Madoff's scheme was simple. Figure 7.1 shows a time line highlighting Madoff's scheme. Starting in the early 1990s, he marketed his scheme as an exclusive investment opportunity, with clients waiting a year to be given the opportunity to invest with him (Healy & Syre, 2008). It was a privilege to have Madoff investing on an investor's behalf. Investors sent him millions, but instead of investing the money, he deposited it in a bank account at Chase Manhattan (Healy & Mandell, 2009). Eventually, thousands of investors had invested $65 billion in Madoff's accounts (Glovin, 2009a). Madoff had a few complaints about his activities, which opened up SEC investigations, but the investigations never substantiated wrongdoing.

Madoff's scheme continued for more than 17 years. Two elements of his scheme allowed it to continue for so long: (1) investors were receiving positive returns on their investments and (2) Madoff was extremely secretive in sharing information about investors' accounts. In terms of positive returns, a hedge fund managed by Madoff averaged a 10.5 percent annual return over 17 years—at least it appeared to average those returns (Appelbaum, Hilzenrath, & Paley, 2008). With returns like that, investors were likely extremely satisfied with their interactions with Madoff.

Regarding his secretiveness, Madoff provided very little information about his "investments" to his investors. When he was asked questions by his investors about how his investment strategy paid so well, he told investors, "secrecy as to information is a key issue for everyone" (Glovin, 2009b, p. C4). Madoff was so extreme in his secrecy that he did not allow clients electronic "access to their accounts" (Appelbaum et al., 2008). This practice was described by the head of a consulting firm as "extremely secretive, even for the non-transparent world of hedge funds" (Appelbaum et al., 2008).

One day in the fall of 2008, clients asked Madoff to withdraw $7 billion. His account, however, did not hold the funds. He called a meeting with his sons and told them about his scheme. The next day, his sons turned their father in to the FBI (Healy & Syre, 2008). Incidentally, his wife "withdrew ten million dollars from a brokerage account the same day her sons turned him in" (Healy, 2009a). On March 12, 2009, Madoff pleaded guilty to the largest Ponzi scheme to date. At his court hearing he very directly admitted, "I operated a Ponzi scheme through the investment advocacy side of my business" (Glovin, 2009b).

Madoff's victims were stunned by the revelations. Both individual and institutional investors lost huge amounts of funds. Victims included nonprofits and charities that had trusted Madoff to manage their foundation's finances. Several philanthropic organizations lost hundreds of millions, and charities experienced large losses. Madoff managed "nearly 45% of Carl and Ruth Shapiro's Family Foundation," which lost $145 million (Healy & Syre, 2008). Jewish charities, in particular, were hit quite hard. The Women's Zionist Organization of America lost $90 million, Yeshiva University lost

$14.5 million, and the Eli Weisel Foundation for Humanity lost the $15.2 million it had invested with Madoff. Mark Charendoff, the Jewish Funders Network president, lamented, "It's an atomic bomb in the world of Jewish philanthropy" (Campbell, 2009, p. 70). Madoff's individual victims included well-known clientele such as Sandy Koufax (baseball Hall of Fame pitcher), Fred Wilpon (owner of the New York Mets), Larry King (Cable News Network, or CNN, anchor), Jeffrey Katzenberg (Hollywood mogul), Kevin Bacon (actor), Zsa Zsa Gabor (actress), and John Malkovich (actor) ("Madoff's Victims," 2009). Thousands of others also lost money to Madoff's scheme.

One task that has proven to be particularly difficult has been to accurately estimate the losses. Initially, Yeshiva University was believed to have lost $110 million to the scheme. However, when examining their losses, they found they had actually lost $14.5 million. Why the discrepancy? Because the university officials (and Madoff's investors) were basing their losses on amounts that Madoff told them they had in their accounts—fictitious amounts for his victims. Yeshiva never actually had $110 million. So, their loss was calculated as the actual amount it had invested. Beyond the economic losses, foundations and charities also experienced negative consequences from having their names attached to Madoff.

As an analogy, imagine that, unbeknownst to you, someone had broken into your white-collar crime professor's grade book online and changed all of the student's grades to make it look as if everyone had an A+. You would not know the other students' grades, but you would "know" (or assume) that you had a perfect score in the class. You would likely be feeling pretty good about the class. Then, if the professor became aware of the scheme and changed everyone's grades back to their actual grade, how would you feel? Would you think that you "lost" points? Many of you probably have legitimate A+ grades, but for those who would have the grade changed to something lower, understanding your actual grade in the class would be somewhat confusing. For Madoff's victims, understanding the precise extent of their losses was confusing—on both an economic level and an emotional level.

Not surprisingly, Madoff was not well liked by Americans. As an indicator of the hatred that Americans had for him, it is significant to note that Madoff wore a bulletproof vest when going to and from court. Somewhat telling of his betrayal to his friends and family, the judge in Madoff's case, Manhattan Federal Judge Denny Chin, "noted he had not gotten a single letter from friends or family testifying to Madoff's good deeds" during his sentencing hearing (Zambito, Martinez, & Siemaszko, 2009). In statements to the court, his victims called him "a psychopathic lying egomaniac," "ruthless and unscrupulous," and "a devil" (Dey, 2009, p. 10).

It is not entirely clear where all of the money went. Madoff lent millions to his family members and paid their corporate credit card bills, even for those family members who worked for a different corporation. He also paid bills for the captain of his boat (Efrati, 2009). But even these expenses would account for only a minuscule amount of the funds. Douglas Kass, a hedge fund manager himself, told a reporter, "It appears that at least $15 billion of wealth, much of which was concentrated in southern Florida and New York City, has gone to 'money heaven'" (Stempel & Plumb, 2008, p. B04).

The fallout from Madoff's fraud continues. Civil charges were filed against his broker, Robert Jaffe, for "knowingly and recklessly participating in Madoff's Ponzi scheme" (Healy, 2009b, p. 1). Stanley Chais, a California investment advisor, was charged with fraud for funneling his clients' funds to Madoff. Frank Dipascali, Jr., Madoff's top aide, pleaded guilty in August 2009 for his role in helping to deceive investors in the scheme. The U.S. Marshall's service auctioned off Dipascali's belongings in an effort to help make up for losses. During an auction preview, one woman attending the auction commented, "For someone who stole millions, this stuff isn't all that nice" (Debusmann, 2010).

The SEC has faced enormous criticism for not stopping the scheme sooner. After all, on six separate occasions, it had received complaints about Madoff's activities. A report by the SEC's Office of Investigations titled *Investigation of the Failure of the SEC to Uncover Bernard Madoff's Ponzi Scheme* noted that

> the SEC received more than ample information in the form of detailed and substantive complaints over the years to warrant a thorough and comprehensive examination and/or investigation of Bernard Madoff . . . for operating a Ponzi scheme, and that despite three examinations and two investigations being conducted, a thorough and competent investigation or examination was never performed. (SEC, 2010)

The 499-page report provides a scathing review of the SEC's failure, but it offers suggestions on how to avoid such a failure in the future.

Strategies for improving the investigation of these offenses will be discussed in a later chapter. At this point, one benefit that has come out of Madoff's actions is that increased attention is being given to the warning signs, or "red flags," of Ponzi schemes. These red flags include the following:

- Complicated trading strategies
- Irregular investment payments
- Unique customer statements
- Delays in withdrawals and transfers
- Promises of high investment returns with little or no risk
- Overly consistent returns
- Unregistered investments
- Unlicensed sellers
- Secretive strategies
- Issues with paperwork
- Difficulty receiving payments (SEC, 2009a)

Wells (2010) suggests that "the flag that flies the highest is a rate of return for an investment that greatly exceeds the norm" (p. 6). Madoff's scheme flew this red flag as high as it could be flown. Recognizing patterns surrounding fraud in the securities and commodities industry should help prevent and facilitate response to these offenses in the future.

● ● ● Patterns Surrounding Investment Fraud

Several patterns characterize various dynamics surrounding investment fraud. Some of these patterns are similar to other forms of white-collar crime, while others seem more specific to cases of investment fraud. These patterns include the following:

- Significant press attention
- Attributions of greed
- Increasing punitiveness
- "White-collar gangs"
- Multiple offenses
- Regulatory changes
- Negative consequences

Addressing these patterns will provide a full understanding of investment fraud.

First, several cases of investment fraud, or related offenses, receiving significant press attention were prominently highlighted in the national media over the past few decades. Table 7.2 shows 12 offenders that I would characterize as "infamous," the offenses they were accused of committing, the specific behaviors they performed, and the outcomes of these behaviors. Each of these individuals received a great deal of press attention for his

▲ **Photo 7.4**   Bernie Madoff operated an enormous Ponzi scheme through the investment advocacy side of his business. When he was sentenced for it, few individuals spoke on his behalf.

U.S. Department of Justice

Figure 7.1 Madoff Time Line

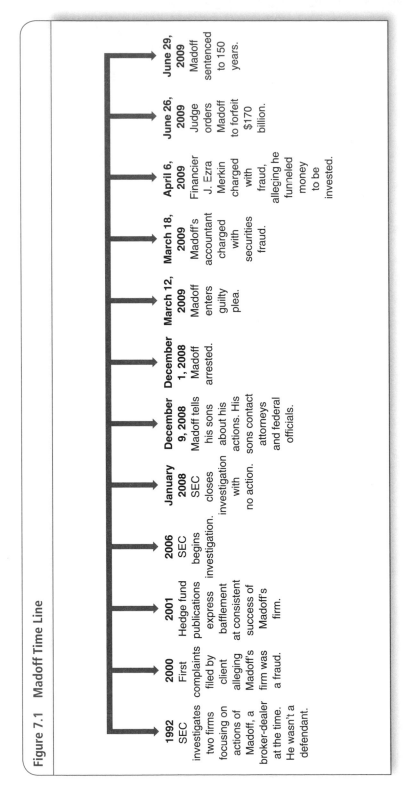

1992 SEC investigates two firms focusing on actions of Madoff, a broker-dealer at the time. He wasn't a defendant.

2000 First complaints filed by client alleging Madoff's firm was a fraud.

2001 Hedge fund publications express bafflement at consistent success of Madoff's firm.

2006 SEC begins investigation.

January 2008 SEC closes investigation with no action.

December 9, 2008 Madoff tells his sons about his actions. His sons contact attorneys and federal officials.

December 1, 2008 Madoff arrested.

March 12, 2009 Madoff enters guilty plea.

March 18, 2009 Madoff's accountant charged with securities fraud.

April 6, 2009 Financier J. Ezra Merkin charged with fraud, alleging he funneled money to be invested.

June 26, 2009 Judge orders Madoff to forfeit $170 billion.

June 29, 2009 Madoff sentenced to 150 years.

Source: Adapted from McCoy (2009).

or her misdeeds. In fact, so much press coverage focused on these scandals that some researchers have focused on how the press reported specific cases of investment fraud. One author team, for example, reviewed media reports about Enron and noted that the reports demonstrated four consistent themes about the scandal: risk, gratification, pride, and fantasy imagery (Knottnerus, Ulsperger, Cummins, & Osteen, 2006). Perhaps partly because of the press coverage given to the Enron fiasco, Friedrichs (2004) notes that Enron became a metaphor for a series of corporate scandals in the past decade. Cases involving executives from WorldCom, Adelphia, Tyco, Rite Aid, and other recognizable companies received significant press attention.

A second pattern has to do with attributions of greed that are used to explain cases of investment fraud. Reporters seemed either directly or indirectly to focus on greed explanations in explaining investment fraud. The high salary of execu-

▲ **Photo 7.5** Economic crime scandals tend to receive a great deal of press attention. Authorities often hold press conferences in the wake of these events.

tives has been a particular source of contention, both in the media and in private discussions. By focusing on their salaries when discussing the offenses by executives, it is as if the reporters are suggesting that the crimes are somehow tied to salary, when—in fact—the root causes of investment fraud are much more complex.

Still, the notion that greed causes investment fraud persists. The movie *Wall Street* (1987), starring Michael Douglas and Charlie Sheen, is illustrative. Douglas stars as Gordon Gekko—a white-collar criminal engaging in a variety of investment frauds, and Sheen plays Bud Fox—a character new to Wall Street and aiming to learn from Gekko. In one scene, Gekko tells a group of shareholders,

> The point is, ladies and gentleman, that greed—for lack of a better word—is good.
> Greed is right.
> Greed works.
> Greed clarifies, cuts through, and captures the essence of the evolutionary spirit.
> Greed, in all of its forms—greed for life, for money, for love, knowledge—has marked the upward surge of mankind.
> And greed—you mark my words—will not only save Teldar Paper, but that other malfunctioning corporation called the USA.

I won't spoil the end of the movie for those who have not yet seen it, but it is important to note that Gekko's speech has been linked to the following comments Ivan Boesky once told a group of University of California, Berkeley, students: "Greed is all right, by the way. I want you to know that. I think greed is healthy. You can be greedy and still feel good about yourself" (Boesky, n.d.).

A third pattern consistent in these investment frauds is that the criminal justice system has demonstrated increasing punitiveness toward these offenders (Payne, 2003b). It is a myth that white-collar offenders are always sentenced more leniently than conventional offenders, and this will be discussed in more detail later in the chapter focusing on corrections. For now, it can simply be stated that judges and prosecutors seem intent on penalizing investment fraud offenders severely, particularly those investment fraud offenders who receive a great deal of attention from the media (Payne, 2003b). Some have attributed the increased punitiveness to the fact that the schemes often bilk elderly persons out of their life savings, as well as the fact that concern about white-collar crime in general has heightened (Hansard, 2007). The stiff "public sentence" allows judges to "send a message" that the (justice) system is not tolerant of these behaviors. In fact, judges and prosecutors often use the phrase "send a message" or some variation when describing the sentence given to investment fraud offenders. Here are a few examples of this practice:

- "The *message must be sent* that Mr. Madoff's crimes were extraordinarily evil," Judge Denny Chin said when he sentenced Madoff (McCoy, 2009b).
- A prosecutor urged a judge "to '*send a message*' to Wall Street that insider trading won't be tolerated, especially when the offender ran a 'billion-dollar hedge fund' and was 'at the pinnacle' of his profession" (Glovin & Hurtado, 2010).
- "The judge said she wanted to *send a message* that those who commit white-collar crimes will be punished severely. . . . The judge said Caplan, who worked at Brean Murray, Carret & Co. LLC, stole from at least seven investors" ("He Made His Own Bed," 2006).
- "Imposing the 121-month sentence, Judge Walter noted the recent 'staggering increase' in investor-advisor frauds and said that he wanted to '*send a message* that these crimes will result in significant prison sentences'" (FBI, 2010a).

Another pattern surrounding these offenses can be called **white-collar gangs**. One criminologist defines a *gang* as

> a self-formed association of peers, bound together by mutual interests, with identifiable leadership, well-developed lines of authority, and other organizational features, who act in concert to achieve a specific purpose or purposes which generally include the conduct of illegal activity and control over a particular territory, facility, or type of enterprise. (Miller, 1975, p. 121)

The very nature of most investment frauds requires that offenders work with other offenders "in concert to achieve a specific purpose" and that their behaviors "include the conduct of illegal activity." Highlighting the themes surrounding the investment scandals of the early 2000s, Friedrichs (2004) drew attention to the "cooperative involvement of a broad network of other parties" (p. 114) that was found in the scandals. While the behaviors of street gangs and white-collar gangs are substantively different, the point is that investment offenders almost always work with other conspirators in committing their crimes.

A related pattern has to do with the fact that investment offenders tend to commit multiple offenses. It is rare that these offenders engage in their illicit behaviors only once or twice, and rarely do they commit just one type of misconduct. As an example, one offender (a) lied to investors about funds, (b) falsely solicited payments from investors, (c) did not tell investors information they needed to know about their accounts, and (d) did not pay his taxes for 4 years (Mclaughlin, 2010). That investment offenders commit crimes in groups and commit these offenses on multiple occasions is useful information for investigators—if they find evidence of one offender committing one offense, by broadening the scope of their investigation, they can identify additional offenses and offenders.

Another pattern concerns regulatory changes enacted to address these offenses. For example, financial institutions have been called upon to help curb financial offenses through identifying customers, improved record keeping, verification processes, and disclosing information to the authorities (Fasanello, Umans, & White, 2011). Other regulatory changes have also been implemented in an effort to limit these crimes. However, it is believed by some that "regulatory gaps and continued lack of adequate oversight . . . [and] non-understanding of the role of fraud . . . virtually guarantee that future financial crises will occur due to fraud" (Pontell & Geis, 2014, p. 70).

A final pattern surrounding investment frauds involves the negative consequences that stem from these offenses. Beyond the direct economic toll for society in general, the offenses negatively impact investors' confidence in their immediate aftermath, and this reduction in confidence may result in fewer investments and lower stock values (Friedrichs, 2004). For specific victims of the investment frauds, different consequences may surface, and these consequences may linger, at least for some victims.

To address the long-term consequences of investment frauds, Shover and his research team (Shover, Fox, & Mills, 1994) interviewed 47 victims of fraud a decade after their victimization. The sample included victims of the Southland Industrial Banking Commission collapse, which was a result of fraudulent and criminal activities committed by the commission's executives. The researchers found that the long-term effects were minimal for many victims, but some described significant effects. Elderly victims, in particular, seemed to experience more negative consequences from the victimization. One victim told an interviewer,

Table 7.2	**Top Twelve Infamous Offenders Committing White-Collar Crime Against the Economic System**		
Name	**Former Job Title**	**Offense Title**	**Offense Description**
Ivan Boesky	Chairman of The Beverly Hills Hotel Corp.	• Insider trading	Boesky made several large stock purchases in the days before corporate takeovers, and he would sell the newly purchased stocks soon after the takeovers were complete and the value of the stock increased. The breadth of his purchases alerted investigators to possible wrongdoing.
Bernard Ebbers	WorldCom CEO	• Conspiracy • Securities fraud • False regulatory filings	Ebbers exaggerated WorldCom's earnings and hid company losses for 2 years. WorldCom went bankrupt, and the investigation uncovered $11 billion in false accounting entries. More than 17,000 employees lost their jobs, and the incident harmed investor confidence.
Andrew Fastow	Enron CFO	• Wire fraud • Securities fraud	Fastow helped hide Enron's debt and exaggerated the company's profits. He conspired with Jeffrey Skilling to lie to investors. Some see him as a scapegoat in the Enron fiasco. Fastow plead guilty and agreed to testify against Kenneth Lay and Skilling.
Walter Forbes	Cendant chairman	• False statements • Conspiracy to commit securities fraud	Forbes was involved in a scheme in which company stock was inflated by $500 million. Upon hearing of the fraud, public confidence dropped and the company's market value decreased $14 billion in a 24-hour period.
Dennis Kozlowski	Tyco CEO	• Grand larceny • Conspiracy • Falsifying records	Kozlowski took $120 million in bonuses without the approval of the board of directors. He also lied about the value of his company to increase stock prices.
Kenneth Lay	Enron chairman and CEO	• Fraud • Conspiracy • Lying to banks	With other Enron executives, Lay lied about Enron's finances. Enron, a Houston-based company that was once the top energy trading company in the United States, eventually collapsed, and 20,000 employees lost their jobs and retirement packages. Lay was convicted but died of heart disease before his sentencing. The judge, following traditional policies in death of offenders presentence, vacated the conviction.
Bernie Madoff	Founder of Bernard L. Madoff Investment Securities Chairman of the NASDAQ Stock Market	• Securities fraud • Ponzi scheme	Madoff stole several million dollars from thousands of investors through a Ponzi scheme he developed. The scheme took place over years, as he did not rapidly increase the amount of positive returns to investors, but he increased the amounts slowly over time. Victims describe him as an angry man. Madoff was quoted by a fellow inmate who was badgering him about his victims: "F--k my victims," Madoff reportedly said. "I carried them for 20 years, and now I'm doing 150 years."

(Continued)

Table 7.2 (Continued)

Name	Former Job Title	Offense Title	Offense Description
Michael Milken	Wall Street financier	• Securities fraud	Milken was involved in the crackdown on Wall Street misconduct in the late 1980s, early 1990s. He pleaded guilty to securities fraud after Boesky indicated he would testify against Milken. Some blame Milken for the savings and loan collapse 30 years ago, a charge he vehemently denies. Milken is now a philanthropist, consultant, and sought-after speaker. Some credit him with making several important changes to the medical field. He has raised hundreds of millions of dollars for medical research, particularly for cancer research. His net worth is $2.5 billion, which is just $200 million below Oprah.
Charles Ponzi	Founder of Old Colony Foreign Exchange Company	• Ponzi scheme	Ponzi persuaded thousands of individuals to invest in a postage stamp program that would provide, according to Ponzi, a 50 percent return in less than 3 months. Ponzi used international mail coupons to begin his scheme and then used incoming investments from new investors to maintain the scheme and pay former investors.
John Rigas	Adelphia CEO	• Securities fraud • Lying to investors • Conspiracy	Rigas hid $2.3 billion of his company's debt. He allegedly "helped himself" to so much of the company's funds that his son limited the elder Rigas's withdrawals to $1,000,000 a month.
Jeffrey Skilling	President and chief operating officer of Enron	• Fraud • Conspiracy • Lying to auditors • Insider trading	Skilling was second in command to Lay at Enron. Part of their scheme included reporting the value of their company based on future rather than current estimates.
Martha Stewart	Martha Stewart Living CEO	• False statements • Obstruction of justice	Stewart sold $228,000 worth of her ImClone stock the day before the Food and Drug Administration (FDA) announced it was not going to approve one of ImClone's cancer drugs. The investigation revealed that she had the same stockbroker as the CEO of ImClone. She was later convicted of lying to investigators (perjury) and obstruction of justice. Ironically, at the time of her sentencing, the stocks she sold had increased in value to $315,000.
Samuel Waksal	ImClone CEO	• Insider trading	Waksal unloaded 79,000 shares of ImClone stock upon hearing that the company's cancer drug, Erbitux, was not being approved by the FDA in 2001. Later, the drug was approved and was instrumental in the sale of ImClone to Eli Lilly for $6.5 billion. Waksal served 5 years in prison, but because he still owned stock options in ImClone, he profited from the sale.

Sources: Information from various news and governmental sources, including Associated Press ("Martha Stewart Reads," 2004), Associated Press ("Accused Dentist," 2007), Cosgrove-Mather (2003), Crawford (2005), Hays (2006), Johnson (2005), Johnson (2006), Kolker (2009), Masters (2005), U.S. Securities and Exchange Commission (n.d.), White (2005).

it's destroying us. It's destroying us. She was trained to look up to and obey an authority figure. I don't necessarily agree with that. Sometimes the authority figures are wrong. So as a result, she's a walking bag of nerves, very short-tempered. (Shover et al., 1994, p. 87)

The results of the Shover research team's study showed that *delegitimation effects dissipated over time, suggesting that investor confidence can be restored.* They also found, though, that when these effects lingered, that tended to be a result of the actions of state officials responding to the misconduct more than the actual misconduct itself.

Others have also commented on the way that investors "get over" investment scandals. A few years after the series of corporate scandals in the early 2000s, one author team wrote the following in a *High Yield Report*: "It was the same story in the U.S. secondary market last week. Everyone was buying everything and anything" (Appin & O'Connor, 2003). The article was appropriately titled "Market Rises as Spectre of Corporate Fraud Fades."

These patterns demonstrate the pervasiveness of investment frauds. As a type of crime in the economic system, investment fraud cases typically involve large profits for offenders and large dollar losses for scammed investors. A similar pattern is found in crimes in the technological system.

● ● ● Student Loan Fraud

Students may think that crimes in the economic system do not closely relate to them. Such an assumption could not be further from the truth. One type of crime occurring in the economic system very closely relates to the lives of college students: fraud in the student loan and financial aid process. According to one author, "fraud schemes have been plaguing higher education for years and have been growing in notoriety" (O'Colmain, 2014). Federal authorities estimated that the number of recipients "potentially participating in this fraud activity had increased 82 percent from award year 2009 (18,719 students) to award year 2012 (34,007 students)" (U.S. Department of Education, 2014). It has also been estimated that during this time period, $187 million of federal aid funds was lost to fraud perpetrated by student aid fraud rings (U.S. Department of Education, 2014, November 14).

Various types of student loan/aid fraud exist. These varieties include the following: (1) lying about intent to take classes, (2) taking out loans with no intent to pay them back, (3) lying about qualifications/income, (3) schemes or fraud rings designed to enroll students in college, (4) identity fraud to enhance qualifications, and (5) schemes targeting students with fee-based financial aid seminars. When applying for loans and federal aid, students and their parents are expected to provide honest information that officials can use to make a determination on whether to award the loan/aid. It is also expected that the student will actually attend the college listed on the aid application. Perpetrators in these cases come from at least five different roles: (1) college officials trying to recruit students to their college, (2) consultants assisting students in college applications, (3) parents helping students apply for financial aid, (4) students applying for financial aid, and (5) traditional offenders organizing fraud rings.

The government employs investigation specialists who are trained how to investigate these (and other) types of loan frauds. The Careers Responding to White-Collar Crime: FDIC Investigations Specialist box on the next page shows the duties carried out by some loan investigation specialists.

Few studies have been conducted on student loan and student aid fraud, but this appears to be growing problem. In a study focusing generally on student loans, but not specifically on fraud, a financial aid counselor commented:

All the advisors at my college are very concerned with the amount of what we consider to be loan fraud at our college. These are students who apply and take out loans and have no intention of getting an education or ever paying back these loans. The advisors here believe this is a silent killer that could sink not only our colleges, but [also] the ability for the federal government to continue to support these loans going forward. We all wish we had more discretion to STOP these students who we suspect and have cause to see [as] NOT serious students. (McKinney Roberts, & Shefman, 2013, pp. 11-12)

CAREERS RESPONDING TO WHITE-COLLAR CRIME

FDIC Investigations Specialist, CG-1101-12

Primary duties include:

- Assists in the responsibility for researching loan proceeds, preparing case write-up for bond claims, directors' and officers' liability claims, accountants' liability claims, and other matters requiring investigation to develop a claim. Responds to subpoenas under procedural guidelines and prepares recommendations concerning viability of a claim.
- Monitors progression of claims, in coordination with FDIC Legal Division Professional Liability Unit (PLU) and outside legal counsel, to ensure that appropriate action is taken and critical statute deadlines are met in an efficient and cost effective manner.
- Collaborates with PLU and outside counsel in the delivery of information to representatives of potential claim defendants.

- Analyzes assigned cases and related documentation, e.g., loan files, financial statements, audit/examination reports, and other failed bank/financial institution records, to determine possible Professional Liability claims. Prepares in final form memoranda concerning such claims. Provides comprehensive work papers to support findings.
- Selects and reviews individual cases for potential recoveries, including analysis of financial transactions, tracing and documentation of loan proceeds, and preparing detailed case write-ups to be forwarded to FDIC Legal Division Professional Liability Unit (PLU).
- Reviews, monitors and prepares monthly management reports pertaining to the status of bond claims, director and officer claims, accountants' and other professional liability claims.
- Other duties as assigned.

Source: Reprinted from USAJobs.Gov

In addition, the federal authorities appear to be identifying more cases of student loan/aid fraud. Here are a few case descriptions excerpted from press releases issued by federal officials:

- When admissions representatives encountered potential students who were ineligible for federal student aid because they had not graduated from high school or earned a GED, the admissions representatives enrolled the potential students anyway, and coached them to lie on their applications to the United States Department of Education for federal student aid, including federal Pell Grants and Direct Loans. Often, FastTrain admissions representatives falsely promised the students they could earn their high school diplomas or GEDs at FastTrain and in some cases, FastTrain admissions representatives actually created fictitious high school diplomas on FastTrain computers. (U.S. Department of Education [USDOE], 2015, November 30)
- According to court documents, ***** participated in a scheme to defraud the United States Department of Education of student aid grants and loans. She submitted false financial aid applications to Axia College at the University of Phoenix and Capella University on behalf of students who did not intend to attend either school. She also used stolen or wrongfully obtained personal identifying information of another person to apply for college financial aid. As a result of the scheme to defraud, more than $370,000 in grants and loans were disbursed. (USDOE, 2015, August 3)
- **** filed fraudulent financial information, including false federal tax returns, in support of applications for financial aid for his daughter while she was a student at Harvard College from 2010 through 2012. Based on the

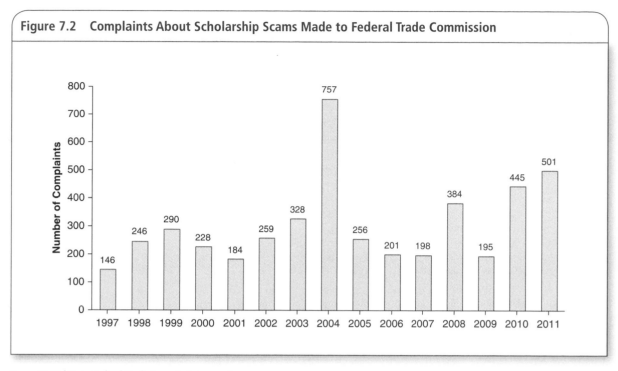

Figure 7.2   Complaints About Scholarship Scams Made to Federal Trade Commission

Source: United States Federal Trade Commission, www.ftc.gov

applications, ****'s daughter was approved for aid totaling more than $160,000 over the three school years. The same false information was used to support a financial aid application in the amount of $46,600 for ****'s second daughter who was attending the University of Rochester in 2010. (USDOE, 2014, December 10)

- A Cleveland man was indicted on charges that he fraudulently received up to $55,000 in federal student financial aid funds . . . The indictment alleges that *** enrolled in approximately six different Ohio colleges between 2007 and 2012 in order to receive Department of Education and Department of Veterans Affairs federal student aid benefits, despite the fact that he had no intention of obtaining a degree. (USDOE, 2014, April 9)

In some cases, students may be targets of student aid fraud. Figure 7.2 shows the number of complaints received related to scholarship scams between 1996 and 2011. As shown in the figure, the number of complaints increased. Potential reasons for this increase include (1) more offenders may have been targeting students, (2) students and families became more aware of complaint processes, (3) a downturn in the economy made students more in need of aid and subsequently more vulnerable, (4) a reduction in the amount of government support given to public universities increased tuition costs and made it harder for students to pay for college (again making them more vulnerable targets), and (5) the market demand for college education expanded.

Various strategies have been suggested for limiting student loan/aid fraud. One suggestion that some colleges have implemented is disbursing student loan funds twice a semester rather than once a semester (Queisser, Sutton, & Fultz, 2015). Another set of recommendations excerpted from another author team includes the following:

- Create an interdepartmental "fraud squad" to monitor potential illegal activity,
- Provide enhanced training to student financial aid staff—give them the confidence to deny financial aid to suspicious students,
- Create a policy to deny aid to suspicious individual(s),
- Wait two weeks before dispersing financial aid,
- Give students partial financial aid payments throughout the term rather than one lump sum payment,
- Record unsatisfactory academic performance,
- Look twice at individuals who have multiple addresses, similar IP or home addresses, or unusual student enrollment clusters,
- Create a system so faculty can report similar student assignments to alert staff about trends,
- Require students to take an orientation when they enroll,
- Require students to provide a copy of their high-school transcript when they enroll. (Lokken & Mullins, p. 6)

Students can also engage in actions to prevent being a victim of a scholarship scam. The Federal Trade Commission (2012) advises students to watch out for the following promises:

- "The scholarship is guaranteed or your money back."
- "You can't get this information anywhere else."
- "I just need your credit card or bank account number to hold this scholarship."
- "We'll do all the work. You just pay a processing fee."
- "The scholarship will cost some money."
- "You've been selected" by a 'national foundation' to receive a scholarship."
- "You're a finalist" in a contest you never entered." (FTC, 2012)

SUMMARY

- A wide range of offenses are committed in the economic system.
- When the term white-collar offender is used, it is often images of offenders from the economic or technological system that come to mind.
- The economic system includes banks, investment companies, stock markets across the world, commodities markets, and other exchanges and markets where individuals are able to make investments, purchase raw materials, and secure goods.
- The phrase "securities and commodities fraud" covers a broad concept, capturing a range of behaviors designed to rip off investors.
- Several specific varieties of these frauds exist, including market manipulation, broker embezzlement, hedge fund fraud, insider trading, futures trading fraud, foreign exchange fraud, high-yield investment schemes, advance-fee fraud, and Ponzi and pyramid schemes.
- Market manipulation refers to situations where executives or other officials do things to artificially inflate trading volume and subsequently affect the price of the commodity or security.
- Three federal statutes restrict market manipulation by energy companies: the Commodity Exchange Act, the Energy Policy Act of 2005, and the Energy Independence and Security Act of 2007.
- Broker fraud occurs when stockbrokers fail to meet their legal obligations to investors. Broker embezzlement occurs when brokers take money that is supposed to be in an investment account and use it for their own personal use.
- Hedge fund fraud refers to fraudulent acts perpetrated in hedge fund systems.
- Insider trading occurs when individuals share or steal information that "is material in nature" for future investments.

- Futures trading fraud refers to fraud occurring in the trading of futures contracts and options on the futures trading market.
- Ponzi and pyramid schemes scam investors by paying them from future investors' payments into the offender's scheme.
- Bernie Madoff was the mastermind behind what has come to be called the largest Ponzi scheme in the history of the United States.
- One benefit that has come out of Madoff's actions is that increased attention is being given to the warning signs, or "red flags," of Ponzi schemes.
- Several patterns characterize various dynamics surrounding investment fraud, including significant press attention, attributions of greed, increasing punitiveness, white-collar gangs, multiple offenses, regulatory changes, and negative consequences.
- To address the long-term consequences of investment frauds, Shover and his research team interviewed 47 victims of fraud a decade after their victimization. The results of the Shover research team's study showed that delegitimation effects dissipated over time, suggesting that investor confidence can be restored.
- Types of fraud occurring in the student financial aid process include (1) lying about intent to take classes, (2) taking out loans with no intent to pay them back, (3) lying about qualifications/income, (3) schemes or fraud rings designed to enroll students in college, (4) identity fraud to enhance qualifications, and (5) schemes targeting students with fee-based financial aid seminars

KEY TERMS

Advance-fee fraud	Front running	Insider trading
Broker embezzlement	Futures contracts	Investment fraud
Broker fraud	Futures trading fraud	Market manipulation
Commodities	Hedge fund fraud	Ponzi schemes
Commodities fraud	Hedge fund systems	Prearranged trading
Foreign exchange fraud	High-yield investment schemes	White-collar gangs

DISCUSSION QUESTIONS

1. Which crimes do you think do more harm—crimes against the economic system or street crimes? Explain.

2. How are crimes in the economic system similar to crimes in the health care system? What are some differences in the two categories of crime?

3. Do you think Martha Stewart's penalty was accurate? Why or why not?

4. What are some patterns surrounding investment fraud?

5. How does investment fraud impact your life as a student?

6. How does student loan fraud impact your life?

7. Is it a crime for a student to register for a class simply so he or she can get federal aid? Explain.

WEB RESOURCES

Investor Tip: http://www.investortrip.com/how-to-recognize-stock-market-manipulation-vs-normal-stock-market-movement/

SEC Law and Insider Trading: http://www.mystockoptions.com/articles/index.cfm/secID/D851C4F4-43AD-450C-A3EEB399AEFDED48

Student Loan Fraud: http://www.stopfraud.gov/report.html#studentloans

Federal Student Aid Rules: https://studentaid.ed.gov/sa/eligibility

STUDENT RESOURCES

The open-access Student Study Site, available at study.sagepub.com/paynewccess2e, includes useful study materials including SAGE journal articles and multimedia resources.

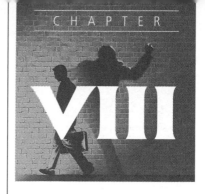

VIII

Crime in the Cyber System

CHAPTER HIGHLIGHTS

- Types of Cybercrime
- Types of Cybercriminals
- Costs of Cybercrime
- Explaining Cybercrime
- Responding to Crime in the Cyber System
- Problems Responding to Computer Crime
- The Interdisciplinary Response to Cybercrime
- Colleges and Cybercrime

I n November 2014, Sony pictures was on the receiving end of what was, at the time, one of the most publicized instances of computer hacking. The movie company was set to release *The Interview*, a comedy starring James Franco and Seth Rogen. The plot of the movie centered on Franco and Rogen's characters, who were ordered by the CIA to assassinate North Korea dictator Kim Jong-Un after they were given the opportunity to interview the leader as part of their journalistic endeavors. During the marketing campaign for the movie, hackers accessed the Sony computer system and began to release all sorts of details related to Sony's employees, actors, and business practices. Embarrassing e-mails about Hollywood stars, unreleased movies, private information, and identities of employees were distributed online by the hackers, who called themselves "Guardians of Peace." It was believed by some that the hackers were North Koreans who were upset about the movie. Eventually, Sony limited the widespread release of the movie and distributed it through online mediums. Sony employees sued the company for the harm they experienced from the **breach**.

In October 2015, the company settled the suit and agreed to pay up to $8 million to employees (with each affected employee receiving $10,000). For a time line of this hack, please see Grisham (2015).

Less than a year later, the dating site Ashley Madison faced a similar nightmare. Hackers accessed the names, contact information, and credit card numbers for those who used the dating site. This dating site differed in its clientele from other sites: it connected married people to those interested in committing adultery. The hackers, a group calling itself "The Impact Team," released the names and e-mail addresses of Ashley Madison customers on the Dark Web (which is a collection of websites accessible only when users have certain types of software). The hack received international attention. While many found the reports to be amusing, the real consequences were devastating for those exposed from the breach. Media reports suggested that at least a handful of suicides occurred as a result of the shame adulterers felt from being exposed internationally. For a time line of this hack see Bisson (2015).

While the Ashley Madison and the Sony cases received widespread attention, in reality they represented just two of the many different types of cyber offenses that target businesses. Many different types of computer-related offenses are perpetrated in workplace settings. Consider the following examples quoted verbatim from their original sources:

- A contract security guard at the North Central Medical Plaza on North Central Expressway in Dallas, pleaded guilty . . . to felony offenses related to his compromising and damaging the hospital's computer system . . . [the defendant], a/k/a "Ghost Exodus," 25, of Arlington, Texas, pleaded guilty to an indictment charging two counts of transmitting a malicious code. . . . [The defendant] gained physical access to more than 14 computers located in the North Central Medical Plaza, including a nurses' station computer on the fifth floor and a heating, ventilation and air conditioning (HVAC) computer located in a locked room. The nurses' station computer was used to track a patient's progress through the Carrell Memorial Clinic and medical staff also used it to reference patients' personal identifiers, billing records and medical history. . . . [The defendant] installed, or transmitted, a program to the computers that he accessed that allowed him, or anyone with his account name and password, to remotely access the computers. He also impaired the integrity of some of the computer systems by removing security features, e.g., uninstalling anti-virus programs, which made the computer systems and related network more vulnerable to attack. (U.S. Department of Justice, 2010a)
- ***** appeared before U.S. Magistrate Judge Nancy A. Vecchiarelli and pleaded guilty to a two-count Information filed on May 14, 2010, which charged ***** with causing damage to a protected computer system and possessing 15 or more unauthorized access devices. According to court documents, ***** admitted that between August 2006, and March 2007, while enrolled as a student at the University of Akron, he used the University's computer network to access IRC channels on the Internet to control other computers and computer networks via computers intentionally infected and taken over, known as "BotNet" zombies, which were located throughout the United States and in other countries. (U.S. Department of Justice, 2010b)
- A federal grand jury has returned an indictment charging former U.S. State Department employee ***** has been engaging in a hacking and cyberstalking scheme in which, using stolen passwords, he obtained sexually explicit photographs and other personal information from victims' email and social media accounts, and threatened to share the photographs and personal information unless the victims provided him with additional explicit photos and videos. (U.S. Department of Justice, 2015, Former U.S. government employee)
- Nine people were charged in two indictments unsealed today in Brooklyn, New York, and Newark federal court with an international scheme to hack into three business newswires and steal yet-to-be published press releases containing non-public financial information that was then used to make trades that allegedly generated approximately $30 million in illegal profits. (FBI, 2015, August 11)

In this chapter, attention is given to computer offenses in the workplace. In addressing these offenses, it is important to note that all types of computer crime are not necessarily white-collar crimes. For example, distributing child pornography on the Internet is a computer crime, but it is not a white-collar crime. As well, many computer crimes target businesses but are not necessarily committed by workers. In effect, one might broadly conceive these offenses as forms of white-collar victimization because they target businesses.

● ● ● Conceptualizing Crime in the Cyber System

Our technological system has made massive strides during our lifetime. Cell phones, liquid crystal display (LCD) televisions, laptops, and handheld technological devices are relatively recent creations. These items all came about as the result of technological advancements. While technological advancements have resulted in new products, the same advancements have also resulted in new types of crimes. In particular, computer crime (or cybercrime) has become an international concern.

The terms **computer crime and cybercrime** refer to a range of computer-related behaviors that are criminally illegal or otherwise harmful. In cases of computer crime, the computer is either a target of the offense (e.g., sabotage) or a tool for the crime (e.g., cyber fraud, piracy), or is incidental to the crime (e.g., containing evidence about a crime; Hale, 2002; Sinrod & Reilly, 2000). While not all "computer crimes" are necessarily illegal—consider times when workers spend the day surfing the Internet rather than working—legal changes beginning in 1978 have provided criminal definitions that prohibit computer crime. In 1978, Florida and Arizona became the first two states to pass laws related to computer crime. Florida's Computer Crime Act "defined all unauthorized access as a third degree felony regardless of the specific purpose" (Hollinger & Lanza-Kuduce, 1988, p. 114). Within 10 years, the majority of states and the federal government had followed suit.

Hollinger and Lanza-Kuduce (1988) note that the

▲ **Photo 8.1** We are so reliant on computers that it is natural to ask whether computers are good for our health. Many believe they are. On the other hand, the types of consequences experienced from cybercrime are hardly good for one's health.

public was somewhat apathetic with regard to the creation of these new laws. They also note that, unlike other legal developments, the media's reporting was "indispensable to the criminalization process" (p. 113). They also wrote that unlike other legal developments that are promoted by advocacy groups, efforts to reform the criminal law so it would respond more directly to computer crimes was led by "computer crime experts and legislators rather than moral entrepreneurs" (p. 101). More than three decades after these laws were first developed, computer crime laws have expanded and are routinely enforced by state and federal authorities.

While the phrase "computer crime" was initially used to characterize offenses involving computers, over the past decade an assortment of terms have been used to describe these behaviors. Among these terms are cybercrime, cyber offense, cyber deviance, digital crime, e-crime, high-tech crime, and Internet crime (see Figure 8.1). In this chapter, the terms" "cybercrime," "computer crime," and "cyber offense" will be used interchangeably. In addition, many different terms and concepts are used to describe various facets of cyber offending. In Focus 8.1 provides definitions of common terms as defined by the National Institute of Standards and Technology. These terms are frequently used to characterize different dimensions of offending in the cyber system. To provide a full understanding of crimes committed in the cyber system, in the following paragraphs attention is given to the following:

- Types of Cybercrime
- Types of Cybercriminals

Figure 8.1   Phrases Used to Describe Computer Crime

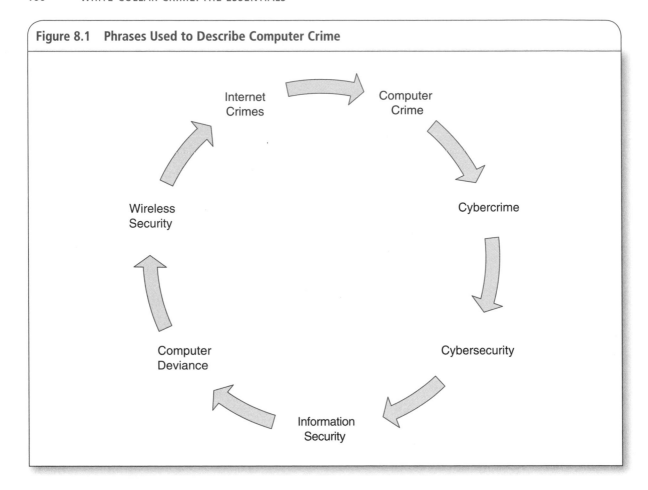

- Costs of Cybercrime
- Explaining Cybercrime
- Responding to Crime in the Cyber System
- Problems Responding to Computer Crime
- The Interdisciplinary Response to Cybercrime
- Colleges and Cybercrime

The dynamic and changing nature of computer crimes will be demonstrated through this discussion, and the way that the systems approach relates to this form of white-collar crime will be particularly evident.

● ● ● Types of Cybercrime

Experts have identified a laundry list of different types of computer crimes. These include hacking, cracking, phishing, extortion, child pornography, software piracy, money laundering, fraud, corporate espionage, cyberterrorism, surveillance, identity theft, cyber trespassing, cyber hoaxing, cyber bullying, online stalking, and hate speech (Minnaar, 2008; Sinrod & Reilly, 2000; Yar, 2006). In Focus 8.1 provides definitions of the many different terms and concepts related to these offenses.

For our purposes, the simplest way to understand computer crimes as white-collar crimes is to focus on general categories of computer crimes that target, or occur in, businesses. The following overlapping types of computer crimes warrant discussion: theft, unauthorized access, virus introduction, software crimes, and Internet crimes.

IN FOCUS 8.1

Key Terms in Cybersecurity

Antivirus Software: A program that monitors a computer or network to identify all major types of malware and prevent or contain malware incidents.

Backdoor: A malicious program that listens for commands on a certain Transmission Control Protocol (TCP) or User Datagram Protocol (UDP) port.

Blended Attack: An instance of malware that uses multiple infection or transmission methods.

Boot Sector Virus: A virus that infects the master boot record (MBR) of a hard drive or the boot sector of removable media, such as floppy diskettes.

Compiled Viruses: A virus that has had its source code converted by a compiler program into a format that can be directly executed by an operating system.

Cookie: A small data file that holds information regarding the use of a particular Web site.

Deny by Default: A configuration for a firewall or router that denies all incoming and outgoing traffic that is not expressly permitted, such as unnecessary services that could be used to spread malware.

Disinfecting: Removing malware from within a file.

Egress Filtering: Blocking outgoing packets that should not exit a network.

False Negative: An instance in which a security tool intended to detect a particular threat fails to do so.

False Positive: An instance in which a security tool incorrectly classifies benign content as malicious.

File Infector Virus: A virus that attaches itself to executable programs, such as word processors, spreadsheet applications, and computer games.

Host-Based Intrusion Prevention System: A program that monitors the characteristics of a single host and the events occurring within the host to identify and stop suspicious activity.

Indication: A sign that a malware incident may have occurred or may be occurring.

Ingress Filtering: Blocking incoming packets that should not enter a network.

Interpreted Virus: A virus that is composed of source code that can be executed only by a particular application.

Keystroke Logger: A device that monitors and records keyboard usage.

Macro Virus: A virus that attaches itself to application documents, such as word processing files and spreadsheets, and uses the application's macro programming language to execute and propagate.

Malware: A program that is inserted into a system, usually covertly, with the intent of compromising the confidentiality, integrity, or availability of the victim's data, applications, or operating system or of otherwise annoying or disrupting the victim.

Mass Mailing Worm: A worm that spreads by identifying e-mail addresses, often by searching an infected system, and then sending copies of itself to those addresses, either using the system's e-mail client or a self-contained mailer built into the worm itself.

(Continued)

(Continued)

Memory Resident: A virus that stays in the memory of infected systems for an extended period of time.

Mobile Code: Software that is transmitted from a remote system to be executed on a local system, typically without the user's explicit instruction.

Multipartite Virus: A virus that uses multiple infection methods, typically infecting both files and boot sectors.

Network Service Worm: A worm that spreads by taking advantage of a vulnerability in a network service associated with an operating system or an application.

Network-Based Intrusion Prevention System: A program that performs packet sniffing and analyzes network traffic to identify and stop suspicious activity.

On-Access Scanning: Configuring a security tool to perform real-time scans of each file for malware as the file is downloaded, opened, or executed.

On-Demand Scanning: Allowing users to launch security tool scans for malware on a computer as desired.

Payload: The portion of a virus that contains the code for the virus's objective, which may range from the relatively benign (e.g., annoying people, stating personal opinions) to the highly malicious (e.g., forwarding personal information to others, wiping out systems).

Persistent Cookie: A cookie stored on a computer indefinitely so that a Web site can identify the user during subsequent visits.

Phishing: Tricking . . . into disclosing sensitive personal information through deceptive computer-based means.

Precursor: A sign that a malware attack may occur in the future.

Proxy: A program that receives a request from a client, and then sends a request on the client's behalf to the desired destination.

Quarantining: Storing files containing malware in isolation for future disinfection or examination.

Remote Administration Tool: A program installed on a system that allows remote attackers to gain access to the system as needed.

Rootkit: A collection of files that is installed on a system to alter the standard functionality of the system in a malicious and stealthy way.

Session Cookie: A temporary cookie that is valid only for a single Website session.

Signature: A set of characteristics of known malware instances that can be used to identify known malware and some new variants of known malware.

Spyware: Malware intended to violate a user's privacy.

Spyware Detection and Removal Utility: A program that monitors a computer to identify spyware and prevent or contain spyware incidents.

Tracking Cookie: A cookie placed on a user's computer to track the user's activity on different Web sites, creating a detailed profile of the user's behavior.

Trigger: A condition that causes a virus payload to be executed, usually occurring through user interaction (e.g., opening a file, running a program, clicking on an e-mail file attachment).

Trojan Horse: A nonreplicating program that appears to be benign but actually has a hidden malicious purpose.

Virus: A form of malware that is designed to self-replicate; make copies of itself; and distribute the copies to other files, programs, or computers.

Web Browser Plug-In: A mechanism for displaying or executing certain types of content through a Web browser.

Web Bug: A tiny graphic on a Web site that is referenced within the Hypertext Markup Language (HTML) content of a Web page or e-mail to collect information about the user viewing the HTML content.

Worm: A self-replicating program that is completely self-contained and self-propagating.

Zombie: A program that is installed on a system to cause it to attack other systems.

Source: Reprinted From Mell, P., Kent, K., and Nusbaum, J. *Guide to Malware Incident Prevention and Handling*. National Institute of Standards and Technology. U.S. Department of Commerce.

Theft as a Computer Crime

Theft as a type of computer crime refers to a variety of computer-related activities that result in the offender stealing something from the business. Items stolen include funds, information, and intellectual property (Carter & Katz, 1996). In terms of theft of funds, computer crimes include computer fraud and computer embezzlement. In computer fraud cases, offenders gain access to an account they are not supposed to enter and steal from the account. In computer embezzlement cases, the offender already has authorized access to the account by virtue of his or her position in the business.

Theft of information occurs when offenders steal information including (a) information that can be used to trade securities and stocks and (b) intellectual property (Carter & Katz, 1996). One type of information theft, the theft of intellectual property, occurs when offenders steal information that is protected by copyright. Estimates suggest that 63 percent of computer theft of proprietary information in the U.S. is done by current employees or employees of other U.S. businesses (Sinrod & Reilly, 2000).

Cyber offenders sometimes use what are called phishing strategies to commit their offenses. **Phishing** refers to the distribution of a large number of e-mails to potential victims, inviting them to participate in a particular scheme. The schemes might include any of the following:

- Advance fee frauds, where victims are promised an extravagant item or service in exchange for a minimal upfront fee
- Refund scams, where victims are promised a refund for something they should have received in the past
- Fake greeting cards
- Fake reimbursements
- Fake lottery winnings
- Promises of assistance with a blocked inheritance (Minnaar, 2008)

Identity theft might also occur as a result of these cyber offenses. In these situations, offenders steal the identity of a victim and use that identity to receive credit, make purchases, and engage in business transactions. Identity theft has been characterized as more of a "social construction" than a "legal construction" on the basis that the behavior is not technically new behavior (Wall, 2013). Sometimes the size of these thefts may make them too small for authorities to investigate, and corporations are increasingly expecting victims to be responsible for protecting their identity (Wall, 2013). Also, according to one estimate, it may take more than two years for victims to recover any goods/funds they lost from identity offenses (Martin & Rice, 2011).

Not all criminologists define identity theft as a form of white-collar crime. The acts are often committed by unemployed and traditional offenders. Also, the behavior has been linked to terrorism, with one author team describing identity theft as "one of the most lucrative enterprises which terrorists have engaged in" (Perri & Brody, 2011, p. 55). In these situations, identity theft provides terrorists many items of value, including money, the ability to hide in plain sight, access across borders, and entrance into airports.

Unauthorized Access as a Computer Crime

Unauthorized access occurs when individuals break into various computer databases to which they do not have legitimate access. *Hacker* is a term used to describe those who have the skills to access various secure computer databases and programs but do so only out of a desire to experiment to see if they are able to access these programs. **Crackers** crack into computer systems "with [the intent] to sabotage and cause chaos to [the] corporation" (Wiggins, 2002, p. 20). Health care providers and utility companies are believed to be especially vulnerable to these incidents (Rogers, 2002).

Two types of crackers exist—those outside the targeted business and those inside the business. Crackers outside the business engage in their activities to "cause disruption to the networks for personal or political motives" (Sinrod & Reilly, 2000, p. 5 [e-version]). Hacktivism is the concept of politically motivated cracking and hacking. Some crackers may commit their acts in order to highlight security problems to the company. Others might commit electronic theft of credit card information, while some may engage in what is called Netspionage (e.g., stealing confidential information) (Philippsohn, 2001).

When insiders are the crackers, a different set of concerns arise. Data breaches by insiders have been found to be more costly than breaches by outsiders (Ponemon, 2015, Cost of Data Breach).

According to Sinrod and Reilly, "disgruntled employees are the greatest threat to a computer's security" (p. 7 [e-version]). Another expert suggested that cyber intrusions are "usually not an 'outside' job" (Minnaar, 2013, p. iii). When insiders break into computer systems, they are believed to do so for any of the following reasons:

- Destroying information valuable to the company
- Finding secrets than can be sold
- Deleting client lists
- Destroying information that the company would find valuable
- Selling lists of clients/consumers to competitors (Minnaar, 2013)

The term extrusion specifically refers to instances when employees access information and provide that information to outsiders. Typically, companies are most vulnerable to this when employees are leaving a company (Finkel, 2014). As a result, companies frequently shut down data access of departing employees as soon as possible.

Even if insiders are not the offenders in the cyber intrusion, employees may be targeted for entry points into a company's databases. One cybersecurity advisor told a journalist, "hackers have increased their focus on trying to enter an enterprise network through 'soft' targets (i.e., users and employees) rather than trying to attack the servers, switches, and networks" (C. Meyer, 2015, p. 34). Indeed, sometimes the threat posed by insiders stems from unintentional but negligent actions. These threats include behaviors such as (1) keeping sensitive information on personal devices that are not safe (e.g., if your professor kept your grades on a public computer), (2) failing to understand how to respond to cyberattacks, (3) sharing passwords with friends or co-workers, and (4) selecting passwords that are easy to identify (Ritchie, 2014). Incidentally, here are the most popular passwords from 2014 according to security firm SplashData:

- 123456
- password
- 12345
- 12345678
- qwerty
- 1234567890
- baseball
- dragon
- football
- 1234567
- monkey
- letmein
- abc123
- 111111
- mustang
- access
- shadow
- master
- michael
- superman
- 696969
- 123123
- batman
- trustno1 (*Sky News*, January 21, 2015)

There is no way of knowing how many data breaches occur each year. These are cases that are especially hard to detect. While virus protection software will alert companies to the introduction of viruses, it is not as easy to detect a cyber intrusion. One estimate suggests that it takes on average 243 days before breaches are detected (Kawalec, 2014). As well, the time it takes to "recover" from intrusions has grown from a two week "recovery time" in 2010 to a one month "recovery time" in 2013 (Kawalec, 2013).

After cyber intrusions occur, companies will decide whether to notify law enforcement. Reasons that companies choose to notify the police about these intrusions include the following:

▲ **Photo 8.2**   User behavior can increase or decrease the likelihood of cyber victimization.

- The police may be able to help catch the cyber offenders and keep them away from the company's computer systems.
- The police are in a position to help the company retrieve the stolen data, if possible. If it is not possible, the police may be helpful in minimizing losses.
- Working with law enforcement can strengthen the skills of the company security team.
- The company may have a legal obligation to report the intrusion (Chabinsky, 2013).

Alternatively, failure to report these incidents may be illegal, open the business up to civil lawsuits, increase their risk of cyber victimization, and lead to negative publicity (Davis, 2003).

In some ways, being a victim of cybersecurity offenses, and failing to report that victimization, may actually result in a company committing a white-collar crime. In these situations, mistakes that companies might make include failing to notify the SEC of cyber incidents, failing to follow protocol established by the company, failing to follow comprehensive breach policies, and failing to monitor cyber risks that surface when working with other business partners or contractors (Reed & Scott, 2013). Companies and employees could be prosecuted for any of these failures.

One author team has identified four pragmatic actions that companies should perform after a data breach: (1) identify the attack, (2) manage the offense, (3) restore operations, and (4) communicate with stakeholders (McNerney & Papadopoulos, 2013). Another expert recommended answering a series of questions that should be asked in order to determine how to respond. These questions include: (1) what kind of cyber-attack occurred?; (2) why did it occur?; and (3) who committed the intrusion? (Brenner, 2007). The answers to these questions will determine whether the action is defined as a type of cybercrime, a type of terrorism, or cyber warfare. In turn, this determination will dictate which officials should be notified about the intrusion.

Recent attention has been given to the confusion that surfaces surrounding data breaches. One issue that arises is that there is no central agency responsible for monitoring data breaches. Some researchers have called for "the creation of a federal agency to deal with national data breaches across all industries [as a] next logical step" (J. D. Collins, Saintano, & Khey, 2011, p. 807). In theory, such an agency would allow government resources to be allocated in a way that protects the most vulnerable industries in a fair way.

Virus Introduction as a Computer Crime

Virus introduction is another type of computer crime. Viruses are introduced for various reasons. Crackers typically introduce viruses for recreational reasons, pride, profit, protection, or cyberterrorism reasons. Recreationally, just as some unsupervised youth might vandalize public property, crackers find pleasure in "vandalizing" computer programs. In terms of pride, successfully sabotaging computer programs that are difficult to break into provides crackers a sense of accomplishment. In terms of profit, crackers can profit either from stealing funds themselves or from being paid by a coconspirator who is unable to carry out the crime alone. Also, viruses are introduced as a form of protection by employees to cover up evidence of their thefts and protect them from being identified (Carter & Katz, 1996).

With regard to cyberterrorists, crackers aim to use viruses to threaten public security. Note that the types of activities of cyberterrorists are much different from the virus introducing activities of traditional crackers. Consider the following two examples described by Barry C. Collin (2001) of the Institute for Security and Intelligence at the 11th Annual Symposium of Criminal Justice Issues:

- A CyberTerrorist will remotely access the processing control systems of a cereal manufacturer, change the levels of iron supplement, and sicken and kill the children of a nation enjoying their food. That CyberTerrorist will then perform similar remote alterations at a processor of infant formula. The key: the CyberTerrorist does not have to be at the factory to execute these acts. (Collin, 2001)
- A CyberTerrorist will attack the next generation of air traffic control systems, and collide two large civilian aircraft. This is a realistic scenario, since the CyberTerrorist will also crack the aircraft's in-cockpit sensors. Much of the same can be done to the rail lines. (Collin, 2001)

Some will question whether cyberterrorism is a form of white-collar crime. To be sure, not all cases would necessarily fit within the types of behaviors typically characterized as white-collar crimes. However, note that some companies might commit cyberterroristic activities against others, and when businesses are targeted, it can be suggested that they have experienced a form of white-collar victimization. The enormous threats that cyberterrorists pose for businesses and governments have led state and federal officials to develop cyberterrorism law enforcement units.

Viruses may also be introduced in the form of denial-of-service attacks. These attacks make programs or websites nonfunctional (Bartolacci, LeBlanc, & Podhradsky, 2014). Generally speaking, two types of denial-of-service attacks exist: permanent denial of service and personal denial-of-service attacks. Permanent denials (also known as phlashing) aim to make software or a computer system permanently inaccessible. In contrast, in personal denials, a specific individual or business is targeted. The differences in the two varieties center on the nature of the victim, the motivation, the consequences, and the processes used by the offender to carry out the attack (Bartolacci et al., 2014).

Ransomware is an example of a personal denial-of-service attack. With ransomware, offenders are able to stop a victim's computer from working and essentially hold that computer hostage until a ransom is paid or the virus is removed. One popular form of ransomware was the Moneypak virus. This virus attaches itself to the victim's computer and threatens to prosecute the victim for a copyright violation, child pornography, or some other offense unless the victim pays a "fine" using an untraceable prepaid Moneypak card. The FBI's seal appears on the frozen computer screen and, in some cases, the camera from the computer is activated and a video of the victim appears in the upper left hand of the computer screen. The official appearance of the virus led many victims to actually pay the offender. Victims would realize they were victimized when the offender never released the virus from the computer.

Software Crime as a Computer Crime

Software crimes refer to situations when computer software is central to the offense. Four overlapping types of software crimes exist: (1) theft of software, (2) counterfeiting software, (3) copyright violations of computer software, and (4) piracy (L. M. Wiggins, 2002). **Theft of software** refers to instances when workers steal computer software that their company owns and use it for their personal use. Imagine a situation where a worker has a copy of a photo editing program. The computer software is supposed to be loaded only on the worker's office computer. If the worker takes the software home and loads it on his or her home computer so family members can use the software for personal reasons, then misconduct has occurred.

Counterfeiting software crimes occur when individuals make counterfeit copies of particular software programs. Microsoft (2010) describes these crimes as resulting from "unauthorized copying, reproduction, or manufacture of software products." Once the counterfeit software is produced, it is sold to consumers (a) by fraudulent business owners, (b) through e-mail scams, (c) in online auction sites like eBay, (d) on websites like Amazon.com, and (e) by street vendors (Microsoft, 2010). In what was called the "most significant crackdown on software piracy," the FBI and Chinese authorities arrested more than two dozen individuals as part of an offense involving "more than $500 million worth of counterfeit Microsoft and Symantec software that was being made in China and distributed worldwide" (Barboza & Lohr, 2007).

Copyright violations of computer software occur when users use software for purposes beyond what was intended under the copyright agreement described on the software. This could include illegally reproducing, altering, selling, or misrepresenting software programs. Piracy is also seen as a type of copyright violation.

Electronic and software piracy refers to theft of copyright-protected electronic information, including software, electronic programs, and electronic files of movies and music. The Digital Millennium Copyright Act of 1998 was passed in an effort to limit piracy and copyright violations. The law stipulates that it is illegal to possess, sell, or distribute code-cracking devices and calls for stiff penalties for offenders (Higgins, 2006). Much more will be written about piracy (see below) when considering students and computer crime. At this point, it is significant to note that the government has been building its efforts to respond to piracy. These efforts are captured in a statement Vice President Joe Biden made to reporters: "Piracy is theft. Clean and simple. It's smash and grab. It ain't no different than smashing a window at Tiffany's and grabbing [merchandise]."

Internet Crimes

Internet crimes are a range of offenses committed by offenders through the use of the Internet. A decade ago, it was estimated that Internet crime losses totaled one trillion dollars across the world (Rataj, 2001). Examples of Internet crimes reported to the FBI (2010c) include the following:

- Fake e-mail messages from the FBI: scammers sending potential victims e-mail messages requesting funds as part of an FBI investigation
- Nondelivered merchandise: not receiving merchandise purchased on an Internet website
- Nonpayment for items sold on the Internet: not being paid for items sold through auction sites or other Internet websites
- Advance-fee fraud: requesting fees for goods or services that will never be provided
- Identity theft: stealing and falsely using someone's personal identity information
- Overpayment fraud: sending a counterfeit check for a purchase and asking for the difference to be returned

Table 8.1 shows the number of complaints the FBI's Internet Crime Complaint Center received and the losses attached to those complaints between 2004 and 2014. As shown in the table, the number of complaints has actually dropped since 2011, though the costs of the offenses have increased. In fact, these financial costs increased from under $500 million to just over $800 million between 2011 and 2014. Recent e-mail scams identified by the FBI include (a) a hit man scheme where individuals receive e-mail messages from an assassin offering not to kill them in exchange for money, (b) pop-ups promising free astrological readings that turn out not to be free, (c) economic stimulus scams where recipients are told how to receive funds from the stimulus package but only after entering their personal information, and (d) fake pop-up ads that download viruses (FBI, 2010c).

● ● ● Characteristics of Cybercriminals

Just as there are different types of cybercrimes, so too there are different types of cybercriminals. The most general characterization can focus on characteristics of cybercriminals in terms of their (1) roles in the offense and (2) the networks to which they are attached. In terms of their role in the offense, some cybercriminals may operate alone, while others may work with other offenders. One criminal justice scholar classified cyber offenders as loners, associates, and

Table 8.1	Internet Crime Complaints to the FBI, 2004–2014	
Year	**Complaints**	**Loss (in millions)**
2004	207,449	$68
2005	231,493	$183
2006	207,492	$198
2007	206,884	$239
2008	275,284	$265
2009	336,655	$559.7
2010	303,809	n/a
2011	314,246	$485.3
2012	289,874	$525.4
2013	262,813	$781.8
2014	269,422	$800.5

Source: Compiled from Federal Bureau of Investigation (n.d.a–n.d.c). Internet Crime Reports. Fairmont, WV: National White Collar Crime Center.

crime networks (Rege-Patwardhan, 2013). From this typology, loners include novice offenders, insiders, and professionals who work alone (Rege-Patwardhan, 2009). An example of professionals are *cyber mercenaries* or "specialists who sell their knowledge and training to whoever is willing to pay" (Valeri, 1998, p. 52). Services are even available online where hackers are rated based on how well they perform (Kawalec, 2014).

The concept of "network" is relevant to cybercriminals in three different ways: (1) these are offenders who are very familiar with computer networks, software, and technology; (2) cyber offenders often work in a network with other offenders; and (3) cyber offenders often are part of a broader distribution network that mimics the way traditional goods are distributed. Regarding their familiarity with computer networks, cyber offenders have the knowledge and skills to access various computer networks. Consider botnets as an illustration. A botnet is a group of infected computers under the simultaneous control of one offender while those computers are connected to the Internet. It is nearly impossible to determine the source of the botnet or the identity of the offender (van der Wagen & Pieters, 2015). It is important to note that their access to these computer networks is not immediate. According to one expert, "successful intrusions almost always occur by hackers who first got away with thousands of unsuccessful intrusion attempts" (Chabinsky, 2015, April 1, p. 46).

These actions frequently occur within an offender network. A review of Department of Justice cases from 2010 found that more than half of the cases involved offenders who collaborated with other offenders (Lusthaus, 2012). In these cases, offenders assume "cybercriminal identities" to maintain anonymity. This is different from conventional crimes where fake identities are rare. Some have drawn attention to "cybergangs" to describe the relationships between these offenders. According to G. S. Smith (2015), the characteristics of cybergangs are the following:

- They are formed because of their expertise.
- They communicate online.
- They have strong technological skills.

- Whereas traditional gangs have reputations across neighborhoods, their reputation is online.
- While traditional gangs control a small part of a neighborhood, these gangs cover international areas.
- They tend to be more flexible than traditional gangs.
- Their motive is profit and information, not violence.
- They tend to have self-taught skills.

Organized crime networks have also been connected to cybercrime. First, in some situations, organized crime groups might use cyber technology to commit crimes such as prostitution, gambling, and so on. Second, some organized crime networks (such as those cited by Smith above) might operate purely online. Third, some organized crime groups might use cyber technology to create havoc in order to promote their political or ideological beliefs.

With regard to the distribution network, when cyber offenders steal information for profit motives, they need to find ways to sell that information. Similar to the way that burglars and other thieves fence their goods, cyber offenders use different strategies to distribute their stolen information. One research team studied 300 threads in a web-based discussion forum to shed light on the way stolen data is marketed online (Holt & Lampke, 2010). Below is an example of what one such post in a web forum looks like:

1) Dumps from all over the world Original Track 1/Track 2

1.1) EUROPE Dumps Track 1/Track 2

Europe and the rest of world (Following countries are not included: Swiss, Spain, France,

Italy, Turkey, Germany, Australia)

Visa Classic, MasterCard Standart - $60 per 1 dump

38 *T.J. Holt and E. Lampke*

Visa Classic, MasterCard Standart (Swiss, Spain, France, Italy, Turkey, Germany,

Australia) - $70 per 1 dump

Visa Gold | Platinum | Business, MasterCard Gold | Platinum - $100 per 1 dump

Visa Gold | Platinum | Business, MasterCard Gold | Platinum (Swiss, Spain, France,

Italy, Turkey, Germany, Australia) - $120 per 1 dump

1.2) USA Dumps Original Track 1/Track 2

DUMPS Visa Gold | Platinum | Business | Signature, MasterCard Gold | Platinum,

American Express, Discover

Dumps with Name,Address,City,State,Zip,Phone - $100 per 1 dump

Dumps with Name,Address,City,State,Zip,Phone,SSN and DOB - $120 per 1 dump

DUMPS Visa Classic, MasterCard Standard

Dumps with Name,Address,City,State,Zip,Phone - $80 per 1 dump

Dumps with Name,Address,City,State,Zip,Phone,SSN and DOB - $90 per 1 dump

1.3) CANADA Dumps Original Track 1/Track 2

Visa Classic, MasterCard Standart

Amount: >10<50 - $19.5 per 1 dump

Amount: >50<100 - $14.5 per 1 dump

Amount: >100 - $12.5 per 1 dump

Visa Gold | Platinum | Business, MasterCard Gold | Platinum

Amount: >10<50 - $34.5 per 1 dump

Amount: >50<100 - $32.5 per 1 dump (Holt & Lampke, 2010, p. 38).

The items sold most often were dumps. Holt and Lampke (2010) explain that the term dump is used to refer to the credit card or bank account information being marketed. Track 1 "dumps" include the credit card number, name of cardholder, and some additional information, while Track 2 "dumps" include the card information, the encrypted pin, and some additional information. Track 2 dumps are more common.

Other items marketed included compromised bank accounts, compromised PayPal accounts, plastics (blank cards that could be converted into credit cards), e-mail databases, and hacking services. As with other online forums, buyers could even rate the data thieves as verified (they have sold before), unverified, or "rippers." Here is a review of a ripper:

THIS GUY IS A RIPPER HE RIP ME FOR A LOT OF MONEY AND SENT ME ALL

BOGUS DUMPS . . . WE HAVE TO HAVE HONOR WITH EACH OTHER IN

ORDER TO KEEP THIS BUSINESS FLOWING YOU HAVE TOOK MONEY

FROMA FEWLLOW CARDER KNOWING YOUR DUMPS ARE BOGUS . . . YOU'RE A MARK IN THE DARK AND A PUNK IN THE TRUNK F**K YOU! (Holt & Lampke, 2010, p. 44)

If you ever purchase stolen data, you are advised not to pay with your credit card! Incidentally, the authorities sometimes infiltrate these networks. (See White-Collar Crime in the News: Cyber Police Break Intro Hacker's Network).

● ● ● Costs of Cybercrime

As noted in Chapter 2, the costs of all white-collar crimes include physical, social, and economic consequences and these consequences can be quite significant. The physical and social costs of cybercrime can be particularly devastating, but they are not well-studied. On one hand, imagine a time when you did not have access to technology and how that impacted you both personally and socially. We have become so dependent on technology that some psychologists have suggested that some individuals may, in fact, become addicted to technology. For those who are addicted, instances when cyber offending stops individuals from accessing their technology will cause both physical and social consequences. More pragmatically, instances when cyber offenses attack the critical infrastructure can also result in both physical and social losses for members of society.

The phrase **critical infrastructure** refers to parts of the public sector that societies rely on in order to provide basic services. The USA Federal Critical Infrastructure Protection Policy identifies the following sectors as critical infrastructures:

- Agriculture
- Banking
- Chemicals and hazardous wastes
- Defense industry
- Energy services
- Food
- Government
- Information technology/telecom

WHITE-COLLAR CRIME IN THE NEWS

Cyber Police Break Into Hacker's Network

https://commons.wikimedia.org/wiki/File:Computer_hacking.jpg.

Cyber offenses are not typically detected through traditional forms of law enforcement, though the traditional strategies may serve as a starting point for investigations.

It was, in effect, a one-stop, high-volume shopping venue for some of the world's most prolific cyber criminals. Called Darkode, this underground, password-protected, online forum was a meeting place for those interested in buying, selling, and trading malware, botnets, stolen personally identifiable information, credit card information, hacked server credentials, and other pieces of data and software that facilitated complex cyber crimes all over the globe.

Unbeknownst to the operators of this invitation-only, English-speaking criminal forum, though, the FBI had infiltrated this communication platform at the highest levels and began collecting evidence and intelligence on Darkode members.

And today, the Department of Justice and the FBI—with the assistance of our partners in 19 countries around the world—announced the results of Operation Shrouded Horizon, a multi-agency investigation into the Darkode forum. Among those results were charges, arrests, and searches involving 70 Darkode members and associates around the world; U.S. indictments against 12 individuals associated with the forum, including its administrator; the serving of several search warrants in the U.S.; and the Bureau's seizure of Darkode's domain and servers.

Said FBI Deputy Director Mark Giuliano, "Cyber criminals should not have a safe haven to shop for the tools of their trade, and Operation Shrouded Horizon shows we will do all we can to disrupt their unlawful activities."

During the investigation, the Bureau focused primarily on the Darkode members responsible for developing, distributing, facilitating, and supporting the most egregious and complex cyber criminal schemes targeting victims and financial systems around the world, including in the United States.

The Darkode forum, which had between 250-300 members, operated very carefully—not just anyone could join. Ever fearful of compromise by law enforcement, Darkode administrators made sure prospective members were heavily vetted.

Similar to practices used by the Mafia, a potential candidate for forum membership had to be sponsored by an existing member and sent a formal invitation to join. In response, the candidate had to post an online introduction—basically, a résumé—highlighting the individual's past criminal activity, particular cyber skills, and potential contributions to the forum. The forum's active members decided whether to approve applications.Once in the forum, members—in addition to buying and selling criminal cyber products and services—used it to exchange ideas, knowledge, and advice on any number of cyber-related fraud schemes and other illegal activities. It was almost like a think tank for cyber criminals.

Source: Reprinted from FBI (2015, July 15). Cyber criminal forum taken down. https://www.fbi.gov/news/stories/2015/july/cyber-criminal-forum-taken-down

- Postal and shipping
- Public health and health care
- Transportation
- Water treatment and drinking water (Skylar, 2012)

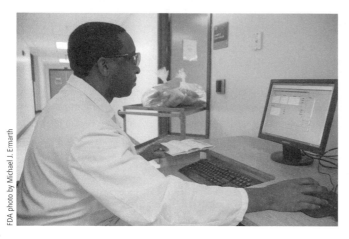

▲ **Photo 8.3**   Health care providers rely heavily on computers to do their jobs. Cyberattacks on hospitals could be devastating.

The operations of each of these sectors relies heavily on technology. Depending on the types of services offered by the critical infrastructure, the consequences from attacks on these entities could range from food poisoning to freezing temperatures to pollution to heat exposure to traffic delays (Rege-Patwardhan, 2009). Concern about a cyberattack on the critical infrastructure led former Secretary of Defense Leon Panetta to warn about the possibility of a "cyber Pearl Harbor" (McNerney & Papadopoulos, 2013, p. 1244).

One of the first publicized cyberattacks on a critical infrastructure involved a teenager's attack on a computer system of the Worcester, Massachusetts, computer system. The attack crippled the airport for six hours (Rege-Patwardhan, 2013). Cases can be true examples of white-collar offenses where employees commit crime as part of their job. In 2006, for example, two disgruntled engineers hacked into the Los Angeles Traffic Surveillance Center's computer system as part of a protest against the wage paid to city engineers. The hackers created havoc by programming traffic lights near major intersections so as to create gridlock (Rege-Patwardhan, 2013). While no injuries occurred from this critical infrastructure attack, the possibility existed. Of course, there were certainly economic costs arising out of the attack in terms of public safety efforts directed toward protecting motorists from the malfunctioning stoplights.

The Ponemon Institute (a cybersecurity think tank) categorizes the costs of cybercrime into internal and external costs. Internal costs refer to costs experienced within the company. These include detection costs, investigation costs, containment costs, recovering costs, and ex-post responding costs. External costs refer to costs involving parties or relationships outside the business. These include information loss, business disruption, damaged equipment, and revenue loss (Ponemon, 2015).

The most recent estimates of the costs of cyber offending come from the Ponemon Institute's (2015) Cost of Cybercrime Survey. The institute interviewed 2,128 employees working in 252 companies across seven countries. The study found that, on average, the companies reported losing $7.7 million a year to cyberattacks. The U.S. had the highest average losses at roughly $15 million per company, while Russia had the lowest average cost at $2.37 million. While all types of organizations incurred losses, the losses were higher in the financial, utility, and energy industries.

The 2015 Ponemon study also found that just over one-third of the companies attributed some of their attacks to a malicious insider. There may be reason to believe that the role of insiders varies across countries. In terms of cost, in the U.S., ten percent of the costs from cyberattacks were attributed to insiders, while in Japan, 19 percent of the costs from cyberattacks were attributed to insiders. In Germany, six percent of the total costs were attributed to insiders. Another important pattern surrounding insider attacks is that they take longer to address than other attacks. Once identified, insider attacks took an average of 54.4 days to address, while other attacks took much less time: web attacks took 27 days, phishing took 22 days, and denial of service attacks took 22 days. The average cost for insider attacks was also higher than all other attacks: they cost $144,542 on average in comparison to an average cost of $1,900 for viruses and worms.

Explaining Computer Crime

Although it is impossible to know for certain why computer crimes occur, a handful of explanations that are routinely cited will likely help clarify the source of many of these offenses. In particular, computer crimes are commonly attributed to human factors, opportunity, structural changes, peer associations, and cultural factors. Each of these explanations will be briefly reviewed here and discussed in more detail when causes of all forms of white-collar crime are considered later in this text.

The explanations of *human factors* focus on the types of activities individuals and businesses engage in and how those activities contribute to offending. For example, research shows that cyber intrusions against universities are more likely to occur during business hours and that the fewest intrusions occur between 5 pm and 12:59 am (Maimon, Kamerdze, Cukier, & Sobesto, 2013). The same study found that attack patterns were related to foreign students' countries of origin, which suggests that "the human element is a key component when dealing with computer security" (p. 337). Another study of 600 students and faculty found that factors involved with cyber victimization included using someone's Internet without their permission, viewing pornography, pirating media, and cyber harassment (Holt & Bossler, 2013). Elsewhere, the same author team found that, for students, engaging in computer deviance may increase individuals' risk of being victimized by malicious software (Bossler & Holt, 2014). The authors suggest that because online behaviors may contribute to victimization risk, "crime and victimization in the real world may be replicated in online environments" (p. 414). In fact, for some types of cyber victimization, it has been found that behaviors and activities of victims are related to victimization, while presence of guardianship (e.g., malware) was not (Holt & Bossler, 2008).

Opportunity explanations center on the ease by which these offenses are committed, particularly for those who have a high degree of knowledge about computers. Offenders can target a high number of victims with great ease and relatively quickly—sometimes with a few key strokes on the computer keyboard. From this perspective, the steady availability of and access to computers provides offenders opportunities to commit all sorts of crimes. Many criminal justice sanctions for convicted computer criminals are based on the belief that opportunity contributes to the crime. As a condition of probation, many offenders are not allowed to own computers or live in a home where computers are present. The assumption is that restricting the opportunity for computer crime will prevent computer crimes from occurring.

Some experts attribute computer crimes to *structural changes*, an explanation that fits well within the ideals of the systems perspective. When I was born in the early 1980s (okay, I'm fibbing about the date), there was virtually no concern about computer crime. Technology was extremely limited. I have fond memories of playing Pong with my brother on our 26-inch black-and-white Zenith television. The television didn't have a remote control—unless you consider my brother and me as my father's remote control. In any event, changes in the technological, educational, social, and political systems resulted in technological advancements that have changed our society. One technological change entailed an increase in the use of computers to the point that virtually all businesses and most individuals in the United States now are computer literate. The increased presence of computers, then, provides new criminogenic opportunities. Consider that the advent of the Internet has resulted in different types of computer crimes (Yar, 2006). It is important to note that the crimes committed with computers are not all necessarily new crimes but that the technologies for committing the crimes are new (Montano, 2001). As shown above, crimes such as theft, trespassing, and vandalism are committed with computers. These are not new crimes per se, though new laws are used to respond to instances where these crimes are committed with the use of computers.

These technological changes may, however, lead to different varieties of crime. Consider, for example "cyborg crime" (van der Wagen & Pieters, 2015). The hybrid nature of human/technological behavior may lead to new interactions, which have been labeled cyborg crime. While a human's actions might initiate a technological action, technology can now act or behave in a way that alters the crime or carries out additional violations. In other words, robots—in the near future—might actually commit crime! Whether one agrees with this possibility, most experts agree that in order to understand cyber offending, attention must be given to both network factors and human factors.

Computer crimes have also been explained by *peer association*, which suggests that the crimes occur as the result of individuals being associated with peers who might be more prone to commit these offenses. Studies of middle school students (Holt, Bossler, & May, 2012) and college students (Gunter, 2009) have supported these explanations. One study found that the seriousness of computer crimes committed by college students was tied to negative peer associations—the more negative peer associations students had, the more serious the types of computer misconduct they committed (Morris & Blackburn, 2009). In another study, a survey of 581 college students found that factors contributing to piracy and illegal access included differential associations, imitation, and differential reinforcement (Skinner & Fream, 1997). The same pattern has been found for cyber victimization: having peers who engaged in cyber deviance has been found to increase the likelihood of experiencing cyber harassment (Holt & Bossler, 2008).

Cultural factors also impact cyber offending. Cybercrime is an international problem, but certain countries may be at a higher risk for different types of cyber offenses. One author, for example, has pointed to five factors that place China and Taiwan at a high risk for cyber offenses between the two countries:

1. Both countries have high populations of Internet users.

2. Residents are not fully aware of appropriate security precautions.

3. A similar language and culture between the two countries makes it easier for offenders to attack one another.

4. Security companies resist developed measures (e.g., malware) that would work only in Chinese systems.

5. Political tensions between the two countries may increase the likelihood of offending (Chang, 2013).

Of course, there is no definitive explanation for why computer crimes occur. Explanations vary across offenders and offense types. For example, factors that lead males to commit computer crimes might be different from the factors that contribute to females' decisions to commit these offenses. As well, the causes of virus introductions might be different from the causes of computer fraud or computer embezzlement. Unfortunately, few studies have focused on the motivations for computer crime. Being unable to accurately pinpoint the causes of these behaviors has made it more difficult for authorities to respond to computer crimes.

Problems Responding to Computer Crimes

In addition to the fact that the causes of computer crime are not clear, other factors have made it more difficult to respond to computer crimes. These problems stem from the dynamics of the offense, awareness issues, offender characteristics, jurisdictional issues, criminal justice dynamics, victim characteristics and decisions, and collaboration issues. With regard to the dynamics of the offense, four issues arise. First, computer crime is an offense that occurs very quickly (Carter & Katz, 1996). Some have referred to the crimes as "hit and run" offenses because of how quickly the offenses occur (McMullan & Perrier, 2007). Second, the offenses, by their very nature, are international in scope, making it difficult to even know where the crime actually occurred (Speer, 2000). Third, the technological nature of the crimes allows the offenses to occur without victims even realizing that they have been victimized until hours, days, weeks, or even months after the offense occurred. Fourth, the nature of computer offenses is constantly changing, making it more difficult to watch for signs of the crimes. Indirectly discussing these offense dynamics, one author wrote: "'Online' is a vast place that promises lots of anonymity as well as eager collectors and conspirators. There is little in the way of a paper trail in these cases, and hardly anyone around to recall a face" (Scullin, 2014, p. 91).

This relates to awareness issues that make it difficult to respond to cybercrime. Common misconceptions about cybercrime are that only tech companies are targeted for these crimes and only IT staff needs to respond (Chabinsky, 2015, April 1; May 1; Davis, 2003). One expert adds the following misconceptions that businesses and employees have about cybercrime:

- It is wrongly assumed that employees should be the first line of defense to cyberattacks, when they should be the last line of defense.
- Companies sometimes erroneously believe they are insulated against cyberattacks.
- Smaller business owners and employees might incorrectly assume they will not be targeted.
- If the federal authorities are notified, a raid will follow.
- Federal oversight will protect all businesses.
- Information sharing is simple and straightforward.
- Companies should devote their efforts toward defense, with little concern given to identifying offenders.
- Businesses can become invincible to attacks.
- Computer patches can be used to stop attacks (Chabinsky, 2015, April 1; May 1).

These misconceptions can leave businesses vulnerable to attacks. It has been suggested that the sources of many misconceptions about cyber offending include inaccurate reporting by the media, the failure of victims to report victimization, conceptual ambiguity regarding cybercrime, and jurisdictional differences in cybercrime definitions (Wall, 2013).

In terms of offender characteristics, computer offenders tend to be highly educated people who are able to go to great lengths to conceal their crime and their identity. When a conventional offender robs a bank, witnesses see the offender, and cameras may even provide pictures of the suspect. When a computer criminal robs a bank, no one sees the criminal, and pictures are certainly not available. Offenders' technical knowledge is the equivalent of the stereotypical ski mask that conventional offenders wear in old cops-and-robbers movies.

Jurisdictional issues also surface and make it more difficult to address cybercrimes, particularly those that cross international borders. If a cybercrime starts in one country and ends in another country, which country has jurisdiction? What if the information "traveled through" the cyberspace of yet another country? These questions make it fundamentally more difficult to address cybercrimes (Bernate & Godlove, 2012). Legal expert Susan Brenner (2006) identified the following additional jurisdictional challenges that may surface in cybercrime cases:

- There may be cases where no government has jurisdiction.
- It may be impossible for a particular government to "assert" jurisdiction.
- Multiple countries might claim jurisdiction over the same offense.

Summarizing these challenges, Brenner (2006) writes that "pieces of the cybercrime occur in territory claimed by several different sovereigns" (p. 189).

Criminal justice dynamics also contribute to problems in responding to computer crimes. Often, criminal justice professionals are not adequately trained in how to respond to computer crimes (Carter & Katz, 1996). Also, solving these offenses requires collaboration between criminal justice agencies, and such collaboration may be difficult to carry out at times (Montano, 2001). In some cases, international collaboration may be necessary (Speer, 2000). Criminal justice officials must grapple with resource deployment issues in deciding the amount of fiscal resources and workload to devote to responding to computer crimes (McMullan & Perrier, 2007).

Victim characteristics and behaviors inhibit the response to computer crimes. On one level, it is difficult in some cases to identify victims of computer crimes, especially when businesses and individuals do not even know they have been victimized (Speer, 2000). On another level, even when businesses are victimized by a computer crime, many will decide not to report the offense to the authorities. If the offense is not reported, authorities cannot respond to the offense.

Collaboration issues refer to problems that criminal justice officials confront in their efforts to work with other officials in responding to cybercrime. Workers from different agencies will often have their own goals, their own professional language, and limited interaction with those from other agencies (see Bolton, 2013). When called upon to work together in responding to cybercrime, collaboration barriers may arise that inhibit effective and efficient responses. In many ways, the bureaucratic "red tape" that surfaces potentially inhibits collaborative responses to crimes committed in the cyber system.

Reasons for this lack of cooperation include the clear lines of authority between different agencies, the "novelty" of cybercrime, the "blurred" jurisdictional lines, and a long history of animosity between organizations (Givens & Busch, 2013). This lack of cooperation is not just between public agencies. Indeed, private agencies may be even less willing to cooperate in cybercrime investigations. As one author notes, private companies providing critical infrastructure services (such as electricity) would be more concerned with continuing to provide services and less concerned with where the offense originated from (Zhang, 2011). Public agencies, on the other hand, would want to know who committed the attack. An unwillingness to share information makes the investigations even more difficult. In the public sector, some believe that information security specialists have the "tendency to over classify documents" (Bolton, 2013, p. 6).

Experts have identified strategies to improve collaboration between agencies in cybercrime investigations. One author suggested the following:

- Officials should avoid jargon, acronyms, and language specific to their profession.
- Interactions should be increased between parties.

- The focus should be on the goals rather than the process.
- Disconnects between parties should be identified (Bolton, 2013).

The federal government has taken a stronger role in promoting information sharing between agencies addressing cyber offenses. To promote communication between agencies and reduce the risk of attacks on government or public systems related to critical infrastructures, President Obama signed executive order 12,636. The order, titled "Improving Critical Infrastructure Cybersecurity," was hailed as "an important step toward protecting critical infrastructures from cyber threats" (Broggi, 2014, p. 676). Strategies for promoting information sharing were described as necessary in order to reduce cyber threats. The order specifically stated:

It is the policy of the United States Government to increase the volume, timeliness, and quality of cyber threat information shared with U.S. private sector entities so that these entities may better protect and defend themselves against cyber threats. Within 120 days of the date of this order, the Attorney General, the Secretary of Homeland Security (the "Secretary"), and the Director of National Intelligence shall each issue instructions consistent with their authorities and with the requirements of section 12(c) of this order to ensure the timely production of unclassified reports of cyber threats to the U.S. homeland that identify a specific targeted entity. The instructions shall address the need to protect intelligence and law enforcement sources, methods, operations, and investigations.

Each of the problems addressed in this section could be at least partially addressed by better preparing professionals for cybersecurity careers. Currently, few university programs focus on cybersecurity, meaning the professionals do not receive the preparation they need (Gogolin, 2011). It is important to note that some colleges and universities have developed academic programs focused on cybersecurity. These courses and programs, however, are sometimes too narrowly construed to effectively address cybercrime.

The Interdisciplinary Response to Cybercrime

Over the past two decades, higher education scholars have increasingly recognized the value of interdisciplinary efforts that provide a broad understanding of societal problems. For cybercrime, experts have noted that cybersecurity curricula should include a focus on technology, people (e.g., human behavior), and processes (LeClair, Abraham, & Shih, 2013). In other words, cybersecurity professionals need to understand (1) the technology behind cyber offenses, (2) the way that human behavior contributes to cybersecurity incidents, and (3) the processes and policies that are used to prevent and respond to cyber offenses.

Scholars have specifically called for more connections between those disciplines studying and teaching about the topic. In 2010, participants in a National Science Foundation workshop on cybersecurity education offered the following conclusion:

Cyber security requires a multi-disciplinary approach. Efforts should be made to educate and partner with disciplines not always thought of as related to cyber security (e.g., decision sciences, forensic sciences, public policy, law). A holistic approach will foster more collaboration across disciplines, increase interest in cyber security as a necessary component of nearly all types of work, and increase resources and support for cyber security. (L. J. Hoffman, Burley, & Toregas, 2011, November 11, p. 5)

Three years later, a group of cybersecurity professionals and academics engaged in a similar NSF workshop and made a similar conclusion: "There is need for a whole variety of academic degree programs in cybersecurity from the technical aspects through to courses based on psychology, psychiatry, criminal justice, business (i.e. policy and economics) and more" (McGettrick, 2013).

The call for interdisciplinary cybersecurity programs is justified given the various types of issues that arise in efforts to prevent and respond to cybersecurity incidents. An early estimate suggested that less than one percent of cyberattacks are detected (Jefferson, 1997). There is little evidence that suggests an increase in our ability to detect cyberattacks.

One of the reasons that efforts lag behind is the death of academic training programs for current and future cybersecurity professionals. Particularly missing from those academic programs that exist are academic programs addressing cybersecurity from an interdisciplinary perspective. Interdisciplinary cybersecurity programs are justified on several practical grounds. Among the most salient justifications are the following:

- In general, interdisciplinary programs are focused on solving a real-world problem from a holistic perspective.
- The complex nature of cybersecurity makes it virtually impossible for one discipline to "claim ownership" over the topic.
- Certain careers that have recently been created, and some that will be developed in the future in response to increases in cybersecurity, will require an interdisciplinary understanding of cybersecurity.
- It is plausible that interdisciplinary programs will increase the number of women and minorities in cybersecurity programming.

This last point warrants additional discussion. It is clear that women and minorities are underrepresented in STEM majors. Women received 57.3 percent of the bachelor's degrees in 2011, but received less than one-fifth of the computer science, engineering, and physics degrees (National Science Foundation [NSF], 2015). As well, minority females graduating with a bachelor's degree appear to be four times more likely to graduate in the social sciences rather than engineering and three times more likely to graduate in the social sciences than in computer sciences. In 2012, 14.2 percent of awarded bachelor's degrees in the social sciences were received by female minorities. That same year, just 3.1 percent and 4.7 percent of bachelor's degrees in engineering and computer science were received by female minorities (NSF, 2015).

While there are fewer women in STEM majors than other majors, there is reason to believe that women may be particularly interested in interdisciplinary STEM initiatives. In general, research shows that females are more open to interdisciplinary research collaborations than males. This includes research in the United States (Payne, 2015), Italy (Abramo, D'Angelo, & Murgia, 2013), and the Netherlands (van Rijnsoever & Hessels, 2011). In some ways, some women might be drawn to opportunities to create new fields, while there is also a possibility that females are pushed away from traditional disciplines into interdisciplinary programs (Rhoten & Pfirman, 2007). Regardless of the mechanisms driving women into interdisciplinary initiatives, it seems reasonable to suggest that interdisciplinary cybersecurity programs are in a prime position to produce more female cybersecurity professionals.

As noted above, certain challenges arise when addressing cybersecurity through an interdisciplinary lens. Perhaps the strongest barrier is the structure of higher education institutions. The 2010 NSF cybersecurity workshop participants concluded the following:

> **Academic silos prevent collaboration and integration.** Cyber security is a relatively new field that does not always integrate neatly with other computing programs. Academic departments are notorious for guarding their resources and are justifiably resistant to giving up faculty spots, laboratory space, or funding opportunities. Most academic programs have tended to build their own tools rather than exchange resources with others, and they tend to hold firm ownership over whatever they create. (Hoffman et al., 2011, November 11, p. 6)

These challenges, however, can be overcome when professors from different academic disciplines work together in developing courses and academic programs focusing on the topic of cybersecurity from a holistic framework.

Colleges and Cybercrime

Colleges and universities are not immune from concerns about cybersecurity. For our purposes, there are two frameworks for understanding the relevance of cybersecurity for college campuses: a data framework and a behavioral framework. The data framework focuses on the various types of data available on college campuses, while the behavioral framework focuses on the behaviors of individuals on those campuses.

Figure 8.2   Types of Data Stored by Colleges

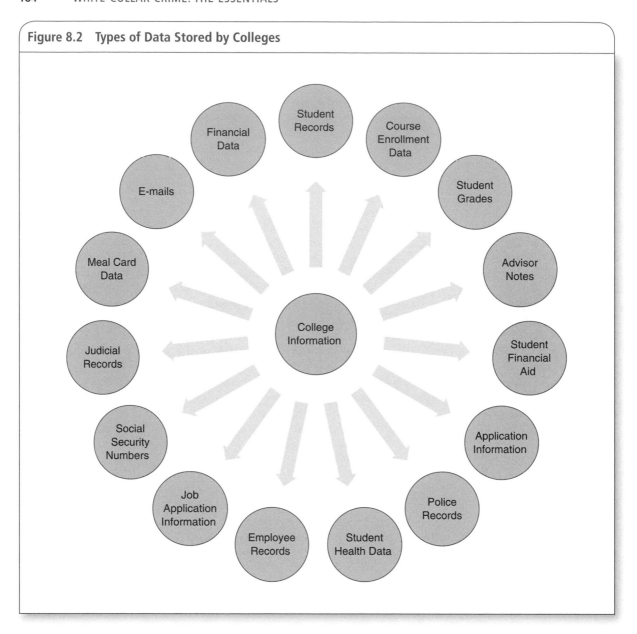

Regarding the data framework, it is important to understand the sheer amount of information that colleges store about students and employees (see Figure 8.2). Think about the types of information that your college has about you. In all likelihood they have the following:

- Your social security number
- Your health records
- Your high school grades

- Your college grades
- Your disciplinary records (for the few of you who have them!)
- Your family's financial records
- Your current bills

Every time you swipe you identification card, your college is able to gather another piece of information about you. How often do you go to the library? How often do you login to your e-mail? How often do you eat at certain places? How often do you login to your online class? What websites did you go to on the college computer? How often did you go to sporting events? How much money do you have left on your account? All of this information (and more) is available on most college computer networks for their students.

Colleges and universities also store an equivalent amount of information about their employees. The sheer amount of information available on computer databases means that these institutions can be targeted for cyber offenses. The security specialists working at your college will not advertise their security strategies because they don't want everyone to know these measures. In some instances, security specialists may work with the campus police department to develop a collaborative information sharing network so the area agencies are prepared for breaches (Aeilts, 2005). In some ways, it's not a matter of if these breaches will occur, but when.

Regarding the behavioral framework as it relates to cybercrimes in colleges and universities in Chapter VI, it was briefly noted that a current concern on college and university campuses is digital and Internet piracy by students. Most colleges have specific policies that prohibit piracy by students. By developing these policies, colleges and universities are able to insulate themselves from blame when students are caught misusing college or university computers. In effect, officials can say that the student was violating an institutional policy, showing that the officials do not support the student's actions.

Internet piracy is "the illegal duplication and distribution of copyrighted materials from the Internet" (Hohn, Muftic, & Wolf, 2006), and digital piracy is the illegal duplication of copyright-protected software. These forms of piracy are believed to cost society between 25 and 30 billion dollars a year (Hohn et al., 2006). The music and movie industries have been particularly vigilant in their efforts to suppress Internet piracy.

Lars Ulrich, drummer from the heavy metal band Metallica, was among the most vocal critics of file-sharing programs that allowed computer users to illegally download and share music. After learning that his band's unreleased music was being distributed on Napster, the band sued Napster for copyright infringement and racketeering. Testifying before the Senate Judiciary Committee on downloading music on the Internet on July 11, 2000, Ulrich said,

> We were startled to hear reports that five or six versions of our work-in-progress were already being played on some U.S. radio stations. We traced the source of this leak to a corporation called Napster. Additionally, we learned that all of our previously recorded copyright songs were, via Napster, available for anyone around the world to download from the Internet in a digital format known as MP3. In fact, in a 48-hour period, where we monitored Napster, over 300,000 users made 1.4 million free downloads of Metallica's music. Napster hijacked our music without asking. They never sought our permission. Our catalog of music simply became available for free downloads on the Napster system. I do not have a problem with any artist voluntarily distributing his or her songs through any means that artist so chooses. But just like a carpenter who crafts a table gets to decide whether he wants to keep it, sell or give it away, shouldn't we have the same options? We should decide what happens to our music, not a company with no rights to our recordings, which has never invested a penny in our music or had anything to do with its creation. The choice has been taken away from us. (Ulrich, 2000)

Metallica and Napster settled out of court.

Over the past few years, high-profile cases of college students being convicted for various forms of digital piracy have made the news headlines. In 2009, Joel Tenenbaum, a Boston University graduate student, was fined $675,000 after the court had found that he had illegally downloaded 30 songs from four record labels (doodlebug, 2009).

▲ **Photo 8.4**   Metallica became embroiled in efforts to control computer crime when drummer Lars Ulrich led efforts of the music industry to stop individuals from illegally downloading music.

Research shows that college students routinely engage in various forms of digital and Internet piracy. A study of 114 students found that 79.8 percent said they had illegally downloaded music, and more than a third said they had pirated software (Hohn et al., 2006). A 2007 survey by SurveyU found that two thirds of the 500 students surveyed were not concerned about illegally downloading music or repercussions from doing so. The survey also found that "only 57% of the students' total libraries had been purchased" (Yoskowitz, 2007).

Researchers have tested various theories in an effort to explain software piracy by students. One author team surveyed 342 students and found support for the idea that low self-control contributes to software piracy (Higgins, Fell, & Wilson, 2006). In another study, of 507 college students, a researcher found that broadband connections combined with prior experience using CD-ROMs increased the risk of Internet piracy (Hinduja, 2001).

● ● ● Responding to Cybercrime

Different strategies are used to address cybercrime. Broadly speaking, these strategies can be characterized as police strategies, legislative strategies, retributive strategies, and general prevention strategies. Each of these strategies is addressed below.

Police Strategies

In this context, the phrase *police strategies* is used to describe a range of activities performed by law enforcement agencies in response to cyber offending. Depending on offense type, different law enforcement agencies may be called upon to respond to different types of cyber offending. Table 8.2 shows the federal law enforcement agencies that have jurisdiction over select types of cybercrimes.

While many agencies may get involved with different types of cyber offenses, in reality the public likely does not distinguish between these agencies. Instead, the public has an expectation that "the police" protect citizens from cyber victimization (Wall, 2007). In reality, the law enforcement response to cyber offending is three-pronged:

- Law enforcement agencies are expected to protect both individuals and businesses from cyber offending and must respond to those offenses when they occur.
- Law enforcement agencies must protect their own computer systems from cybercrimes.
- Law enforcement agencies must work with state and federal agencies to coordinate investigations (Golban, 2015).

While members of the public may expect the police to protect them against cyber offending, law enforcement officers may not be adequately prepared to respond to these crimes. A study of 268 patrol officers found that although nearly 80 percent of the officers viewed computer crime as serious, roughly ten percent of them had received computer crime training (Holt & Bossler, 2012). The officers demonstrated a great deal of uncertainty about the dynamics of computer crime. Echoing this concern, one author commented, "the structure within which law enforcement operates does not lend itself to effective investigations of digital crimes" (Gogolin, 2011, p. 469).

Table 8.2 Federal Law Enforcement Agencies Responding to Different Types of Cybercrimes	
Type of Crime	**Appropriate Federal Investigative Law Enforcement Agencies**
Computer intrusion (i.e. hacking)	• FBI local office • U.S. Secret Service • Internet Crime Complaint Center
Password trafficking	• FBI local office • U.S. Secret Service • Internet Crime Complaint Center
Counterfeiting of currency	• U.S. Secret Service
Child Pornography or Exploitation	• FBI local office • If imported, U.S. Immigration and Customs Enforcement • Internet Crime Complaint Center
Child Exploitation and Internet Fraud matters that have a mail nexus	• U.S. Postal Inspection Service • Internet Crime Complaint Center
Internet fraud and SPAM	• FBI local office • U.S. Secret Service • Federal Trade Commission (online complaint) • If securities fraud or investment-related SPAM e-mails, Securities and Exchange Commission (online complaint) • Internet Crime Complaint Center
Internet harassment	• FBI local office
Internet bomb threats	• FBI local office • ATF local office
Trafficking in explosive or incendiary devices or firearms over the Internet	• FBI local office • ATF local office

Source: Adapted from Richardson. (n. d.). *15th Annual 2010/2011 cyber crime and security survey.*

Some officers have described the response to cybercrime as "good, old fashioned police work" (Garrett, 2010, p. 45). While technology allows offenders access into spaces they would not have accessed in the past, law enforcement can gain access to those same spaces. One expert suggests that law enforcement authorities ask these questions in the early stages of their investigation:

- Was the attack launched from the Internet or from the internal network?
- Did the attacker have access to the [local] system?
- If the attacker was an outsider . . . how did he manage to have the first access?
- Did he take advantage of any vulnerability?
- Was he helped by any employee?
- Did he use some kind of blackmail? (Donato, 2009, p. 189)

Obviously, different types of cybercrimes will require different investigation techniques. Those crimes that involve e-mails, for example, might involve an analysis of the e-mails to determine if they were all written by the same suspect. Writers often use the same punctuation and characters in the same way. Investigators will review e-mails much as handwriting might be analyzed. How did the writer set the tab function? How long were the sentences? Were numbers spelled out or listed numerically? How many numbers were used? How many spaces were after the period? Were there common spelling errors? Asking these questions will allow investigators to group together anonymous e-mails to determine if they were written by the same suspect (Iqbal, Binalleeh, Fung, & Debbabi, 2010). Instant messages can also be analyzed to determine who wrote them. According to one author team, "the real time, casual nature of instant messages produces text that is conversational in style and reflects the author's true writing style and vocabulary" (p. 193).

For law enforcement officers, responding to cybercrime requires a set of skills not commonly found among criminal justice professionals (Bolton, 2013). Cybersecurity careers are flourishing in both the private and public arena. (See the Careers Responding to White-Collar Crime: Information Security Specialist box below.)

CAREERS RESPONDING TO WHITE-COLLAR CRIME

Information Security Specialist

Major duties up to the full performance level include, but are not limited to:

- Effectively communicate, orally and in written from, the breadth and depth of intrusion activity based on team findings from incident response engagements, potential risks presented due to intrusion activity, cyber security architectural recommendations, best practices, guidance and strategies to client stakeholders including technical staff, operations staff, and executive leadership.
- Provide a professional interface with private sector critical infrastructure asset owners and operators while performing control system network architecture assessments as well as verification and validation of said network traffic.
- Field voluntary reports of incidents as well as conduct victim notification duties to evaluate incidents for triage, prioritization, and initial scoping of response efforts.
- Gather incident data (such as host and network log data) to validate initial reports and escalate as needed; oversee and prepare technical reports for incident victim companies as well as broader, anonymized reports that identify key data points (technical indicators) or shifts in behavior that are suitable for inclusion in information products to improve shared situational awareness.

- Manage relationships with private and public sector companies at multiple levels (technical SMEs, Agency head, CIO, CEO, Board of Directors, etc) to shepherd them through the process of responding to cyber incidents of major significance. (This includes being knowledgeable on the business aspects and process control elements of critical infrastructure.)
- Deploy to victim company or agency locations for incident response (IR) engagements, work long hours (12+ hours per day) for the first few days of an incident until a steady-state pace is established; gather incident data (protecting victim data from improper disclosure) and conduct technical analysis functions such host and network-based analysis, log review, and author indicators of compromise.
- Monitor and review multiple data sources, including intelligence, media, and law enforcement reporting, to identify control system cybersecurity incidents, threats, and vulnerabilities and apply knowledge of the tactics, techniques, and procedures of these actors to identify and validate threats; periodically participate in industry or government outreach and engagement through briefings or presenting at conferences in both classified and unclassified settings at all levels (from technical exchanges through supporting congressional briefings).

Source: Reprinted from USAJobs.Gov

Legislative Strategies

Legislative strategies are also used in an effort to respond to cybercrime. As noted above, in the U.S., the Computer Fraud and Abuse Act of 1984 was the first law in U.S. to specifically address computer offenders. This law was initially passed to protect government information on government computers. It was broadened in 1996 to offer protections to the private sector (Davis, 2003). The act makes the following behaviors federal crimes:

- Hacking into government or bank computers
- Damaging computers through viruses, worms, or other software crimes
- Committing fraud through computer access
- Threatening computer damage against a bank or government computer
- Password trafficking related to government computers
- Using computers to spy on the government (Doyle, 2014)

Other countries have passed similar laws. England, for example, passed the Computer Misuse Act of 1990, which, among other things, made it illegal to create or possess certain hacking tools (Furnell, 2008). States have passed their own laws governing cybersecurity and other federal policies and executive orders have followed. One federal policy, for example, now requires businesses receiving government contracts to demonstrate how the business protects information related to the government contract (Bancroft, 2013). In addition, a recent executive order from President Barack Obama mandated that the National Institute of Standards and Technology develop a framework to minimize cyber risks confronting critical infrastructures. NIST identified five functions that are a part of the government's comprehensive framework:

- Identifying systems, assets, and data that need protection
- Providing safeguards to protect those systems, assets, and data
- Detecting cyber offenses
- Responding to cyber events
- Recovering from cyber events (Levi, 2014)

The cybersecurity laws have been criticized on different grounds. For example, the information security regulations are seen as potentially making it more difficult for small businesses to compete for government contracts (Bancroft, 2013). Also, laws requiring Internet service providers to support law enforcement activities have been viewed as "a larger move by governments to establish policing networks 'beyond the state'" (Huey & Rosenberg, 2004, p. 599).

Retributive Strategies

Retributive strategies refer to efforts to punish individuals in order to keep them from committing cybercrimes. One philosophical question that arises is whether the punishment for cybercrimes should be proportionate to the pleasure/harm from the offense. This would mean that the penalties for these crimes would be far more severe than for conventional crimes. After all, the harm from cybercrimes can be quite severe. According to one scholar, proportional sanctions for some cyber offenders might potentially "offend our sense of justice" (Jetha, 2013, p. 20).

General Prevention Strategies

Three different types of strategies are used to prevent computer crimes by white-collar offenders. These include employer-based strategies, employee-based strategies, and situational crime prevention strategies. In terms of *employer-based strategies*, employers use a range of tactics to protect their businesses from computer crimes. Most commonly, these tactics include encryption, firewalls, employee training, routine audits, and physical surveillance (Carter & Katz, 1996). Many large private businesses have security personnel whose sole efforts are directed toward preventing and/or identifying cases of computer crime.

Steve McNally, NSF

*Security Blanket
Quilt by Lorrie Faith Cranor*   IEEE★USA

▲ **Photo 8.5**   Employees play an important role in protecting their company's computer networks. Selecting a secure password is one of the most important steps employees can take. Some passwords are far too common.

Employee-based strategies call upon employees to make active efforts to prevent computer crimes. The phrase "security hygiene" is used to characterize efforts where workers learn and carry out safe computer behaviors (Pfleeger, Sasse, & Furnham, 2014). Such strategies include updating virus protection programs, conducting employee-initiated audits of computer use, taking additional precautions to protect one's work computer from victimization, and initiating formal agreements whereby employees agree to use computers only for work-related activities (Carter & Katz, 1996). Including employees in prevention strategies ensures that well-rounded prevention programs are in place.

Situational crime prevention strategies refer to specific actions that can be taken that are directly related to those factors that promote offending. Companies can use specific strategies to limit opportunities for cyber offending. Examples relevant to cybercrime include the following:

- Requiring biometric credentials (eyes, fingerprints, voice recognition) for employees to gain access to certain types of data
- Using entry screening measures that grant access only to certain individuals
- Developing formal surveillance strategies that monitor the behavior of employees
- Identifying property with codes so the property can be recovered if misplaced or stolen
- Removing the temptation by hiding data systems
- Setting rules that are clear and enforceable
- Implementing target hardening strategies, such as information security standards, secure passwords, and encryption (Hinduja & Kooi, 2013)

Encryption refers to the process of coding information so that only the original codes are able to understand the information.

Other specific strategies that have been suggested include spam filters, honey nets, self-initiated Google hacking, and security banners. *Spam filters* are e-mail tools that catch unwanted bulk e-mails. One estimate suggests that 97 percent of all e-mail sent through the Internet was spam (Carucci, Overhuls, & Soares, 2011). Users set their spam filters so that e-mails scoring above a certain level or identified by the user as spam are sent to the user's spam folder. For some reason, the author receives an e-mail almost weekly from a user called "6 Pack Abs." It doesn't take a sophisticated spam filter to recognize that this e-mail is either spam or meant for someone else!

Honey nets (or honey pots) are websites or datasets that are designed to "attract and entrap offenders" (Wall, 2008, p. 57). These sites do not include any data of real value to the company. There are at least three reasons why honey nets are used by businesses. First, some businesses may do this so they can catch offenders and turn them in to law enforcement. Second, some businesses (including researchers) may create these honey nets so they can study the behavior of hackers. Third, some businesses may use honey nets simply as a decoy or distraction for hackers. In this case, the hope is that hackers would spend their time and energy on the "fake" site and stay away from the data that is truly of value to the company.

Self-initiated Google hacking refers to instances when companies or businesses google themselves in order to identify vulnerable networks that might be uncovered from Google searches. It is well accepted that hackers search certain terms in order to locate vulnerable networks. The presence or lack of certain features on a company's website increases its vulnerability. The phrase "Google Dork" characterizes "the search terms used to discover vulnerabilities" (Mansfield-Devine, 2009, p. 4). For instance, the following search would reveal files that contain passwords: inurl:wp-content/uploads filetype:xls | filetype:xlsx password (Exploit Database, n. d., https://www.exploit-db.com/google-hacking-database/). Security experts encourage companies to Google hack their websites in order to identify potential vulnerabilities (Mansfield-Devine, 2009).

Security banners or warnings have also been used by companies in an effort to prevent cybercrime. In these cases, a box appears on the computer screen advising workers they are in a part of the network that they should not be in. The usefulness of these banners is debatable. Some have suggested that workers ignore the banners unless there is an immediate consequence (Pfleeger et al., 2014). David Maimon and his colleagues (2014) conducted an experiment in which computers were set up with the expectation that they would be targeted for intrusions or trespassing. After cyber offenders hacked into the computers, they were randomly assigned to one of two groups. One group received a warning in the form of a banner and the other did not receive anything. Maimon found that the banner did not reduce the number of intrusions, but it did reduce the amount of time that offenders spent in the targeted computer database. This research suggested that banners won't keep offenders from entering databases, but they won't stay as long. As an analogy, a "Stay Off the Grass" sign may not keep people from standing in my yard, but they won't stay as long!

▲ **Photo 8.6** Society has changed dramatically through the recent technological revolution led by masterminds such as Steve Jobs. These changes have had ramifications for the criminal justice system as well.

Identifying prevention strategies can be problematic given the changing nature of cyber offenses. Efforts to develop prevention plans face financial, personnel, and structural barriers. In addition, it is believed by some that cybercrime has changed over time. Whereas past hackers more frequently committed offenses out of the desire to "brag," more cyber offenses are now committed for profit motives. Describing this shift, one author has suggested that "cybercriminals have become an international plague" (G. S. Smith, 2015, p. 104). Despite this change, others have argued that, in some ways, the presence of computers have only provided "a new medium . . . to commit traditional crimes" (Viano, 2006). As Viano notes, the advent of the phone, television, and audio resulted in different strategies to commit crime. Others agree that technology has simply provided new ways of committing "old" crimes. One author team explained, "health care fraud provides an example of a traditional crime that has been upgraded and enhanced by new computer and Internet technologies" (Gray, Citron, & Rinehart, 2013, p. 749).

That technological changes have enhanced traditional crimes has implications for the way that officials prevent and respond to cybercrime. New prevention and response strategies are not necessarily needed; instead, enhanced response strategies are justified. In line with this point, it has been suggested that cybersecurity efforts have been "iterative rather than linear" (Harknett & Stever, 2009, p. 2). Within this iterative change, it has been recognized that the key to successful cybersecurity efforts is cooperation between government agencies, citizens, and businesses.

Do As I Say, Not As I Do

In what can be filed under the category of "Do as I say, not as I do," an interesting anecdote about my own experience with computer victimization comes to mind. While working on this chapter for the first edition, I decided that I would search the Internet for additional information about computer viruses. I found a few useful websites and took some notes on the material I read. About 2 hours later, I realized that my computer had become infected by a computer virus called the *control center virus*. Somehow, during my search, I had clicked on a website that downloaded this virus to my laptop. I had to stop work immediately, save my work to that point, and shut down the computer. The next day I delivered my computer to one of the computer tech employees in my college. He confirmed that my computer had become infected and that he would need to take a few days to get rid of the virus and restore the computer to its appropriate state. Fortunately, I didn't lose any files or data—I just lost some time.

So, if you are writing a paper about computer viruses for your white-collar crime class, do not search the Internet for information—make sure you search your library database and rely on scholarly journal articles published by top publishing companies, such as SAGE. This little bit of advice will take you a long way in your academic career.

SUMMARY

- The phrases *computer crime* and *cybercrime* refer to a range of computer-related behaviors that are criminally illegal or otherwise harmful.
- In 1978, Florida and Arizona became the first two states to pass laws related to computer crime.
- Not all computer crimes are white-collar crimes.
- The following overlapping types of computer crimes are often cases of white-collar crime: theft, unauthorized access, virus introduction, software crimes, and Internet crimes.
- Theft as a type of computer crime refers to a variety of computer-related activities that result in the offender stealing something from the business. Items stolen include funds, information, and intellectual property.
- Theft of information occurs when offenders steal information, including (a) information that can be used to trade securities and stocks and (b) intellectual property.
- Unauthorized access occurs when individuals break into various computer databases to which they do not have legitimate access.
- Crackers typically introduce viruses for recreational reasons, pride, profit, protection, or cyberterrorism reasons.
- Four overlapping types of software crimes exist: (1) theft of software, (2) counterfeiting software, (3) copyright violations of computer software, and (4) piracy.
- The phrase *Internet crimes* refers to a range of offenses committed by offenders through the use of the Internet.
- Different types of cybercriminals exist, including loners, associates, and networks.
- The costs of cybercrime include physical, social, financial, and emotional.
- Computer crimes are commonly attributed to opportunity, structural changes, and peer associations.
- Problems in responding to computer crime stem from the dynamics of the offense, offender characteristics, jurisdictional issues, criminal justice dynamics, victim characteristics, and general crime prevention issues.
- The best way to respond to cybercrime involves an interdisciplinary response system.
- Colleges house a great deal of information that could be targeted by cyber offenders.
- Most colleges have specific policies that prohibit piracy by students. One author team surveyed 342 students and found support for the idea that low self-control contributes to software piracy (Higgins et al., 2006).
- Strategies used to prevent computer crimes by white-collar offenders include police strategies, legislative strategies, retributive strategies, and general prevention strategies.

KEY TERMS

Breach	Internet crimes	Theft of software
Computer crime	Internet piracy	Unauthorized access
Counterfeiting software crimes	Phishing	Virus
Crackers	Ransomware	Worm
Critical Infrastructure	Situational crime prevention	
Electronic and software piracy	Software crimes	

DISCUSSION QUESTIONS

1. Which crimes do you think do more harm—crimes against the cyber system or street crimes? Explain.

2. How are crimes in the economic system similar to crimes in the technological system? What are some differences in the two categories of crime?

3. How is "being hacked" a crime rather than a form of victimization?

4. How does cybercrime impact your life as a student?

5. How serious are computer crimes on your campus?

6. Why do you think hackers engage in computer crime behaviors?

7. How do you think computer crimes will change in the next decade?

WEB RESOURCES

Identity Theft: http://www.ftc.gov/bcp/edu/microsites/idtheft/

Internet Crime Complaint Center: http://www.ic3.gov/default.aspx

IT Crime Prevention: http://www.interpol.int/public/technologycrime/crimeprev/itsecurity.asp

Security: http://www.consumer.ftc.gov/media/video-0056-protect-your-computer-malware

STUDENT RESOURCES

The open-access Student Study Site, available at study.sagepub.com/paynewccess2e, includes useful study materials including SAGE journal articles and multimedia resources.

CHAPTER

IX

Crimes in the Housing System

CHAPTER HIGHLIGHTS

- Mortgage Fraud
- Types of Mortgage Fraud
- Consequences of Mortgage Fraud
- Patterns Surrounding Mortgage Fraud
- Slumlords as White-Collar Criminals

In September 2015, the Houston mayor and police chief held a joint press conference. While joint press conferences are relatively routine, the topic of this event was out of the ordinary. The two city leaders had come together to declare that they were planning to arrest a landlord for forcing his tenants to live in deplorable conditions. According to news reports, "Residents said they were forced to live with cockroaches, holes in walls, leaking faucets, without power and their food rotting in their homes for weeks" (KHOU, 2015). The mayor boldly announced to reporters: "If this guy comes to Houston, we will be waiting to arrest him. . . . This is wrong. Again, these are not people who are trying to get something for nothing. These are people who live in bad conditions with a bad landlord and paid their rent and have been shafted by a millionaire" (KHOU, 2015).

What made this case stand out was not the presence of poor living conditions. Instead, it was the willingness of the authorities to bring the criminal justice system into the process to address the slum conditions. Complaints about poor living conditions in rental units are common. There are even websites where tenants can rate their landlords. Here are two entries from college students describing the slum-like conditions of their apartments:

- The landlord is loud and obnoxious. . . . My biggest problem has been there is a hole in my roof. The hole allows water in and the ceiling collapsed. It took them 2 months to fix my ceiling. As far as I know they still haven't fixed the roof. . . . The day I moved in the microwave in the apartment did not work. I notified them and there response was we aren't going to replace those because people keep breaking them. So I do not receive a microwave because other people before me broke it. Finally the exhaust fan in my bathroom does not work. This causes water damage to the walls that I'm sure will be taken out of my security deposit. I could go on but I think you get the picture. https://www.housing.purdue.edu/OffCampus/Survey/LandlordRatingBreakdown?landlordID=bba22198-70f2-41ea-8ff7-bda5711966d9

- Linda was not at all professional with us as tenants. I went in to complain about electrical problems and mold in the house and she would cut me off while talking and didn't care at all that my roommates and I were completely unsatisfied with the way things were. We would call constantly about things not being fixed and no one ever showed up or if they did nothing was ever fixed. I felt like I constantly had to harass her to get anything done. Even then, they didn't take electrical problems seriously until I had the fire marshal come and inspect it and call them. Same with problems with mold. First time with mold, maintenance was not going to remove the panels covering the wall until I demanded they do so, only to find the mold was EVERYWHERE on the walls. Nothing was done about all the damaged clothes and belongings that were covered in mold. The second time, I called in Jan about mold and no one came to LOOK at it until late Feb and then nothing was done until early May. I was never allergic to anything and am now seriously allergic to mold because of these two experiences. They also took an unreasonably large amount of our deposit out for things that had never been fixed when we moved in and will likely not fix them for the next tenants. In summation, the landlord and maintenance were TERRIBLE and I would NEVER recommend them. https://www.housing.purdue.edu/OffCampus/Survey/LandlordRatingBreakdown?landlordID=1ff6ba29-8de6-472b-bd74-c7b7a41b1085

Some readers may have lived in shoddy conditions themselves at some point during their college years, but did you think of your landlord as a white-collar criminal? Most likely, if we encountered them, we did not define slumlords as criminal. However, their actions fall within the domain of white-collar crime. They are not alone in committing crimes in the housing system. In fact, an increase in mortgage fraud has made crimes by slumlords seem rare by comparison. Consider the following examples, quoted verbatim from their original sources, as additional illustrations of crimes by slumlords, officials in the mortgage industry, and other professionals:

- On Aug. 14, 2015, ****** was sentenced to 60 months [for convictions] on 13 counts of mortgage fraud, passing fictitious financial instruments and tax fraud. According to court records and evidence introduced at trial, from 2007 to 2010, ****** targeted distressed homeowners who owed more on their mortgage loan than the market value of the home with false promises of financial recovery. ****** acquired the distressed homeowners' properties in her own name or under entities she controlled, made false representations to mortgage lenders in order to induce approval of the short sales and then resold the properties to new buyers at a price above the short sale amount in violation of agreements made with mortgage lenders. (IRS, 2015)

- On June 22, 2015, ****** was sentenced to 60 months in prison and ordered to pay $568,413 in restitution. ******, a former Realtor, and his co-conspirators embarked on an 11-year mortgage fraud scheme that resulted in losses just under $2 million. Among other things, the defendants provided false information to lenders and used straw buyers to perpetrate the scheme. During the course of the conspiracy, the defendants obtained at least 14 loans on 11 properties that totaled over $3 million and resulted in nine foreclosures. (IRS, 2015)

- On June 9, 2015, ******* was sentenced to 63 months in prison, five years of supervised release and ordered to pay $47,908 in restitution. According to court documents, between approximately December 2006 and March 2008, ********* conspired with her daughter ******* to obtain more than $47,000 in real estate appraisal fees to which they were not entitled. *****submitted falsified work logs to the Connecticut Department of Consumer

▲ **Photo 9.1** Is it a crime for landlords not to maintain their apartments?

Protection purporting to show that *********, a provisional appraiser, completed dozens of real estate appraisals under the supervision of a certified appraiser when, in fact, ******* had not performed such work and was not entitled to such appraisal fees. (IRS, 2015)

Tenants living inside apartments on Taillon Street in Bristol will have to find new homes after Christmas. The Building Department condemned their building on Friday, citing a multitude of issues, including: extensive mold; no working smoke detectors; broken storm doors, windows and tiles; rotting door frames; combustible materials in the basement; and sidewalks in disrepair. (Corrado, 2015)

In this chapter, attention is given to crimes committed in the housing system. As will be shown, a number of different types of white-collar crimes occur in this system. Generally speaking, these crimes can be classified as (a) mortgage fraud and (b) renting unsafe properties (e.g., being a slumlord).

● ● ● Mortgage Fraud

Mortgage fraud involves cases of "intentional misrepresentation to a lender for the purpose of obtaining a loan that would otherwise not be advanced by the lender" (Financial Crimes Enforcement Network [FinCEN], 2009). Mortgage fraud has always been a problem in the United States, but it has increased in recent years. In a 2005 press release describing a mortgage fraud operation called Quick Flip, the FBI (2005) described mortgage fraud as "one of the fastest growing white-collar crimes in the United States." For the first time ever, losses to mortgage fraud exceeded one billion dollars in 2005 (Federal Deposit Insurance Corporation [FDIC], 2007). Not long after that, it was estimated that mortgage fraud costs banks and lenders more than $4 billion a year (Creswell, 2007).

Experts have tied increases in mortgage fraud to the cooling real estate market. According to Vickers (2007), "as business dries up, there's increasing pressure on lenders, brokers, title companies, and appraisers to be profitable." Federal responses demonstrated an increase in mortgage fraud. In fact, the number of mortgage fraud investigations by the FBI doubled from 2008 to June 2010 (Pelofsky, 2010). As evidence of the breadth of these cases, consider that in June 2010, federal officials "charged 1,215 people in hundreds of mortgage fraud cases that resulted in losses of 2.3 billion dollars" (Pelofsky, 2010).

Reports from banking institutions also demonstrate a significant increase in mortgage fraud cases. Suspected cases of mortgage fraud are reported by banking officials "through Suspicious Activity Reports (SARs) required under the Bank Secrecy Act" (FinCEN, 2009). SARs have been described as "one of the most important sources of lead information for law enforcement in fighting financial crimes" (FinCEN, 2010d). To put in perspective the increase in mortgage fraud cases, at least suspected mortgage fraud cases, consider that in fiscal year 2004 banks across the United States filed 17,127 SARs about mortgage fraud. In fiscal year 2009, bank officials filed 67,190 SARs about mortgage fraud. This means that the number of suspected mortgage fraud cases nearly quadrupled within a 5-year time frame! As of March 2010, the FBI had 2,989 active investigations related to mortgage fraud. More than two-thirds of the cases involved losses exceeding a million dollars.

It is important to stress that not all cases of mortgage fraud are necessarily white-collar crimes committed by employers. Indeed, some cases entail situations where consumers scam banks by committing fraud in order to benefit from deceiving the lender. Many cases of mortgage fraud, particularly those that are the most pervasive, can be classified as white-collar crimes. Between June 1, 2009, and June 30, 2009, the Financial Crimes Enforcement Network (2010d) reported that 32,926 SARs describing mortgage fraud cases were filed by banks. While many of the reports focused on allegations against consumers, about half clearly implicated white-collar offenders. Real estate professionals, brokers, and appraisers were listed in more than half of all the reports. In fact, broker-facilitated mortgage fraud has been hailed as "the most prevalent segment of mortgage fraud nationwide" (FDIC, 2007).

Beyond focusing on type of offender in these cases, researchers can give attention to the types of mortgage fraud committed by professionals working in the housing system. Accordingly, a fuller understanding of the nature of mortgage fraud will be possible. After discussing these types of mortgage fraud, attention will be given to the patterns surrounding these cases and the consequences of these behaviors.

At the most general level, experts distinguish between "mortgage fraud-for-profit" and "mortgage fraud-for-housing." **Fraud-for-housing** cases occur when borrowers lie about their financial information in order to secure the mortgage so they can purchase a home (Glink & Tamkin, 2008). In contrast, **fraud-for-profit** occurs when offenders commit the fraud in order to reap a monetary benefit from the mortgage transaction. Mortgage fraud-for-profit is also known as "industry insider fraud" because the vast majority of cases involve schemes with employers inside the business transaction playing a prominent role (FBI, 2009b). In these situations, offenders could be real estate professionals, employees of property management companies, appraisers, financial advisors, loan officers, processors, underwriters, closing attorneys, or bank employees. The underlying thread across fraud-for-profit cases is that they involve multiple participants who commit an assortment of schemes over time (Fannie Mae, 2007). Box 9.1 includes the press release from a recent for-profit scheme busted by authorities.

Several different types of mortgage fraud exist. In regard to types of for-profit fraud, the following warrant discussion: (a) straw buyer fraud, (b) short sale fraud, (c) appraisal fraud, (d) equity skimming, (e) reverse mortgage fraud, (f) fraud during closing and settlement, (g) foreclosure rescue scams, (h) builder-initiated fraud, (i) flipping, (j) qualifications fraud, and (k) real estate agent/investor fraud. Each of these is discussed below.

Straw Buyer Fraud

Straw buyer fraud occurs when individuals who do not plan on living in or even owning a house purchase the house and then deed it over to the person who will live there. In many cases, the straw buyers do this for a fee (Fannie Mae, 2007). In other cases, the straw buyers do this with the intent of unloading the mortgage on an unsuspecting homeowner who is unaware of the true costs of the home and, in most cases, probably unable to pay the actual mortgage amount. Based on these dynamics, Curry (2007) identified two types of straw buyers: (1) conspirator straw buyers who are in on the scheme and the (2) victim straw buyers who are not in on the scheme but who believe they will either legitimately own the home or be able to rent it. In the latter cases, the victim is often an "unsophisticated buyer, without cash or good credit" (V. Martin, 2004).

A few examples will help distinguish between these different strategies used in straw buying fraud. In terms of coconspirator straw buyers, consider a case where a loan officer worked with a coconspirator to "take out more than $38 million in bank loans by recruiting strangers to fill out applications" (J. C. Anderson, 2010). All individuals involved in the scheme were aware of the straw buying fraud. On one side of the transaction, straw buyers purchase homes. The funds provided by the bank are given to the conspirator in the scheme. The straw buyer who owns the home either sells the home to another straw buyer or simply defaults on the loan. In these situations, the straw buyers are often offenders who have been convicted of other offenses. This dynamic somewhat blurs the line between street offenders and white-collar offenders.

The case of Lessie Towns provides an example of unsuspecting victims getting involved in a straw buying scheme. The 75-year-old Chicago homeowner learned that her house was being foreclosed on even though she "never missed a payment." In 2005, Towns "signed what she thought was a refinancing agreement with Oak Based Trust One Mortgage"

WHITE-COLLAR CRIME IN THE NEWS

Home Is Where the Fraud Is:
Mortgage Fraud Scheme Broken Up

https://commons.wikimedia.org/wiki/File:Context_sensitive_cuplex_(822860518).jpg.

Fraud can occur during any transaction . . . Even when a person buys a home.

ATLANTA—**** have been sentenced for their roles in a scheme to defraud mortgage lenders of over $2 million in mortgage loans. "Mortgage fraud has dragged down our economy, blighted our communities, and put in jeopardy the financial security of many Americans. We will diligently pursue those who misuse the dream of home ownership to line their own pockets by fraud and deceit," said United States Attorney Sally Quillian Yates.

"The U.S. Postal Inspection Service is committed to protecting the American Public from individuals who make misrepresentations to prey on innocent victims," said Thomas L. Noyes II, Inspector in Charge of the Charlotte Division of the U.S.

Postal Inspection Service. "The collaborative effort between federal agencies in this case is an excellent example of the partnerships that focus on bringing those to justice who violate the law and defraud hardworking citizens." J. Britt Johnson, Special Agent in Charge, FBI Atlanta Field Office, stated: "Today's sentencing of this group engaged in mortgage fraud represents the federal government's commitment toward combating such criminal activities. The FBI will continue to work with its various law enforcement partners in identifying such individuals engaged in this activity."

According to United States Attorney Yates, the charges and other information presented in court: ****, a licensed real estate agent, and **** were long time business partners, operating an office rental business on Covington Highway in DeKalb County, Ga. In late 2007 or 2008, **** and **** began working out of **** and **** office space. Beginning in 2008, ****, and **** worked together to locate properties, recruit straw borrowers, and obtain mortgage loans using false information about the borrowers' employment, income, and assets. **** created false W-2s and pay stubs (or earning statements) that were submitted to the lenders to obtain mortgage loans, along with fake bank statements that the co-conspirators obtained from other sources. The false documents represented that the straw borrowers earned significant salaries working for a company owned by **** and ****. When lenders attempted to verify the straw borrower's employment by contacting the company, ****, or their co-conspirators falsely verified the straw borrower's employment, posing as a human resources manager or other high-level employee of **** and **** company.

Source: FBI (2014, November 9). Members of Mortgage Fraud Ring Sentenced. Reprinted from https://www.fbi.gov/atlanta/press-releases/2014/members-of-mortgage-fraud-ring-sentenced.

(Meincke, 2009). What had actually occurred was that she had transferred her home to another owner without knowing it. In fact, her home was sold twice without her knowledge through straw buyers. "I'm not angry," she told a reporter. "I'm disgusted. Just tired of fraud, tired of people using people" (Meincke, 2009). This victimization almost resulted in Towns losing her home. She had to enlist the services of a real estate attorney and spend a significant amount of time recovering ownership of her home. She was able to stop the foreclosure process on her home on the stipulation that she prove that she had not meant to sell her home when she signed the paperwork 4 years earlier. Incidentally, an Illinois law was passed in August 2009 in an effort to crack down on mortgage fraud and strengthen homeowners' rights. The governor signed the bill in Lessie Towns's backyard (Kass, 2009). He referred to the law as the "Lessie Towns Act" to honor the older woman's efforts to save her home. Towns lamented that she knew the governor was coming to her home only 20 minutes before he arrived.

Short Sale Fraud

The phrase *short sale* refers to instances where lending institutions allow homes to be sold for amounts that are lower than what the homeowner owed on the home's mortgage. These sales typically occur for houses that have been foreclosed on or those that are nearing foreclosure. To put this in perspective, a homeowner might have a $400,000 mortgage. Unable to sell the home for that amount, the bank may allow the homeowner to sell it for less, even waiving any additional future costs to the homeowner in some cases. Short sales in and of themselves are entirely legal and offer homeowners a way to get out from a mortgage and home they are no longer able to afford. These sales allow lending institutions to avoid lengthy and costly foreclosure processes. Still, the lending institution loses money on a short sale. Consider the following example:

1. Susan buys a home from Chandra and gets a $300,000 mortgage.

2. The bank gave $300,000 to Chandra as part of the transaction.

3. Susan is unable to pay her mortgage and asks for a short sale.

4. The home is sold for $270,000 to Randy.

5. The bank loses $30,000.

Short sale fraud occurs when parties involved in the short sale manipulate the process in order to persuade the lending institution to permit the short sale to occur. One variety of short sale fraud is *premeditated short sale fraud*. This occurs when the offender "uses straw buyers to purchase and ultimately default on a home loan, creating a short sale situation so that the perpetrator himself can take advantage and purchase the home at a steep discount" (FBI, 2009b). Consider the example above. If Susan is a straw buyer and Randy asked her to buy the home and default on the loan so he could buy the home at a lower price, then premeditated short sale fraud has occurred.

Another variety of short sale fraud can be coined "secondary short sale fraud." Secondary short sale fraud involves situations in which the home has a second mortgage or equity loan attached to it. If a short sale occurs on a home with a second mortgage or an equity loan, by law, the entire proceeds from the short sale go to the primary mortgage holder. Secondary short sale fraud occurs when the owner of the secondary mortgage contacts settlement agents and asks for a cut that will not be shown on the settlement statement (Olick, 2010). One executive who arranges short sales told Olick that he had been contacted by 200 settlement agents who had been asked by bank employees to do this. The victim in these cases would be the primary lending institution, which would get even less from the short sale.

Appraisal Fraud

Appraisal fraud occurs when appraisers misrepresent the actual value of a home (Curry, 2007). Appraisers are called upon to determine a home's value so the lending institution can determine if the home is worth the amount of money that the lending institution would need to lend the buyer for the purchase. Four types of appraisal fraud occur. First, **inflated appraisals** overestimate the value of a home in order to allow it to be sold at an inflated price. This is also known as value fraud (Rudra, 2010). Second, **deflated appraisals** underestimate the value of the home in order to force the seller to lower the home price. Third, **windshield appraisal fraud** occurs when appraisers fail to do a thorough appraisal of a home (and may not even go into the home to determine its value—hence they determine its value by looking through the windshield of their automobile) (FDIC, 2007). Fourth, **conspiracy appraisal frauds** occur when appraisers work with other offenders as part of broader mortgage schemes. For example, for straw buying or flipping schemes to be successful, appraisers must provide inflated appraisals of targeted homes on a regular basis for their coconspirators. In Focus 9.1, When Real Estate Appraisers Go Bad, is a press release from the Department of Justice describing the conviction of an appraiser involved in a complex conspiracy that was designed to artificially inflate property values in order to defraud lenders.

IN FOCUS   9.1

When Real Estate Appraisers Go Bad

Department of Justice Press Release

For Immediate Release

January 29, 2010

United States Attorney's Office

Central District of California

Contact: (213) 894-2434

Real Estate Appraiser Sentenced to Three Years in Prison in Mortgage Fraud Scheme That Led to $46 Million in Losses

LOS ANGELES—A former state-licensed real estate appraiser was sentenced today to three years in federal prison and ordered to pay more than $46 million in restitution for her role in a massive mortgage fraud scheme that caused tens of millions of dollars in losses to federally insured banks.

****, 43, of Rancho Santa Margarita, received the three-year prison term after her conviction last summer on conspiracy, bank fraud and numerous loan fraud charges.

**** was sentenced by United States District Judge Dean D. Pregerson, who warned that other professional real estate appraisers should know that if they inflate appraisals and lie about the value of homes, "there is an overwhelming likelihood that they will be caught and go to prison."

The evidence presented at **** trial last summer showed that she was part of a wide-ranging and sophisticated scheme that obtained inflated mortgage loans on homes in some of California's most expensive neighborhoods, including Beverly Hills, Bel Air, Holmby Hills, Malibu, Carmel, Mill Valley, Pebble Beach, and La Jolla. Members of the conspiracy sent false documentation, including bogus purchase contracts and appraisals, to the victim banks to deceive them into unwittingly funding mortgage loans that were hundreds of thousands of dollars more than the homes actually cost. Lehman Brothers Bank alone was deceived into funding more than 80 such inflated loans from 2000 into 2003, resulting in tens of millions of dollars in losses.

The evidence presented at trial showed that **** profited by collecting hundreds of thousands of dollars in fees for providing inflated appraisals in the scheme. Her appraisals typically valued the homes three times higher than what the homes really cost. In order to supposedly justify these inflated values, **** used "comps," or comparable homes, that were far bigger, more luxurious, and in better neighborhoods than the homes she appraised. Once she had inflated a few dozen homes, she then used those homes as "comps" to supposedly justify inflated prices for homes later in the scheme.

Ten other real estate professionals have been convicted of federal charges related to the scheme.

This case is the result of an investigation by the Federal Bureau of Investigation and IRS–Criminal Investigation.

Source: Reprinted From United States Attorney's Office. (2010).

Equity Skimming/Equity Fraud

Equity skimming occurs when investors persuade financially distressed homeowners to use their home equity to "hire" the investor to buy the home, or part of the home, from the homeowner and rent it back to the homeowner. The investor receives funds from the equity loan, collects fees for rent, and then defaults on the mortgage (Donohue, 2004). Figure 9.1 shows the stages of equity skimming. Here is the foundation of the equity skimming process:

> Homeowners facing foreclosure sell their homes to a third-party investor, typically located by a foreclosure consultant, but continue living in them for one year. The original homeowners use that time to build their credit or otherwise improve their financial position. Fees for the investor and the foreclosure consultant are paid from equity in the property, and at the end of the year, the property is sold back to the original owner if that person can obtain a new mortgage. (Londoño, 2007)

If the process unfolds as described, then fraud has not necessarily occurred. Fraud occurs when the investor decides not to pay the equity loan or the mortgage, resulting in the homeowner's losing his or her home to foreclosure.

A related variety of **equity fraud** occurs when offenders steal the equity of a home by forging a homeowner's signature on equity loan forms and then direct the funds from the equity loan to the offenders' bank account. Sometimes, the funds are maneuvered through several different bank accounts, including offshore and international accounts, making it virtually impossible to track the funds. As an analogy, think of a home that has a $30,000 theater system installed. The theater system has significant monetary value. If an offender breaks in and steals the theater system, then the homeowner has been victimized by theft. Now, think of a home that has $30,000 in equity (meaning that the home is worth $30,000 more than the amount of money the homeowner owes the lending institution). Just as burglars could break in and steal a theater system, offenders can steal a homeowner's equity by committing fraud against a lending institution using the homeowner's property information. Homeowners know they have been burglarized when they enter an empty home, but they may not learn of their equity theft victimization until they "receive an eviction notice" (Fannie Mae, 2007).

Reverse Mortgage Fraud

A reverse mortgage is a transaction whereby homeowners over the age of 62 sell their homes back to the lending institution and are able to live in their homes until they move or pass away. The homeowner can receive either a lump sum or monthly payments from the bank. The use of reverse mortgages has increased over the past decade, partly because of the higher number of older persons seeking strategies to increase their income. As a result, reverse mortgage frauds tend to target the elderly (FBI, 2010b). In general, **reverse mortgage fraud** refers to situations where fraudulent activities occur as part of the reverse mortgage transaction. One financial expert cites the following types of reverse mortgage fraud: charging for free information, misrepresenting pre-loan counseling, forgery of homeowner's signature, posing as government officials hired to help seniors get reverse mortgages, and bundling unnecessary services with reverse mortgage transactions (Paul, 2006). Another scheme occurs when closing agents fail to pay off the homeowner's original mortgage and pocket funds from the reverse mortgage transaction, instead of sending those funds to the lending institution (Tergesen, 2009).

Some offenders have been known to actively engage in the real estate process with the aim of committing reverse mortgage fraud. In these situations, the offenders target a foreclosed or distressed home, purchase the home with a straw buyer who lives in the home for a short while, and then get a reverse mortgage in which the bank gives the schemers a lump sum of money for the equity in the home. Then, the conspirators disappear and stop making payments on the original mortgage (Glink, 2009).

Concern exists that reverse mortgage fraud is increasing (Carswell, Seay, & Polanowski, 2013). These mortgages are particularly attractive to those with limited retirement incomes. Here are the steps followed in one type of reverse mortgage fraud targeting older adults:

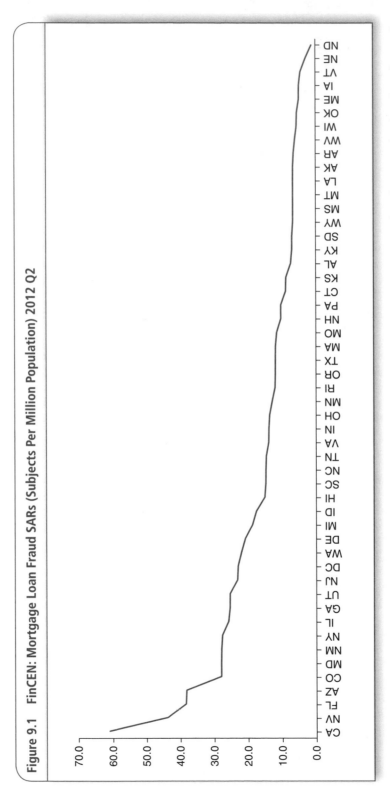

Figure 9.1 FinCEN: Mortgage Loan Fraud SARs (Subjects Per Million Population) 2012 Q2

Source: Financial Enforcement Crime Network (n.d.). *FinCEN fraud SAR dataset.* Washington, DC: U. S. Department of the Treasury. Retrieved October 30, 2015 from https://www.fincen.gov/mlf_sar_data/

1. Fraudulent offender buys a run-down home for a low price.

2. Offender promises the home to an older person at new price.

3. The offender backdates documents and makes it appear that the price paid for the house was much higher than it actually was.

4. A reverse mortgage is taken out on the house for the higher price.

5. The offender pockets the funds from the reverse mortgage.

6. The older person is given the home, but it may not be habitable. (Carswell et al., 2013)

▲ **Photo 9.2** Reverse mortgage frauds may disproportionately target older people.

The result of these behaviors have been described in this way: "The fraudster is then able to walk away with a significant profit, while the senior is left with an often unsuitable home" (Carswell et al., 2013, p. 153).

Fraud During Closing/Settlement

Real estate closings or settlements refer to the end of the real estate transaction, when buyers and sellers sign the paperwork transferring ownership and agreeing to the terms of the sale and mortgage. Types of fraud that are possible during this phase of the real estate transaction include the following:

- Closing fee kickback fraud in which settlement agents give kickbacks to real estate professionals who persuaded the parties to use the settlement agent
- Failure to reveal settlement costs that one of the parties will have to pay the lending institution, real estate professionals, or the other party
- Overstating settlement costs and pocketing the difference between the stated costs and the actual costs
- Increasing fees above those promised for real estate services provided to the buyer or seller
- Providing kickbacks to lenders (Castillo, 2007)

A related type of fraud during closing is called **dual settlement statements fraud** In these cases, settlement agents send one settlement statement to the bank and a different copy to the seller. The one given to the seller has the actual sales price agreed to by the seller. The one given to the bank has a higher selling price. The bank gives the higher amount to the settlement agent. The settlement agent gives the seller the amount he or she expected. The agent, and conspirators if there are any, keep the difference. In some cases, the buyer and seller are aware of the scheme (IRS, 2010).

Foreclosure Rescue Scams

Foreclosure rescue scams include various illicit activities designed to use impending foreclosures or a homeowner's financial distress as an element of the offense. These scams include arson, unauthorized bankruptcy filings, advance-fee frauds, and stimulus frauds. Arson as a type of foreclosure rescue scam occurs when investors, flippers, or homeowners destroy their property by fire in order to have the insurance company pay off the debt that has accumulated with the mortgage (Glink, 2009). If homeowners do this on their own, the action would not necessarily be a white-collar crime. If investors or business owners destroy their business or investment properties, these behaviors could be classified as white-collar crimes.

Unauthorized bankruptcy filings occur after a homeowner has hired a financial consultant who is paid to help the homeowner overcome his or her financial distress. The financial consultant promises to get the lending institution to stop bothering the homeowner to make mortgage payments. Without the homeowner's knowledge, the consultant files for bankruptcy on behalf of the homeowner. The homeowner stops receiving calls from the lending institution and assumes that the consultant has fixed the situation. When the homeowner fails to show up for the bankruptcy hearing (which he or she does not know about), the foreclosure process begins (FBI, 2009b).

Advance-fee fraud occurs when financial consultants or other individuals charge fees in advance to help homeowners address their financial problems. In many cases, the fraud occurs when offenders charge homeowners up front for help refinancing their mortgage. Federal officials have noted that these schemes have become increasingly popular over the past few years (FinCEN, 2010c). The popularity of advance-fee schemes led some states to pass laws to address the offenses. In California, for instance, a law was passed that stated

> it is illegal for . . . any person including lawyers, real estate brokers, real estate professionals, corporations, companies, partnerships, or any other licensed or unlicensed person or party to demand, charge, or collect any advance, up-front, or retainer fees, or any other type of pre-payment compensation, for loan modification work or services, or any other form of mortgage loan forbearance. (California Department of Real Estate, 2009)

Stimulus frauds occur when offenders use government stimulus programs as a tool for foreclosure rescue frauds (FinCEN, 2010b). Offenders hide behind the guise of government support and recruit potential victims through well-organized "clinics" they hold at luxury hotels or other posh settings. One approach that is used is the "redemptionist" approach where distressed homeowners are promised that their debt will go away if they participate in a redemption program (FinCEN, 2010b). Those in financial distress, a vulnerable state, trust the "financial consultants" and end up passing along private information that the offenders use to steal from the homeowner. Foreclosure schemes "are particularly evil because they prey on people with big enough financial problems that they're in danger of losing their home" (Curry, 2007).

Builder-Initiated Fraud

Builder-initiated mortgage frauds occur when builders or developers engage in behaviors that are designed to defraud the lender or the buyer. Such behaviors include (a) pump-and-pay schemes, (b) builder bailout schemes, and (c) faulty credit enhancements. With regard to pump-and-pay schemes, some builders work with others in the housing system to fraudulently increase their property's value. The builder has the property refinanced and collects the fraudulently obtained equity (Glink, 2009). The builder might actually repay the equity loan, but the fact remains the equity was fraudulently created.

In **builder bailout schemes**, builders offer buyers "excessive incentives" but hide those offers from the mortgage company to make it appear that the property is worth more than it is actually worth (FBI, 2010b). It has become increasingly common, for example, for builders to give homeowners a new car to get them to purchase a new home. As long as the builder reports this incentive to the lender, such practices are legitimate. When builders hide these incentives, they are able to increase the amount of profit they actually get from the lender.

Faulty credit enhancements by builders occur when builders engage in measures that make it appear as if buyers have better credit than they actually have. They do this to ensure that buyers are able to secure a mortgage. For instance, builders might put money in a buyer's account to make it appear that the buyer has a strong credit rating and the funds needed for the down payment (Glink, 2009). The problem is that the buyer actually does not have good credit and his or her risk of not being able to repay the mortgage is higher than the lending institution realizes. The builder sells the home, gets the money, and then the lending institution may in the not-so-distant future end up having to begin the foreclosure process on the home.

Flipping

Flipping occurs when scammers buy and resell properties with inflated prices. Sometimes, the same home will be sold over and over at escalating prices as part of these schemes. This should not be confused with legitimate flipping businesses, whereby investors purchase homes, fix them up, and then sell the homes for a profit (Curry, 2007). In the illegal flip, the home is bought, sold, resold, resold, and so on, with no changes made to the property. Fraudulent appraisals are used to resell the property at inflated prices (FBI, 2009b).

Reselling the same property creates numerous problems for neighborhoods. Typically, these homes are not well maintained, and the presence of dilapidated structures potentially breeds additional problems. Also, when the home is resold at higher prices, those who legitimately own their homes will have their property values artificially inflated. This is problematic for at least two reasons. First, the homeowners' property taxes will increase as the result of the artificially inflated prices. Second, if homeowners purchase neighboring homes based on appraisals including the flipped home's artificially inflated price, they will be purchasing their home at an inflated price. At some point, the home will potentially be worth less than the amount of money the homeowner owes on mortgage. This is known as the mortgage being *under water*. In Focus 9.2, Flip This, provides a detailed description of the way that the flipping process is carried out.

IN FOCUS 9.2

Flip This

Here is a case description of property flipping excerpted from an FDIC (2007) publication:

During a routine examination of a $1 billion financial institution, examiners became suspicious when they noticed that one loan officer worked apart from other loan originators and had processing personnel dedicated to his loan originations. Bank management indicated the loan officer was the bank's highest producer and that "even a bad month was a good month" for that loan officer. The loan officer maintained a high number of loan originations, even though he took no referrals from the phone queue. On further investigation, the FDIC discovered that the loan officer had an undisclosed relationship with a local mortgage broker. Examiners' review of the officer's lending activity revealed several loans that had been originated, sold, and then quickly fell into foreclosure. Properties were also refinanced rapidly, with an affiliate of the broker placing second mortgages on the property that would immediately be paid from the next refinance. A sample of the officer's loan documentation discovered altered or falsified account statements, purchase and sale agreements, income figures, credit reports, and verification of deposit forms. The loan officer has since resigned from the institution and is the subject of an ongoing criminal investigation. Total loss exposure to the bank is still being determined; however, the bank has already had to repurchase several loans as a result of this officer's actions.

Source: Reprinted From Federal Deposit Insurance Corporation. (2007). Staying alert to mortgage fraud. Available from http://www.fdic.gov/regulations/examinations/supervisory/insights/sisum07/aritcle02_staying-alert.html

Qualifications Fraud

Qualifications fraud refers to situations where professionals lie about a buyer's qualifications in order to secure a mortgage that allows the buyer to purchase the home. Industry professionals will lie about or exaggerate any of the following: income, assets, collateral, length of employment, employment status, and property value (FBI, 2005). Those items most commonly misrepresented are "employment, income, and occupancy intentions" (FDIC, 2007). In some cases, professionals might help buyers appear to be qualified when they are not (IRS, 2010). For instance, real estate developers or agents might tell buyers to have their names added to a family member's or friend's bank account so they look as if they have more funds available for the home purchase than they do (FBI, 2009b). Not surprisingly, income overstatement has been empirically tied to "poor performance during the mortgage credit boom" (Mian & Sufi, 2015, p. 1).

Real Estate Agent/Investor Fraud

Real estate agent/investor fraud refers to a variety of scams committed by agents and investors. For example, **home improvement scams** include instances when agents or investors conceal problems with homes that should be disclosed to potential buyers. **Fraudulent loan origination** scams occur when professionals help buyers qualify for loans even though the buyers are not actually qualified. **Chunking** occurs when investors buy several properties without telling banks about properties other than the one the bank is financing. **Liar loans** refer to situations where investors lie about loans they have or are trying to get. **Churning** refers to "excessive selling [of the same property] for the purpose of generating fees and commissions" (Fannie Mae, 2007). Many of these scams occur as part of a broader scheme involving several coconspirators. As an illustration, churning may occur as part of a flipping scheme where homes are sold and resold. The agent's role in these schemes is to broker the deal and collect commissions. As well, in many appraisal fraud cases, "unscrupulous real estate agents . . . conspire with appraisers to fraudulently declare artificially high market values for homes" (Bennett, 2007).

Another variety of real estate agent fraud—which involves the help of fraudulent appraisers—is "inflate and crash" schemes (Bennett, 2007). In these situations, homes are sold at inflated prices (thousands of dollars above the listing price), and when the bank gives the seller the funds from the transaction, the seller gives the amount of funds that was over the listing price back to the coconspirators. Here are the steps in this fraud:

1. Randy lists his house for sale for $400,000.

2. Susan offers Randy $600,000 for his house on the condition that he gives $180,000 back to her at closing. This would mean that Randy is selling the house for $420,000.

3. Real estate agents negotiate the deal and approve it because it increases their commissions.

4. The appraiser appraises the house value at an inflated value of $600,000.

5. After closing the sale, Randy gives Susan the $180,000, and she divides the proceeds with the real estate agents and the appraiser.

6. Susan lives in the home for a short period, but then she stops paying the mortgage and is evicted. The lending institution is unable to recover its losses as the home is not worth more than $400,000.

One mortgage fraud investigator alone said he had encountered 400 cases of "inflate and crash" fraud (Bennett, 2007).

● ● ● Consequences of Mortgage Fraud

The consequences of mortgage fraud are widespread. To fully understand these consequences, it is necessary to focus on the consequences for (a) individual victims of mortgage fraud, (b) business victims of mortgage fraud, (c) communities and neighborhoods where the frauds occur, and (d) the real estate market. In terms of individual victims of mortgage fraud, homeowners victimized by mortgage fraud experience tragic consequences as a result of these crimes. Consumers who have lost their homes due to these offenses offer "stories of financial ruin" (J. C. Anderson, 2010). James Frois, director of the federal government's Financial Crime Enforcement Network lamented that the most "troubling aspect" of some types of mortgage fraud is that the fraudulent actions "take advantage of senior citizens who have worked hard over their entire lives to own their homes" (FinCEN, 2010a).

When businesses are victimized by mortgage fraud, similar stories of financial ruin may surface. Beyond the dollar losses that lending institutions experience from fraud, many businesses face problems with morale and potential business failures as a result of fraud. After Lee Farkas, chairman of the bankrupted mortgage lender Taylor, Bean, and Whitaker Mortgage Corporation, perpetrated a mortgage scheme that resulted in millions in overdrafts to the bank, the fraud "contributed to the downfall of Colonial Bank" ("Ex U.S. Mortgage Executive Charged," 2010). Many employees lost their jobs, and the bank ceased to exist because of the illicit actions of Farkas.

Communities will also experience negative consequences from mortgage fraud. Abandoned homes used in various mortgage frauds become targets of vandals (Fannie Mae, 2007), and the vandalism results in neighboring homes having lower property values (Creswell, 2007). The abandoned homes also increase levels of disorganization in the neighborhood, which may serve to breed conventional crime. Alternatively, as noted above, some types of mortgage fraud, like variations of appraisal fraud, may artificially increase property values and subsequently raise homeowners' property taxes (Fannie Mae, 2007).

The real estate market also experiences consequences from mortgage fraud. At the simplest level, increased mortgage rates and fees and difficulties determining actual home values have been linked to fraud (Fannie Mae, 2007). Federal officials suggested that "a direct correlation between fraud and distressed real estate markets [exists]" (FBI, 2009b). Others have suggested that the inflated home prices found during the real estate boom of the early to mid-2000s could be attributed to mortgage fraud (J. C. Anderson, 2010). In somewhat of a cyclical pattern, then, the current housing crisis can be seen as stemming at least partly from potentially fraudulent activities. Many homeowners now have mortgages that are higher than the value of their homes. The high rate of foreclosures has dropped home values even further. Ironically, the lack of business for mortgage industry insiders is now being seen as a motivating factor for current fraudulent activities.

● ● ● Patterns Surrounding Mortgage Fraud

Because mortgage fraud is a recent social and crime problem, virtually no criminological studies have examined the offense type. Still, news reports and government studies reveal three patterns that characterize these offenses. First, somewhat similar to other white-collar crimes, the offenses generally involve large dollar losses. The offenses can range from thousands of dollars to millions of dollars, depending on the size of the mortgage and value of the home.

Second, and also similar to other white-collar crimes, mortgage fraud cases often occur over long periods of time. Offenders committing these schemes do not tend to commit the offense just once and stop. Rather, they appear to commit the offenses over time as a part of their occupational routines.

Third, these are offenses that typically involve coconspirators. The very nature of the mortgage process requires that individuals work with other professionals to process the mortgage loans. When fraud occurs, more than one offender is likely involved in the incident. Here is how one mortgage broker described his role in mortgage fraud:

As a mortgage broker, you have lenders so you set up your accounts with different lenders. When dealing with lenders, you have to meet certain guidelines in order for them to accept the package which is you put together an application, you get an appraisal, and you get all of the documents together for them to be able to say that they are going to finance this loan. Sometimes the lender will walk you through certain things and tell you what you are supposed to do; they are not always ethical, but we still do them. I feel that because I allowed myself to be persuaded by listening and adapting to what I knew was wrong but I didn't act on what I felt was

Table 9.1	Top Ten Regions With SARs for Mortgage Fraud in 2012 (Second Quarter)
Location	**Subjects**
Los Angeles-Long Beach-Santa Ana, CA	4,028
Miami-Fort Lauderdale-Pompano Beach, FL	2,364
New York-Northern New Jersey-Long Island, NY-NJ-PA	2,326
Chicago-Naperville-Joliet, IL-IN-WI	1,738
Riverside-San Bernardino-Ontario, CA	1,385
San Francisco-Oakland-Fremont, CA	1,060
Phoenix-Mesa-Scottsdale, AZ	1,002
Atlanta-Sandy Springs-Marietta, GA	837
Washington-Arlington-Alexandria, DC-VA-MD-WV	806
San Diego-Carlsbad-San Marcos, CA	778

Note: Subjects Reported in MLF SARs, by Core Based Statistical Area (CBSA)

Source: Financial Enforcement Crime Network (n.d.). *FinCEN fraud SAR dataset.* Washington, DC: U.S. Department of the Treasury. Retrieved October 30, 2015 from https://www.fincen.gov/mlf_sar_data/

the right way of doing it, I went along with what as they say going along with the program, I went along with the program so that's why I'm here. I made a mistake actually. . . . It's standard for it for sure; you will talk with any other mortgage company, you will find that in doing your mortgages when you call the company they have what's called AE's and you talk to them and they walk you through step by step or they have what's called the underwriter so they are gonna tell you the exact documents that they need or what you need to do in order to make this loan fly. Now I'm by no means trying to blame anyone else because I take full responsibility for my actions, there's that line, that gray area that you should know, you know this doesn't sound right and you are the one that is responsible so not at all that I am trying to say that I'm not responsible. I still think responsibility needs to go others who gave me this knowledge; it's still going on so it doesn't make sense to me. (Klenowski, 2012, p. 473)

Fourth, government studies show that mortgage fraud is distributed differently across the country. Table 9.1 shows the top 10 regions where suspicious activity reports for mortgage fraud occurred in the second quarter of 2012. As shown in the table, the top three areas where suspicious reports come from include regions of Miami, Los Angeles, and New York City. Figure 9.2 shows the breakdowns by states in the second quarter of 2012.

Historically, states that are believed to have significant mortgage problems include (1) Florida, (2) New York, (3) California, (4) Arizona, (5) Michigan, (6) Maryland, (7) New Jersey, (8) Georgia, (9) Illinois, and (10) Virginia (Mortgage Asset Research Institute, 2010). State laws have been somewhat successful in curbing mortgage fraud. Georgia, for example, dropped from being the state with the highest ranking for mortgage fraud to eighth after the state passed laws addressing mortgage fraud and increased its efforts to become more vigilant in responding to these crimes (Glink & Tamkin, 2008).

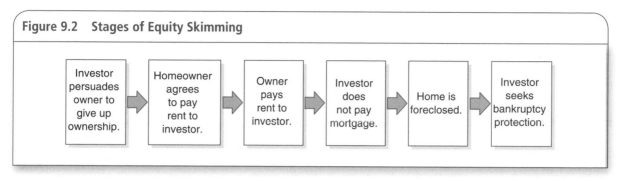

Figure 9.2   Stages of Equity Skimming

Investor persuades owner to give up ownership. → Homeowner agrees to pay rent to investor. → Owner pays rent to investor. → Investor does not pay mortgage. → Home is foreclosed. → Investor seeks bankruptcy protection.

Source: Adapted from Donahue, K. (2004 October 7). "*Statement of Kenneth Donuhue, Inspector General Department of Housing and Urban Development.*" Before the United States House of Representatives Subcommittee on housing and Community Opportunity Committee on Financial Services.

Based on the patterns surrounding mortgage fraud, warning signs for these offenses have been identified. These warning signs include the following:

- Inflated appraisals
- Increased commissions for brokers and appraisers
- Exclusive use of one appraiser
- Requests to sign blank forms
- Higher than customary fees (FBI, 2009c)

The Mortgage Bankers Association (MBA, 2007) called for a number of changes to increase efforts to prevent and more easily identify cases of mortgage fraud. In particular, the MBA supports these changes:

- Mandatory reporting requirements to law enforcement about certain types of transactions
- Better communication between the mortgage industry and law enforcement
- A database of censored or debarred mortgage officials
- Increased funding for preventing and prosecuting these offenses
- Assigning law enforcement responsibility to one specific U.S. Department of Justice office
- Enhancing intergovernmental collaborations in prosecuting mortgage fraud cases

The relative newness of the mortgage fraud crisis has forced criminal justice officials to respond using strategies and tools built for other types of crimes. These agencies have adapted and continue to change in an effort to improve the response to these cases. For example, in March 2010, the Financial Fraud Enforcement Task Force (created by President Barack Obama in fall 2009) held a summit in Phoenix, Arizona, to address mortgage fraud. At that summit, U.S. Attorney General Eric Holder announced that an additional $8 million would be provided to agencies to step up their efforts to address mortgage fraud. Similar summits have been held in other cities with high rates of mortgage fraud. The summits brought together criminal justice officials, community leaders, officials from lending institutions, and other real estate professionals to promote the coordinated response needed to address mortgage fraud effectively.

The conditions leading to mortgage fraud during the housing crisis have been called a "perfect storm" (Patterson & Koller, 2011). The subprime mortgage market was seen as ripe for fraud with lax laws, securitization of high-risk mortgages, a housing boom, and new players entering the mortgage market. Describing this perfect storm, Patterson and Koller (2011) wrote as follows:

▲ **Photo 9.3**   Slumlord behavior may lead to homelessness.

Combined with escalating housing prices and equity accumulations, this represented a regime shift with an upward credit cycle. Homebuyers, brokers, lenders, securitizers, and investors all enjoyed eased entry conditions, which in turn increased competition, risk taking, predatory lending, and fraud. All the while, housing values, origination volumes, and investment profits soared, and what appeared to be manageable debt continued to accumulate across the board (p. 42).

Some criminologists have suggested that the practices underlying the fraud in the housing crisis disproportionately impacted minorities (Nguyen & Pontell, 2011). Through predatory loan practices, minorities who could not actually afford homes were given loans after dumping their life savings into the new home. Many of them later lost their homes and their livelihoods because they should not have been given the loan in the first place. Nguyen and Pontell (2011) described opening up the home market to minorities as a "latent and sinister element that has little to do with equality and more to do with continued victimization and exploitation" (p. 20). Another author team echoed similar sentiments stating, "The tendency to blame the recent financial crisis on lending to 'risky applicants,' however, masks underlying problems of predation and deregulation in the housing market (Velez, Lyons, & Boursaw, 2012, p. 1049).

● ● ● Slumlords as White-Collar Criminals

Another pervasive crime in the housing system is the failure of landlords to provide adequate housing. The concept **slumlord** is used to describe landlords who profit from renting run-down apartments that are not maintained by the property owner. While some may think that these behaviors are not criminal, the **Uniform Residential Landlord and Tenant Act (URLTA)** is a federal law stipulating that homes must be inhabitable, up to code, safe, and capable of providing the necessary utilities (Richter, 2010). States and localities have similar laws and codes. One issue that arises, though, is that local officials must decide which is worse: (1) forcing impoverished tenants to move out of their homes and perhaps end up homeless or (2) doing nothing and allowing the slumlord's activities to continue (M. Thomas, 2005).

In some instances, local officials are excluded from decision-making processes designed to respond to slumlords. Lawsuits against slumlords are a perfect example. Adam Murray, executive director of the Inner City Law Center in California, described a case where one landlord was sued by 56 tenants after the landlord had been cited for 2,700 code violations. Here are some of the problems uncovered as described verbatim from the out-of-court settlement:

- Dilapidated plumbing that caused a ceiling to collapse onto a tenant
- Cockroach infestations so overwhelming that roaches lodged themselves in the ears of sleeping tenants and mothers had to stand watch over their sleeping babies
- An elevator that was out of service for 3 years, requiring mothers of small children to carry their baby's strollers up as many as four flights of stairs
- Sewage pipes that had leaked into an apartment, soaking the tenant's living room rug with raw sewage (Murray, 2009b)

The case was settled out of court with the slumlord agreeing to pay the tenants $3.3 million.

Imagine the horror of the parents who found a cockroach lodged in their child's ear. The consequences of such filth are enormous. In the following paragraphs, attention is given to the numerous types of negative consequences that slumlords' activities have on individuals, communities, and society.

Consequences of Slumlord Behavior

Few criminological studies have focused on the consequences of slumlords' behaviors. However, using sociological, public policy, and public health literature, one can identify a host of different consequences that are likely to arise when landlords fail to maintain their property. These consequences include the following:

- Health consequences
- Financial consequences
- Dehumanization
- Emotional consequences
- Decreased property values
- Social disorganization
- Crime
- Legislative consequences
- Grassroots efforts

Each of these consequences is addressed below.

With regard to *health consequences*, public health scholars have long noted that individuals' health outcomes are tied to the types of environments in which the individuals live. Those who live in run-down apartments that are not well maintained are more likely to experience negative health outcomes. As one expert notes, "ill health and living in slums are intrinsically interwoven" (Sheuya, 2008, p. 298). According to one estimate, in Los Angeles, 48,000 people "get sick each year from living in slum conditions" (Murray, 2009a).

To be sure, landlords are not to blame for all of the problems that arise in slums, but if they actively choose not to maintain their property, then one can suggest that they have at least some blame in the negative health outcomes that are tied to slum conditions.

Financial consequences also arise from the behaviors of slumlords. On one level, it must be stressed that the health conditions are tied to financial consequences for those exposed to slum conditions. Individuals who get sick from living in slums will have health care bills to pay. They also will miss work as a result of the health conditions. Health care bills and missing work result in very real financial consequences for those living in slums. On another level, it is important to note that living in slums can actually cost residents and members of society significantly. As a simple example, for residents, utility bills for utilities operating through broken appliances can be exorbitant. A leaky faucet or broken toilet not fixed by the landlord can drastically raise the tenant's water bill. Or, an outdated furnace or air conditioner can add precious dollars to the tenant's heating and cooling bill. While tenants will "pay more" to live in a slumlord's property, residents and city officials will also pay more as a result of the slumlord's behavior. Four decades ago, the National Commission on Urban Problems (1972) noted that "slums are expensive to city administrations" (p. 5). The same comment remains true today.

Dehumanization is another consequence of the slumlord's behaviors. Residents of slums are in positions of powerlessness, whereas the property manager and landlords have significant power over the tenants. The degree of control given to property owners is such that the lives of tenants are truly in the landlord's hands. For those who don't maintain their properties, it can be suggested that the landlords are, in effect, treating human beings in dehumanizing ways. Arguing for the need for laws to protect residents, Colorado Representative Michael Merrifield commented that the living conditions of pets and animals are better protected than humans' living conditions are. He pleaded before the state legislature: "It's time—it's past time for Colorado's human animals to have the same rights as Colorado's dogs and cats" (Gathright, 2008).

Tenants will also experience *emotional consequences* from living in a slumlord's property. Perhaps the simplest way to explain how slum residents experience emotional consequences is to apply Maslow's *hierarchy of needs* to tenants. Maslow argued that all individuals have certain needs, and these needs could be categorized as a hierarchy including lower-level needs and higher-level needs (see Figure 9.3). According to Maslow, we direct our behaviors toward meeting our lower-level needs, and once those needs are fulfilled, we then direct our behaviors toward fulfilling the higher-level needs. The most basic needs individuals have are physiological needs—the need for food, clean air, water, usable toilets, and so on. The next level of needs is security needs—the need to feel safe. If we have our physiological and security needs met, then we are able to focus on meeting higher-level needs—including belonging, self-esteem, and self-actualization. It is very likely that those who live in slums will face problems with food, air, water, and other physiological needs. As well, many will feel threatened by crime. As a result, most of their efforts will be spent on behaviors targeting physiological and security needs, meaning they won't be able to address their emotional needs.

A simple example might clarify how slumlords' behaviors contribute to these processes. In one case in which a landlord was convicted for not making repairs ordered by code officials, one of the residents described how his "girlfriend's seven-year-old missed school because of a lack of water to bathe in" (Yaniv & Moore, 2008, p. 18). In effect, the child could not go to school and work toward meeting his higher-level needs because he was not able to have his lower-level needs fulfilled.

Another consequence of slumlords' behaviors are *decreased property values.* As noted above, property values in a particular neighborhood are tied to the value of nearby properties. If landlords fail to maintain their property, the value of the property will plummet, and the value of the neighboring properties will go down as well.

Slumlords' behaviors also contribute to *social and physical disorder.* Social disorder refers to social activities of residents that lack order and cohesion. Activities such as open-market drug dealing, unsupervised youth, public drunkenness, and so on are examples. Physical disorder refers to changes in properties or other physical structures. Graffiti, burglar bars, vandalism, litter, and other physical changes to the environment are examples. In this context, it is reasonable to suggest that when landlords fail to maintain their properties, the likelihood for social and physical disorder increases. Said one representative to a reporter, "these slumlords destroy a block, and that destroys a neighborhood" (Singer, 1999). Describing this phenomenon, Justice William O. Douglas once said in a court option, "The misery of housing may despoil a community as an open sewer may ruin a river" (cited in Murray, 2009a).

Slumlords' behaviors may also contribute to *crime* in a particular neighborhood. This notion is related to broken windows theory. Broken windows theory suggests that disorder leads to crime because disorder sends a "signal that no one cares" (Wilson & Kelling, 1982, p. 31) to potential offenders. As an example, when I was in the second grade, my family lived in a home near the railroad tracks and across the street from an abandoned milk factory. I was with some kids playing ball in the street when a baseball went through one of the windows in the abandoned building. Like many (unsupervised) youth might do, we all ran home. A few months later a group of kids (again unsupervised) was hanging out and looking at the broken window on the old factory. The kids assumed that "no one cares" about the building and, out of boredom, proceeded to throw rocks at the windows and break virtually every window in the building. In effect, one broken window, left unfixed, led to dozens of broken windows.

With regard to slumlords, when landlords fail to maintain their property, it is possible that the degraded property sends messages to potential offenders that "no one cares." Some problem-oriented policing practices have integrated landlords into efforts to restore neighborhoods, and in some places landlords are held criminally liable for contributing to neighborhood decay. Interestingly, while it is possible that slumlords' behaviors (white-collar crimes) lead to street crimes, no criminological studies have assessed how this form of white-collar misconduct potentially breeds additional crimes. This is a fruitful area of study. Perhaps readers looking for capstone, thesis, or future dissertation topics will find this area of research interesting enough to address. The potential implications—for theory, policy, and future research—from such a study are laudable.

Legislative consequences have also resulted from the pervasiveness of slumlords' behaviors. States have passed a number of different laws in an effort to control slumlords. In Washington state, legislators passed a tenant relocation assistance bill that stipulated that landlords had to pay tenants three times their monthly rent (up to $2,000) if the tenants were displaced because housing code violations forced the residence to be condemned. If landlords do not pay the tenants, the law stipulates that local governments may pay and then collect funds plus interest from landlords. The new law also requires landlords to return deposits in these situations (Thomas, 2005).

In Colorado, HB 1356, passed in 2008, stipulated, "In every rental agreement, the landlord is deemed to warrant that the premises are fit for human habitation" (Kopel, 2008). Arizona's Residential Landlord and Tenant Act offered a little more direction in defining expectations of landlords. This law requires landlords or rental properties to fulfill the following:

- Meet building and health codes
- Make repairs to make the home inhabitable
- Keep common areas clean and safe
- Keep appliances supplied by the landlord working and safe
- Provide for trash removal
- Supply water, heating, and cooling (Volunteer Lawyers Program Community Legal Services, 2009)

Failure to meet these expectations can result in civil penalties for landlords.

Grassroots responses are a final type of consequence resulting from slumlords' behaviors. In some cases, tenants and community members may come together in an effort to address specific slumlords. In other cases, advocacy groups have been formed to help residents exposed to slumlords. One rather interesting grassroots effort is the use of the Internet to share information about bad landlords. Websites have been developed where renters are able to evaluate or rate their landlords. If you still live with your parents, you may want to think twice about rating them.

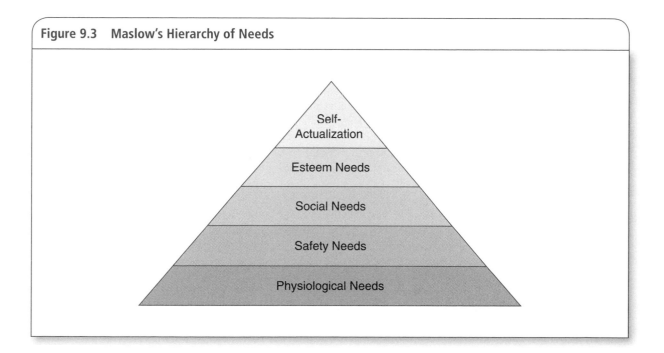

Figure 9.3 Maslow's Hierarchy of Needs

Responding to Slumlords

Tenants who encounter slumlords are advised to follow a formal and written process in addressing their concerns. In reporting complaints to the local housing authority, tenants will find tremendous variation in the way that localities respond to misconduct by landlords. Many major cities now have housing courts where these disputes are heard. Typically, the sanctions administered in these courts are fines and directives to fix up the property. The fines are collected by the city (and are not necessarily given to the victims). Ideally, such funds can be used to address slumlord behavior on a community scale. In Brooklyn, New York, the Housing Preservation and Development court collected $4.52 million in fines in 2007 ("Landlord Jailed," 2008). Box 9.2 describes one career related to these efforts.

CAREERS RESPONDING TO WHITE-COLLAR CRIME

Housing Management Specialist (Air Force)

The primary purpose of this position is:

- To perform a variety of housing assignments related to maintainability, habitability, and cleanliness of housing units; and to provide contract surveillance, performing inspector duties related to maintenance, repair, and janitorial requirements.
- Performs installation housing facilities services.

- Monitors service contracts within this functional responsibility.
- Performs surveys of housing units, streets, utility systems, roofs, and other conditions for input to housing improvements, maintenance, alterations, modification, and construction programs and projects.
- Reviews all self-help work orders and recommends approval or disapproval.

Source: Reprinted from USAJobs.Gov

Criminal penalties are applied less often to slumlords, but they are occasionally used. Not long ago, Hamid Khan was sentenced to 9 days in jail and ordered to pay $156,000 in fines after a 94-unit Bronx apartment building he owned racked up more than 2,000 code violations (E. Brown, 2008). Note that his sanction was not for the violations but for the failure to fix the violations after he was ordered to do so.

In what *Newsweek* called "the prescription to fit the crime," some judges have sentenced slumlords to live in the slums they owned. Milton Avol's tenants "repeatedly complained of horrors: rats roaming through bedrooms, frayed electrical wiring, foul water seeping through cracked plaster." Avol earned the nickname "ratlord" ("R[X] for the 'Ratlord,'" 1987, p. 54). Other landlords have faced similar sanctions. In Boston, a judge ordered a slumlord to live in his rental property until the property was repaired, *and* the judge said the family living in the rental property could live in the slumlord's own home (Zeman & Howard, 1992). In Washington, DC, a landlord who pleaded guilty to 70 building code violations was sentenced to live for 2 months "where his tenants lived without heat, hot water, and basic sanitation" (Leonning, 2001, p. B1). Later, officials recommended that the landlord be placed on electronic monitoring to ensure that he actually lived on the decayed property (Kovaleski, 2002).

Clearly, the behavior of slumlords presents numerous problems for residents, community members, city administrators, and the rest of society. Efforts to control slumlords have been largely unsuccessful. Still, the continuing local, state, and federal activities are warranted. Without some form of intervention, slums could be in even more dire straits than they currently are.

SUMMARY

- In this chapter, attention was given to crimes committed in the housing system.
- The most commonly committed crimes in the housing system include mortgage fraud and renting unsafe properties (e.g., being a slumlord).
- Mortgage fraud involves cases of "intentional misrepresentation to a lender for the purpose of obtaining a loan that would otherwise not be advanced by the lender" (FinCEN, 2009).
- It is important to stress that not all cases of mortgage fraud are necessarily white-collar crimes committed by employers.
- At the most general level, experts distinguish between mortgage fraud-for-profit and mortgage fraud-for-housing.
- In terms of types of for-profit fraud, the following types of mortgage fraud were discussed: (1) straw buyer fraud, (2) short sale fraud, (3) appraisal fraud, (4) equity skimming, (5) reverse mortgage fraud, (6) fraud during closing and settlement, (7) foreclosure rescue scams, (8) builder initiated fraud, (9) flipping, (10) qualifications fraud, and (11) real estate agent/investor fraud.
- Curry (2007) identified two types of straw buyers: (1) the conspirator straw buyers who are in on the scheme and the (2) victim straw buyers who are not in on the scheme but who believe they will either legitimately own the home or be able to rent it.
- The phrase *short sale* refers to instances where lending institutions allow homes to be sold for amounts that are lower than what the homeowner owed on the home's mortgage.
- Appraisal fraud occurs when appraisers misrepresent the actual value of a home.
- One variety of equity fraud occurs when offenders steal the equity of a home by forging a homeowner's signature on equity loan forms and then direct the funds from the equity loan to the offender's bank account.
- Reverse mortgage fraud refers to situations where fraudulent activities occur as part of the reverse mortgage transaction.
- Foreclosure rescue scams include various illicit activities designed to use impending foreclosures or a homeowner's financial distress as an element of the offense.
- Builder-initiated mortgage frauds occur when builders or developers engage in behaviors that are designed to defraud the lender or the buyer including (1) pump-and-pay schemes, (2) builder bailout schemes, and (3) faulty credit enhancements.
- Flipping occurs when scammers buy and resell properties with inflated prices. Sometimes, the same home will be sold over and over at escalating prices as part of these schemes.
- Qualifications fraud refers to situations where professionals lie about a buyer's qualifications in order to secure a mortgage and allow the buyer to purchase the home.
- Real estate agent/investor fraud refers to a variety of scams committed by agents and investors.
- To fully understand these consequences, attention was given to (1) individual victims of mortgage fraud, (2) business victims of mortgage fraud, (3) communities and neighborhoods where the frauds occur, and (4) the real estate market.
- Because mortgage fraud is a recent social and crime problem, virtually no criminological studies have examined the offense type.
- The concept *slumlord* is used to describe landlords who profit from renting run-down apartments that are not maintained by the property owner.
- These consequences of failing to maintain rental properties include health consequences, financial consequences, dehumanization, emotional consequences, decreased property values, social disorganization, crime, legislative consequences, and grassroots efforts.
- Tenants who encounter slumlords are advised to follow a formal and written process in addressing their concerns.

KEY TERMS

Advance-fee fraud

Appraisal fraud

Builder bailout schemes

Builder-initiated mortgage fraud

Chunking

Churning

Conspiracy appraisal fraud

Deflated appraisals

Dual settlement statements fraud

Equity fraud

Equity skimming

Flipping

Foreclosure rescue scams

Fraud-for-housing

Fraud-for-profit

Fraudulent loan origination

Home improvement scams

Inflated appraisals

Liar loans

Mortgage fraud

Qualifications fraud

Real estate agent/investor fraud

Reverse mortgage fraud

Short sale fraud

Slumlord

Straw buyer fraud

Uniform Residential Landlord and Tenant Act (URLTA)

Windshield appraisal fraud

DISCUSSION QUESTIONS

1. Which type of mortgage fraud do you think is the most serious type?

2. What are three similarities between mortgage fraud and the behaviors of slumlords? What are three differences between the two types of crimes?

3. You are elected mayor of a large city that has several properties that appear to be run by slumlords. If you close the slums down, your homeless population will increase. If you allow the slumlords to continue their practices, other negative consequences will surface. What will you do?

4. Describe how mortgage fraud and slumlord activity might actually cause street crime.

5. List four concepts that come to mind when you think of the word *slumlord*. What do these concepts have to do with white-collar crime?

6. What does the systems approach have to do with mortgage fraud and slumlord activities?

7. If you could choose a career responding to either mortgage fraud, slumlord behavior, or other types of white-collar crime, which career would you choose? Why?

WEB RESOURCES

Flipping Frenzy: http://www.flippingfrenzy.com/

Mortgage Assistance Relief Scams: http://www.ftc.gov/bcp/edu/pubs/consumer/credit/cre42.shtm

Slumlord Laws: http://definitions.uslegal.com/s/slumlord/

Mortgage Fraud Prevention: https://www.fanniemae.com/singlefamily/mortgage-fraud-prevention

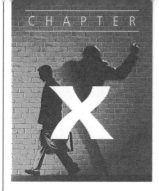

CHAPTER

X

Crimes by the Corporate System

CHAPTER HIGHLIGHTS

- Conceptualizing Corporate Crime
- Types of Corporate Crime
- Dynamics of Corporate Offending
- Public Concern About Crimes by the Corporate System

A student interested in learning more about a specific for-profit college completed a website registration form indicating interest in the college. Minutes later, the individual received a phone call from a marketing specialist from the college. The student told that marketer that he was interested in criminal justice. The marketer told the student that he should consider a medical assistant certificate instead because he would potentially earn $70,000 a year after just 9 months of course work. In reality, 9 out of 10 employees in the medical assisting field make under $40,000 a year. And the marketer knew this. What the marketer did not know, however, was that the "student" was actually an undercover employee working on an investigation focusing on the marketing practices of for-profit colleges for the U.S. Government Accountability Office (U.S. Government Accountability Office [USGAO], 2010).

In this case, the marketer's illicit actions were conducted to benefit the company for which he worked. This distinguishes the misconduct from those discussed earlier in this work. Indeed, all of the offenses discussed in the prior chapters were conducted by the employee and for the employee's benefit. Other white-collar offenses either benefit—or are committed by, an employer or business. Consider the following quotes from press releases distributed by different government agencies:

- LifeLock will pay $100 million to settle Federal Trade Commission contempt charges that it violated the terms of a 2010 federal court order that requires the company to secure consumers' personal information and prohibits the company from deceptive advertising. This is the largest monetary award obtained by the Commission in an order enforcement action . . . Second, the filing alleged that during this period LifeLock falsely advertised that it protected consumers' sensitive data with the same high-level safeguards used by financial institutions. Third, the FTC alleged that, from January 2012 through December 2014, LifeLock falsely advertised that it would send alerts "as soon as" it received any indication that a consumer may be a victim of identity theft. Finally, the FTC alleged that the company failed to abide by the order's recordkeeping requirements. (FTC, 2015,December 17)

- The [California] Attorney General's lawsuit alleges that Corinthian has violated consumer protection and securities laws. For example, Corinthian misrepresented job placement rates to students and investors, advertised for programs that it did not offer, and subjected students to unlawful debt collection practices. The Attorney General filed the lawsuit in October 2013, and the case is still in progress. (California Attorney General's Office, 2015)

- DB Group Services (UK) Limited, a wholly owned subsidiary of Deutsche Bank AG (Deutsche Bank), has agreed to plead guilty to wire fraud for its role in manipulating the London Interbank Offered Rate (LIBOR), a leading benchmark interest rate used in financial products and transactions around the world. In addition, Deutsche Bank entered into a deferred prosecution agreement to resolve wire fraud and antitrust charges in connection with its role in both manipulating U.S. Dollar LIBOR and engaging in a price-fixing conspiracy to rig Yen LIBOR. Together, Deutsche Bank and its subsidiary will pay $775 million in criminal penalties to the Justice Department. (U.S. Department of Justice, 2015)

- The U.S. Equal Employment Opportunity Commission has settled a disability discrimination suit with OHM Concessions Group, LLC of Baltimore, MD. An employee who managed the company's Dunkin' Donuts stores in the Baltimore-Washington International Airport requested unpaid leave for breast cancer surgery and treatment. Dunkin' Donuts allegedly violated the Americans with Disabilities Act by refusing to provide a reasonable accommodation of medical leave and firing the employee because of her disability. (Disability.gov, 2015)

- The U.S. Consumer Product Safety Commission (CPSC) is announcing that phil&teds USA, of Fort Collins, Colo., has agreed to a $3.5 million civil penalty to settle charges that the company knowingly failed to report to CPSC, as required by federal law, a defect and an unreasonable risk of serious injury concerning their MeToo high chair. In addition, the penalty settles CPSC's claim that phil&teds knowingly made material misrepresentations to agency staff during an investigation of the high chair in 2011. (CSPC, 2015)

In this context, the phrase *crimes by the corporate system* is used to characterize the body of offenses that are committed to benefit the corporation for which the employee (or employees) works. To provide an understanding of this body of offenses, this chapter gives attention to conceptualizing corporate crime, types of corporate crime, dynamics of corporate offending, and public concern about crimes by the corporate system. By addressing these areas, readers will see how corporations also commit, and benefit from, various types of misconduct.

● ● ● Conceptualizing Corporate Crime

As noted in Chapter I, the term *corporate crime* was initially discussed by Clinard and Quinney, who, in *Criminal Behavior Systems,* showed how white-collar crime can be classified into "corporate crime" and "occupational crime." From this perspective, the crimes discussed in the prior chapters can be seen as occupational crimes. To understand what is meant by corporate crime, it is useful to first define *corporation*.

The concept of corporation can be seen four different ways (see Figure 10.1). First, one can suggest that a corporation is a *business*. Second, one can also point to the *physical or structural location* where a business exists as a corporation (or an organization). Third, if businesses become incorporated, that *legally recognized status* can be seen as indicating the presence of a corporation that is separate from the presence of a specific person or persons owning or running an organization. Fourth, a corporation can be seen as a *collection of employees* who work for an employer.

The employment arrangement in a corporation is hierarchal in nature. At the bottom of the corporate hierarchy are workers with no supervisory responsibilities. Direct supervisors are at the next level of the corporation. Managers and administrators are above the supervisors. Many corporations also have a specific corporate board. A chief executive officer or president of the board is ultimately the highest ranking individual in a corporation. In theory, the corporation exists to meet its goals—which typically include profit, growth, and success.

Understanding these levels helps shed light on the concept of corporate crime and the persistence of misconduct in businesses. As Ermann and Lundman (2002) note, corporations are not technically "collections of people," but are collections of "replaceable people." What this means is that individuals can lose their jobs if they are not performing in a way that helps the corporation to meet its goals. Consequently, individuals—through direct or indirect pressures—might break rules or violate the law in order to promote corporate growth. In some cases, criminal decision making might be clearly intentional in nature. In other cases, harm arising from corporate misdeeds might be the result of organizational processes that do not actually intend for the harmful behavior to occur.

The abstract nature of corporate offending has resulted in an assortment of terms and definitions to describe these behaviors. One author has suggested that corporate crime "includes the vast majority of regulatory offenses subsumed under regulatory law" (Snyder, 1990, p. 439). Frank and Lynch (1992) describe corporate crime as including behaviors that are "socially injurious and blameworthy acts, legal or illegal that cause financial, physical, or environmental harm, committed by corporations and businesses against their workers, the general public, the environment, other corporations or businesses, the government, or other countries" (p. 17).

Some scholars have used phrases such as organizational crime (Schrager & Short, 1978), organizational deviance (Ermann & Lundman, 1978), and organizational misconduct (Vaughan, 2001) to describe similar behaviors. **Organizational misconduct**, for example, refers to "violations of laws, rules, or administrative regulations by an individual or group of

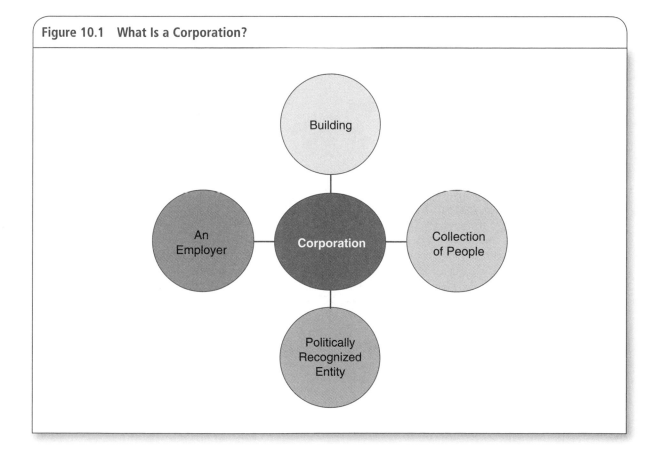

Figure 10.1 What Is a Corporation?

individuals in an organization who, in their organizational role, act or fail to act in ways that further the attainment of organizational goals" (Vaughan, 2001, p. 46).

These behaviors can be distinguished from the other forms of white-collar crime (discussed earlier in this text) in at least four different ways. First, the offenses are committed either *for the organization* or *by the organization*. Many of the crimes discussed earlier are committed *against the organization* and *by an individual*. Second, many corporate crimes are committed in groups, as part of an organizational decision-making process. Third, while the consequences of all forms of white-collar crime are serious, the consequences of corporate misdeeds can be particularly devastating. Fourth, the misdeeds of corporations are more rarely defined as criminally illegal.

Because corporate crime is different from the other forms of white-collar crime, it is best seen as a distinct form of white-collar crime. As a distinct form of white-collar crime, one can point to several specific types of corporate crime.

● ● ● Types of Corporate Crime

In a classic corporate crime study, Clinard and Yeager (1980) reviewed 1,553 corporate offenses and uncovered the following varieties: (1) administrative violations, (2) environmental violations, (3) financial violations, (4) labor violations, (5) manufacturing violations, and (6) unfair trade practices. Their research was useful in showing that the concept of corporate crime could be subdivided into types of corporate misdeeds. Depending on the level of analysis, it would be possible to list hundreds of different types of corporate misconduct. To keep the discussion manageable, it is useful to focus on general types of corporate wrongdoing. Therefore, the following seven types of corporate crimes warrant attention:

- Antitrust offenses
- False advertising
- Deceptive sales
- Unfair labor practices
- Unsafe work environments
- Harmful consumer products
- Harmful treatment of consumers

Antitrust Offenses

Our economy is based on principles of open market competition. The price of goods and services is tied to supply and demand. Businesses compete with one another by selling goods and services at prices that can be determined by a competitive marketplace. This helps keep prices low and stimulates new businesses that form to enter the competitive marketplace (USDOJ, n.d.a., p. 2). Such a process, in theory, ensures that consumers pay fair prices for goods and services. Some corporations, however, commit crimes known as antitrust offenses to control competition. Put simply, antitrust offenses are those that restrict competition. **Antitrust laws** are designed to promote and protect competition. In the United States, antitrust laws cover business activities in the areas of (1) pricing distribution, (2) mergers, (3) joint ventures, and (4) intellectual property use (Jacobsen, Seat, Shugarman, & Gildea, 1991).

The most prominent laws that control antitrust offenses are the Sherman Antitrust Act, the Clayton Act, and the Federal Trade Commission (FTC) Act (see Table 10.1). The **Sherman Antitrust Act,** often called the Sherman Act, passed in 1890, is the broadest antitrust law. This act makes it illegal for competitors to engage in activities that restrict competition. The Antitrust Division of the U.S. Department of Justice has the responsibility for prosecuting these crimes. Common types of antitrust offenses include the following:

- Price fixing
- Bid rigging
- Price discrimination

Table 10.1	Major Antitrust Laws
Law	**Descriptions**
Sherman Antitrust Act	The Sherman Act outlaws all contracts, combinations, and conspiracies that unreasonably restrain interstate and foreign trade. This includes agreements among competitors to fix prices, rig bids, and allocate customers. The Sherman Act also makes it a crime to monopolize any part of interstate commerce. An unlawful monopoly exists when only one firm controls the market for a product or service, and it has obtained that market power, not because its product or service is superior to others, but by suppressing competition with anticompetitive conduct. This Act is not violated simply when one firm's vigorous competition and lower prices take sales from its less efficient competitors—that is competition working properly. Sherman Act violations involving agreements between competitors usually are punished as criminal felonies.
Clayton Act	The Clayton Act is a civil statute (carrying no criminal penalties) that was passed in 1914 and significantly amended in 1950. The Clayton Act prohibits mergers or acquisitions that are likely to lessen competition. Under the Act, the government challenges those mergers that a careful economic analysis shows are likely to increase prices to consumers. All persons considering a merger or acquisition above a certain size must notify both the Antitrust Division and Federal Trade Commission. The Act also prohibits other business practices that under certain circumstances may harm competition.
Federal Trade Commission Act	The Federal Trade Commission Act prohibits unfair methods of competition in interstate commerce, but carries no criminal penalties. It also created the Federal Trade Commission to police violations of the Act.
Other Laws	The Department of Justice also often uses other laws to fight illegal activities, including laws that prohibit false statements to federal agencies, perjury, obstruction of justice, conspiracies to defraud the United States, and mail and wire fraud. Each of these crimes carries its own fines and imprisonment terms, which may be added to the fines and imprisonment terms for antitrust law violations.

Source: U.S. Department of Justice (USDOJ). (n.d.a). *Anti-Trust Enforcement and the Consumer.* Retrieved November 27, 2015 from http://www.justice. gov/sites/default/files/atr/legacy/2015/03/06/antitrust-enfor-consumer.pdf

- Price gouging
- Market allocation
- Group boycotts

As will be shown below, it is extremely difficult to determine whether these crimes occur or behaviors in the corporate system simply reflect fluctuations in the economy.

Price Fixing

Price fixing offenses occur when competitors agree on a price at which goods or services should be sold. The competitors do not need to agree on the same price; they simply need to agree to set prices. Other examples of price fixing include instances where competitors agree to "(1) establish or adhere to price discounts; (2) hold prices firm; (3) eliminate or reduce discounts; (4) adopt a standard formula for computing prices; (5) maintain certain price differentials between different types, sizes, and quantities of products; (6) adhere to a minimum fee or price schedule (7) fix credit terms; and (8) not advertise prices" (U.S. Department of Justice, n.d.b.).

A distinction can be made between horizontal and vertical price fixing. **Horizontal price fixing** involves situations where competing businesses conspire to charge prices at a similar level. **Vertical price fixing** refers to situations where parties from different levels of the production and distribution chain agree to set prices. Traditionally, vertical price fixing has been regarded as illegal. A manufacturer, for example, is not allowed to tell retailers and distributors how much to charge for products produced by the manufacturer. In a U.S. Supreme Court case, *Leegin Creative Leather Products, Inc. v. PSKS, Inc.* (2007), this premise was changed and the Court ruled that the "rule of reason" should be used to determine whether agreements between various levels of the production distribution chain are illegal. The rule of reason refers to the premise that "courts must weigh all of the circumstances of the restraint, and the restraint's history, nature and effect in the market involved, in order to ascertain whether anti-competitive effects outweigh any pro-competitive benefits" (Martin, 2007, p. 1). The Court cited "a growing consensus in economic theory that vertical pricing agreements, while sometimes anti-competitive, can often have pro-competitive effects" (as cited in Martin, 2007).

Bid Rigging

Bid rigging (or collusion) occurs when competitors conspire to set specific bids for goods or services they would supply in response to a request for bids. At least four types of bid rigging exist. First, **bid suppression** refers to instances where competitors agree not to submit a bid for a particular job on the understanding that a specific competitor will likely be selected for that job. Second, **complementary bidding** exists when competitors submit bids with artificially high estimates or specific demands that cannot be met so that a specific competitor with a lower price or without the demands is selected. Third, **bid rotation** occurs when competitors agree to take turns submitting the lowest bid on different bids. Fourth, **subcontracting** occurs when competitors hire one another on subcontracts after the winning bid has been selected (USDOJ, n.d.b, p. 2).

It is believed that bid rigging is more likely to occur if (1) there are fewer competitors, (2) the products or services are standardized, (3) competitors know one another, and (4) bidders or businesses submit their bids in the same physical location at the same time (USDOJ, n.d.b, p. 5). This last item refers to the possibility that competitors will meet one another in the building when submitting their bids, and this "chance meeting" will give them the opportunity to "compare notes," or otherwise discuss their bids. Imagine a professor telling students to turn their take-home exams in at a specific time and in a specific location. The possibility that students might run into one another and engage in wrongdoing potentially increases by creating a situation where it is likely they will see one another.

Price Discrimination

On the surface, one might assume that the term **price discrimination** means that businesses cannot charge individuals two different prices based on protected classes such as gender, race, religion, and so on. While civil rights laws do prohibit charging for goods based on the characteristics of the consumer, price discrimination actually refers to practices where different prices are charged simply to restrict competition between competitors (Knopp, 1966). It is problematic, however, to determine whether different prices are being offered to limit competition or price differences are just a natural part of business. Indeed, in many instances consumers can legally be charged two different prices. Rakowski (2004) uses the example of charging business travelers more for airfare. One can point to several other examples where consumers are charged different prices:

- Two consumers buy the same car on the same day, with one paying more than the other.
- Two consumers stay in a hotel on the same day, with one paying more than the other.
- Two concertgoers pay two different prices to see Justin Bieber in concert.
- Two students in the same class are charged two different prices for the class (one student is a graduate student, and the other is an undergraduate student).
- A grocery store charges two consumers two different prices for the same goods because one of the consumers has a "grocer card" that allows discounts.
- On "Ladies'" night, women are admitted free to a bar, but men have to pay a cover charge.

What it comes down to is the fact that price discriminations "are generally lawful, particularly if they reflect the different costs of dealing with different buyers or are the result of a seller's attempts to meet a competitor's offering" (FTC, 2010b). Made illegal under the **Robinson-Patman Act,** price discrimination is illegal if it is done to lessen competition.

Price Gouging

Price gouging refers to situations where businesses conspire to set artificially high prices on goods and services. Check cashing businesses have been implicated in price gouging. These businesses, which exist primarily in minority neighborhoods, charge consumers relatively high fees to cash their paychecks. Some states have passed laws capping the amount that these businesses can charge for cashing checks. Such laws have been found to reduce the number of minority households that do not have bank accounts (Washington, 2006).

Price gouging claims often surface after disasters because of seemingly inflated prices for goods and services such as gas, hotel rooms, food, and so on. After Hurricane Katrina, politicians were quick to blame the oil industry and local gas stations for the high gas prices consumers were forced to pay in the hurricane's aftermath. State attorneys general charged gas stations with gouging, although "it was later found by the FTC that gas prices were being set in competitive markets" (Carden, 2008, p. 531).

Some states have passed laws making it illegal for businesses to raise prices if a state of emergency has been declared. Critics of such laws suggest that selling commodities at prices below market value will actually create more problems and cause shortages on a quicker basis. The higher price, it is believed, helps to prevent shortages. Indeed, after Hurricane Katrina, a call for federal antigouging laws was opposed by FTC Chairwoman Deborah Platt Majoras because such a law "could hurt consumers by causing fuel shortages" (McNamara, 2006). Other experts have also warned against federally mandated price controls, suggesting that such practices harm consumers by increasing the amount of time it would take goods to reach consumers (Montgomery, Baron, & Weisskopf, 2007). Montgomery and his colleagues note that price controls on gasoline after Hurricanes Katrina and Rita would have increased economic damage by 1.5 to 2.9 billion dollars.

Other critics of federal price controls suggest that such laws and policies would keep many businesses from "providing goods and services after natural disasters" (Carden, 2008, p. 531). If there is no economic incentive to deliver goods to a disaster area where it may take more resources to deliver the goods, businesses may choose to deliver their goods elsewhere. Critics also suggest that the policies assume that the government better knows how to "allocate resources more efficiently than the market" (Culpepper & Block, 2008, p. 512). To these critics, price controls place artificial constraints on demand and supply, which makes it difficult to promote a free market economy. Culpepper and Block further suggest that "government regulation is nothing short of a disaster as far as satisfying customers is concerned" (p. 512).

Of course, some scholars support the use of price controls in responding to disasters. The assumption is that while natural laws of supply and demand exist during routine days,

> in times of disaster, this assumption is often void. A gouger has a local monopoly on the scarce commodity and exploits this monopoly. Gougers violate social norms that dictate that one should help out in times of disaster, not seek profit from them. (Angel & McCabe, 2009, p. 283)

Based on the premise that gougers violate social norms, some have also suggested that gougers are immoral. Drawing on principles of supply and demand, one economist, however, argues that (1) antigouging laws are not morally justified, (2) price gouging is not necessarily morally reprehensible, and (3) gouging "offenders" are not necessarily immoral (Zwolinski, 2008). The ambiguity surrounding the utility of these laws reflects the general difficulties that arise when defining white-collar crime (discussed earlier in this text).

Market Allocation

Market allocation refers to divide markets according to territories, products, goods, or some other service (USDOJ, n.d.b, p. 4). Perhaps an analogy can be made to drug dealing. It is well known that drug dealers have specific territories where they sell their drugs. Efforts to deal drugs in a rival drug dealer's neighborhood would likely be met with a violent response from the rival dealer. In effect, the drug dealers have engaged in market allocation. As regards legitimate goods and services, market allocation is illegal because it restricts competition and potentially allows one business to have a monopoly over the jurisdiction or territory it serves or the product or services it provides.

Group Boycotts

Group boycotts are situations where competitors agree not to do business with specific customers or clients. Consider a case in which a group of competing attorneys in the District of Columbia agreed not to provide services to indigent defendants unless the District paid the attorneys more for their services. The FTC investigated the case and found the attorneys in violation of antitrust laws, group boycotting in particular. The attorneys appealed the decision and the case eventually made its way to the Supreme Court. The Supreme Court upheld the FTC's decision (FTC, n.d.).

Dynamics Surrounding Antitrust Offenses

Several varieties of antitrust offenses exist, and four patterns are consistent across these offenses. These patterns include (1) the way that "agreement" is conceptualized, (2) the seriousness of harm arising from the offenses, (3) globalization, and (4) difficulties proving (and punishing) offenses.

First, in terms of the way "agreement" to limit competition is conceptualized, some might assume that agreements occur only through verbal or written agreements. This is not the case. In each of the antitrust offenses discussed above, agreements can be in writing, verbally agreed, or *inferred from the conduct of businesses.* As a result, to prove an antitrust offense, officials may rely on either direct evidence—such as testimony of participants or witnesses—or circumstantial evidence, such as expense reports, fluctuations, or bidding histories (USDOJ, n.d.b, p. 4). Note also that if the behaviors of competitors result in an antitrust offense, like price fixing, competitors can be found in violation of the laws. Consider the following example provided by the FTC (n.d.):

> A group of competing optometrists agreed not to participate in a vision care network unless the network raised reimbursement rates for patients covered by its plan. The optometrists refused to treat patients covered by the network plan, and eventually the company raised reimbursement rates. The FTC said that the optometrists' agreement was illegal price fixing, and that its leaders had organized an effort to make sure other optometrists knew about and complied with the agreement.

Second, it is important to draw attention to the serious harm that arises from antitrust offenses. Estimates suggest that antitrust offenses "can raise the price of a product by ten percent . . . and that American consumers and taxpayers pour billions of dollars each year into the pockets of [those participating in these schemes]" (USDOJ, n.d., p. 4). As evidence of this harm, consider that 6 of the top 10 corporate offenders from the 1990s, as defined by the *Corporate Crime Reporter,* were convicted of antitrust offenses (see Table 10.2).

One of the most prominent antitrust offenses involved vitamin producers in the late 1990s. Firms across the world conspired to set caps on how many vitamins each firm would produce, how much they should charge, and whom they would sell the vitamins to. The scheme was so large that the U.S. Department of Justice suggested that "in the end, for nearly a decade, every American consumer—anyone who took a vitamin, drank a glass of milk, or had a bowl of cereal—ended up paying more so that the conspirators could reap hundreds of millions of dollars in additional revenue" (USDOJ, n.d.a, p. 4). Those involved in the conspiracy included executives from F. Hoffmann-LaRoche, Ltd., and BASF AG.

A third pattern surrounding antitrust offenses centers on the globalization of our economy. As the world has become more global in nature, the types of antitrust offenses have become more globally oriented. The federal response to antitrust offenses has shifted to adjust to the types of issues arising in a global economy. For example, historically, the United States would apply only civil actions against businesses from other countries that engaged in violations of U.S. antitrust laws. In the 1990s, however, U.S. officials began to apply criminal sanctions to businesses in other countries. The criminalization of foreign antitrust cases through an application of the Sherman Act was upheld in *U.S. v. Nippon Paper Industries* (M. S. Lee, 1998).

The fourth pattern surrounding antitrust cases centers on the difficulties officials have establishing that crimes occurred and subsequently applying appropriate punishments. Interestingly, difficulties convicting antitrust offenders

Table 10.2	Top Ten Corporate Offenders, 1990s		
Corporation	**Type of Crime Committed**	**Criminal Fine**	**Where to Read More**
1.F. Hoffmann-LaRoche	Antitrust	$500 million	12 *Corporate Crime Reporter 21*(1), Map 24, 1999
Daiwa Bank Ltd.	Financial	$340 million	10 *Corporate Crime Reporter 9*(3), March 4, 1996
BASF Aktiengesellschaft	Antitrust	$225 million	12 *Corporate Crime Reporter 21*(1), Map 24, 1999
SGL Carbon Aktiengesellschaft (SLG AG)	Antitrust	$135 million	12 *Corporate Crime Reporter 19*(4), May 10, 1999
Exxon Corporation and Exxon Shipping	Environmental	$125 million	5 *Corporate Crime Reporter 11*(3), March 18, 1991
UCAR International, Inc.	Antitrust	$110 million	12 *Corporate Crime Reporter 15*(6), April 13, 1993
Archer Daniels Midland	Antitrust	$100 million	10 *Corporate Crime Reporter 40*(1), October 21, 1996
(tie) Banker's Trust	Financial	$60 million	12 *Corporate Crime Reporter 11*(1), March 15, 1999
(tie) Sears Bankruptcy Recovery Management Services	Fraud	$60 million	13 *Corporate Crime Reporter 7*(1), February 15, 1999
Haarmann & Reimer Corp.	Antitrust	$50 million	11 *Corporate Crime Reporter 5*(4), February 3, 1997

Source: Adapted from Mokhiber, R. (n.d.). Top 100 Corporate Criminals of the Decade. In *Corporate Crime Reporter.*

have been traced to efforts to "get tougher" against this group of offenders. In particular, some scholars have argued that it became harder to convict antitrust offenders in the 1980s after a 1970s law made offenses such as price fixing a felony rather than a misdemeanor (Snyder, 1989, 1990). The rationale for this argument is that offenders put a lesser defense when they were charged with misdemeanors. Facing a felony conviction, alternatively, potentially raises the bar for the kinds of penalties convicted offenders would receive and, as a result, may cause defendants to seek more remedies to avoid a conviction.

False Advertising

False advertising occurs when businesses make inaccurate statements about their products or services in order to facilitate the sale of those items or services. Put more simply, false advertising laws prohibit "untrue or misleading information given to you to get you to buy something, or to come to visit their store" (County of Los Angeles Department of Consumer Affairs, 2010). False advertising is illegal through the Federal Trade Commission Act, which stipulates the following:

- Advertising must be truthful and nondeceptive.
- Advertisers must have evidence to back up their claims.
- Advertisements cannot be unfair (FTC, 2001).

The concept of *deceptive* suggests that businesses cannot mislead or provide irrelevant information in their efforts to promote products. The concept *unfair* means that businesses cannot use advertisements to injure or harm consumers. Types of false advertising include the following:

- **Bait and switch practices**, where customers are lured into the store with the promise of a sale item that does not exist, or, is not available in an appropriate amount
- **Resale fraud**, where used items are sold as new
- Misuse of on sale phrases, where regular prices are presented as if they are sale prices
- Misrepresenting the product's capability, where consumers are told that the product can do things that it cannot
- Misrepresenting items as made in the United States, when parts of the product were made elsewhere (County of Los Angeles Department of Consumer Affairs, 2010)

The FTC regularly addresses cases of false advertising. In 2004, Kentucky Fried Chicken settled charges with the FTC that the company "made false claims in a national television advertising campaign about the relative nutritional value and healthiness of its fried chicken" (FTC, 2004). The company was also charged with comparing the nutritional value of its chicken to "certain popular weight loss programs." KFC promoted its chicken breasts as having less fat than a Burger King Whopper, which, while true, hides the facts that because of the way they were cooked, the chicken breasts in fact did "have more than three times the trans fat and cholesterol, more than twice the sodium, and more calories" (FTC, 2004).

More recently, the FTC announced complaints and judicial orders finding four national retailers in violation of advertising rules. The FTC alleged that the companies (JC Penney, Nordstrom, Bed Bath and Beyond, and Backcountry.com) advertised certain products as being made of bamboo when the products were actually made of rayon. The FTC sent the companies warning letter in 2010 about these practices, but the practices reportedly continued. Court orders were issued to the companies stipulating that the following payments would settle the allegations: Bed Bath & Beyond Inc. ($500,000), Nordstrom, Inc. ($360,000), J.C. Penney Company ($290,000), and Backcountry.com ($150,000) (FTC, 2015, December 9). According to the FTC, the types of advertisements that will receive the most scrutiny from the federal government are those that (1) make claims regarding the consumer's health or safety or (2) include statements that consumers could not realistically be able to evaluate on their own (FTC, 2001). Consider the following false advertising cases as examples:

- The FTC charged that athletic apparel company Tommie Copper Inc. was engaging in false advertising practices by claiming that their clothing helped to provide pain relief. Among other advertising practices, in infomercials selling their products, the company featured celebrity Montell Williams stating "Tommie Copper truly is pain relief without a pill" (FTC, 2015, December 1). The company agreed to pay $1.35 million to settle the charges.
- The state of Connecticut and FTC filed a lawsuit against the marketers of LeanSpa for their use of fake websites to market colon cleansing products and their deceptive ads for a free product trial if customers paid a small shipping and handling fee. Customers were actually charged $79.95 for the "free" trial, and they had great difficulty trying to cancel the order after the "trial" finished. After settling the charges with the marketers, the FTC mailed 23,046 checks to each customer impacted by the fraud. The average check was for $160.10. (FTC, 2015, October 1)
- A company purporting to have created an app (the Ultimeyes app) was charged by the FTC with violating advertising rules. The company agreed to stop claiming that its app improved vision and surrendered $150,000. Jessica Rich, the FTC's Director of the Bureau of Consumer Protection, said, "This case came down to the simple fact that 'Ultimeyes' promoters did not have the scientific evidence to support their claims that the app could improve users' vision." (FTC, 2015, September 17)

Two common trends in advertising include going-out-of-business sales and the use of celebrities to promote goods. Laws exist to govern these advertising practices. For example, a business cannot advertise that it is going out of business unless it is actually going out of business. With regard to celebrity ads, the advertisement must accurately reflect the celebrity's view of the product. If a celebrity states that he or she uses a product in an ad, he or she must actually use that product. If the celebrity decides at a later date not to support the product any longer, the advertiser can no longer promote the product as if it were endorsed by the celebrity (FTC, 2001). For example, if P. Diddy endorsed this book upon its release, the book could be promoted with his endorsement. If P. Diddy later writes his own white-collar crime book and decides not to support this one, later promotions would not be able to use the music mogul's endorsement.

Some have suggested that the recession starting in 2008 contributed to an increase in false advertising by businesses trying virtually anything to offset the negative consequences of the downturn in the economy (A. Cooper, 2009). Another author suggested that the Internet provides easier opportunities to commit false advertising (Sarna, 2012). While these suggestions are speculative, they are in line with the assumption of the systems perspective, which suggests that changes in the one system (e.g., the economic system) will have ramifications for other systems (e.g., marketing practices in the corporate system).

One author team found that after false claims are sanctioned by federal authorities, it appears that the misleading claims "primarily affect newcomers and not the loyal users" (Rao & Wang, 2015, p. 5). This same author team estimated using a "back of the envelope" calculation that a company's false advertisement "gained $105 million in revenue because of the false claims [which is] a substantial amount compared to the $4 million it settled in a recent class action lawsuit" (p. 3).

Deceptive Sales

Deceptive sales are illicit sales practices that are driven by corporate policies and directives. Certainly, corporate policies and pressures can promote deceptive sales practices by employees. Consider a 1991 undercover investigation by California's Department of Consumer Affairs that found that the commission structure used in Sears Auto Centers appeared to promote fraud by sales staff. The undercover visitors posed as customers seeking automobile services 38 different times. Of those 38 visits, sales staff recommended unnecessary services 34 times, with one of the visits resulting in needless repairs costing nearly $600 (L. M. Fisher, 1992). Interviews with the workers found that under the commission structure, which was instituted in 1990, employees were reportedly expected to sell a certain number of services and products over an 8-hour shift. Failure to sell the expected amounts would result in punitive responses from employers, including having their hours cut or being moved to another department. After the fraud charges by the Department of Consumer Affairs surfaced, the company changed its policy and now pays its auto center salespersons hourly wages (Halverson, 1992).

Despite the change in corporate policy, charges against the company were not dropped, and similar charges against Sears were filed in 41 other states. Eventually, Sears settled the charges, paying out $23 million, with California receiving $8 million to pay for "reimbursement costs, new employee training, and coupons for discounts at the service center" (Jennings, 2008, p. 507). Sears's net loss that year was $3.9 billion, the worst year for the company in 60 years. Since then, the amount of sales in auto centers has been below the pre-1992 levels (Jennings, 2008). In the interest of full disclosure, I should note that I worked for Sears from 1989 through 1992, not in the auto centers but in hardware, sporting goods, and lawn and garden. The fall in auto center sales probably had more to do with the fraud investigation than with my departure.

In another case involving deceptive sales practices, and one many students might be able to relate to, a large for-profit college came under fire in 2004 after a federal investigation by the Department of Education (DE) revealed that the college recruiters systematically lied to students about how courses would transfer, the amount of financial aid available, and class size (Coutts, 2009). The DE report said that the college "based its recruiters' pay on the number of students they brought in, and punished underperforming recruiters by isolating them in glass-walled rooms and threatening to fire them if they failed to meet management goals" (E. Brown, 2004). Here's how a recruiter from the college described the process:

> One thing we would be told to do is call up a student who was on the fence and say, "all right, I've only got one seat left. I need to know right now if you need me to save this for you, because this class is about to get full." Well, that wasn't true. We were told to lie. . . . One of the things we were to do was . . . say we are regionally accredited, which means that [credits] are transferred anywhere. (Coutts, 2009)

Those of you who have transferred know that transfer decisions are made by the college or university to which the student is transferring, not by an accreditation standard. Such deceptive practices were done to benefit the college, not the employee.

The DE ruled that the recruiting strategies violated Title II of the Higher Education Act. A subsequent audit found that other violations related to the use of financial aid funds were also allegedly committed by the college. The parent company of the for-profit college eventually paid the Department of Education $9.8 million. Later, it was ordered to pay shareholders $280 million because investors were reportedly fraudulently misled about the school's recruiting practices ("University of Phoenix Parent," 2008).

Problems with deceptive practices in recruiting students were not limited to this one for-profit college. In a U.S. Government Accountability Office (USGAO, 2010) investigation, four undercover employees registered on the websites of 15 different for-profit colleges. After registering on the websites, they began receiving phone calls from recruiters. Some calls were made within 5 minutes after the employee registered on the website. One received an average of six calls a day for an entire month.

The active recruiting by the for-profit recruiters was not problematic in and of itself. After all, they were hired to recruit students to their colleges. Instead, the problems arose when recruiters made deceptive statements about (1) accreditation, (2) graduation rates, (3) employment possibilities, (4) expected salaries, (5) program duration, and (6) cost. Four of the colleges encouraged the undercover applicant to lie about their income and savings in order to gain federal support for their education. All 15 of the colleges "made some type of deceptive or otherwise questionable statement to undercover applicants" (USGAO, 2010, p. 7). Table 10.3 summarizes the deceptive practices.

The types of deceptive statements made by recruiters might resonate some with readers who, as students, have their own set of expectations about the value of their education. Consider the following examples quoted from the GAO report:

- A college owned by a publicly traded company told our applicant that, after completing an associate's degree in criminal justice, he could try to go work for the Federal Bureau of Investigation or the Central Intelligence Agency. While other careers within those agencies may be possible, a position as a FBI special agent or CIA clandestine officer requires a bachelor's degree at a minimum.
- A small beauty college told our applicant that barbers can earn $150,000 to $200,000 a year. While this may be true in exceptional circumstances, the Bureau of Labor Statistics (BLS) reports that 90% of barbers make less than $43,000 a year.
- A representative at a college in Florida owned by a publicly traded company told an undercover applicant that the college was accredited by the same organization that accredits Harvard and the University of Florida when in fact it was not. The representative told the undercover applicant: "It's the top accrediting agency—Harvard, University of Florida—they all use that accrediting agency. . . . All schools are the same; you never read the papers from the schools." (USGAO, 2010, p. 91)

The undercover investigation revealed that deceptive sales practices by college recruiters seemed to occur far too regularly. To date, no charges have been filed against the colleges, but charges remain possible. Go to www.gao.gov/products/gao-10-948t to view a video of the undercover applicants talking with recruiters.

Some for-profit colleges have also been accused of engaging in harmful practices that may not technically be illegal, but may bend the rules. For example, attorneys general raised concerns that some for-profit colleges were pushing the envelope on the 90/10 rule, which states that no more than 90 percent of a student's education can be paid for with federal student aid funds from the Department of Education's Title IV program. The rule is based on the premise that someone other than the federal government should pay for at least some of a student's college education. The attorneys general expressed concern that for-profit colleges were aggressively targeting military students and using the student's military aid to count in the "10 percent" rather than the "90 percent" (Blumenstyk, 2012). Proponents of changing the rule argue that the application of the rule has placed "a dollar sign on the backs of veterans, service members and their families and led unscrupulous for-profit colleges to aggressively and deceptively recruit veterans, service members and their families to enroll in high-priced, low-quality programs" (Institute for College Access and Success, 2015).

Table 10.3	Fraudulent Actions Encouraged by For-Profit Colleges		
Location	**Certification/ Course of Study**	**Type of College**	**Fraudulent Behavior Encouraged**
California	Certificate– computer- aided drafting	Less than 2-year, privately owned	• Undercover applicant was encouraged by a financial aid representative to change the FAFSA [Free Application for Federal Student Aid] to falsely increase the number of dependents in the household in order to qualify for Pell Grants. • The representative told the undercover applicant that by the time the college would be required by Education to verify any information about the applicant, the applicant would have already graduated from the 7-month program.
Florida	Associate degree– radiologic technology	2-year, privately owned	• This undercover applicant indicated to the financial aid representative that he had $250,000 in the bank and was therefore capable of paying the program's $15,000 cost. The fraud would have made the applicant ineligible for grants and subsidized loans. • Financial aid representative suggested to the undercover applicant that he not report $250,000 in savings on the FAFSA. The representative told the applicant to come back once the fraudulent financial information changes had been processed. • This change would not have made the applicant eligible for grants because his income would have been too high, but it would have made him eligible for loans subsidized by the government. However, this undercover applicant indicated that he had $250,000 in savings— more than enough to pay for the program's $39,000 costs.
Pennsylvania	Certificate– webpage design	Less than 2-year, privately owned	• Financial aid representative told the undercover applicant that he should have answered "zero" when asked about the money he had in savings—the applicant had reported a $250,000 inheritance. • The financial aid representative told the undercover applicant that she would "correct" his FAFSA form by reducing the reported assets to zero. She later confirmed by e-mail and voicemail that she had made the change. • This change would not have made the applicant eligible for grants, but it would have made him eligible for loans subsidized by the government. However, this applicant indicated that he had about $250,000 in savings—more than enough to pay for the program's $21,000 costs.
Texas	Bachelor's degree– construction management	4-year, privately owned	• Admissions representative encouraged applicant to change the FAFSA to falsely add dependents in order to qualify for Pell Grants. • Admissions representative assured the undercover applicant that he did not have to identify anything about the dependents, such as their Social Security numbers, nor did he have to prove to the college with a tax return that he had previously claimed them as dependents. • Financial aid representative told the undercover applicant that he should not report the $250,000 cash he had in savings.

Source: U.S. Government Accountability Office. (2010).

A group of state attorneys general also recommended legislation limiting the amount of federal funds that for-profit colleges can use to advertise their services. In 2009, fifteen for-profit education corporations received roughly 86 percent of their revenue from federal sources and spent $3.7 billion on marketing. This amount represented one-fourth of the total budget for these colleges. In comparison, nonprofit colleges had marketing budgets that were less than one percent of their total budget (Wallack, 2013). In their defense, proponents of the for-profit schools pointed out that the schools provide access to education for a large number of nontraditional students who otherwise would not have education. Limiting marketing was viewed as limiting access. Steve Gunderson, president of the Association of Private Sector Colleges and Universities, told a reporter, "Advertising can shine a light on available opportunities for all citizens and should be encouraged rather than restricted. What this legislation does is limit information, and by doing so it limits access" (Wallack, 2013). The proposed law, while introduced in 2012, has yet to make it out of congressional committees. According to one author, these activities are expected to continue because "market structures and government policies play crucial roles in facilitating crime in these organizations and . . . such behavior is likely to continue despite tougher regulations, since the same elements will continue to influence for-profit colleges" (Beaver, 2012, p. 274).

In a more recent case, the second largest for-profit education company in the United States (Education Management Corporation) settled charges centering on deceptive recruiting practices where the company allegedly paid its recruiters based on the number of students they recruited. The company agreed to pay $95.5 million to settle the allegations. In the words of one of the deputy assistant attorney generals who worked on the case, "Improper incentives to admissions recruiters result in harm to students and financial losses to the taxpayers" (U.S. Department of Justice, 2015, November 16).

Unfair Labor Practices

Unfair labor practices refer to corporate violations where workers are subjected to unethical treatment by their bosses and corporate leaders. In this context, two general types of unfair labor practices can be identified: (1) exploitation and (2) systemic discrimination.

Exploitation

Exploitation refers to situations where businesses take advantage of their workers. Pay exploitation is an example. An assignment I give my white-collar crime students asks them to write about types of white-collar crimes they have experienced. Each semester, at least a handful of students write about jobs where they work parts of their shifts for free. From my students' reports, this seems to be particularly popular in the restaurant industry—where waiters and waitresses stick around after their shifts to help clean the restaurants, being paid the standard waiter-waitress wage of $2.13 an hour if they are paid at all.

Sweatshops are examples of unfair labor practices. Such businesses "regularly violate both wage and child labor laws and safety or health regulations" (Foo, 1994, p. 2179). In many sweatshops, undocumented workers are hired and paid reduced wages. Such practices are criticized because they cheat the government out of tax dollars and deprive workers of necessary benefits (Foo, 1994). These activities are not simply a modern phenomenon. In 1892, Florence Kelley identified three types of sweatshops in the garment industry:

- *Inside shops* are those created by manufacturers inside a factory.
- *Outside shops* include contractors hired to produce goods or materials to be used by the manufacturer.
- *Home shops* (also known as family groups) are run out of the exploited worker's home (F. Kelley, 2005).

Even then, she drew attention to the problems of infection and disease that stemmed from such practices.

Some may point to greed and profit as the primary motivators for the creation and persistence of sweatshops. However, the reasons for the development of sweatshops are more complex than this. Foo (1994) cites a GAO report that attributed the existence of sweatshops to the following:

- The presence of a vulnerable population
- The presence of an exploitable population
- Labor intensive industries
- Low profit margin industries
- Lack of inspection staff
- Weak penalties
- Inadequate cooperation among enforcement agencies

Barnes and Kozar (2008) examined the types of exploitation targeted at pregnant workers in the textile industry in China, Mexico, Nicaragua, and the Philippines. Their research identified an assortment of types of exploitation, including forced abortions, unpaid overtime, forced job requirements harmful to the fetus, and lack of appropriate benefits. The authors note that U.S. firms are linked to these practices in that "governments of developing nations continue to lure [U.S. firms] in with promises of tax breaks, no duties, longer work weeks, and low minimum wage requirements" (p. 291).

Discrimination

Discrimination is another type of unfair labor practice committed in the corporate system. Some may question whether these offenses are actually corporate crimes. It is significant to note that Clinard and Yeager (1980) cited discrimination under the category of labor violations in their discussion of corporate crime. What this suggests is that discrimination has been considered a type of corporate misconduct ever since scholars first began to discuss these misdeeds.

Four federal statutes prohibit employment discrimination: Title VII, the Americans with Disabilities Act, the Age Discrimination Act, and the Equal Pay Act of 1963 (Goldman, Gutek, Stein, & Lewis, 2006). These laws prohibit the unfair treatment of employees based on their membership in a protected class including race, sex, religion, national origin, and disability status (Chien & Kleiner, 1999). Table 10.4 shows the number of discrimination complaints individuals filed with the Equal Employment Opportunity Commission (EEOC) between 1996 and 2013. One trend stands out: The number of complaints was higher in 2008 and 2009 than any other time and the number of complaints has decreased since then. However, there were still more charges in 2014 than in 2007. When releasing the 2009 data, officials from the EEOC attributed the differences to several possible factors, including "greater accessibility of the EEOC to the public, economic conditions, increased diversity and demographic shifts in the labor force, [and] employees' greater awareness of their rights under law" (Equal Employment Opportunity Commission, 2010).

Women are more likely than men to experience discrimination because of stereotypes, perceptions of a lack of fit in the workforce, and the inability of recruiters to identify with women (Chien & Kleiner, 1999). Chien and Kleiner argue that these factors "inhibit women's career development and advancement and subsequently undermine women's contributions to the labor market" (p. 34).

Basing employment decisions on stereotypes has been regarded as a form of discrimination. In *Price Waterhouse v. Hopkins* (1989), a woman was denied a promotion in an accounting firm because she was seen as "too macho" (Malos, 2007, p. 97). Managing partners of the company said she needed to act more feminine and wear more makeup. The Supreme Court ruled that businesses could not base promotion decisions on gender stereotypes. Courts have also held that employers can be held liable for discrimination if they make employment decisions based on a woman's status as a mother. If employers assume, for instance, that a job would be too difficult because the employee is a new mother, the employer could be held liable for discrimination (Malos, 2007).

Discrimination does not just stem from employment decisions; instead, hostile or harassing behaviors of employees against other employees can be seen as discriminatory. Consider the following illustration:

An African American employee at an East Coast Company took the day off to celebrate Martin Luther King Jr. Day. Upon returning from work, he discovered a note that had been scribbled on his desk calendar. It read: "Kill four more, get four more days off." (Solomon, 1992, p. 30)

Table 10.4 Complaints Filed With EEOC, 2004–2014

Fiscal Year	2004	2005	2006	2007	2008	2009	2010	2011	2012	2013	2014
Total charges	79,432	75,428	75,768	82,792	95,402	93,277	99,922	99,947	99,412	93,727	88,778
Race	27,696	26,740	27,238	30,510	33,937	33,579	35,890	35,395	33,512	33,068	31,073
	34.90%	35.50%	35.90%	37.00%	35.60%	36.00%	35.90%	35.40%	33.70%	35.30%	35.00%
Sex	24,249	23,094	23,247	24,826	28,372	28,028	29,029	28,534	30,356	27,687	26,027
	30.50%	30.60%	30.70%	30.10%	29.70%	30.00%	29.10%	28.50%	30.50%	29.50%	29.30%
National origin	8,361	8,035	8,327	9,396	10,601	11,134	11,304	11,833	10,883	10,642	9,579
	10.50%	10.70%	11.00%	11.40%	11.10%	11.90%	11.30%	11.80%	10.90%	11.40%	10.80%
Religion	2,466	2,340	2,541	2,880	3,273	3,386	3,790	4,151	3,811	3,721	3,549
	3.10%	3.10%	3.40%	3.50%	3.40%	3.60%	3.80%	4.20%	3.80%	4.00%	4.00%
Color	930	1,069	1,241	1,735	2,698	2,943	2,780	2,832	2,562	3,146	2,756
	1.20%	1.40%	1.60%	2.10%	2.80%	3.20%	2.80%	2.80%	2.70%	3.40%	3.10%
Retaliation—all statutes	22,740	22,278	22,555	26,663	32,690	33,613	36,258	37,334	37,836	38,539	37,955
	28.60%	29.50%	29.80%	32.30%	34.30%	36.00%	36.30%	37.40%	38.10%	41.10%	42.80%
Retaliation—Title VII only	20,240	19,429	19,560	23,371	28,698	28,948	30,948	31,429	31,208	31,478	30,771
	25.50%	25.80%	25.80%	28.30%	30.10%	31.00%	31.00%	31.40%	31.40%	33.60%	34.70%
Age	17,837	16,585	16,548	19,103	24,582	22,778	23,264	23,465	22,857	21,396	20,588
	22.50%	22.00%	21.80%	23.20%	25.80%	24.40%	23.30%	23.50%	23.00%	22.80%	23.20%
Disability	15,376	14,893	15,575	17,734	19,453	21,451	25,165	25,742	26,379	25,957	25,369
	19.40%	19.70%	20.60%	21.40%	20.40%	23.00%	25.20%	5.80%	26.50%	27.70%	28.60%
Equal Pay Act	1,011	970	861	818	954	942	1,044	919	1,082	1,019	938
	1.30%	1.30%	1.10%	1.00%	1.00%	1.00%	1.00%	0.90%	1.10%	1.10%	1.10%
GINA							201	245	280	333	333
							0.20%	0.20%	0.30%	0.40%	0.40%

Source: U.S. Equal Employment Opportunity Commission (n. d.). Charge statistics FY 97 to FY 2014. Retrieved October 30, 2015 from http://eeoc.gov/eeoc/statistics/enforcement/charges.cfm

In many cases, such attitudes stem from the top of the corporation and reflect corporate culture. Indeed, one court has recognized that "top level officials are 'in a position to shape the attitudes, policies, and decisions of corporate managers'" (Sorensen, 2009, p. 194, citing *Ercegovich v. Goodyear Tire and Rubber Co., 1998*). It is through this perspective that corporations can be held accountable for discriminatory practices of its employees. Consider, as an illustration, a survey of nearly 700 business leaders focusing on hiring disabled workers that found that "86% agreed that employers would pick a non-disabled candidate, while 92% said there was still discrimination against disabled people in employment and recruitment" (Faragher, 2007, p. 22).

In a case highlighting how corporate leaders are involved in discrimination, an investigation by the Office of Inspector General (USOIG) and the Office of Professional Responsibility found that U.S. Deputy Assistant Attorney General Bradley S. Schlozman "considered political and ideological affiliations in hiring career attorneys and in other personnel actions affecting career attorneys in the Civil Rights Division" (USOIG, 2008, p. 64). As part of the evidence to substantiate the investigation, investigators found email messages with comments such as "I have an interview with some lefty who we'll never hire but I'm extending a courtesy interview as a favor," "[I] just spoke with [the attorney] to verify his political leanings and it is clear he is a member of the team," (p. 24) and in response to a request to hire an attorney, Schlozman e-mailed, "Conservative?" Ironically, while the Civil Rights Division exists to protect against civil rights violations, in this case a top-ranking official from the division committed multiple civil rights violations.

Discrimination has negative consequences for individuals, groups, and organizations. At the individual level, discrimination can negatively impact one's health, self-esteem, and job performance. At the group level, groups receive unfair pay differences and are assigned to different jobs based on group identities. At the organizational level, the corporation suffers from a negative reputation, law suits, and fines from the EEOC (Goldman et al., 2006).

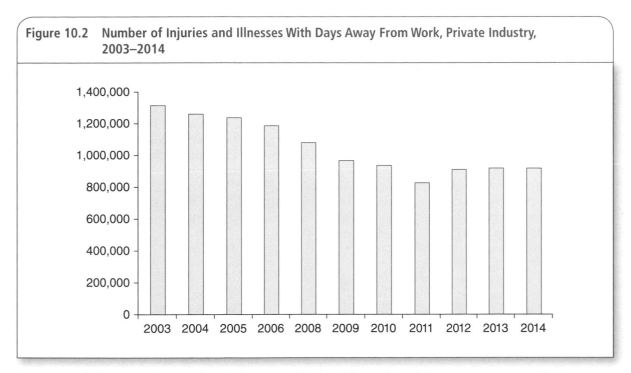

Figure 10.2   Number of Injuries and Illnesses With Days Away From Work, Private Industry, 2003–2014

Source: Bureau of Labor Statistics. (2009-2015). *Nonfatal occupational injuries and illnesses: Private industry, state government, and local government.* Available online.

Unsafe Work Environments

Crime also occurs in the corporate system when employers place employees at risk of harm in *unsafe work environments*. Labeled corporate violence by Frank and Lynch (1992), unsafe work environments can result in death, illnesses, and injuries. In terms of death, one author describes corporate murder as including deaths from industrial "accidents" and "occupationally related diseases, the majority of which are caused by the knowing and willful violation of occupational health and safety laws by corporations" (Kramer, 1984, p. 7). One scholar has suggested that "managers and corporations commit far more violence than any serial killer or criminal organization" (Punch, 2000, p. 243).

Prior to the creation of OSHA, roughly 14,000 workers in the U.S. were killed on the job annually. This has improved dramatically, with 4,679 workers dying on the job in 2014. Daily fatal injuries have decreased from 38 per day to 12 a day (OSHA, 2015b). When focusing on work-related illnesses, the number of deaths increases. It is more difficult, however, to track these numbers. OSHA (2006) estimates that 50,000 employees die each year from work-related illnesses. Depending on how one defines "work-related illnesses," this number may be far higher.

Consider stress-induced illnesses, for example. Did the stress come from the workplace or some other aspect of the individual's life? One author points to three issues that make it difficult to link illness to the workplace. First, determining the precise cause of illnesses and linking the illness to the workplace are difficult. Second, disease is seen as a normal part of the aging process. If individuals develop a workplace illness after years of work, the assumption is that the illness came from "getting old" rather than working. Third, and somewhat related, diseases are "considered normal" and accepted as a part of our lives (Frank, 1993, p. 110).

Workplace injuries can be either acute or chronic. Acute injuries are immediate injuries that one might experience on the job. Chronic injuries refer to those that occur over time. The nature of some types of jobs can lead to long-term injuries. Standing on a cement floor and packing boxes in a 100°F factory for 40 hours a week over 30 years (a job my dad had) can lead to knee and shoulder problems. Bending over and serving schoolchildren lunch for 22 years (a job my mom had) can lead to back problems. Typing on a computer over several years (a job I have) can result in carpal tunnel syndrome, a disease that makes it difficult to move one's hands (see Frank, 1993).

In terms of acute injuries, in 2014, 107.1 out of 10,000 full-time workers missed at least one day of work as the result of an occupational injury or illness (Bureau of Labor Statistics [BLS], 2015). This was a slight decrease from the prior year when the rate was 109 workers per 10,000 workers. The injuries may have been more serious, as the median days away from work increased to 9 days from 8 days between 2013 and 2014.

Figure 10.2 shows the number of injuries and illnesses between 2003 and 2014. As shown in the figure, 2009 was the first year that there were fewer than a million workplace injuries and the number has stayed under a million each year since. Somewhat in line with the systems perspective and the assumption that changes in one system will lead to changes in other systems, experts attribute this decrease to the downturn in the economic system. In particular, because of problems in the economic system, beginning in 2009 there were fewer hours worked in construction and manufacturing—two industries that typically have more injuries (BLS, 2010). Because fewer workers were in these industries, the number of possible injuries would also decrease. Changes in the economic system, in this case, reduced the number of workplace injuries in the corporate system. Whether those changes contributed to long-term decreases remains to be seen.

Despite this reduction, certain industries seem to be more at risk for workplace injuries than others. Table 10.5 shows the number of injuries in various industries. One clear pattern, and one that is not entirely surprising, is that "blue-collar" industries have more workplace injuries and illnesses than "white-collar" industries. According to OSHA, in 2014, there were just six occupations where the incidence rate was more than 300 (per 10,000) workers and the missed work days was greater than 10,000 days. These occupations included police officers, correctional officers, firefighters, nursing assistants, construction laborers, and truck drivers.

The top 10 most frequently cited OSHA standards in fiscal year 2015 included (1) fall protection; (2) hazard communication; (3) scaffolding; (4) respiratory protection; (5) lockout/tagout ; (6) powered industrial trucks; (7) ladders; (8) electrical, wiring; (10) machine guarding; and (10) electrical, general requirements (OSHA, 2016, https://www.osha.gov/Top_Ten_Standards.html). Where these problems exist, the possibility of workplace injuries increases. Note that I made an intentional decision not to refer to injuries as "accidents." As will be shown below, injuries occurring in the corporate system are often far from accidental.

Beyond the physical costs, the costs of workplace injuries and illnesses are significant. These costs include (1) settlement costs to victims and family members, (2) negative publicity, (3) increases in insurance premiums, (4) higher worker compensation rates, and (5) increased attention from government agencies (Yakovlev & Sobel, 2010). In terms of economic costs, it is estimated that "the cost of occupational injuries and illnesses totals more than $156 billion" (OSHA, 2006, p. 5).

Some authors have suggested that corporations are more concerned with profit than worker health and safety. One author even suggests that such a statement "seems incontrovertible" (Tombs, 2008, p. 26). However, economists have found that companies actually maximize profit if they provide safer working environments for their employees. In some cases, this means replacing workers with technological devices that are safer and "reduce worker exposure to danger and lead to lower injury rates over time" (Yakovlev & Sobel, 2010, p. 435). This may mean fewer jobs in "dangerous" occupations but more jobs in technologically oriented occupations that develop the technologies to make workplaces safer.

A summer job I had in college comes to mind. For 4 years, I spent my summers working in the bottle factory where my dad worked. College students had various summer jobs in the factory, including painting, packing bottles in boxes, driving forklifts, cleaning, and so on. One job was called "snapping." In this job, workers waited on the basement floor of the factory to stack packed bottles of boxes on a pallet. The packed boxes were carried on a conveyor belt, with as many as 30 boxes a minute coming before the "snapper." The snapper would grab several boxes at once, "snap" the lids of the boxes strategically, and flip them over while turning around to place them in a predetermined pattern on a pallet. The job was actually somewhat exciting to those of us who rarely did it. Trying to stack all of the boxes without creating a mess made the task more like a game than a job. If we fell behind, a full-time worker was there to help us out (while making fun of us for being unable to keep up). Each summer, someone got hurt from either dropping boxes (filled with bottles—which would become broken bottles) or from trying to lift too many boxes at once.

Years later, I learned that the snapper job no longer existed. A machine was created that would simultaneously pack the bottles in boxes and then stack the packed boxes on a pallet. A worker had to watch the machine to make sure it was working properly. Sitting and watching a machine stack boxes is much safer than stacking the boxes yourself!

The Occupational Safety and Health Administration, situated in the Department of Labor, is the federal agency charged with addressing health and safety issues in businesses. OSHA exists to "ensure safe and healthful working conditions for working men and women by setting and enforcing standards and by providing training, outreach, education, and assistance" (OSHA, 2011a). About 2,400 inspectors work for OSHA and related state agencies. In 2014, OSHA completed 36,163 inspections and identified 67,941 violations (OSHA, 2014). The types of violations OSHA issues citations for are outlined in Table 10.6.

OSHA was created in 1970 as part of the Occupational Safety and Health Act. This act covers all employees working in the private sector. State and local government workers are covered under specific state occupational acts, which by law must be similar to the federal law. The act does not cover (1) self-employed workers, (2) immediate family members of self-employed farmers, and (3) workers covered by another federal agency (OSHA, 2010a). The act stipulates that workers have the following rights (see OSHA, 2011b):

1. Receive information and training about hazards, methods to prevent harm, and the OSHA standards that apply to their workplace

2. Observe testing that is done to find hazards in the workplace and get the testing results

3. Review records of work-related injuries and illnesses

4. Get copies of their medical records

5. Request that OSHA inspect their workplace

6. Use their rights under the law to be free from retaliation and discrimination

Table 10.5 Number, Incidence Rate, and Median Days Away From Work for Nonfatal Occupational Injuries and Illnesses

Occupation	Total private, state, and local government[4,5,6]			Private industry[4,5,6]			State government[5,6]			Local government[5,6]		
	Number	Incidence rate	Median days away from work	Number	Incidence rate	Median days away from work	Number	Incidence rate	Median days away from work	Number	Incidence rate	Median days away from work
Total	1,157,410	107.1	9	916,440	97.8	9	67,400	170.3	12	173,570	166.4	10
Management occupations	24,390	36.9	7	20,510	34.6	7	910	42.8	5	2,970	61.4	8
Business and financial operations occupations	8,770	15.7	7	6,560	13.0	9	1,580	52.1	6	630	26.7	5
Computer and mathematical occupations	2,740	8.3	6	2,100	6.8	6	240	18.7	7	410	31.9	7
Architecture and engineering occupations	3,960	18.8	19	3,580	18.1	16	220	29.0	31	170	24.5	14
Life, physical, and social science occupations	3,300	37.1	7	2,240	35.4	5	530	34.4	16	520	53.5	21
Community and social services occupations	14,370	94.9	6	7,010	74.8	5	4,480	189.0	9	2,880	87.9	3
Legal occupations	1,400	15.5	10	980	13.2	10	170	22.2	5	260	29.7	13
Education, training, and library occupations	36,540	59.0	5	9,890	69.3	5	1,080	16.9	6	25,570	66.3	5
Arts, design, entertainment, sports, and media occupations	6,410	47.9	7	5,740	46.2	7	120	30.1	10	550	90.8	5
Healthcare practitioners and technical occupations.	64,500	103.6	7	51,060	92.9	7	6,070	227.3	11	7,370	153.8	9
Healthcare support occupations	64,240	220.6	6	55,200	201.3	6	5,120	575.3	9	3,930	390.7	7
Protective service occupations	78,910	298.7	12	9,270	97.5	8	17,600	454.4	14	52,030	426.0	11
Food preparation and serving related occupations	76,450	96.9	6	69,690	91.6	5	1,530	454.4	9	5,230	160.5	9
Building and grounds cleaning and maintenance occupations	84,090	258.5	9	58,570	214.2	8	4,360	522.0	10	21,160	490.2	10

Occupation	Total private, state, and local government[4,5,6]			Private industry[4,5,6]			State government[5,6]			Local government[5,6]		
	Number	Incidence rate	Median days away from work	Number	Incidence rate	Median days away from work	Number	Incidence rate	Median days away from work	Number	Incidence rate	Median days away from work
Personal care and service occupations	30,370	110.3	6	26,090	103.9	5	2,640	585.9	14	1,640	75.0	9
Sales and related occupations	55,900	51.8	9	55,460	51.1	9	260	169.6	9	180	44.2	2
Office and administrative support occupations	81,750	50.4	10	70,750	49.0	10	3,910	62.5	4	7,090	58.5	10
Farming, fishing, and forestry occupations	15,160	149.8	6	14,780	147.8	6	220	181.7	5	160	188.0	9
Construction and extraction occupations	88,910	189.5	12	73,460	168.9	11	4,460	503.2	8	10,990	400.6	18
Installation, maintenance, and repair occupations	94,430	202.9	11	81,730	189.6	10	2,640	328.8	12	10,060	354.4	11
Production occupations	108,130	136.5	8	104,980	133.6	8	520	298.7	9	2,630	234.2	10
Transportation and material moving occupations	203,180	–	14	182,800	246.7	14	3,500	–	21	16,880	464.9	13

[1]The incidence rates represent the number of injuries and illnesses per 10,000 full-time workers and were calculated as (N/EH) x 20,000,000, where N = number of injuries and illnesses EH = total hours worked by all employees during the calendar year 20,000,000 = base for 10,000 equivalent full-time workers (working 40 hours per week, 50 weeks per year).

[2]Median days away from work is the measure used to summarize the varying lengths of absences from work among the cases with days away from work. Half the cases involved more days and half involved fewer days than a specified median. Median days away from work are represented in actual values.

[3]Days-away-from-work cases include those that resulted in days away from work, some of which also included job transfer or restriction.

[4]Excludes farms with fewer than 11 employees.

[5]Data for Mining (Sector 21 in the *North American Industry Classification System*– United States, 2012) include establishments not governed by the Mine Safety and Health Administration rules and reporting, such as those in Oil and Gas Extraction and related support activities. Data for mining operators in coal, metal, and nonmetal mining are provided to BLS by the Mine Safety and Health Administration, U.S. Department of Labor. Independent mining contractors are excluded from the coal, metal, and nonmetal mining industries. These data do not reflect the changes the Occupational Safety and Health Administration made to its recordkeeping requirements effective January 1, 2002; therefore, estimates for these industries are not comparable to estimates in other industries.

[6]Data for employers in rail transportation are provided to BLS by the Federal Railroad Administration, U.S. Department of Transportation.

Source: U.S. Bureau of Labor Statistics, Survey of Occupational Injuries and Illnesses, in cooperation with participating state agencies.

Note: Dash indicates data do not meet publication guidelines. Because of rounding and data exclusion of nonclassifiable responses, data may not sum to the totals.

Table 10.6	Types of OSHA Violations
Violation	**Definition**
Willful	The employer knew that a hazardous condition existed but made no reasonable effort to eliminate it, and the hazardous condition violated a standard, regulation, or the OSH Act.
Serious	The workplace hazard could cause injury or illness that would most likely result in death or serious physical harm, unless the employer did not know or could not have known of the violation.
Other-than-serious	A situation in which the most serious injury or illness that would be likely to result from a hazardous condition cannot reasonably be predicted to cause death or serious physical harm to exposed employees but does have a direct and immediate relationship to their safety and health.
De minimis	Violations that have no direct or immediate relationship to safety or health.
Failure to abate	The employer has not corrected a violation for which OSHA has issued a citation, and that abatement date has passed.
Repeated	Employer may be cited for a repeated violation if that employer has been cited previously for a substantially similar condition.

Source: Occupational Safety & Health Administration (OSHA), United States Department of Labor. (2015b). *Employer rights and responsibilities following an OSHA inspection.* Available from https://www.osha.gov/Publications/osha3000.pdf.

Under this last provision, employees cannot be punished by employers for exercising their rights. If employers engage in any form of adverse action, the corporation or business could face additional penalties from OSHA. Types of adverse actions that would warrant a response from OSHA include any of the following actions directed toward the employee who reported a concern to OSHA: firing or laying off, making threats, blacklisting, reassigning, reducing pay or hours, demoting, denying overtime, disciplining, denying benefits, failure to rehire, and intimidation (OSHA, 2010b).

Workplace injuries and illnesses are rarely treated as crimes. A study of Finnish police officers found a systematic lack of interest in responding to workplace safety offenses (Alvesalo & Whyte, 2007). In this study, one officer told an interviewer that such cases were "worthless shit" that should not receive police intervention.

Typically, workplace injuries and illnesses are handled within the regulatory environment. This presents problems in that victims' needs may not be fully addressed through an administrative response system. One expert has suggested expanding workers' compensation policies as well as filing civil lawsuits and criminal prosecutions in cases where companies harm their workers.

With regard to workers' compensation, the specific features of the policies are not "worker friendly" policies. Under worker compensation systems, it is up to workers to prove that their ailment was caused by the occupational setting. If workers agree to the compensation, they typically give up their right to sue their company for negligence (Frank, 1993). The pursuit of criminal remedies is complicated by perceptions of workplace injuries as accidents rather than avoidable injuries inflicted by the corporate system employing the injured employee.

Some have criticized the use of the word *accidents* to describe workplace injuries (Alvesalo & Whyte, 2007). The basis for the criticism is fourfold. First, many of the injuries are foreseeable and can be attributed to decisions made by managers and supervisors to place workers at risk. Second, the term *accident* implies that the injured party is to blame. Keep in mind that injured parties more often work in blue-collar occupations. Third, by construing injuries as accidents, the managers increase their power over the workers, who get blamed for getting hurt on the job. Finally, by defining injuries as accidents, workers are less likely to pursue civil and criminal remedies to address their injuries. As an example of how defining workplace injuries as accidents helps keep the cases out of the justice system, consider the following comments from one police officer: "It's not the responsibility of the employer if some idiot blunders by oneself, does something stupid. There cannot be someone looking over every Tom, Dick, and Harry" (Alvesalo & Whyte, 2007, p. 69).

Reflecting the connections between constructions of definitions of deviance, workplace injury, and the system's response, author Maurice Punch (2000) observed the following:

> Corporations can create an environment that leads to risk-taking, even recklessness, resulting in high casualties and severe harm. Companies then get away with "murder" because the courts are not geared to organizational deviance and corporate violence. (p. 243)

Discussing these ideas in the abstract may make it difficult for some students to fully appreciate the dynamics of workplace injuries and illnesses. However, many students are likely already employed in either full- or part-time jobs. Students must recognize that in their role as "worker" they too have certain rights that their employer is expected to recognize. In Focus 10.1 includes information about these rights from an OSHA publication (n.d.a) titled "Young Workers."

IN FOCUS 10.1

Young Workers' Rights: What Every College Student Needs to Know

You Have a Right to a Safe and Healthy Workplace and a Responsibility to Be Safe

You may work to earn spending money, buy a car, save for college or gain work experience. Whatever the reason, plans for your job and for your future don't include getting hurt.

Each year, 60–70 teens die from work-related injuries and about 200,000 young workers seek emergency medical treatment.

It doesn't have to be this way. You have the right to be safe and healthy at work and you have a responsibility to be safe. And there are simple, practical steps that you and your employer can take to help make sure that your job helps you build a better future.

Employer Responsibilities

Provide a workplace that protects workers from injuries, illnesses, and fatalities.

Know the law about working limits for teens, including the number of hours they can work and the kinds of jobs that can be performed.

Emphasize the importance of safety.

Make sure that young workers are trained properly.

Teach workers to recognize hazards and use safe work practices.

Teen Worker Responsibilities

Trust your instincts about dangerous situations.

Follow all safety rules.

Wear proper safety equipment.

Ask questions about potentially dangerous situations or equipment.

Tell your supervisor or parent if you suspect unsafe conditions.

Be aware of your work environment.

Work safely.

Stay sober and drug-free.

Know your workplace rights.

(Continued)

(Continued)

What Is OSHA?

OSHA is the Occupational Safety and Health Administration. Its role is to assure the safety and health of America's workers by setting and enforcing standards; providing training, outreach, and education; establishing partnerships; and encouraging continual improvement in workplace safety and health.

Finding Answers

Employers are responsible for providing a safe and healthy workplace for their employees. If you are worried about a specific workplace hazard or interested in learning more about keeping yourself and others safe and healthy at work, visit the OSHA Teen Workers website at www.osha.gov/teens. Or call OSHA toll-free at 1-800-321-OSHA to report a problem, ask questions or request information.

To protect yourself:

Know your workplace rights.

Talk to your employer.

Stay alert and work safely.

Get safety and health training.

Visit the OSHA Teen Workers website at www.osha.gov/teens.

Common workplace hazards and injuries:

Slips, trips and falls

Strains and sprains

Chemical exposure

Burns and cuts

Eye injuries

Hearing loss

Motor vehicle crashes

Electrocution

Machinery malfunctions

Source: Reprinted From OSHA. (n.d.). Available from http://www.osha.gov/Publications/teen_worker_brochure.html.

Harmful Consumer Products

Crimes also occur in the corporate system when corporations create **harmful consumer products**. Companies produce all sorts of goods for our use. In most cases, these goods are safe. Occasionally, however, goods enter the marketplace that create significant harm to consumers. Consider that in 2013, the U.S. Consumer Product Safety Commission (CPSC) issued 373 recalls for millions of goods "that either violated mandatory standards or were defective and presented a substantial risk of injury to the public" (CPSC, 2013).

While virtually any product can be unsafe if used inappropriately, goods that have been linked to serious harm include the following:

- Harmful toys
- Certain automobiles
- Types of food
- Specific types of construction material
- Recalled goods from China

These goods are discussed further.

Harmful Toys

Children's products are those that are often found to be the least safe. One advocacy group, Kids in Danger, lamented that children are "used as guinea pigs for unsafe products" because government "safety tests aren't required for children's products" (Sorkin, 2008). Interestingly, the number of toy-related injuries has continued to consistently grow since 2005. Table 10.7 shows the number of toy injuries requiring emergency room treatment between 2005 and 2013. During this time, the number of toy injuries increased roughly 30 percent—from 202,300 to 256,700. Incidentally, approximately 130,000 toy injuries requiring emergency room treatment occurred in 1996. This means that the number of injuries nearly doubled from 1996 to 2013. In 2013, nonmotorized scooters caused the most injuries for children under the age of 15. They accounted for more than one-fourth (28%) of the injuries (Tu, 2014). Nine children (all under the age of 12) died as a result of toy-related injuries in 2013 (Tu, 2014).

▲ **Photo 10.1**   The number of kids who required emergency room treatment for injuries they experienced from playing with toys in the United States nearly doubled between 1996 and 2014.

Certain Automobiles

On August 28th, 2009, a 911 operator received a call from Mark Saylor, an off-duty California highway patrol officer. He told the operator, "We're in a Lexus . . . and we're going north on 125 and our accelerator is stuck . . . we're in trouble . . . there's no brakes . . . we're approaching the intersection . . . hold on . . . hold on and pray . . . pray" (Frean & Lea, 2010). He and three family members were killed in what was later attributed to a problem with the accelerator sticking to the floor mat.

Table 10.7	Number of Toy-Related Injuries Requiring Emergency Room Intervention, 2005–2013		
Year	**All Ages**	**Under 15**	**Under 5**
2005	202,300	152,400	72,800
2006	220,500	165,100	78,400
2007	232,900	170,100	80,200
2008	235,300	172,700	82,300
2009	250,100	185,900	90,600
2010	251,700	181,500	89,200
2011	262,300	193,200	92,200
2012	265,000	192,000	89,500
2013	256,700	188,400	83,700

Source: Tu, Y. (2014). *Toy-related deaths and injuries calendar year 2013.* Bethesda, MD: U. S. Consumer Product Safety Commission. Retrieved November 1, 2015 from http://www.cpsc.gov/Global/Research-and-Statistics/Injury-Statistics/Toys/ToyReport2013.pdf

Initially, National Highway Traffic Safety Administration (NHTSA) investigators found that the mat in Saylor's vehicle was longer than it should have been, and it was believed that this potentially contributed to the crash. Until Toyota found a fix, owners of certain models were advised to remove the mats from the driver's side ("Fatal Crash Spurs Review," 2009). Another review of the incident found that the design of the gas pedal could have forced it to get lodged with the mat (Bensinger & Vartabedian, 2009). A subsequent investigation revealed that similar problems in other cars made by Toyota "led to thousands of accidents and nineteen deaths" (Frean & Lea, 2010).

In response to these concerns, in 2009 Toyota recalled 4.26 million automobiles. The recall resulted in Toyota's shares dropping 0.9 percent (Keane & Kitamura, 2009). It is estimated that the recall cost Toyota $900 million (Glor, 2010), and U.S. sales of Toyota vehicles dropped to under 100,000 vehicles for the first time since the late 1990s ("There's No Brakes," 2010). Obviously, this drop in sales was the result of a reduction in consumer confidence. In Focus 10.2 includes the testimony Toyota's chief executive made before the U.S. House Committee on Oversight and Reform on February 24, 2010.

Toyota was not the first automobile company to face concerns about safety. In the early 2000s, the Ford Explorer faced public scrutiny after it was found that tread separation problems on the Explorer's Firestone tires resulted in the deaths of 134 individuals in the United States. The investigation found that separately the tires and the vehicles were safe. However, when combined, they were a "toxic cocktail," according to Rep. Edward Markey (D. Mass.) (White, Power, & Aeppel, 2001). Ford and Firestone recalled more than 27 million tires in a 10-month time frame, and in 2001, Ford cut its 100-year supply relationship with Firestone (Ackman, 2001).

Of course, this was not the first time that the safety of a Ford vehicle was called into question. Recall the discussion of the Ford Pinto case earlier in this text. The Pinto was linked to a series of deaths "because of gas-tank explosions in rear-end collisions" (Glazer, 1983, p. 37). Ford was sued in 50 different lawsuits between 1971 and 1978 as a result of these collisions. One employee, Frank Camps, a design engineer, "questioned the design and testing procedure and later charged publicly that his superiors who knew of this danger were so anxious to produce a lightweight and cheap car . . . that they were determined to overlook serious design problems" (Glazer, 1983, p. 36).

Most automobile companies, as well as the state and federal government, now employ individuals to monitor the safety of automobiles. The Careers Responding to White-Collar Crime: Motor Safety Specialist box describes the duties performed in one such job.

Types of Food

Certain types of food can also be seen as unsafe consumer products. Walters (2007) notes that genetically modified food has the potential to harm consumers. He also draws attention to the "sale of contaminated meat" and "the illegal use of chemicals" on food items. Whereas the Consumer Product Safety Commission has the authority to recall many products, consumable products, such as food, are under the authority of the Food and Drug Administration.

In September 2008, concern surfaced over potentially contaminated peanut butter. An investigation revealed that Peanut Butter Corporation of America, a peanut butter producer in Georgia, had distributed peanut butter contaminated with salmonella. Initially, the FDA concluded that the company actually knew about the tainted peanut butter but engaged in "lab shopping" to find another lab that would approve the peanut butter before distribution. A subsequent report by the FDA found that the company had actually distributed the peanut butter before even receiving approval from the second laboratory. Congress held a hearing, inviting food safety experts and subpoenaing representatives from Peanut Butter Corporation. Officials from the corporation did not testify, invoking their Fifth Amendment right against self-incrimination ("FDA: Georgia Plant Knowingly Sold," 2009). By April 2009, at least 9 individuals had allegedly died from eating the peanut butter, and more than 700 had become seriously ill (Centers for Disease Control [CDC], 2009). The company filed for bankruptcy, and the entire peanut butter industry experienced economic losses as consumers cut back on their peanut butter consumption. In September 2015, the CEO was sentenced to 28 years in prison after a jury found him guilty of 72 fraud and conspiracy charges the year before. This was reportedly the first time a food safety case resulted in a felony conviction, let alone a prison sentence. The company's food broker and quality assurance manager received prison sentences of 20 and 5 years respectively.

CAREERS RESPONDING TO WHITE-COLLAR CRIME

Motor Carrier Safety Specialist

As a Motor Carrier Safety Specialist (Border Investigator), you will:

- Analyze compliance review, enforcement, and inspection results, accident and incident reports, complaints, and other information to identify safety and compliance problems or trends among the motor carriers and shippers in the assigned State; assists in developing an annual area work planning guide consistent with national, regional, and division goals.

- Plan and carry out a schedule of safety, economic, security, and hazardous materials investigations of carrier and shipper operations; through personal interviews, examination of various records, and comparison with other known facts, determines whether the company is in compliance or whether the violations found indicate deliberate and conscious disregard of applicable regulations; makes a preliminary determination whether prosecution is warranted and evidence is sufficient to support enforcement action.

- Conduct investigations into alleged violations either as follow-up to an investigation or in response to complaints; upon advice and approval by the supervisor, initiates enforcement investigations to develop supportive evidence of the kinds and volume needed to sustain criminal or civil forfeiture actions, cease and desist orders, or other proceedings.

- Plan and conduct unannounced roadside inspections of interstate commercial motor vehicles and driver's documentation to determine carrier or driver compliance with applicable regulations; notes deficiencies and declares out-of-service any vehicle or driver in accordance with the established Out of Service Criteria.

- Conduct in-depth investigations into the causes of highway accidents and hazardous material incidents involving motor carriers to determine whether applicable regulations or laws have been violated; develop information for use in furthering the agency's accident prevention program.

Source: Reprinted from USAJobs.Gov

Many cases of food poisoning from harmful food products likely go unnoticed. Research by CDC scientists estimates that 48 million individuals (or one in six Americans) get sick from food poisoning each year (Scallan et al., 2011). Also, it is estimated that approximately 128,000 individuals are hospitalized in the United States from food poisoning each year, and approximately 3,000 die from tainted food (CDC, 2011). See Box 10.2 for a recent case where authorities fined an egg company for unsafe practices.

Specific Types of Construction Material

Certain types of construction materials have also been shown to be unsafe products. Asbestos is perhaps the most well-known construction material deemed to be unsafe. Asbestos is a mineral used in the past in various construction processes and products, including insulation, siding, roofing materials, shipyard construction materials, and so on. Initial concern about asbestos can be traced to the 1920s, when physicians wrote about the potential for harm from exposure to this product. It was not until the mid-1970s, however, that widespread concern about the product surfaced. Workers in various industries exhibited different illnesses that were traced to exposure to asbestos. It is now known that asbestos exposure can lead to asbestosis (an illness making it difficult to breathe), lung cancer, and mesothelioma. Between the early 1970s and 2002, 730,000 individuals filed asbestos claims at a cost of

IN FOCUS   10.2

Toyota Chief Executive Akio Toyoda's Remarks to the House Committee on Oversight and Reform

I am Akio Toyoda of Toyota Motor Corporation. I would first like to state that I love cars as much as anyone, and I love Toyota as much as anyone. I take the utmost pleasure in offering vehicles that our customers love, and I know that Toyota's 200,000 team members, dealers, and suppliers across America feel the same way. However, in the past few months, our customers have started to feel uncertain about the safety of Toyota's vehicles, and I take full responsibility for that. Today, I would like to explain to the American people, as well as our customers in the U.S. and around the world, how seriously Toyota takes the quality and safety of its vehicles. I would like to express my appreciation to Chairman Towns and Ranking Member Issa, as well as the members of the House Oversight and Government Reform Committee, for giving me this opportunity to express my thoughts today.

I would like to focus my comments on three topics—Toyota's basic philosophy regarding quality control, the cause of the recalls, and how we will manage quality control going forward. First, I want to discuss the philosophy of Toyota's quality control. I myself, as well as Toyota, am not perfect. At times, we do find defects. But in such situations, we always stop, strive to understand the problem, and make changes to improve further. In the name of the company, its long-standing tradition and pride, we never run away from our problems or pretend we don't notice them. By making continuous improvements, we aim to continue offering even better products for society. That is the core value we have kept closest to our hearts since the founding days of the company.

At Toyota, we believe the key to making quality products is to develop quality people. Each employee thinks about what he or she should do, continuously making improvements, and by doing so, makes even better cars. We have been actively engaged in developing people who share and can execute on this core value. It has been over 50 years since we began selling in this great country, and over 25 years since we started production here. And in the process, we have been able to share this core value with the 200,000 people at Toyota operations,

dealers, and suppliers in this country. That is what I am most proud of.

Second, I would like to discuss what caused the recall issues we are facing now. Toyota has, for the past few years, been expanding its business rapidly. Quite frankly, I fear the pace at which we have grown may have been too quick. I would like to point out here that Toyota's priority has traditionally been the following: First; Safety, Second; Quality, and Third; Volume. These priorities became confused, and we were not able to stop, think, and make improvements as much as we were able to before, and our basic stance to listen to customers' voices to make better products has weakened somewhat. We pursued growth over the speed at which we were able to develop our people and our organization, and we should sincerely be mindful of that. I regret that this has resulted in the safety issues described in the recalls we face today, and I am deeply sorry for any accidents that Toyota drivers have experienced.

Especially, I would like to extend my condolences to the members of the Saylor family, for the accident in San Diego. I would like to send my prayers again, and I will do everything in my power to ensure that such a tragedy never happens again.

Since last June, when I first took office, I have personally placed the highest priority on improving quality over quantity, and I have shared that direction with our stakeholders. As you well know, I am the grandson of the founder, and all the Toyota vehicles bear my name. For me, when the cars are damaged, it is as though I am as well. I, more than anyone, wish for Toyota's cars to be safe, and for our customers to feel safe when they use our vehicles. Under my leadership, I would like to reaffirm our values of placing safety and quality the highest on our list of priorities, which we have held to firmly from the time we were founded. I will also strive to devise a system in which we can surely execute what we value.

Third, I would like to discuss how we plan to manage quality control as we go forward. Up to now, any decisions on conducting recalls have been made by the Customer Quality Engineering

Division at Toyota Motor Corporation in Japan. This division confirms whether there are technical problems and makes a decision on the necessity of a recall. However, reflecting on the issues today, what we lacked was the customers' perspective. To make improvements on this, we will make the following changes to the recall decision making process. When recall decisions are made, a step will be added in the process to ensure that management will make a responsible decision from the perspective of "customer safety first." To do that, we will devise a system in which customers' voices around the world will reach our management in a timely manner, and also a system in which each region will be able to make decisions as necessary. Further, we will form a quality advisory group composed of respected outside experts from North America and around the world to ensure that we do not make a misguided decision. Finally, we will invest heavily in quality in the U.S., through the establishment of an Automotive Center of Quality Excellence, the introduction of a new position—Product Safety Executive, and the sharing of more information and responsibility within

the company for product quality decisions, including defects and recalls.

Even more importantly, I will ensure that members of the management team actually drive the cars, and that they check for themselves where the problem lies as well as its severity. I myself am a trained test driver. As a professional, I am able to check on problems in a car, and can understand how severe the safety concern is in a car. I drove the vehicles in the accelerator pedal recall as well as the Prius, comparing the vehicles before and after the remedy in various environmental settings. I believe that only by examining the problems on-site, can one make decisions from the customer perspective. One cannot rely on reports or data in a meeting room. Through the measures I have just discussed, and with whatever results we obtain from the investigations we are conducting in cooperation with NHTSA, I intend to further improve on the quality of Toyota vehicles and fulfill our principle of putting the customer first.

My name is on every car. You have my personal commitment that Toyota will work vigorously and unceasingly to restore the trust of our customers.

Source: Reprinted From House Committee on Oversight and Reform

---

$70 billion. Estimates suggest that by 2029, a half million Americans will have died from asbestos-related diseases (J. Morris, 2010).

Asbestos is rarely used in building products today, though materials containing it are still found in older buildings and homes. Left alone in the construction material, the asbestos poses little harm. However, when cut, damaged, or moved, the asbestos fibers can become airborne and cause health problems.

Chinese drywall is another type of unsafe building material. In 2008, the U.S. Consumer Product Safety Commission began receiving complaints about problems homeowners were having with drywall installed in their homes. The drywall was imported from manufacturers in China between 2003 and 2007 when the U.S. levels of drywall were low because of the building boom and the need for drywall to repair homes after Hurricanes Katrina and Rita. Residents with the drywall in their homes reported (1) rotten egg smells or odors that

▲ **Photo 10.2** In general, consumers expect their food to be safe, and most give little thought to the possibility that they could be consuming unsafe meals.

WHITE-COLLAR CRIME IN THE NEWS

Yoke's on the Business:
Egg Company Fined for Unsafe Practices

https://commons.wikimedia.org/wiki/File:Chicken_Farm_034.jpg

It's no game of chicken when lives are at risk. One company was fined $6.79 million for distributing harmful eggs.

The 81-year-old owner of an Iowa egg production company and his son, a top executive in the business, are going to prison for bribing a federal food inspector and distributing eggs that contained Salmonella bacteria, which caused hundreds of consumers to become sick.

A federal judge in Iowa last month ordered the Quality Egg company to pay a $6.79 million fine and sentenced company owner Austin "Jack" DeCoster, and his son, Peter DeCoster, who was Quality Egg's chief operating officer, to serve time in prison.

During the spring and summer of 2010, adulterated eggs produced and distributed by Quality Egg were linked to nearly 2,000 consumer illnesses in a nationwide outbreak of salmonellosis that led to the recall of millions of eggs produced by the defendants.

"This was a classic case of putting profits over public safety," said Special Agent Grant Permenter, who helped investigate the case from the FBI's Omaha Division.

Quality Egg pled guilty to bribing an inspector of the U.S. Department of Agriculture (USDA) to release eggs that had been retained for quality issues. The eggs had been "red

tagged" for failing to meet minimum USDA quality grade standards. The company also pled guilty to introducing misbranded eggs into interstate commerce with the intent to defraud. From approximately 2006 until 2010, Quality Egg employees affixed labels to egg shipments that indicated false expiration dates with the intent to mislead state regulators and retail egg customers regarding the true age of the eggs.

In the government's sentencing memorandum prepared for the court, it was noted that Quality Egg personnel had for years disregarded food safety standards and misled customers about the company's food safety practices.

"As with a lot of fraud cases," Permenter said, "Quality Egg's crimes were committed over and over for years, and, eventually, these illegal practices caught up with them." But this case was not just about deception, he said. "People got sick. There was a serious public safety issue here. Quality Egg's business practices put the public at risk—at times, substantial risk."

Permenter explained that the FBI assisted in the investigation led by the USDA's Office of Inspector General and the Food and Drug Administration's Office of Criminal Investigations. He added that the USDA inspector who received bribes from Quality Egg was in ill health and died before he could be charged. "The inspector was a federal employee. Had he lived," Permenter said, "he would have been charged and, in all likelihood, would have gone to jail as well." In June 2014, Quality Egg and Jack and Peter DeCoster pled guilty to bribery and other charges related to adulterated egg distribution.

In the end, Permenter said, "it seems obvious that company profits outweighed other concerns." By being able to circumvent the inspection process through bribes and not having to remove the tainted eggs from its inventory, the company saved a significant amount of money. "When you start bending your ethical and moral fibers because there are dollar signs in front of you," he said, "a lot of bad things are likely to happen."

Source: Reprinted from FBI (2015, May 8). Profits over safety. Available online at https://www.fbi.gov/news/stories/2015/may/profits-over-safety/profits-over-safety

smelled like fireworks, (2) corroded or black metals, (3) corroded electrical wiring, and (4) an assortment of health problems. The health problems they described included "irritated and itchy eyes, difficulty breathing, persistent coughing, bloody noses, runny noses, headaches, sinus infections, fatigue, asthma attacks, loss of appetite, poor memory, and irritability;" testing of the homes with the drywall found that the Chinese drywall emitted 100 times the amount of hydrogen sulfide than non–Chinese drywall emitted (U.S. Consumer Product Safety Commission [CPSC], 2010a; Hernandez, 2010).

It is estimated that 7 million sheets of the tainted drywall were installed in thousands of homes in the United States and that property damage from the defective drywall will rise to $3 billion. By March 2010, approximately 2,100 home-owners had filed lawsuits over the drywall against builders, insurers, manufacturers, and others ("Insurers' Recent Success," 2010). Around the same time, the CPSC recommended that homeowners remove the drywall from their homes, an expense that would need to be covered by the homeowners. Estimates suggested that such a process would cost an average of $100,000 per home (Hernandez, 2010).

In the fall of 2010, a judge held that insurers could not be held liable because of traditional exclusions found in insurance policies ("Insurers' Recent Success," 2010). In October 2010, Knauf Plasterboard Tianjin Co., the company responsible for some of the tainted drywall, agreed to fix the homes that had its drywall installed in them (Burdeau, 2010). By January 2011, the CPSC had received 3,770 complaints from consumers in 41 states saying that the defective drywall caused problems in their homes. At present, the agency is still conducting an investigation; it is described as "the largest compliance investigation in agency history" (CPSC, 2010b).

Recalled Goods From China

The drywall was not the first imported good from China deemed to be unsafe. The year 2007, deemed "Year of the Recall," saw a particularly high number of Chinese goods recalled by the Consumer Product Safety Commission. To put this in perspective, in 2007, the CPSC issued 473 recalls. Of those 473, 82 percent were for imported goods, most of which included toys and jewelry from China (CPSC, 2010c). Many of the recalls centered on what was deemed to be an unsafe level of lead paint in the goods. In September 2007, the CPSC signed an agreement with China's equivalent agency stipulating that China would no longer export toys containing lead paint to the United States ("Chinese Goods Scare Prods Regulators," 2007). The CPSC's Office of International Programs and International Affairs enhanced its efforts to work with China and other foreign manufacturers to focus on product safety. Part of their efforts entailed the coordination of U.S.–China Consumer Product Safety Summits. The agency also staffed an employee in China for the first time beginning in December 2009 (CPSC, 2010c).

To be sure, globalization has had ramifications for the way that corporations create and distribute unsafe products. On the one hand, it is hard to hold manufacturers in other countries accountable "because attorneys can't establish jurisdiction" (PR Newswire, 2007). On the other hand, the way that goods are now created, a specific product may include parts that were created in several different countries. It becomes particularly difficult to determine where the faulty part of an unsafe product was made (Wahl, 2009).

▲ **Photo 10.3** The FDA trains Chinese manufacturers and regulators how to promote safety. In this photo, the FDA's Daniel Geffin is showing Chinese regulators the way that he inspects manufacturing equipment designed to sterilize canned foods.

US Government Work

Harmful Treatment of Consumers

Harmful treatment of consumers refers to situations where businesses either intentionally or unintentionally put consumers who are using their services at risk of harm. Institutional neglect in nursing homes is one example. Offenses that have been known to occur in nursing homes include instances where nursing homes fail to

1. check and update each resident's assessments every 3 months;

2. have a program to keep infection from spreading;

3. give proper treatment to residents with feeding tubes to prevent problems;

4. make sure that each resident gets a nutritional and well-balanced diet;

5. resolve each resident's complaints quickly;

6. make sure each resident is being watched and has assistance devices when needed to prevent accidents;

7. make sure that residents are well nourished;

8. keep residents free from physical restraints, unless needed for medical treatment;

9. keep the rate of medication errors (wrong drug, wrong dose, wrong time) to less than 5 percent (Payne, 2011).

Note that these offenses in and of themselves may not produce harm. However, they raise the likelihood that consumers might experience harm.

Businesses have a duty to ensure that consumers are as safe possible. A landmark case demonstrating this involved pop singer Connie Francis. In 1974, she was raped at a Howard Johnson's hotel in New York. After her victimization, she sued the hotel for failing to provide her adequate security after learning that the lock on the door of the room where her rape occurred had not been fixed six months after she was raped (Barrows & Powers, 2009; Shuler, 2010).

Another case demonstrating how businesses and corporations can commit misconduct by failing to keep consumers safe involves the band Great White. The 1980s band is best known for its hit, "Once Bitten, Twice Shy." Like many '80s bands, Great White was still entertaining audiences two decades later by playing in nightclubs and local establishments across the country. On February 20, 2003, they were playing at The Station, a popular nightclub in West Warwick, Rhode Island. To start the show, the band's tour manager, Dan Biechele—with the approval of the owners of the establishment—set off a fireworks display that shot flames into the soundproofing foam installed in the ceiling (Kreps, 2010; Kurkjian, S. Ebbert, T. Ebbert, & Farragher, 2003).

The establishment erupted in fire. Concertgoers could not even see the exit signs at the doors because of the smoke. Some of them had problems getting past a local television camera person who was there, ironically, to film a story about nightclub safety. Within 3 to 5 minutes, The Station was engulfed in flame. By the time the fire was over, 100 people had been killed (Kurkjian et al., 2003).

Band manager Biechele later pleaded guilty to 100 counts of manslaughter. In May 2006, he was sentenced to 15 years in prison with 11 years suspended. He was paroled in March 2008. The owners of the club—brothers Michael and Jeffery Derderian—pleaded no contest after Biechele, while still claiming that they did not know that the soundproofing was flammable. Several entities involved in the concert were sued, including the band, the installer of the soundproofing foam, the promoters, alcohol suppliers, the owners, their insurance companies, and the television station doing the story on nightclub safety. In 2010, the case was settled for $176 million ("Great White Band Manager," 2006; Kreps, 2010). That so many defendants were listed in the lawsuit demonstrates the complexity of these cases. The Great White case also shows that the failure to keep consumers safe is defined as a criminal wrong for those directly involved in the event and a civil wrong for those indirectly involved.

● ● ● Dynamics of Corporate Offending

It is clear that several varieties of corporate crime exist. At least four patterns run through these varieties of crime. These patterns include the following:

- The benefits of corporate crime
- The complexity of intent
- The breadth of victimization
- Problems responding to corporate crime

With regard to the *benefits of corporate crime*, it is clear that corporations benefit from wrongdoing, assuming they don't get caught. Even when they get caught, many believe that the low penalties given to offenders result in corporations still benefiting from the misconduct. It is important to stress that some individuals benefit from corporate offending. The discussion has tended to suggest that it is the corporation that benefits from these misdeeds (Glasberg & Skidmore, 1998a). However, employees may also benefit, particularly if the misdeeds result in promotions, favorable job evaluations, and bonuses.

The *complexity of intent* is another dynamic of corporate crimes. Punch (2000) categorized three levels of knowledge to describe managerial involvement in corporate violence: (1) fully conscious conspiratorial behavior over time; (2) incompetent and negligent; and (3) unaware of criminal risks, or perceived as legitimate behavior. This third level may be particularly difficult to grasp. In effect, it is entirely reasonable that no one did anything wrong, but a corporate harm nonetheless occurred. As Vaughan (2001) notes, "traditionally, when things go wrong in organizations, individuals are blamed." Vaughan goes on to say that organizations "have their dark side" and that organizational processes can produce "harmful outcomes, even when personnel are well-trained, well-intentioned, have adequate resources, and do all the correct things" (p. 57). Ermann and Lundman (2002) offer a similar perspective: "Well-intentioned individuals in organizational settings may produce deviant actions, even though none of them have deviant knowledge, much less deviant motivations. Indeed, individuals may do their jobs well and nevertheless produce deviance" (p. 9).

Consider the Ford Pinto case, the first time a prosecutor tried to criminally prosecute an automobile company for corporate misconduct tied to the gas tank explosions of the Pinto. While many may want to place blame on the Ford executives and attribute the misdeeds to profit-seeking motivations, Lee and Ermann (1999), after a thorough review of the case, "argue[d] that institutionalized norms and conventional modes of communication at the organizational and network level better explain available data" (p. 33). They also note that "routine processes can generate unintended tragedy" (p. 43) and concluded that the accidents were the result of "unreflective action," writing, "the Pinto design emerged from social forces both internal and external to Ford. There was no 'decision' to market an unsafe product, and there was no decision to market a safe one" (p. 45).

As another example, recall the Great White tragedy. The tour manager and bar owners were simply doing their jobs—trying to entertain the concertgoers. They did not intend to create the harm that arose that winter night. But their actions did nonetheless result in harm.

One can also point to the **breadth of victimization** as another corporate crime dynamic. One single corporate offense could harm thousands, if not millions, of individuals. One author has classified corporate crime victims into primary, secondary, and tertiary victims (Shichor, 1989). Primary victims are those directly harmed by the corporate offense (i.e., the individual who used the unsafe product). Secondary victims are impersonal victims, typically not individuals (e.g., businesses that are harmed by the misdeeds of a corporation). Tertiary victims include members of the community harmed by victimization. Another author has noted that victims of corporate crime include workers, consumers, investors, taxpayers, and other corporations (H. C. Barnett, 1981). In addition, scholars have noted that corporations can victimize themselves through what is called collective embezzlement, defined as "crimes by the corporation against the corporation" (Calavita & Pontell, 1991, p. 94). Instances where top executives allow a corporation to fail, knowing that they will profit from the failure, are examples of collective embezzlement.

Another dynamic surrounding corporate crime has to do with *problems responding to corporate crime*. Corporations "possess an economic and political power that is great relative to that generally possessed by victims of corporate crime" (H. C. Barnett, 1981, p. 4). With this power, corporations are believed to be able to influence criminal justice decision making and use their resources to "manipulate politicians and the media" (Garoupa, 2005, p. 37). As an example, one expert has shown how some types of corporate misconduct are not defined as crime but as "risky business" by various parties (Pontell, 2005).

Figure 10.3   Topics Addressed in Criminal Justice Journals

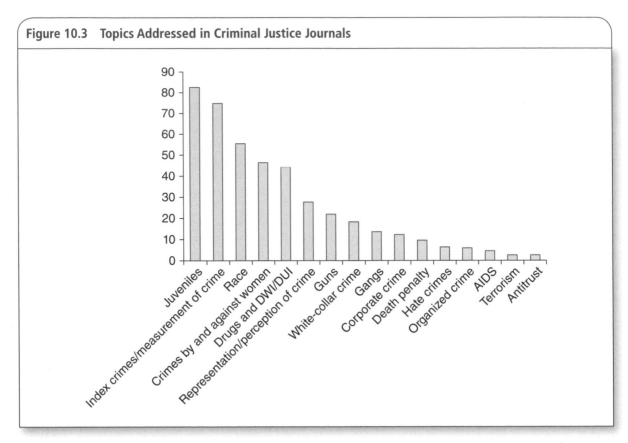

Source: Adapted from Lynch, M. J., McGurrin, D., & Fenwick, M. (2004). "Disappearing act: The representation of corporate crime research in criminology journals and textbooks." *Journal of Criminal Justice, 32*(5), 389–398.

● ● ●   Public Concern About Crimes by the Corporate System

Corporate crimes do not typically receive the same level of public scrutiny that other crimes do. One author attributed this to the belief that these offenses "are usually less sensational, better concealed, and harder to prove" (Minkes, 1990, p. 128). Members of the public often do not know they have been victims of corporate offenses, nor are they aware of the harm from these offenses or of possible strategies for recovering the costs of the harm (Tombs, 2008).

Some have attributed the lack of understanding about corporate crime to media coverage of these offenses. Research by R. G. Burns and Orrick (2002) suggested that (1) corporate crime coverage is less frequent than traditional crime coverage, (2) when corporate crime is covered in the media, the coverage will influence policymakers, (3) the public receives a distorted image of corporate crime, and (4) reporters do not define corporate misconduct as deviant or criminal. The authors also suggested that when corporate crime is addressed in the media, the focus is on the harm and the incident—but not on the criminal or the factors contributing to the crime.

A recent study by Cavendar and Miller (2013) confirms this suggestion. They examined how three newspapers—the *New York Times*, the *Washington Post*, and the *Wall Street Journal*—reported on the 2002 corporate crime scandals. Analyzing 227 articles published in the three newspapers, they found that the media tended to focus narrowly on the offense and assign blame on the individual level. They wrote: "The media covered the scandals to be sure, but the newspapers that we analyzed did not connect the dots that would have revealed how these scandals were emblematic of the larger economy" (p. 926). Others have argued that the portrayal of fraud in this way "deflects attention to one of the actors, the business and its directors, without clear recognition of the role played by the government itself" (Haines, 2013, p. 1).

News reporters are not the only ones to ignore corporate crime. Criminologists also pay relatively little attention to the topic. Figure 10.3 shows the subjects of articles in criminal justice journals from a study by Lynch, McGurrin, and Fenwick (2004). As Lynch's study shows, compared to articles and studies on other forms of crime, few studies focused on corporate crime. In fact, articles on antitrust offenses were the least frequent type of article.

SUMMARY

- The phrase *crimes by the corporate system* is used to characterize the body of offenses that are committed to benefit the corporation for which the employee (or employees) works.
- The concept of corporation can be seen four different ways—as a business, a location, a legally recognized status, and a collection of employees.
- Frank and Lynch (1992) describe corporate crime as including behaviors that are "socially injurious and blameworthy acts, legal or illegal that cause financial, physical, or environmental harm, committed by corporations and businesses against their workers, the general public, the environment, other corporations or businesses, the government, or other countries" (p. 17).
- Antitrust offenses are offenses that restrict competition. Antitrust laws are designed to promote and protect competition.
- Price fixing offenses occur when competitors agree on a price at which goods or services should be sold.
- Bid rigging (or collusion) occurs when competitors conspire to set specific bids for goods or services they would supply in response to a request for bids.
- Made illegal under the Robinson-Patman Act, price discrimination is illegal if it is done to lessen competition.
- Price gouging refers to situations where businesses conspire to set artificially high prices on goods and services.
- Market allocation occurs when competitors agree to divide markets according to territories, products, goods, or some other service (U.S. Department of Justice, n.d., p. 4).
- Group boycotts refer to situations where competitors agree not to do business with specific customers or clients.
- Four patterns are consistent across these antitrust offenses—(1) the way that "agreement" is conceptualized, (2) the seriousness of harm arising from the offenses, (3) globalization, and (4) difficulties proving (and punishing) offenses.
- False advertising occurs when businesses make inaccurate statements about their products or services in order to facilitate the sale of those items and services.
- Two common trends in advertising include going out of business sales and the use of celebrities to promote goods.
- Deceptive sales refers to illicit sales practices that are driven by corporate policies and directives.
- Unfair labor practices refer to corporate violations where workers are subjected to unethical treatment by their bosses and corporate leaders. Two general types of unfair labor practices can be identified: (1) exploitation and (2) systemic discrimination.
- Discrimination has negative consequences for individuals, groups, and organizations.
- Labeled corporate violence by Frank and Lynch (1992), unsafe work environments can result in death, illnesses, and injuries.
- Crimes also occur in the corporate system when corporations create harmful consumer products. In 2010, the United States Consumer Product Safety Commission issued 427 recalls for millions of goods "that either violated mandatory standards or were defective and presented a substantial risk of injury to the public" (CPSC, 2010c).
- The year 2007, deemed "Year of the Recall," saw a particularly high number of Chinese goods recalled by the Consumer Product Safety Commission.
- Globalization has ramifications for the way corporations create and distribute unsafe products.
- *Harmful treatment of consumers* refers to situations where businesses either intentionally or unintentionally put consumers who are using their services at risk of harm.
- At least four patterns run across these varieties of crime—the benefits of corporate crime, the complexity of intent, the breadth of victimization, and problems responding to corporate crime.
- Corporate crimes do not typically receive the same level of public scrutiny that other crimes receive.

KEY TERMS

Antitrust laws

Bait and switch practices

Bid rigging

Bid rotation

Bid suppression

Breadth of victimization

Complementary bidding

Deceptive sales

Exploitation

False advertising

Group boycotts

Harmful consumer products

Harmful treatment of consumers

Horizontal price fixing

Market allocation

Organizational misconduct

Price discrimination

Price fixing

Price gouging

Resale fraud

Robinson-Patman Act

Sherman Antitrust Act

Subcontracting

Unfair labor practices

Vertical price fixing

DISCUSSION QUESTIONS

1. Watch the GAO video showing college recruiters lying to undercover applicants available online at www.gao.gov/products/gao-10-948t. Do you think any crimes were committed? How can the recruiters' behaviors be characterized as corporate crime?

2. Write two personal ads for yourself: one that is accurate and one that is a "false advertisement." What is it that makes the advertisement false?

3. Visit the Federal Trade Commission's website and find an example of an antitrust offense. Search the World Wide Web to find how often the specific offense was discussed on various websites. How does the attention given to the antitrust offense compare to the attention given to other offenses?

4. What do you think should be done to companies that produce unsafe products? Explain.

5. How can companies save money by providing a safer work environment? What factors would influence a business leader to provide an unsafe environment?

6. Is food poisoning a crime? Explain.

7. Review the types of corporate crime discussed in this chapter. Rank the offenses from least serious to most serious.

8. Describe a way that you have been a victim of a corporate crime.

9. Review the testimony provided by Toyota Chief Executive Akio Toyoda in In Focus 10.2. Do you think his statements reflect suggestions by Ermann and Lundman that corporate harm sometimes comes from unreflective action and organizational processes? Explain.

WEB RESOURCES

Consumer Product Safety Commission. http://www.cpsc.gov/

Food and Drug Administration: http://www.fda.gov/

FTC Guide to Antitrust Laws: http://www.ftc.gov/bc/antitrust/index.shtm

Reporting Corporate Crimes: http://www.quackwatch.com/02ConsumerProtection/complain.html

U.S. Labor Laws. http://www.dol.gov/general/aboutdol/majorlaws.

XI

Environmental Crime

CHAPTER HIGHLIGHTS

- Conceptualizing Environmental Crime
- Varieties of Environmental White-Collar Crime
- The U.S. Environmental Protection Agency (EPA)
- Problems Addressing Environmental Crimes

O n April 20th, 2010, an explosion on British Petroleum's (BP's) Deepwater Horizon rig occurred in the Gulf of Mexico. Eleven rig workers were killed, and oil began to spill out of the Macondo well into the Gulf of Mexico. The oil poured into the Gulf for 3 months, with some estimates suggesting that a million gallons of oil flowed into the Gulf every day. By most measures, this seemed to be the "world's worst oil spill" (Randall, 2010). Referring to the harm from the spill, one reporter called the Gulf an "unsolved crime scene" (Sutter, 2010).

It is still too early to know all the consequences of the spill. As of August 2010, the National Science Foundation provided $7 million in research funding to study the long-term effects of the disaster. BP pledged to spend $500 million to address the consequences of the disaster, though it may be some time until we fully understand the effects of the unprecedented spill. After all, the consequences of the *Exxon Valdez* disaster are still being identified two decades after that oil spill occurred (Sutter, 2010).

Some consequences are obvious. Eleven men died. Fishermen in the Gulf were forced to give up their livelihoods. Birds, fish, and oysters died from the exposure to oil. Some have argued that the disaster will impact ecosystems across the world (Adams, 2010). Said the editor of naturalnews.com, "We may have just done to ourselves . . . what a great meteorite did to the dinosaurs" (M. Adams, 2010). The cleanup effort cost an estimated $6 million a day, and a long-term focused financial analysis estimated that cleanup costs alone would amount to $7 billion (Condon, 2010).

BP received criticism on a daily basis. The criticism targeted BP for misrepresenting various aspects of the response, underestimating the extent of the problem, paying out claims too slowly to affected workers, and having a flawed response plan (Searcey, 2010; Webb & Pilkington, 2010). The response plan received the brunt of the criticism. One rather disturbing criticism was that the response plan listed "a wildlife expert who died in 2005" (Webb & Pilkington, 2010). Also, the response plan listed marine animals (walruses, seals, etc.) as "sensitive biological resources," despite the fact that these mammals do not "[live] anywhere near the Gulf" (Mohr, Pritchard, & Lush, 2010). Mohr and his coauthors (2010) referred to BP's response as "on-the-fly planning." It did not help when the world saw BP chief executive Tony Hayward vacationing on his 52-foot yacht just weeks after the explosion. Hayward explained that he just "wanted to get [his] life back." He was removed as chief executive not long after making those comments.

One news headline that comes to mind read "Officials dismayed with BP's response." A colleague of mine cut this headline from the paper and hung it on my door, referring to my own initials (and maybe my own response to departmental issues). Suddenly, my initials weren't as cool as they used to be.

BP established a $20 billion fund that was to be used to respond to claims that individuals brought against the company (Searcey, 2010). The confusing nature of the claims process made it difficult to process the claims. Ironically, those involved with administering the fund on behalf of BP noted that they "had to sift through fraudulent claims" against the company (Searcey, 2010).

Some have argued that the blame for the disaster cannot be placed solely on BP. One author noted that it was "American firms that owned the rig AND the safety equipment that failed" (Pendlebury, 2010). This same author noted that the United States uses more oil than any other country and that the United States leased drilling rights in coastal waters to BP to generate revenue. It is safe to suggest that several companies were involved in the disaster.

On December 15, 2010, the U.S. Department of Justice filed a lawsuit against BP and eight other companies for their role in the rig explosion. Filed under the Oil Pollution Act and the Clean Water Act, the lawsuit alleged the following:

- Failure to take necessary precautions to secure the Macondo well prior to the April 20th explosion
- Failure to use the safest drilling technology to monitor the well conditions
- Failure to maintain continuous surveillance of the well
- Failure to utilize and maintain equipment and materials that were available and necessary to ensure the safety and protection of personnel, property, and the environment ("Attorney General Holder Announces," 2010)

The lawsuit sought costs for governmental removal efforts, the damage to the environment, and the impact on the economy. On July 2, 2015, it was announced that BP settled with the government and agreed to pay an $18.7 billion penalty. This penalty made it the largest penalty ever given in the U.S. for an environmental crime (Gilbert & Kent, 2015). Previously, the company had pleaded guilty to criminal manslaughter charges and was fined $4.5 billion for those charges. In all, the company had incurred settlement and legal costs totaling $54 billion "pushing its tab for the spill higher than all the profits it has earned since 2012" (Gilbert & Kent, 2015).

In terms of specific criminal charges against workers, charges were filed against some of the workers. Manslaughter charges against two of the rig supervisors were dropped in December 2015, prompting one of the parents of a worker killed in the spill to say, "As a result of this court proceeding today, no man will ever spend a moment behind bars for killing 11 men for reasons based entirely on greed" (McConnaughey & Kunzelman, 2015). In the end, it appears that just two criminal convictions were obtained against individuals for the offense, and those were for charges related to obstructing justice after the investigation began. BP and the other companies implicated in the spill are not the only businesses to harm the environment. Consider the following, quoted verbatim from the press release or media description of the environmental crime cases:

- A Clean Air Act settlement with Hyundai-Kia netted a $100 million fine, forfeiture of emissions credits and more than $50 million invested in compliance measures to help level the playing field for responsible companies and reduce greenhouse gas emissions fueling climate change (EPA, 2015, December 16a).
- On May 14, 2015, three subsidiaries of Duke Energy Corporation were sentenced in federal court for multiple criminal violations of the Clean Water Act . . . [and] were sentenced five years' probation for each charged count; fined $68 million; and will pay $34 million for environmental projects in North Carolina and Virginia. In the plea agreement, the defendants admitted that they had unlawfully failed to maintain equipment at the Dan River and

Cape Fear facilities and unlawfully discharged coal ash and/or coal ash wastewater from impoundments at the Dan River, Asheville, Lee, and Riverbend facilities. The fine that Duke has agreed to pay would be one of the largest ever levied under the landmark Clean Water Act (EPA, 2015, December 16b).

- An oilfield production company employee pleaded guilty and was sentenced July 16, 2015, for dumping polluted water into West Cote Blanche Bay, off the Louisiana coast. **** pleaded guilty in Lafayette federal court to one count of negligent discharge of pollutants. He was then sentenced to one day in prison and one year of supervised release and was ordered to perform 200 hours of community service (EPA, 2015, December 16b).

- On January 29, 2015, Matson Terminals, Inc., was sentenced in U.S. District Court in Honolulu to pay a $400,000 fine plus restitution of $600,000 based on previously entered guilty pleas to two criminal charges of unlawfully discharging molasses into Honolulu Harbor. The restitution will be divided equally to support coral protection programs and beach clean-ups. According to information provided to the court, Matson Terminals loaded molasses from storage tanks into ships in Honolulu Harbor (EPA, 2015, December 16b).

- **** was sentenced in federal court in Florence, South Carolina, for violation of the Clean Air Act, 42 U.S.C. §7412. United States District Judge R. Bryan Harwell of Florence sentenced **** to six months in prison, six months house arrest, three years supervised release and a $10,000.00 fine. Evidence presented at the change of plea hearing in October established that the defendant ran CoolCote, a construction and renovation company in the Myrtle Beach area. The defendant was contracted to remove and replace siding on a high rise beach front condominium complex in Myrtle Beach. The defendant was made aware that the existing siding contained asbestos material and agreed to do the job for a lower price. The defendant did not provide the proper protection to his employees or obtain the proper permits to allow for the removal of asbestos (EPA, 2014, May 22).

In each of these cases, businesses or employees harmed the environment as part of their work efforts. To fully understand environmental crime within the context of white-collar crime, it is necessary to consider the following topics: the conceptualization of environmental crime, types of environmental crime, consequences of environmental crime, the EPA and environmental crime, and problems addressing environmental crime. A full understanding of these topics will help students understand how environmental crime fits within the broader concept of white-collar crime.

● ● ● Conceptualizing Environmental Crime

Pollution is a problem that affects all of us. Several different types of pollution exist, including water pollution, air pollution, noise pollution, soil pollution, waste disposal, and so on. Concern about environmental pollution escalated in the United States in the 1970s, a decade labeled the "environment decade in reference to the increase in environmental legislation and political support for laws regulating pollution" (H. C. Barnett, 1993, p. 120). Elsewhere, H. Barnett (1999) refers to this time period as "a decade long surge of environmental concern" (p. 173). As a result of this public and political concern, hundreds of environmental protection laws were passed by state and federal governments. At the federal level, the best known environmental protection laws include the following:

▲ **Photo 11.1** Crime scene or accident scene. . . . Emergency responders work to put the fire out that was caused by the explosion on BP's Deepwater Horizon rig.

U.S. Coast Guard photo

- Atomic Energy Act
- Chemical Safety Information, Site Security, and Fuels Regulatory Relief Act
- Clean Air Act
- Clean Water Act
- Comprehensive Environmental Response, Compensation, and Liability Act
- Emergency Planning and Community Right to Know Act
- Endangered Species Act
- Energy Independence and Security Act
- Energy Policy Act
- Federal Food, Drug, and Cosmetic Act
- National Environmental Policy Act
- Noise Control Act
- Occupational Safety and Health Act
- Ocean Dumping Act
- Oil Pollution Act
- Pollution Prevention Act
- Safe Drinking Water Act
- Resource Conservation and Recovery Act
- Shore Protection Act
- Toxic Substance Act (EPA, 2010e)

These acts provide a foundation from which one can consider criminal and civil definitions of environmental crime. In particular, violations of these acts are environmental crimes. Some environmental crime scholars have called for broader, more philosophical conceptualizations of environmental crime. H. Barnett (1999) used Aldo Leopold's land ethic to conceptualize environmental crime: "A thing is right when it tends to preserve the integrity, stability, and beauty of the biotic community. It is wrong when it tends otherwise" (p. 161). Such an approach highlights the fact that many behaviors that harm the environment are often not codified in law. As a result, some authors have argued that a need exists to distinguish between those behaviors labeled as environmental crime and those that are "serious instances of ecological destruction" (Halsey, 1997, p. 121).

Two fundamental statements about environmental crime need to be made to adequately discuss this concept within the context of white-collar crime. First, pollution in and of itself is not an environmental crime. Many individuals and businesses routinely pollute the environment without actually committing environmental crimes. When we drive our automobiles to get to class, we pollute the environment. If we are running late for our white-collar crime class and speed to make up for lost time, we pollute the environment even more, but we have not committed an environmental crime. Indeed, routine activities we engage in on a daily basis produce different levels of pollution or destruction. Here is how one author described the seemingly routine nature of environmental harm:

> Not only is it profitable to be environmentally destructive (in the sense of mining, manufacturing cars, clearfelling forests), it feels good too (in the sense of purchasing a gold necklace, driving on the open road, looking at a table, chair, or house constructed from redwood, mahogany, mountain ash, or the like). (Halsey, 2004, p. 844)

U.S. Coast Guard photo by Petty Officer 2nd Class Rob Simpson

▲ **Photo 11.2** A massive effort was put in place to clean up the oil spill in the Gulf.

Second, it is important to understand that not all environmental crimes are white-collar crimes. If an individual throws an old washer and dryer away along the side of a rural road, that person has committed an environmental crime, but not a white-collar crime because the offense was not committed as part of work efforts. As another example, if an individual buys new tires for his or her automobile, asks to keep the old tires, and then dumps the old tires in an empty field, the individual has committed an environmental crime but not a white-collar crime.

White-collar environmental crimes, then, involve situations where individuals or businesses illegally pollute or destroy the environment as part of an occupational activity. Here are a few examples quoted from the U.S. Environmental Protection Agency (2010e) that demonstrate what is meant by white-collar environmental crimes:

▲ **Photo 11.3** Chances are that something you own or are wearing was on a ship or in a tractor trailer. Simply getting that item from one place to another required a certain amount of air pollution.

- A plant manager at a metal finishing company directs employees to bypass the facility's wastewater treatment unit in order to avoid having to purchase the chemicals that are needed to run the wastewater treatment unit. In so doing, the company sends untreated wastewater directly to the sewer system in violation of the permit issued by the municipal sewer authority. The plant manager is guilty of a criminal violation of the Clean Water Act.
- In order to avoid the cost of paying for proper treatment of its hazardous waste, the owner of a manufacturer of cleaning solvents places several dozen 5-gallon buckets of highly flammable and caustic waste into its Dumpster for disposal at a local, municipal landfill that is not authorized to receive hazardous waste. The owner of the company is guilty of a criminal violation of the Resource Conservation and Recovery Act.
- The owner of an apartment complex solicits bids to remove 14,000 square feet of old ceiling tiles from the building. Three bidders inspect the building, determine that the tiles contain dangerous asbestos fibers, and bid with understanding that, in doing the removal, they would be required to follow the work practice standards that apply to asbestos removal. The fourth bidder proposes to save the owner money by removing the tiles without following the work practice standards. The owner hires the fourth bidder on this basis, and, so, the work is done without following the work practice standards. The owner is guilty of a criminal violation of the Clean Air Act (no pagination, available online; see EPA, 2010f).

In each of these cases, the offender committed the offense as part of an occupational routine. Note that although each of these cases could be handled as violations of criminal law, in many cases white-collar environmental offenses are handled as civil wrongs or regulatory violations. As you read through these types of environmental white-collar crimes, one point to bear in mind is that many careers are available for criminal justice students battling these offenses. The Careers Responding to White-Collar Crime: Environmental Protection Specialist box on the next page provides insight into one such career.

● ● ● Varieties of Environmental White-Collar Crime

Recognizing the distinction between environmental crime and environmental white-collar crime helps to identify the roles of workplace and class status in the commission of these offenses. The distinction also helps us recognize that several varieties of environmental white-collar crimes exist. These varieties include the following:

- Illegal emissions
- Illegal disposal of hazardous wastes

CAREERS RESPONDING TO WHITE-COLLAR CRIME

Environmental Protection Specialists

Environmental protection specialist positions require specialized knowledge of the principles, practices, and methods of program or administrative work relating to environmental protection programs. This entails (1) an understanding of the philosophy underlying environmental regulation; (2) knowledge of environmental laws and regulations; (3) knowledge of the planning, funding, organization, administration, and evaluation of environmental programs; (4) practical knowledge of environmental sciences and related disciplines, the effects of actions and technology on the environment, the means of preventing or reducing pollution, and the relationship between environmental factors and human health and well-being; and (5) practical knowledge of important historic, cultural, and natural resources (including land, vegetation, fish, wildlife, endangered species, forests) and the relationship between the preservation and management of these resources and environmental protection. Environmental protection specialists apply specialized knowledge of one or more program or functional areas of environmental protection work, but do not require full professional competence in environmental engineering or science.

Source: Reprinted from U.S. Office of Personnel Management. *Position classification standard for environmental protection specialist series*, GS-0028 https://www.opm.gov/policy-data-oversight/classification-qualifications/classifying-general-schedule-positions/standards/0000/gs0028.pdf

- Illegal dumping
- Harmful destruction of property and wildlife
- Environmental threats
- Environmental state crime
- International environmental crimes

It is important to note that these varieties are not mutually exclusive because there is overlap between them.

Illegal Emissions

Illegal emissions, as a variety of environmental white-collar crime, refer to situations where companies or businesses illegally allow pollutants to enter the environment. Water pollution and air pollution are examples of illegal emissions. Sometimes, water and air pollution occur as a result of the production process. The smoke billowing out of factory towers contains pollutants that are the result of the production process. Companies are permitted to allow a certain amount of pollutants into the environment. They pay what is called a *sin tax* to cover the perceived costs of polluting the environment. If they exceed the "permissible" amount of pollution, then civil and criminal laws can be applied.

Other times, the pollution might be the result of unintended processes or neglectful behavior by employees. Consider the *Exxon Valdez* incident in March 1989, when the ship ran aground on Bligh Reef off the Alaskan shore. The crash spilled more than 11 million gallons of oil into Prince William Sound. It has been reported that the ship was on autopilot while the ship's captain was sleeping off a drunken stupor below deck and the third mate ran the ship on less than 5 hours' sleep. Exxon did not technically intend for the disaster to occur, but because the company overworked ship employees (not giving them enough rest) and allowed someone with an alcohol problem to serve as the captain of the ship, the company eventually settled both criminal and civil charges resulting from the incident.

Under the **Federal Water Pollution Control Act**, companies are required to self-disclose to the EPA instances when they have discharged potentially harmful substances into navigable waters. After disclosing the incident, they can still be assessed civil penalties, like fines. Criminal justice students might quickly ask if this is a violation of the Fifth Amendment right against self-incrimination. In an early test of the self-disclosure rule, the owner of an oil refinery in Arkansas, who had self-disclosed that oil from his property had leaked into a nearby tributary, appealed a $500 fine on the grounds that his Fifth Amendment right had been violated (*U.S. v. Ward*). The U.S. Supreme Court upheld the fine on the grounds that the self-disclosure resulted in a civil penalty and not a criminal penalty (D. G. Beck, 1981; Melenyzer, 1999).

Illegal Disposal of Hazardous Wastes

Illegal disposal of hazardous wastes involves situations where employees or businesses dispose of wastes in ways that are potentially harmful to individuals and the environment. These offenses are actually quite easy to commit. For example, it is easy to mix hazardous substances with nonhazardous substances, but it is difficult to detect (Dorn, Van Daele, & Vander Beken, 2007). Often, the cases are detected through witnesses who anonymously report the misconduct. In one case, for instance, an anonymous caller contacted the Maryland Department of Environment to reveal "that asbestos debris was being dumped [by contractors] through a trash chute into an open [D]umpster on the street below, potentially exposing both workers and the community to toxic asbestos fibers" ("Maryland Contractor Fined," 2010). Officials recovered 7,000 bags full of asbestos debris. The contractor was fined $1.2 million. In another case, a company was fined $819,000 after its workers threw asbestos into public trash receptacles, including one located at a high school (Hay, 2010).

In the past, illegal hazardous waste disposal cases were attributed to private truckers or waste management contractors hired to get rid of waste via illegally dumping of the waste, and there were no repercussions for the businesses that created the waste. The Resource Conservation and Recovery Act, passed in 1976, provided greater controls over the way that hazardous waste was created, monitored, and discarded. Of particular relevance is the "Cradle to Grave" provision of the act, which requires a "manifest system" to keep track of the waste from the time it is created through its disposal. The *manifest system* refers to the record-keeping process used to monitor the waste. The creator of the waste must monitor the waste when it is created and keep track of the waste all the way through its disposal. The law states that those who create the waste are accountable for all aspects of the disposal of the waste. The business can be held liable if it doesn't complete the manifest forms, if it hires an unlicensed contractor to get rid of the waste, or if the waste is eventually dumped illegally by the contractor hired to dispose of it (Stenzel, 2011).

One of the most well-known environmental crimes involving hazardous wastes is the Love Canal tragedy. Located in Niagara Falls, New York, the Love Canal was initially designed to be a canal, but it ended up being a waste disposal site for Hooker Chemical. After Hooker filled the canal with waste—and covered the waste in ways the company thought were safe, it sold the property to the Niagara Falls school board for one dollar in the mid-1950s. The company never hid the fact that the property was on top of a waste site (E. Beck, 1979).

The school board developed a school, and several homes were built on and around Love Canal. In the late 1970s, chemicals from the abandoned site leaked into the homes, and residents began to experience a number of different health problems (Baldston, 1979). An EPA report cited "a disturbingly high rate of miscarriages" among pregnant women in the neighborhood (E. Beck, 1979). One EPA administrator wrote:

> I visited the canal area. Corroding waste disposal drums could be seen breaking up through the grounds of backyards. Trees and gardens were turning black and dying . . . puddles of noxious substances were pointed out to me by the residents. . . . Everywhere the air had a faint, choking smell. Children returned from play with burns on their hands and faces. (E. Beck, 1979)

Eventually, the federal government and the state of New York declared an emergency and provided a temporary relocation of 700 families (In Focus 11.1 includes a press release from the White House describing the declaration of emergency).

In 1979, the EPA and USDOJ (U.S. Department of Justice) filed four suits against Hooker Chemical alleging violations of Resource Conservation and Recovery Act, the Clean Water Act, the Safe Drinking Water Act, and the Refuse Act. The basis for the suits was that Hooker had illegally disposed of its waste, which included 21,000 tons of chemical waste. The State of New York filed a similar lawsuit against the company. By the mid-1990s, the company had settled for $20 million, and its parent company agreed to pay $129 million to the federal government and $98 million to the state of New York to support cleanup efforts (W. Moyer, 2010).

IN FOCUS   11.1

EPA, New York State Announce Temporary Relocation of Love Canal Residents

[EPA press release—May 21, 1980]

President Carter today declared an emergency to permit the Federal government and the State of New York to undertake the temporary relocation of approximately 700 families in the Love Canal area of Niagara Falls, New York, who have been exposed to toxic wastes deposited there by Hooker Chemical company.

Barbara Blum, Deputy Administrator of the U.S. Environmental Protection Agency, in announcing the President's action—taken at the request of Governor Carey of New York—said that the Federal government and the State will jointly fund the relocation effort.

"This action is being taken," said Blum, "in recognition of the cumulative evidence of exposure by the Love Canal residents to toxic wastes from Hooker Chemical company and mounting evidence of resulting health effects.

"Health effects studies performed by others so far are preliminary. Taken together, they suggest significant health risks. Ordinarily, we would not subject the public and affected families to the disruption of temporary relocation unless conclusions on adverse health have been fully documented and confirmed after independent review," she said.

"But this is not an ordinary situation. This case presents special circumstances warranting this extraordinary action. The studies completed to date are sufficiently suggestive of a threat to public health that prudence dictates the residents be relocated while further definitive studies are being completed," Blum declared.

The families eligible for temporary relocation assistance live in the area from 103rd Street on the east to both sides of 93rd Street on the west, Black Creek on the north to Frontier Avenue on the south.

The temporary relocation will last until long-range studies of the environmental exposures and resulting health effects suffered by the affected families are completed. These studies, which will be conducted by EPA, will be completed within the next few months.

Governor Carey's request to declare an emergency will make funds available on a matching basis with the State of New York to fund the temporary relocation under the Federal Disaster Relief Act.

The temporary relocation will be assisted by the Federal Emergency Management Agency and the New York Department of Transportation. Personnel from these two agencies are currently at the Love Canal site to begin assisting families.

Under existing Federal law, this temporary housing may be provided rent free for a period of up to one year. Pending the location of such temporary housing, residents may seek shelter with family members or in hotels, motels or other transient accommodations and will be reimbursed by the Federal government.

"The Hooker Chemical Company's dumping of toxic wastes at Love Canal," said Blum, "and the resulting health and environmental damages are a stark symbol of the problems created by the improper disposal of hazardous wastes by our society. The implementation of the regulatory program by EPA and the States under the Resource Conservation and Recovery Act should prevent new Love Canals. But Americans will not be free of the effects of our toxic waste heritage without the passage of Superfund legislation to give EPA the authority and funds to clean up hazardous waste sites before they damage public health."

The complaint in the Governor's suit against Hooker Chemical Company will be amended to seek reimbursement for costs expended in this effort. The Justice Department has requested that Hooker pay the costs of temporary relocation, but the company has refused.

EPA believes this action is required at Love Canal even though it may not be necessary at other hazardous waste sites. A review by EPA's Hazardous Waste Enforcement Task Force indicates that a larger number of people in Love Canal are directly exposed to a broader range of toxic chemicals at high levels than now known at other abandoned hazardous waste sites around the country. In addition, President Carter has previously declared an emergency at Love Canal, the only hazardous waste site to be identified as such. Finally, the Government's lawsuit against Hooker Chemical Company requests relocation of the affected families, the only case involving a hazardous waste site where such relief has been requested.

Source: Reprinted From U.S. Environmental Protection Agency (EPA), Office of Enforcement and Compliance. (1980, May 21). EPA, New York State announce temporary relocation of love canal residents. Retrieved December 1, 2015 from http://www2.epa.gov/aboutepa/epa-new-york-state-announce-temporary-relocation-love-canal-residents

Illegal Dumping

Illegal dumping, in this context, is different from illegal disposal of hazardous waste. Also known as "fly dumping" "wildcat dumping," and "midnight dumping," **illegal dumping** refers to situations where employees or businesses dump products they no longer need in sites that are not recognized as legal dump sites (U.S. Environmental Protection Agency [EPA], 1998). Common products that are illegally dumped include automobile tires, construction waste (such as drywall, roofing materials, plumbing waste), landscaping waste, and automobile parts.

These materials present different types of risk than might be found with the illegal disposal of hazardous wastes. For example, many of the products are not biodegradable and will destroy the usefulness of the land where they are dumped. Also, the site where offenders dump these products will

▲ **Photo 11.4** Zoo owners can be found criminally or civilly liable for mistreating or neglecting animals housed at their zoo.

become an eyesore and attract future illegal dumpers. In addition, some of the products such as tires will trap rainwater and attract mosquitoes, thus becoming a breeding ground for disease (EPA, 1998). In one case, the owner of a used tire shop in Ohio was sentenced to 6 years in prison after he was caught illegally dumping tires on five separate occasions (Futty, 2010).

Illegal dumping is primarily done for economic reasons. Business owners wanting to avoid the costs of waste disposal dump their goods in the unregulated open dump areas. The offenses also present significant economic costs, particularly in terms of cleanup costs. In Columbus, Ohio, for example, city crews "cleaned up 621 tons of illegally dumped tires in 2009" (Futty, 2010). Assuming that the average city worker makes $30,000 a year, this suggests that three full-time employees were hired solely to clean up illegally dumped tires in Columbus. And this estimate accounts for only one type of illegal dumping.

Harmful Destruction of Property/Wildlife

Harmful destruction of property and wildlife by companies or workers during the course of their jobs can be seen as environmental white-collar crime. Before businesses can clear land for development, thus destroying habitat, they must gain approval from the local government. Failing to gain such approval would be a regulatory violation. Also, instances where workers destroy wetlands are examples of environmental crimes. Additional examples of harmful destruction of property include using unsafe chemical pesticides, using chemical fertilizers, and logging on public land (Barnett, 1999).

Harmful treatment of animals can be seen as an environmental white-collar crime. This could include illegal trading of wildlife or illegal fishing by companies or sailors (Hayman & Brack, 2002) and overharvesting sea life (H. Barnett, 1999). Illegal fishing also includes unregulated and unreported fishing. These activities include "fishing in an area without authorization; failing to record or declare catches, or making false reports; using prohibited fishing gear; re-supplying or re-fueling illegal, unregulated, or unreported vessels" (National Oceanic and Atmospheric Administration, 2010). In October 2010, a new federal rule was passed stipulating that the United States would deny foreign vessels suspected of illegal fishing entry into U.S. ports.

Harmful treatment of animals, as an environmental white-collar crime, includes instances where those whose work centers on animals do things to harm the animals. Two examples include harmful treatment of animals in zoos and crimes by big-game operators. In one case of the former, a zoo owner was fined $10,000 and ordered to shut down his zoo for 30 days after the U.S. Department of Agriculture found the owner in violation of the Animal Welfare Act for failing to build appropriate fences around the animals, failing to keep the food safe from contamination, and failure to provide the animals proper housing (Conley, 2007). Just 3 years before, the same owner was fined after two Asiatic bears that escaped from the zoo had to be shot and killed (Chittum, 2003).

Crimes by big-game operators include situations where they or their clients kill endangered species or hunt on protected land. In one case, a big-game operator and his sons pleaded guilty "for illegally guiding clients on Brown bear hunts on federal property" (U.S. Department of Justice, Environment and Natural Resources Division, 2010, p. 28).

The owner was fined $71,000, and his sons were sentenced to 3 months of house arrest. Those getting paid to help individuals in these hunts commit a white-collar crime when they intentionally perform activities that harm animals. For the hunters (e.g., clients involved in a big-game hunt), a crime is also committed, but it would not be characterized as a white-collar crime because the activities were not committed during work). Note that the crime is not when the hunters actually harm the animals, but it is the act of intending to harm the protected animals that is illegal (USDOJ, Environment and Natural Resources Division, 2010, p. 28).

Environmental Threats

A number of environmental threats exist that have the potential to harm the environment. The federal government has identified five "significant threats" to the environment. First, **knowing endangerment** refers to situations where individuals or businesses intentionally mishandle hazardous wastes or pollutants that pose risks to their workers or community members. Second, *repeat offenders* are a threat inasmuch as the government recognizes that some businesses repeatedly violate environmental laws on the assumption that it is cheaper to pay the fine and harm the environment rather than fix the problem. Third, the federal government closely monitors *misuse of federal facilities and public lands* to protect properties from further environmental harm. Fourth, the government has called attention to the need to be prepared for catastrophic events. Finally, *organized crime entities* like the Mafia are believed to be intimately involved in the waste disposal industry (U.S. Department of Justice, 1994).

Scholars have drawn attention to the way organized crime groups are involved in illegal waste offenses. In fact, some have used the phrase "environmental organized crime" to describe the Mob's involvement in these crimes (T. S. Carter, 1999). The organized nature of the illegal waste disposal enterprise has allowed authorities to use Racketeer Influenced and Corrupt Organization (RICO) statutes to prosecute environmental offenders.

In New York City, the Mafia had such a strong hold on the waste disposal industry that other businesses rarely tried to enter the waste disposal marketplace. In the early 1990s, Browning Ferris Industries (BFI) began its efforts to become one of the businesses responsible for collecting waste in the city. T. S. Carter (1999) quotes a *Fortune* magazine writer who described the Mob's reaction shortly after learning of BFI's intentions:

> The freshly severed head of a large German Shepherd [was] laid like a wreath on the suburban lawn of the one of the company's top local executives. A piece of string tied to the dog's mouth around a note . . . read, "Welcome to New York." (p. 19)

Fans of the former Home Box Office (HBO) hit *The Sopranos* might recall the following exchange between Tony Soprano and his daughter Meadow in an episode where the crime boss and his daughter were visiting colleges during Meadow's senior year in high school:

Meadow Soprano: Are you in the Mafia?

Tony Soprano: Am I in the what?

Meadow Soprano: Whatever you want to call it. Organized crime.

Tony Soprano: That's total crap, who told you that?

Meadow Soprano:	Dad, I've lived in the house all my life. I've seen the police come with warrants. I've seen you going out at three in the morning.
Tony Soprano:	So you never seen Doc Cusamano going out at three in the morning on a call?
Meadow Soprano:	Did the Cusamano kids ever find $50,000 in Krugerrands and a .45 automatic while they were hunting for Easter eggs?
Tony Soprano:	I'm in the waste management business. Everybody immediately assumes you're mobbed up. It's a stereotype. And it's offensive. And you're the last person I would want to perpetuate it. . . . There is no Mafia. (Manos, Chase, & Coulter, 1999)

A braver white-collar crime text author might follow up this exchange with a joke about the Mafia and the waste management industry. This author does not want to find the head of a German shepherd in his front yard, so he will pass on the opportunity for a joke.

Environmental State Crime

In Chapter V, the way that governments are involved in corporate offending was discussed. One type of crime that governments can commit can be called **environmental state crimes**. In this context, environmental state crime refers to criminal or deviant behaviors by a governmental representative (or representatives) that result in individuals and/or the environment being harmed by pollutants and chemicals. Examples include situations where government officials illegally dispose of waste or use harmful chemicals in unjustified ways.

As an illustration, R. White (2008) describes how depleted uranium was used in the Gulf Wars. The product was used in armor and as weapons, and it has been linked to various illnesses in Iraq and Gulf War veterans. Government officials have denied that the use of the product was criminal, which is not surprising given that, as White notes, "one of the features of state crime is in fact denial on the part of the state that an act or omission is a crime" (p. 32). White quotes the former director of the Pentagon's Depleted Uranium Project, Dough Rokke, to highlight the criminal nature of the use of depleted uranium. Rokke remarked:

This war was about Iraq possessing illegal weapons of mass destruction, yet we are using weapons of mass destruction ourselves. Such double standards are repellent. . . . A nation's military personnel cannot willfully contaminate another nation, cause harm to persons and the environment, and then ignore the consequences of their actions. To do so is a crime against humanity (p. 42)

White points out that Rokke has, himself, suffered negative health effects from exposure to depleted uranium.

International Environmental Crimes

International environmental crimes include environmental offenses that cross borders of at least two different countries or occur in internationally protected areas. Instances where companies ship their waste from an industrialized country to a developing nation are an example (Dorn et al., 2007). In some cases, companies might bribe "Third World government officials to establish toxic waste dumps in their countries" (Simon, 2000, p. 633).

Other examples of international environmental crimes include illegally trading wildlife, illegally trading substances harmful to the ozone, illegal fishing, and illegal timber trading and logging (Hayman & Brack, 2002). International environmental crimes are potentially more difficult for regulatory agencies to address because of issues surrounding jurisdiction, economic competition, and language barriers. Still, it is clear that environmental crime has become an international issue that has evolved as the process of globalization has unfolded in our society. As evidence of the globalization of environmental crime, consider that more than 100 countries have passed laws stipulating that environmental assessments must be conducted before a business will receive approval to begin a construction project (McAllister, 2008). Indeed, world leaders have recognized that environmental crime has serious consequences.

Consequences of Environmental Crime

It is overly simplistic to say that the consequences of environmental crime are devastating. But it must be stated that these crimes threaten the existence of human life (Comte, 2006). Not surprisingly, environmental crime has more victims than other crimes, but these victims are often not aware of their victimization (Hayman & Brack, 2002). O'Hear (2004) provides a useful taxonomy that outlines the following types of harm potentially arising from environmental crime: (1) immediate physical injury from exposure to harmful products that may burn or kill individuals, (2) future physical injuries, (3) emotional distress, (4) disrupted social and economic activities, (5) remediation costs, (6) property damage, and (7) ecological damage. In general, the types of consequences can be classified as *physical costs*, *economic costs*, and *community costs*.

With regard to physical costs, there are absolutely no studies that show that pollution is good for one's health. It is impossible to accurately determine the precise extent of physical injuries from environmental crimes, but estimates are somewhat startling:

- It is estimated that up to 50,000 deaths in the United States are caused by pollution every year (WorldWatch Institute, 2015).
- The EPA estimates between 130,000 and 320,000 people died from small particle matter in the atmosphere in 2005 (A. C. Brown, 2013).
- Worldwide, in 2012, an estimated seven million people died prematurely because of air pollution exposure. Air pollution is now recognized as the most significant environmental health risk in the world (World Health Organization, 2015).
- Estimates from one study that considered all forms of pollution suggest that as many as 60 million deaths can be attributed to pollution, suggesting that 40 percent of all deaths are pollution related (Pimentel et al., 2007).

Of course, it is not just deaths that increase with pollution; physical illnesses are also tied to the problem. One estimate suggests that 38,000 people have heart attacks each year that were caused by pollution from U.S. power plants (Schneider, 2004). Schneider also suggests that pollution causes hundreds of thousands of individuals to have respiratory problems. As well, research shows that lead exposure causes "intellectual and behavioral deficits in children and hypertension and kidney disease in adults" (Schwemberger et al., 2005, p. 513). Rather than listing ill effects from all pollutants, it can be stated that for virtually any pollutant, researchers can point to potentially harmful health effects.

Like other forms of white-collar crime, environmental crime has enormous economic costs. A study by a research team at California State University, Fullerton, found that the state of California loses $28 billion a year to the consequences of pollution (Hall & Brajer, 2008). Costs stem from a variety of sources, including missed work, missed school days, visits to the doctor, and visits to the emergency room. One can also note that taxpayers pay for enforcement and cleanup costs associated with white-collar environmental crime. In addition, employees end up "paying for" the violations of corporations and businesses when—after a company is caught engaging in environmental offending—they lose their jobs, become unemployed, and must find other ways to make a living (H. C. Barnett, 1981).

Environmental crime presents different costs to the community. In communities where these crimes occur, quality of life is reduced. These offenses create public eyesores and reduce property values around the areas exposed to environmental pollution. Also, consistent with other corporate crimes, environmental crimes have the potential to "erode the moral base" of the community (Kramer, 1984, p. 8). While not specifically tested, it is plausible that environmental crime is correlated with traditional crimes. Criminologists have noted that socially disorganized communities have higher crime rates than other communities. Environmental pollution has the potential to produce social disorganization and, therefore, potentially contributes to conventional crimes.

Environmental crimes also harm the community by posing a number of risks to those around the "environmental crime scene." For example, illegal waste disposals create the following risks for the immediate area surrounding the site where the illegal disposal occurred:

- Fire and explosion
- Inhaling toxic gases
- Injury to children playing around the site
- Soil or water contamination
- Plan or wildlife damage (Illinois Environmental Protection Agency, 2010)

A large body of research has shown that minorities and minority communities are more at risk for experiencing the ill effects of environmental crime.

▲ **Photo 11.5** Environmental crimes can also harm animals.

The term **environmental racism** is used to describe this heightened risk of victimization for minorities. Consider, for example, that research shows that minority children are significantly more likely than nonminority children to have higher levels of lead in their blood (Schwemberger et al., 2005). One author describes the placement of environmentally unsafe companies near minority communities as "the path of least resistance" (McDowell, 2013, p. 395). These situations do not go unnoticed by residents. McDowell (2013) provides the following quote one resident made to the county board of supervisors:

I personally feel our area has more than done its share. This area they are proposing has historic value, a fact that needs to be considered. . . . I feel it's extremely unfair to push another landfill on a small, poor rural area, simply because they most likely haven't the means to fight back. We are a small rural area, but there are enough of us to stand up and be heard! Please hear our voices! [Email communication to MCBS] (p. 400)

Various efforts have been promoted to address environmental racism. For example, the Southern Center on Environmentally Driven Disparities in Birth Outcomes was created at Duke University to study the links between environmental, social, and individual factors and how those factors contribute to health disparities in birth outcomes. The Center's ongoing projects include "Mapping Disparities in Birth Outcomes," "Peri-natal Environmental Exposure," and "Healthy Pregnancy, Healthy Baby." The Center is funded by the U.S. Environmental Protection Agency (EPA) (Duke University, 2010).

The EPA has also addressed concerns about environmental racism by developing an Office of Environmental Justice in the early 1990s and giving the office the responsibility of promoting environmental justice activities in the agency. According to the EPA (2010d), environmental justice is "the fair treatment and meaningful involvement of all people regardless of race, color, national origin, or income with respect to the development, implementation, and enforcement of environmental laws, regulations, and policies." The two assumptions of the federal Environmental Justice Initiative are fair treatment and meaningful involvement. Fair treatment refers to the notion that no group should be disproportionately impacted by pollution. In the words of the EPA, meaningful involvement refers to the following assumptions:

- People have an opportunity to participate in decisions about activities that may affect their environment and/or health.
- The public's contribution can influence the regulatory agency's decision.
- Their concerns will be considered in the decision-making process.
- The decision makers seek out and facilitate the involvement of those potentially affected (EPA, 2010b).

On December 15, 2010, the first White House Forum on Environmental Justice was held, with five cabinet secretaries and several other senior agency officials participating in the discussion. Much of the discussion focused on the way that poor and minority communities experience more pollution than other communities, a fact that led to the development of the Office of Environmental Justice in the first place nearly two decades earlier. Indeed, not all environmental activists in attendance viewed the forum favorably. Suzie Canales, who helped create the Texas-based advocacy group Citizens for Environmental Justice after her sister died from what Canales believed was environmentally induced breast cancer, told the director of the EPA, "We need to stop being studied to death. . . . What I'm saying to you is that with all these powerful agencies . . . instead of giving us more documents that have no value to us, you need to roll up your sleeves." She gave the EPA a report in which she wrote of the forum, "There's no cause for celebration. . . . All the executive order has really done to date is spawn more bureaucracies that give false hope to communities with promises and words" (McArdle & Nelson, 2010).

To be sure, the consequences of environmental crime are serious and warrant a response from formal control agencies. Local police are not trained or equipped to respond to these offenses, which are complex and potentially harmful to those responding to environmental crimes involving hazardous materials (Dorn et al., 2007). Some have noted that criminal penalties are rarely applied and that while enforcement is done by local, state, and federal regulatory agencies, the law enforcement response is not as aggressive as compared to other crimes (Shover & Routhe, 2005). At the federal level, the U.S. Environmental Protection Agency (EPA) is the largest agency, with 17,000 employees, responsible for addressing environmental crimes.

● ● ● The U.S. Environmental Protection Agency (EPA)

The **Environmental Protection Agency** was created in 1970 when President Richard Nixon reorganized several federal agencies to create one federal agency responsible for addressing environmental pollution. In developing his message to Congress about the EPA, President Nixon stated that the agency's roles and functions would include the following:

- The establishment and enforcement of environmental protection standards consistent with national environmental goals
- The conduct of research on the adverse effects of pollution and on methods and equipment for controlling it, the gathering of information on pollution, and the use of this information in strengthening environmental protection programs and recommending policy changes
- Assisting others, through grants, technical assistance, and other means in arresting pollution of the environment
- Assisting the Council on Environmental Quality in developing and recommending to the president new policies for the protection of the environment (EPA, 1992)

Four decades later, the roles and functions have not changed a great deal, though the authority of the agency has expanded significantly. Today, the actions of the EPA can be characterized in four overlapping ways: (1) as an enforcer of criminal and civil laws, (2) as an agency trying to protect public health, (3) as an agency aiming to deter future misconduct, and (4) as a facilitator of fund generation and cost savings. As you read about these areas, consider whether you would want to work in environmental protection careers. Each of these areas is addressed below.

EPA as an Enforcer of Criminal and Civil Laws

The EPA works with other federal and state agencies to enforce environmental crime laws. The EPA's Office of Criminal Enforcement responds to (1) Clean Water Act and Clean Air Act violations, (2) Resource Conservation and Recovery Act (RCRA) violations, (3) illegal disposal of waste, (4) exporting hazardous waste, (5) illegal discharge of pollutants, (6) illegal disposal of asbestos, (7) illegal importation of chemicals, (8) tampering with drinking water supplies, (9) mail fraud, (10) wire fraud, and (11) money laundering (EPA, 2010f).

Figure 11.1 shows the number of criminal cases opened by the EPA between 1999 and 2015 (fiscal years). As shown in the table, the number of investigations has fluctuated throughout the years. However, there has been a general downward trend. These fluctuations can be attributed to changing priorities, changes in workload, and shifts in administrative structures. In its 2015 annual enforcement report, the agency points out the following: "The criminal program continued in FY15 to focus on complex cases that involve a serious threat to human health and the environment or that undermine program integrity. The focus on high impact more complex cases results in fewer investigations overall" (EPA, 2015).

The EPA takes an active stance toward detecting environmental criminals. In 2008, it borrowed from the traditional fugitive posters that other federal agencies used and began to publish fugitive posters of "wanted" environmental offenders. Figure 11.2 shows the wanted poster of environmental crime suspect Raul Chavez-Beltran, whose company was accused of illegally transporting soil that was contaminated with mercury. You can check out the other wanted environmental crime fugitives online at http://www.epa.gov/compliance/criminal/fugitives/index.html.

It is important to note that the EPA works with other agencies in its efforts to enforce criminal and civil laws. The cases will be adjudicated by the Department of Justice. The process for criminally prosecuting these types of crimes will be discussed later in the text.

EPA as a Protector of Public Health

The adverse health effects of pollution were discussed above. Activities of the EPA can be seen as protecting public health in three ways. First, a significant portion of the agency's efforts are directed toward educating members of the public about environmental issues. The agency's website (http://www.epa.gov) includes a wealth of information about the environment, causes of pollution, the consequences of pollution, and effective remedies. Various types of search tools are available,

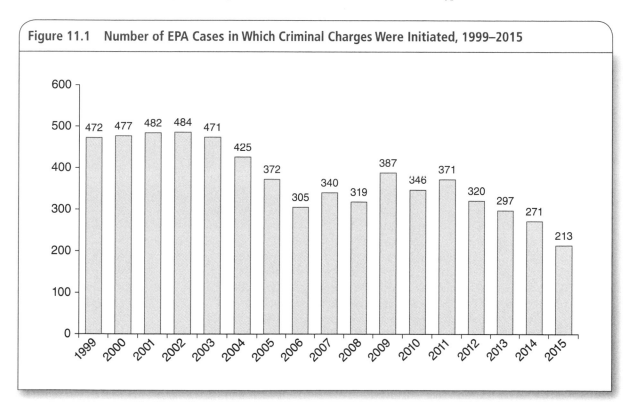

Figure 11.1   Number of EPA Cases in Which Criminal Charges Were Initiated, 1999–2015

Source: Data compiled from EPA Office of Enforcement and Compliance. (n.d.). In *Annual Reports.*

Figure 11.2 Environmental Protection Agency Wanted Poster

WANTED

by the
U.S. Environmental Protection Agency
CRIMINAL INVESTIGATION DIVISION

Name:	Chavez-Beltran, Raul
ALIAS:	
SEX:	MALE
RACE:	WHITE
DATE OF BIRTH:	07/20/1961
PLACE OF BIRTH:	SALTILLO, COAHUILA, MEXICO
HEIGHT:	5'08"
WEIGHT:	180 LBS
EYES:	BROWN
HAIR:	BLACK
SCARS/TATTOOS:	
FBI #:	
NIC #:	W724108332

LAST KNOWn ADDRESS: MEXICO

Case Summary:
- CHAVEZ-BELTRAN WAS CHARGED IN THE WESTERN DISTRICT OF TEXAS - EL PASO DIVISION.
- Chavez-Beltran's alleged VIOLATIONS INCLUDE:
  - RESOURCE CONSERVATION AND RECOVERY ACT (RCRA)
  - CONSPIRACY
  - MAIL FRAUD
- CHAVEZ-BELTRAN'S COMPANY IS CALLED EN-CON ENVIRONMENTAL SERVICES, INC. ILLEGALLY TRANSPORTED MERCURY CONTAMINATED SOIL.
- CHAVEZ-BELTRAN HAS BEEN A FUGITIVE LIVING AND WORKING IN MEXICO.

ANYONE WITH INFORMATION REGARDING THIS FUGITIVE SHOULD CONTACT THE U.S. ENVIRONMENTAL PROTECTION AGENCY, CRIMINAL INVESTIGATION DIVISION – DALLAS TEXAS OFFICE AT 1-214-665-6600 OR COMPLETE THE FORM LOCATED AT HTTP://WWW.EPA.GOV/COMPLIANCE/CRIMINAL/FUGITIVES/REPORT-LOCATION-FORM.HTML

U.S. EPA/CID WANTED POSTER NOVEMBER 1, 2008   www.epa.gov/fugitives

Source: U.S. Environmental Protection Agency. (n.d.). Available from http://www.epa.gov/compliance/criminal/fugitives/posters/beltran-08-wanted-poster.pdf

allowing website visitors to gather information about an assortment of environmental topics. As well, one search tool allows visitors to determine the quality of air in their city, county, or state. Many of you have likely heard of sex offender registries and may have even searched them. A similar tool, called AirNow, exists for air pollution. The tool provides users insight into the quality of air in different locations across the year. It is available online at airnow.gov. Another tool includes a mapping tool that provides users details on EPA enforcement actions each year. Users can use the map to click on the location where each enforcement action occurred. When doing so, they will access the address of the business/individual charged with the action, a detailed case enforcement report, and facility report. The 2015 data for this tool is available online at http://www.epa.gov/enforcement/enforcement-annual-results-fiscal-year-fy-2015.

A second way that the agency protects public health is through research programs that investigate how various chemicals and pollutants harm individuals and the environment. The EPA's Office of Research and Development (ORD) conducts and oversees various scientific studies on different aspect of pollution. ORD oversees several research centers, laboratories, and research programs, including the National Center for Environmental Research, the National Center for Computational Toxicology, the National Center for Environmental Assessment, the National Health and Environmental Effects Research Laboratory, and the National Homeland Security Research Center. Research by ORD is focused on assessing environmental risks, characterizing harm from the pollutants, and developing management practices to deal with risk (EPA, 2010a).

Environmental risk assessment research encompasses three domains. *Hazard identification* refers to efforts to identify the negative health consequences of various pollutants. *Exposure assessment* refers to efforts to identify specific locations where the pollutants exist, how much of the pollutants exist, and how long they have existed. *Dose-response assessment* refers to efforts to determine how much of specific pollutants produce specific effects (EPA, 2010a). Using this risk assessment process as a foundation, researchers can then assess how to characterize environmental risks and how best to manage them.

A third way that EPA protects public health is through its enforcement efforts. When cases are resolved, agency representatives include a discussion on the way various chemicals or pollutants involved in that particular settlement or case harmed individuals and the environment. For example, in December 2010, North America's largest lead producer, Doe Run Resources Corporation of St. Louis, Missouri, settled charges that it violated several federal laws, including the Clean Air Act, the Clean Water Act, the Resource Conservation and Recovery Act, the Emergency Planning and Community Right-to-Know Act, and the Comprehensive Environmental Response, Compensation, and Liability Act. The settlement required Doe Run Resources to implement measures to reduce the amount of the following pollutants in the environment: lead, sulfur dioxide, nitrogen oxides, volatile organic compounds, carbon monoxide, carbon dioxide, particulate matter, arsenic, cadmium, copper, and zinc. Table 11.2 shows the adverse effects of these pollutants. The amount of pollution reduced in this case was significant. In fact, estimates suggest that the settlement actions will reduce the amount of lead pollution by the company by 822 tons annually (EPA, 2010c).

EPA as a Deterrent

Settlements are designed not just to punish environmental offenders but also to ensure that the offenders develop measures to stop future offending. Consider the case of three subsidiaries of Duke Energy Corporation. A federal investigation uncovered evidence of harmful actions the subsidiaries were committing through the use of coal-fired power plants that were in violation of the Clean Water Act. In September 2015, the corporation entered into a consent decree agreeing with the EPA to settle the case under certain conditions.

Table 11.1 Deaths and Illnesses Prevented From the 1990 Clean Air Act Amendments		
	Year 2010 (in cases)	**Year 2020 (in cases)**
Adult Mortality - particles	160,000	230,000
Infant Mortality - particles	230	280
Mortality - ozone	4,300	7,100
Chronic Bronchitis	54,000	75,000
Heart Disease - Acute Myocardial Infarction	130,000	200,000
Asthma Exacerbation	1,700,000	2,400,000
Emergency Room Visits	86,000	120,000
School Loss Days	3,200,000	5,400,000
Lost Work Days	13,000,000	17,000,000

Source: EPA

Table 11.2	Types of Harm From Pollutants in the Doe Run Resources Corporation Case
Pollutant	**Harm**
Lead	At high levels can cause convulsions, coma, and even death. Lower levels of lead can cause adverse health effects on the central nervous system, kidney, and blood cells. Fetuses, infants, and children are more vulnerable to lead exposure than adults since lead is more easily absorbed into growing bodies, causing delays in physical and mental development, lower IQ levels, shortened attention spans, and increased behavioral problems.
Sulfur dioxide	High concentrations affect breathing and may aggravate existing respiratory and cardiovascular disease. Sensitive populations include asthmatics, individuals with bronchitis or emphysema, children, and the elderly. Sulfur dioxide is also a primary contributor to acid rain.
Nitrogen oxides	Can cause ground-level ozone, acid rain, particulate matter, global warming, water quality deterioration, and visual impairment. Nitrogen oxides play a major role, with volatile organic chemicals, in the atmospheric reactions that produce ozone. Children, people with lung diseases, such as asthma, and people who work or exercise outside are susceptible to adverse effects such as damage to lung tissue and reduction in lung function.
Volatile organic compounds	Play a major role in the atmospheric reactions that produce ozone, which is the primary constituent of smog. People with lung disease, children, older adults, and people who are active can be affected when ozone levels are unhealthy. Ground-level ozone exposure is linked to a variety of short-term health problems, including lung irritation and difficulty breathing, as well as long-term problems, such as permanent lung damage from repeated exposure, aggravated asthma, reduced lung capacity, and increased susceptibility to respiratory illnesses such as pneumonia and bronchitis.
Carbon monoxide	Colorless, odorless gas that is formed when carbon in fuel is not burned completely. It is a component of motor vehicle exhaust, which contributes about 56% of all carbon monoxide emissions nationwide. Carbon monoxide can cause harmful health effects by reducing oxygen delivery to the body's organs (like the heart and brain) and tissues.
Particulate matter	Short-term exposure to PM can aggravate lung disease, cause asthma attacks and acute bronchitis, may increase susceptibility to respiratory infections, and has been linked to heart attacks.
Arsenic	A carcinogen, and chronic exposure can result in fatigue, gastrointestinal distress, anemia, neuropathy, and skin lesions that can develop into skin cancer in mammals.
Cadmium	A probable carcinogen, and can cause pulmonary irritation and kidney disease.
Copper	Drinking water containing large concentrations of copper can cause gastrointestinal distress and liver or kidney damage. High concentrations of copper can become toxic to aquatic life.
Zinc	Can cause stomach cramps, nausea, vomiting, and anemia.

Source: EPA Office of Enforcement and Compliance. (2010, October 8). In Doe Run Resources *Corporation Settlement.*

The company agreed to pay a $925,000 fine as a result of the consent decree. But perhaps more important, it agreed to engage in practices that would prevent future violations. In particular, the consent decree stipulated that the corporation would spend $4.4 million in developing or exploring certain mitigation projects. As quoted in the case summary, these included the following:

- Forest Service/National Park Service (NPS):
  - Duke must pay $175,000 each to the U.S. Forest Service and the National Park Service. The Forest Service project will involve the restoration of soil calcium to support healthy forests on lands on the Cherokee, Nantahala, and/or Pisgah National Forests. The NPS project will involve the restoration of native brook trout and/or the revegetation of Red Spruce trees in Great Smoky Mountains National Park. These projects will help mitigate some of the harmful effects of acid deposition on plants and animals. Duke also has the option to pay an additional $175,000 to these agencies to support the same projects.

- Installation of Electric Vehicle Charging Infrastructure:
  - Duke has the option to submit a plan to the EPA for a project to enhance electric vehicle charging infrastructure in North Carolina. Battery powered and some hybrid vehicles need plug-in infrastructure to recharge the batteries. Lack of a charging infrastructure is a major barrier to adoption of electric vehicles. Establishment of electric vehicle charging stations could expand the useful driving range of electric vehicles as well as encourage drivers to purchase electric vehicles for local and commuting use.

- Advanced Truck Stop Electrification Project:
  - Duke has the option to submit a plan to the EPA for the installation of advanced truck stop electrification equipment in North Carolina. Long-haul truck drivers often idle their engines during rest stops to power vehicle systems, such as to supply heat or cooling in their sleeper cab compartments, and to maintain vehicle battery charge while electrical appliances such as TVs, computers and microwaves are in use. Modifications to rest areas to provide access to electrical power will allow truck drivers to turn their engines off. Truck driver utilization of the advanced truck stop electrification will result in reduced idling time and therefore reduced fuel usage, reduced emissions of PM, NOx, VOCs and toxics, and reduced noise, as idling trucks typically use about 1 gallon of diesel fuel/hour, creating emissions and noise pollution.

- Residential Wood-burning Appliance Change-Out Program:
  - Duke must submit a plan to the EPA for a minimum of $500,000 to sponsor a wood burning appliance (*e.g.*, stoves, boilers and fireplaces) replacement and retrofit program that would be implemented by one or more third-parties. This project must give priority to areas located within a geography and topography that make them susceptible to high levels of particle pollution and that have a significant potential for replacement of older and/or higher-polluting wood or coal-burning appliances, such as the Eastern Band of Cherokee Indians community in North Carolina including the counties of Jackson, Cherokee, Graham, Haywood, and Swain, as well as Mecklenburg county.

- Clean Energy/Energy Efficiency:
  - Duke must submit a plan to the EPA, at a maximum of $600,000, for the purchase and installation of clean air energy generation resources and/or environmentally beneficial energy efficiency measures in economically distressed counties within Duke's service territory (EPA, 2015, September 10).

In theory, these initiatives would reduce the likelihood of future offending.

On another level, it is important to note that the ability of the EPA (and other agencies for that matter) extends beyond stopping specific offenders from committing new offenses. Indeed, the hope is that these agencies will keep businesses who have never offended from doing so as well. Surveys of 70 workers from two companies (a steel business and a paper/pulp business) and 91 environmental decision makers found that the likelihood of an environmental crime is lowest when "there is a credible legal threat for non-compliance and/or when one perceives information consequences associated with offending, such as losing the respect of one's significant others, to be certain and costly" (Simpson et al., 2013, p. 266). As Sally Simpson and her coauthors (2013) point out, "formal sanctions do not work in isolation" (p. 65).

EPA as a Fund Generator and Cost-Saving Entity

The EPA can be seen as a resource generator and a cost-saving entity. The agency generates resources through the fines that are imposed in cases it investigates. Table 11.3 shows the amount of fines in EPA cases between 1974 and 2015 (fiscal years). Since 1996, the EPA cases have recovered more than $130 million every year, and the amount was even more than $250 million for a few years. In 2015, the EPA cases recovered $405 million in fines.

The EPA is also instrumental in collecting fines to help with cleanup costs of environmental pollution sites in the United States. The **Comprehensive Environmental Response Compensation and Liability Act**, also known as the Superfund Act, was passed in 1980 "to clean up past environmental sins" (Barnett, 1993, p. 120). This law placed the economic onus of fixing environmental harm on corporations and provided a legislative remedy that assisted in determining how funds should be collected and distributed. Funds come from taxes and enforcement-initiated penalties on corporations and companies (H. C. Barnett, 1993). In fiscal year 2015, the EPA received commitments of $2.2 billion to support the investigation and cleanup of environmental crime sites. Sites selected to use Superfund dollars are referred to as Superfund sites.

The EPA also helps save future costs through its compliance efforts. By ensuring that companies are in compliance with environmental laws, in theory, the agency is reducing future costs of pollution. Though it is difficult to gauge the degree to which these savings occur, it nonetheless seems safe to suggest that fewer environmental crimes in the future

Table 11.3 | **EPA, FY 1974–FY 2015 Penalties Assessed**

Fiscal Year	Civil Judicial	Administrative	Criminal	Total
1974	$5,000	NA	NA	$5,000
1975	$75,250	NA	NA	$75,250
1976	$314,500	NA	NA	$314,500
1977	$4,423,960	NA	NA	$4,423,960
1978	$1,313,873	$25,000	NA	$1,338,873
1979	$4,028,469	$56,800	NA	$4,085,269
1980	$10,570,040	$159,110	NA	$10,729,150
1981	$5,634,325	$742,910	NA	$6,377,235
1982	$3,445,950	$949,430	NA	$4,395,380
1983	$5,461,583	$2,419,898	$369,500	$8,250,981
1984	$3,497,579	$3,385,344	$198,000	$7,080,923
1985	$13,071,530	$9,707,480	$1,526,000	$24,305,010
1986	$13,178,414	$7,449,993	$1,936,150	$22,564,557
1987	$17,507,499	$6,818,374	$2,475,051	$26,800,924
1988	$25,001,221	$11,908,300	$8,660,275	$45,569,796

Fiscal Year	Civil Judicial	Administrative	Criminal	Total
1989	$21,473,087	$13,778,859	$11,601,241	$46,853,187
1990	$38,542,015	$22,747,652	$5,513,318	$66,802,985
1991	$41,235,721	$31,868,407	$14,120,387	$87,224,515
1992	$50,705,071	$28,028,260	$62,895,400	$141,628,731
1993	$85,913,518	$29,219,896	$29,700,000	$144,833,414
1994	$65,635,930	$48,020,941	$36,812,000	$150,468,871
1995	$34,925,472	$35,933,856	$23,221,100	$94,080,428
1996	$66,254,451	$29,996,478	$76,660,900	$172,911,829
1997	$45,966,607	$49,178,494	$169,282,896	$264,427,997
1998	$63,531,731	$28,041,562	$92,800,711	$184,374,004
1999	$141,211,699	$25,509,879	$61,552,874	$228,274,452
2000	$54,851,765	$29,258,502	$121,974,488	$206,084,755
2001	$101,683,157	$23,782,264	$94,726,283	$220,191,704
2002	$63,816,074	$25,859,501	$62,252,318	$151,927,893
2003	$72,259,713	$24,374,718	$71,000,000	$167,634,431
2004	$121,213,230	$27,637,174	$47,000,000	$195,850,404
2005	$127,205,897	$26,731,150	$100,000,000	$253,937,047
2006	$81,807,757	$42,007,029	$43,000,000	$166,814,786
2007	$39,771,169	$30,696,323	$63,000,000	$133,467,492
2008	$88,356,149	$38,197,194	$63,454,493	$190,007,837
2009	$58,496,536	$31,608,710	$96,000,000	$186,105,246
2010	$70,200,000	$33,400,000	$70,200,000	$175,800,000
2011	$104,390,628	$47,800,937	$41,000,000	$193,191,565
2012	$155,539,269	$52,022,612	$44,000,000	$251,461,881
2013	$1,100,000,000	$48,000,000	$1,500,000,000	$2,648,000,000
2014	$56,000,000	$44,000,000	$63,000,000	$163,000,000
2015	$163,000,000	$42,000,000	$200,000,000	$405,000,000

Source: Compiled from EPA Office of Enforcement and Compliance. *Enforcement and compliance numbers at a glance.*

means reduced costs of environmental crimes (controlling for business growth and inflation). The EPA website boasts the following specific savings in fiscal year 2015:

- $7 billion in investments by companies in actions and equipment to control pollution and clean up contaminated sites
- $404 million in combined federal administrative, civil judicial penalties, and criminal fines
- $4 billion in court-ordered environmental projects resulting from criminal prosecutions
- 129 combined years of incarceration for sentenced defendants
- $1.975 billion in commitments from responsible parties to clean up Superfund sites
- $39 million for environmental mitigation projects that provide direct benefits to local communities across the country (EPA, 2015, December 16a)

It is important to reiterate that state and local environmental protection agencies also respond to environmental crimes, particularly those that are more manageable given the resources of those agencies. These local and state agencies

WHITE-COLLAR CRIME IN THE NEWS

Dumper Dumped on Probation

https://commons.wikimedia.org/wiki/File:Sithalapakkam_Garbage_Dump_1.jpg.

Illegal dumping has serious consequences for individuals and the community.

A Northborough man has been sentenced to serve one year in jail with the sentence suspended with five years of probation for operating an illegal dumping site, Attorney General Martha Coakley announced today.

The judge also ordered that Santo Anza Jr., age 52, of Northborough, remove all solid waste from the site. Anza is also prohibited from working with any solid waste in any community for the next five years.

"This defendant operated an illegal dump that unlawfully accepted more than 2 million pounds of solid waste, fouling the air and polluting the environment," AG Coakley said. "He repeatedly disregarded solid waste and clean air laws for his own personal gain while putting the public's health at risk and damaging the environment."

"This case sends a strong signal that the rules we have in place to protect public health and the environment, cannot be ignored," said Martin Suuberg, MassDEP's deputy commissioner. The sentence was imposed today by Worcester Superior Court Judge Richard T. Tucker. Judge Tucker also ordered that Anza, within 60 days, develop a plan and schedule to remove all the solid waste from the site, subject to approval by the Massachusetts Department of Environmental Protection (MassDEP). Anza was sentenced to serve an additional five years of probation for violations of the Massachusetts Clean Air Act.

The Commonwealth recommended that Santo Anza be incarcerated for one year in the House of Correction, and to serve five years of probation upon completion of his sentence. Several residents from the surrounding community delivered impact statements in court today describing the negative effect that Anza's illegal dump site on his Whitney Street property had on their lives, including details on how they suffered from the sights, sounds and smells of the illegal operation that emitted rotten odors.

Source: Reprinted from Massachusetts Attorney General's Office (2013, August 22). Northborough Man Sentenced for Multiple Environmental Violations in Connection with Operating Illegal Dump. http://www.mass.gov/ago/news-and-updates/press-releases/2013/2013-08-22-anza-sentence.html

can be seen as fulfilling functions similar to those of the federal agency. The box White-Collar Crime in the News shows a recent criminal case handled by a state agency. More will be written about how these agencies identify and respond to these crimes in a later chapter.

Criticisms of EPA

In discussing the functions of the EPA, it important to draw attention to the criticisms that individuals and groups have made about the agency. In particular, the EPA has been criticized for the following:

- An ineffective response to the September 11, 2001, terror attacks
- Overregulating rural areas
- Overstepping its boundaries regarding state issues
- Politicizing the science process

In terms of an ineffective response to September 11, the EPA was criticized for not providing enough information about the harmful effects of the air around New York City's "Ground Zero" after the September 11 terror attacks. The agency was also criticized for not providing enough assistance in cleanup efforts. Rep. Jerrold Nadler (D-NY) commented that "New York was at the center of one of the most calamitous events in American history and the EPA has essentially walked away" (Lyman, 2003b). The EPA's Office of Inspector General conducted its own investigation into the EPA's response to September 11. The report claimed that "the White House reviewed and even changed EPA statements about public health risks to make them sound less alarming" and that the EPA understated the potential health effects of the attack (Lyman, 2003a).

The EPA has been accused of overregulating in rural areas and making it difficult for farmers to make a living by producing goods they have been producing for centuries. With changes in rules, including one proposed rule that would have supposedly allowed the EPA to regulate dust, farmers and their advocates were in an uproar about the EPA's actions. Tamara Thies, the National Cattlemen's Beef Association chief environmental counsel, accused the EPA of "waging an unprecedented war to end modern production of animal agriculture" (K. Anderson, 2010). In September 2010, Senate Agriculture Committee Chairman Blanche Lincoln (D-AR) held a committee hearing to "examine the impact of the U.S. Environmental Protection Agency regulation on agriculture" (Clayton, 2010). At the hearing, Lincoln was critical of the EPA, stating, "Farmers need certainty and stability, not additional burdensome and costly regulation" and said that many of EPA's initiatives reflected "dubious rationales and . . . they will be of questionable benefit" (Kopperud, 2010).

Critics have also claimed that the EPA oversteps its boundaries into states' issues all too often. Texas Governor Rick Perry has been especially critical of the EPA. In a statement released on May 26, 2010, Perry made the following comments:

> An increasingly activist EPA is ignoring the 22 percent reduction in ozone and 46 percent decrease in NO_x emissions that Texas has achieved since 2000. On behalf of those Texans whose jobs are threatened by this latest overreach, and in defense of not only our clean air program but also our rights under the 10th Amendment, I am calling upon President Obama to rein in the EPA and instruct them to study our successful approach for recommended use elsewhere. (Office of the Governor Rick Perry, 2010)

In Fall 2010, federal regulations changed in terms of how greenhouse gas permits should be issued to businesses, a task that had been done by state agencies previously. A spokesman from Perry's office told reporters, "The existing permits in Texas have helped our state achieve dramatic improvements in air quality and we believe they will ultimately be upheld in the courts. In their latest crusade, the EPA has created massive job-crushing uncertainty for Texas companies" (Plushnick-Masti, 2010). In December 2010, Perry vowed to "defend Texas' freedom to continue our successful environmental strategies free from federal overreach" (Powell, 2010). The battle reached the point where six Texas legislators developed a proposal to establish autonomy from the federal government.

The EPA has faced criticisms of politicizing the science process. A 2008 survey of 1,586 EPA scientists administered by the by Iowa State University's Center for Survey Statistics and Methodology on behalf of the Union of Concerned Scientists found that 889 of the scientists (60%) "reported personally experiencing what they viewed as political interference in their work over the last five years" ("Meddling at EPA?" 2008). Additional findings from the survey showed that about one-fourth of the scientists witnessed EPA officials misrepresenting findings, 284 witnessed situations where officials selectively used data, and 224 scientists said they had been told to engage in such activities. One EPA scientist made the following comments in the study: "Do not trust the Environmental Protection Agency to protect your environment. Ask questions. Be aware of political and economic motives. Become politically active. Elect officials with motives to protect the environment and hold them accountable" (Union of Concerned Scientists [UCS], 2008, p. 6). Francesca Grifo, senior scientist with the Union of Concerned Scientists, presented a summary of the findings in a hearing titled *Oversight Health on Science and Environmental Regulatory Decisions* before the U.S. Senate Committee on Environment and Public Works Subcommittee on Public Sector Solutions to Global Warming, Oversight, and Children's Health Protection. In her testimony, Grifo said,

> Science is not the only element of effective policy making. However, because science enjoys widespread respect, appointed officials will always be tempted to manipulate or suppress scientific findings to support predetermined policies. Such manipulation is not only dishonest; it undermines the EPA's credibility and affects the health and safety of Americans. (UCS, 2008, p. 8)

● ● ●   Problems Addressing Environmental Crimes

Like other white-collar crimes, environmental white-collar offenses are complex, with a number of barriers making it difficult for control agencies to respond to the problem. In general, the three barriers are (1) media portrayals of environmental crime, (2) evidentiary issues, and (3) an empirical void.

Media Portrayals of Environmental Crime

With regard to the *media portrayals of environmental crime,* it is safe to suggest that the media provide little information about environmental crimes, and the information provided may give the public and policymakers a distorted image of environmental crime. One author team examined how often chemical spills were reported in the *Tampa Tribune*—the largest newspaper in Hillsborough County, Florida—between 1987 and 1997 (Lynch, Stretesky, & Hammond, 2000). The study showed that 878 chemical spills were reported to the EPA in the county over the decade. Of those 878, nine were reported in the newspaper. The authors note that newspapers fail to focus on environmental crimes because they do "not fit the public's image of crime" (p. 123). Another study, this one of 162 EPA cases between 2001 and 2002, showed that the cases received little scrutiny from the press. The cases that did receive press attention were deemed as more serious, which was determined by the penalty given to the offender (Jarrell, 2007).

Another problem related to the media and environmental crime is that environmental disasters tend to be politicized by commentators in the media. After the BP disaster, President Barack Obama was criticized for not doing enough to respond to the environmental situation in the Gulf. Fox News showed a daily description of Obama's White House schedule and compared the president's schedule with the daily activities in the Gulf in the aftermath of the oil spill ("Disaster in the Gulf," 2010). In a similar way, President George W. Bush was vilified by commentators for what was perceived to be a lackadaisical response to Hurricane Katrina. One photo that created controversy showed President Bush looking out of the window of *Air Force One* as it flew over New Orleans. Five years later, in his memoir, the former president said he regretted having that photo taken.

Evidentiary Issues and Environmental Crime

Evidentiary issues also make it difficult to address environmental crimes. Environmental crime pioneer Gerhard Mueller (1996) identified 10 such problems that hindered the criminal justice response to environmental crime (see Table 11.4). These problems include the following:

- Identifying the harm from environmental crimes
- Determining the amount of "permissible" pollution
- Identifying liability
- Issues around vicarious liability (e.g., holding an employer responsible for an employee's actions)
- Determining ways to hold corporations liable
- Establishing proof
- Lack of enforcement
- Power abuses
- Changing priorities
- Decriminalization and/or determining the appropriate penalty

Of course, the criminal justice system cannot respond to environmental crime by itself. Some have argued that better controls in the form of self-regulation, improved marketing of safe products, and improved communication about environmental risk will help address environmental crime (Grabosky & Gant, 2000).

Empirical Issues and Environmental Crime

Empirical issues have made it difficult to address environmental crime. On a general level, one can point to a dearth of research on the topic, which is surprising given the wealth of compliance and violations data available from the EPA that could be used to study various types of white-collar crime (Burns & Lynch, 2004). Indeed, the data available are virtual gold mines for future researchers. Perhaps those of you doing theses or dissertations in the near future could "mine" some of the EPA data to help generate empirical understanding about environmental crime.

A related empirical issue has to do with the way that environmental crime is conceptualized. Focusing solely on a legal orientation may ignore much of the harm done by corporations. Some researchers who see pollution as contributing to climate change define the behavior of the government—its reluctance to address the problem in particular—as a form of state-corporate crime (Kramer, 2013). Recall from chapter 5 that state-corporate crimes are defined as harmful acts perpetrated by the government.

On a related point, the existing environmental crime research has given limited attention to "the place of the upper class in environmental research" (Simon, 2000, p. 633). What this means is that the research has failed to adequately address environmental crime *as a white-collar crime*. In doing so, opportunities for contextualizing, characterizing, and explaining "environmental white-collar crime" have been missed.

Another issue that surfaces concerns a lack of research on why certain companies do an outstanding job in terms

▲ **Photo 11.6** Political leaders are expected to protect the environment and are held accountable in the media when they appear to respond too lightly to environmental disasters. Former President Bush took a lot of flack in the media for this picture, taken of him flying over New Orleans in the aftermath of Hurricane Katrina. President Obama received similar criticism from members of the media for his response to the BP oil spill.

▲ **Photo 11.7** Evidence gathering in environmental crime cases is different from that in other types of crime. Environmental crime agents have a different tool kit from that of other law enforcement officers.

Table 11.4 Problems Responding to Environmental Crime

Problem	Why It's a Problem	Can This Problem Be Addressed?
Problem of qualification	Harm is not always immediately visible, causing some criminal justice officials and policymakers to misunderstand the problem.	Through education and awareness, improved response systems have evolved.
Problem of quantification	It is difficult to determine how "much" pollution is permissible, and how much harm is appropriate, with decisions somewhat arbitrary.	Laws have placed a "sin tax" on companies exceeding permissible pollution, but this may not help.
Problem of strict liability	Laws too narrowly defined on intent make it difficult to prove intent.	Laws became more flexible in the U.S., focusing on mens rea, but not in other countries.
Problem of vicarious liability	Can be counterproductive to deterrence if offenders are held accountable for things they did not intend.	Responsible corporate officers can be held accountable for environmental offending.
Corporate criminal liability	Identifying specific corporate officers with the decision-making power that was abused is difficult, with "blame passed downward."	Through complex investigations and plea bargains, officers can be identified.
Problem of proof	Hard to prove damage, effects, guilt, mens rea, and connection between the crime and the consequences.	With time and resources, cases can be proven, but it is complex. Also, corporations can't plead the fifth (must provide information)
Problem of abuse of power	Powerful businesses might control policy makers and regulators.	Must be addressed on a case-by-case basis.
Problem of inadequate enforcement	In the 1970s, only 130 cases were referred by EPA to DOJ for criminal prosecution.	The EPA has been opening more criminal investigations this decade.
Problem of changing priorities	Industrialization is seen as progress, and consequences are virtually ignored.	Advocates must continue efforts to generate awareness about environmental issues.
Problem of decriminalization	Cases were routinely kept out of the justice system in the past.	The criminal justice system has increased its efforts responding to environmental crime cases.
Problem of penalization	Mixed evidence on the deterrent potential of punitive policies.	Need more research to determine appropriate sentences.

Source: Adapted from Mueller, G. (1996). An essay on environmental criminality, pp. 3–32. In Edwards, S. M., Edwards, T. D., & Fields, C., *Environmental crime and criminality*. New York: Garland.

of environmental compliance. Carole Gibbs (2012) reminds us of this important fact. She writes that "many companies comply and even overcomply with environmental regulations by polluting significantly less than legally allowed" (p. 345). Gibbs offers several reasons for this compliance. Some companies may have installed incredibly effective pollution equipment. Other companies may "over abide" in an effort to develop positive relationships with policymakers and thereby influence the way that regulations are developed in the future. Still others might over abide in order to avoid any harm to their reputation. Or, some might overestimate the risk of prosecution and be cautious to avoid getting in trouble. Regardless of the reason, research is needed to focus on why many corporations do not break environmental laws.

Simon (2000) also draws attention to the lack of research on global aspects of environmental offending. In a similar way, one can point to a lack of research on the way that environmental crime is influenced by various societal systems. Certainly, the environmental system can be seen as a system that interacts with other societal systems on various levels. As noted earlier in this text, the interrelated nature of systems is central to the systems perspective. Put another way, changes in one system will lead to changes in other systems. Some have argued that as our industrial system developed, the environmental system "has been cast in the role of a commodity for use in the production and consumption" (H. Barnett, 1999, p. 167). Then, as our technological system grew, new forms of chemical wastes were created, and new areas of concern for the environmental system arose. The task at hand is to recognize how our changing societal systems have changed the nature of environmental white-collar crimes occurring in communities across the world.

SUMMARY

- On April 20, 2010, an explosion on BP's Deepwater Horizon rig occurred in the Gulf of Mexico. Eleven rig workers were killed, and oil began to spill out of the Macondo well into the Gulf of Mexico.
- On December 15, 2010, the U.S. Department of Justice filed a lawsuit against BP and eight other companies for their role in the rig explosion.
- Concern about environmental pollution escalated in the United States in the 1970s, a decade labeled the "environment decade in reference to the increase in environmental legislation and political support for laws regulating pollution" (H. Barnett, 1993, p. 220).
- It is important to understand that not all environmental crimes are white-collar crimes.
- White-collar environmental crimes involve situations where individuals or businesses illegally pollute or destroy the environment in the course of occupational activity.
- The varieties of environmental white-collar crime include illegal emissions, illegal disposal of hazardous wastes, illegal dumping, harmful destruction of property and wildlife, environmental threats, environmental state crime, and international environmental crimes.
- Illegal emissions, as a variety of environmental white-collar crime, refer to situations where companies or businesses illegally allow pollutants to enter the environment.
- Illegal disposal of hazardous wastes involves situations in which employees or businesses dispose of harmful wastes in ways that are potentially harmful to individuals and the environment.
- One of the most well-known environmental crimes involving hazardous wastes is the Love Canal tragedy.
- Also known as "fly dumping," "wildcat dumping," and "midnight dumping," illegal dumping refers to situations where employees or businesses dump products they no longer need in sites that are not recognized as legal dump sites (EPA, 1998).
- Harmful destruction of property and wildlife by companies or workers during the course of their jobs can also be seen as environmental white-collar crimes.
- The federal government has identified five "significant threats" to the environment: knowing endangerment, repeat offenders, misuse of federal facilities, catastrophic events, and organized crime.
- Environmental state crime refers to criminal or deviant behaviors by a government representative (or representatives) involving the intentional use of pollutants and chemicals to harm individuals and the environment.
- International environmental crimes include those environmental offenses that cross borders of at least two different countries or occur in internationally protected areas.
- Environmental crime has more victims than other crimes, but victims are often not aware of their victimization (Hayman & Brack, 2002). In general, the types of consequences can be classified as *physical costs*, *economic costs*, and *community costs*.
- The Environmental Protection Agency has addressed concerns about environmental racism by developing an Office of Environmental Justice in the early 1990s and giving the office the responsibility of promoting environmental justice activities in the agency.

- The EPA was created in 1970 when President Richard Nixon reorganized several federal agencies to create a single federal agency responsible for addressing environmental pollution.
- The actions of the EPA can be characterized in four overlapping ways: (1) as an enforcer of criminal and civil laws, (2) as an agency trying to protect public health, (3) as an agency aiming to deter future misconduct, and (4) as a facilitator of fund generation and cost savings.
- The EPA has been criticized for the following: an ineffective response to the aftermath of September 11, overregulating rural areas, overstepping its boundaries regarding state issues, and politicizing the science process.
- Three barriers to addressing environmental crime include (1) media portrayals of environmental crime, (2) evidentiary issues, and (3) an empirical void.

KEY TERMS

Comprehensive Environmental Response Compensation and Liability Act

Environmental Protection Agency (EPA)

Environmental racism

Environmental state crime

Federal Water Pollution Control Act

Illegal dumping

Illegal emissions

International environmental crimes

Knowing endangerment

White-collar environmental crimes

DISCUSSION QUESTIONS

1. Check out the EPA fugitives at http://www.epa.gov/enforcement/epa-fugitives. Categorize them based on (a) whether they are white-collar offenders, (b) the type of offense they committed, and (c) the harm from their offenses. What patterns do you see regarding gender, race, age, and geography? Explain.

2. Go to http://www.epa.gov/air/data/. Check to see how much air pollution exists in your hometown as well as your college town (if it is different from your hometown). Compare and contrast the amount of pollution in the two places.

3. Watch Doug Rokke's presentation about depleted uranium on YouTube: http://www.youtube.com/watch?v=e-VkpRwka8. How can depleted uranium be characterized as white-collar crime? Is its use an environmental crime?

4. What is it that makes big-game hunting illegal in some situations? Do you think these crimes are serious? Explain.

5. Rank the various types of environmental crime from least serious to most serious. Explain your rankings.

6. Would you be interested in working for the Environmental Protection Agency? Explain.

7. How can scientists commit environmental crime? Explain.

8. Imagine the world 20 years from now. What do you think environmental crime will be like then?

WEB RESOURCES

Department of Environmental Protection: http://www.ct.gov/dep/site/default.asp

Environmental Protection Agency, Criminal Enforcement Program. http://www.epa.gov/enforcement/criminal-enforcement

Interpol Environmental Crime: http://www.interpol.int/public/environmentalcrime/default.asp

Zero Waste America: http://www.zerowasteamerica.org/RefuseNewsIllegalDumping.htm

Explaining White-Collar Crime

CHAPTER HIGHLIGHTS

- Culture and White-Collar Crime
- Deterrence Theory/Rational Choice Theory and White-Collar Crime
- Strain Theory and White-Collar Crime
- Learning Theory and White-Collar Crime
- Neutralizing and Justifying White-Collar Crime
- Control Theory and White-Collar Crime
- Self-Control Theory and White-Collar Crime
- Routine Activities Theory and White-Collar Crime
- Conflict Theory and White-Collar Crime
- Explaining Corporate Crime
- Theories Ignored in the White-Collar Crime Literature
- Integrated Efforts to Explain White-Collar Crime
- Systems Theory

I n the movie *Office Space,* the workplace experiences of a group of coworkers who are not entirely enthusiastic about their employer are chronicled in a rather humorous manner. The lead character Peter Gibbons, played by Ron Livingston, decides to put in as little effort as possible at his job and is rewarded for this effort with a significant promotion. Later in the movie, he and his disgruntled coworkers, who learn they are going to be fired, concoct a scheme to embezzle a small amount of money that should go unnoticed from the company on a regular basis until they have collected millions over time. The plan goes awry when they embezzle a large amount of funds that is noticed by company officials. Fearing the repercussions that they will experience once they are caught, they write a letter confessing their workplace misconduct and telling where the embezzled funds are located. After they slide their confession under their boss's door, Milton Waddams, another disgruntled coworker, played by movie director Mike Judge, decides to burn the business to the ground because he is fed up with the emotional abuses perpetrated by his bosses. Subsequent scenes show Milton enjoying the spoils of the embezzlement scheme and the offending team moving on in their respective careers.

A close look at the movie shows how various criminological theories can be used to explain the behaviors of workers in the movie. According to Sutherland (1941), "many white-collar crimes are made possible because a businessman holds two or more incompatible and conflicting positions of trust, and is analogous to a football coach who umpires a game in which his own team is playing" (p. 112). In the *Office Space* example, the workers used the trust placed in them by their employers to steal money from company accounts. In reviewing the movie, readers can likely identify how several other theories are relevant to the story line.

Criminological theory is central to the study of white-collar crime. Five comments about using criminological theory to understand and explain white-collar crime will help create a foundation from which readers can gain an appreciation of white-collar crime explanations. First, it is important to stress that theories are potential explanations of behaviors or phenomena. Recall the principle of skepticism discussed in Chapter I: There are no truths when it comes to social science theories. Or, maybe there is one truth: We do not know for certain what causes white-collar crime. Still, theories are useful because they help us research white-collar crime and determine appropriate responses to the problem.

Second, for white-collar crime explanations to have practical utility, the theories or explanations must point to changes that would reduce (rather than increase) white-collar misconduct. For example, based on his review of the multidimensional causes of white-collar crime, Passas (2001) identified the need to (1) watch for fraud among high-level managers—especially when competition and corporate pressures are high, (2) develop strong internal control mechanisms to strengthen companies, (3) institutionalize internal and external strategies that can limit the ability of offenders to make excuses for or rationalize their misconduct, (4) improve publicity surrounding incidents of white-collar crime victimization, and (5) increase the amount of accountability given to external auditors. In essence, his explanations for white-collar crime led to specific policy implications.

Third, it is important to realize that multiple factors likely contribute to white-collar crime. We cannot say that one variable or one event automatically leads to white-collar misconduct. Although theories are discussed separately below, the most accurate explanations combine various theoretical assumptions and explanations to address human behavior.

Fourth, a great deal of theory building centers on explaining individual motivations for white-collar crime. Attempts to explain white-collar crime often center on identifying individual motivations for white-collar offending. Consider how two offenders explained their crimes in the following two examples:

- Everybody does it. It's 100% legal. We are in sales. This is the name of the game. We were very aggressive during our collections, almost like the mafia. We would go after individuals to make sure that they would pay what they owed us. I am telling you, it was all about the money and in our mentality our justification was that everybody is doing it. We thought it was 100% legal, everybody was doing it, why couldn't we? We don't sell light bulbs, we don't sell cleaners, we sell gifts. Organized bribery, that's exactly what it is. I learned this on the job my very first day back in the late 1970s. This is the way of sales. . . . Of course, but well, it is not an official process. I mean, people talk, tell you what works, what doesn't. That's it, you observe, listen and do what you're told, if you do you will be successful. If you don't, well, one should look to find employment elsewhere. So to answer your question, yes the industry promotes language that makes it easier to deal with it (Klenowski, 2012, p. 471).
- The laws are too strict. Federal and state governments force people in this field to be criminal. Let's face it; we have to make money too—to earn a living. I would say 5% of this is my fault, 95% is my partner's fault, but the government acts like it plays no part, when in fact, it motivates us to do what we do. Why should we follow regulations that the government itself does not follow (Klenowski, 2012, p. 468)?

Fifth, while explanatory attempts often focus on individual behavior, it is important to realize that structural variables and macro-level features are useful in explaining and understanding white-collar crime. Consider, for example, that structural factors of the medical profession have been used to explain health care fraud (P. R. Wilson, Lincoln, Chappell, & Fraser, 1986). As well, structural features of other occupations might promote or inhibit white-collar offending in those occupations. Put another way, reasons that one occupational group engages in wrongdoing might be different from the reasons that other occupational groups engage in wrongdoing. Of course, some criminologists would dispute this statement vehemently and suggest that the phenomena that cause any specific type of crime are that same phenomena that cause all types of crime (Hirschi & Gottfredson, 1987). The key to keep in mind is that micro-level theories will address individual-level motivations for white-collar offending while macro-level theories will address societal factors that contribute to rates of white-collar offending.

Criminologists have devoted a great deal of effort to trying to identify the causes of white-collar crime. In this chapter, the following topics are addressed to provide readers with a basic understanding about the potential causes of white-collar crime: culture, deterrence theory and rational choice theory, strain theory, learning theory, neutralizing and justifying white-collar crime, control theory, self-control, routine activities theory, conflict theory, an explanation of corporate crime, theories ignored in the white-collar crime literature, integrated efforts to explain white-collar crime, and systems theory. This should give readers a general understanding of the efforts to explain white-collar misconduct.

● ● ● Culture and White-Collar Crime

Some criminologists attribute white-collar crime to cultural influences that seemingly promote wrongdoing by workers and corporations. James Coleman (1987), for example, argued that industrial capitalism promotes a "culture of competition." Within the social structure that has developed in our industrialized capitalist society, upper-class workers are presented with various types of opportunities for white-collar crime. Based on this, Coleman suggested that white-collar crime "results from a coincidence of motivation and opportunity" (p. 407). The culture of competition is not just about competing to succeed; it is also reflective of a fear of failing that rests on apparent insecurities individuals have about their careers and their roles in their respective organizations. In effect, workers might bend, or even break, workplace rules in an effort to compete in the workplace.

As evidence of the presence of this culture of competition, consider a study in which Jenkins and Braithwaite (1993) reviewed violations in 410 nursing homes in Australia. They found that for-profit nursing homes had more violations than nonprofit nursing homes, and that nonprofit homes, when they do commit violations, often do so in response to the broader goals of the nursing home (e.g., their violations result from competing toward the organization's goals).

Greed is an often-cited explanation for white-collar misconduct that fits within this notion of a culture of competition. Both practitioners (G. Miller, 1993) and researchers (Braithwaite, 1991; Robinson & Murphy, 2009) have attributed corporate wrongdoing to greed that stems from cultural influences. Braithwaite (1991) wrote that "greed motivates crime even after a need has been satisfied" (p. 42). G. Miller (1993), a former federal probation officer who

▲ **Photo 12.1**   Greed is frequently cited as a motivation for white-collar crime.

worked extensively with white-collar probationers, wrote the following reflections upon his retirement after a career that spanned 30 years:

> I am often asked what the offenders I supervised had in common. A large portion were professionals—doctors, pharmacists, lawyers, accountants, stockbrokers, and even a few former judges and high-level politicians. And the one common thread I noted, year after year, was greed. . . . This common denominator has changed society's priorities and damaged the nation's value system. One goal now dominates—to achieve material things at any cost. (p. 22)

Tied into this competitive culture is ego seeking by workers. As Wheeler, Weisburd, Waring, and Bode (1988) wrote, the corporate "ladder is shaped like a pyramid," and competition for advancement becomes stiffer as employees move up the workplace ladder (p. 356). When the competition becomes extremely tight, some individuals might "slip over the boundary of legality" (p. 356). Also reflective of the ties between a competitive culture and greed, a study of 91 companies over a 3-year period found that executive compensation was a factor in manager-controlled firms. In particular, more compensation for executives meant more crime in these firms (Bilimoria, 1995).

Poverty can be seen as a cultural influence that potentially promotes white-collar crime. Criminologists have long suggested that a culture of poverty is correlated with street crime. Historically, though, it has been assumed that poverty explanations were not relevant in terms of white-collar crime. Indeed, when Sutherland first discussed white-collar crime, he rejected poverty explanations as causes of the behavior because poverty, on the surface, does not seem to cause white-collar offending. After all, white-collar offenders are not impoverished. In an effort to broaden our understanding of poverty and crime, criminologist John Braithwaite (1991) has argued that poverty explanations may actually be useful in explaining how power is used to perpetrate white-collar crime if one considers the ties between poverty and inequality. He explained:

> When needs are satisfied, further power and wealth enable crime motivated by greed. New types of criminal opportunities and new paths to immunity from accountability are constituted by concentrations of wealth and power. Inequality thus worsens both crimes of poverty motivated by need for goods for use and crimes of wealth motivated by greed enabled by goods for exchange. (p. 43)

In other words, poverty is correlated with both street crime and white-collar crime. For poor individuals, crimes are motivated by a need for goods that arises out of poverty. For white-collar offenders, crimes are motivated by greed, and poverty provides them power to commit offenses. The more powerful those wealthy individuals become, the more pathways they have to white-collar crime, particularly in the face of limited responses to crimes committed by those with power.

Hirschi and Gottfredson (1987) have been extremely critical of cultural theories. On the most basic level, they argue that white-collar crime is far rarer than would be expected if culture actually caused white-collar crime. From their perspective, if a culture of competition or culture of poverty led to white-collar crime, then more professionals should be involved in workplace offending. Most doctors do not commit crime. Most accountants are honest. Most textbook authors do not plagiarize. Most lawyers are ethical. Most investors are law abiding. They also implied that if white-collar crime were caused by cultural values, then coworkers and citizens should be more accepting of the offenders, and the offenders would not feel the need to hide their crimes or their criminal identities. To Hirschi and Gottfredson, if white-collar crime emanated from values central to our society, then we would not expect the offenders to experience shame, embarrassment, or stigma when their crimes are exposed.

● ● ● Deterrence Theory/Rational Choice Theory and White-Collar Crime

Deterrence theory can be traced to Cesare Beccaria's *On Crimes and Punishments* (1764), a work that many have defined as the foundation of the classical school of criminological thought. In this brief work, Beccaria outlined his theory of punishment, which was based on the assumption that punishment can stop individuals from offending. For punishment to be effective, however, he argued that it must meet three criteria: (1) Punishment must be swift so that the offender links the behavior of crime with the response of punishment in his or her mind; (2) punishment must be certain so that offenders know if a crime is committed, then a negative consequence will occur; and (3) punishment must be proportional to the crime so that the punishment outweighs the positive benefits individuals experience from committing crime.

The underlying assumption of deterrence theory is that individuals are rational beings. This assumption has direct bearing on the theory's applicability to white-collar crime. John Braithwaite (1982) wrote, "White-collar criminals are more deterrable than common criminals because their crimes are more rational and calculating and because they have more of all of the things that can be lost through criminal justice sanctions" (p. 760). Somewhat in line with this assumed rationality, interviews with judges found that the judges tended to view punishment as necessary in order to deter white-collar misconduct (Pollack & Smith, 1983).

Research by Sally Simpson and various colleagues (Simpson & Koper, 1992; Elis & Simpson, 1995; Piquero, Exum, & Simpson, 2005) has been instrumental in demonstrating how deterrence ideals can be used to explain various forms of workplace misconduct. One of her studies found some evidence that stiffer sanctions might deter corporations from future wrongdoing, though the likelihood of repeat offending in corporate crime cases was found to be more influenced by industry type than sanction severity (Simpson & Koper, 1992). In particular, automobile and oil industry firms were found to be more likely to reoffend than firms in the aircraft industry.

In another study, surveys of 96 business school graduates and executives conducted by Elis and Simpson (1995) examined the importance of punishment threat and morality in preventing corporate misconduct. Their findings showed that risk of informal detection and costs from informal sanctions did not deter corporate misconduct; however, the research team did find four factors that appeared to prevent intentions to commit corporate misconduct: (1) certainty of informal sanctions, (2) beliefs about immorality, (3) corporate climate, and (4) pressures from the boss.

Rational choice theory, the modern variation of deterrence theory, considers the limits of human rationality while still considering humans as rational and suggests that offenders will consider the benefits of offending and weigh those benefits against possible negative consequences that arise from misconduct (Clarke & Cornish, 1985). Piquero, Exum, and Simpson (2005) integrated rational choice theory with the idea of "desire for control" to explain how such a desire influences decision making that may lead to corporate offending. To test this premise, Piquero and her research team surveyed 13 business executives and 33 master of business administration (MBA) students. They found that desire for control was related to support for white-collar misconduct. From this finding, they suggested that corporate crime is committed to "gain control over environments that are uncertain or irrational" (p. 272). They also found a vicarious effect of internal reprimands. If coworkers were reprimanded, individuals were less likely to indicate intentions to engage in white-collar crime. In addition, they found that informal sanctions deterred intentions to offend, but formal sanction threats did not.

Some authors have used deterrence ideals to speculate why white-collar crime persists. Albrecht and Searcy (2001) attributed white-collar misconduct to a failure to identify the crimes in the workplace, the absence of formal efforts to respond to fraud, and inadequate control mechanisms. Each of these elements has to do with the certainty of punishment: If offenders are not identified and they know there is little likelihood of getting caught, then they will be more likely to engage in workplace misconduct. Other authors have suggested that lenient sanctions promote wrongdoing. For example, one author noted that it is cheaper for some businesses to break the law than it is to abide by the law (Millspaugh, 2001). From this perspective, fines are seen as providing very little deterrent power. Still other authors have suggested that deterrence strategies alone are not enough to prevent white-collar misconduct and that deterrence strategies and theories must consider values of individuals, businesses, and communities (Payne & Gainey, 2004).

● ● ● Strain Theory and White-Collar Crime

In general, **strain theory** focuses on the way stresses and strains contribute to offending. The source of strain varies across types of strain theories. Some theories point to the social and economic structures as the source of strain, others point to the individual, and others point to the organization. In terms of white-collar offending, three types of strain theories warrant discussion: classical strain theory, institutional anomie theory, and general strain theory.

Classical Strain Theory

Classical strain theory traces the source of strain to interactions between the social and economic structures. As a macro-level theory, classical strain theory addresses how macro-level variables influence individual behavior. Robert Merton (1938) developed his version of strain theory in "Social Structure and Anomie," a brief article published in *American Sociological Review*. Merton based this theory on four assumptions:

- Capitalism promotes financial success as a goal.
- Individuals are socialized to follow legitimate means such as working hard and getting an education to meet financial goals.
- Some individuals face barriers or strain in their efforts to attain financial success.
- When individuals experience strain, they change either the goals or the means to address the strain.

Merton's theory was developed to explain why poor individuals engage in crime, and this has led some to question whether the theory can be used to explain crimes by white-collar workers. The assumption of Merton's theory is that being unable to achieve economic success makes some individuals engage in illegitimate activities. White-collar workers have already achieved economic success. As Langton and Piquero (2007) wrote, "the basic focus on the stresses associated with being poor was incompatible with studies of white-collar crime" (Langton & Piquero, 2007, p. 1). Despite this focus of Merton's theory, Langton and Piquero demonstrate how the theory can explain white-collar offending.

According to Merton, five modes of adaptation characterize how individuals adapt to the way goals and means are prescribed. **Conformists** accept the goals prescribed by society and follow legitimate means to attain the goals. Most white-collar professionals can be characterized as conformists. I am a conformist. I want material success, and I am awfully concerned about doing things the right way to attain it.

Innovators accept the goal of financial success but replace legitimate means with illegitimate means. Consider how embezzlers steal funds after experiencing strain caused by financial problems (Cressey, 1953; G. S. Green, 1990). Or consider how computer criminals find ways to get around the rules to attain material success. They maintain the goal of financial success but use illegitimate means to attain their goals. Interviews with sixteen convicted white-collar offenders showed that some of the offenders attributed their misdeeds to the economic climate (Gill, 2011). In particular, when times were "bad," they said the likelihood of offending increased. In other words, they had to be innovators to deal with the "bad" times.

Ritualists are white-collar workers who do not accept the goals of society but go through the motions of engaging in the means prescribed by society. Companies that violate the law repeatedly and pay fines because the fines are seen as costs of doing business have been described as ritualists (Braithwaite, 1993). These companies go through the motions with regulators in a ritualistic way to make it seem as if they are playing by the rules, but in reality, they have no intention of actually following the rules.

Retreatists are white-collar workers who accept neither the goals of society nor the means to attain those goals. Merton noted that this is the least common adaptation. He wrote that retreatists are "*in* the society, but not *of* it" (1938, p. 677). To Merton, ritualists included those with drug and alcohol addictions. One could also suggest that workers who allow their drug and alcohol problems to influence their workplace activities are retreatists. Also, one could point to workers who show up for work but do not do any work as retreatists. They are "*in* the workplace," but they are not a part "*of* the workplace."

Rebels are workers who reject the goals and means of society and replace the societal-prescribed goals and means with their own goals and means. Recall the notion of collective embezzlement developed by Kitty Calavita and her coauthors (Calavita, Pontell, & Tillman, 1997). They described **collective embezzlement** as crime committed by the organization against the organization. Rather than focusing on success as the goal, workers developed failure as the goal so that the government insurance programs would bail out the failed business. As I have noted elsewhere, "those participating in collective embezzlement reject the standard goal of success, replace it with the goal of failure, and reject the legitimate ways to attain success" (Payne, 2003b, p. 45).

Merton's strain theory can be used to understand deviance by Olympic athletes, which, with a bit of a stretch, can be conceptualized as occupational deviance (Payne & Berg, 1999). Most Olympic athletes can be described as conformists—they want success, and they work hard in legitimate ways to attain success. Those who use performance-enhancing strategies like blood doping and the consumption of illegal substances can be seen as innovators. Ritualists would be those athletes who have little interest in winning or succeeding. Retreatists include former athletes who "drop out of organized sports to become 'beer-belly' softball players" (p. 139) or develop substance abuse problems. Rebels include athletes who defy the rules of the sport and replace the sport's rules with their own. Consider examples of "podium politics" where athletes make symbolic gestures while they are receiving their Olympic medals (Cardinal, 2010). Such gestures, prohibited by Olympic rules, are committed with the aim of meeting the athlete's own political or social goals (rather than the Olympic Games' apolitical and prosocial goals). In 1968, for example, gold medalist Tommie Smith and bronze medalist John Carlos were suspended from the U.S. Olympic team after they raised their fists on the Olympic podium to protest against racism.

Institutional Anomie Theory

Another variety of strain theory, **institutional anomie** theory, is a more modern macro-level approach to explaining how societal institutions promote crime (Messner & Rosenfeld, 2007). In *Crime and the American Dream,* Steve Messner and Richard Rosenfeld describe how society promotes values related to financial success but fails to promote values consistent with using legitimate means to attain financial success. Culture, as it is described by the authors, affects societal institutions. Messner and Rosenfeld note that four values central to the American culture are a breeding ground for crime (see Table 12.1). First, the focus on achievement encourages Americans to always want more. Once we achieve a goal, new goals are developed. Second, universalism suggests that everyone should want material success, despite the fact that

Table 12.1 Values That Are Central to the American Dream

Value	What It Means	How It Relates to White-Collar Crime
Achievement	Individuals are socialized to work hard and direct their efforts toward achieving financial goals. Once certain goals are achieved, new goals are developed.	Individuals keep working toward getting more and more. Eventually a fear of failure may cause some individuals to engage in wrongdoing in the workplace.
Universalism	All individuals are encouraged to strive for monetary success regardless of whether that is realistic.	As individuals move up the workplace ladder, advancement becomes more competitive. It is unrealistic to assume that everyone can be promoted. Individuals might engage in wrongdoing to increase their likelihood of advancement.
Individualism	Individuals are socialized to believe that they can succeed on their own.	Efforts to build careers on one's own can be stressful and counterproductive. Individuals might resort to wrongdoing to address the shortfalls of working alone.
Materialism	Individuals are socialized to want material goods.	The desire for better and new goods in order to "keep up with the neighbors" might cause individuals to engage in wrongdoing to have the finances needed to acquire the goods and services, and it may cause corporations to use shortcuts and provide products desired by the public but that are unsafe.

such a goal is unrealistic. Third, individualism suggests that we should be able to attain our financial goals on our own, which is also unrealistic. Fourth, materialism refers to the way that our society encourages us to be enamored of material goods and the acquisition of the best new products.

The underlying assumption of institutional anomie theory is that individuals are socialized to succeed at any cost, but not all individuals are (1) given the opportunities to succeed or (2) socialized in how to succeed in legitimate ways. Hence, anomie (e.g., normlessness) exists at the institutional level between the prescription of societal goals and legitimate means. The result of this anomie is unbridled aspirations to "get rich." According to one white-collar crime scholar, "regardless of their social background and social capital available to them, people are encouraged to desire more than they presently have" (Passas, 2001, p. 122). Describing these aspirations, one author team wrote:

> Monetary success has no limit. There are always possibilities to acquire more. When money has inherent value as it does in America, and a person's "success" is measured in financial terms, there is also no limit to a person's status. American culture perpetuates these assumptions because to do so is productive to its advancement as a corporate nation. If American citizens become satiated with wealth at a certain level, American industry can move no further than this limit. (Trahan, Marquart, & Mullings, 2005, p. 606)

Messner and Rosenfeld's early editions of their work made little mention of white-collar crime, though they began their book with a description of Michael Milken's experiences as a white-collar offender. Schoepfer and Piquero (2006) point out that because institutional anomie theory "assumes that criminal activity relates to the pursuit of monetary success . . . white-collar crimes should not only be able to be explained under this theoretical framework, but also should expand the generalizability of the theory" (p. 228). In later editions, Messner and Rosenfeld (2007) added a significant amount of discussion about the way white-collar crime was tied to the American dream, and they began their book with a discussion of how the Enron scandal created a foundation for understanding institutional anomie theory. They also noted that "the same social forces that lead to higher levels of serious crime also produce the contrasting social responses to street crime and suite crime" (p. 32).

Schoepfer and Piquero (2006) tested institutional anomie theory through a consideration of embezzlement cases included in the FBI's *Uniform Crime Reports* in 1991. They used 1990 census data to determine how well structural variables related to institutional anomie predicted embezzlement cases in 1991. The researchers found some support for institutional anomie: More high school dropouts (a sign of increased anomie) meant more embezzlement, and more voters (a sign of decreased anomie) meant less embezzlement.

Institutional anomie theory has also been used to understand victim behavior in white-collar crime cases. Adam Trahan and his research team (2005) used data from a survey of 434 victims of a Ponzi scheme and information from investor files contained in prosecutors' case files to determine how the "American dream" influenced victim behavior. The survey revealed that a desire for money influenced decisions to invest in the scheme for 86 percent of the victims. Victims found it difficult to believe that they were victimized by a crime or that the offender had actually done anything criminal. After all, their efforts to invest were simply part of their American dream. The authors concluded:

> The victims of the Ponzi scheme examined here clearly sought financial success with no apparent stopping point. Prior to their involvement in the scheme, they were relatively successful. . . . Some would argue that they had already achieved the American dream. However, the American dream is entirely unattainable because it is always possible to acquire more money, status, and so forth. (p. 616)

General Strain Theory

Developing what is known as **general strain theory**, Robert Agnew (1985, 1992) used a social psychological approach to explain how crime is an adaptation to stress and frustration. Agnew highlighted three sources of strain that could lead to crime:

1. The failure to achieve positively valued goals

2. The removal or expected removal of positively valued stimuli

3. Confronting or expecting to confront negative stimuli

Agnew argued that stress leads to crime if the stress leads to negative affective states, such as anger.

First, the *failure to achieve positively valued goals* could lead to strain. In terms of white-collar crime, not being promoted, given raises, or paid fairly could result in offending. White-collar workers direct a great deal of effort toward meeting the organization's goals. If the organization meets its goals but the worker is not rewarded for his or her efforts in working toward those goals, strain occurs, and this strain could result in offending.

Second, *the removal or expected removal of positively valued stimuli* results in strain because individuals must confront losing something they find valuable. With regard to white-collar crime, individuals, who have invested so much in their careers and moved up the organizational ladder, might face stress maintaining their status. Donald Cressey's (1953) classic study of embezzling found that the embezzlers engaged in offending because they developed an "unshareable financial problem." In other words, they lost the amount of "positively valued stimuli" they needed to address their financial needs. Wheeler and his coauthors (Wheeler, Weisburd, & Bode, 1988) noted that the "fear of failing"—the fear of "losing what they have worked so hard to gain" (p. 356)—might lead these offenders to engage in misconduct. They also suggested that these types of offenders feel remorse (or "social pain") when they are caught.

Third, *confronting or expecting to confront negative stimuli* refers to instances where individuals confront negative events in their lives. Those who experience unpleasant work settings, for example, would be more prone to commit misconduct from this perspective (Van Wyk, Benson, & Harris, 2000). Surveys of 1,116 nursing home employees found that employees who reported being abused by patients were more likely to steal from patients and physically abuse them (Van Wyk et al., 2000). The authors found that motivations (confronting negative stimuli) were more important than opportunities because offenders would find or create the opportunities to commit the misconduct if they wanted to.

Langton and Piquero (2007) used data from the "Nature and Sanctions of White-Collar Criminals Study" (see Wheeler, Weisburd, & Bode, 2000) to assess the ties between strain and white-collar offending. They found that the presence of strain was related to financial motivations to offend. In addition, they found that types of strain experienced by white-collar offenders possibly vary across white-collar offenders by status. Lower-status white-collar offenders might respond more to one type of strain while higher-status white-collar offenders might respond more to other types of strain. For lower-status offenders, financial motives seemed to be more likely types of strain. For white-collar offenders, like security violators, strain appeared to be linked more often to the fear of losing one's status. The authors compared this suggestion to Wheeler et al.'s (2000) conclusion that a "fear of failing in their professional careers" might lead some upper-status workers to engage in wrongdoing.

The role that "fear of failing" plays is somewhat complex. More recently, Piquero (2012) suggested that the impact the "fear of failing" has on an offender's intentions to offend may depend on situational factors. In particular, she noted that if offenders perceive negative consequences from the offense, the "fear of failing" may actually stop individuals from offending because the negative consequences would themselves be signs of failure.

● ● ● Learning Theory and White-Collar Crime

Some criminologists have focused on the way that white-collar crime can be understood as learned behavior. The most prominent learning theory is **differential association theory**, which was developed by Edwin Sutherland. Differential association theory includes a series of nine propositions (see In Focus 12.1) that describe how individuals learn criminal behavior. The general thrust of the theory is that individuals learn from their peers through a process in which they learn how to commit crimes, why to commit those crimes, and why laws restricting those crimes are inappropriate. An often-cited example of the way that Sutherland (1949) viewed his differential association theory as explaining crime in the workplace is the comment of a shoe salesman who said that his manager conveyed the following message to him when he was hired:

> My job is to move out shoes, and I hired you to assist in this. I am perfectly glad to fit a person with a pair of shoes if we have his size, but I am willing to misfit him if it is necessary in order to sell him a pair of shoes. I expect you to do the same. If you do not like this, someone else can have your job. While you are working for me, I expect you to have no scruples about how you sell shoes. (p. 238)

Although Sutherland created both the concept of white-collar crime and the differential association theory, few studies have tested the theory's ability to explain white-collar crime. In one of the few studies, Nicole Piquero and her colleagues (Piquero, Tibbetts, & Blankenship, 2005) used data from a survey of 133 MBA students to see whether the theory would explain students' decisions to market and produce a hypothetical drug that was about to be recalled (and respondents knew this about the drug). They found support for differential association. Decisions to market the drug even though it was going to be recalled were tied more to corporate climate and coworkers' attitudes, and were not tied to connections with peers and friends outside the workplace. Put simply, if I am Bernie Madoff's coworker, I would be more likely to offend than if I were his friend or family member.

Learning theory is relevant in terms of the skills needed to commit white-collar offenses and the motives for offending. In terms of skills, many white-collar crimes involve "highly complex and technically skilled acts" (Robin, 1974, p. 259). Computer crimes, for example, often require a level of technological skills that many do not possess. Cases of embezzlement involving computers might require a similar level of skills. Physicians need certain skills to commit unnecessary surgery. Researchers need skills to fudge data. In essence, one needs the skill set required to do a job in order to commit crime on that job.

Learning theorists have suggested that in addition to learning the skills to commit white-collar crimes, white-collar offenders learn motives or reasons for committing crime on the job. Some researchers have examined how academic training influences attitudes supportive of white-collar offending. As an illustration, one author team surveyed 350 medical students to examine how the students perceived public health insurance programs and found that "the students viewed Medicare and Medicaid in the same unflattering light as physicians" (Keenan, Brown, Pontell, & Geis, 1985, p. 171). One-third of the students attributed health care fraud to structural aspects of health care programs, and many students called for structural changes of the programs to improve the ability of doctors to deliver health care to impoverished groups. What this suggests is that the students had learned to attribute fraud to an external source even before they became practicing health care professionals. In another study, a survey of 537 students compared MBA students to nonbusiness students and found that the business students "were more likely to be tolerant of business practices with ethical issues" (Yu & Zhang, 2006, p. 185). Business students tended to follow "a law-driven approach to business ethics," which suggests that "if it is legal, it is ethical" (p. 185). Somewhat ironically, the authors suggest that teaching business law classes may result in students' becoming more accepting of unethical practices (e.g., if they learn that certain behaviors are technically legal, they would be more supportive of those behaviors regardless of whether the behaviors are ethical).

Learning theory has been criticized on a number of grounds. Some have questioned the source of learning: Whom did the first "white-collar criminal" learn the skills and motives from (see R. Martin, Mutchnick, & Austin, 1990)? Randy Martin and his colleagues (1990) also note that learning theory, differential association in particular, is difficult to test empirically. Researchers have found that the actual relevance of learning from coworkers is overstated. Research by Spahr and Alison (2004) on 481 fraud offenders found that most offenders worked alone, and when there were collaborators, the co-offenders tended to come from outside the white-collar offenders' workplace.

IN FOCUS   12.1

Sutherland's Differential Association Theory

1. Criminal behavior is learned.

2. Criminal behavior is learned in interaction with other persons in a process of communication.

3. The principal part of the learning of criminal behavior occurs within intimate personal groups.

4. Learning criminal behavior includes learning the techniques of committing the crime, which are sometimes very complicated and sometimes very simple, and learning the specific direction of motives, drives, rationalizations, and attitudes.

5. The specific direction of motives and drives is learned from perceptions of various aspects of the legal code as being favorable or unfavorable.

6. A person becomes criminal when he or she perceives more favorable than unfavorable consequences to violating the law.

7. Differential associations may vary in frequency, duration, priority, and intensity.

8. The process of learning criminal behavior by association with criminal and anticriminal patterns involves all of the mechanisms involved in any other learning.

9. While criminal behavior is an expression of general needs and values, it is not excused by those general needs and values since noncriminal behavior is also an expression of the same needs and values.

Source: Excerpted From Sutherland, E. (1939). *Principles of criminology*, 3. Philadelphia: J.B. Lippincott.

● ● ● Neutralizing and Justifying White-Collar Crime

Neutralization theory was developed by Gresham Sykes and David Matza (see Matza, 1964; Sykes & Matza, 1957) in an effort to explain how juvenile delinquents drift in and out of delinquent behavior. They argued that juveniles understand right from wrong and that before they commit delinquent acts, they neutralize or rationalize their behavior as appropriate. Researchers have highlighted the difference between neutralization and accounts. Neutralizations occur before the criminal act and provide offenders the mental strength they need to commit the crime. Accounts are offered after the act and allow the offender to minimize the criminal label (Benson, 1985a). After an examination of how neutralizations are used to commit white-collar misconduct, attention will be given to the types of accounts offered by white-collar offenders to describe their behaviors and the purposes served by these accounts.

Neutralizations and White-Collar Offending

Sykes and Matza (1957) described five techniques of neutralization they believed juveniles used to rationalize their misconduct. Given that white-collar workers are rational beings, it is plausible that white-collar offenders use similar types of neutralizations. First, denial of injury refers to situations where offenders justify their actions on the grounds that no one was harmed or injured as a result of their misconduct. One study found that individuals neutralized the marketing of unsafe products by suggesting that the government overstates the degree of harm to consumers (Piquero et al., 2005).

Denial of victim refers to situations where the offenders convince themselves that victims deserve the harm they experience. As an illustration, Bernie Madoff told a fellow inmate about his misdeeds: "F*ck my victims. I carried them for 20 years and now I'm doing 150 years" (Ruiz, 2010). In embezzlement cases, this denial arises when offenders convince themselves that "the victim mistreated the offender and deserved to be victimized, the money belonged to the offender anyway" (G. Green, 1993, p. 102).

Appeal to higher loyalties neutralizations occur when offenders justify their wrongdoing by suggesting that the misbehavior was done for the good of a larger group. Instances where white-collar offenders attribute their misdeeds to efforts to help their company make a profit are indicative of an appeal to a higher loyalty (Piquero, Tibbetts, & Blankenship, 2005). As another example, situations where prosecutors allow witnesses to lie on the grounds that the lie will help achieve justice can be seen as appeals to higher loyalties. In these cases, prosecutors possibly "neutralize misconduct because they believe they are prosecuting guilty defendants" (Schoenfeld, 2005, p. 258).

Denial of responsibility refers to situations where offenders neutralize their behaviors by suggesting that they are not responsible for their misconduct. An auto repair shop owner, for example, told a colleague: "You can't be honest in this business and make a decent living" (Seibel, 2009). In another example, an offender involved in a complex fraud told investigators, "My mandate was to keep the bank running until a final solution to the financial problems is found. That was the mandate given to me by the president . . . when the security is involved . . . you do not always go by the rule of the book" (Passas, 2001, p. 130).

Condemnation of condemners is a neutralization where offenders blame the criminal justice and social control systems for their misdeeds. They argue that those who are persecuting them for their misdeeds also engage in wrongdoing. This rationalization is closely aligned with "claims that everyone does it" rationalizations. In addition, from their perspective, lenience would be a natural response from a system that is perceived to be run by individuals who engage in misconduct themselves. One offender convicted after defrauding victims in a $14 million commodities fraud scheme said that "he deserved mercy for helping fellow alcoholics like himself" ("Kingpin of Commodities Fraud," 2006).

Several studies have considered how different types of white-collar offenders justify their misdeeds with neutralizations. Paul Klenowski (2012) interviewed forty convicted white-collar offenders (20 men and 20 women) and found that each offender offered at least one neutralization. Here is how often each neutralization was offered in the interviews:

- appeal to higher loyalties (35)
- denial of injury (14)
- condemnation of the condemners (10)
- denial of victim (9)
- denial of responsibility (10)
- defense of necessity (8)
- claim of normality (11)
- claim of entitlement (10)

Research shows that older individuals are more likely to neutralize their misconduct than younger workers are (Piquero, Tibbetts, & Blankenship, 2005). Research also shows that workers learn the types of rationalizations to use on the job from their coworkers (Dabney, 1995; Klenowski, 2012) or from family and friends (Klenowski, 2012). Incidentally, of the 40 white-collar offenders interviewed by Klenowski, just over one-fourth of them learned their neutralizations on the job.

One team of researchers conducted an ethnographic study using participant observation, in-depth interviews, and survey methodologies to examine how speech therapists, occupational therapists, and physical therapists neutralized Medicaid fraud (Evans & Porche, 2005). Findings showed that "claims everyone else does it" were the most common neutralizations offered. Denials of responsibility and injury were the second and third most commonly used types of neutralization. Table 12.2 shows how these different neutralizations were offered by health care providers in situations when the providers billed for more time than was actually provided to the care recipient (e.g., they would bill for an hour after spending only 45 minutes with the patient) or submitted individual bills after providing group services.

An ethnographic study of three private veterinary practices over a 5-year time span focused on "ethical lapses" made by workers in this industry and the role of various neutralizations in promoting these misdeeds (Gauthier, 2001). The study found evidence of rationalizations paralleling those offered by Sykes and Matza (1957). For example, like a denial of responsibility, the defense of necessity was found to be "the primary justification invoked for professional lapses" (Gauthier, 2001, p. 475). This defense was frequently used to justify dishonest billing procedures. For instance, in one case, a veterinarian billed a client for euthanizing a dog when the dog had in fact died on its own. The vet wanted the dog owner to feel that the owner had made the decision to put the dog down.

Gauthier also found claims of "everyone else is doing it," particularly with regard to price fixing. The vets engaged in denial of injury, denial of victim, claims of entitlement, condemnation of condemners, and appeal to higher loyalties. In

▲ **Photo 12.2** One study examined how veterinarians use rationalizations to engage in workplace offending.

the latter case, Gauthier provides the example of billing for euthanizing a healthy animal when in fact the vet had put the pet up for adoption. Gauthier suggested this happened on at least a few occasions. In these cases, vets did not believe it was appropriate to put down a healthy animal, and their loyalty to animals led them to not euthanize the animal, even though they billed for it.

Criminologist Dean Dabney (1995) interviewed 25 nurses with a view toward identifying how differential association, social learning, and neutralization theories work together to explain deviance by nurses. His interviews showed a significant amount of deviance (23 reported engaging in theft, and all 25 said they saw their coworkers steal). Items stolen included supplies, over-the-counter medicines, and narcotics. Comments from the nurses suggested that neutralizations are learned from the workgroup "through an informal socialization process" (p. 328), and nurses used the neutralizations before committing a deviant act. They also used the neutralizations to condone misconduct by their peers.

Some researchers have found that white-collar offenders' use of neutralizations does not vary from that of traditional offenders (Stadler & Benson, 2012). In addition, researchers have explored whether there are gender differences in the use of neutralizations by white-collar offenders. Results are somewhat mixed. Surveys of 133 MBA students asking about their intentions to offend for a hypothetical corporate crime found that denial of injury impacted men's intentions more than women's, while condemnation of condemners had a stronger influence on women's intentions to offend (Vieraitis, Piquero, Piquero, Tibbetts, & Blankenship, 2012). These relationships existed at the bivariate level but disappeared when other variables were entered into the equation. The authors concluded that "there were more similarities than differences found between men and women" (p. 487).

Others have suggested that there may be qualitative differences underlying the nature of the neutralization offered by men and women (Klenowski, Copes, & Mullins, 2011). For instance, research on the data collected by Klenowski showed that when offering appeals to higher loyalties, men tended to describe their need to fill a role of breadwinner and females tended to use narratives describing a caregiver role. The accounts paralleled gendered expectations. Consider the following two appeals to higher loyalty from a man and woman respectively:

- I guess when I was committing my acts, I believed that maybe I was doing some of this for my family. I wanted to have the time and the financial security to be around my family to make sure I would be there for my children, so I guess family also subconsciously played into why I did what I did. It all boils down to power and greed and decisions you make in life, in my case, my family was part of my decision making for why I did what I did. (p. 55)

- Well what really happened is my two daughters when they were three and five years old in 1990, 1991 they were sexually abused by their father and I aligned myself with somebody that was able to pay my legal bills to fight for custody and to fight for justice in that regard so I guess I'm here because of what I did and I should be here but I don't think I should be here because of my motive. I feel like I was only doing what I had to do as a mother. (p. 59)

Similar differences were found for the other neutralizations. The authors note, for example, that for males denial of responsibility centered on the men not wanting to lose "masculine capital," while women's denials of responsibility "were culturally situated where they could safely rely upon denial of responsibility and its associated loss of agency without having their gender identity challenged" (p. 63).

Accounts and White-Collar Crime

While offenders use neutralizations to give them the mental fortitude to engage in wrongdoing, accounts are offered after the fact to describe their behaviors. An account is "a statement made by a social actor to explain unanticipated or untoward behavior" (Scott & Lyman, 1968, p. 46). Three types of accounts exist: denials, justifications, and excuses. Denials involve situations where offenders deny a specific aspect of the crime: They deny that they committed the crime, or they deny knowing anything about the crime. Types of denials attributed to white-collar offenders include the following:

- Denial of crime: Offenders say they did not commit the crime they are accused of.
- Denial of fact: Offenders deny specific aspects of the crime.
- Denial of awareness: Offenders indicate that they did not understand that their actions were violations of workplace rules.
- Denial of guilt: Offenders admit doing something but deny that the action was criminal (Payne, 2003b).

The denial of guilt may be particularly common among white-collar offenders. For example, former governor of Illinois Rod Blagojevich was convicted of using his position to "sell off" Barack Obama's senate seat, which he was charged with filling after Obama was elected president. Blagojevich never denied having conversations about filling the seat. He argued that his actions were "business as usual" in the political arena and that he was being persecuted. As another

Table 12.2	Neutralizations Offered by Speech, Occupational, and Physical Therapists
Neutralization	**Verbatim Comments Quoted by Evans and Porche (2005)**
Everyone does it	• I feel it is very accepted around here. You see it all the time. • I think it is very acceptable. It may not be right, but we all do it. (p. 260)
Denial of responsibility	• Sometimes the patient just won't work with you, especially if their family is visiting. Patients' families really interfere also. • Sometimes my patients are sick and coughing all over so I cut the session short. Other times they are just uncooperative. (p. 262)
Denial of injury	• It's not like the patients care when I end their session 5 or 10 minutes early. Most of them are eager to leave and get back to their family or the activities the nursing home has going on. • Besides, we do actually give each patient individual attention. The patients are still getting their therapy. (p. 265)

Source: Evans & Porche. (2005). Adapted from *Deviant Behavior*. Taylor & Francis.

example, John Rigas, the former chairman of Adelphia Communications, was sentenced to 15 years in prison for fraudulent accounting practices. After his conviction, he maintained that his case was not "about fraud" (Cauley, 2007). He told a reporter, "because you know, there was no fraud. . . . It was a case of being in the wrong place at the wrong time. If this had happened a year before, there wouldn't have been any headlines" (Cauley, 2007, p. 1B).

Interviews with 30 white-collar offenders by Benson (1985a) focused on the types of denials offered by white-collar offenders for their misconduct. Within the context of "denying the guilty mind," Benson showed how different types of white-collar offenders used different denials that, on the surface, seemed to be tied to the nature of each occupation where the misdeeds occurred. Antitrust offenders, for example, told Benson about the "everyday character and historical continuity of their offenses" (p. 591). They described their actions as "blameless" and condemned prosecutors, while showing how their alleged crimes were not like street crime. Tax offenders, on the other hand, commonly made claims that everyone engages in the offenses. Those who committed financial trust violations were more likely to accept responsibility for their behavior. Fraud and false statement offenders denied "committing any crime at all," and suggested that prosecutors were politically motivated and inept. Because of the nature of fraud, Benson suggested that "defrauders are most prone to denying any crime at all" (p. 597). The nature of fraud is such that offenders lie to commit the crime. They continue to lie after the crime in an attempt to conceal their offending.

In contrast to denials where offenders reject responsibility for the act, justifications are "accounts in which one accepts responsibility for the act in question but denies the pejorative quality associated with it" (Scott & Lyman, 1968, p. 47). Types of justifications offered by white-collar offenders include the following:

- Denial of law: Professionals describe the law as unfair (Coleman, 1994).
- Defense of entitlement: Workers indicate that they are underpaid, overworked, and entitled to the funds.
- Borrowing: Workers say that they planned to return the money (Coleman, 1987).
- Metaphor of the ledger: Workers suggest that occasional wrongdoings are okay (Minor, 1981).
- Denial of wrongfulness: Offenders suggest that there was nothing wrong with their behavior (Payne, 2003b).

Excuses are different from justifications and denials. Scott and Lyman (1968) defined excuses as "socially approved vocabularies for mitigating or relieving responsibility" (p. 47). Examples of excuses Scott and Lyman described that are relevant to white-collar crime include appeal to accidents, appeal to defeasibility, and scapegoating. Appeal to accidents refers to excuses where offenders describe the outcome as an accident. The portrayal of the BP oil spill by BP executives and the way that OSHA violations are constructed as accidents are examples of the "appeal to accidents" excuse type.

Appeal to defeasibility includes situations where offenders deny intent, deny knowledge, or minimize the harm surrounding the offense. Consider a case where a white-collar offender said, "I would never have done this business if I wasn't told by my lawyers that it was legal. I didn't believe in my heart of hearts that I did anything wrong" ("Kingpin of Commodities Fraud," 2006). At his sentencing, Madoff tried to minimize his intent. He told the court: "When I began the Ponzi scheme, I believed it would end shortly and I would be able to extricate myself and my clients. But, that ended up being impossible" (Healy, 2009b, p. 1).

Scapegoating refers to excuses where white-collar offenders blame others for their wrongdoing. In some cases, for example, white-collar offenders blame their billing directors and administrative staff for wrongdoing. Also, cases where corporate executives blame lower-level workers or "disgruntled" workers for corporate harm can be seen as examples of scapegoating.

Gibson (2000) discussed four types of excuses that workers make for workplace misconduct:

- "I was told to do it" (let's call this the authority excuse).
- "Everybody is doing it" (we can call this the institutional excuse).
- "My actions won't make a difference" (this can be called the minimization excuse).
- "It's not my problem" (the ostrich excuse) (p. 66).

Those who use the authority excuse might actually believe that their misconduct was the result of their being ordered by their boss to engage in the wrongful behavior. Gibson (2000) cites the power of authority as demonstrated in Stanly Milgram's *Obedience to Authority* study as an example of this power.

With regard to institutional excuses, Gibson notes that offenders know their actions are wrong, so they look around the workplace to find others who are engaging in similar acts. The minimization excuse parallels Sykes and Matza's (1957) denial of injury neutralization. Finally, the "ostrich" excuse refers to situations where workers ignore their coworkers' misdeeds because they believe that is not their responsibility to stop misconduct.

Purposes of Rationalizations and Accounts

Rationalizations and accounts serve four purposes for white-collar offenders (Payne, 2003b). First, given that white-collar offenders know right from wrong, rationalizing behavior allows them to engage in behavioral drifting: They can drift in and out of acceptable and unacceptable behavioral patterns (see Matza, 1964). Second, rationalizations and accounts promote intrinsic identity management, which simply means that they allow offenders to "maintain a positive self-image" (Payne, 2003b). Third, rationalizations and accounts promote extrinsic identity management, meaning that offenders are able to control that others see them in a positive way. Fourth, accounts allow offenders to try to minimize the types of sanctions given to them. In effect, by making excuses or using justifications, offenders can avoid punishment, reduce the sanction, and delay the sanction altogether (Payne, 2003b).

● ● ● Control Theory and White-Collar Crime

Control theory approaches the question of crime causation somewhat differently than other criminological theories. Rather than asking "why do people commit crime," the question from a control theory perspective is "why don't people commit crime" (Hirschi, 1969). Travis Hirschi (1969) answered this question in *Causes of Delinquency* by suggesting that individuals' bonds to society keep them from engaging in criminal behavior. According to Hirschi, four elements make up an individual's bond to society: attachment, belief, involvement, and commitment. Attachment refers to the degree of attachment that individuals have to their parents, schools, and other prosocial institutions. Belief refers to whether individuals believe in social rules and laws. Involvement refers to whether individuals are involved in prosocial activities, because those who are would have less time to commit criminal or delinquent acts. Commitment refers to whether individuals are committed to the values and goals prescribed by society. According to Hirschi, society is largely organized around conventional behavior, with supports and rewards given to promote conventional behavior. The theory is quite simple—the stronger an individual's societal bond is, the less likely the person will engage in criminal behavior; the weaker the bond, the more likely criminal behavior will follow. Hirschi's research confirmed his theory with the exception of his focus on involvement. He found that involvement in prosocial activities does not reduce likelihood of offending, possibly because it does not take that much time to commit a crime.

Finding that involvement in prosocial activities does not reduce criminal activities has direct implications for applying his theory to crime in the workplace. In particular, having a job is a prosocial activity, yet the fact that one has a job does not reduce the likelihood that the one will commit a white-collar crime. In fact, the very definition of white-collar crime requires that individuals have jobs at which to commit crimes. Also, one does not have to be involved in a number of outside activities in order to keep from engaging in white-collar crime (Makkai & Braithwaite, 1991).

Lasley (1988) conducted surveys of 435 executives employed by a large multinational auto manufacturing company to consider how well Hirschi's control theory explained white-collar crime. He used Hirschi's theory to develop four "theorems of white-collar offending." These theorems included the following:

- Executives with stronger attachments to their company and coworkers will have lower workplace offending rates.
- Executives with stronger commitments to "lines of action" will have lower workplace offending rates.
- Executives with stronger involvement in corporate activities will be less likely to engage in white-collar crime.
- Executives who believe in workplace rules will be less likely to violate those rules.

The results of Lasley's (1988) study showed support for Hirschi's control theory. Executives with stronger (1) attachments to their corporation, (2) commitment to "corporate lines of action," (3) stronger involvement in corporate activities, and (4) stronger belief in organizational rules were less likely to commit white-collar crime. Lasley emphasized the importance of attachment to one's organization (or the lack of attachment) as being problematic for organizations. He wrote,

> It cannot be denied, in most cases, that unpleasant attitudes held by an executive toward his or her employing organization will result in some denial of legitimacy of the controlling organization's rules and policies. For some, white-collar criminality may even be a means for relieving organizational pressures brought about by unpleasant working conditions. (p. 359)

Not all studies have found support for an application of control theory to explain white-collar crime. One study found that white-collar offenders have stronger social bonds to society, as is evidenced through participation in religious activities and membership in community organizations (Benson & Kerley, 2001). To some, bonds to a company might actually promote lawbreaking rather than inhibit it. This would be particularly likely in cases where individuals commit crime on behalf of their business. Some regard loyalty as central to corporate decision making. According to Robinson and Murphy (2009), "the reason loyalty is so important . . . is simple: loyalty means moving up in the corporate organization; disloyalty means failing" (p. 63).

● ● ● Self-Control Theory and White-Collar Crime

Self-control theory was created by Michael Gottfredson and Travis Hirschi (1990), who argued in *A General Theory of Crime* that all types of crime were caused by the presence of low self-control. Self-control was described by the theorists as "the individual characteristic relevant to the commission of criminal acts" (p. 88). They characterized individuals with low self-control as "impulsive, insensitive, physical (as opposed to mental), risk-taking, short-sighted, and non-verbal" (p. 90). According to Gottfredson and Hirschi (1990), self-control levels are tied to parenting, with bad parenting resulting in low self-control, and levels of self-control are stable throughout one's life after early childhood.

The authors put a great deal of effort into arguing that their theory explains white-collar crime and street crime, and they critiqued white-collar crime theories for being narrow in scope (see Hirschi & Gottfredson, 1987). In their first effort to describe how their general theory of crime explained white-collar crime, the authors used the concept of "criminality" to describe what is now known as self-control. They wrote that

> criminality is the tendency of individuals to pursue short-term gratification with little consideration for the long-term consequences of their act. . . . People high on this tendency are relatively unable or unwilling to delay gratification; they are relatively indifferent to punishment and to the interests of others. (p. 960)

As evidence of the ties between criminality and white-collar crime, and their suggestion that white-collar crime and street crime are caused by criminality, Hirschi and Gottfredson compared arrest data for fraud and embezzlement with murder arrests. They suggested that similar age distributions for offenders across offense types showed evidence for a general theory, with their premise being that "a major correlate of ordinary crime is similarly correlated with white-collar crime" (p. 966). They also compared gender and race data for the three offense types and found that arrest rates were similar across the offenses.

Hirschi and Gottfredson (1987) were extremely critical of white-collar crime theories that explained the behavior by focusing on the nature of the occupation rather than the characteristics of the individual offender. They argued that focusing on motives and opportunities limited to the workplace "confuse[s] social location with social causation" (p. 971). In their view, the cause of white-collar crime lies within the individual: Those with low self-control should be more prone to engage in white-collar misconduct. They also suggested that when low self-control interacts with opportunity, misconduct results (Gottfredson & Hirschi, 1990).

Several different studies have examined the utility of self-control theory in explaining various forms of occupational misconduct. Some of these studies offer support for self-control theory's applicability to white-collar crime. For example, one study found that low self-control of corporate managers was tied to corporate crime (Mon, 2002). As well, a study of 522 "fraud" and "force" offenders examined the self-control levels of the offenders and found that lower levels of self-control were more likely among those who committed more offenses (Longshore & Turner, 1998). The authors of this study found an important distinction between the two offense types: self-control was tied to fraud by the presence of criminal opportunity, but opportunity was not a factor in force crimes. In another study, surveys of 342 undergraduates revealed that the tie between low self-control and digital piracy was mediated by learning theory (Higgins, Fell, & Wilson, 2006). The authors suggested that those with low self-control must learn how to commit white-collar crimes, and they must also be presented with opportunities to offend.

Alternatively, research by Grasmick, Tittle, Bursik, and Arneklev (1993) found that self-control predicted fraud, but the presence of opportunity had independent effects on fraud. They noted that opportunity is tied to social structure and that their findings "direct attention back toward features of the social environment that influence the number and distribution of criminal opportunities" (p. 24). The authors suggested that researchers look more closely at motivations and cautioned not to assume that motivations are the same for all low self-control offenders.

In addition to being linked to offending, low self-control has been described as "a powerful predictor of victimization" (Holtfreter, Reising, & Pratt, 2008, p. 208). In terms of white-collar crime victimization, a study of 922 Florida residents by Holtfreter and her colleagues found that low self-control increases consumers' risks of fraud victimization. The authors explained that "individuals who lack self-control tend to make impulsive decisions that are associated with negative life outcomes" (p. 207). Another study found that some types of cybercrime victimization (cyber harassment, computer viruses, and stolen passwords) are tied to a low self-control among victims (Holt & Bossler, 2012).

Some studies offer mixed support for using self-control theory to explain white-collar crime. Benson and Moore (1992) analyzed presentence reports to compare 2,462 convicted white-collar offenders to 1,986 convicted conventional offenders, all of whom were convicted in federal court between 1973 and 1978. Addressing Gottfredson and Hirschi's assumption that white-collar offenders and conventional offenders share similar characteristics, Benson and Moore uncovered several differences between the two types of offenders. For instance, white-collar offenders exhibited fewer past problems in school and less excessive drinking. However, they found that white-collar offenders with more extensive criminal histories were, in fact, similar to conventional offenders.

Based on their findings, Benson and Moore suggested that self-control operates differently based on circumstances and situational factors. First, some occupational offenders with low self-control levels engage in misconduct just as conventional offenders do. These offenders commit criminal and delinquent acts somewhat frequently in the workplace. Second, high self-control offenders commit white-collar crime in order to meet organizational-economic goals that arise from our culture of competition. Third, opportunistic self-control offenders engage in misconduct as a result of personal situations (like unshareable financial problems) and do so only when opportunities are presented. Benson and Moore (1992) described this group of offenders in the following way: "If their positions in life are somehow threatened, a formerly adequate level of self-control may become inadequate and criminal opportunities that once were resisted are now accepted" (p. 257).

At least a handful of studies have found virtually no support for using self-control theory to explain various types of white-collar crime. For example, research shows that the theory does not explain corporate offending (Simpson & Piquero, 2002). Also, surveys of 1,116 nursing home workers found that self-control was not related to occupational offending in cases of theft or patient abuse (Van Wyk et al., 2000). In another study, N. L. Piquero and her coauthors (Piquero, Schoepfer, & Langton, 2010) surveyed 87 working adults enrolled in business courses using a vignette survey to determine how well self-control and desire for control explained "intentions to destroy damaging workplace documents" (p. 640). While they found that desire for control predicted intentions to offend, they also found that self-control level was not a significant predictor of offending intentions. They suggested that "self-control offers little by way of helping criminologists better understand corporate offending" (p. 642).

More recently, Schoepfer and her co-authors (2014) found that the desire for control—in comparison to low self-control—is a stronger predictor of corporate and white-collar crime, but not traditional crime. They also found that those who have a high self-control also tended to have a high desire for control. Based on this, the authors suggest that the way that self-control interacts with other variables (such as desire for control) may be a stronger predictor of white-collar crime.

Several criticisms have been cited regarding the theory's application to white-collar crime. In general, these criticisms can be classified as conceptualization issues, empirical concerns, and problems with logical consistency. With regard to conceptualization issues, scholars have noted that Gottfredson and Hirschi conceptualize crime as an irrational act, though white-collar crime is generally rational behavior (Simpson & Piquero, 2002). Also, Gottfredson and Hirschi have been critiqued for oversimplifying the complex nature of white-collar crime in their efforts to conceptualize the relationship between self-control and workplace offending (Geis, 2000; Simpson & Piquero, 2002). Criminologist Gilbert Geis (2000) noted the complexities of explaining white-collar crime and highlighted the fact that many workplace decisions are driven by complex organizational processes and structural factors. He said, "to say an absence of self-control prods the decisions of top-level business officers who violate the law is to trivialize the roots of their actions" (p. 44).

Empirical criticisms of Gottfredson and Hirschi's efforts to explain white-collar crime as based on self-control centered on the way that the authors operationalized white-collar offending (Geis, 2000; G. E. Reed & Yeager, 1996). In particular, their reliance on arrest data and their focus on the offenses of fraud and embezzlement were seen as both narrowly and ambiguously defining white-collar crime. Their empirical effort was regarded as narrow because it focused only on arrests (excluding acts that did not result in arrests) for two specific types of offenses. Their effort was also seen as ambiguous because many offenders arrested for these crimes were likely not actually white-collar offenders.

Self-control theory's application to white-collar crime has been criticized on the grounds of logical consistency. In effect, it is illogical to some to suggest that white-collar crime can be caused by low self-control because most white-collar workers would not achieve their levels of status unless they possessed high self-control (Piquero, Exum, & Simpson, 2005; Spahr & Alison, 2004). Employees higher up in the workplace theoretically should have higher levels of self-control and more job stability, and they tend to be older than conventional offenders described by Gottfredson and Hirschi (Spahr & Alison, 2004). In other words, white-collar offenders are different from conventional offenders.

Gottfredson and Hirschi (1990) addressed the issue of whether executives have high levels of self-control by critiquing white-collar crime studies. They noted that their theory would not predict a great deal of offending by white-collar employees because they recognized that most white-collar employees need a high level of self-control to ascend the workplace ladder. They suggested that some white-collar crime authors misinterpret statistics and exaggerate the extent of the problem to make white-collar crime seem more prevalent than it actually is. They also follow a strictly "legal" approach in defining white-collar crime.

● ● ● Routine Activities Theory and White-Collar Crime

Routine activities theory was developed by Cohen and Felson (1979) as a structural theory to explain how different societal changes work together to impact crime rates. In particular, the theorists contended that crime occurs when the following three elements exist at the same time and place: (1) the presence of motivated offenders, (2) the absence of capable guardians, and (3) the availability of suitable targets. As an example of their theory, they described how changes in the 1960s involving more televisions in homes (as a result of technological influences) and fewer individuals at home during the day (as a result of more women entering careers) resulted in an increase in burglaries by motivated offenders.

Various features of different types of white-collar crime discussed earlier in this text can be understood through an application of routine activities theory. Consider, for example, the following:

- A decrease in the number of workers in retail settings means that more workers are working alone in retail jobs. This means that there will not be as many capable guardians available to keep the workers from engaging in misconduct.
- The number of individuals injured in the workplace decreased significantly between 2007 and 2010. This decrease is potentially attributed to fewer individuals in manufacturing jobs. This means that there are fewer vulnerable targets for workplace injuries.
- With a downturn in the economy, businesses have been forced to become more competitive. This may mean that some businesses are more motivated to engage in such wrongdoing as false advertising or price fixing.

The theory is particularly useful for analyzing specific occupational situations to determine the likelihood of workplace crime. For example, experts have noted that the "presence of other employees close by is assumed to act as a form of guardianship" (Van Wyk et al., 2000, p. 35). In addition, research has shown that higher rates of unemployment are tied to lower rates of embezzlement (suggesting there are fewer motivated offenders available to embezzle when fewer individuals are employed) (Schoepfer & Piquero, 2006). Also, researchers have noted that consumers who engage in certain types of risky behaviors (like remote buying on the phone or Internet) are more at risk for fraud victimization (Holtfreter, Reisig, & Pratt, 2008). Another study showed that theory helped to understand white-collar crime in the European carbon market (Gibbs, Cassidy, & Rivers, 2013). As well, scholars have used the theory as a guide to determining how vulnerable different groups are for white-collar victimization and which strategies to use to reduce vulnerability (either by developing capable guardians or limiting the presence of motivated offenders). Some careers are designed to prevent white-collar crime. The Careers Responding to White-Collar Crime: General Safety and Health Inspector box provides one such career.

CAREERS RESPONDING TO WHITE-COLLAR CRIME

General Safety and Health Inspectors

General safety and health inspections typically include the following functions:

- reviewing the mine operator's records of safety inspections, health sampling, and accident reports;
- examining the condition of the roof (underground) and high wall or slope (surface) for stability and conformity with the roof or ground control plans;
- measuring the flow of air and airborne contaminants;
- examining the condition of equipment and machinery for proper maintenance and for permissibility in coal and other gassy mines;
- observing worker habits including whether workers follow good safety practices in performing duties and wear or use appropriate protective equipment;
- measuring noise levels;
- examining electrical systems, cables, and equipment for adequacy, maintenance, proper grounding, permissibility, and protection from live currents;
- examining the storage and transportation of explosives for regulatory agencies such as the Bureau of Alcohol, Tobacco, and Firearms;

- examining hoisting facilities, such as lifts and conveyors;
- examining the condition of service or haul roads for adequate clearances, grading, and maintenance;
- holding opening and close-out conferences with mine operators and labor representatives to discuss inspection; and
- advising the mine operator on methods of improving operations and/or correcting violations.

Inspectors also investigate accidents, disasters, and complaints to determine whether laws and regulations have been violated. They identify the causes of accidents and disasters and determine how they might be prevented. Sometimes the cause(s) of accidents are apparent from a few simple observations and discussions. Other times there may be no apparent explanation. Inspectors specializing in various areas of mining (such as electrical and ventilation) may be requested to make an in-depth technical analysis of the conditions and circumstances surrounding an accident.

Source: Reprinted from *Job Family Position Classification Standard for Administrative Work in the Inspection, Investigation, Enforcement, and Compliance Group, 1800.* Available online at https://www.opm.gov/policy-data-oversight/classification-qualifications/classifying-general-schedule-positions/standards/1800/1800a.pdf

Several researchers have suggested that elderly persons are more likely to be vulnerable targets or "attractive targets for consumer fraud" (Braithwaite, 1991, citing research by Fattah & Sacco, 1989). A study of medical fraud found that the vast majority of the fraudulent acts were "directed at elderly persons, regardless of whether they were receiving therapy in nursing homes, hospitals, or through home health agencies" (Evans & Porche, 2005, p. 266). Evans and Porche went on to state, "this population seemed to be viewed as the ideal population to defraud," primarily because they are seen as unlikely to report fraud. The White-Collar Crime in the News: Camera Provides Guardianship in Fraud Case box shows how one type of security effort was a capable guardian.

WHITE-COLLAR CRIME IN THE NEWS

https://commons.wikimedia.org/wiki/File:Security_Camera.JPG

Cameras are routinely used to detect crime in the workplace.

Camera Provides Guardianship in Fraud Case

Attorney General DeWine announced on November 20 that Hope Connolly was sentenced to 30 days in jail and ordered to pay $1,067.91 in restitution after she pleaded guilty to Medicaid fraud.

Connolly billed for home health aide services not rendered to two Medicaid recipients. Surveillance cameras were installed at the homes of the Medicaid recipients and Connolly was observed not providing home health aide services during times reported in her time sheets. Connolly explained that she thought her hours were flexible as long as she was "basically" working her hours. She acknowledged that it was wrong to leave early and claim the time as though she worked.

Source: National Association of Medicaid Fraud Control Units

Because of these age-related vulnerabilities, it should not be surprising that the theory has been used to address crimes in nursing homes (see Payne & Burke-Fletcher, 2005). Randy Gainey and I (see Payne & Gainey, 2006) used routine activities theory as a guide to understanding the nature of crime and victimization in a sample of 801 cases of patient abuse perpetrated by different types of occupational offenders against nursing home residents. Our research found that the image of a stressed worker as a "motivated offender" mischaracterized the apparent dynamics underlying these offenses. We identified three types of motivated offenders:

- The *serial-abuser* committed multiple offenses. Serial abusers were identified in 47.9 percent of the cases where motivation could be assessed.
- The *pathological tormentor* committed offenses to torment or control the victim. This involved 27.5 percent of the cases.
- The *stressed out caregiver* appeared to commit abuse as a reaction to something the patient did to the worker. Just under one fourth of the offenders were characterized this way.

While stress played a role in less than a fourth of the cases as a motivation for offending, in three-fourths of the cases, offenders were motivated by other factors, including histories of employee misconduct and the desire to torment patients. Here are two case descriptions of motivated offenders that we categorized as pathological tormentors:

- An aide "taped a resident's buttocks together with masking tape" (*Medicaid Fraud Report March,* 1996, p. 10).
- "A certified nursing assistant found the . . . resident with a washcloth stuffed inside her tracheotomy mask, which effectively cut off her oxygen supply. . . . Interviews with employees placed defendant in the resident's room approximately ten minutes prior to the discovery of the washcloth. [The aide] was not assigned to this resident and was under orders she was not to care for the resident because of past incidents. . . . Interviews with facility employees stated the parents of the victim would leave a note on a chalk board in the victim's room saying, 'Terri, we love you.' When the family would leave, [the aide] would go into the victim's room and erase the message. Employees have seen her turn the television set away from the resident so she could not see the screen and turn family photographs face-down so the resident could not see the photographs" (*Medicaid Fraud Report September,* 1998, p. 13).

From our analysis, we characterized vulnerable targets based on their age (older patients had increased vulnerability) and presence of cognitive impairments (which also increased vulnerability). We focused on the presence of mandatory reporting laws, which require officials to report suspected cases of elder abuse, and on penalty enhancement laws, which provide for stiffer penalties for those who abuse the elderly. Our analysis suggested that mandatory reporting laws did not affect victimization rates, and states with penalty enhancement statutes actually gave shorter prison or jail sentences than those states without the statutes. This finding calls into question whether certain types of policies can be seen as capable guardians.

● ● ● Conflict Theory and White-Collar Crime

Conflict theorists explain white-collar crime from a more critical perspective, focusing on the way that those with power exert influence in order to use the law as an instrument of power. Several different types of conflict theory exist, including but not limited to Marxist conflict theory, conservative conflict theory, radical conflict theory, anarchist criminology, left realist theory, feminist criminology, critical criminological theory, and peacemaking criminology (Bohm & Vogel, 2011; Williams & McShane, 2009). These theories tend to be macro-level theories, focusing on the way institutional forces (controlled by those with power) shape wrongdoing. While various themes are presented with these different types of conflict theories, one common theme is an assumption that power differences between classes (upper vs. lower) result in differential treatment of those without power.

Richard Quinney's *The Social Reality of Crime* (1974) is a classic work that accurately shows how class differences potentially result in differential applications of the law. In this work, Quinney outlines six propositions that demonstrate how the powerful classes exert their power to define behaviors as criminal. These propositions are as follows:

Proposition 1: Definition of crime: Crime is a definition of human conduct that is created by authorized agents in a politically organized society.

Proposition 2: Formulation of criminal definitions: Criminal definitions describe behaviors that conflict with the interests of the segments of society that have the power to shape public policy.

Proposition 3: Application of criminal definitions: Criminal definitions are applied by the segments of society that have the power to shape the enforcement and administration of criminal law.

Proposition 4: Development of behavior patterns in relation to criminal definitions: Behavior patterns are structured in segmentally organized society in relation to criminal definitions, and in this context persons engage in actions that have relative probabilities of being defined as criminal.

Proposition 5: Construction of criminal conceptions: Conceptions of crime are constructed and diffused in the segments of society by various means of communication.

Proposition 6: The social reality of crime: The social reality of crime is constructed by the formulation and application of criminal definitions, the development of behavior patterns related to criminal definitions, and the construction of criminal conceptions (Quinney, 1974, pp. 15–23, as cited in Martin et al., 1990, pp. 389–390).

Quinney's thesis is that powerful classes use the law to exert influence over less powerful classes. In particular, the way law is developed, enforced, and applied is seen as a tool for increasing the amount of power that controlling groups have over minority groups. This assumption parallels many aspects of white-collar crime. Consider that many types of white-collar offending are not typically defined as criminally illegal. Doctors, for example, do not go to jail for making medical errors. Corporate executives are not sent to prison for creating unsafe products. Environmental pollution is defined as a cost of doing business, and those exposed to the pollutants are defined as unfortunate but are not defined as crime victims. As criminologist Ronald Kramer and his colleagues (Kramer, Michalowski, & Kauzlarich, 2002) note, "the social process of naming crime is significantly shaped by those who enjoy the economic and political power to ensure that the naming of crime . . . will reflect . . . their worldview and interests" (p. 266).

Conflict theorists are concerned not only with how crime is defined but also with how crime is perceived and addressed by criminal justice officials. With regard to perceptions about crime, conflict theorists would draw attention to the misguided perception that white-collar offenders are less serious offenders than conventional offenders. For example, some criminal justice officials have justified shorter prison sentences for white-collar offenders in the following two ways: (1) "Prison is much harder" on white-collar offenders than it is on conventional offenders, and (2) "it is not class bias to consider prison a greater hardship for the middle class because the loss of reputation is very serious" (Pollack & Smith, 1983, p. 178). To conflict theorists, such perceptions are inaccurate, unfair, and reflective of the influence that powerful classes have over those that are less powerful.

In a similar way, conflict theorists are critical of the criminal justice system's response to white-collar offending. Some criticize the system for punishing white-collar offenders too leniently, though it will be shown in a later chapter that convicted white-collar offenders may not be receiving sentences as lenient as believed. Others point out that most white-collar offenders commit a "prison escape" by preventing their cases from being brought into the criminal justice system in the first place (Gerber, 1994). Conflict theorists also point out that the overemphasis on street crimes (like the war on drugs) and lack of emphasis on white-collar crimes are indicative of unfair treatment of less powerful groups. They further stress that large companies control how laws are made, how businesses are regulated, and the amount of resources devoted to battling different types of crime (Pontell, Black, & Geis, 2014).

More than a quarter century ago, Kramer (1984) pointed to six proposals to control corporate crime that had been identified in studies conducted between 1975 and 1982. Quoted verbatim from Kramer, these proposals included the following:

- New criminal laws that deal specifically with harmful actions engaged in by corporate (organizational) entities;
- The adoption of a proactive enforcement stance with regard to corporate crime;
- The creation of special corporate crime units within enforcement agencies;
- Changing the law to make it easier to convict corporations in a criminal court;
- Increasing the level of fines for corporations;
- The creation of new sanctions which penetrate the corporate structure, that is, reach inside and attempt to restructure its management structure and decision making process. (p. 9)

Those approaching white-collar crime from a conflict theory orientation would note that only one of these six proposals has been fulfilled over the past three decades: The size of fines has increased. Interestingly, these fines can be used by the criminal justice system to increase the power that it has over less powerful groups. Indeed, one could envision a study concluding this year with these same implications. In effect, conflict theorists draw attention to the apparent lack of interest that some officials have in treating behaviors "close to home" as criminal behavior.

● ● ● Explaining Corporate Crime

Thus far, the discussion of theories has focused primarily on explaining individual behavior in white-collar crimes. Recall from the discussion in the corporate crime chapter that in some cases, the crime is committed either by the organization or for the good of the organization. The nature of corporate crime is such that individual-level variables may not sufficiently explain the misconduct. As a result, several theorists have devoted specific attention to explaining corporate crime. One thing is clear from these efforts—while it is difficult to explain individual behavior, it may be even more difficult to explain corporate behavior (Albanese, 1984). Describing the conceptual roadblocks that arise when trying to explain corporate crime, Tillman and Pontell (1995) said that organizations "have a dual nature." They explained organizations this way: "They both structure and constrain action by providing a context in which decisions are made, while at the same time existing as resources to be used by individual actors or groups to further their interests" (p. 1459).

Punch (2008) suggested that the "corporate setting provides MOM—motive, opportunity, and means." He described motives as including power, growth, profit, and so on. He said that the opportunity for offending occurs in boardrooms and executive offices that are not policed. The means for offending refers to the strategies employers use to carry out corporate offending. While Punch provides a simple framework for explaining corporate crime, the nature of the offending is so complex that identifying precise predictors of the behavior is not a simple task. In general, explanations of corporate crime have focused on (1) the structure of the organization, (2) organizational processes, and (3) dynamic organizational explanations.

Organizational Structure and Corporate Crime

Some theorists have noted how variables related to an organization's structure are also related to corporate crime. For example, Tillman and Pontell (1995) suggested that corporate crime is more often found in larger organizations, organizations growing quickly, and organizations with complex ownership structures. Other authors have also suggested that size and complexity influence corporate crime (Punch, 2008). One author suggested that corporate crime is more likely in larger organizations because larger businesses (1) see penalties as a cost of doing business and (2) are more resistant to any stigma that arises from misconduct (Yeager, 1986).

Organizational Processes and Corporate Crime

Theorists have also described the way that organizational processes influence wrongdoing. From this orientation, one can consider the definition of corporation offered by Ermann and Lundman (2002): "Organizations are collections of positions that powerfully influence the work-related thoughts and actions of the replaceable people who occupy positions in them" (p. 6). The notion of "replaceable people" is particularly important. Coleman (1982) described the "irrelevance of persons," writing that "persons have become, in a sense, that [which] was never before true, incidental to a large fraction of the productive activity in society" (p. 26).

Corporations have goals, and rules are assigned that prescribe behaviors corporate actors are expected to follow in their efforts to attain corporate goals. Although goals and rules are prescribed, there is evidence that pressure from the top of an organization may encourage wrongdoing by employees. Describing this top-down pressure, it has been suggested that "organizations, like fish, rot from the head down" (Jenkins & Braithwaite, 1993, p. 220). Another way to suggest it is that those with power influence "replaceable people" to engage in misconduct so that they, the replaceable people, do not become *replaced*. Simpson and Piquero (2002) note that "when employees are ordered to do something by a supervisor, most will do what is expected of them because they are only partial moral agents, limited in their responsibility and liability" (p. 537).

Figure 12.1 shows the cycle of corporate crime following a process-oriented explanation of corporate crime. Employees learn rules of what is expected in their corporation. In some cases, organizational rules may come into conflict with societal laws. The employees' behaviors, because the employees are replaceable, may break societal laws to further the organization's goals. Employees are rewarded for helping the organization move toward its goals. If they are caught

Figure 12.1   The Cycle of Corporate Crime

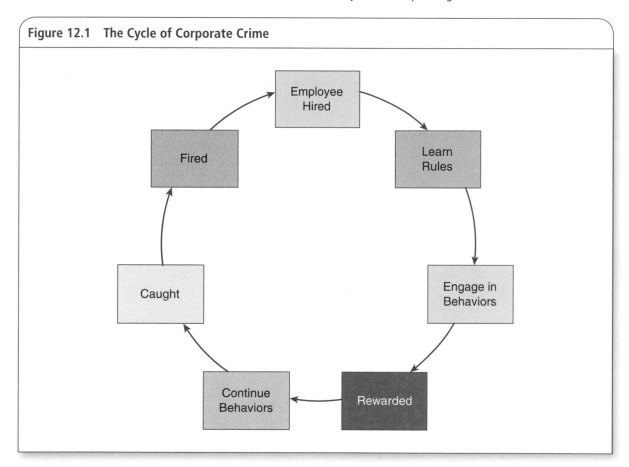

breaking the rules, they may be fired. In such cases, new employees are hired into the position (after all, employees are replaceable people), and the cycle begins anew.

Dynamic Organizational Explanations and Corporate Crime

Dynamic organizational theories explore the links among societal factors, organizational processes, and individual motivation. These approaches recognize the limited nature of other organizational theories in explaining corporate crime. Simpson and Piquero (2002) called for an integration of organizational theories in order to develop stronger explanations of corporate misconduct. They theorized that less successful firms might engage in misconduct in order to become more successful; however, individuals in those firms must accept and conduct wrongdoing in order for misconduct to occur. Based on this, they call for the integration of macro- and micro-level theories and develop their own organizational contingency theory to "explain the circumstances and conditions under which corporate crime is likely" (p. 515). In line with this thinking, Simpson and Koper (1997) demonstrated how both external (political changes, market pressures, competition levels, legal changes) and internal dynamics (changes in organizational management) potentially influence corporate wrongdoing.

Simpson and Piquero (2002) conducted a factorial survey with 96 students to examine the impact of organizational factors and self-control on attitudes about offending. They found that self-control and organizational factors (e.g., corporate offending propensity) were not tied together; however, they also found that "variables consistent with an integrated materialistic and cultural organizational theory predicted managers' offending intentions" (p. 309). They found additional support for integrating macro- and micro-level explanations. Managers were more likely "to offend if they perceived career benefits," and concerns about job security kept some from offending. They summarized their findings:

> Offending is more likely when companies are not doing well economically and when illegality is apt to garner significant financial gains for the firm. . . . Managers who believed their illegal act would negatively affect the firm's reputation were significantly less willing to offend. (p. 536)

Diane Vaughan (1992) has also noted the importance of bringing together the micro- and macro-levels to explain corporate offending. According to Vaughan, "the link between individual choice and the structural determinants of those choices is paramount to understanding misconduct both in and by organizations" (p. 134). Vaughan's theory of organizational offending uses Merton's theory as a framework to link together individual and institutional motivations. According to Vaughan, three features of the interactions between individuals and the organizations where they work promote crime in the organization:

- A competitive environment generating pressures for organizational law violations
- Organizational characteristics, including processes that provide opportunities for offending
- A relationship with regulators that minimizes the likelihood of detection and prosecution

When these elements are present in an organization, the likelihood of corporate misconduct increases. If a corporation, for example, places a great deal of pressure on its employees and there is little likelihood that regulators will catch employees breaking rules for the good of the organization, then employees will be more prone to commit wrongful acts.

● ● ● Theories Ignored in the White-Collar Crime Literature

At least a handful of criminological theories have received very little, if any, attention in white-collar crime studies. This is unfortunate because the strength of these "ignored" theories can be assessed by determining whether the theories explain white-collar crime and our understanding about white-collar crime could be advanced through an application of different theories to the behavior. Theories that warrant more attention in the white-collar crime literature include the following:

- Life course theory
- Social disorganization theory
- Gender theories
- Labeling theory
- Biological theories

Life Course Theories and White-Collar Crime

Life course theory uses a social psychological orientation to identify how events early in one's life course shape experiences later in one's life (Payne & Gainey, 2009). The theory is regularly used to explain violence, with a great deal of research showing that many, but not all, individuals who have violent childhoods also have violent adulthoods. As Michael Benson and Kent Kerley (2001) note, white-collar crime researchers have not used life course theory to address white-collar crime, and life course theorists have not used white-collar crime to test the theory. The authors note that such a gap between the two areas of research is problematic because of research showing relatively lengthy criminal histories among many white-collar offenders and evidence that white-collar offenders do not fit "the stereotypical image of the white-collar offender as a person who comes from the privileged sectors of society" (p. 121). In other words, a need exists to consider the past lives of white-collar offenders in order to understand how past experiences influenced decision making in offending.

To address this obvious gap in the white-collar crime literature, Benson and Kerley (2001) compared the life histories of a sample of convicted conventional offenders with a sample of convicted white-collar offenders. The authors culled data from the presentence investigation reports of offenders convicted in eight federal districts between 1973 and 1978. Their analysis showed that the life histories of white-collar and conventional offenders were different. White-collar offenders were much more likely to come from intact families and less likely to have problems in school. They were more likely to be involved in prosocial activities, had fewer prior arrests, and were older when their criminal careers began.

Benson and Kerley (2001) point to the need to consider how turning points later in life contribute to white-collar offending. Possible turning points they identify include dire family consequences, stressors related to occupational dynamics, and changes in business revenues. In addition to calling for more attention being directed toward the causes and consequences of white-collar crime for individual offenders, the authors suggest that white-collar crime be examined "as a social event in the life course" (p. 134).

Piquero and Benson (2004) described the need to expand the use of life course theory to address white-collar crime. They highlighted the differences between white-collar and conventional offenders, and also the similarities, to provide a framework that future researchers could use to address white-collar crime from a life-course perspective. As Piquero and Benson (2004) pointed out, "we simply need more information about the life histories of white-collar offenders" (p. 160).

In an effort to fill this void, Morris and El Sayed (2013) used longitudinal data over a sixteen-year time frame from the National Youth Survey Family Study in order to identify white-collar crime patterns over the life course. In general, the authors identified three patterns of white-collar offending: intermittency, periodic amplified offending, and persistent offending. They found that intermittency was a particularly common characteristic with rates of offending going up and down over time.

Social Disorganization Theory and White-Collar Crime

Social disorganization theory suggests that a neighborhood's crime rate is shaped by the ability of its members to agree on and work toward a common goal, such as crime control. The ability of a neighborhood to be organized is predicted to be determined by neighborhood structural characteristics, in particular the mobility of its population, racial and ethnic heterogeneity, and poverty. Thus, neighborhoods that are less able to agree to work together toward controlling criminal behavior tend to have the following in common: A large percentage of the residents do not stay very long (a mobile population), residents are a diverse mix from different racial and ethnic origins, and many of the residents are poor. Many studies have found strong support for the idea that social disorganization breeds street crime.

At least one study used social disorganization theory to assess the factors that business owners take into account when deciding which types of crime-prevention tools to use (Casten & Payne, 2008). Not surprisingly, business owners consider neighborhood factors in deciding how to develop loss-prevention strategies.

What is not clear is whether social disorganization contributes to white-collar crime. Such a question could be addressed several different ways. For example, it would be useful to identify whether retail settings in disadvantaged areas have more employee theft than retail settings in more advantaged areas. In addition, it would be interesting to determine

▲ **Photo 12.3**   Would you expect white-collar crime to occur in this neighborhood? Why or why not?

whether corporations located in disadvantaged areas have different rates of regulatory violations than corporations located in non-disadvantaged areas. As well, more research needs to be done on the way white-collar crime promotes social disorganization in disadvantaged communities. It seems as though the application of social disorganization theory to white-collar crime is an area ripe for empirical efforts.

Gender Theories and White-Collar Crime

Gender theories are also underrepresented in the white-collar crime literature. These theories call attention to the need to consider crime from the perspective of women (Danner, 1998). In "Three Strikes and It's *Women* Who Are Out: The Hidden Consequences for Women of Criminal Justice Policy Reforms," Mona Danner outlines the way that laws such as three strikes policies negatively impact women. Similar questions arise with regard to white-collar crime theories and policies: (1) how do white-collar crime policies impact women? (2) do patriarchal values contribute to white-collar crime? (3) are women disproportionately victims of certain types of white-collar crime? and (4) how can the feminist perspective promote understanding about white-collar crime?

Research by Kathleen Daly (1989) shows that theories used to explain women's involvement in white-collar crime may need to be different from those traditionally used to explain men's involvement in workplace offending. Reviewing data from Wheeler et al.'s data set of white-collar offenders, Daly found significant differences between male and female white-collar criminals. She found that many of the women did not fit the image of the typical upper-class white-collar offender. A third of the women were unemployed, and many who worked were in clerical positions, while many of the men worked in managerial positions.

In addition, the women were less likely to have college degrees and more likely to non-white. Daly found that that their crimes were better described as "occupational marginality" as opposed to mobility (the women worked on the fringes of the organization rather than in its upper echelons). She also found that women were more likely to work alone in their offending, and financial need was more commonly a motive for them. Daly notes that individuals do not need a white-collar job to commit the crimes of embezzlement, fraud, and forgery. Citing research by Howe (1977), she notes that a "'pink-collar world' suffices, as does having no ties to the labor market" (p. 179). Daly argues that white-collar crimes by women should be addressed with theories—not with a focus on how the crimes "deviate" from men's white-collar crimes; instead, "women's illegalities should be explained on their own terms" (p. 790).

Recent research shows that women are more likely to (1) support regulations in the corporate environment (Piquero, Vieraitis, Piquero, Tibbetts, & Blankenship, 2013) and (2) have lower intentions to commit corporate crime (Vieraitis et al., 2012). In the most comprehensive study on the topic to date, Darrell Steffensmeier and his co-authors (2013) developed a database including 436 defendants from 83 corporate crimes. They found that women were infrequently involved in these offenses and pointed to two pathways that brought women into the offenses: (1) relational pathways where women were involved because of a personal relationship with a coconspirator and (2) utility pathways where women held a "financial-gateway corporate position" that offenders had to go through in order to commit the offense (p. 448). In all, 91 percent of the offenders were men and three-fourths of the corporate crime groups were all-male groups. Mixed-sex offending groups were more common in industries where women tended to be employed more, such as health care, real estate, and insurance. Over half of the female corporate offenders received no profit from their offenses. Those women were primarily in the "utility role" because the male offenders had to "go through" them to commit the crime. Prosecutors then appeared to also use women in a "utility role," using them to make a case against other offenders.

Labeling Theory and White-Collar Crime

Labeling theory focuses on the way that individuals develop criminal labels. Some labeling theorists have suggested that the process of labeling individuals certain ways results in behaviors consistent with those labels. The notion of "self-fulfilling prophecy" comes to mind. It is widely accepted, for example, that if children are treated as intelligent, then they will be more likely to show signs of intelligence. If children are labeled as bad, then they will be more likely to misbehave. Criminologist Ruth Triplett (1993) has noted that it is not simply the process of being labeled that results in deviant outcomes; instead, negative labels increase the number of delinquent peers one has, which can increase support for subsequent misconduct. In other words, some individuals are able to reject negative labels, while others might respond to the labels by joining forces with others who have the same delinquent or criminal label.

The way labeling relates to white-collar crime has been only tangentially addressed in the literature. Research by Benson (1985a) shows how white-collar offenders reject the criminal label and use that as a coping strategy to deal with the consequences of their sanction. Elsewhere, Benson (1990) wrote the following:

> Few events produce stronger emotions than being publicly accused of a crime. Especially for the individual who has a stake in maintaining a legitimate persona, the prospect of being exposed as a criminal engenders "deep emotions" (Denzin, 1983): shame, humiliation, guilt, depression, and anger. (p. 515)

Consistent with Triplett's hypothesis, if convicted white-collar offenders avoid contacts with other offenders and reject the criminal label, they should be less prone to reoffend. Alternatively, the labeling of white-collar offenders as criminals may serve to increase their offending if the strength of the labeling is such that white-collar offenders are not able to reject the label. Such a label could create additional opportunities for offending. David Weisburd and his colleagues (Weisburd, Waring, & Chayet, 1995) described this process in the following way:

> Once prestige and status are lost, they may be perceived as difficult to regain. Once the cost of illicit behavior has been minimized, recidivism may be more likely. In some sense, the model of a spiraling process of deviance set into play by a labeling experience (Wilkins, 1965, cited in Weisburd et al., 1995) may be more appropriate for white-collar criminals than for the common criminals for whom the concept was initially developed. (p. 590)

It is plausible that labels attach differently based on offender type. Labeling a young male in a disadvantaged community as a gang member or criminal may serve to increase his social status in his community, and the rewards that come along with being labeled a criminal could perpetuate wrongdoing (Triplett, 1993). Labeling an older male in an affluent community a white-collar criminal would not increase his social status in his neighborhood. The negative consequences of the "white-collar criminal" label, as opposed to the rewards that others might get from the criminal label, might actually serve to promote future wrongdoing. Such an assumption has not yet been addressed in the white-collar crime literature. Indeed, research on how labels affect white-collar criminality is needed.

Biological Theories

Early explanations of crime cited biological factors as contributing to criminal behavior among traditional criminals. These explanations fell out of favor in the early 1900s when sociological theories became the more preferred explanations. In recent years, a small group of criminologists have reintroduced the possibility that biological factors contribute to criminal behavior (see Armstrong & Boutwell, 2012; Madden, Walker, & Miller, 2008; Rader, 2008; Robinson, 2004; Walsh, 2002; D. E. Wright, Titus, & Cornelison, 2008; J. P. Wright, Tibbetts, and Daigle, 2008). It makes sense that biological explanations might contribute to criminal behavior; after all, our biological make-up contributes to "normal" behavior. Why wouldn't it then contribute to criminal behavior?

Photo Courtesy of ICE.

▲ **Photo 12.4**   Sometimes, being labeled a criminal creates rewards in terms of increased status for conventional offenders. For white-collar offenders, the label of "criminal" is unlikely to result in status-related rewards.

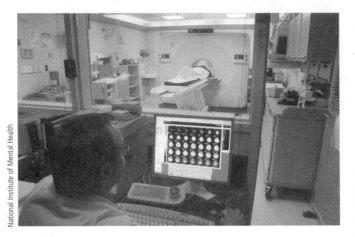

National Institute of Mental Health

▲ **Photo 12.5**   Do you think white-collar offenders' brains are different from nonoffenders' brains?

A study conducted on white-collar crime and biological factors was recently conducted by Adrian Raine and his co-authors (2012). The research team compared neurobiological traits of 21 white-collar offenders and 21 nonoffenders, who were matched based on demographic variables. They hypothesized that certain neurobiological factors might make it easier for white-collar individuals to offend. These included superior executive functioning, attentional functions, and enhanced brain cortical thickness. The researchers conducted a series of medical tests, including MRIs, on the sample group. Interestingly, their research found that white-collar offenders' neurobiological factors (and brains) were different from nonoffenders. In particular, the researchers found "White-collar criminals demonstrate better executive functions, increased and sustained orienting, increased arousal, and increased cortical thickness in multiple brain regions subserving decision-making, social cognition, and attention" (Raine et al., 2012, p. 2937).

This study marked one of the first (if not the first) study applying biological factors to white-collar crime. Many other questions remain fodder for future biological criminologists. In particular, researchers could examine whether neurobiological factors vary across types of white-collar offenders. Also, researchers could explore whether white-collar crime creates biological consequences that may lead to further crime. For example, does pollution lead to birth defects, and if it does, do those defects lead to higher levels of aggression among those with the birth defects? Examining questions such as these will provide a broader picture of those factors contributing to white-collar crime.

● ● ● Integrated Efforts to Explain White-Collar Crime

Thus far, the various theoretical perspectives addressing white-collar crime have been discussed separately. Many scholars, however, have suggested that the best way to explain white-collar crime is to use an integrated approach that brings together multiple perspectives (Gerber, Jensen, & Fritsch, 1996). Even among specific types of occupations, misconduct by employees is likely not "a unidimensional phenomenon" (Hollinger, Slora, & Terris, 1992, p. 155).

The call for integrated theories gained popularity in criminology in the mid- to late-1980s, so the importance of bringing together multiple perspectives is not a new idea. The value of theoretical integration is demonstrated in the way that Donald Cressey (1953) explained the causes of embezzlement in *Other People's Money*. Later, summarizing Cressey's research, Green (1993) highlighted four steps that Cressey saw as leading to embezzlement:

- An unshareable financial problem
- Embezzlement defined as a means to fix the financial problem
- An offender with the skills to commit the crime
- Neutralizations to give the offender the mental strength to commit the crime

In these steps, one can point to the linking together of four different theoretical perspectives: (1) The unshareable financial problem relates to strain theory, (2) the values suggesting that it is OK to steal can be linked to cultural theory, (3) the skills needed to steal can be linked to learning theory, and (4) the neutralization can be linked to neutralization theory.

Other researchers have noted the need to use integrated models to explain different forms of white-collar misconduct. Makkai and Braithwaite (1991) conducted a multimethod study involving interviews with regulatory officials, surveys of nursing home directors, and reviews of compliance data to determine how well four theories addressed violations by nursing homes: control theory, opportunity theory, subcultural theory, and differential association theory. They found that none of the theories on their own predicted compliance rates and called for theory integration to explain regulatory violations by nursing homes. As well, describing how strain (or greed) leads to white-collar crime, one author team showed how various factors, such as individual personality characters, social controls, personal controls, reward and punishment, loyalty, executive ideology, and opportunity, work together to foster misconduct in the workplace (Robinson & Murphy, 2009).

● ● ● Systems Theory

As noted throughout this book, **systems theory** offers a foundation from which white-collar crime can be addressed. The theory does not explain why white-collar crime occurs on an individual level; instead, it provides insight into the interconnections among various societal systems and the way that various systems influence white-collar wrongdoing.

As an illustration, activities in the political system have a direct influence on white-collar misconduct. For example, changes in the political system routinely lead to changes in the health care system. These systemic changes are tied to changes in the social, educational, and technological systems. Together, these changes influence the types of crimes committed in the health care system. Consider the nature of crimes committed in the home health care field:

> In the late 1980s and early 1990s, changes in health care payment plans encouraged hospitals to shorten hospital stays, technological advancements allowed hospital equipment to be mobile, and a graying population led to an explosion in the use of home health care services. . . . In the state-operated Medicaid system, which serves the impoverished population, home health care spending quadrupled between 1985 and 1992. (Payne & Gray, 2001, p. 210)

During this same time frame, the amount of fraud occurring in the home health care industry increased dramatically as well.

Also, showing how the political system influences white-collar crime, some have attributed white-collar crime to types of economic policies developed in legislation (Mon, 2002). From this perspective, researchers have blamed the rampant fraud found in the savings and loan industry in the late 1980s on federal policies promoting deregulation (Glasberg & Skidmore, 1998a). Under deregulation policies, rules governing thrifts and savings and loan companies were changed "so that the behaviors that previously fell within the definition of corporate or executive crime were no longer violations but, rather, were enabled by the structure of the legislation" (Glasberg & Skidmore, 1998b, p. 124). Among other things, deregulation policies relaxed federal control over interest rates, provided federal insurance on deposits up to $100,000 for thrift institutions, and removed "restrictions on the intermingling of commercial banking, real estate, and securities investing," thereby encouraging the institutions to engage in risky behaviors (Glasberg & Skidmore, 1998a, p. 432). Pontell (2005) suggested that financial policies were too lax and wrote: "Public policies that 'white-wash' white-collar crime and that do not explicitly recognize the potential devastation of control fraud, will not only be ineffective, but will serve as virtual blueprints for financial disasters" (p. 319). Indeed, scholars argued that the deregulation policies resulted in the collapse of the thrift industry, with billions lost to fraud perpetrated by those employed in the industry (Calavita et al., 1997).

Glasberg and Skidmore (1998a) attributed the failure of deregulation and the fraud that resulted to "unintended consequences of the dialectics of state projects" (p. 424). They pointed to the need to look at how external factors came together to foster misbehavior by organizations in the thrift industry and called attention to the need to address how policies are implemented and the consequences of those policies (Glasberg & Skidmore, 1998b). In other words, in line with systems theory, they recognized that policymaking in the political arena will impact other societal systems.

The activities of other systems and behaviors of individuals in those systems also demonstrate how white-collar crime can be understood from a systems perspective. Consider the following:

- It has been argued that the criminal justice system's crackdown on different types of white-collar crime in the 1980s occurred because the government viewed white-collar crime as "undermin[ing] the legitimacy of the political and financial systems" (Newbold & Ivory, 1993, p. 245).
- With changes in the economic system, it is possible that "downsizing will promote more corporate crime because corporate personnel will be especially pressured to take risks to maximize profits as an alternative to the public trauma associated with downsizing" (Friedrichs, 1997, p. 360). Friedrichs also noted that economic changes could inhibit wrongdoing because people are more afraid of losing their jobs in times of downsizing. Whether corporate downsizing leads to, or prevents, white-collar crime, it seems safe to suggest that such changes at the broader economic and corporate system levels have direct bearing on white-collar offending.
- Technological changes in the technological system influence the commission of white-collar crime and the way the justice system responds to the crimes (Croall, 1989). One author team noted that the "criminal law cannot keep up with a technologically advanced, constantly changing business environment" (Simpson & Koper, 1992, p. 367). In a similar way, highlighting how changes in the technological system influence the criminal justice system, Albanese (1984) wrote, "increasing sophistication of law enforcement techniques may produce only more sophisticated forms of organized crime" (p. 18).

Again, the main premise of systems theory is that all systems are interrelated. Changes in one system will lead to changes in other systems. Such changes have direct implications for the commission of white-collar crime and appropriate response strategies.

SUMMARY

- Criminological theory is central to the study of white-collar crime. It is important to stress that theories are potential explanations of behaviors or phenomena, and for white-collar crime explanations to have practical utility, the theories or explanations must point to changes that would reduce (rather than increase) white-collar misconduct.
- Some criminologists attribute white-collar crime to cultural influences that seemingly promote wrongdoing by workers and corporations. James Coleman (1987), for example, argued that industrial capitalism promotes a "culture of competition."
- Deterrence theory can be traced to Cesare Beccaria's *On Crimes and Punishments*, a work that many have defined as the foundation of the classical school of criminological thought. Research by Sally Simpson and various colleagues has been instrumental in demonstrating how deterrence ideals can be used to explain various forms of workplace misconduct.
- Three types of strain theories were discussed: classical strain theory, institutional anomie theory, and general strain theory.
- Classical strain theory traces the source of strain to interactions between the social and economic structures.
- In *Crime and the American Dream,* Steve Messner and Richard Rosenfeld (2007) describe how society promotes values related to financial success but fails to promote values consistent with using legitimate means to attain financial success.
- Developing what is known as general strain theory, Robert Agnew (1985, 1992) used a social psychological approach to explain how crime is an adaptation to stress and frustration.
- Some criminologists have focused on the way that white-collar crime can be understood as learned behavior. The most prominent learning theory is differential association theory, which was developed by Edwin Sutherland.
- Sykes and Matza (1957) described five techniques of neutralization they believed juveniles used to rationalize their misconduct. Given that white-collar workers are rational beings, it is plausible that white-collar offenders use similar types of neutralizations.

- While offenders use neutralizations to give them the mental fortitude to engage in wrongdoing, accounts are offered after the fact to describe their behaviors.
- Rather than asking, "why do people commit crime," the question from a control theory perspective is, "why don't people commit crime" (Hirschi, 1969). Some have regarded loyalty as central to corporate decision making.
- Self-control theory was created by Michael Gottfredson and Travis Hirschi (1990), who argued in *A General Theory of Crime* that all types of crime are caused by the presence of a low self-control. Hirschi and Gottfredson (1987) were extremely critical of white-collar crime theories that explained the behavior by focusing on the nature of the occupation rather than the characteristics of the individual offender.
- Routine activities theory suggests that crime occurs when the following three elements exist at the same time and place: (1) the presence of motivated offenders, (2) the absence of capable guardians, and (3) the availability of suitable targets.
- Conflict theorists explain white-collar crime from a more critical perspective, focusing on the way those with power exert influence in order to use the law as an instrument of power.
- The nature of corporate crime is such that individual-level variables may not sufficiently explain the misconduct. In general, explanations of corporate crime have focused on (1) the structure of the organization, (2) organizational processes, and (3) dynamic organizational explanations.
- Theories that warrant more attention in the white-collar crime literature include life course theory, social disorganization theory, gender theories, and labeling theory.
- Many scholars have suggested that the best way to explain white-collar crime is to use an integrated approach that brings together multiple perspectives.
- As noted throughout this book, systems theory offers a foundation from which white-collar crime can be addressed. The theory does not explain why white-collar crime occurs on an individual level; instead, it provides insight into the interconnections among various societal systems and the way that various systems influence white-collar wrongdoing.

KEY TERMS

Appeal to higher loyalties	Differential association theory	Rebels
Biological theory	General strain theory	Retreatists
Collective embezzlement	Innovators	Ritualists
Condemnation of condemners	Institutional anomie	Routine activities theory
Conflict theorists	Labeling theory	Scapegoating
Control theory	Learning theory	Self-control theory
Denial of responsibility	Life course theory	Social disorganization theory
Denial of victim	Neutralization theory	Strain theory
Deterrence theory	Rational choice theory	Systems theory

DISCUSSION QUESTIONS

1. Which theory do you think most accurately explains white-collar crime? Which one is least effective? Why?

2. Watch the movie *Office Space* and apply four different theories to the movie.

3. How can theory influence the criminal justice system's response to white-collar crime? Explain.

4. Select two theories and explain how white-collar crime prevention strategies might be developed using those theories.

5. Are white-collar offenders born to be bad? Explain.

6. Find two examples of white-collar crimes in recent news articles. Apply two theories of white-collar crime to the articles.

7. Which types of rationalizations do you think are most commonly used by white-collar offenders? Are there any rationalizations that you think justify white-collar misconduct?

8. Do you think corporations cause people to commit crime? Explain.

WEB RESOURCES

Factors Which Allow the Problem to Continue: http://www.crimes-of-persuasion.com/laws/problems.htm

Criminological Theory on the Web: http://www.umsl.edu/~keelr/200/Diane_Demelo/diane.pdf

STUDENT RESOURCES

The open-access Student Study Site, available at study.sagepub.com/paynewccess2e, includes useful study materials including SAGE journal articles and multimedia resources.

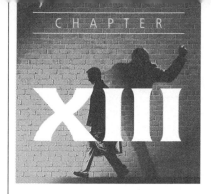

XIII

Policing White-Collar Crime

CHAPTER HIGHLIGHTS

- Agencies Involved in Responding to White-Collar Crime
- Law Enforcement Strategies and White-Collar Crime
- Suggestions for Improving the Law Enforcement Response to White-Collar Crime
- Self-Policing and White-Collar Crime
- Regulatory Policing and White-Collar Crime
- The Global Police and White-Collar Crime

In his senior year of college, criminology student Garrett Speaks was approached by his professor and told about an opportunity that ultimately shaped his career. In particular, Speaks was told that the attorney general's office was searching for a possible undercover agent to send into nursing homes in an effort to detect misconduct by nursing homes. After meeting with the investigator overseeing the investigation, Speaks was selected to participate in the undercover investigation. He had to change his identity from criminology student to nurse's aide. He went through a nurse's aide training program to receive the necessary certification. A fictional employment history was created for him. Eventually, he was hired as a nurse's aide in a nursing home. Working in the nursing home for a short period, he did not see any evidence of wrongdoing. So, he sought employment at another nursing home. In the second home, where he was paid just $3.75 an hour, he uncovered several horrific examples of misconduct. Eventually, his undercover investigation resulted in the criminal prosecution of the nursing home (Speaks, 1997).

It was no coincidence that the attorney general sought out the services of a graduating senior rather than a seasoned officer. First, it would likely have been very difficult to persuade more experienced police officers to give up their careers to work in a nursing home. Second, the excitement of undercover activities is likely higher among those new to the career. Third, in a case such as this, it is easier for a younger individual to become an undercover operative than it would be for an older agent (alternatively, a new graduate would not be able to pull off an undercover investigation in many other white-collar settings where one's level in the corporation is based on experience and age). Finally, most new college graduates have a clean slate when it comes to law enforcement practices. If they are new to law enforcement, then they are not yet cynical, and they are possibly easier to train than those who already have experience and a set of expectations that may not match the reality of the undercover assignment.

As an example, a police trainer once told me that he would rather train someone who has never shot a gun how to shoot a gun, as opposed to training someone who was raised as a hunter. The trainer's rationale was that many people learn the wrong way to shoot guns, and it is harder to teach them the right way than it is to teach someone who has never even touched a gun. In a very real sense, Speaks was like the "new gun owner" who had never touched a gun. Training him how to go into a corporation and serve as an undercover agent was likely much simpler because of that.

While Speaks's experience as a lone undercover investigator is illustrative of a successful way to police white-collar crime, several different types of policing efforts and strategies are used to uncover white-collar crime. Consider the following cases excerpted from their original sources:

- The FBI, along with investigators from the Las Vegas Metropolitan Police Department and Internal Revenue Service – Criminal Investigations, used a variety of investigative techniques—including confidential sources, multiple undercover operatives, and forensic accountants—and conducted hundreds of interviews to piece together the extent of the crimes committed by ****** and his co-conspirators. In January 2015, ****** pled guilty to multiple counts of conspiracy to commit mail and wire fraud and tax evasion (FBI, 2015, October 29).

- Based on a joint investigation, an undercover FBI agent contacted ***** by telephone on Sept. 18, 2014, and asked to meet him the following day. Without seeking additional information from the caller, ***** agreed. The next day, ***** met with the undercover FBI agent, who was posing as an Egyptian intelligence officer, in a park in Hampton, Virginia. During the meeting, ***** claimed it was his intention to utilize his position with the U.S. Navy to obtain military technology for use by the Egyptian government, including but not limited to the designs of the USS *Gerald R. Ford* nuclear aircraft carrier, a new Navy "supercarrier." ***** agreed to conduct clandestine communications with the undercover FBI agent, and to conduct "dead drops" in a concealed location in the park.

- The Department of Justice Medicaid Fraud Control Unit performed a "lengthy investigation" into ********'s billing practices between November 2012 and September 2013 at the clinic following a tip to the division's hotline in 2013, according to the release. Through the investigation, the DOJ established and identified "extensive patterns of alleged fraud throughout 2012 and 2013," according to the release (Horn, 2015).

- An investigation into the City of Neola has revealed more than $230,000 in city funds were allegedly misspent over a five-year period, with a former city clerk now running for mayor at the center of the controversy. State Auditor Mary Mosiman released a report Tuesday investigating transactions from Jan. 1, 2009 through Dec. 31, which found $230,795.55 of improper and unsupported disbursements and undeposited utility collections (Brownlee, 2015).

- According to the arrest affidavit in the case, BCT President Peter Posk first discovered ****'s fraudulent activities in casual conversation with a friend. Posk asked his friend why he wasn't attending the same local conference **** was at, and the friend said there was no conference. Posk contacted the American Institute of Certified Public Accountants and confirmed there was no conference. Posk began to research past conferences dating back to 2009 and discovered more inconsistencies, the affidavit stated (Roustan, 2015).

These examples highlight four important themes regarding the policing of white-collar crimes. First, white-collar crimes come to the attention of the police through several different avenues. Second, a number of different agencies are involved in the police response to white-collar crime. Third, the notion of "police response" describes different forms of policing, including criminal policing, private policing, and regulatory policing. Fourth, the specific police techniques used to address white-collar crimes are tied to the types of white-collar crime under investigation. An official responding to pollution, for example, performs one set of activities, while an officer responding to stock fraud would perform another set of activities.

● ● ● Agencies Involved in Responding to White-Collar Crime

Generally speaking, three types of agencies are involved in responding to white-collar crime. These include private agencies (or self-policing by corporations or businesses), formal criminal police agencies, and governmental regulatory agencies. Private agencies are involved in policing misconduct inasmuch as a specific business guards against employee misconduct through the development of security and prevention measures. Formal criminal policing agencies at all levels of government respond to white-collar crime, though local police more rarely respond to these cases. State police agencies may become more involved, while federal law enforcement is engaged in even more policing of white-collar misconduct (see Figure 13.1). With regard to regulatory responses, at the local level, different government agencies have responsibility for ensuring that businesses are not in violation of local ordinances. At the state level, regulatory agencies enforce state health-, safety-, and sales-related laws. The federal government has several regulatory agencies whose purpose is to make sure that businesses and their workers are abiding by federal laws and regulations.

It is important to note that many white-collar crime cases are addressed through joint policing efforts by agencies from each level of government (local, state, and federal) and each type of policing agency (criminal policing, regulatory policing, and self-policing). Table 13.1 shows some of the federal agencies involved in responding to white-collar crime. Note that this list is not exhaustive. Dozens of other federal agencies are involved in responding to different forms of white-collar crime. Perhaps one way to think of it is to recognize that for each profession and industry, a different type of policing or regulatory agency guards against occupational misconduct in that occupation. A discussion of the FBI's response to white-collar crime helps frame an understanding of the way that law enforcement agencies address these offenses.

The FBI and White-Collar Crime

In the FBI, the **Financial Crimes Section (FCS)**, located in the agency's Criminal Investigative Division, investigates cases of white-collar crime. The FCS is composed of the Economic Crime Unit (ECU), Health Care Fraud Unit (HCFU), Forensic Accountants Unit, National Mortgage Fraud Unit, and Asset Forfeiture/Money Laundering Unit. The ECU addresses fraudulent behavior (excluding health care fraud). The HCFU investigates various forms of health care fraud committed

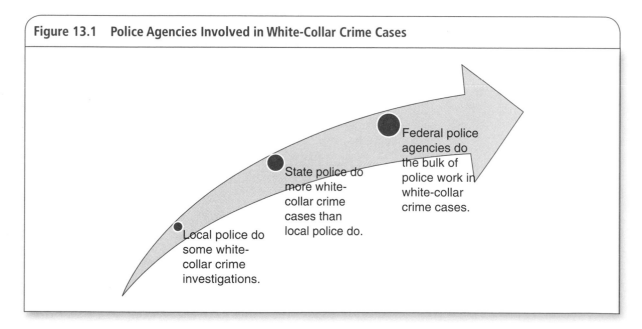

Figure 13.1 Police Agencies Involved in White-Collar Crime Cases

Federal police agencies do the bulk of police work in white-collar crime cases.

State police do more white-collar crime cases than local police do.

Local police do some white-collar crime investigations.

Table 13.1   Some Federal Agencies Involved in Policing/Regulating White-Collar Crime

Agency	What the Agency Does That Is Related to White-Collar Crime*	Where to Learn More
Consumer Product Safety Commission	Regulatory agency responsible for protecting the public from unreasonable risk of injury from thousands of products	www.cpsc.gov
Commodities Futures Trading Commission	Regulatory agency responsible for regulating U.S. commodities and futures markets and preventing fraud and abuse in the markets	www.cftc.gov
Environmental Protection Agency	Government agency responsible for protecting the environment through compliance efforts and criminal and civil law enforcement practices	www.epa.gov
Equal Employment Opportunity Commission	Federal agency responsible for enforcing federal employment discrimination laws; it has authority to file lawsuits if necessary	www.eeoc.gov
Federal Bureau of Investigation	Federal law enforcement agency that addresses white-collar crime through its Financial Crimes Section	www.fbi.gov
Federal Deposit Insurance Corporation	Independent agency that insures bank deposits, supervises financial institutions and examines their activities, and manages failed banks	www.fdic.gov
Federal Trade Commission	Addresses antitrust laws, anticompetitive practices, and false advertising practices by businesses	www.ftc.gov
Financial Crimes Enforcement Network (FinCEN)	Has regulatory duty to administer the Bank Secrecy Act. Assists law enforcement through analysis of information gathered as part of the Bank Secrecy Act.	www.fincen.gov
Financial Industry Regulatory Authority	Independent regulatory agency regulating more than 4,500 securities firms operating in the United States (largest of its kind)	www.finra.org
Food and Drug Administration	Ensures safety and effectiveness of certain food and drug products and investigates potential manufacturing violations	www.fda.gov
HHS Center for Medicare and Medicaid Services (CMS)	Administers nursing home inspections by contracting with states, which hire inspection teams and provide inspection data to CMS	www.cms.gov
HHS Office of Research Integrity	Has regulatory authority to promote the responsible conduct of research and monitors college and university reviews of research misconduct cases	http://ori.dhhs.gov/
Internal Revenue Service	Federal agency enforcing tax laws; it becomes involved in white-collar crime cases when businesses/corporations break tax laws.	www.irs.gov
National Labor Relations Board	Independent agency administering the National Labor Relations Act, addressing unfair labor practices	www.nlrb.gov
National Highway Traffic Safety Administration	Federal agency that develops and enforces motor vehicle performance standards, including gas mileage standards, investigates motor vehicle safety, and detects odometer fraud	www.nhtsa.gov
Occupational Safety and Health Administration	Federal agency that sets and enforces safety and health standards for work settings and maintains data on workplace injuries and illnesses	www.osha.gov

Agency	What the Agency Does That Is Related to White-Collar Crime*	Where to Learn More
Office of the Comptroller of the Currency	Independent agency responsible for chartering and regulating national banks and for ensuring fairness and equal access to the banks	www.occ.treas.gov
Office of Thrift Supervision	Independent agency that regulates savings associations and their holding companies	www.ots.treas.gov
Public Company Accounting Oversight Board	Ensures that publicly registered accounting firms are in compliance with various federal laws	http://pcaobus.org/Pages/default.aspx
Securities and Exchange Commission	Regulates the U.S. securities market, using civil enforcement actions and administrative proceedings	www.sec.gov
U.S. Army Corps of Engineers	Has responsibility of protecting nation's water from harmful and illegal discharge of dredged and fill material	www.usace.ary.mil
U.S. Department of Agriculture	Inspects and monitors poultry, eggs, and meat products sold in the United States	www.usda.gov
U.S. Department Education (DE), Office of Inspector General	Conducts independent investigations, audits, and inspections of DE personnel, activities, and programs receiving DE funding	www2.ed.gov/about/offices/list/oig/programs.html
U.S. Department of Health and Human Services, Office of Inspector General (OIG)	Conducts independent audits, investigations, and inspections to guard against fraud and abuse in Health and Human Services programs and to protect program beneficiaries	http://oig.hhs.gov/
U.S. Department of the Interior, Office of Inspector General	Provides oversight of programs, employees, and operations occurring in the Department of Interior	www.doioig.gov
U.S. Department of Justice Office of Inspector General	Conducts independent investigations of DOJ personnel and programs to determine whether fraud, abuse, or waste is occurring	www.justice.gov/oig
U.S. Fish and Wildlife Service	Administers Endangered Species Act and responds to white-collar crimes when businesses/corporations harm endangered species	www.fws.gov
U.S. Postal Inspection Service	Federal law enforcement agency addressing fraud conducted through the mail	https://postalinspectors.uspis.gov/
Wage and Hour Division of Department of Labor	Enforces federal labor laws, including minimum wage laws, overtime laws, and family and medical leave laws	www.dol.gov/whd

Source: *Information in this column adapted from agency's website. All agencies do activities other than those listed here.

against insurance companies and individuals. The National Mortgage Fraud Team (NMFT) investigates mortgage frauds perpetrated against banks. The Asset Forfeiture/Money Laundering Unit assists agents in using asset forfeiture laws to support their investigations of white-collar crimes. The Forensic Accountants Unit, created in 2009, assists in white-collar crime investigations that require the services of a financial accountant or financial analyst (FBI, 2010b). Currently, the FBI is seeking to hire more cyber police (See the White-Collar Crime in the News box on the next page).

WHITE-COLLAR CRIME IN THE NEWS

FBI Hiring More Cyber Police

https://commons.wikimedia.org/wiki/Category:Hacker_culture#/media/File:Bomba_L%C3%B3gica.jpg.

More than ever before, the FBI is recruiting agents to help respond to cybercrimes.

Since its earliest days, the FBI has looked for recruits with specialized skills to fill its special agent ranks: lawyers, accountants, scientists, and engineers, to name a few. Today, however, the most sought-after candidates possess a uniquely 21st century quality: cyber expertise.

Investigating cyber crimes—such as website hacks, intrusions, data theft, botnets, and denial of service attacks—is a top priority for the FBI. To keep pace with the evolving threat, the Bureau is appealing to experienced and certified cyber experts to consider joining the FBI to apply their well-honed tradecraft as cyber special agents.

"The FBI seeks highly talented, technically trained individuals who are motivated by the FBI's mission to protect our nation and the American people from the rapidly evolving cyber threat," said Robert Anderson, Jr., executive assistant director for the Bureau's Criminal, Cyber, Response, and Services Branch. "What we want are people who are going to come and be part of a team that is working different, very complex types of investigations and to utilize their skillsets in that team environment."

The Bureau recently launched a campaign to bring aboard more technical talent, including computer scientists, IT specialists, and engineers.

"One thing that no one else can offer is the mission and the camaraderie and the teamwork the FBI brings to the table," Anderson said. "Cyber agents will be integrated into all the different violations that we work. So whether it's a counterterrorism or counterintelligence investigation, they could be the lead agent in the case."

"Cyber permeates every aspect of what we do, whether it's counterterrorism, criminal investigations, or traditional cyber attacks, as we've seen in the recent past," Anderson said.

"That's why these types of people are so important to get into the pipeline and come into our organization." Bank robberies help illustrate how the landscape has shifted.

Traditionally, a team of agents responding to an armed bank robbery would cordon off a crime scene, interview witnesses, and collect evidence, such as fingerprints and security video. However, if the money was stolen through a cyber intrusion into the bank's holdings, the approach would be very different: a cyber agent would request firewall logs and forensic copies of hard drives, in addition to interviews.

The FBI already has a lengthy track record fighting cyber crimes. In June, the FBI announced its role in the multinational effort to disrupt the GameOver Zeus Botnet, believed to be responsible for the theft of millions of dollars from businesses and around the world. A month earlier, the FBI announced charges against distributors of malicious software that infected millions of computers. Forty FBI field offices executed more than 100 search warrants and seized more than 1,900 domains used by Blackshades users to control victims' computers.

But the FBI wants to grow to meet tomorrow's challenges. "We're looking to hire a lot of cyber agents now," Anderson said. "It's an area where the FBI and the whole U.S. government will be looking for this talent for years to come."

Source: Reprinted from FBI

Initiatives by the FBI include the agency's Health Care Fraud Initiative and the Forensic Accounting Program. The former initiative included expanded efforts to address frauds involving (a) durable medical equipment (beginning in December 2006), (b) infusion therapy (beginning in April 2008), and (c) home health care (beginning in January 2010). The Forensic Accounting Program (FAP) is an initiative that started in March 2009 with the purpose of attracting and retaining **forensic accountants** in the battle against white-collar crime (FBI, 2010b). Initiatives of the FAP are outlined in Table 13.2.

Figure 13.2 shows the number of FBI white-collar crime cases between 2005 and 2011 for four types of white-collar crime. As shown in the figure, while some types of cases have increased, others have decreased. Note that these fluctuations are potentially a reflection of law enforcement behavior rather than changes in the prevalence of white-collar crimes.

"Long standing partnerships" are hailed by the FBI as "one of the best tools in its arsenal" for addressing various types of white-collar crime (FBI, 2010b) as well as various local and state agencies. In Focus 13.1 provides an overview of the NMFT as an example of such a partnership. In some cases, the FBI is the leading partner in the effort, while in others, the agents are members of a supporting cast.

Other federal law enforcement agencies recognize the benefits of partnerships in addressing white-collar crimes for which they are responsible. Consider the Health Care Fraud and Abuse Program, which is jointly administered by the U.S. Attorney General and U.S. Department of Health and Human Services (HHS). The program was created as part of the Health Insurance Portability and Accountability Act of 1996. Since its creation, it has "returned over $27.8 billion to the Medicare Trust Funds" accounts (Health Care Fraud and Abuse Program, 2015). One active partnership that grew out of this program is the Health Care Prevention and Enforcement Action Team (HEAT), which includes officials from the HHS Office of Inspector General and U.S. Department of Justice (DOJ). This initiative builds on past partnerships and has developed initiatives, including the Medicare Fraud Strike Force, which was created in the spring of 2007. The strike force coordinates federal, state, and local investigations related to Medicare fraud. In 2010, the strike force charged 88 individuals or businesses with crimes, convicted 89 defendants of fraud, and recovered "$71.3 million in investigative resources" (U.S. Department of Health and Human Services, 2010).

A few points about the agencies involved in responding to white-collar crime need to be stressed. First, a plethora of different agencies are involved in controlling and responding to white-collar crimes, and these agencies go by different names depending on the state or locality where they exist. It can be somewhat confusing to keep track of jurisdictional issues and determine who is responsible for preventing and policing specific types of white-collar crime. Here is how one author described this issue:

> There is no reason to believe that decisions as to which agency responds to a white-collar crime challenge are in any way related to resources or other capabilities of that agency. Rather, who becomes involved is likely to reflect which agency moved first, or which has greater clout or resources. Agencies have overlapping jurisdiction and there is little to prevent dysfunctional duplication of effort or significant matters falling through the gaps. (Edelhertz, 1983, p. 128)

▲ **Photo 13.1**   The majority white-collar crime law enforcement is done at the federal level.

Table 13.2	Initiatives of the FBI's Forensic Accounting Program
Initiative	**Description**
Forensic accountant core training session training course	In FY 2009, the FAU [Forensic Accounting Unit] initiated development of a rigorous training curriculum titled the Forensic Accountant Core Training Session ("FACTS"). FACTS is a comprehensive introductory program of instruction designed to increase a FoA's [forensic auditor] proficiency in the critical areas necessary to conduct a financial investigation. This extensive course develops the FoA's aptitude and knowledge in handling a financial investigation according to pertinent rules and regulations across a wide variety of subject matters. The FAU developed the FACTS training curriculum and is responsible for administering the training. The material covered will focus primarily on providing an overview of FBI programs and systems, financial investigative topics and techniques, resources available to develop an investigation, legal training, and expert witness-testifying techniques.
BankScan initiative	BankScan is an in-house-created software application, which translates physical bank and credit card statements into an electronic medium, thus dramatically decreasing the time-consuming data-entry process. In FY 2009, FAU deployed the BankScan training initiative Train the Trainer with the goal of full field office deployment by the end of FY 2010. The Train the Trainer Initiative was completed, and each field office "Trainer" received the requisite training and was supplied with the necessary software and equipment to implement the BankScan Project. Since its implementation, the FBI has benefited through an exponential increase in financial investigative efficiency and productivity.
Electronic subpoena production	The Electronic Subpoena Production initiative represents a joint undertaking of the FBI's Criminal Investigative Division (CID), DOJ's Criminal Division Fraud Section, and the IRS. Electronic Subpoena Production requires financial institutions to digitally produce account data stored electronically by relying on existing Rule 17 of the Federal Rules of Criminal Procedure. When used in conjunction with BankScan, the introduction of this new process will substantially increase the efficiency and effectiveness of FBI forensic financial investigations.
Financial analyst conversion	In FY 2009, the FAU developed a selective conversion process to transition qualified FAs [forensic accountants] to the FoAP [Forensic Accounting Program] to provide the FBI's investigative programs with the highest caliber of financial investigative work-product and support. This effort will ensure that only those individuals who meet the FoA requirements be selectively converted to the FoAP.

Source: Reprinted from FBI (2010, 2009). In *Financial Crimes Report.* Available from http://www.fbi.gov/stats-services/publications/financial-crimes-report-2009/financial-crimes-report-2009#forensic

A second issue has to do with the way that agencies have historically defined "white-collar crime." In the 1970s, the Department of Justice declared white-collar crime "an investigative priority." Poveda (1992) argued that in their declaration of "priority," agencies reconceptualized what scholars meant by white-collar crime in a way that resulted in the importance of class status, in defining white-collar crime, being cast aside. He wrote: "We need to consider whether the justice department's institutionalization of a white-collar crime represents a 'real' effort at combating the crimes of the elite or simply a 'symbolic' gesture" (p. 240). Simon and Swart (1984) offered a similar observation, stating that the DOJ's definition of white-collar crime was "so non-specific that it could include everything from welfare cheating by the poor to antitrust violations by upper-class businessmen" (p. 109).

Recognizing the conceptual and jurisdictional issues that surface with regard to law enforcement efforts to address white-collar crime should help us appreciate the complexities surrounding the police and regulatory response

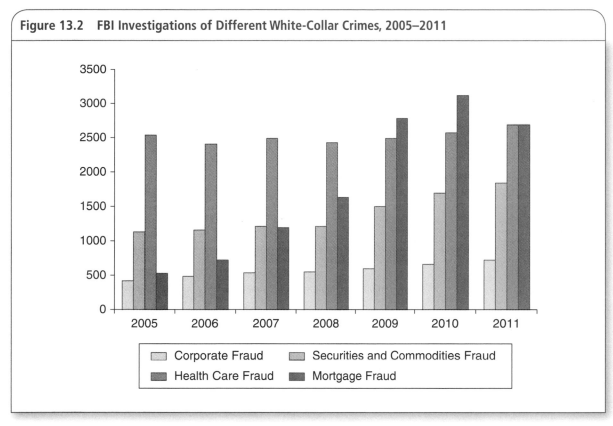

Figure 13.2 FBI Investigations of Different White-Collar Crimes, 2005–2011

Sources: Adapted from Federal Bureau of Investigation (n.d.e). *Financial crimes reported to the public: Fiscal years 2009 (October 1, 2008-September 30, 2009).* Retrieved November 7, 2015, from https://www.fbi.gov/stats-services/publications/financial-crimes-report-2009

Federal Bureau of Investigation (n.d.f). Financial crimes reported to the public: Fiscal years 2010-2011 (October 1, 2009-September 30, 2011). Retrieved November 7, 2015, from https://www.fbi.gov/stats-services/publications/financial-crimes-report-2010-2011

to occupational misconduct. These complexities are particularly evident when considering the use of traditional polic-ing strategies for addressing white-collar crime.

● ● ● Law Enforcement Strategies and White-Collar Crime

A major portion of the police response to white-collar crime involves law enforcement strategies carried out by officials in the justice system. The law enforcement response to white-collar crime is similar to how the police respond to traditional crimes in several ways. For example, police use both reactive and proactive strategies in both types of cases. **Reactive strategies** entail situations where the police respond to reports of criminal incidents, and **proactive strategies** entail situ-ations where the police develop criminal cases in an active way. An enormous amount of power is afforded police officers who respond to both types of cases. In addition, law enforcement officers have an enormous amount of discretion in deciding how to proceed in both types of cases.

IN FOCUS 13.1

The FBI National Mortgage Fraud Team

In December 2008, the FBI established the NMFT to assist field offices in addressing the financial crisis from the mortgage fraud problem and loan origination scams to the secondary markets and securitization. The NMFT provides tools for identifying the most egregious mortgage fraud perpetrators, prioritizes investigative efforts, and provides information to evaluate resource needs.

The FBI continues to support 18 mortgage fraud task forces and 53 working groups; it participates in the National Mortgage Fraud and National Bank Fraud Working Groups, the National Securities and Commodities Fraud Working Group, and the President's Corporate Fraud Task Force to maximize intelligence sharing between stakeholder agencies and coordinate multiagency, multijurisdictional mortgage fraud initiatives. Task forces and working groups include, but are not limited to, representatives of the [Department of Housing and Urban Development-OIG] HUD-OIG, the U.S. Postal Inspection Service, the U.S. Securities and Exchange Commission, the Commodities Futures Trading Commission, the IRS, FinCEN, the Federal Deposit Insurance Corporation, and other federal, state, and local law enforcement officers across the country. Additionally, representatives of the Office of Comptroller of the Currency, the Office of Thrift Supervision, the Executive Office of U.S. Trustees, the Federal Trade Commission, and others participate in national and ad-hoc working groups.

The FBI continues to foster relationships with representatives of the mortgage industry to promote mortgage fraud awareness and share intelligence information. FBI personnel routinely speak at and participate in various mortgage industry conferences and seminars, including those sponsored by the MBA [Mortgage Bankers Association]. Collaborative efforts are ongoing to educate and raise public awareness of mortgage fraud crimes with the publication of the annual *Mortgage Fraud Report*, the *Financial Crimes Report to the Public*, and press releases and through the dissemination of information with and between various industry and consumer organizations. Analytical products are routinely disseminated to a wide audience to include public- and private-sector industry partners, the intelligence community, and other federal, state, and local law enforcement.

Source: Reprinted From FBI (2009d). In *2008 Mortgage Fraud Report*. Available from http://www.fbi.gov/stats-services/publications/mortgage-fraud-2008

Despite these similarities, as will be shown below, a number of specific features of white-collar crime investigations make them substantively different from responses to traditional forms of crime. To provide insight into the law enforcement response to white-collar crimes, attention is given to the following:

- Stages of the white-collar crime investigation
- Evidence-gathering strategies
- Problems addressing white-collar crime through a law enforcement response
- Suggestions for improving the law enforcement response to white-collar crime

Stages of the White-Collar Crime Investigation

White-collar crime investigations can be discussed as part of the broader criminal justice process. In discussing investigations from this perspective, one can point to the fact that white-collar crime investigations begin one of two ways. First, some white-collar crime investigations begin when cases are referred to law enforcement agencies that are responsible for addressing specific forms of white-collar crime. Such referrals come from consumers who are victims of white-collar crime, coworkers of the individual or individuals committing white-collar crime, competitors of the white-collar or corporate offender, the suspect's employer, and local, state, and federal agencies that uncover evidence of wrongdoing (Payne, 2003a). With regard to local agencies in particular, in some cases, individuals might contact the local police to report white-collar offenses. In these situations, it is entirely likely that the local police do not have the resources to investigate or jurisdiction over the misconduct. In these cases, the local police will refer the report to the appropriate agency charged with addressing that specific form of misconduct, which could be a state or federal agency.

A second way that white-collar crime investigations begin is as the result of evidence uncovered as part of routine reviews of financial records by agencies proactively searching for evidence of wrongdoing. For example, auditors in Medicaid Fraud Control Units routinely review insurance claims submitted by health care providers in an effort to identify signs of misconduct. If the auditor finds signs of fraud, the investigation officially begins.

Once a white-collar crime investigation begins, a series of stages are followed. One expert suggested that white-collar crime investigations be conducted in the following stages:

- Identify target, including conspirators
- Locate documents
- Review and confirm false statements in the records
- Interview participants (Bradley, 2008, p. 4)

Bradley draws attention to the need to gather information through records reviews before interviewing participants. This is somewhat different from traditional investigations, perhaps because of the how the crimes are reported.

Compare a domestic violence incident to a white-collar crime, for example. In the domestic violence incident, the police are called, they arrive on the scene, and they immediately question participants about the incident. Records (e.g., threatening notes the offender wrote, phone records), if needed, might be gathered at a later date. If a banking employee is suspected of embezzling money from the bank, however, the investigators will wait until they have reviewed the records before interviewing participants.

In many white-collar crime cases, multiple suspects might be involved. For example, mortgage fraud cases might involve appraisers, real estate agents, mortgage brokers, developers, home builders, and other conspirators. In these situations, Bradley (2004) suggests that investigators "begin with the least culpable and work . . . toward the primary suspects" (p. 4). There are a number of possible reasons to start with the "least culpable" participant. For example, the person who has done the "least amount of harm" is not going to want to take the blame for the harm committed by conspirators. Somewhat related, the least culpable suspect will be in a better position to receive plea bargain offers later in the criminal justice process.

As an illustration of the *least culpable* recommendation, consider an incident of academic dishonesty that occurred in my class not long ago. Two students had written exactly the same wrong answers on their quizzes. Their wrong answers were so preposterously incorrect that it was clear to me that academic dishonesty had occurred. It was also clear that student B had copied from student A (because student A was an "A" student and student B . . . well, let's just say it was obvious). I asked student A to come by my office and asked her about the situation. In my view, student A was the least culpable because this student was not the "copier" but was the "supplier" who had the answers correct on her own. After I asked her about the incorrect answers, student A immediately confessed that student B had copied her answers. I asked student B to come by my office. Initially, he insisted that he did not copy but that he and student A had simply studied together. I asked if he really wanted to stick with that story. Shortly later, he confessed to the academic dishonesty. Had I started my "investigation" with student B, it is entirely likely that the process would not have flowed as smoothly.

Evidence-Gathering Strategies

White-collar crime investigations differ from traditional crime investigations in the way that evidence is gathered. Common strategies for gathering evidence in white-collar crime cases include (1) audits, (2) record reviews, (3) undercover strategies, (4) the use of whistleblowers, and (5) the use of technological devices. Each of these strategies is discussed below.

Audits

As noted above, some agencies routinely conduct **audits** in search of evidence of white-collar misconduct. Sometimes audits are done through data-mining techniques, which involve searching data sets for patterns that might indicate fraud (Rejesus, Little, & Lovell, 2004). Whether conducted in a proactive or reactive manner, audits are typically conducted by financial fraud accountants with specific skills designed to enhance their abilities to identify fraud.

Recall once again the principle of skepticism discussed in Chapter 1. This principle encourages individuals to have an open mind and to question and re-question everything, to never assume that anything is true. Financial fraud investigators are skeptical by nature and review cases from the perspective that the records are not accurate (Wells, 2003b). Such a perspective is believed to help find evidence of wrongdoing. Describing this skeptical approach to conducting audits, one investigator said, "audits are like an onion. You keep peeling away the different levels until you get to that level where you know what happened" (Payne, 2003a, p. 121).

Audits can be complex and time consuming, but the payoff is significant. In most cases, however, an audit by itself is not necessarily enough to establish that a white-collar crime was committed or to identify who the white-collar offender is. Instead, as one investigator said, audits are "an indicator of the problem; . . . they do not indicate automatically that a crime occurred" (Payne, 2003a, p. 121). While not always sufficient by themselves, when combined with other forms of evidence-gathering strategies, audits can provide the evidence needed to substantiate wrongdoing.

Record Reviews

White-collar crime investigators will review an assortment of records in building their case. The number of records law enforcement investigators will need to review in these cases can be enormous. Investigators will review all sorts of records, including financial records, banking records, sales records, e-mail correspondence, phone records, property deeds, loan applications, and any other records that are relevant to the case under investigation.

As part of the search for records, white-collar crime investigators will examine whether suspects tried to destroy records, which would be a separate offense as well as evidence supporting the belief that they engaged in the offense under investigation. In one case, for example, nine employees were convicted of neglecting an at-risk child who was in their care. An autopsy revealed that the child had starved to death. In the course of the investigation, officials from the HHS Office of Inspector General found that the employees "attempted to conceal the incident by destroying old records and creating new false records" (U.S. Department of Health and Human Services [HHS], 2010, p. v). The fact that they destroyed records was used to show that they knew that they had done something wrong. Had the records been left alone, it would have been more difficult to establish intent.

E-mail messages are a relatively recent type of record that can be used in white-collar crime investigations. Two misconceptions about them exist. First, some assume that once e-mail is deleted it is gone forever. However, e-mail servers save deleted messages for set periods of time, and investigators have been able to access deleted messages to use as evidence in white-collar crime cases. Second, many people assume that their e-mail is private; however, most businesses have e-mail use policies that allow employers to access workers' e-mail without their consent. Also, for government workers who work in states with liberal open records laws, any of the workers' e-mail can be made public through freedom of information requests.

Undercover Investigations

Undercover investigations are also used in white-collar crime cases. On the surface, these investigations are no different from undercover criminal investigations in conventional criminal cases. However, as will be shown below, important differences exist between white-collar and conventional undercover investigations.

One basic difference is that **white-collar undercover investigations** are not typically begun unless there is already evidence of wrongdoing by the suspect or the corporation. Whereas many undercover drug investigations involve "reverse sting" activities where undercover officers pose as drug dealers and arrest whoever happens to try to purchase drugs, white-collar crime investigations are rarely conducted without already knowing who the specific target of the investigation is. In other words, typically, "there are no random spot checks" of white-collar employees (Payne & Berg, 1997, p. 226).

As an illustration of how undercover investigations are "built into" the broader criminal investigation in white-collar crime cases, consider the following stages of one white-collar crime investigation:

1. A senior official at PepsiCo receives an envelope offering to sell him confidential, private information about Coca-Cola.

2. The Pepsi executive contacts Coca-Cola.

3. Coca-Cola executives call the FBI and tell them about the case.

4. The FBI opens the investigation and interviews witnesses.

5. Undercover agents offer to buy the secret information from the suspect, a Coca-Cola employee.

6. Agents give the employee $30,000 stuffed in a Girl Scout cookie box.

7. A Coca-Cola employee provides information to the undercover agents.

8. A review of Coca-Cola video surveillance finds proof of the employee stealing documents and product samples.

9. The employee and two coconspirators are arrested (McKay, 2006).

All of this happened in a 3-month time span. Note that the undercover investigation was just one component of the case, albeit a significant component.

Criminologist Gary Marx (1982) has discussed several criticisms of undercover policing. While he focused on all types of undercover policing (e.g., undercover prostitution stings, drug stings), Marx used several examples of undercover white-collar crime investigations to frame his discussion. One criticism he levied against these investigations was that they deceive individuals and may coerce individuals into offending. He also noted the significant amount of stress police officers experience from undercover policing, and he argued that the independence given to law enforcement officers in these cases may be a breeding ground for corruption. In addition, over-relying on informers may give informers too much power and become problematic if informers take advantage of the undercover investigation. Marx also suggested that undercover work may promote poor police-community relationships.

One can envision how these criticisms have merit in undercover investigations involving street crimes and organized crime. The criticisms may not be as relevant when considering undercover investigations of white-collar crimes. Table 13.3 shows the similarities and differences between the two types of investigations. First, in terms of danger, there is very little risk for undercover agents in white-collar crime cases. Consider a case where an undercover officer goes to a pharmacist suspected of committing prescription fraud. There is virtually no danger in that assignment. Alternatively, for undercover investigations of street crimes, the investigations occur in dangerous areas and often target dangerous offenders.

Another difference between the two types of undercover assignments has to do with the time element given to the undercover investigation. For many undercover investigations of street crimes or organized crime, undercover agents infiltrate the criminal subculture and spend significant amounts of time in the dangerous settings. For white-collar crime investigations, it is rare that an undercover agent would join the occupational subculture under investigation for an extended period of time.

Somewhat related, one can also distinguish the two types of investigation based on the role that the undercover work has in the broader investigation. For investigations of drug crimes or organized crime, the undercover work is central to the investigation. The centrality of the undercover work to the investigation is what justifies spending the extended amount of time on the case. For white-collar crime cases, the undercover investigation is typically a "supplemental component" to the investigation. This is not to diminish the importance of undercover work in these cases, as the cases may not be solved without the undercover work.

Another difference between the two types of investigation has to do with the nature of the role playing in white-collar and conventional undercover investigations. In undercover investigations of conventional crimes, the undercover agent must often act as if he or she is a criminal—a drug dealer, prostitute, thief, mobster, gang member, or some other

Table 13.3	Distinguishing Undercover Investigations of White-Collar Crime and Conventional Crime Cases	
	White-Collar Undercover Investigation	**Conventional Undercover Investigation**
Potential for danger	Minimal	High
Time to complete undercover investigation	Short period of time	Lengthy period of time
Centrality to the case	Supplemental evidence	Evidence central to case
Role playing	Some (as consumer)	Identity change (as criminal)
Stress potential	Unlikely	Likely

identity relevant to the investigation. In white-collar crime investigations, the agent often does not have to take on the role of the criminal, but the agent may take on the role of a consumer. Consider a case in which a broker is suspected of stealing clients' funds. If an undercover investigation is initiated, the agent simply poses as someone interested in investing. Or if a doctor is being investigated for submitting fraudulent bills to insurance companies, then the investigator just has to act sick. Who among us has not acted sick at some point in our lives? Maybe some of us have acted sick to get out of work. For undercover investigations in health care fraud cases, undercover investigators act sick as part of their work.

Based on the dynamics noted above, one can assume that level of stress in the two types of cases varies. Undercover investigations of conventional crimes are dangerous and time consuming and involve situations where individuals have to pretend to be criminals. Certainly, one can accept Marx's premise that such activities would potentially stress undercover police officers. As well, these dynamics could potentially contribute to police corruption. For white-collar crime investigations, the fact that the investigations are short, in safe settings, and do not involve a great deal of role playing should reduce the amount of stress arising from these cases.

Gerald L. Nino

▲ **Photo 13.2**   It is safe to suggest that traditional policing is much more dangerous than white-collar crime policing.

Whistleblower Evidence

White-collar crime investigations often involve the collection of whistleblower evidence. **Whistleblowers** are individuals who notify authorities about wrongdoing in their organization. Two types of whistleblowers exist: internal whistleblowers and external whistleblowers (Vinten, 1994). **Internal whistleblowers** share information with officials within the organization where they work, often reporting the misconduct to the company's security program. **External whistleblowers** share the information with outside organizations such as law enforcement agencies or the media. Table 13.4 shows some whistleblowers whose stories eventually made it to Hollywood.

Table 13.4	You're Going to Hollywood: Whistleblowers Who Made It to Hollywood			
Whistleblower	Description		Name of Movie or Show	Actor Who Played Whistleblower
W. Mark Felt	Felt was "Deep Throat," the individual who fed information about the Watergate scandal to reporters Bob Woodward and Carl Bernstein. He announced his role in Watergate three decades after the scandal.		*All the President's Men*	Hal Holbrook
Frank Serpico	Serpico told the *New York Times* about NYPD corruption and was subsequently suspiciously shot in the face during a drug bust. He also provided testimony in the Knapp Commission's investigation of corruption.		*Serpico*	Al Pacino
Karen Silkwood	Silkwood, a nuclear plant worker, was providing information about her factory's safety violations to a reporter. One night when she was delivering evidence to a coworker, she was suspiciously killed in a car accident. The evidence documents were not found in the wrecked car.		*Silkwood*	Meryl Streep
Linda Tripp	Tripp tape-recorded conversations she had with Monica Lewinsky about Lewinsky's sexual relations with President Clinton and provided the tapes to Independent Counsel Kenneth Starr.		*Saturday Night Live*	John Goodman
Sherron Watkins	Watkins sent a letter to Enron's CEO, Ken Lay, detailing Enron's misdeeds. She was named "2002 Person of the Year" by *Time* magazine, along with two other whistleblowers.		*Enron: The Smartest Guys in the Room*	Self (documentary)
Mark Whitacre	Whitacre was the FBI's highest level executive whistleblower in the early 1990s when he provided evidence about price fixing at Archer Daniels Midland (ADM). ADM settled the case for $100 million and alleged wrongdoing by Whitacre. An FBI investigation revealed that Whitacre had stolen $9 million himself. He served 8 years in prison for his fraud.		*The Informant*	Matt Damon

Working with whistleblowers can strengthen white-collar crime investigations significantly. One author team argued that such evidence "may be the best evidence for proving a case" (Botsko & Wells, 1994, p. 21). The same author team suggested that investigators must make sure that the emotional impact of participating in the investigation be minimized. One strategy they suggested for minimizing the emotional impact on whistleblowers was to not ask for too much information until the worker is at a place where he or she is comfortable providing the information. They wrote:

Effective management of witnesses represents one of the most challenging responsibilities for white-collar crime investigators. To overcome such barriers as anger and fear and to collect and preserve the most accurate testimony possible from . . . whistleblowers, investigators should focus on the informer's emotional agenda. (p. 21)

Research shows that whistleblowers decide to report their coworker's or organization's misconduct for several reasons (Latimer, 2002). Some workers report white-collar misconduct out of a sense of obligation or duty. Other workers report misconduct because they want to see the offender punished for the misconduct. Still other employees report misconduct so they will not get into trouble themselves. In many cases, whistleblowers are able to collect monetary awards, and these awards can be sizable. Some whistleblowers report misconduct because of the positive attention they get from participating in the investigation. These whistleblowers "have aspirations to become a hero" (Latimer, 2002, p. 23).

A study of whistleblowers found that workers were more likely to blow the whistle on evidence they saw, as opposed to evidence they heard about (Near & Miceli, 2008). This same study found that workers who perceived their company as retaliatory in nature were more likely to report misconduct than those who did not see their company in this light. In addition, compared to nonwhistleblowers, whistleblowers were more likely to be (a) supportive of cash rewards, (b) paid more, and (c) more educated.

Technological Devices and White-Collar Crime Evidence

Various types of technological devices are used to search for evidence in white-collar crime cases. Several types of software, for example, are used to search for evidence of computer crimes against corporations. As well, cameras and tape recorders are sometimes used to substantiate wrongdoing. As an illustration, in one case, a senior financial analyst for WellCare—Sean Hellein—alerted authorities that his coworkers had defrauded Medicaid of approximately a half billion dollars. After alerting authorities about the misconduct, he was asked to wear "hidden microphones and miniature cameras disguised as buttons" (Hundley, 2010). He collected 1,000 hours of evidence that led the authorities to raid the company's headquarters.

In another case, a physician, two nurses, and six aides were arrested after a camera was hidden in a nursing home resident's room for 5 weeks. The video from the hidden camera revealed the following:

- To prevent contractures, this patient's physician ordered that the patient receive 30 minutes of range of motion therapy twice a day. The camera revealed that the patient consistently did not receive this therapy.
- To prevent the development of dangerous pressure sores or promote their healing, the patient was required to be turned and repositioned every 2 hours and to receive incontinence care every 2 hours as well, but the camera revealed that the patient often went without this care.
- To ensure proper nutrition and hydration, the patient was supposed to receive total assistance while eating. The camera further revealed that the patient often failed to receive assistance in eating and often went without eating or drinking at all.
- To avoid seizures, combat pressure sores, prevent depression, reduce pain, and maintain proper nutrition, the patient was required to receive a series of medications, including Tegretol, an antiseizure medication; Celexa and Remeron, antidepressants; Baclofen, a muscle relaxant and pain reducer; and a liquid protein nutritional supplement. The camera revealed that the nurses charged to do so often failed to administer these medications as prescribed. (*Medicaid Fraud Report November*, 2006, p. 1)

In these cases, the presence of audio and video recordings provides valuable evidence that will increase the likelihood of a conviction.

Other forms of computer technology may also be used for some white-collar crime investigations. Some cyber policing strategies may rely on remote forensic software to detect offending and gather evidence (Abel, 2009). These strategies either (1) place software on a suspect's computer and monitor the suspect's activities or (2) place the software on a website and monitor who visits the website. Known as "police trojans," this type of software "require[s] the unwitting cooperation of the target" (p. 100). Internationally, companies are grappling with the question of whether law enforcement agencies should use remote forensic software tools "as a standard investigation method to combat cybercrime" (Abel, 2009, p. 99).

Problems Addressing White-Collar Crime Through a Law Enforcement Response

Few criminal cases are actually simple to detect and investigate. White-collar crime cases are no exception. Problems that surface in criminal white-collar crime investigations include the following:

- Resource problems
- Relationship dynamics
- Time
- Complexity
- Proof
- Perceptions of white-collar crime police work

Resource Problems

Resources are a problem inasmuch as white-collar crime police units are grossly under-resourced in comparison to police units focusing on conventional crimes. To be sure, police departments are underfunded in general, and many recent budget cuts have forced departments to eliminate various programs and services. It is likely much easier to reduce services addressing crimes like white-collar crime,

▲ **Photo 13.3** White-collar crime police officers are more apt to use technology in their investigations than other officers.

which is often viewed as less serious than conventional crime. State and federal agencies have also experienced funding problems when it comes to responding to various types of white-collar crimes (Payne, 2006).

Resource problems are a little different for white-collar crime investigations than they are for conventional crime investigations. In particular, whereas most conventional offenders have limited resources that they can use to build their defense against the charges, white-collar offenders typically have significant resources that can be devoted to defending against the allegations. During investigations, corporations will often "lawyer up" as soon as the investigation begins (Williams, 2008, p. 322). Said one investigator, "This is one of the biggest things I've noticed in every interview we do. There's lawyers, upon lawyers, upon lawyers" (Williams, 2008, p. 322).

To be sure, many interviews with conventional offenders are conducted without defense attorneys present. This is less common in white-collar crime investigations. Williams (2008) highlights a process called *litigotiation,* where corporate lawyers engage with police in a way that makes it seem that they are cooperating through "interaction rituals." But they are simply protecting their client through "legal gamesmanship" (p. 322). Examples of litigotiation would include participating in interviews but stalling the case by making unnecessary requests of the police—requests that are not typically made in investigations of conventional criminal cases.

Varying amounts of resources will need to be assigned to different types of cases. Agencies must make decisions about the amount of resources they will devote to different cases. The SEC, the federal agency responsible for addressing securities fraud through civil actions, provides its enforcement division guidance in the Division of Enforcement's enforcement manual. In particular, home office associate directors and regional directors are asked to prioritize their top three cases and list their top 10 cases based on three criteria: "programmatic importance of enforcement action," "magnitude of potential violations," and "resources required to investigate potential violations" (Securities and Exchange Commission, Division of Enforcement, 2010, p. 9). Table 13.5 shows what is meant by each of these items.

Table 13.5	Criteria Used to Decide Resource Allocation in Securities Fraud Investigations	
Programmatic Importance Indicators	**Indicators of Magnitude Potential**	**Indicators of Resources Required**
• whether the subject matter is an SEC priority • whether the subject matter is a Division priority • whether an action would fulfill a programmatic goal of the SEC or the Division • whether an action would address a problematic industry practice • whether the conduct undermines the fairness or liquidity of the U.S. securities markets • whether an action would provide an opportunity for the SEC to address violative conduct targeted to a specific population or community that might not otherwise be familiar with the SEC or the protections afforded by the securities laws • whether an action would present a good opportunity to work together with other civil and criminal agencies • whether the conduct can be addressed by any other state or federal regulators • whether an action would alert the investing public of a new type of securities fraud	• the egregiousness of the conduct • the length of time the conduct continued or whether it is ongoing • the number of violations • whether recidivists were involved • whether violations were repeated • the amount of harm or potential harm to victims • the amount of ill-gotten gains to the violators • whether victims were specifically targeted based on personal or affinity group characteristics • for issuers or regulated entities, whether the conduct involved officers, directors, or senior management • whether gatekeepers (such as accountants or attorneys) or securities industry professionals were involved	• the complexity of the potential violations • the approximate staff hours required over the course of the investigation • the number of staff assigned • the amount of travel required • the duration of the relevant conduct • the number of potential violators • the number and locations of potential witnesses • the number and location of relevant documents to be reviewed

Source: Securities and Exchange Commission, Division of Criminal Enforcement. (2015). In *Enforcement Manual.* Available from http://www.sec.gov/divisions/enforce/enforcementmanual.pdf

Relationship Dynamics

Relationship dynamics also present problems in white-collar crime investigations. Three types of relationships are relevant: (1) the victim-offender relationship, (2) the offender-witness relationship, and (3) the officer-offender relationship. First, in terms of the victim-offender relationship, recall that in many cases, white-collar crime victims are not aware of their victimization, perhaps partly because of the trust that the victim (consumer, client, coworker, etc.) places in the offender (Bucy, 1989). As a result, they are unable to report the victimization to the police and subsequently unable to participate as a witness in the investigation.

With regard to the offender-witness relationship, many of the witnesses that investigators want to interview will be in trusting relationships with the offender. These relationships might be work relationships or personal relationships. Either way, the relationship makes it more difficult for investigators to get accurate information from witnesses. For example, if the witness is a coworker or subordinate of the suspect, the witness has a level of trust in the suspect but may not trust the white-collar crime investigator (Payne, 2003a). As well, in certain professions, the occupational subculture is perceived as protecting members of that subculture in law enforcement investigations (Wilson, Lincoln, Chappell, &

Fraser, 1986). When witnesses are interviewed, they often tell investigators that the suspects are "pillars of the community," making white-collar offenders, in the words of one investigator, "sympathetic defendants who do not look like criminals" (Payne, 2003a, p. 145). In other cases, witnesses might actually be colluding or conspiring with the suspect, thereby making it less likely that they will be cooperative witnesses (Payne, 2006).

The police officer-offender relationship may also present barriers in white-collar crime investigations. The relationship dynamics between officers and offenders are different in white-collar crime and conventional crime cases (see Table 13.6). First, one can note that class status differences between officers and white-collar offenders make these white-collar crime cases different from conventional crime cases. In white-collar crime cases, offenders typically come from a higher social class than most officers do. Alternatively, officers are in a higher social class than conventional offenders are in. This is potentially problematic when white-collar suspects try to use their class status to gain power over officers.

Educational differences might also exist between officers and white-collar offenders. While more and more police officers are required to have college degrees, especially at the federal level, the vast majority of white-collar offenders will have higher educational levels than conventional offenders, and their educational expertise will be different from police officers' expertise. This can be problematic in that officers will need to be acquainted with the offender's occupational specialization in order to understand the nature and dynamics of the occupational misconduct. While those of us trained in criminology and criminal justice are well versed in our own fields, understanding the intricacies of careers in other fields is a difficult task.

White-collar offenders will have more political and economic power than police officers, while police officers have more economic and political power than conventional offenders. This becomes problematic when offenders use their expertise to try to call in favors from politicians, business leaders, and community leaders. In a case involving a 16-year-old kid from an inner-city neighborhood, few outsiders might try to intervene on behalf of the kid. In a case involving a powerful white-collar offender, officers will sometimes need to take more precautions to ensure that the offender is not able to exert political power over the investigation. For example, they might wait longer to proceed with a white-collar case in order to have the strongest case possible.

One can point to the familiarity that police officers have with conventional offenders (as opposed to white-collar offenders) as another relationship barrier in these cases. Conventional offenders are typically more "familiar" with the criminal justice system, having longer arrest records and more contacts with law enforcement officers. Scholars have long talked about a courtroom workgroup to describe familiarity between actors in the courts. For offenders arrested many times, police officers and offenders have—in a very real sense—an informal relationship, albeit one that is based on formal control mechanisms. No such relationship exists between police officers and white-collar offenders, most of whom have

Table 13.6	Relationship Dynamics Between Police Officers and White-Collar and Conventional Offenders	
	White-Collar Offenders	**Conventional Offenders**
Class status	Have a higher class status than police officers	Have a lower class status than police officers
Education	Have either more or a different type of education than police officers	Tend to be less educated than police officers
Economic power	Have more economic power than police officers	Have less economic power than police officers
Political power	Have more political clout and political contacts than police officers	Have less political power than police officers
Familiarity with criminal justice	Very little prior contacts with police	Have longer criminal histories and more contacts with the police

had few prior contacts with the police. In the end, police officers lack familiarity with white-collar offenders. Ironically, the familiarity element might actually result in officers "liking" conventional offenders more than white-collar offenders. Said one white-collar crime investigator, "You cannot trust these white-collar criminals. They are not 'honest criminals' like traditional ones" (Alvesalo, 2003, p. 129).

Time

Time is another problem in white-collar crime investigations. Time becomes problematic in three ways. First, because white-collar crime victims often do not know they were victimized, a long period of time may pass between the time the crime was committed and the time the investigation begins. The longer the amount of time that elapses between the commission of the offense (whether a white-collar crime or conventional crime) and the time police become aware of the offense, the less likely that an arrest will occur in the case.

Second, time is problematic in that it can take an inordinate amount of time to collect all of the necessary records in white-collar crime cases (Payne, 2003a). While the collection of electronic evidence has made record collection more efficient, it still takes time to identify which records are needed and then to review all of the records. As well, writing up the results of the record review can be quite time consuming.

Third, some have argued that it takes longer to prepare for a white-collar crime interrogation than it takes to prepare for an interrogation of a conventional offender (Alvesalo, 2003). Alvesalo notes that interrogations of conventional offenders are usually not prepared ahead of time. Investigators, perhaps because they routinely complete such interrogations, are able to conduct the interrogations "by free narration" (p. 127). Describing the interrogation of white-collar offenders, he quotes one investigator who said:

> In the uniformed police . . . you never had to prepare for the . . . interrogation at all. You just went in there and asked, "What is going on?" and took the statements. In cases of economic crime, you might write questions for a week and you have to do background work for a month and when you start to interrogate, you check the questions, and prepare yourself with all kinds of documents that you have to show the suspects . . . a totally different world. (p. 127)

As an analogy, think of a class you could attend, never study, and then ace the exams. This would be like interrogating conventional offenders. Alternatively, think of a class you have to work hard in, such as most of your criminal justice classes. This would be like interrogating white-collar offenders.

Complexity

Complexity is another problem in white-collar crime investigations. Three issues that make the cases particularly complex include (1) complex record searches, (2) extensive collaborations with partners, and (3) the lack of a systematic approach. In terms of complex record searches, the number of records collected in white-collar crime cases can be overwhelming to the investigations. It is estimated that the "average fraud case can entail fifty boxes of evidence" and 150,000 to 250,000 pages of information (Taylor, 2001, p. 22). Not only is sifting through all of those records time consuming, but a complex endeavor arises in efforts to take that information and narrow it down to evidence indicating that a crime has been committed.

The extensive collaborations with partners in white-collar crime cases can also make the investigations more complex than might be found in investigations of conventional crimes. In home health care fraud cases, for example, investigators will work with the following agencies to pursue the white-collar crime investigation:

- Adult protective services
- Auditor of state
- Crime Victims' Coordinator
- Department of Family Services
- Department of Health
- Division on Aging

- Division on Medical Assistance
- Federal Bureau of Investigation
- Internal Revenue Service
- Local law enforcement
- Local county and prosecuting attorneys
- State Medicaid agency
- State police
- State professional licensing boards (e.g., Board of Nursing, Pharmacy)
- U.S. Attorney's Office
- U.S. Postal Inspection Service
- U.S. Department of Health and Human Services, Office of Inspector General (Payne, 2003a)

Collaboration is necessary in many white-collar crime investigations and can result in adding complexities to the investigation (Middlemiss & Gupta, 2007). For example, it may be difficult to determine which agencies should be involved in the investigation. As well, statutes may keep agencies partnering with one another from sharing relevant information (Payne, 2011). In addition, turf wars may erupt during the course of the investigation. Also, participants in the partnership might have different goals—some might be obsessed with crime statistics, while others might be involved in the effort because they want a part of the funds recovered through the investigation. Also, bureaucratic inertia, which refers to situations where a large group of individuals is unable to move for-

▲ **Photo 13.4**   White-collar crime investigations can involve complex record searches.

ward, may keep the partnership from attaining its goal (Middlemiss & Gupta, 2007). In effect, having to partner with other agencies can make white-collar crime investigations more complex.

The lack of systematic approaches has also contributed to complexity in some white-collar crime investigations. For example, some authors have contended that environmental crime investigations do not always follow systemic approaches (Van den Berg & Eshuis, 1996). Without a systematic approach, the investigatory process becomes more difficult than it needs to be. Remember the principle of parsimony discussed earlier in the text. This principle suggests that theorists must keep their explanations of white-collar crime as simple as possible. In a similar way, investigators must try to simplify the complexities of white-collar crime investigations. To do so, it has been argued that white-collar crime investigations need to be better planned, prioritized, and sensitive to group dynamics (Van den Berg & Eshuis, 1996).

Keep in mind that the police processing of white-collar crime cases varies across offense types. Some white-collar crime cases will be less complex and subsequently easier to investigate than other white-collar crime cases. FBI agent Daniel Bradley (2008) has suggested that records in real estate fraud cases are easier to review than those found in other white-collar crimes. According to Bradley, "these false statements are clear and simple, provable through documentation and witness testimony, and therefore easily conveyed. For example, it is easy to compare a home value estimate from an appraisal form to the estimate actually listed on a mortgage document" (p. 3).

Establishing Proof

It is also difficult for investigators to gather evidence that prosecutors will be able to use to prove various aspects of the misconduct. In some white-collar crime cases, it is so difficult to establish intent that investigators might end up having

▲ **Photo 13.5**   Traditional police work is seen as exciting. White-collar crime investigations are not held in the same regard. Rarely do you see kids playing "white-collar crime cops and robbers."

to "devote their endeavors to less serious charges" (Wilson et al., 1986, p. 139). Consider Martha Stewart's case. She was accused of insider trading but ultimately convicted of perjury.

In a similar way, it is difficult to prove that specific suspects are responsible for the misconduct. This is particularly the case in corporate crimes where it is difficult to determine which employees participated in the offense. In investigations of conventional crimes, "the police ask 'Who did it?' In [white-collar] crime cases, they ask 'which one of the known suspects is responsible?'" (Alvesalo, 2003, p. 124). One criminal justice official commented, "as in any white-collar crime . . . defendants usually assert that they did not understand the complicated regulations, were bad record keepers, etc., but had no criminal intent. Absent a confession, that defense is difficult to overcome" (Payne, 2003a, p. 137).

Perceptions of White-Collar Crime Police Work

Another barrier in the response to white-collar crime is that police work in these cases is often perceived pejoratively, as if the activity is not real police work. On the one hand, such perceptions become problematic when funding for these activities is withheld or reduced based on perceptions such police work is not "real" police work. On the other hand, given that even some police officers view white-collar crime police work as "not real police work" (see Alvesalo & Whyte, 2007), it may be difficult to recruit and retain seasoned criminal justice professionals in policing careers targeting white-collar offenders.

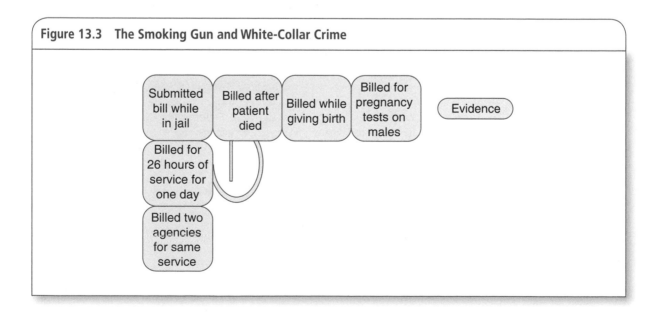

Figure 13.3   The Smoking Gun and White-Collar Crime

- Submitted bill while in jail
- Billed after patient died
- Billed while giving birth
- Billed for pregnancy tests on males
- Evidence
- Billed for 26 hours of service for one day
- Billed two agencies for same service

● ● ● Suggestions for Improving the Law Enforcement Response to White-Collar Crime

A number of suggestions have been made for improving the law enforcement response to white-collar crime. For example, just as the media show celebrated white-collar offenders doing the "perp walk" to the police car, police department, or courthouse, some researchers have suggested that efforts should be undertaken to make sure that arrests are "publicized" to those in the workplace by arresting suspects when a lot of people are at work, as during shift changes (Payne & Gray, 2001). This same author team warns officers against assuming that labels given to white-collar crime are accurate descriptors of the behavior. For instance, some believe that "financial crimes" are not harmful, and this would, in turn, diminish the value that officers give to the work. Recognizing the seriousness of the offenses potentially increases the value that officers would place on law enforcement activities targeting white-collar crimes.

The search for a **"smoking gun"** has been suggested as a strategy for improving investigations in white-collar crime cases (Payne & Gray, 2001). In this context, the phrase *smoking gun* refers to indisputable evidence that substantiates that a crime has been committed. One contracted employee, for example, billed an employer for 800 consecutive days of work. Think about that. That's 27 straight months with no day off from work. Incidentally, this employee held a separate full-time job and took three vacations to New York, Aruba, and Mexico during the 27-month scam (Payne, 2003a). Figure 13.3 shows some additional smoking gun cases.

Another recommendation for improving the police response to white-collar crime is related to the popular movie *Jerry Maguire.* Even if you have not seen the movie, you have probably heard the tag line by Rod Tidwell, played by Cuba Gooding, Jr., who said to Jerry, "Show me the money." The quote is among the most recognized movie lines. There's another quote that financial investigators recognize: "Follow the money" (Wells, 2003a, p. 84). Certainly, in many white-collar crime cases, money is the target. If investigators can find the money, then they find evidence that substantiates the crime. As Wells (2003b) wrote, "Money from any source—lawful or not—can be dispersed only four ways: It can be spent, saved, used to acquire assets, or to pay debts" (p. 76). Thus, investigators will review the suspects' assets (e.g., their possessions), liabilities, sources of funds, and expenditures.

Improved educational programs have also been hailed as strategies for helping law enforcement officers respond to white-collar crime. Over the past decade, efforts have expanded to involve colleges and universities in preparing current and future investigators to address white-collar crime. One example is the Internal Revenue Service Criminal Investigation's (IRS CI) Adrian Project. In this project, the IRS CI partners with a college and assigns a coach to work with students on an applied learning exercise. The students are given crime scene scenarios, including white-collar crime scenarios, and asked to investigate the offenses. The program has been found to improve students' detection skills, abilities to gather and organize data, abilities to use multiple investigative tools, and interviewing and communication skills (Brickner, Mahoney, & Moore, 2010).

At the University of West Virginia, the College of Business and Economics developed a Fraud Accounting and Fraud Investigator program to improve the skills of future fraud fighters. This is a certificate program that includes four courses: "Fraud Investigation, Fraud Data Analysis, Criminology and Legal Issues, and Advanced Fraud Investigation" (H. Richardson, 2010, p. 10). Assignments include hands-on crime scene investigation.

At Gonzaga University, the Justice for Fraud Victims project was created as a joint effort between forensic accountants, faculty, the police, and local prosecutors. Accounting students assigned to teams work on real fraud cases involving small businesses and nonprofit organizations. The students help gather evidence, recover money for businesses, and prosecute offenders (Sowa, 2010). The number of college-level fraud courses grew significantly (from 19 to 150) between the 1990s and 2003 (Wells, 2003b). These courses aim to teach students the following skills that are needed among fraud investigators:

- Expertise with financial matters
- Understanding motivations for white-collar crime
- Understanding the laws surrounding white-collar crime

- Insight into legal and ethical issues
- Communication and writing skills, particularly report writing
- Critical thinking skills (Peterson, 2004)

Following this same line of thinking, some have called for a more proactive educational response to white-collar crime that addresses the changing nature of societal systems. Said one official employed in a statistical financial analysis unit:

> The authorities find themselves in this position of running after the problems and their perpetrators—the robbers always keeping the advantage over the cops. With the advantage and with the ever-increasing innovations in technology that can be used for illicit ends, the risk grows that the criminal act cannot be [stopped]. (Nardo, 2004, p. 139)

Increasing technological awareness about white-collar crime should help improve the police response to white-collar crime.

● ● ● Self-Policing and White-Collar Crime

Self-policing refers to efforts by companies and businesses to develop their own policing responses to white-collar crime. Businesses develop self-policing strategies for practical and economic reasons. Practically speaking, it is impossible for law enforcement agencies to police businesses on a daily basis, so businesses develop their own private policing systems. Economically, self-policing strategies help businesses protect their bottom lines by minimizing the economic costs of employee misconduct. Options available to businesses who identify crime as a result of self-policing strategies include (1) reporting the crime to the police, (2) filing civil charges, (3) negotiating a settlement with the offender, (4) sanctioning the offender with an internal reprimand, and (5) negotiating a nondisclosure agreement with the offender (Meerts, 2013). Types of self-policing efforts used by business to detect or prevent white-collar crime include loss prevention strategies, compliance programs, audits, and forensic accounting.

Loss Prevention Strategies

Loss prevention strategies are efforts that businesses use to keep employees from stealing from the business. Traub (1996) cites three types of loss prevention strategies. Category I strategies refer to efforts where businesses emphasize security. Security officials perform a number of different activities, including "surveillance, plain-clothes detective work, and undercover operations directed at criminal activity and other forms of misconduct" (p. 248). Some businesses have increased their reliance on security strategies to detect and prevent workplace crimes. Consider that the number of investigators hired in some accounting firms doubled in the wake of the Enron and WorldCom scandals in the early 2000s (Wells, 2003b).

Category II loss prevention strategies emphasize screening and education (Traub, 1996). During recruiting stages, workers are screened intensively in an effort to weed out those who have a likelihood of engaging in criminal acts on the job. Background checks and reference checks have long been used to screen out applicants that employers think might steal from the workplace. With the advent of technology, some employers now also conduct media and Internet searches to learn more about prospective employees. These searches can be quite enlightening. In one media search, the following information was uncovered:

> A candidate said he had been working in the family business for a few years, when in fact he had been in prison. A Kroll media search found out that the candidate had been in prison because he had shared a cell with mass murderer Fred West at some point and on being released, sold his story to a newspaper. (Huber, 2010, Labour Market Lies section, para. 3)

Facebook and similar social network sites have also been searched to determine the employability of job candidates. Criminal justice students should take note of this particular statement. In a conference presentation titled "What Were You Thinking? Criminal Justice Students and Their Social Networking Sites," a criminal justice professor and his graduate student discussed a research project where they reviewed public Facebook pages of criminal justice students at their university (J. Lee, 2010). The research team showed some of the pictures they found on students' Facebook pages. Many of the criminal justice majors included pictures of drunken celebrations and marijuana use. One that stood out showed two students in a bathroom, with one of them bent over the toilet. Even if the pictures were not of the students themselves, simply having these pictures on one's Facebook page might be enough to raise concern in future employers. (Note to readers—after you read this chapter, review your Facebook page to make sure it won't keep you unemployed in the future. Make sure you finish this chapter first, though.)

Category III strategies emphasize getting employees to share information about their coworkers' misconduct through efforts such as whistleblowing and anonymous hotlines (Traub, 1996). Anonymous hotlines have been found to be particularly effective "if accompanied by positive support from management" (Holtfreter, 2004, p. 89). What this means is that the leaders of the business must promote a culture that advances and supports ethical decision making in the workplace.

In conducting workplace investigations, it is imperative that information be secured and not shared with coworkers of suspects until necessary. Most workplace settings have tight-knit relationships among coworkers. Coworkers will share information—whether accurate or not—with one another. If information about an ongoing investigation becomes public, the internal investigation could be derailed.

The internal investigation process will follow stages similar to those followed in law enforcement investigations of white-collar crime (discussed above). Some differences are worth noting. For example, if a business catches an employee engaging in misconduct, it may simply fire the employee and not refer the case to the authorities. This is often done to avoid negative publicity or simply to minimize the amount of time that would be spent in the criminal justice process.

Another difference has to do with the way interviews are conducted in self-policing and law enforcement investigations. Public law enforcement officers are held to a higher standard with regard to the rights of the individual they are interrogating. If, for example, a suspect "pleads the Fifth" and says that he or she will not answer specific questions in a criminal investigation, this cannot be held against that person at trial. If a suspect refuses to cooperate in an internal investigation, the person's employer can make decisions about the outcome of the investigation by inferring from the employee's refusal to answer questions (Schiff & Kramer, 2004).

Some also make a distinction between a "custodial interrogation" of arrested offenders and a **workplace interview** conducted in internal investigations. One expert advised:

> The interview is not a forum for cross-examination, but for information gathering. If cross-examination techniques are used, then often little is achieved. However, it is important for the investigator to use assistance language, "can you help me?" "can you be of assistance to me?" or "I do not understand some issues." (Coburn, 2006, p. 348)

The key distinction centers on a more inquisitorial approach found in internal investigations, as opposed to the adversarial approach used in criminal investigations.

Like criminal investigations, internal investigations might entail a significant number of records that need to be collected, analyzed, and secured. Coburn (2006) recommended that organizations develop policies for collecting and securing records. In particular, Coburn suggested the following:

- "Have a written procedure for the collection of evidence;
- Document the collection of evidence, detailing, time, place of origin, and circumstances of collection;
- Identify documents;
- Obtain relevant primary documents, i.e., contracts, invoices, share certificates, financial transaction documents, etc.;
- Obtain relevant secondary documents, e.g., entry documentation to buildings, telephone, facsimile and computer information;

- Verify primary and secondary documents;
- Secure documents inside the organization" (Coburn, 2006, p. 348).

Whereas a criminal investigation secures records in the law enforcement agency, self-policing efforts keep their records in-house. Whether those records become public depends on the seriousness of the offending and whether the business decides to report the case to the authorities.

Compliance Strategies

Compliance strategies are another form of self-policing. A **compliance program** is an "organizational system aimed at comprehensively detecting and preventing corporate criminality" (Goldsmith & King, 1997, p. 9). Such programs provide a mechanism for identifying and reporting misdeeds with a view toward keeping the misconduct from occurring in the first place. Strategies used in compliance programs include "audits, employee training, reporting mechanisms, and sanctions for illegal actions" (Goldsmith & King, 1997, p. 10).

Under the 1991 U.S. Sentencing Guidelines, corporations with strong compliance programs are eligible to receive lighter sanctions for misconduct. The sentencing guidelines offer guidance to organizations to indicate what is expected in compliance programs in order to be eligible for reduced sanctions. The guidelines state:

1. The organization must have established compliance standards and procedures to be followed by its employees and other agents that are reasonably capable of reducing the prospect of criminal conduct.

2. Specific individual(s) within high-level personnel of the organization must have been assigned overall responsibility to oversee compliance with such standards and procedures.

3. The organization must have used due care not to delegate substantial discretionary authority to individuals whom the organization knew, or should have known through the exercise of due diligence, to have a propensity to engage in illegal activities.

4. The organization must have taken steps to communicate effectively its standards and procedures to all employees and other agents, for example, by requiring participation in training programs or by disseminating publications that explain in a practical manner what is required.

5. The organization must have taken reasonable steps to achieve compliance with its standards, for example, by using monitoring and auditing systems reasonably designed to detect criminal conduct by its employees and other agents and by having in place and publicizing a reporting system whereby employees and other agents could report criminal conduct by others within the organization without fear of retribution.

6. The standards must have been consistently enforced through appropriate disciplinary mechanisms, including, as appropriate, discipline of individuals responsible for the failure to detect an offense. Adequate discipline of individuals responsible for an offense is a necessary component of enforcement; however, the form of discipline that will be appropriate will be case specific.

7. After an offense has been detected, the organization must have taken all reasonable steps to respond appropriately to the offense and to prevent further similar offenses—including any necessary modifications to its program to prevent and detect violations of law. (U.S. Federal Sentencing Guidelines available from http://www.ethics.org/resource/federal-sentencing-guidelines)

Beyond allowing a lighter sanction if a corporation is found liable for corporate misconduct, compliance programs are valuable because they can potentially deter workplace transgressions. Scholars have offered suggestions for how to ensure that compliance programs effectively police workplace misconduct. Nestor (2004) argued that executives should "drive compliance from the top" (p. 348). He called for the development of a corporate code of ethics and mandated reporting by officials. If executives show they are serious about preventing corporate misconduct, Nestor suggested, the compliance program will serve as an effective self-policing strategy.

Audits

Audits are included as a part of many organizations' compliance programs and can be seen as an effective self-policing strategy. In this context, audits are different from those discussed above. Criminal investigation audits are conducted by law enforcement representatives for the purpose of searching for wrongdoing. **Self-policing audits** are done by the organization, and as a result, the organization has more control over the direction and timing of the audit.

Audits have been described as "a widely used organizational defense against fraud" (Holtfreter, 2004, p. 89). Audits are done as part of routine procedures, or they may be initiated out of a concern that fraud is occurring in the organization. Organizations will conduct either internal or external audits. **Internal audits** are conducted by the organization's accounting department, while **external audits** are conducted by consultants hired by the corporation (Holtfreter, 2004). Some red flags that surface from audits include the following:

- A lack of documentation for new projects
- Significant payments to new vendors
- Larger payments than usual
- Signs of managers systematically overriding internal controls (Heslop, 2004)

It is believed that, when fraud is discovered during a routine audit, the detection is typically "by chance" (Hemraj, 2002, p. 85). **Fraud audits**, or audits conducted for the purpose of exposing fraud, are more likely to reveal fraud. The objectives of a fraud audit include (1) identifying control mechanisms in a business, (2) identifying weaknesses in a business that place the business at risk for fraud, and (3) identifying those with access who have taken advantage of the weaknesses (Buckhoff, Higgins, & Sinclair, 2010). Some estimates suggest that nearly half of frauds against businesses are uncovered through audits (Peterson, 2004).

Audits are useful in helping companies identify parts of the company that are not profitable as well as potential areas of concern. In addition, audits help companies determine whether they are at risk of criminal and civil liability, and if conducted as part of a strong compliance program, audits allow companies more control over the direction of any subsequent criminal or civil investigation (Goldsmith & King, 1997).

In July 2002, the Sarbanes-Oxley Act (SOX) was passed in reaction to the scandals that were occurring at the time, including Enron's and WorldCom's crimes. Among other things, the act, known as SOX, developed standards for auditor independence in publicly traded companies and public accounting firms. The act states that an external auditor must meet these provisions:

- Cannot have been an employee of the company being audited in the prior year
- Must be approved by the company's audit committee
- Cannot offer additional services (such as bookkeeping) without the approval of the audit committee
- Cannot perform audits more than 5 years in a row for the same company
- Must communicate policies and changes to the audit committee
- Must publicly disclose fees (Nestor, 2004)

The SOX act included a number of other provisions relevant to the criminal and civil processing of corporate crimes. These other provisions will be discussed later in the text.

Forensic Accounting

Students are likely familiar with television shows like *CSI: Crime Scene Investigation*, where forensic scientists review crime scene evidence and solve the crime by the end of the show. Just as forensic scientists are able to piece together evidence to identify suspects, forensic accountants are able to review financial records and determine whether evidence indicates that a crime has been committed. Accordingly, forensic accounting is another self-policing strategy some businesses use to detect fraud.

When using forensic accountants, businesses will typically hire external consultants to perform the investigation. Just as a large private investigator business exists in the United States, an industry called "Forensic Accounting and Corporate

Investigation" also exists (Williams, 2005). This industry has been described as "a diverse and loosely coupled network of private firms and professional groups providing investigative, advisory, and adjudicative service to clients embroiled in cases of economic and financial wrongdoing, whether as 'victims' or 'offenders'" (Williams, 2005, p. 188). Williams described three tiers in this industry: (1) specialized forensic accounting units in large accounting firms, (2) large forensic accounting firms devoted solely to corporate investigations, and (3) small private investigation agencies. When hired, forensic accountants can do investigative accounting, searching for evidence of fraud, economic loss calculations determining how much a company has lost to fraud or other events, and appraisals of the business to determine whether the company made or lost money as a result of misconduct (Rasmussen & Leauanae, 2004). For corporate offenders, forensic accounting firms offer services as expert witnesses, consulting about federal policies and laws, witness preparation, and a number of other services.

It is important to note that forensic accountants will also collect and scrutinize evidence other than financial records. They will review work schedules, read e-mail messages, interview workers and bosses, gather and review other available evidence, and develop a report detailing their conclusions about the presence of fraud in the business: (1) whether it is occurring in the business, (2) why it is occurring, and (3) who is possibly committing the fraud. A survey of 252 academics and forensic accountants found that the most necessary skills for forensic accountants included deductive reasoning, critical thinking, and the ability to serve as an expert witness (DiGabriele, 2008). The author of this study notes that an accounting education often focuses on a structured way to do accounting, but forensic accounting is different because the practitioners need to be able to improvise.

● ● ● Regulatory Policing and White-Collar Crime

Regulatory agencies are government agencies responsible for making sure that regulations are followed in industries and businesses across the United States. In this context, regulations are rules that guide workplace activities. Note that the violation of a "rule" may not necessarily be treated as a violation of the criminal law, but these violations can be seen as white-collar crimes. To provide a framework for understanding regulatory policing, the following areas will be addressed:

- Conceptualizing regulatory policing
- Regulatory officials as police officers
- Regulatory policing styles
- Criticisms of regulatory policing

Conceptualizing Regulatory Policing

Different types of businesses are regulated by different regulatory agencies, depending on the different types of products and/or services the business provides. In reality, most businesses are regulated by multiple regulatory agencies. For example, restaurants and bars are regulated by (1) local and state agencies responsible for ensuring that food safety laws are not violated, (2) state alcohol control agencies to make sure that liquor laws are not violated, (3) occupational safety and health agencies to make sure businesses are not violating workers' rights or making them unsafe, and (4) local, state, and federal agencies charged with ensuring waste is disposed of correctly.

Regulatory agencies engage in policing activities in different ways that are tied to the specific agency's mission statement. Regulatory enforcement has been defined as "the consistent application of formal rules and sanctions to secure compliance with the enabling legislation and promulgated regulations" (Snider, 1990, p. 374). As Hazel Croall (1989) points out, regulatory officers "proceed very much like police" (p. 166). Others have added that regulators "are required to set in motion a process to identify . . . and punish those who have been irresponsible" (Jayasuriya & Sharp, 2006, p. 51). The Careers Responding to White-Collar Crime: Consumer Safety Officer box shows the duties performed by one type of regulatory officer.

CAREERS RELATED TO WHITE-COLLAR CRIME

Consumer Safety Officer

Consumer safety officers are concerned with enforcing and obtaining voluntary compliance with laws and regulations protecting consumers from products that are impure, harmful, unwholesome, ineffective, improperly labeled, or in some other way dangerous, defective or deceptive. The products that come under their jurisdiction are numerous and varied. They include foods, drugs, therapeutic devices, cosmetics, toys and equipment used by children, flammable fabrics, and hazardous substances (a broad category that includes such things as household cleaning products, pottery foodware, and household appliances).

Regulations and programs relating to these products primarily concern:

1. Ingredients in food and drug products. – Standards of identity are set for many common food products and tolerances are set for the use of certain chemical substances, food additives, preservatives, color additives, and artificial ingredients. Packaging and other materials coming in direct contact with foods and drugs are monitored for possible reactions with and adulteration of products.

2. Sanitation and contamination of products. – This includes microorganisms; insect infestation; contamination by rodent, bird, insect, or other animal excreta; foreign materials; decay; and deterioration that render products unfit for human consumption.

3. Labeling and packaging. – Labels must include specific information on the ingredients, weights, and directions for use. Packaging must be appropriate for the nature and quantity of the contents.

4. Safety. – Products must meet certain standards for safety under normal or prescribed use. Labels must warn consumers about possible hazards.

5. Effectiveness of drug products. – Firms that produce drugs and therapeutic devices must have sufficient scientific evidence to prove that their products are effective for the purpose intended.

6. Good manufacturing practices. – This primarily relates to manufacturing processes, equipment, facilities, quality control systems, and work performance standards that are conducive to producing commodities that meet prescribed standards of identity, purity, quality, and strength.

Source: Reprinted from Position Classification Standard for Consumer Safety Series, Available online at: https://www.opm.gov/policy-data-oversight/classification-qualifications/classifying-general-schedule-positions/standards/0600/gs0696.pdf

Some have said that the financial crisis of the early 2000s actually served to "awaken the world to the role of the regulator in the fight against financial crimes" (Pusey, 2007, p. 300). Pusey draws attention to the changing nature of the regulator's role. The Obama administration increased regulatory efforts. Describing crackdowns on unsafe products and unsafe workplace settings, one reporter commented, "The new regulators display a passion for rules and a belief that government must protect the public from dangers lurking at home and on the job—one more way the new White House is reworking the relationship between government and business" (Layton, 2009).

The more recent financial crises of the late 2000s also awakened some politicians to the need for additional regulation in the financial markets. After the economic collapse, which was compared to the Great Depression, the Dodd-Frank Wall Street Reform and Consumer Protection Act was passed in 2010. This act essentially overhauled the financial regulation system. Its stated purpose was

To promote the financial stability of the United States by improving accountability and transparency in the financial system, to end "too big to fail," to protect the American taxpayer by ending bailouts, to protect consumers from abusive financial services practices, and for other purposes.

The 848-page act was a piece of sweeping legislation aiming to prevent another situation where the economy would collapse as a result of poor decisions by financial institutions. Various federal agencies were called upon to create new strategies to regulate the financial industry. For example, after the passage of the act, the SEC created the following offices:

- Office of the Whistleblower
- Office of Credit Ratings
- Office of the Investor Advocate
- Office of Minority and Women Inclusion
- Office of Municipal Securities

The act also created the Consumer Finance Protection Bureau, which was developed as a strategy to prevent consumer fraud. The bureau is tasked to:

- Write rules, supervise companies, and enforce federal consumer financial protection laws
- Restrict unfair, deceptive, or abusive acts or practices
- Take consumer complaints
- Promote financial education
- Research consumer behavior
- Monitor financial markets for new risks to consumers
- Enforce laws that outlaw discrimination and other unfair treatment in consumer finance (Consumer Finance Bureau, 2015)

Figure 13.4 shows the organizational chart for this bureau. As shown in the figure, many different offices were created in the bureau to address the many different types of consumers in the United States.

Regulatory Officials as Police Officers

In general, agencies receive information about violations through referrals, site inspections, news reports, and record reviews. In terms of referrals, regulatory agencies receive information about potential rule breaking from investors, consumers, anonymous tips, competitors, and other government agencies that uncover potential wrongdoing (Rutledge, 2006). Regulatory officials will review the referral by using traditional investigatory techniques, including interviewing witnesses, visiting the site of the alleged violation, reviewing records, and so on.

In addition to visiting business sites to follow up on complaints, regulatory officers will carry out routine site visits to conduct periodic reviews of businesses. Inspectors from local or state health departments, for example, will visit restaurants to ensure that the businesses are in compliance with food safety and health regulations. The inspectors assign the restaurant a score based on the inspection. In some places, the inspection reports are posted online. Inspectors can force a business to shut down until the violations are addressed. Consider a case in which an inspector temporarily closed a restaurant in south Florida for 17 violations uncovered as part of the inspection. Among other things, the inspection found "raw sewage in the back yard of the restaurant; more than 100 fresh rodent droppings in the kitchen; a live roach in the kitchen; ready-to-eat, potentially hazardous food prepared on site and held more than 24 hours and not properly date-marked" (Trischitta, 2011). In another case, a restaurant was shut down by inspectors who found employees butchering a deer in the kitchen when they visited the establishment to follow up on an anonymous tip ("Restaurant Closed Briefly," 2008).

As another example of site visits as part of regulatory policing of white-collar crime, the Center for Medicare and Medicaid Services contracts with states to have state inspectors visit nursing homes receiving Medicare or Medicaid at least once a year and conduct health and safety inspections. The inspectors conduct a thorough investigation assessing the degree to which the business is adhering to more than 150 different rules. Based on their findings, the team can fine the nursing homes, deny payments, and suspend the nursing home from participation in Medicare and Medicaid if it fails to address violations found by inspectors (Medicare.Gov, 2008). See In Focus 13.2 for a description of the thoroughness of the site visits.

Regulatory investigations sometimes stem from news reports demonstrating how a particular agency or industry is violating regulations. In July 2010, for example, the Department of Housing and Urban Development (HUD) initiated an investigation after a *New York Times* article titled "Need a Mortgage? Don't Get Pregnant," by reporter Tara Bernard (2010), showed that pregnant women and new moms were being denied loans because of their new babies. After the article appeared in print, HUD released a statement to the press that included the following comments:

A published report in the *New York Times* indicated that some mortgage lenders may be denying credit to borrowers because of a pregnancy or maternity leave. As a result, HUD's Office of Fair Housing Equal Opportunity is opening multiple investigations into the practices of lending institutions to determine if they are violating the Fair Housing Act.

"This report is profoundly disturbing and requires immediate action," said John Trasviña, HUD's Assistant Secretary for Fair Housing and Equal Opportunity, the office that will be directing these investigations. "Lenders must not carry out due diligence responsibilities in ways that have the practical effect of discriminating against recent or expectant mothers." (U.S. Department of Housing and Urban Development [HUD], 2010)

Regulatory agencies also learn about violations through record reviews. For businesses that receive payments from the government, regulatory officials review the bills submitted by the business to ensure the business is in compliance and to determine whether regulatory rules were violated. If officials detect errors in the claims, an additional examination is conducted to determine whether the error was intentional or accidental. For accidental errors, the funds are recovered from the business. For intentionally submitted false bills, the case is referred to another office for criminal and civil investigations. In securities fraud investigations, federal and "state regulators have authority to issue subpoenas for documents" (Rutledge, 2006, p. 340).

IN FOCUS 13.2

The Nursing Home Inspection Process

The inspection team observes resident care processes, staff-resident interaction, and environment. Using an established protocol, the team interviews a sample of residents and family members about their life within the nursing home, and interviews caregivers and administrative staff. The team reviews clinical records.

The inspection team consists of trained inspectors, including at least one registered nurse. This team evaluates whether the nursing home meets individual resident needs. In addition,

fire safety specialists evaluate whether a nursing home meets standards for safe construction. When an inspection team finds that a home does not meet a specific regulation, it issues a deficiency citation.

The regulations cover a wide range of aspects of resident life, from specifying standards for the safe storage and preparation of food to protecting residents from physical or mental abuse or inadequate care practices. (Medicare.gov, 2008)

Source: Reprinted From Medicare.Gov. (2008). In *About nursing home inspections.* Available from http://www.medicare.gov/nursing/aboutinspections.asp

---

Regulatory Policing Styles

Generally speaking, two types of regulatory strategies exist—persuasion or cooperation strategies and retributive or punishment strategies (Frank, 1984; Snider, 1990). Persuasion strategies promote "education, negotiation, and cooperation" to

Figure 13.4 Consumer Protection Finance Bureau Organizational Chart

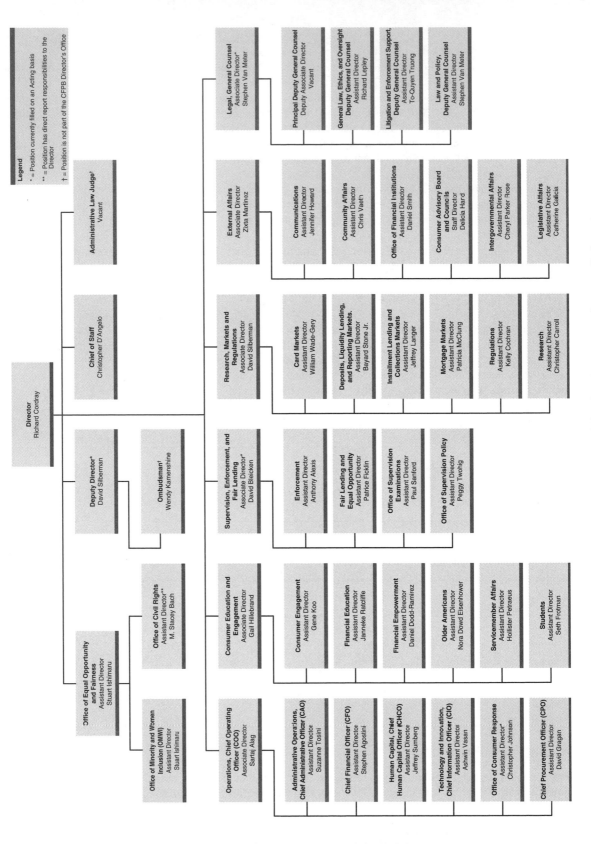

Source: Reprinted from Consumer Financial Protection Bureau (no date). About Us. Organizational Chart. http://www.consumerfinance.gov/the-bureau/.

▲ **Photo 13.6a and 13.6b**   Regulatory officers act in many ways as police officers do, though they may be searching for different types of evidence.

get businesses and corporations to comply with regulations (Frank, 1984, p. 237). Retributive strategies emphasize finding violations and punishing offenders. An analogy to traffic enforcement helps distinguish between the two strategies. If your campus police develop strategies to educate and persuade students to obey traffic laws, this would be a persuasion strategy. If your campus police focus solely on catching traffic violators and giving them stiff fines, this would be a retributive strategy. Among regulatory agencies, some are more persuasion oriented, while others are more punishment oriented.

A question that often arises is whether regulatory officers are police officers. Using James Q. Wilson's typology of police officers, criminologist Nancy Frank (1984) shows how regulatory policing styles are similar to traditional law enforcement styles. First, some regulatory agencies follow a "service style" where the agencies serve the community through the provision of various services. According to Frank, administrators in these agencies see themselves as serving the government and not the public.

Second, some agencies follow a "watchman" style in their efforts to regulate corporate behavior—using discretion and staying out of the way, with officers who are described by Frank as possessing "only marginal competence" (Frank, 1984, p. 242). Consider the movie *Larry the Cable Guy: Health Inspector*, which one or two readers may have seen. In the movie, Larry the Cable Guy is portrayed as a health inspector letting businesses get away with all sorts of atrocities and enforcing laws only as a last resort. I won't give away the plot because it truly is worth watching to learn more about regulatory policing.

Third, "legalistic" agencies address regulatory violations more aggressively. Officers are more competent and more professional in such agencies, and the agencies "have formal guidelines instructing enforcement officers when to bring actions" (Frank, 1984, p. 245). These officers likely see their occupations as being oriented toward law enforcement and play by the book in their efforts to regulate businesses and corporations.

Fourth, the "free agent" style is similar to the legalistic style, but regulatory officers are given more leeway in deciding how to proceed with the case. Imagine Clint Eastwood's Dirty Harry character as a regulatory officer. Instead of a .44

magnum, he would be armed with a clipboard, rule book, and BlackBerry, but his efforts to root out corporate rule breaking would be similar to the way the fictional officer sought out criminals in the five movies about the detective's crime fighting.

As long as we are using a Dirty Harry analogy, in the 1983 Dirty Harry movie *Sudden Impact*, Detective Harry Callahan was pointing his gun at his nemesis when he said, "Go ahead, make my day"—a quote that has become part of our lexicon. Callahan was, in effect, communicating a very clear message to the offender—he wanted to shoot the suspect in the head. In a no-nonsense way, regulatory officers are expected to communicate messages to the businesses and organizations they regulate.

Researchers have suggested that how compliance messages are communicated to managers in the business or corporation may have an impact on how they respond to the regulatory activity (Makkai & Braithwaite, 1994). If the regulator's behaviors and messages are perceived as overly punitive, the business might continue to engage in rule breaking. Makkai and Braithwaite call for a reintegrative shaming model to notify businesses about misconduct. They suggest that regulators do the following:

(a) communicate noncompliance in a way that is perceived as procedurally fair, (b) communicate noncompliance in a way that does not communicate distrust, (c) communicate noncompliance in a way that shows respect for professionalism, (d) give praise to low self-efficacy actors when they fix one of the problems, and (e) encourage disengagers to become reengaged. (p. 365)

In other words, the "Dirty Harry style of communicating" may not be the best way for regulators to communicate with corporations.

Criticisms of Regulatory Policing

A number of different criticisms have been levied against regulatory policing, with most of these criticisms suggesting that the regulatory efforts do little to stop misconduct. In fact, some say that rather than stopping misconduct, such efforts may actually breed rule breaking. For example, one author team suggested that "much regulation . . . represents a facilitation, rather than diminishment, of environmental harm" (Halsey & White, 1998, p. 347). Others have blamed regulatory agencies for recent economic woes on the grounds that "light-handed" regulation allowed corporate misconduct to escalate to the point that markets collapsed and criminal prosecutions were inevitable (Tomasic, 2011).

Scholars have also argued that corporate power weakens the regulatory system. Snider (1990) suggested that "the entire agenda of regulation is the result of a struggle between the corporate sector opposing regulation and the much weaker forces supporting it" (p. 384). Another criticism that has been levied is that regulatory efforts are too lenient and corporate misconduct should be handled as violations of the criminal law, with more severe sanctions given to offenders.

While some have said the corporations, businesses, and offenders should be criminally punished rather than regulated, criminologist Susan Shapiro (1985) has argued that a clear sign that regulatory agencies have failed is the use of the criminal law to respond to corporate misconduct. From this perspective, if regulatory agencies were working, then companies would be abiding by corporate regulations, and there would be no need for the criminal law in these cases.

● ● ● The Global Police and White-Collar Crime

As noted throughout this book, white-collar offending occurs internationally. One author summed up this pattern stating, "with the globalization of the world economy, white collar crime is increasingly transnational in nature" (Lardo, 2006, p. 867). Consequently, police agencies from across the world have been called upon to use law enforcement strategies to detect, respond to, and prevent white-collar crime. A number of issues arise in efforts to address international white-collar crimes. Such issues include the following:

- Countries vary in the types of records they maintain.
- Linguistic barriers make it difficult for officers to communicate with one another.
- Cultural barriers create situations where misconduct and offenders might be perceived differently.
- Gaining cooperation between agencies from different countries is difficult.
- Variation in international laws results in misconduct being defined differently across the world.
- Determining whether international enforcement policies are effective is an arduous task (Passas, 2004).

Barriers also arise when international companies do internal investigations within their own company. Different data protection laws between countries, for example, may limit a company's ability to transfer documents between countries (Dervan, 2011). In addition, the regulations governing how internal security officials can interview employees may vary across countries and make it more difficult to conduct these interviews in some cases (Dervan, 2011).

These barriers can be overcome, or at least minimized. For example, cooperation can be enhanced if officers are aware of cultural differences between countries (Larsson, 2006). Also, resource commitments by specific agencies involved in international partnerships would help to demonstrate that countries are committed to responding to white-collar crime (Berkman et al., 2008). Larsson (2006) suggested that international cooperation can be improved if officials do the following: (1) create networks where police officers can develop a "common language" (p. 463), (2) provide appropriate education and training to those involved in the international response to white-collar crime, (3) ensure that police agencies have the information they need to prevent crime, and (4) identify communication channels.

SUMMARY

- White-collar crimes come to the attention of the police through several different avenues, and a number of different agencies are involved in the police response to white-collar crime.
- The notion of *police response* to white-collar crime describes different forms of policing, including criminal policing, private policing, and regulatory policing.
- Three types of agencies are involved in responding to white-collar crime. These include private agencies (or self-policing by corporations or businesses), formal criminal police agencies, and governmental regulatory agencies.
- In the FBI, the Financial Crimes Section (FCS), located in the agency's Criminal Investigative Division, investigates cases of white-collar crime.
- A major portion of the police response to white-collar crime involves law enforcement strategies carried out by officials in the criminal justice system.
- White-collar crime investigations begin one of two ways—from referrals or as a part of a proactive policing initiative.
- Common strategies for gathering evidence in white-collar crime cases include (1) audits, (2) record reviews, (3) undercover strategies, (4) the use of whistleblowers, and (5) the use of technological devices.
- While not always sufficient by themselves, when combined with other forms of evidence-gathering strategies, audits can provide the evidence needed to substantiate wrongdoing.
- White-collar crime investigators will review an assortment of records in building their case. The number of records law enforcement investigators will need to review in these cases can be enormous.
- On the surface, undercover white-collar crime investigations are no different from undercover criminal investigations. However, important differences exist between white-collar and conventional undercover investigations.
- Compared to conventional undercover investigations, white-collar crime undercover investigations are less dangerous, less time consuming, involve lower degrees of role playing by officers, and are not as central to the case as undercover investigations in criminal cases.
- Whistleblowers are individuals who notify authorities about wrongdoing in their organization. Two types of whistleblowers exist: internal whistleblowers and external whistleblowers (Vinten, 1994).
- Various types of technological devices are used to search for evidence in white-collar crime cases.

- Problems that surface in criminal white-collar crime investigations include the following resource problems: relationship dynamics, time, complexity, proof, and perceptions of white-collar crime police work.
- Resources are a problem inasmuch as white-collar crime police units are grossly under-resourced in comparison to police units focusing on conventional crimes.
- Three types of relationships present obstacles in white-collar crime investigations: (1) the victim-offender relationship, (2) the offender-witness relationship, and (3) the officer-offender relationship.
- Three issues that make white-collar crimes particularly complex are (1) complex record searches, (2) extensive collaborations with partners, and (3) the lack of a systematic approach.
- It is difficult for investigators to gather evidence that prosecutors will be able to use to prove various aspects of the misconduct.
- Police work in these cases is often perceived pejoratively, as if the activity is not real police work.
- A number of different suggestions have been made to improve the law enforcement response to white-collar crime, including searching for the "smoking gun," "following the money," and educating officials.
- Self-policing refers to efforts by companies and businesses to develop their own policing responses to white-collar crime.
- Types of self-policing efforts used by business to detect or prevent white-collar crime include loss prevention strategies, compliance programs, audits, and the use of forensic accountants.
- Loss prevention strategies are efforts that businesses use to keep employees from stealing from the business.
- A compliance program is an "organizational system aimed at comprehensively detecting and preventing corporate criminality" (Goldsmith & King, 1997, p. 9).
- Criminal investigation audits are conducted by law enforcement representatives for the purpose of searching for wrongdoing. Self-policing audits are done by the organization.
- Forensic accountants are able to review financial records to determine whether there is evidence indicating that a crime has been committed. Forensic accounting is another self-policing strategy some businesses use to detect fraud.
- Regulatory agencies are government agencies responsible for making sure that regulations are followed in industries and businesses across the United States.
- Different types of businesses are regulated by different regulatory agencies, depending on the different types of products and/or services the business provides.
- In general, agencies receive information about violations through referrals, site inspections, news reports, and record reviews.
- Two types of regulatory strategies exist: persuasion or cooperation strategies and retributive or punishment strategies (Frank, 1984; Snider, 1990).
- A number of different criticisms have been levied against regulatory policing, with most of these criticisms suggesting that the regulatory efforts do little to stop misconduct.
- Police agencies across the world have been called upon to use law enforcement strategies to detect, respond to, and prevent white-collar crime.
- Larsson (2006) suggested that international cooperation can be improved if officials do the following: (1) develop networks where police officers can create a "common language" (p. 463), (2) provide appropriate education and training, (3) ensure that police agencies have the information they need to prevent crime, and (4) identify communication channels.

KEY TERMS

Audits	External whistleblower	Fraud audits
Compliance program	Financial Crimes Section (FCS)	Internal audits
External audit	Forensic accountant	Internal whistleblower

Loss prevention strategies

Proactive strategies

Reactive strategies

Record reviews

Regulatory agencies

Self-policing

Self-policing audits

Smoking gun

Whistleblower

White-collar undercover investigations

Workplace interview

DISCUSSION QUESTIONS

1. How are white-collar crime investigations different from investigations of conventional crimes?

2. Review the police and regulatory agencies that respond to white-collar crimes. Which of those agencies would you want to work for? Explain.

3. Compare and contrast law enforcement strategies and regulatory strategies to control white-collar crime.

4. What would you like most about being a white-collar crime investigator? What would you like the least?

5. Should businesses be required to report their employees to the police if they catch them stealing from the business? Explain.

6. Compare and contrast self-policing efforts with traditional policing efforts.

7. Which types of evidence-gathering strategies do you think are the most effective for building white-collar crime cases?

8. Why is white-collar crime so difficult to address with law enforcement and regulatory efforts?

9. You are elected president. A representative from the banking industry, which helped get you elected, asks you to sign an executive order calling for deregulation. What do you do?

10. How would you feel if you found out that one of your coworkers is an undercover investigator posing as an employee in your work setting? Explain.

WEB RESOURCES

Cisco Loss Prevention: http://www.cisco.com/web/strategy/docs/retail/Video_Surveillance_BR.pdf

COPS website: http://www.cops.usdoj.gov/

Whistleblower Laws: http://www.whistleblowerlaws.com/whistleblower-protections-act/

STUDENT RESOURCES

The open-access Student Study Site, available at study.sagepub.com/paynewccess2e, includes useful study materials including SAGE journal articles and multimedia resources.

CHAPTER XIV

Judicial Proceedings and White-Collar Crime

CHAPTER HIGHLIGHTS

- Types of Judicial Proceedings Responding to White-Collar Misconduct
- The Role of Judges in Addressing White-Collar Crime
- The Role of Prosecutors in Addressing White-Collar Crime
- The Role of Defense Attorneys in White-Collar Crime Cases
- Other Actors Involved in White-Collar Judicial Proceedings
- Civil Lawsuits and White-Collar Crime
- Issues in White-Collar Judicial Networking and the Judicial Process

Bernie Madoff stood before Judge Denny Chin, having pled guilty to defrauding investors out of billions of dollars. Several individuals were in the court with him. His defense attorney, Ira Sorkin, stood by his side. At the table to his right were U.S. attorneys, including Marc O. Litt, one of the lead prosecutors of the case. Behind him were victims of his schemes, members of the press, family members, and other members of the public wanting to see how justice would be served. Some victims were given the opportunity to address the court and describe the devastating impact of Madoff's crimes. Discussing the sentence he was giving to Madoff, Judge Chin remarked, "Here the message must be sent that Mr. Madoff's crimes were extraordinarily evil and that this kind of manipulation is not just a bloodless crime that takes place on paper, but one instead that takes a staggering toll" (Zambito, Martinez, & Siemaszko, 2009). The judge sentenced Madoff to 150 years in prison. Several viewers in the court cheered and applauded when the sentence was announced. The next day, Sorkin was on television news shows arguing that the sentence was "absurd" (McCoy, 2009a).

This one court hearing was scrutinized across the world. In some ways, it may have seemed as if this hearing was the most important part of the judicial process. However, the bulk of the criminal justice system's judicial process in Madoff's case, and every other criminal case for that matter, occurs before the actual sentencing. In other ways, it may have seemed as if this hearing marked the end of the judicial process. But, as is the case with many white-collar crime convictions, a series of civil proceedings followed in an effort to determine how to recover as much money as possible for victims.

Madoff's white-collar crime case is just one of many that made its way through the courts. Consider a few recent examples that show the actors and processes as they were described in press reports:

- "Through his position as a high-ranking executive at Qualcomm, **** gained unique access to information about the company's earnings and intended acquisitions and illegally exploited that inside information for personal gain," said Assistant Attorney General Caldwell. "He then enlisted the services of others—his stockbroker and his brother—to cover up the scheme. This prosecution demonstrates the Criminal Division's commitment to holding accountable corporate executives who would undermine the integrity of the financial marketplace." (U.S. Department of Justice, 2015, June 26)
- Warner Chilcott U.S. Sales LLC, a subsidiary of pharmaceutical manufacturer Warner Chilcott PLC, has agreed to plead guilty to a felony charge of health care fraud, the Justice Department announced today. The plea agreement is part of a global settlement with the United States in which Warner Chilcott has agreed to pay $125 million to resolve its criminal and civil liability arising from the company's illegal marketing . . . Warner Chilcott agreed to plead guilty in the District of Massachusetts to criminal charges that the company committed a felony violation by paying kickbacks to physicians throughout the United States to induce them to prescribe its drugs, manipulating prior authorizations to induce insurance companies to pay for prescriptions of Atelvia° that the insurers may not have otherwise paid for and making unsubstantiated marketing claims for the drug Actonel° . . . "The Justice Department is committed to protecting the integrity of physician prescribing decisions and ensuring that financial arrangements in the healthcare marketplace comply with the law," said Principal Deputy Assistant Attorney General Benjamin C. Mizer, head of the Justice Department's Civil Division. (U.S. Department of Justice, 2015, October 29)
- Based upon the evidence and findings of an investigation report by the University of Minnesota (UMN), an investigation conducted by another Federal agency, and additional information obtained by the Office of Research Integrity (ORI) during its oversight review of the UMN investigation, ORI found that ****, former Graduate Student, Department of Chemistry, UMN, engaged in research misconduct in research that was included in grant application R01 GM095559-01A1, submitted to the National Institute of General Medical Sciences (NIGMS), National Institutes of Health (NIH). ORI found by a preponderance of the evidence that the Respondent intentionally and knowingly engaged in research misconduct by falsifying and/or fabricating data that was provided to his mentor to include in [a] grant application. (Department of Health and Human Services, 2015)
- A Zachary man was sentenced Wednesday, Feb. 4, in the 18th Judicial District Court for violating Louisiana's Environmental Quality Act . . . Information received by the DEQ-Criminal Investigation Division revealed that *** drove a tanker truck for ACM Transportation at the time of the incident. While loading gasoline and diesel fuel into his tanker truck at Placid Refinery on the night of Jan. 25, 2013, **** mistakenly mixed several hundred gallons of diesel with several thousand gallons of gasoline already in the tanker truck. In an effort to conceal his mistake from his employer, ***** then drove to the Super Lucky Louie Casino and dumped an unknown portion of the gasoline and diesel mixture at the rear of the facility. (Louisiana Department of Environmental Quality, 2015, February 9)
- ***** pleaded guilty Feb. 4, 2015, in 18th Judicial District Court and was sentenced. In accepting Wallace's plea, Judge J. Robin Free, 18th Judicial District Judge, ordered him to pay a $5,000 fine and reimburse the Louisiana Department of Environmental Quality in the amount of $970 for the cost of its investigation. Judge Free sentenced Wallace to two years of probation. The contaminated property has since been remediated in accordance with DEQ regulations. (Louisiana Department of Environmental Quality, 2015)

▲ **Photo 14.1** Judge Denny Chin sentenced Bernie Madoff to 150 years in prison, describing Madoff's actions as "extraordinarily evil" and hoping to send a message to others that such behavior would not be tolerated.

The scrutiny that Madoff's court hearing received and the four others highlighted above demonstrate several important facts regarding the judicial response to white-collar crime. In particular, these cases show that white-collar crimes (1) are processed through several different judicial proceedings, (2) involve the efforts of many different actors in the judicial process, and (3) present numerous complexities to those involved in adjudicating the cases. To shed some light on the way the judicial system responds to white-collar crimes, in this chapter, attention is given to the following: types of judicial proceedings; the roles of judges, prosecutors, and defense attorneys; other actors involved in white-collar crime judicial proceedings; civil lawsuits; and issues in white-collar judicial proceedings. Addressing these areas will help students appreciate the complexities surrounding the judicial response to white-collar crime.

● ● ● Types of Judicial Proceedings Responding to White-Collar Misconduct

White-collar misconduct cases are adjudicated in at least five different types of judicial or quasi-judicial proceedings: (1) criminal proceedings, (2) civil proceedings, (3) administrative proceedings, (4) professional-disciplinary proceedings, and (5) workplace-disciplinary proceedings (see Figure 14.1). In **criminal proceedings**, criminal charges are filed against the defendant, and sanctions could include imprisonment, fines, probation, community service, and restitution. Because an individual's liberty is at stake (through incarceration), criminal proceedings offer offenders more protections than other proceedings, and the standard of proof is higher. The bulk of this chapter addresses criminal judicial proceedings as they relate to white-collar offenders.

In **civil proceedings**, an individual or government representative, referred to as a *plaintiff*, files civil charges against an individual or business. The charges focus on violations, allegedly committed by the defendant, which brought some sort of harm to the plaintiff. In some white-collar crime cases, the government will file motions in civil court that seek injunctive remedies. For instance, officials routinely ask civil courts to issue *cease and desist* orders, which tell a business or corporation to refrain from the activities under judicial review until the proceeding is completed. In civil proceedings, the standard of proof is less (e.g., plaintiffs must prove by a preponderance of evidence), and defendants are not afforded the same level of protection (e.g., while they may refuse to testify, the judge and jury are permitted to make inferences about such a refusal). Also, sanctions are primarily monetary in nature. More on civil proceedings will be provided below.

Administrative proceedings are different from criminal justice and civil proceedings. Technically, these proceedings are not designed to punish but are designed "to restrict . . . certain future actions" (M. Cohen, 1992, p. 1059). These proceedings are used more commonly for white-collar offenses than for conventional offenses. Many regulatory agencies use administrative proceedings to adjudicate cases brought to their attention. Depending on the laws that govern the regulatory agency, the types of decisions made in administrative proceedings could include the following:

- Issue civil fines
- Issue cease and desist orders to protect the health and safety of workers, consumers, citizens, and others
- Prevent specific individuals or groups from participating in corporate activities
- Prohibit the corporation from participating in specific types of government programs (Van Cleef, Silets, & Motz, 2004)

CAREERS RESPONDING TO WHITE-COLLAR CRIME

Administrative Law Judge

The Administrative Law Judge (ALJ) function was created by the Administrative Procedure Act (APA) in 1946 to ensure fairness in administrative proceedings before Federal Government agencies.

ALJs serve as independent impartial triers of fact in formal proceedings requiring a decision on the record after the opportunity for a hearing. In general, ALJs prepare for and preside at formal proceedings required by statute to be held under or in accordance with provisions of the APA, codified, in relevant part, in sections 553 through 559 of title 5, United States Code (U.S.C.). ALJs rule on preliminary motions, conduct pre-hearing conferences, issue subpoenas, conduct hearings (which may include written and/or oral testimony and cross-examination), review briefs, and prepare and issue decisions, along with written findings of fact and conclusions of law.

The Federal Government employs ALJs in a number of agencies throughout the United States. Cases may involve Federal laws and regulations in such areas as admiralty, advertising, antitrust, banking, communications, energy, environmental protection, food and drugs, health and safety, housing, immigration, interstate commerce, international trade, labor management relations, securities and commodities markets, social security disability and other benefits claims, and transportation.

Source: Reprinted from Position Classification Standard for Consumer Safety Series. *Classification & Qualifications General Schedule Qualification Standards* https://www.opm.gov/policy-data-oversight/classification-qualifications/general-schedule-qualification-standards/specialty-areas/administrative-law-judge-positions/

As an illustration, the Securities and Exchange Commission (SEC) will hold administrative proceedings before the Commission or an administrative law judge. The SEC has the authority to impose administrative sanctions, including cease and desist orders and monetary penalties. One issue that arises in the judicial processing of white-collar crime cases is that the boundaries between criminal, civil, and administrative proceedings "are often very fuzzy" (M. Cohen, 1992, p. 1060). The Careers Responding to White-Collar Crime: Administrative Law Judge box above shows the duties performed by the judges.

Professional-disciplinary proceedings are used to address different types of white-collar misconduct. Recall the discussion of the ways bar associations discipline lawyers in Chapter V. These proceedings are administered through the state bar association, with the professional disciplinary association processing the case and deciding whether and how to sanction the attorney. Other professions have similar proceedings. For instance, medical professionals accused of misconduct could have their cases adjudicated by state medical boards, which are responsible for licensing different types of medical professionals. Other occupations that have professional boards reviewing their allegations of wrongdoing include but are not limited to social workers, counselors, barbers, teachers, and clergy.

Workplace-disciplinary proceedings are similar to the professional-disciplinary proceedings, except they are conducted entirely within the workplace where the misconduct was alleged. Cases heard in the workplace (quasi-judicial hearings) often include labor violations and discrimination. The cases are typically handled through a company's equal opportunity office or human resources department. These cases may not necessarily be resolved in the workplace because the offended party might file a claim in civil or administrative court once the workplace proceedings are completed.

While white-collar misconduct cases are adjudicated in different ways, from a criminological perspective, the role of the criminal court is particularly important in understanding how white-collar crime cases are handled as crimes. In the following chapter, attention is given to various actors involved in criminally adjudicating white-collar offenses. This will be followed by a discussion of civil lawsuits and issues that arise in the judicial processing of white-collar offenders.

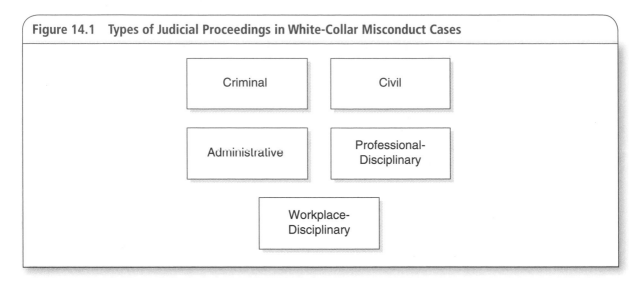

Figure 14.1   Types of Judicial Proceedings in White-Collar Misconduct Cases

Criminal

Civil

Administrative

Professional-
Disciplinary

Workplace-
Disciplinary

● ● ●   The Role of Judges in Addressing White-Collar Crime

Judges play an extremely important role in processing white-collar crime cases through the justice system. Among other things, it is their responsibility to ensure that the justice process unfolds in a way that is fair to the defendant and the state. Judges oversee cases from the time they are filed until they are resolved. They approve plea negotiations and oversee trials. They also sentence convicted offenders and even make recommendations about where incarcerated offenders will serve their sentences. Clearly, judges are afforded a great deal of power in the criminal justice system.

Unfortunately, few recent studies have examined the judicial role in white-collar crime cases, though a few classic studies create a foundation from which understanding about judges and white-collar crime can evolve. These earlier studies focused on how judges perceive white-collar offenders, offenses, and sanctions. With regard to studies on perceptions about offenders, one early study found that judges perceive public officials (e.g., politicians) as deserving of more severe sanctions than other offenders (Pollack & Smith, 1983).

Stanton Wheeler, Kenneth Mann, and Austin Sarat (1988) authored the seminal work *Sitting in Judgment: The Sentencing of White-Collar Criminals,* which was based on interviews with 51 federal judges who had significant involvement with hearing white-collar crime cases. Among other things, their research showed that judges varied in how they received information and used the information available to them. Their research also showed that the three most salient factors influencing judicial decision making in white-collar crime cases were (1) harm from the offense, (2) blameworthiness, and (3) consequences of the punishment.

In terms of harm, the more harm caused by the offense, the less favorably judges perceived white-collar offenders. In the words of the authors, for some judges, "if an offense is more serious, its perpetrator is therefore more culpable" (Wheeler et al., 1988, p. 54). Judges determined harm by considering how much was lost, the duration of the offending, whether there were identifiable victims and the types of victims, and whether trust violations occurred. In assessing blame, judges considered prior records, offender motive, the offender's life history, and evidence presented at the trial.

In terms of sentencing, the author team noted elsewhere that the judges perceived white-collar offenders as having a special sensitivity to imprisonment (Mann, Wheeler, & Sarat, 1980). They viewed this special sensitivity as providing a powerful general deterrent that would keep white-collar employees from engaging in future misconduct. As a result, the judges viewed publicity as an important ingredient in increasing the deterrent potential of jail. One judge indicated that "he had tried to make sure" that certain types of cases would receive publicity (p. 479). Others have also suggested that judicial sanctions, such as jail, have the ability to deter white-collar misconduct (Pollack & Smith, 1983).

More will be written about sentencing of offenders in the next chapter. At this point, attention can be given to factors contributing to judges' sentencing behaviors and judges' perceptions of criminal sanctions. With regard to the former, a study of U.S. federal antitrust sentences from the mid-1950s through the early 1980s showed that sentences appeared to be tied to judges' goals. For example, those seeking promotion to higher courts sentenced differently than those who did not aspire to a higher court (M. A. Cohen, 1992).

A number of researchers have drawn attention to the short sentences that white-collar offenders receive (Payne, 2003b). According to Mann and his colleagues (1980), judges justified these shorter sentences on three grounds. First, the judges did not want to do additional harm to the offender's family. Second, a shorter sentence was seen as providing offenders the opportunity to contribute back to the community. Third, with shorter sentences, offenders would be in better positions to pay victims back and make reparations for their misdeeds. The judges did not see fines as being useful for white-collar offenders.

Early legal scholars highlighted the difficulties that judges faced in sentencing corporate offenders. Orland (1980), for example, wrote, "Often judges find it difficult to condemn the acts of corporate executives which are undertaken not only to advance personal career goals, but also to maximize the profits of the corporation" (p. 511). He continued, "Many judges find it less difficult to punish criminal conduct undertaken at the expense of the corporation than conduct in which the corporation and its stakeholders are the ultimate beneficiaries of the criminal act" (p. 511). As will be shown below, corporations make better "victims" than "offenders."

Federal and state sentencing guidelines now give judges less discretion in deciding how to punish white-collar offenders. Under these guidelines, judges refer to the guidelines to determine the sentence recommended for a specific offense. The sentence (time to be served) is typically offered as a range (e.g., 6 months to 1 year). Judges can depart from the recommended range, either increasing or decreasing the actual sentence given to the offender. In white-collar crime cases, upward departures usually result from significant monetary harm, emotional harm, offenses targeting vulnerable groups, and abuses of trust (J. Barnard, 2001). Judges don't always view the guidelines as helpful. One judge told a *Newsweek* reporter that the federal guidelines "are just too goddamn severe" (Goodman, 2014). The judge elaborated: "The arithmetic behind the sentencing calculations is all hocus-pocus—it's nonsensical, and I mean that sincerely. It gives the illusion of something meaningful with no real value underneath" (Goodman, 2014).

Departures have been found to be related to white-collar crime type. For example, a review by the U.S. Sentencing Commission (1996) found that computer criminals were more likely than other white-collar offenders to receive downward departures from the guidelines range, and no computer criminal had received an upward departure. The Commission suggested that computer criminals were more educated than other white-collar criminals and all federal defendants in general.

It is important to note that guidelines exist at the federal level for sentencing individuals and corporations. The guidelines, designed for informing sentences for corporations, are known as Organizational Guidelines. These guidelines are based on four principles:

- The corporation is responsible for addressing the harm it causes.
- The corporation that exists for criminal purposes will lose all of its assets in an effort to repay victims and society.
- The corporation that exists for legitimate reasons should be fined according to the seriousness of the offense.
- Corporations can be placed on probation, if necessary, for compliance. (Thompson & Yong, 2012)

▲ **Photo 14.2** Judges oversee the criminal justice process. Regarding white-collar defendants, judges may hold the defendants to a higher set of expectations than conventional defendants.

US National Archives

▲ **Photo 14.3**   The prosecutor is one of the most powerful officials in the criminal justice process.

The Role of Prosecutors in Addressing White-Collar Crime

Prosecutors have a central role in processing white-collar crime cases through the justice system. At the federal level, U.S. attorneys are the prosecutors responsible for prosecuting federal offenses. At the state and local level, prosecutors go by different names, including district attorney, commonwealth's attorney, solicitor, attorney general, and so on. In some jurisdictions, specific units devoted to white-collar crimes exist, while other jurisdictions rely on prosecutors who seem to have more expertise with white-collar crimes. Regardless of what they are called and their levels of expertise, these officials are responsible for making several important decisions about white-collar crime cases. Decisions prosecutors make include the following:

- Deciding whether to prosecute a white-collar crime case
- Deciding what to charge offenders with
- Deciding whether to accept plea bargains
- Deciding whether to charge corporations
- Deciding whether to defer prosecution

Each of these areas is addressed below.

Deciding Whether to Prosecute a White-Collar Crime Case

The prosecution of white-collar criminals is seen as necessary in order to demonstrate "moral outrage" for white-collar misconduct (Cohen, 1992). Obviously, not all white-collar crimes are prosecuted in the justice system (see Figure 14.2). Some crimes never come to the attention of authorities, others are detected but not investigated, and others are investigated but not prosecuted. The question that arises is how prosecutors decide which cases to prosecute. Kitty Calavita and Henry Pontell (1994) noted that "major cases" are determined based on dollar amount. Major cases would be those selected for prosecution. Table 14.1 shows the types of cases heard in state district courts in fiscal year 2012. As shown in the table, by the time these cases make it to court, it is unlikely that the verdict will be not guilty.

In a 1994 memo, Earl Devaney, director of the Environmental Protection Agency's (EPA's) Office of Criminal Enforcement, offered environmental law enforcement agents guidance in determining which cases should be treated as criminal as opposed to civil or administrative wrongs. He suggested that the decision to handle cases criminally be guided by two factors: **significant environmental harm** and **culpable conduct**. He specified that harm includes (1) actual harm, (2) threat of harm, (3) failure to report potentially harmful activities, and (4) the possibility that the behavior will escalate if it is not handled criminally. Delaney did not define culpable conduct as intent per se but as including (1) an offender's history of misconduct, (2) deliberate misconduct, (3) concealing misconduct, (4) tampering with monitoring equipment, and (5) practicing business without a license.

While Devaney's memo focused solely on environmental crime, other researchers have cited similar factors that are believed to guide prosecutorial decision making. For example, Cohen (1992) argued that prosecutors will consider the following factors when deciding whether to prosecute white-collar offenders: the defendant's knowledge and intent, harm from the offense, whether misconduct continued after the regulatory agency initiated its investigation, amount of evidence, and how much the defendant benefited from the wrongdoing. A survey of state attorneys general found that seriousness of the offense was the most important factor prosecutors considered when deciding whether to prosecute

Table 14.1	Defendants in U. S. State District Courts, Fiscal Year Ending 2012				
	Filed	**Terminated**	**Guilty**	**Not Guilty**	**Other**
Bank fraud/embezzlement	1,303	1,418	1,314	6	98
Corporate fraud	92	109	99	1	9
Health care fraud	892	982	826	15	141
Environmental	360	441	375	8	58
Health and safety	22	23	20	0	3
State corruption	237	242	195	7	40
Local corruption	93	69	64	0	5
Labor management	89	107	98	2	9
Civil rights	245	209	168	15	26

Source: U.S. Department of Justice

white-collar crimes (Ayers & Frank, 1987). Incidentally, this same study found that political factors were among "the least important factors."

Some have noted that decisions to prosecute may be tied to the way the referral is made to the prosecutor. According to one group of white-collar crime experts, referral agencies must "sell a case to a prosecutor" (Pontell, Jesilow, & Geis, 1984, p. 413). Pontell and his colleagues quote one fraud investigator who said of U.S. attorneys:

> Their priorities are bank robberies, drugs, immigration, and terrorists. . . . Somebody goes and blows up nine airplanes and then you come in the next day with a doctor who is [stealing] from Medicare or Medicaid. Where are their priorities? They will be more concerned with violent crimes. (p. 413)

Federal statistics support the suggestion that white-collar crime cases are declined for prosecution by U.S. attorneys more often than other types of crimes. In 2004, a total of 148,229 cases were referred to U.S. attorneys for review and to be considered for prosecution. Of those cases, 22 percent were declined for prosecution. Consider the declination rates based on the agency referring the case to the U.S. attorneys:

- Small Business Administration—69 percent of cases declined for prosecution
- Land Management Bureau—68 percent of cases declined for prosecution
- U.S. Environmental Protection Agency—54 percent of cases declined for prosecution
- U.S. Army—5 percent of cases declined for prosecution
- Citizen and Immigration—2 percent of cases declined for prosecution

Also, supporting this suggestion that white-collar crime cases are declined more often, here are the declination rates for offenses:

- Food and drug cases: 50.3 percent of cases declined for prosecution
- Regulatory offenses: 62.2 percent of cases declined for prosecution

- Embezzlement offenses: 32 percent of cases declined for prosecution
- Fraud: 39.7 percent of cases declined for prosecution
- Drug offenses: 15.3 percent of cases declined for prosecution
- Immigration offenses: 1.5 percent of cases declined for prosecution (Bureau of Justice Statistics, 2006)

It should not automatically be assumed that cases are declined out of some sort of intentional bias on the part of prosecutors toward lower-class offenders. Three traditional explanations addressing why prosecutors choose not to prosecute include the organizational advantage argument, the alternative sentencing argument, and the system capacity argument (Tillman, Calavita, & Pontell, 1997). The **organizational advantage argument** suggests that "organizational structure may serve as a buffer between the white-collar offender and social control mechanisms" (p. 55). The **alternative sanctions argument** points to the use of less costly civil and administrative procedures to respond to misconduct. The **system capacity argument** points to the difficulties officials face in responding to these crimes (Tillman et al., 1997).

Tillman and his research team (1997) examined how the criminal justice system responded to the savings and loan crisis to see which argument might best address the system's response to the fiasco. The researchers found limited support for the first two arguments and moderate support for the third argument—at least in some jurisdictions. They added a fourth possible explanation, for which they coined the term **damage control argument**. This orientation emphasizes the importance of "symbolic, high-visibility prosecutions in restoring public confidence" (p. 72).

Prosecutors face a number of other issues that may influence their decision-making process in white-collar crime cases. Issues include (1) that trials may be harder to win in white-collar crime cases, (2) the time to complete the cases is significant, (3) resource issues, (4) establishing intent, and (5) practical issues. With regard to trials, several features of the white-collar criminal trial mean that the cases may be harder for the prosecutor to win. The cases use complex evidence, the trials last a long time, and the defense attorneys are often among the most talented attorneys prosecutors will face. Brickey's (2006) review of the white-collar crime trials of the executives involved in the scandals that occurred in the early 2000s found that 18 defendants were convicted, 11 were acquitted, and 15 had their cases result in mistrials. By comparison, in conventional cases, trials almost always result in a victory for prosecutors.

The time to complete white-collar crime cases is also significant. These cases take far longer to complete than prosecutions of conventional crimes. An investigation by the Government Accounting Office (USGAO, 2003) found that more than half of the Medicaid fraud cases prosecuted by fraud control units took more than 2 years to process from identification through adjudication. A review by the Bureau of Justice Statistics (2006)—focusing on the amount of time it took U.S. attorneys to file charges (or decline the case) from the time they received notification about the case from the referral agency—found the following:

- The median amount of time for fraud cases was 14.6 months.
- The median amount of time for regulatory offenses was 15.9 months.
- The median amount of time for drug offenses was 6.6 months.
- The median amount of time for immigration offenses was 1.1 month.
- The median amount of time for violent offenses was 6.5 months.

In other words, it took more than twice as long to decide how to proceed with white-collar crimes as it took to decide how to proceed with drug crimes and violent offenses.

Resource issues potentially influence prosecutors' decisions about white-collar crime cases. In this context, *resources* refer to time, funds, staff, and materials needed to process the case through the justice system. Particularly at the local level, prosecutors lack the resources they need to address white-collar crimes. As a result, when prosecuted, the cases are more often handled by federal prosecutors (Benson, 1990). As illustrated above, even at the federal level many cases are not prosecuted.

Problems establishing intent may influence prosecutors' decisions to prosecute white-collar crime cases. As one author noted, "it is quite difficult to judge the motivation and behavior" of many white-collar offenders (Punch, 2000, p. 251). In fact, surveys from fraud prosecutors revealed that "the burden of the commonwealth/government to prove the

Figure 14.2   The White-Collar Crime Criminal Justice Funnel

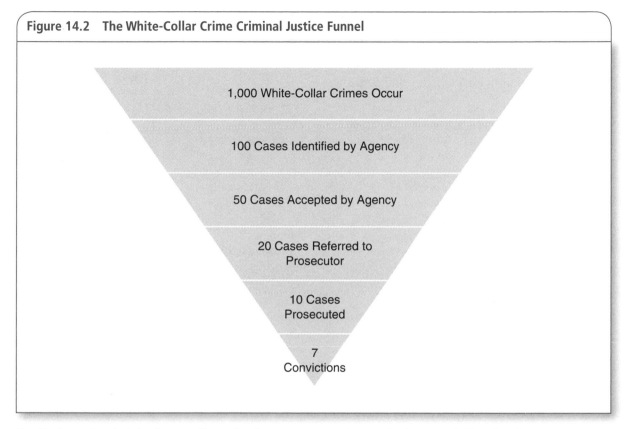

1,000 White-Collar Crimes Occur

100 Cases Identified by Agency

50 Cases Accepted by Agency

20 Cases Referred to Prosecutor

10 Cases Prosecuted

7 Convictions

Note: Numbers are hypothetical and meant to illustrate how few cases are prosecuted compared to the amount of white-collar crime.

mental state . . . beyond a reasonable doubt (knowledge and intent) . . . is the most difficult element of [white-collar] crime to establish" (Payne & Berg, 1997, p. 228).

Practical issues refer to an assortment of issues that commonly arise in the prosecution of most white-collar crime cases. For example, the cases typically require much more expertise to prosecute than conventional crimes might require (Jesilow, Pontell, & Geis, 1986). Also, prosecutors will often need technical assistance in these cases, and many have not been trained adequately in how to prosecute white-collar crimes (Payne, 2011). One topic for which prosecutors need specific training is deciding which charges to file against white-collar offenders. Also, a decline in resources to support these efforts is believed to have reduced the number of prosecutions. Pontell, Black, and Geis (2014) cite estimates that suggest white-collar crime prosecutions dropped 50 percent while George W. Bush was president and attribute these reductions to declines in FBI agents assigned to these cases after 9/11.

Deciding Charges

Prosecutors must decide what charges to file against white-collar criminals. These decisions follow rather lengthy investigations designed to inform prosecutors whether a charging decision is warranted. (See White-Collar Crime in the News: Score One for the Feds for the press release highlighting the decision to charge FIFA officials with an assortment of crimes.) At the federal level, prosecutors have hundreds of possible statutes to choose from. In some instances, white-collar offenders are charged with violations of the **Racketeer Influenced and Corrupt Organizations (RICO) Act.**

WHITE-COLLAR CRIME IN THE NEWS

Score One for the Feds in Soccer Investigation: FIFA Officials Indicted

Caption Missing

The U.S. government... unsealed indictments in a New York federal court against high-ranking officials and corporate executives affiliated with FIFA, the governing body of international soccer, for their roles in a decades-long scheme to corrupt the sport through bribes, kickbacks, and other criminal activity aimed at controlling lucrative marketing rights to international tournaments such as the World Cup.

Nine FIFA officials—including two current vice presidents—along with five corporate executives were charged with racketeering, wire fraud, and money laundering, among other offenses.

"The indictment alleges corruption that is rampant, systemic, and deep-rooted both abroad and here in the United States," said Attorney General Loretta E. Lynch. "It spans at least two generations of soccer officials who, as alleged, have abused their positions of trust."

Related guilty pleas of an additional four individuals and two corporate defendants were unsealed today as well. The investigation, which is ongoing, has also snared U.S. sports marketing executives. In all, it is alleged that more than $150 million in bribes and kickbacks were paid or agreed to be paid to obtain media and marketing rights to international soccer tournaments.

"The defendants fostered a culture of corruption and greed that created an uneven playing field for the biggest sport in the world," noted FBI Director James B. Comey. "Undisclosed and illegal payments, kickbacks, and bribes became a way of doing business at FIFA," he said.

FIFA—the Fédération Internationale de Football Association—is the organization responsible for the regulation and promotion of soccer worldwide. It also oversees officials of other soccer governing bodies that operate under the FIFA umbrella.

The organization is composed of 209 member associations, including six continental confederations that assist it in governing soccer in different regions of the world. The U.S. Soccer Federation is one of 41 member associations of the confederation known as CONCACAF, which has been headquartered in the U.S. throughout the period charged in the indictment.

A key way FIFA makes money is by selling media and marketing rights associated with flagship tournaments such as the World Cup. Rights are typically sold through multi-year contracts. Sports marketing companies, in turn, sell the rights downstream to TV and radio broadcast networks, major corporate sponsors, and other sub-licensees who want to broadcast the matches or promote their brands. According to FIFA, 70 percent of its $5.7 billion in total revenues between 2011 and 2014 was attributable to the sale of TV and marketing rights to the 2014 World Cup.

The indictment alleges that between 1991 and present, the defendants and their co-conspirators corrupted the enterprise by engaging in various criminal activities. Two generations of soccer officials abused their positions of trust for personal gain, frequently through alliances with sports marketing executives who shut out competitors and kept highly lucrative contracts for themselves through the systematic payment of bribes and kickbacks.

The wide-ranging corruption at FIFA, said Lynch, "has profoundly harmed a multitude of victims, from the youth leagues and developing countries that should benefit from the revenue generated by the commercial rights these organizations hold, to the fans at home and throughout the world whose support for the game makes those rights valuable. Today's action," she added, "makes clear that this Department of Justice intends to end any such corrupt practices, to root out misconduct, and to bring wrongdoers to justice. We look forward to continuing to work with other countries in this effort."

Source: Reprinted from FBI

Because it is Title IX of the Organized Crime Control Act, many have assumed that RICO is limited to prosecutions of mobsters and other participants in organized crime ventures. However, as Beare (2002) notes, Robert Blakey who drafted the law, supported the use of controlling white-collar crime with the RICO act. In Blakey's words,

> there is nothing in RICO that says that if you act like a racketeer you will not be treated like a racketeer. Whatever the color of your shirt or your collar . . . people who run groups by extortion or violence or fraud ought to be called racketeers. (p. 225)

When considering the text of the RICO act, one can see how the act can be used in white-collar crime prosecutions. As one author team notes,

> Section 1962 of RICO prohibits "any person" from (i) using income derived from a pattern of racketeering activity, or from the collection of an unlawful debt, to acquire an interest in an enterprise affecting interstate commerce; (ii) acquiring or maintaining through a pattern of racketeering activity, or through collection of an unlawful debt, an interest in an enterprise affecting interstate commerce; (iii) conducting, or participating in the conduct of, the affairs of an enterprise affecting interstate commerce through a pattern of racketeering activity or through collection of an unlawful debt; or (iv) conspiring to participate in any of these activities. (Argust, Litvack, & Martin, 2010, p. 961)

Clearly, the breadth of this statute is such that many white-collar crime cases fall within the realm of RICO violations. Other common charges against white-collar offenders at the federal level include violations of mail fraud statutes, the False Statements Act, the False Claims Act, and specific acts targeting specific forms of white-collar misconduct (Altschuler, Creekpaum, & Fang, 2008). **Mail fraud statutes** prohibit the use of the U.S. mail service to commit crimes. The **False Statements Act and False Claims Act** govern against the submission of fraudulent claims or bills for services. The False Claims Act was passed during the Civil War to guard against situations where individuals tried to defraud the government. It has gone through several changes since then, but it covers situations where individuals or businesses bill for goods that were not delivered or services that were not provided. In Focus 14.1 shows some specific laws targeting specific forms of white-collar misconduct. As shown in these statutes, the laws stipulate minimum and maximum sentences. Thus, the type of charge prosecutors file will have ramifications for the sentence convicted offenders receive. Charge type also influences decisions about plea bargaining.

IN FOCUS 14.1

U.S. Laws Governing Against White-Collar Crimes

§ 1344. Bank fraud—Whoever knowingly executes, or attempts to execute, a scheme or artifice—(1) to defraud a financial institution; or (2) to obtain any of the moneys, funds, credits, assets, securities, or other property owned by, or under the custody or control of, a financial institution, by means of false or fraudulent pretenses, representations, or promises; shall be fined not more than $1,000,000 or imprisoned not more than 30 years, or both.

§ 1347. Health care fraud—Whoever knowingly and willfully executes, or attempts to execute, a scheme or artifice—(1) to defraud any health care benefit program; or (2) to obtain, by means of false or fraudulent pretenses, representations, or promises, any of the money or property owned by, or under the custody or control of, any health care benefit program, in connection with the delivery of or payment for health care benefits, items, or services, shall be fined under this title or imprisoned not more than 10 years, or both. If the violation results in serious bodily injury (as defined in section 1365 of this title), such person shall be fined under this title or imprisoned not more than 20 years, or both; and if the violation results in death, such person shall be fined under this title, or imprisoned for any term of years or for life, or both.

§ 1348. Securities and commodities fraud—Whoever knowingly executes, or attempts to execute, a scheme or artifice—(1) to defraud any person in connection with any commodity for future delivery, or any option on a commodity for future delivery, or any security of an issuer with a class of securities registered under section 12 of the Securities Exchange Act of 1934

(15 U.S.C. 78l) or that is required to file reports under section 15(d) of the Securities Exchange Act of 1934 (15 U.S.C. 78o (d)); or (2) to obtain, by means of false or fraudulent pretenses, representations, or promises, any money or property in connection with the purchase or sale of any commodity for future delivery, or any option on a commodity for future delivery, or any security of an issuer with a class of securities registered under section 12 of the Securities Exchange Act of 1934 (15 U.S.C. 78l) or that is required to file reports under section 15(d) of the Securities Exchange Act of 1934 (15 U.S.C. 78o (d)); shall be fined under this title, or imprisoned not more than 25 years, or both.

Source: Reprinted From U.S. Code. (n.d.).

Deciding About Plea Bargains

Prosecutors will also make decisions about **plea bargains** in deciding whether to allow a defendant to plead guilty in exchange for a reduced sentence or some other incentive. A common estimate is that 90 percent of offenders (white-collar and conventional) plead guilty (O'Hear, 2004). Consider that 90 percent of those involved in the corporate scandals of the early 2000s (Adelphia, WorldCom, HeathSouth, Enron, etc.) entered guilty pleas (Brickey, 2006). After pleading, nearly all of them became cooperating witnesses "who assisted the government in developing the case against their peers" (Brickey, 2006, p. 403).

▲ **Photo 14.4**   Being a part of the criminal justice process is embarrassing for white-collar defendants. Many will plead guilty to avoid the publicity.

While similar proportions of white-collar and conventional offenders plead guilty, their reasons for pleading guilty might vary. For conventional offenders, a common reason is to avoid the costs of a trial that come along with paying the defense attorney higher fees for trial services. For white-collar offenders, many likely plead guilty in order to avoid the stigma and shame that would come along with a public trial. For both groups of offenders, a lighter sentence drives the decision to accept a plea bargain offered by prosecutors.

Deciding Whether to Charge Corporations

Dating back as far as Sutherland (1941), some criminologists have claimed that prosecutors are reluctant to prosecute corporations or businesses. A common explanation for this refusal is that prosecutors are "persuaded by the argument that punishing a corporation in effect punishes innocent shareholders" (Plimton & Walsh, 2010, p. 331) and workers. Another explanation offered is that such prosecutions might harm the economic system. Former attorney general Eliot Spitzer chose the civil settlement route in response to securities fraud allegations against banks in 2003 in order to minimize the possibility of significant economic fallout (Tillman, 2013). Tillman explains why such a reason is problematic:

> The fact that prosecutors are often reluctant to pursue organizational defendants out of fear of the economic consequences suggests a situation in which, as Tillman and Indergaard (2005:263) have put it, America is being "held hostage" by corrupt corporations whose executives can operate with a sense of impunity knowing that they and their firms are not only too big to fail but also too big to prosecute and too big to jail. This situation also raises questions about the state's interests and goals in responding to financial crimes. (p. 32)

In the face of this resistance to prosecuting corporations, one can point to three reasons justifying the prosecution of corporations. First, the harm from many corporate crimes is more severe than the harm from other crimes. Second, it is believed that corporate criminals are "just as morally culpable as traditional criminals" (Page, Savage, Stitt, & Umhoffer, 1999, p. 520). Third, corporate prosecutions send a message to other corporations that misconduct will not be tolerated.

Another reason corporations were not prosecuted was that it was not always clear when such a prosecution would be appropriate. To offer guidance to U.S. attorneys in determining when to prosecute corporations, the deputy attorney general sent a memo in November 2006 offering federal prosecutors guidance in making this determination. The factors McNulty (n.d.) addressed included offense characteristics, organizational characteristics, and the consequences of different types of reactions by the justice system. In terms of offense characteristics, the memo drew attention to the seriousness of the offense, the consequences of the offense, as well as the risk of harm from the offense. Attention was also given to whether the nature of the offense fit in with national priorities. Table 14.2 shows the types of questions prosecutors might now ask in determining whether to prosecute corporations.

In terms of organizational characteristics, McNulty (n.d.) urged prosecutors to consider the pervasiveness of wrongdoing in the corporation, with specific attention given to past misconduct by the business. Also, whether the corporation disclosed the misconduct in a timely manner was noted as a factor to consider along with whether the corporation had a strong compliance program. In addition, prosecutors were encouraged to consider the remedial actions taken by company officials to address the wrongdoing (e.g., replacing corporate leaders, disciplining workers, revising compliance policies, etc.).

In addition to addressing offense and corporate characteristics, attention was drawn to the consequences of the system's intervention. For example, if a prosecution would have a disproportionately adverse effect on those not responsible for the misconduct, prosecutors were encouraged by McNulty (n.d.) to take that into consideration. He also encouraged prosecutors to consider the adequacy of prosecution as well as "the adequacy of remedies such as civil or regulatory enforcement actions" (p. 4).

Despite these guidelines, or maybe because of them, corporations are still rarely prosecuted in the criminal justice system. According to one author, structural features of the criminal justice system assigning responsibility for handling these cases to regulatory agencies results in infrequent use of criminal laws to address corporate offenses (Slapper, 1993). This same author notes that corporate offenses are often framed as accidents, thereby allowing companies to hide behind this conceptual frame. Consider the British Petroleum (BP) oil disaster in the Gulf of Mexico in July 2010. The disaster was routinely portrayed as an "accident," implying that corporate wrongdoing did not occur.

Local and state prosecutors also have authority to prosecute corporate crimes. Michael Benson and Frank Cullen (1998) described the most detailed study on how local prosecutors responded to corporate crime in *Combating Corporate Crime: Local Prosecutors at Work*. Among other things, they examined the impact of resources, the presence of alternative remedies, legal and technical difficulties, and political factors on local prosecutors' decisions to prosecute corporate crime. In terms of resources, attention was given to the lack of staff, funds, and time to prosecute corporate crime. With regard to alternative remedies, attention was given to deferring the cases to federal officials, relying on regulatory agencies, and filing civil suits against corporate criminals. Legal and technical difficulties considered included investigatory problems, proving intent, inappropriateness of criminal sanctions, and lack of expertise. Political factors included state of the local economy, the corporation's level of resources, and the prosecutor's career goals.

Part of their research efforts included a survey of district attorneys in California to determine how local prosecutors perceived corporate crime, how often they prosecuted these cases, and how community factors might contribute to decision making (see Benson, Cullen, & Maakestad, 1988). Their research found that "a significant majority of the district attorneys had prosecuted a variety of corporate crimes" (p. 505). The main barriers prosecutors confronted had to do with the limited resources available to respond to corporate misdeeds. They also found that rural prosecutors were more sensitive to prosecuting businesses that the community relied on, presumably because the rural prosecutors did not want to lose a business and harm the entire community. Elsewhere, Benson, Cullen, and Maakestad (1990) reported that half of the urban district attorneys said that corporate crime was "not serious", and only 11 percent of rural prosecutors said that the misconduct was serious or somewhat serious. Prosecutors described harm and blameworthiness as influencing their decisions to prosecute along with other factors such as multiple offenses, victim preference, and regulatory inaction at the federal level.

Scholars have noted other problems that arise when prosecuting corporations. For example, it is extremely difficult to identify the decision-making processes that led to the corporate misconduct (Punch, 2000). Take BP's, case, for example. What decisions were made by executives that contributed to the explosion in the Gulf of Mexico? Who made those decisions? Were those decisions made in good faith? Identifying this decision-making process is complex and sometimes impossible. In addition, laws are written and interpreted as applying to individuals and not organizations, resulting in atypical offenders in corporate crime prosecutions (Punch, 2000).

Although these obstacles exist, some corporate offenses are prosecuted in the criminal justice system. Geis and Dimento (1995) point to six principles of **corporate crime liability** that support the need to prosecute corporations criminally. These principles include the following:

- A corporation is the sum of the actors in the organization.
- It is ineffective to punish individuals for corporate misconduct.
- It is more shameful for a corporation to be prosecuted than it is for an individual.
- Corporations can change more than individuals.
- It is easier to prove intent in corporations than it is with individuals.
- The corporation has resources to pay fines.

Geis and Dimento (1995) stress that the principles are not empirically grounded and are potentially misguided and harmful (e.g., if executives continue their misconduct). They conclude:

Punishing the corporation alone might well induce it to clean up its act, but such punishment, almost always a fine, could be regarded as not much more than an unfortunate consequence. . . . Punishing perpetrator and corporation together appears to offer the best deterrence, although it remains to be demonstrated that such punishment produces the kinds of results claimed for it. (p. 84)

When corporations are prosecuted, different legal standards apply to the prosecution. For example, business entities do not have the right to "plead the Fifth" (e.g., the Fifth Amendment of the U.S. Constitution offers protection against self-incrimination). This is an individual right, not an organizational right (Nakayama, 2007). Also, intent is determined somewhat differently in corporate crimes. For example, in corporate crime cases intent is (1) demonstrated through uncovering evidence of conspiracies, (2) inferred in a new corporation after two corporations merge, (3) applied if corporate officials actively try to conceal a felony, and (4) present if corporate officials actively ignore criminal activity (Plimton & Walsh, 2010).

Common defenses that corporations use are "rogue employee" defenses and due diligence defenses (Plimton & Walsh, 2010). The **rogue employee defense** argues that the corporate misconduct was the result of an individual employee and not the result of any corporate activities. To counter this defense, prosecutors must show that the employee was acting within the scope of employment, that the employee's actions were done to benefit the corporation, and that "the act and intent can be imputed to the organization" (Plimton & Walsh, 2010, p. 332).

Table 14.2	Factors U.S. Attorneys Are Urged to Consider in Deciding to Prosecute Corporations		
Factor			
Is the offense serious with a high risk of harm?	Yes	No
Was misconduct pervasive in the organization?	Yes	No
Has the corporation been involved in past allegations of misconduct, whether criminal, civil, or regulatory violations?	Yes	No
Did the corporation voluntarily disclose wrongdoing in a timely way?	Yes	No
Does the corporation have an adequate compliance program that was in place before the misconduct occurred?	Yes	No
Did the corporation address this misconduct through appropriate remedial actions?	Yes	No
Are there collateral consequences for groups that were not responsible for the misconduct?	Yes	No
Would prosecuting individuals responsible for the misconduct be adequate?	Yes	No
Would civil or regulatory actions be adequate?	Yes	No

Source: U.S. Department of Justice

Under the **due diligence defense,** the corporation contends that it did everything it could do, in good faith, to abide by the law. In determining whether the organization acted with due diligence, the court will consider seven factors. In particular, the organization must have met the following conditions:

- An established compliance program
- Assigned the responsibility for supervising the compliance program to a high-ranking employee
- Demonstrated that it did not give significant responsibility to an employee prone to misconduct
- Communicated compliance messages to employees
- Made a reasonable effort to meet compliance
- Enforced compliance standards when wrongdoing occurred
- Responded to wrongdoing and initiated measures to keep that misconduct from recurring (Goldsmith & King, 1997, p. 20)

Some have argued that prosecutors have become "unjustifiably heavy-handed" in corporate crime cases, "compelling corporations to cooperate in criminal investigations" (Bharara, 2007, p. 54). Strategies that have come under fire include situations where prosecutors (1) force companies to waive attorney-client privilege, (2) require corporations to fire employees, and (3) make unrealistic requests in exchange for leniency (Bharara, 2007). Bharara quotes several other legal scholars who used the following concepts to describe the notion of holding corporations criminally liable: "unprincipled, pointless, counterproductive, indiscriminate, incoherent, illogical, puzzling, and extreme" (p. 67).

Deciding Whether to Defer Prosecution

Another decision prosecutors will make is whether to enter into deferred prosecution agreements or non-prosecution agreements with corporations or businesses. Prosecutors have used pretrial diversion programs routinely over the last several decades for individual offenders. Their use for corporate offenders has been somewhat sparing until recently.

In a **deferred prosecution agreement (DPA)**, the prosecutor agrees not to prosecute the corporation if the corporation agrees to certain conditions to be completed over a probationary period. In a **non-prosecution agreement (NPA)**, the prosecutor indicates that the prosecution will not occur based on the corporation's agreement to certain conditions. A DPA is filed with the court, while an NPA is not (USGAO, 2009). Conditions that are imposed on corporations include the development of improved compliance programs, removal of certain personnel, fines, and a waiver of privileges (Spivack & Raman, 2008).

The number of DPAs and NPAs doubled between 2002 and 2005, as compared to the number of agreements the entire decade before. The agreements have become so frequent that some have suggested they have "become the standard means for concluding corporate crime prosecutions" (Spivack & Raman, 2008, p. 159). Deferrals are seen as advantageous because they save prosecutorial resources and protect "innocent" employees from experiencing collateral consequences that stem from corporate crime prosecutions (Spivack & Raman, 2008). They have been critiqued because it is not always clear that the agreements are used consistently (USGAO, 2009).

Table 14.3 shows the number of corporate crime prosecutions, DPAs, and NPAs by U.S. attorneys and the Department of Justice's Criminal Division between 2004 and 2014. There was an increase in their use in the years since 2004. Overall, prosecutions are down, but DPAs and NPAs are up. The funds recovered through the DPAs have increased substantially. An investigation by the U.S. Government Accountability Office (2009) concluded that while the DOJ has improved its ability to monitor the number of DPAs and NPAs, the next step is to determine the actual effectiveness of the agreements in controlling corporate misconduct.

● ● ● The Role of Defense Attorneys in White-Collar Crime Cases

The defense attorney is responsible for defending the accused offender against the criminal charges. One legal scholar indicated that defense attorneys have four goals in defending white-collar defendants, depending on where the case is in the judicial process. These goals include (1) keeping the defendant from being indicted; (2) if indicted, keeping the defendant from being convicted; (3) if convicted, keeping the defendant from being imprisoned; and (4) if imprisoned, keeping the sentence shorter (Lawless, 1988). These goals demonstrate that the role of the defense attorney extends throughout the criminal justice process. Indeed, their work may begin very early in the criminal justice process (Gottschalk, 2014a).

Kenneth Mann (1985), author of *Defending White-Collar Crime: A Portrait of Attorneys at Work,* has provided the most descriptive overview of the defense attorney's role in white-collar crime cases. Conducting interviews with 44 defense attorneys experienced with defending white-collar offenders, Mann demonstrated how some attorneys have made a career out of white-collar crime defense work. Mann's research showed how attorneys worked to control the flow of information and to prepare white-collar offenders in how to act in the criminal justice process. A student from Norway found that lawyers "become more famous if [they] handle more white-collar crime cases" (Gottschalk, 2014b).

Several features of the white-collar criminal case make these cases different from traditional criminal cases for defense attorneys. Just as the complex record search creates problems for prosecutors and investigators, the sheer number of records can be difficult for defense attorneys to review (Leto, Pogrebin, & Stretesky, 2007). Also, the cases typically involve more witnesses than might be found in conventional crimes (Leto et al., 2007). In addition, defense attorneys will need to direct efforts toward dealing with the media more than they might in other cases (Preiser & Swisher, 1988). Somewhat related, defense attorneys will spend more time preparing the white-collar defendant for the emotional impact of the trial and for the attention the case will get from the media (Lawless, 1988). Note also that prosecutors will select only white-collar crime cases that are very strongly in their favor (Lawless, 1988).

Stereotypes about white-collar offenders can also make the cases a little more challenging for defense attorneys. For instance, one author team noted that the cases are harder for defense attorneys because juries are predisposed to assume that white-collar defendants are guilty (Preiser & Swisher, 1988). Also, some defense attorneys perceive white-collar offenders as "defendants who are manipulative and [who] attempt to influence their defense team" (Leto et al., 2007, p. 106). In short, white-collar defense attorneys may have quite a task in front of them when they agree to defend white-collar defendants.

Table 14.3	Number of Corporate Prosecutions Compared to Deferred Prosecution Agreements or Non-Prosecution Agreements Entered Into by the U. S. Department of Justice 2004-2014*
Year	
2004	
Number of Prosecutions	335
Number of DPAs and NPAs	8
Prosecutions per DPA or NPA	41.9
2005	
Number of Prosecutions	398
Number of DPAs and NPAs	14
Prosecutions per DPA or NPA	28.4
2006	
Number of Prosecutions	345
Number of DPAs and NPAs	24
Prosecutions per DPA or NPA	21.6
2007	
Number of Prosecutions	300
Number of DPAs and NPAs	39
Prosecutions per DPA or NPA	7.7
2008	
Number of Prosecutions	299
Number of DPAs and NPAs	19
Prosecutions per DPA or NPA	15.7
2009	
Number of Prosecutions	284
Number of DPAs and NPAs	21
Prosecutions per DPA or NPA	13.5
2010	
Number of Prosecutions	239
Number of DPAs and NPAs	40
Prosecutions per DPA or NPA	5.9

(Continued)

Table 14.3	(Continued)
Year	
2011	
Number of Prosecutions	256
Number of DPAs and NPAs	34
Prosecutions per DPA or NPA	7.5
2012	
Number of Prosecutions	279
Number of DPAs and NPAs	38
Prosecutions per DPA or NPA	7.3
2013	
Number of Prosecutions	298
Number of DPAs and NPAs	28
Prosecutions per DPA or NPA	10.6
2014	
Number of Prosecutions	237
Number of DPAs and NPAs	30
Prosecutions per DPA or NPA	7.9
2004 through 2014	
Number of Prosecutions	3,270
Number of DPAs and NPAs	295
Prosecutions per DPA or NPA	11.1

*Prosecutions reflect calendar year numbers and DPAs/NPAs reflect fiscal year numbers, so caution should be used in interpreting the ratio.

Sources: Gibson Dunn (2015). 2014 year-end update on corporate non-prosecution agreements (NPAs) and deferred prosecution agreements (DPAs).

Trac Reports (2015) *Justice department data reveals 29 percent drop in criminal prosecutions of corporations*

U. S. Department of Justice (2015). *Criminal program update 2015*

In-depth interviews of five federal public defenders by Jessica Leto and her colleagues (2007) found that defense attorneys used three strategies to manage their cases and their clients. First, the **process-oriented defense** strategy is guided primarily by a process that flows from one step to the next step (e.g., 1. read the indictment, 2. contact the defendant, 3. contact the prosecutor, 4. construct the defense). The attorneys "process" these cases the same way regardless of case or offender characteristics.

Second, the **discovery-oriented defense** is a more flexible defense strategy that is dictated by the characteristics of the charges, with no set formula used to respond to the cases. Attorneys using this strategy rely more on records and may not view the defendant (or the case) in a favorable light. The authors quote one attorney who—when asked about the first thing he did when assigned a white-collar crime case—responded, "Go tell [the chief] to kiss my ass for giving it to me. Then, I don't know beyond that" (Leto et al., 2007, p. 97).

Third, the **client-oriented defense** strategy involves situations where the client "direct[s] the way the attorney defends the case" (Leto et al., 2007, p. 100). In these situations, the client is given a little involvement in the beginning stages of the judicial proceedings and then more and more as the case progresses. The underlying assumption is that white-collar defendants have a great deal to offer in building and orchestrating their own defense strategies.

Leto and her research team (2007) note that strategies may change as the case proceeds. For example, sometimes a defense case may begin using process- or discovery-oriented strategies and then shift to a client-oriented defense case. They note that the attorneys in Mann's (1985) seminal research project tended to use "mistake of fact" defenses, but none of the attorneys in their research project used this defense. The strategy they used if the case made it to trial was to "find flaws in the government's case in order to cast doubt upon their client's guilt" (Leto et al., 2007, p. 104).

Part of the defense attorney's role will be devoted to information control where attorneys will limit the amount of information that the press and others have about the defendant (Gottschalk, 2014a). Because these cases receive more press attention than traditional criminal cases, attorneys will try to find a way to use their information control strategies to their advantage. These strategies "are normally kept hidden as a secrecy to other parties, including the client [because] success is often dependent upon the lack of awareness among other parties (Gottschalk, 2014a, p. 62).

Mann (1985) suggested that defense attorneys will "portray the [white-collar] defendant as an innocent victim of circumstance" (p. 40). Benson (1989) argued that defense attorneys will paint a picture of the defendant as an upstanding member of the community who, through the publicity surrounding the case, has already been punished enough. To be sure, white-collar crime defense attorneys will use a variety of defenses that are tailored to the specific type of white-collar crime the defendant is charged with. Some of the common types of defenses used to defend white-collar defendants include the following:

1. The **good faith defense** is based on the argument that defendants lack knowledge and intent. They did not know the crime was being committed; therefore, they could not have formed the intent to commit the crime. The "ostrich instruction" means that this defense does not apply if defendants actively avoided finding out about the crime by simply ignoring behaviors they should have been monitoring (Fischer & Sheppard, 2008).

2. The **meeting competition defense** is raised in price discrimination cases to show that a business's price discriminations were done "in good faith to counter actions of a competitor" (Hill & Lezell, 2010, p. 257).

3. The **isolated occurrence defense** argues that the misconduct was a rare event done by a single employee and not part of any systematic criminal activity. This defense is "one of the most frequently litigated defenses in OSH Act citations" (Trumka, 2008, p. 348). The business must show that measures were implemented to stop similar incidents from occurring in the future.

4. The **lack of fraudulent intent defense** argues that the defendant did not intend to commit a criminal act (Heenan, Klarfeld, Roussis, & Walsh, 2010).

5. The **withdrawal from conspiracy defense** is used in offenses to argue that the defendant withdrew his or her involvement from the misconduct before the illegal actions occurred. The defendant must demonstrate active efforts to stop the conspiracy. Reporting the crime to authorities is seen as one strategy for demonstrating withdrawal from a conspiracy (Hill & Lezell, 2010).

6. The **reliance on the advice of counsel defense** is raised when defendants argue that their actions were carried out simply because they were following the advice of their attorneys. This is technically not a defense that would mitigate guilt, but this information may sway a jury to side with the defendant (Heenan et al., 2010).

7. The **ignorance defense** is raised to show that the defendant did not know that the criminal acts were occurring (Altschuler et al., 2008).

8. The **multiplicity of indictment defense** argues that the offender is being charged for one single offense on several different counts in the indictment. This defense suggests that the defendant is being tried twice and the defendant's double jeopardy rights are violated (Fischer & Sheppard, 2008).

Denial of criminal intent is among the most common denials offered by white-collar defendants (Benson, 1985a). In fact, one group of legal scholars wrote that "a typical defense . . . begins with a denial that the defendant carried out any violations with a criminal or fraudulent purpose" (Heenan et al., 2010, p. 1027). In addition to serving as a legal defense, such a denial allows white-collar offenders to shield themselves from the social stigma of a criminal label.

In cases where a corporation, business, or organization is the defendant, the company may rely on its internal general legal counsel for assistance and advice. In these situations, defendants sometimes raise the attorney-client privilege in an effort to keep information out of court (Yohay & Dodge, 1987). **Attorney-client privilege** has been described as "the oldest and most widely applied doctrine protecting confidential information" (Goldsmith & King, 1997, p. 24). There are restrictions regarding what type of information is protected under this privilege. Judges will occasionally use the "subject matter" test to see if the privilege applies. Under this test, five elements are necessary for the privilege to apply:

1. The communication must be made for the purpose of securing legal advice.

2. The employee making the communication must do so at the direction of a supervisor.

3. The direction must be given by the supervisor to obtain legal advice for the corporation.

4. The subject matter of the communication must be within the scope of the employee's corporate duties.

5. The communication may not be disseminated beyond those persons who need to know information (Goldsmith & King, 1997, p. 27).

Corporate attorneys often direct their efforts toward delaying the investigation and prosecution by filing motions and using an assortment of tactics to give them more time to build their own cases. One expert suggested that legal counsel should not see settling as a rational decision if a corporate executive is facing both criminal and civil charges (Zane, 2003).

One legal scholar argues that white-collar defense attorneys have done a poor job making a case for reducing sentences due to mitigating factors (Haugh, 2012). Drawing on the way that mitigating factors are used in death penalty cases to argue for life imprisonment rather than a sentence of capital punishment, Haugh offers the following suggestions to fellow defense attorneys:

- Defense attorneys should change their mind-set about the weight that sentence guidelines have in determining the final sentence given to offenders.
- Defense attorneys should use a team approach to defend white-collar defendants so that the expertise of different attorneys is used to help make a case for a reduced sentence.
- Defense attorneys should begin thinking about mitigation factors early in the case.
- Defense attorneys should build trust with clients, using a mitigation specialist who will approach all involved in a warm and friendly manner.
- Defense attorneys should develop a mitigation defense tailored to the specific details of the case and the defendant.
- Defense attorneys should present the case for mitigation as strongly and passionately as possible.
- Defense attorneys should stay focused on the goal of mitigation.

Of course, prosecutors will not necessarily agree with these tactics, and they will engage in their own efforts to call for stiffer sentences for white-collar offenders.

● ● ● Other Actors Involved in White-Collar Crime Judicial Proceedings

When watching an episode of *Law & Order* or another television show depicting the trial process, viewers will always see other "actors" involved in the courts. These other actors include (1) jurors, (2) witnesses, (3) defendants, and (4) victims. While these actors are involved in all types of court proceedings, certain dynamics of white-collar crime cases mean that the roles of these participants is substantively different in white-collar versus traditional cases.

Jurors

In cases where trials are held before juries, jurors will determine guilt or innocence of accused offenders. In some places, juries may play a role in sentencing, and they may make recommendations about the amount of damages to be awarded in civil trials. Some have argued that juries are harsher than judges—in determining guilt and in meting out penalties (Levine, 1983).

Some researchers have hypothesized that offenders who do not have specific characteristics of what would be expected for different types of crimes will be judged by external or situational factors, meaning that jurors might be assessing offenders based on whether they look like the "typical offender" in a certain type of crime (Gordon, Michels, & Nelson, 1996). Gordon and his coauthors' mock juror study found that respondents sentenced white embezzlers to longer sentences than black embezzlers, but black burglars were given longer sentences than white burglars. The authors suggest that mock jurors "viewed a white defendant committing the white-collar crime as a more typical event than the black defendant committing the white-collar crime" (p. 159).

Such a finding is relevant to other forms of white-collar crime as well. In effect, jurors might be reluctant to see certain types of white-collar defendants as capable of engaging in wrongdoing (Jesilow, Pontell, & Geis, 1985). It may be difficult, for example, for jurors to accept that a trusted physician actually engaged in fraud. Fraud by some types of professionals is not a "typical event" among those professionals. Hence, jurors' perceptions are influenced by cognitive processes that define and assess defendants by preconceived notions.

Juries will occasionally "make mistakes" in white collar crime cases—either failing to come to a unanimous agreement or engaging in behavior that allows defendants to appeal a conviction. In the Tyco case, for example, a mistrial was declared after a juror gave a thumbs-up sign to the defense table. In the first Enron trial, which lasted 3 months, a mistrial was declared after the jury was unable to come to an agreement on nearly 180 of the 202 charges filed against the executives (Brickey, 2006). The jury deliberated for only 4 days.

The complexity of white-collar crime cases sets them apart from many traditional criminal cases decided by jurors. Consider a robbery as opposed to a securities fraud case. In the robbery, the jury hears one type of evidence, and the evidence is typically easy to follow. In securities fraud cases, the jury will hear different types of evidence, which may not always be easy to follow. In some cases, the evidence—particularly environmental crime and corporate crime cases—might include material which is new to the jurors, or potentially even harmful to the public.

On the one hand, prosecutors will make efforts to simplify proceedings so all can understand the evidence. On the other hand, defense attorneys may use the complexity of the cases to help demonstrate why the defendant should not be convicted. Brickey (2006) quotes a securities lawyer who said, "If you look at Bernie Ebbers, Adelphia, and Martha Stewart, the government has done an exceptional job when they keep it simple so juries understand" (p. 417).

The amount of time that jurors must devote to white-collar crime cases is also different from other types of cases. The time estimates for different types of white-collar crimes have been provided elsewhere. At this point it is important to suggest that *time* can influence juror decision making in that some jurors might vote certain ways out of a desire to end their involvement in the case.

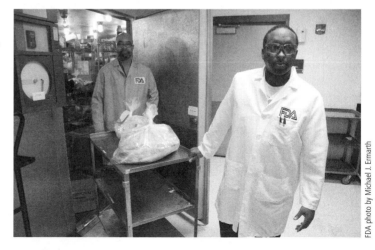

▲ **Photo 14.5** In some cases, evidence from environmental and corporate crime cases might actually include unsafe materials that must be handled with caution.

FDA photo by Michael J. Ermarth

Witnesses

Witnesses are also involved in white-collar crime trials. Generally speaking, types of witnesses include government witnesses, lay witnesses, cooperating witnesses, character witnesses, and expert witnesses. **Government witnesses** are police officers, investigators, auditors, and other officials who developed the case as part of the investigation process. These witnesses are trained in how to share information so that the evidence best reflects the government's interests. In terms of white-collar crimes, much of the testimony of government witnesses will be directed toward the records reviewed as part of the investigation.

Lay witnesses are individuals who have some relevant information to share about the white-collar crime case based on something they saw or experienced. Two issues arise in white-collar crime cases that limit the use of lay witnesses. First, white-collar crimes are not committed openly; few witnesses are available to describe the offense. Second, white-collar crime victims were often not aware of the victimization when it occurred and may, as a result, have little to offer at a trial.

Cooperating witnesses are witnesses who are cooperating with the prosecution as a result of some involvement they had in the case. In terms of white-collar crime cases, cooperating witnesses often include coworkers, subordinates of the defendant, supervisors, or informants who participated in the criminal investigation. Cooperating witnesses are sometimes offered a reduced sentence in exchange for their testimony.

Character witnesses are individuals who share information about the defendant that demonstrates, in theory, that it is not in the defendant's "character" to engage in wrongdoing. For white-collar crime trials, character witnesses are called upon to demonstrate that the defendant's work ethic, long history of contributions to the community, and good citizenship are not consistent with evidence that suggests wrongdoing. White-collar offenders, in particular, may have access to well-known and powerful character witnesses such as celebrities and politicians. There is debate surrounding the utility of such witnesses. After former Los Angeles Mayor Richard Riordan testified in the criminal case of an executive accused of fraud, one former prosecutor turned white-collar criminal defense attorney told a reporter, "High-profile character witnesses never concerned me. . . . While they are interesting to watch testify, they by definition don't know the facts of the case being prosecuted, and therefore the impact of their testimony is usually quite limited" (Pfiefer, 2010).

Expert witnesses are witnesses who share their professional insight and interpretation of the evidence used in the case. Typically hired for a fee, these witnesses are actually involved throughout the justice process (see Figure 14.3). At the pretrial phase, expert witnesses review evidence and provide advice about how the evidence can be used at trial. During the trial, the expert will testify and educate the jury about the evidence under review. After the trial, the expert will assist in filing appeals and helping to identify the grounds for appeal. Also, experts will be called upon to help white-collar offenders prepare for their punishment experience.

Perhaps the more important part of an expert witness's role involves his or her testimony in court. The individuals will discuss the strength of evidence for the side that hired them and will also address the limitations of the other side's evidence. In white-collar crime cases, they will communicate complex financial information or other industry-specific information in a way that jurors can understand.

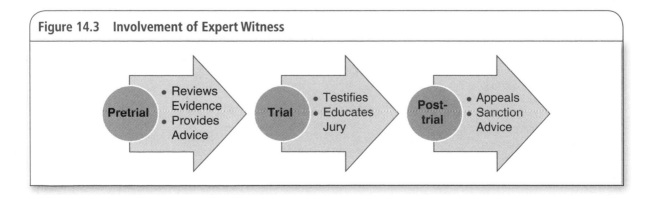

Figure 14.3   Involvement of Expert Witness

Pretrial — • Reviews Evidence • Provides Advice

Trial — • Testifies • Educates Jury

Post-trial — • Appeals • Sanction Advice

Expert witnesses must exhibit a level of scientific expertise that is consistent with what would be expected in the expert's scientific area of study (Summerford, 2002). The judge determines whether someone is able to serve as an expert witness. In selecting experts for white-collar crime cases, one author team suggests that those hiring the expert consider the following: (1) the expert's academic training, (2) whether the expert is accredited by an accreditation body, (3) the expert's match to the specific type of case, (4) the expert's level of expertise, and (5) what the expert looks like (Rasmussen & Leauanae, 2004). This fifth factor might surprise readers. The authors use the phrase "beauty contest" in suggesting that "better looking" experts who have "charisma" will be better received by jurors.

One defense attorney team has noted that prosecutors will try to sneak expert testimony into white-collar crime cases by submitting written opinions from experts as part of nontestimonial documents (Frongillo, Simons, Essinger, & Knowles, 2014). This is done, they suggest, in order to get information before the judge or jury without allowing the defense to question the expert. They further suggest that defense attorneys should use the constitutional Confrontation Clause to try to keep the evidence out where warranted, or at least to allow the opportunity to cross-examine the expert. Specific steps they suggest include the following:

- Scrutinize the discovery documents to determine if the government intends to use a non-testifying expert
- Establish the purpose of the non-testifying expert option as testimony or litigation
- Establish that the information is being used to legally define the offense

Following these steps, they argue, will make it easier to keep expert testimony from being introduced without being cross-examined.

The Role of White-Collar Defendants

White-collar defendants play a role in judicial proceedings. Many scholars have pointed to the way that white-collar offenders deflect blame from themselves and onto others in an effort to portray themselves as honest professionals (Croall, 1993). This blame deflection is particularly evident during the judicial process when defendants blame the wrongdoing on administrative errors, coworker errors, unclear policies, or unfair regulations (Jesilow, Pontell, & Geis, 1986). Some white-collar defendants will describe their misdeeds as if they are analogous to what can be called a *Robin Hood defense* (e.g., their crimes help the poor). Here is how Paul Jesilow and his colleagues (1986) described efforts to shape perceptions about physicians accused of fraud: "Physicians are many times able to cast shady actions in a positive light. For example, providers who knowingly bill for unnecessary services can argue that the procedures were necessary for the health of the patient" (p. 17).

In most trials, white-collar defendants will not take the stand. The messages of denial and blame deflection are communicated through their attorneys. If white-collar defendants take the stand, then their efforts to lie and minimize would be frowned on by the judge (Mann, 1985). Consider Judge Marian Cedarbaum's comments to Martha Stewart at her sentencing hearing: "Lying to government agencies during the course of an investigation is a very serious matter, regardless of the outcome of the investigation" ("Martha Stewart Reads a Statement," 2004). Jurors also look unfavorably on white-collar defendants when they lie or blame others for their transgressions (Brickey, 2006).

For white-collar defendants, the trial experience will be different from the trial experience of many traditional offenders in four ways. First, in some cases, the corporation or business is on trial, not an individual offender. Second, many white-collar trials will have multiple defendants; one study showed that two thirds of the celebrated corporate fraud cases of the mid-2000s had more than one defendant (Brickey, 2006). Third, recall that many white-collar offenders have no criminal record, meaning that they have never been on trial before. Presumably, this could make the trial more stressful. Fourth, the longer length of white-collar crime trials can be particularly problematic for white-collar defendants (R. Wright, 2006). Depression, anxiety, and mental health problems have anecdotally been found among white-collar defendants. These problems can be attributed to the following: (1) Their lack of prior exposure to the trial process creates added stress, (2) they are used to being in control as leaders and executives but are not in control in court, (3) they have a great deal to lose if they are found guilty, and (4) a significant amount of shame or stigma is part of the trial process.

Where appropriate, defense attorneys may encourage defendants to take responsibility for their actions. This is done because accepting responsibility reduces the sentence that defendants receive if they are found guilty. In the words of one legal expert, "sentencers credit defendants who are contrite and demonstrate they would not commit future crimes" (Haugh, 2012, p. 51). This is borne out in research that shows that embezzlers who accepted responsibility for their sentences received sentences one month shorter on average than those offenders who did not accept responsibility (Madden, Hartley, Walker, & Miller, 2012). Accepting responsibility is also believed to reduce penalties given to corporations (Thompson & Yong, 2012).

While they typically will not take the stand, if convicted, white-collar offenders will go to great lengths to convince the judge why they should be punished leniently. For example, many white-collar offenders will send the judge a letter expressing remorse and begging for lenience. They will also call upon their family members and friends to write letters to the judge to appeal for a light sentence (Mann, 1985). In Martha Stewart's case, the judge received 1,500 letters from supporters who urged the judge to issue a light sentence to Stewart. One of the letters was from Stewart herself. In Focus 14.2 includes an excerpt of the letter Stewart sent ("Martha Stewart Reads a Statement," 2004). Note the direct appeal to the judge where Stewart said, "My hopes that my life will not be completely destroyed lie entirely in your hands."

IN FOCUS 14.2

It's a Good Thing: Excerpt of Martha Stewart's Letter to Her Judge

Dear Judge Cedarbaum:

We have never had the opportunity to speak one on one, you and I, despite the fact that I sat before you for five weeks. I am sorry that the legal system is such that even when a person's life is at stake—and for me that means my professional and personal life, not my physical being—the constraints prohibit conversation, communication, true understanding and complete disclosure of every aspect of the situation. I am not a lawyer, I am not skilled in legal processes, I am not even knowledgeable about many legal terms and legal procedures. I am still, after two and a half years of legal maneuverings and countless hours of preparation and trial time, abysmally confused and ill prepared for what is described to me as the next step in this process.

I am a 62 year old woman, a graduate of the excellent Nutley, New Jersey public school system and Barnard College. I have had an amazing professional life and several exciting careers, and I am grateful for that. I have a lovely family and a beautiful, upright, intelligent daughter (also a graduate of Barnard College), and I feel blessed and proud.

For more than a decade I have been building a wonderful company around a core of essential beliefs that are centered on home, family values and traditions, holidays, celebrations, weddings, children, gardening, collecting, home-making, teaching and learning. I have spent most of my professional life creating, writing, researching, and thinking on the highest possible level about quality of life, about giving, about providing, so that millions of people, from all economic strata, can enjoy beauty, good quality, well made products, and impeccably researched information about many hundreds of subjects which can lead to a better life and more rewarding family lifestyle.

I ask that in judging me you consider all the good that I have done, all the contributions I have made and the intense suffering that has accompanied every single moment of the past two and a half years. I seek the opportunity to continue serving my community in a positive manner, to attempt to repair the damage that has been done and to get on with what I have always considered was a good, worthwhile and exemplary life.

My heart goes out to you; my prayers are with you, and my hopes that my life will not be completely destroyed lie entirely in your hands.

Respectfully and most sincerely,
Martha Stewart

Source: Reprinted From Stewart, M. (2004 July 15). In Martha Stewart's Letter to Judge Cedarbaum.

The Role of Victims in White-Collar Judicial Proceedings

Victims also have a role in white-collar judicial proceedings, though their role is limited. Criminologist Gilbert Geis (1975) has observed that the victim's role in the criminal justice process can be compared to the role that an expectant father has in the delivery room during the birth of his child. The father had a major role in the beginning of the pregnancy, but when the baby is being born, the father is tangential to the process. According to Geis, the victim has a similar role in the criminal justice process.

In white-collar crime proceedings at the federal level, historically, victims were not permitted to participate in the allocution process. **Allocution** refers to the part of the trial process where individuals are permitted to address the court prior to sentencing. Federal law reserved allocution for victims to those who had been victimized by violent crimes. This changed in 2004 with the passage of the **Crime Victims Rights Act**, which permitted victims of all types of federal offenses to participate in the allocution process.

The importance of victim allocution cannot be overstated. A sampling of the comments victims made in Bernard Madoff's sentencing hearing include the following:

- "Last year, my mother died. Now I don't have my mother or my money."
- "Your sons despise you. . . . [You] are an evil lowlife."
- "For the first time in my life, I'm very, very frightened about my future."
- "I calculate again and again how long it is I can hold out." (R. Barnard, 2009, "Madoff Case")

Hearing victims' voices and seeing them in court reinforces that white-collar crimes are not victimless crimes.

It is certainly plausible that the voices could actually provide support for increasing offenders' sentences. Beyond the sentencing enhancement, participating in the process can be empowering and rehabilitative to victims (J. Barnard, 2002). Drawbacks include time and resources, identifying which victims should participate, how to deal with emotional outbursts, revictimization in the justice process, inarticulate victims, and emotional letdowns for victims (J. Barnard, 2001).

In some cases, the victim may be a business or corporation. A question that has come up is the degree to which the business or corporation can contribute to the prosecutorial efforts in terms of financial support. In one case involving insurance fraud, an insurance company paid for some of the prosecutorial costs (see *People v. Eubanks*). The defendant appealed the case, and the California Supreme Court ruled that such activity has the potential to result in unfair treatment of the defendant and that the activity could lead to a conflict of interest. Courts do allow victims to provide assistance to the prosecution in some cases (e.g., they may hire a private investigator), though financial contributions are generally not permitted (Nahra, 1999).

● ● ● Civil Lawsuits and White-Collar Crime

As noted above, white-collar crime cases can be adjudicated in civil court through the use of lawsuits. Types of lawsuits can be categorized by the plaintiff-defendant relationship. The following types of lawsuits are relevant to white-collar crime:

- Individuals suing businesses
- Businesses suing businesses
- Government agencies suing individuals
- Government agencies suing businesses
- *Qui tam* lawsuits
- Class action suits

Within these types of lawsuits, different varieties of lawsuits exist. Two that are particularly relevant for white-collar crimes include tort lawsuits and contract lawsuits. A **tort lawsuit** involves "one party alleging injury, damage, or loss stemming from the negligent or intentional acts of another party" (T. Cohen, 2009, p. 1). **Contract lawsuits** "involve fraud, employment discrimination, tortious interference, or allegations of unfulfilled agreements between buyers and sellers [and] lenders and borrowers" (Farole, 2009, p. 1). These lawsuits can be filed in either state or federal court.

The Civil Justice Survey of State Courts collects information on types of tort and contract trials held in state general jurisdiction courts. The survey was conducted in 1991, 1996, and 2005. In 2005, 7.4 million claims were filed in all types of state courts. Just under 27,000 cases were heard in courts of general jurisdiction, which are the trials that hear more serious cases (Langton & Cohen, 2008). Table 14.4 shows the types of defendants (individual, government, or business) in state court tort and contract trials in 2005 by misconduct type. Businesses were defendants more often for each case type, except for medical malpractice cases (which had hospitals as defendants most often).

Table 14.5 shows the types of defendants in contract and tort cases for the same year and whether the case was decided by a judge or a jury. Lawsuits for failing to provide services were more likely to be heard through a bench trial (with 80% of the cases heard in this manner), while lawsuits for medical practice were more likely to be decided by jury trials (nearly 99% of medical malpractice cases were jury trials). Additional findings from the 2005 Civil Justice Survey of State Courts include the following:

- 80 percent of torts were individuals suing businesses or other individuals.
- Jury trials lasted, on average, 2 days longer than bench trials in both tort and contract cases.
- Plaintiffs won two thirds of contract trials.
- Half of all plaintiffs in tort trials received $24,000 or less in damages.
- Half of the tort cases were completed within 2 years after the complaint was filed (T. Cohen, 2009; Farole, 2009).

Table 14.4   **Types of Defendants in State Court Tort and Contract Trials, 2005**

	% Individual	% Government	% Business	% Hospital
Tort trials				
Fraud	34.9	0.8	64.2	0.1
Failure to provide services	19.3	0.0	80.6	0.0
Employment discrimination	0.6	35.4	59.9	4.1
Other employment disputes	23.0	8.1	58.3	10.6
Interfering with contractual relationship	32.0	4.6	61.4	0.0
Contract trials[a]				
Medical malpractice	38.5	0.4	5.2	55.6
Professional malpractice	36.0	0.0	37.3	2.7
Asbestos	6.0	2.4	88.0	0.0
Other product liability	1.1	0.0	89.9	0.0

[a]Includes only cases where an individual is the plaintiff. The percentage refers to percentage of all cases.

Source: U.S. Department of Justice

Table 14.5	Types of Defendant Trials in State Court Tort and Contract Trials, 2005			
	Number	Percentage of Total[a] (%)	Jury (%)	Bench (%)
Tort trials				
Fraud	1,113	12.5	50.1	49.9
Failure to provide services	2,591	29.1	16.6	83.4
Employment discrimination	319	3.6	91.2	8.8
Other employment disputes	558	6.3	62.9	37.1
Interfering with contractual relationship	15.2	1.7	61.8	38.2
Contract trials				
Medical malpractice	2,449	14.9	98.7	1.3
Professional malpractice	150	0.9	60.0	40.0
Asbestos	87	0.5	95.4	4.6
Other product liability	268	16.3	92.5	7.5

[a]Refers to percentage of total trials

Source: U.S. Department of Justice

At the federal level, 512,000 civil cases were completed in district courts in 2002 to 2003, the most recent year for which data were available. About one-fifth of the cases were tort claims where the plaintiffs sued alleging that they were injured or damaged by the defendant's negligent actions (T. Cohen, 2005, August). Additional characteristics of federal lawsuits over this time frame include the following:

- 90% of tort cases were personal injury cases.
- 71% of cases were decided by juries.
- 48% of cases were won by the plaintiff.
- 84% of the plaintiffs who won received monetary awards, with the median award being $201,000 (T. Cohen, 2005, August).

Government agencies, particularly regulatory agencies, might also file civil lawsuits against individuals and businesses in an effort to stop white-collar offending, punish the individual or offender for the wrongdoing, and recover the economic costs arising from the misconduct. Recall the discussion in an earlier chapter of the billions of dollars that the EPA recovered from environmental criminals. Most of these funds were recovered through civil enforcement actions.

In other cases, known as ***qui tam* lawsuits**, an individual can actually sue a corporation or company on behalf of the government. These lawsuits give private citizens the authority to take on the role of the government and sue corporations that have defrauded the government. Citizens who bring the charges can receive 25 percent to 30 percent of the damages received from the lawsuit. These are also known as *whistleblower lawsuits* in reference to the economic incentive given to whistleblowers to bring charges against a company (Payne, 2003a). Citizens must show that the information they are using to file their suit did not come from public disclosures made by other parties. In other words, the citizen must be the "original source of the information" (Pacini, Qiu, & Sinason, 2007, p. 68).

As long as the lawsuits are filed in good faith, employees cannot be punished by their companies for filing the lawsuits. Employers, of course, do not see *qui tam* policies favorably. Beyond getting employees to report misconduct, the lawsuits "supplement the strained resources of government attorneys and investigators" (Pacini et al., 2007, p. 65). In one case, John Kopchinski and five others were awarded $51.5 million after they filed a lawsuit against Pfizer Inc. for defrauding Medicaid through its marketing practices for various drugs. Pfizer settled the case without admitting wrongdoing (Neil, 2009).

Class action lawsuits are used to address corporate wrongdoing. In these situations, a group of victims sues a business or corporation jointly for the harm caused by the corporation. Victims agree to be a part of the lawsuits with the understanding that any damages received would be split in a predetermined way. These lawsuits can be quite lucrative for attorneys and plaintiffs. A website even exists that publishes current class action suits—http://classactionworld.com/.

● ● ● Issues in White-Collar Judicial Networking and the Judicial Process

A number of different issues arise concerning the judicial processing of white-collar offenders through the justice system. Some of these issues exist throughout the entire criminal justice system's processing of white-collar offenders, while others are unique to the judicial processing of white-collar offenders. These issues include the following:

- The need for networking
- Class bias
- The use of parallel proceedings
- Conceptual ambiguity surrounding corporate crime prosecutions

Each of these issues is discussed below.

Networking and the Judicial Process

As with the police response to white-collar crime, prosecutors must work with a number of different agencies in their efforts to battle white-collar misconduct. Unfortunately, interagency conflict and a lack of information sharing prohibit collaboration in some instances (Hammett & Epstein, 1993). Benson, Cullen, and Maakestad (1990) commented that the "continued rarity of intergovernmental cooperation is troubling" (p. 371).

In effect, some prosecutors would likely pass on white-collar crime prosecutions simply to avoid the headache of collaboration. As an analogy, think of group projects in courses. Many students despise such projects and may even drop courses simply to avoid group projects. Prosecutors do the same thing in white-collar crime cases.

Class Bias

Class bias is also implicit throughout the judicial processing of white-collar crime cases. Such bias is evident in four ways: (1) the hiring of high-powered defense attorneys, (2) complacency of criminal justice officials adjudicating the cases, (3) the disparate treatment of corporations, and (4) inadequate laws. In terms of *hiring high-powered defense attorneys,* some white-collar defendants are able to assemble powerful defense teams that are paid hundreds of thousands, if not millions, of dollars to defend the white-collar defendant. These defense teams are able to use resources that far outweigh the types of resources prosecutors have available. Traditional defendants, by comparison, have few, if any, resources available to support their defense.

Class bias is evident regarding the *complacency* that some officials show toward the judicial processing of white-collar crimes. Some authors have noted that white-collar crimes are not a priority for prosecutors (Hammett & Epstein, 1993), while others have suggested that the failure to take action potentially contributes to future misconduct (Van den Berg & Eshuis, 1996). Consider the war on drugs. Prosecutors devote tremendous resources to battling drug crimes. These prosecutions tend to focus more on poor and minority suspects. So white-collar crimes are ignored while drug crimes are "attacked" in a warlike fashion. In terms of a lack of enforcement contributing to future misconduct, one can point to the way that drivers speed on certain highways because police officers never stop speeders on those highways. In Atlanta, Georgia, where I live, you have to go 20 miles an hour over the speed limit on some roads just to keep from being run over. The lack of traffic enforcement results in drivers speeding. The lack of white-collar crime prosecutions may contribute to future white-collar misconduct.

One can also recognize bias when considering the *disparate treatment of corporations*. Criminologist John Hagan drew attention to the dual role that corporations can have in the criminal justice system: (1) They can be victims of white-collar crime, or (2) they can be perpetrators of crime. Hagan (1982) wrote, "Corporate entities not only have successfully avoided large-scale prosecutions, they also have proven themselves effective in using criminal prosecutions to penalize those who offend them" (p. 994). Hagan suggested that prosecutors spend significant resources protecting corporations, but by comparison, fewer resources are devoted to prosecuting corporate entities. Hagan concluded that the criminal justice system "better serves corporate than individual interests" (p. 1016). Another scholar noted that businesses have a significant amount of "power" to get out of trouble (Punch, 2000, p. 273). Or, as suggested above, they make great victims but lousy offenders.

Inadequate laws are another indicator of class bias in the judicial response to white-collar crimes. Conflict theorists have argued that laws are developed in a way that protects the powerful and weakens the poor and minority groups. This assumption will be discussed later. At this point, it is sufficient to point out that the consequences of inadequate laws are borne out in the judicial process. To be fair, it is important to note that efforts have been made to improve the laws to better address white-collar offending. For example, states have expanded their laws to make them apply to different types of white-collar crime. In New York, for example, a "scheme to defraud" statute was passed because it was recognized that the "false pretense larceny" statute was not sufficient for many white-collar crime cases (Clarey, 1978).

Still, problems remain that make traditional laws weak when processing white-collar crime cases. In one case, for example, a prosecutor charged contractors who tried to defraud an older woman with burglary. His rationale—the contractors committed the elements of "breaking" and "entering" into a home with "the intent to commit a crime." Incidentally, this prosecution was successful. More often than not, other prosecutors would have forgone charging the offenders because of the very real perception that the laws do not always cover the behavior of the white-collar offender.

The Use of Parallel Proceedings

Another issue that arises is the use of **parallel proceedings** in adjudicating a white-collar crime case. What this means is that a specific white-collar crime can be heard in more than one court simultaneously. There are different ways that proceedings might occur simultaneously. A criminal case could be processed with a civil or administrative proceeding, or a civil proceeding could be processed along with an administrative proceeding. Parallel proceedings are warranted under two circumstances: (1) Criminal proceedings may need to parallel civil or administrative hearings that address immediate needs to protect health and safety, and (2) simultaneous proceedings may be necessary to respond to cases that are especially serious (Nakayama, 2007).

Table 14.6 shows the advantages and disadvantages of using parallel proceedings in white-collar crime cases. Reasons criminal proceedings might be completed on their own include the following: (1) the ability to use evidence from the criminal proceeding in the civil case, (2) ensuring the civil case does not negatively impact the criminal case, (3) gaining an evidentiary advantage by not disclosing evidence too early, and (4) avoiding the surfacing of unnecessary issues. Reasons proceedings might occur simultaneously include (1) the need to address an immediate threat, (2) the threat of losing assets or bankruptcy, (3) the civil case was already under way when the criminal case began, and (4) the civil case fits within a national priority (Nakayama, 2007).

Table 14.6	Pros and Cons of Parallel Proceedings Instead of Completing Criminal Proceedings First
Pros of Parallel Proceedings	**Cons (Reasons Criminal Prosecution Should Be First)**
• Immediate threats to health and safety can be dealt with through injunction • Defendant's assets could "disappear" • Pending statute of limitations • Pending deadline for bankruptcy • Civil case is further along in justice process when criminal proceeding begins • Civil case directly relates to a national priority, and failing to address the case would jeopardize the national priority	• Criminal sanctions have potential to deter and punish offenders • Civil sanction could undermine criminal case and lessen penalty given to offender • Civil proceedings could expose ongoing investigation • Defendant could gain prosecutor's evidence prematurely • Officials from one proceeding may need to address unnecessary issues arising from other proceeding • Witnesses would be interviewed too frequently within short period of time

Source: Adapted from Environmental Protection Agency

The use of parallel proceedings has been questioned on various grounds such as concerns about double jeopardy, excessive fines, and due process violations (McDade & O'Donnell, 1992). Despite these questions, the use of parallel proceedings remains a popular alternative. Note that the proceedings are expected to remain separate. For example, it is deemed unethical for authorities to "use the threat of a criminal enforcement to resolve a civil matter" (Nakayama, 2007, p. 8).

Conceptual Ambiguity Surrounding Corporate Crime Prosecutions

Another issue surrounding corporate crime prosecutions centers on our lack of understanding about the number of corporate crime prosecutions and how to define them, measure them, and study them. Legal scholar Leonard Orland (1980) expressed great disgust over the way that criminologists discussed corporate crime adjudications. He argued that criminologists considered some adjudications as corporate crimes when, he believed, those acts were not truly corporate crimes. For example, criminologists often include civil and administrative judicial proceedings that result in violations, warnings, and injunctions as indicators of corporate crime. Orland contended that by wasting its time studying these sorts of behaviors, the criminal justice system is given the freedom to ignore serious acts of wrongdoing that should be handled criminally. Describing these beliefs, Orland (1980) wrote:

> Ultimately, the investigative power of the government, and not the musings of criminologists, should be used to quantify the actual amount of reported corporate crime. These data will permit criminologists to estimate the prevalence of underreported corporate crime, and it is likely they will discover that the amount of "hidden" corporate crime is vast and that true corporate crime is substantially underreported. (p. 518)

SUMMARY

- White-collar misconduct cases are adjudicated in at least five different types of judicial or quasi-judicial proceedings: (1) criminal proceedings, (2) civil proceedings, (3) administrative proceedings, (4) professional-disciplinary proceedings, and (5) workplace-disciplinary proceedings.
- Judges play an extremely important role in processing white-collar crime cases through the justice system.
- The three most salient factors influencing judicial decision making in white-collar crime cases are (1) harm from the offense, (2) blameworthiness, and (3) consequences of the punishment.

- At the federal level, U.S. attorneys are the prosecutors responsible for prosecuting federal offenses.
- The prosecution of white-collar criminals is seen as necessary in order to demonstrate "moral outrage" for white-collar misconduct (Cohen, 1992).
- Cohen (1992) argued that prosecutors will consider the following factors when deciding whether to prosecute white-collar offenders: the defendant's knowledge and intent, harm from the offense, whether misconduct continued after the regulatory agency initiated its investigation, amount of evidence, and how much the defendant benefited from the wrongdoing.
- Prosecutors face a number of other issues that may influence their decision-making process in white-collar crime cases, including (1) that trials may be harder to win in white-collar crime cases, (2) the time to complete the cases is significant, (3) resource issues, (4) establishing intent, and (5) practical issues.
- Dating back as far as Sutherland (1941), some criminologists have claimed that prosecutors are reluctant to prosecute corporations or businesses.
- The factors prosecutors are encouraged to address in deciding whether to prosecute corporations include offense characteristics, organizational characteristics, and the consequences of different types of reactions by the justice system.
- Common defenses that corporations use are "rogue employee" defenses and due diligence defenses (Plimton & Walsh, 2010).
- Another decision prosecutors will make is whether to enter into deferred prosecution agreements or non-prosecution agreements with corporations and businesses.
- The defense attorney is responsible for defending the accused offender against the criminal charges.
- Kenneth Mann (1985), author of *Defending White-Collar Crime: A Portrait of Attorneys at Work,* has provided the most descriptive overview of the defense attorney's role in white-collar crime cases.
- In-depth interviews of five federal public defenders by Jessica Leto and her colleagues (2007) found that defense attorneys used three strategies to manage their cases and their clients: *process-oriented, discovery-oriented, and client-oriented strategies.*
- Denial of criminal intent is among the most common denials offered by white-collar defendants.
- Other actors in the court include (1) jurors, (2) witnesses, (3) defendants, and (4) victims.
- Jurors might be reluctant to see certain types of white-collar defendants as capable of engaging in wrongdoing (Jesilow et al., 1986).
- Types of witnesses include government witnesses, lay witnesses, cooperating witnesses, character witnesses, and expert witnesses.
- Many scholars have pointed to the way that white-collar offenders will deflect blame from themselves and onto others in an effort to portray themselves as honest professionals (Croall, 1993).
- The 2004 Crime Victims Rights Act permitted victims of all types of federal offenses to participate in the allocution process.
- Two types of lawsuits that are particularly relevant for white-collar crimes are tort lawsuits and contract lawsuits.
- In *qui tam* lawsuits, an individual can actually sue a corporation or company on behalf of the government.
- Issues arising in the adjudication of white-collar crime cases include the need for networking, class bias, the use of parallel proceedings, and conceptual ambiguity surrounding corporate crime prosecutions.

KEY TERMS

Administrative proceedings	Civil proceedings	Cooperating witnesses
Allocution	Class action lawsuits	Corporate crime liability
Alternative sanctions argument	Class bias	Crime Victims Rights Act
Attorney-client privilege	Client-oriented defense	Criminal proceedings
Character witnesses	Contract lawsuits	Culpable conduct

Damage control argument

Deferred prosecution agreement (DPA)

Discovery-oriented defense

Due diligence defense

Expert witnesses

False Statements Act and False Claims Act

Good faith defense

Government witnesses

Ignorance defense

Isolated occurrence defense

Lack of fraudulent intent defense

Lay witnesses

Mail fraud statutes

Meeting competition defense

Multiplicity of indictment defense

Non-prosecution agreement (NPA)

Organizational advantage argument

Parallel proceedings

Plea bargains

Process-oriented defense

Professional-disciplinary

proceedings

Qui tam lawsuits

Racketeer Influenced and Corrupt Organizations (RICO) Act

Reliance on the advice of counsel defense

Rogue employee defense

Significant environmental harm

System capacity argument

Tort lawsuit

Withdrawal from conspiracy defense

Workplace-disciplinary proceedings

DISCUSSION QUESTIONS

1. Describe the roles of various actors involved in the judicial response to white-collar crimes.

2. Do you think class bias exists in prosecuting white-collar crimes? Explain.

3. What are the advantages and disadvantages of prosecuting corporations?

4. How are civil proceedings different from criminal justice proceedings? How are different types of judicial proceedings punitive?

5. Would you want to defend white-collar offenders as a defense attorney? Why or why not?

6. Go to Classactionworld.com. Review five cases. How are those cases like white-collar crimes? How are they different?

7. If you were called for jury duty, would it matter to you whether the type of case was a white-collar crime case or a conventional case? Explain.

8. How is prosecuting white-collar offenders similar to group projects your professors give you in your college courses?

9. What factors influence prosecutorial decision making?

10. What types of defenses are most commonly used by defense attorneys in white-collar crime trials?

WEB RESOURCES

SEC Administrative Proceedings. https://www.sec.gov/litigation/admin.shtml

Lawyers.com. White Collar Crime: http://white-collar-crime.lawyers.com/

Legal Information Institute. White Collar Crime: http://topics.law.cornell.edu/wex/White-collar_crime

The Corrections Subsystem and White-Collar Crime

CHAPTER HIGHLIGHTS

- Sentencing Dynamics and White-Collar Offenders
- The Prison Experience for White-Collar Offenders
- The Probation and Parole Experience for White-Collar Offenders
- Monetary Fines and White-Collar Offenders
- Alternative Sanctions and White-Collar Offenders
- Punishing Corporations for White-Collar Crimes
- Reasons for Punishing White-Collar Offenders

On July 11, 2015, Dr. Farid Fata stood before a judge waiting to be sentenced for fraud. His offenses were no ordinary fraud, though. The cancer doctor ruined the lives of hundreds of patients. Some of them he provided more treatment than he should have, simply for the profits from the insurance companies. More disconcerting, he even told some people they had cancer when they did not so that he could perform cancer treatments on them and receive payment from insurance companies. While he stole more than $17 million through these activities, the harm from his offenses was not the money lost, but the lives he destroyed.

Prosecutors asked the judge to sentence the disgraced doctor to the maximum sentence of 175 years. The defense attorney asked for 25 years on the basis that the doctor—at age 50—would likely not outlive even that sentence. After the judge announced a sentence of 45 years, victims expressed outrage. The sentence, in their view, did not demonstrate the severity of the offense, even though it ensured that the doctor would never be free again. In the words of the daughters of one the over-treated victims who lived the end of her life being exposed to harmful medical treatment, "Of course, everybody would want to see life. . . . No matter what happens, nobody wins in this situation. There will never be justice" (R. Allen, 2015). Among other things, what this case shows is that the sentencing of white-collar offenders is complex and necessary in order for ideals of justice to be met. Whether justice is met through sentencing depends on one's perspective and experiences.

The horrific doctor was not the only white-collar offender sentenced that month. Consider the following excerpts of news articles describing sentences handed down to less popular white-collar offenders who were sentenced around the same time:

- The mayor of Pine Lawn, Missouri, ********, was sentenced to 33 months in prison on charges involving the extortion of cash payments from the owner of a local towing company and from the owner of a Pine Lawn convenience store. In addition to the prison sentence, he was also ordered to pay $5500 restitution. (FBI, 2015, July 6)
- A Cincinnati man has been sentenced to three years in federal prison after pleading guilty to his role in a Kentucky oil investment scheme that defrauded more than 200 victims nationwide out of more than $3 million. (WLWT.com, 2015)
- A New York federal judge sentenced a former Wilson Sonsini Goodrich & Rosati PC information technology employee to two years in prison Wednesday for trading on inside information about the firm's clients, calling it a "crime of temptation." ********** pled guilty in New York federal court in November to securities fraud, admitting he traded ahead of mergers and acquisitions on which Wilson Sonsini was advising. (Credit: AP) Judge Paul Engelmayer ordered ********* to serve 100 hours of community service after completing the sentence. (Stendahl, 2015)
- A former employee of The Vacation Ownership Group LLC of Pleasantville, New Jersey, was sentenced today to 30 months in prison for conspiring to defraud owners of timeshare properties by offering phony consulting services, U.S. Attorney Paul J. Fishman announced. (FBI, 2015, July 31)
- A former Chelsea Housing Authority manager and a consultant were sentenced on Thursday to short prison terms for their roles in rigging federal inspections of apartments that were managed by the housing agency. (Murphy, 2015)
- *********, 68, of Battlefield, Mo., and his son, ********* II, 43, of Springfield, pleaded guilty in separate appearances before U.S. Magistrate Judge David P. Rush. ********* pleaded guilty to bank fraud and money laundering. ********* II pleaded guilty to misprision of a felony . . . Under the terms of today's plea agreement, ******** must forfeit to the government $5,592,583, which constitutes the proceeds obtained from his criminal activity. (KY3.com, 2015)

Other than being sentenced around the same time or released from a sentence at the same time, these examples demonstrate several patterns relevant to the sentencing of white-collar offenders. First, white-collar offenders are subject to a wide range of sentencing alternatives. Second, some white-collar offenders are indeed sentenced to prison. Third, organizations—as well as individuals—can be sanctioned in white-collar crime cases. Fourth, fines can be quite substantial in these cases. Sixth, these cases often receive significant press attention from the local media. Box 15.1 shows a press release from one recent case illustrating this point.

While these patterns are evident in the punishment of white-collar offenders, to fully address how punishment is meted out against this group of offenders, in this chapter, attention is given to sentencing dynamics, prison, probation and parole, fines, alternative sanctions, the punishing of corporations, and reasons for punishing white-collar offenders. By addressing these areas, readers will gain insight into the dynamics guiding the sanctioning of white-collar offenders and an appreciation of the underlying factors that contribute to the punishment experience for white-collar offenders.

WHITE-COLLAR CRIME IN THE NEWS

Public Officials Sentenced to Jail for Corruption

Local, state, and federal officials respond to public corruption quite aggressively when these cases surface

In the run-up to the 2012 primary elections in Mingo County, West Virginia, a group of officials adopted a campaign slogan to promote their political slate: Team Mingo. But the judge, sheriff, and county prosecuting attorney who were part of the alliance—among the most powerful men in the local judicial system—used their authority to serve their own interests rather than those of the citizens who elected them.

"These men essentially ran the county's legal system," said Special Agent Jim Lafferty, who investigated the case out of our Pittsburgh Field Office. The ringleader was Circuit Court Judge Michael Thornsbury. "The judge and his team were the power in Mingo County," Lafferty explained. "They didn't like anyone who tried to oppose them. If you were an attorney or an individual who wanted to get a fair shake in the court system, you had to play whatever game they wanted you to play. It was a toxic environment."

We opened a case in September 2012. Lafferty and retired Special Agent Joe Ciccarelli—with the help of West Virginia State Police investigators—uncovered evidence that Thornsbury, then-Sheriff Eugene Crum (who had formerly been the county's chief magistrate judge), and Michael Sparks, then the county's prosecuting attorney, had been engaging in corrupt activities

Specifically, the judge coerced a local drug defendant into firing his defense counsel because Thornsbury and other Team Mingo officials, including former County Commissioner David Baisden, learned that the drug defendant was prepared to testify that Sheriff Crum had illegally received prescription pain medication and obtained unlawful campaign contributions. To protect Crum, Thornsbury and his colleagues pressured the defendant into firing his defense attorney and replacing him with another attorney handpicked by Team Mingo. After switching lawyers and pleading guilty to lesser charges, the defendant dropped his allegations against Crum and was sentenced to up to 15 years in prison.

In addition, Thornsbury was later charged with trying to frame the husband of a woman with whom he was having an affair. The judge tried to have drugs planted in the husband's car. When that plan failed, he arranged to have the man arrested for stealing scrap metal—even when it was determined the man had been given permission to take the material.

In June, Thornsbury was sent to prison for more than four years for denying residents their constitutional rights. The federal judge who sentenced him compared Thornsbury's abuses of office to the actions of a Third World dictator.

Sparks, the former prosecutor who later cooperated with our investigation, was recently sentenced to a year in prison for his role in Team Mingo's illegal activities. Others previously jailed as a result of the corruption probe include Baisden, sentenced in January to 20 months' imprisonment, and former Mingo County chief magistrate Dallas Toler, sentenced in March to 27 months in prison.

"Team Mingo controlled the legal system, and they may have thought no one would stand up against them," said Lafferty, who has been investigating public corruption and white-collar crime for more than a decade. "That didn't turn out to be the case. No matter how much power you wield," he added, "when you violate the public trust and engage in corruption, sooner or later, you will get caught."

Source: Reprinted from FBI (2014, August 5), Violation of Public Trust. https://www.fbi.gov/news/stories/2014/august/violation-of-public-trust/violation-of-public-trust

● ● ● Sentencing Dynamics and White-Collar Offenders

To some, the sentencing of offenders is the most important part of the justice process in that it is through sanctioning offenders that goals of the justice system can be addressed and equal treatment of offenders can be promoted. Indeed, the ideals of justice are borne out through the application of just and fair punishments that are tied to the nature of the offense rather than to the class or status of the offender. The ability of the justice system to actually achieve "blind justice" can be assessed through an examination of the sentencing dynamics surrounding white-collar offenses. These dynamics can be understood through a consideration of sentencing practices, sentencing policies, and sentencing patterns.

Sentencing Practices and White-Collar Offenders

Research on the sentencing of white-collar offenders has provided mixed messages about issues related to the dispositions given to this group of offenders. The conventional assumption has been that white-collar offenders are sentenced more leniently than other offenders. Some studies on specific types of white-collar offenders have uncovered evidence of leniency. For example, a study of offenders convicted of Medicaid fraud in California found that this type of white-collar offenders received more lenient sentences than comparable conventional offenders (Tillman & Pontell, 1992). Tillman and Pontell (1992) cite three factors that contribute to the leniency afforded white-collar offenders. First, white-collar offenders have a "status shield" as a result of their occupational prestige, and this prestige is seen as protecting them from the stiff sentences given to street offenders. Second, white-collar offenders are able to hire better attorneys than conventional offenders. Third, the complexity of white-collar crime cases potentially creates enough doubt that more lenient sanctions are justified by criminal justice officials. Incidentally, the authors' own research found that when civil and administrative sanctions were added to the "total sentence," sanctions were more equitable.

Wheeler and his colleagues' (1982) interviews with judges found that the judges considered how the white-collar offender experienced the criminal justice process, and some viewed participation in the process as a punishment in and of itself for white-collar offenders. The judges also reported considering the sanctions imposed on white-collar offenders by civil, administrative, and professional proceedings. In addition, the age of the offender, his or her health, and the impact that the sentence might have on family members were considered by judges.

Interestingly, while the judges reported considering extralegal variables in sentencing white-collar offenders, some studies have found that white-collar offenders actually receive longer sentences than comparable conventional offenders—they are sentenced more severely than people think. One study, for example, found that after Watergate, white-collar offenders "were more likely to be sentenced to prison, but for shorter periods of time than less educated persons convicted of common crimes" (Hagan & Palloni, 1986, p. 603). Examining presentence investigation of 1,094 crimes occurring in seven federal districts between 1976 and 1978, Wheeler, Weisburd, and Bode (1982) found that white-collar offenders were more likely to go to prison and to be sentenced for longer periods of time than comparable conventional offenders were.

Another study showed that the type of sanction given to offenders was not tied to their status, but it was tied to the occupation in which the white-collar defendant worked (Hagan & Parker, 1985). Based on this perspective, Hagan and Parker suggested "that the substitution of class for status measures is crucial" (p. 312). In essence, the structure of certain occupations (which are related to the class of occupations) provides different opportunities for offenders, as well as different types of remedies from the criminal justice system.

Examining the influence of class position, Benson (1989) reviewed the sanctions given to 174 white-collar offenders sentenced in the 1970s. He found that informal social control sanctions were influenced by class position, but class position did not influence formal social control responses. Focusing on how loss of a job impacted sentencing, he found that losing one's job did not influence the sentence given in the justice process. Managers and employers (as white-collar offenders) were less likely to lose their jobs than nonmanagers and employees. He also found that public officials and professionals were "more vulnerable to informal sanctioning than employers and managers," leading Benson to conclude "the advantage of certain class positions seems to be more pronounced outside rather than inside the legal system" (p. 475).

Using the same data that they used in their 1982 study but adding a social class variable, Weisburd, Waring, and Wheeler (1990) found that class and occupational status were "complementary not competing indicators" (p. 237).

They found that offenders "with high class positions receive the most severe prison sanction" (p. 237). In a subsequent study, Weisburd Wheeler, Waring, and Bode (1991) found that most offenders convicted of offenses labeled white-collar offenses are not actually upper-class offenders but middle-class white-collar offenders.

Researchers have identified factors other than class and status that seemed to influence the sentencing of white-collar offenders. One study showed that the judicial district where the white-collar case was tried influenced sentencing outcomes at the federal level (Hagan, Negal, & Albonetti, 1980). Another study found that the combination of sanctions available to punish different types of white-collar offenders influenced the type of sentence given to them (Waldfogel, 1995). Research by Albonetti found that the sanctioning of white-collar offenders was tied to the complexity of the cases and to pleading guilty (Albonetti, 1999). In terms of guilty pleas, she noted that "pleas vary in their worth to prosecuting attorneys" (p. 321). In other words, in exchange for some guilty pleas, prosecuting attorneys are willing to offer a more greatly reduced sentence. For example, a complex case that could be difficult to prove might receive a greater sentence reduction in exchange for a plea as opposed to a "smoking gun" case where the case should be easy to prove.

Sentencing Policies and White-Collar Offenders

The Sentencing Reform Act was passed in 1984 as part of the Comprehensive Crime Control Act. One aim of the act was "to remedy individualized disparity in federal criminal sentences and to equalize sentences for 'street criminals' and 'white-collar offenders'" (Ryan-Boyle, Simon, & Yebler, 1991, p. 739). The **U.S. Sentencing Commission** was created as part of the act; it has the responsibility of developing strategies to promote fairer sentencing at the federal level through the development of sentencing guidelines. As initially envisioned, judges were expected to sentence offenders within a certain range based on the recommendation found in the guidelines. Judges could decrease or increase sanctions through departures if circumstances warranted. For white-collar offenders, the guidelines promoted imprisonment because incarceration was seen "as the most effective deterrent for white-collar offenders" (Ryan-Boyle et al., 1991, p. 756). As a result, the guidelines "increased both the probability of imprisonment and the length of the sentence for most white-collar offenses" (Cohen, 1992, p. 1100).

When first created, the federal guidelines were seen as mandatory in nature, with judges required to provide a justification for departing from the guidelines. After the U.S. Supreme Court reviewed the guidelines in *Booker v. Washington*, the guidelines were revised to be advisory in nature, thus, theoretically giving judges back the discretion that had been taken away when the guidelines were first created.

For some white-collar crimes, sentences at the federal level became even stiffer with the passage of the Sarbanes-Oxley Act in 2002. Passed in reaction to the corporate scandals that had just occurred, the act called for a number of restrictive strategies to prevent white-collar crime. In terms of penalties, the act doubled prison sentences from up to 10 years to up to 20 years for managers who falsified financial statements. In addition to stricter penalties, the act called for improved ethics training, improved corporate governance strategies, and better understanding of internal control efforts (Canada, Kuhn, & Sutton, 2008). The act has been described as "the most comprehensive economic regulation since the New Deal" (Vakkur, McAfee, & Kipperman, 2010, p. 18).

Surveys of 43 corporate executives and 130 graduate students in accounting found that the threat of jail time that is prescribed in the Sarbanes-Oxley Act has limited effectiveness in deterring financial statement fraud (Ugrin & Odom, 2010). The authors found that changing from one to 10 years' incarceration had a deterrent effect but changing from 10 to 20 years did not. Respondents indicated they would be no more deterred by a 20-year sentence than they would by a 10-year prison sentence. While research shows that the sanctions would not deter criminal behavior, research also shows that corporate risk taking declined after the act was passed; however, the decrease is possibly attributed to other types of regulations, including internal controls and increased board oversight (A. Dey, 2010).

Sentencing Patterns

Figure 15.1 shows the types of penalties given for different types of offenses at the federal level between October 1, 2011, and September 20, 2012 (Motivans, 2015).). As shown in the figure, variation exists among white-collar offenders and between white-collar and conventional offenders. Among specific types of white-collar offenders, the following patterns are shown:

- About 63 percent of fraud offenders were sentenced to prison, and roughly one-fourth were given probation.
- Roughly 47 percent of embezzlers were sent to prison, and 43 percent were given probation.
- Roughly 42 percent of antitrust offenders were sent to prison, and just over one-fifth were given probation.
- About a fifth of food and drug offenders were sent to prison, and more than two-thirds were given probation.

In reviewing the figure, it becomes obvious that, with the exception of bribery, a higher percentage of burglars get prison sentences than any of the white-collar offense types. On the surface, this may seem to suggest that white-collar offenders are less likely to be sentenced to prison than conventional offenders. However, these estimates do not control for past criminal histories or other factors that might influence sentencing decisions.

Table 15.1 shows the types of federal sentences and average lengths of sentences for various offense types during the same time frame. A few points are worth highlighting. First, roughly 6,000 offenders were incarcerated for offenses that could be characterized as white-collar offenses (though they may not all actually be white-collar offenders). Second, white-collar offenders tend to receive shorter prison sentences than other offenders. Third, the average probation sentence for white-collar offenders tended to be comparable to the average probation sentence given to other offenders.

Some have argued that the sentencing of white-collar offenders has gotten a little out of control, with some sentences seemingly far too severe. Noting that the sentences are the result of the development of sentencing guidelines, Podgor (2007) writes:

> In an attempt to achieve a neutral sentencing methodology, one that is class-blind, a system has evolved in the U.S. that fails to recognize unique qualities of white-collar offenders, fails to balance consideration of both the acts and the actors, and subjects offenders to draconian sentences that for some cases exceed their life expectancy. (p. 734)

Jonathan Simon, a law professor at the University of California, Berkeley, compared the severe prison sentences given to white-collar offenders to the types of sentences given to drug offenders, stating that "both represent increasingly irrational levels of punishment" (L. Moyer, 2009a).

Prison sentences for some first-time white-collar offenders "can exceed the sentences seen for violent street crimes, such as murder and rape" (Podgor, 2007, p. 733). Podgor contrasts white-collar sentencing with so-called three strikes laws. In the three strikes policies, the primary emphasis is on the actor. If the actor commits three offenses, a strict penalty results. In white-collar sentencing practices, attention is on the action of committing a white-collar offense. If an offender commits one white-collar offense, a stricter penalty results. According to one author team, these long sentences for white-collar offenders do not exist in other countries, such as Norway and Germany (Gottschalk & Glase, 2013).

Some have suggested that the apparent disparate sentencing resulting in long sentences for white-collar offenders might simply reflect the fact that the vast majority of white-collar offenders are kept out of the justice system in the first place. Gerber (1994) commented, "The apparent harshness of sentencing of white-collar offenders proves to be the result of a diversion of less serious offenders from the criminal court" (p. 164). For those white-collar crime cases that make their way into the justice system, by the time the offenders get to the judge, the government often has substantial evidence showing that the white-collar offenders have done something remarkably harmful (Wheeler et al., 1982). In other words, white-collar offenders do not go to court unless they have done something "really really bad."

The white-collar offender with the longest prison sentence on record is Shalmon Weiss. Weiss, whose misdeeds resulted in the collapse of National Heritage Life Insurance, was sentenced in 2000 by a Florida judge to 845 years in prison. According to the Bureau of Prisons, Weiss is scheduled to be released on November 23, 2754 (Moyer, 2009b). Chances are he will not live until his release date.

Other studies have suggested that there is very little evidence that white-collar offenders are sentenced more severely than other offenders. A study comparing auto thieves and embezzlers sentenced in U.S. district courts in 1993 found that auto thieves were four times more likely than embezzlers to go prison and their average prison sentence was five months longer (Madden, Hartley, Walker, & Miller, 2012). Another study of white-collar offenders sentenced in Florida between 1994 and 2004 found that white-collar offenders tended to receive more lenient sentences than burglars

Table 15.1 Type and Length of Federal Sentences Imposed, by Offense, October 1, 2011–September 30, 2012

Most serious offense of conviction			Type of sentence				Average sentence length	
			Total	Incarceration	Probation	Fine only	Incarceration	Probation
	All offenses		87,908	67,582	9,709	1,985	54.9	34.8
Felonies			80,764	65,187	7,380	254	56.6	39.9
	Violent offenses		2,359	2,193	121	3	123	45
	Property offenses		11,975	7,346	3,307	83	35	38.3
	Fraudulent		10,691	6,671	2,753	80	35.2	37.6
		Embezzlement	459	217	197	5	23.9	36.3
		Fraud	9,429	5,897	2,360	69	36.4	37.6
		Forgery	28	13	15	0	48.3	29.6
		Counterfeiting	775	544	181	6	26.2	39.4
	Other		1,284	675	554	3	36.7	41.8
		Burglary	42	31	11	0	18.1	35.3
		Larceny	936	413	481	3	21.5	42.3
		Motor vehicle theft	10	8	2	0		
		Arson and explosives	135	117	15	0	96.3	35.2
		Transportation of stolen property	115	78	33	0	40.4	41.3
		Other property offenses	46	28	12	0	25.9	39
Drug offenses			26,806	24,247	1,294	76	75.5	41.6
	Trafficking		26,724	24,219	1,266	71	75.5	42.1

(Continued)

Table 15.1 (Continued)

Most serious offense of conviction		Type of sentence				Average sentence length	
		Total	Incarceration	Probation	Fine only	Incarceration	Probation
Possession and other drug offenses		82	28	28	5	26	25.1
Public-order offenses		6,597	5,166	1,120	58	74	38
	Regulatory	865	466	302	31	33	34.8
	Agriculture	2	2	0	0		
	Antitrust	45	19	10	15	15.3	
	Food and drug	39	8	28	1		28.4
	Transportation	95	29	56	1	35.8	36.2
	Civil rights	46	39	7	0	50.1	
	Communications	46	23	21	0	18	38.3
	Customs laws	137	98	24	3	39.6	31.5
	Postal laws	25	6	16	1		28.5
	Other regulatory offenses	430	242	140	10	30.3	36.9
	Other	5,732	4,700	818	27	77.8	39.5
	Tax law violations	524	345	158	5	30.1	40.5
	Bribery	111	86	22	0	28.1	38.9
	Perjury, contempt, and intimidation	233	166	57	3	58	35.8
	National defense	60	46	12	0	105.7	33.6
	Escape	736	472	175	5	18.2	33.3

Most serious offense of conviction	Type of sentence				Average sentence length	
	Total	Incarceration	Probation	Fine only	Incarceration	Probation
Racketeering and extortion	1,814	1,546	192	7	82.3	39.3
Gambling	32	9	22	0		28.6
Nonviolent sex offenses	2,006	1,941	64	3	102.5	78.8
Obscene material	10	9	1	0		
Traffic offenses	5	3	1	0		
Wildlife	47	12	34	0	17.5	36.9
Environmental	43	8	30	3		25.4
All other felonies	111	57	50	1	49.4	51.3
Weapon offenses	7,332	6,689	474	10	79.6	40.7
Immigration offenses	25,695	19,546	1,064	24	21.6	44
Misdemeanors						
Fraudulent property offenses	6,568	1,883	2,295	1,728	6.1	18.5
Larceny	900	454	162	21	3.9	24
Drug possession	596	43	380	144	8.3	20.4
Immigration offenses	1,476	919	416	76	7	16.2
	446	176	38	16	5.8	22
Traffic offenses	1,834	102	673	1,045	3.4	13.7
Other misdemeanors	1,316	189	626	426	8	22

Source: U.S. Department of Justice

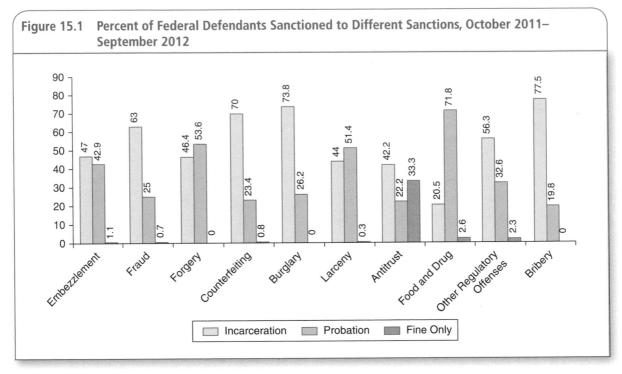

Figure 15.1   Percent of Federal Defendants Sanctioned to Different Sanctions, October 2011– September 2012

Source: Bureau of Justice Statistics, US Department of Justice

and thieves (Van Slyke & Bales, 2012). In this same study, among white-collar offenders, some received stiffer sentences than others, suggesting differential treatment among white-collar offenders (not between white-collar offenders and street offenders). Comparing those convicted of Medicaid provider fraud to those convicted of public assistance fraud (a low status white-collar crime), the researchers found that the odds of imprisonment were 98.7 percent lower for the upper class providers.

It is plausible that sanctioning is not determined solely by type of offense. A study of sentencing in six judicial circuits in Florida found that "female street offenders sentenced by male judges received the most lenient sentences—not female white-collar offenders sentenced by male judges" (Van Slyke & Bales, 2013, p. 188). The authors of this study posit that while white-collar offenders might try to use their status to protect themselves, judges might be more likely to show mercy to disadvantaged offenders.

One question that needs to be addressed, though, is whether recent changes (since 2005) have altered the sentencing dynamics associated with white-collar crime. Research by Van Slyke and Bales (2013), which found that white-collar offenders' likelihood of going to prison increased 30 percent after the Enron scandals, begins to answer this question. More research, though, is needed on the topic.

Summing up the sentencing research on white-collar offenders, one author has identified two types of sentencing studies: (1) advantage-focused studies comparing upper class and lower class offenders and (2) time-oriented studies that examine how sanctions have changed over time. One limitation Simpson (2013) identifies with the advantage studies is that they ignore other types of penalties, such as civil and administrative sanctions. Many white-collar offenders are punished; they are just punished differently. Whether this is fair is a philosophical and theoretical question.

● ● ● The Prison Experience for White-Collar Offenders

While a handful of studies have considered sentencing issues related to white-collar offenders, very few studies have focused on the experience of white-collar offenders in prison. Part of this lack of research has to do with the relatively few white-collar inmates in prison at any given time in the United States. It is extremely difficult to gain access to these inmates, and even if access is granted to a prison, it is even more unlikely that white-collar inmates would agree to participate in a study while incarcerated. Some researchers have done an excellent job locating and interviewing white-collar inmates after they have been released (Benson & Cullen, 1988). Others have relied on anecdotal accounts and media reports to generate understanding about how white-collar offenders experience prison (Payne, 2003b). From these efforts, one can point to five dynamics of the white-collar prison experience: (1) depression, (2) danger, (3) deprivations, (4) deviance, and (5) doldrums (see Payne, 2003b, for a thorough discussion of each of these dynamics). It is important to stress that the experience of incarceration for conventional offenders might be described through a discussion of similar dynamics. However, these characteristics and their consequences likely vary between the two types of offenders. After discussing these dynamics, attention will be given to the way that white-collar offenders adjust to prison.

▲ **Photo 15.1** White-collar inmates will wear the same uniform as other inmates. They will lose their identity as a white-collar employee and gain a new identity as an inmate.

Depression and the White-Collar Offender

For some white-collar offenders, it is likely that various degrees of depression will be experienced, particularly in the initial stages of incarceration. While all inmates likely experience different forms of depression, the sources of depression for white-collar offenders manifest themselves differently. Their sources of depression include (1) stressful changes coming from one's first exposure to prison life, (2) loss of job, (3) loss of status, (4) isolation, and (5) sentencing dynamics (Payne, 2003b).

With regard to *stressful changes* as a source of depression, white-collar offenders who have never been to prison experience an enormous amount of anxiety that exists both before their incarceration and in the early stages of the incarceration. As Michael Benson and Frank Cullen (1988) point out, "For the first-time offender, the stress created by the prospect of going to prison probably exceeds any other that the person may have experienced" (p. 209). Another expert told a reporter that for white-collar offenders, "prison is equivalent to shock therapy, suddenly exposing [white-collar] offenders to people and circumstances they never would have imagined" ("Is Martha Stewart Truly a Changed Woman?" 2005). Prison administrators have been encouraged to watch for signs of depression in an effort to prevent possible suicide attempts among white-collar offenders. For those who experience stress in their initial stages of incarceration, as time passes, they will better adjust to the incarceration experience (Benson & Cullen, 1988).

Another source of depression for white-collar offenders is the *loss of their jobs*. Although their crimes were often committed against their employers and as part of their jobs, individuals define themselves by their careers. For convicted

▲ **Photo 15.2**   White-collar inmates have little in common with other incarcerated offenders. They are older, have different life histories, have had little exposure to violence, and have not led the traditional criminal lifestyle.

white-collar inmates, their loss of a career identity can be particularly problematic. They go from having a respectable job title to having an inmate number. Former California Republican Randy "Duke" Cunningham went from being a member of the U.S. House of Representatives to inmate 94405-198 after being sentenced to prison for accepting bribes from military contractors. Some inmates will have prison jobs to replace their former white-collar jobs. Not surprisingly, the pay is not so good in prison. White-collar inmates will go from making hundreds of thousands, if not millions, of dollars to making 12 cents an hour "for scrubbing floors and toilets" (S. Green, 2007). In the end, these changes in career identities can potentially be a source of depression, at least initially in the incarceration experience.

Somewhat related, *loss of status* can be another potential source of depression for white-collar inmates. These are individuals who go from being in charge in their occupations and businesses to individuals who are ordered around by prison officials and intimidated by fellow inmates. In other words, they go from being at the top of the social and occupational hierarchy outside of prison to the bottom of the social hierarchy inside of prison. Benson's (1990) interviews with white-collar offenders found that inmates experience what he referred to as *status degradation* as a result of their conviction. He notes that white-collar inmates even lose "control over the presentation of self" (p. 522).

Isolation is another potential source of depression for white-collar inmates. Because so few white-collar offenders are in prison at any given time, it may be difficult for them to find peers with whom they can interact in prison. Much of their time may be spent alone until they find ways to communicate with fellow inmates. For example, Bernie Madoff reportedly doled out financial advice to fellow inmates who sought it and spent his time with a fellow white-collar inmate and an organized crime boss (Searcey & Efrati, 2011).

Interestingly, *sentencing dynamics* can be a source of depression in white-collar inmates. Recall from above that white-collar inmates receive shorter sentences than conventional inmates. What makes this particularly ironic is that depression and adjustment problems are more prone to occur in the first 6 months or so of incarceration (Payne, 2003b). After that initial introduction to incarceration, inmates are able to adjust to the incarceration experience (Benson & Cullen, 1988). By the time white-collar inmates are released from prison, many have, in effect, likely become accustomed to the incarceration experience.

Danger and the White-Collar Offender

Another dynamic surrounding the incarceration experience of white-collar offenders centers on their concerns about being injured. Four themes arise regarding danger and white-collar offenders: (1) celebrity bashing, (2) prison placement, (3) prison culture and socialization, and (4) exaggerated concerns (Payne, 2003b). With regard to **celebrity bashing**, some celebrity offenders are attacked by inmates seeking fame and notoriety. John Geoghan, a Catholic priest well known for sexually abusing more than 130 children over his career, was beaten and strangled to death by inmate Joseph Druce in August 2003. Bernie Madoff was allegedly beaten up in prison and treated for broken ribs and multiple bruises in the first year of his incarceration. While receiving widespread media attention, the story was never confirmed by prison officials or Madoff, which is not surprising given that reporting victimization would potentially place Madoff at risk for subsequent victimization.

In terms of prison placement, some prisons and jails are more dangerous than others for white-collar offenders. Between sentencing and admissions, offenders are often held in a detention center that may include all types of offenders. White-collar offenders, particularly those who might be targeted for an attack, might be placed in solitary confinement for their protection (Moyer, 2009b). Also, while many white-collar offenders are sentenced to minimum-security prisons, where the risk of violence is much lower, with the growing trend of longer prison sentences for white-collar offenders, some are being sent to higher-security-level prisons, which are more dangerous (J. O'Donnell, 2004).

Prison culture and socialization are relevant to the danger faced by white-collar inmates in that this offender group is not typically aware of the prison culture, nor have these offenders been socialized in how to behave in prison. The prison subculture includes offenders who have been exposed to, and have histories of, a great deal of violence in their lives. This is most likely not the case for white-collar offenders. One reporter quoted a prison consultant to white-collar offenders who said, "These guys have never been in a fight in their lives—they don't know what violence is, and now they're entering a world where anything can happen" (R. Schapiro, 2009). Describing the importance of prison socialization, another prison consultant advised that white-collar offenders do not know prison rules, such as that "changing the television channel can start a fight" (O'Donnell & Willing, 2003).

Though danger exists, from a scientific perspective, one can note that the concerns about danger are somewhat exaggerated. Violence is relatively infrequent in minimum security prisons, where most white-collar offenders are housed. As well, the rate of prison assaults against inmates is much lower today than in the past (Bureau of Justice Statistics, 2011). In some ways, the fear of harm is likely more inhibiting and significant than the actual experience of harm for white-collar offenders. With time, they adjust to the prison environment, and anxiety decreases (Benson & Cullen, 1988). Here is how one incarcerated white-collar offender described this process to an interviewer: "The inmates see me as someone they can talk to because . . . I've worked with the general public. . . . I expected to be ridiculed because I've been to school. And I expected to be bullied, but I haven't been" (Dhami, 2007, p. 68).

Deprivations and the White-Collar Offender

Prison deprives inmates of liberties, rights, freedom, and lifestyles to which they were previously accustomed. For white-collar inmates accustomed to certain lifestyles, the experience of deprivation might be particularly problematic. Something as basic as food consumption will be very different for white-collar inmates. One reporter team said that the food at one low-security prison was so bad that inmates "prefer microwaved groundhogs captured in the prison yard" (O'Donnell & Willing, 2003). A law professor told a reporter the following about a white-collar offender who was preparing for a prison stint: "His meal choices will not be what he's used to. . . . His diet will be prison food, which probably makes military or college dorm food look good" (S. Green, 2007). As the son of a cafeteria worker, I won't disparage cafeteria food. But the point is worth reiterating—those not accustomed to this environment will experience it differently from those who have been in similar situations in the past.

Of course, it is not just bad food that is a deprivation for white-collar offenders. The enormous status deprivation—or degradation, as Benson (1990) calls it—is particularly salient for white-collar offenders. This degradation can be experienced as a punishment in and of itself. Trying to use this perspective as an argument for a more lenient sentence, Tom DeLay's attorney pointed out in DeLay's sentencing hearing that DeLay "has fallen from the third most powerful position in this country to a man who is unemployed and unemployable" (P. Meyer, 2011).

For some offenders, the deprivations may be more significant than the danger they are concerned about in prison. Consider the following comments from former New York Chief Judge Sol Wachtler about his 13-month stay in prison as told to an interviewer:

Believe it or not, the worst moment was not when I was stabbed and put in solitary confinement—although if you put splints under my fingernails and told me to tell you what happened in solitary, I couldn't, because the human mind locks these unpleasant thoughts out. No, the worst moment was when I was flown from one prison to another, with my wrists shackled together and a waist chain on, and I had to walk across the airport tarmac with everyone staring at me. And then the two sets of guards from the different prisons argued as to whom the chains belonged to. ("Judge Not," 1997, p. 2)

The judge was used to being above (and in control of) correctional officers. Upon his imprisonment, they were in control of him.

Prison Deviance and the White-Collar Offender

As many sociologists have noted, any time you have a group of individuals together, someone in that group will engage in some form of deviance. With a group of convicted offenders together, it seems safe to suggest that some will engage in deviant acts while incarcerated. Many offenders have long histories of rule breaking. They are not going to decide to "behave" simply because they are behind bars. Three types of violations are relevant with regard to white-collar inmates: rule violations, deviant use of the justice process, and jailstripe crimes (Payne, 2003b). In this context, the phrase *rule violations* simply refers to situations where inmates break prison rules. Sometimes, the rule violations seem relatively minor. Martha Stewart, for example, supposedly made more ceramic figures per month than prison rules allowed. She made 12 figures in 5 months, but should have made only one per month (Waller, 2007). Other times, the rule violations might be more significant. For example, Washington, DC, Mayor, Marion Barry, allegedly received oral sex from a prostitute in a crowded visiting room while he was incarcerated ("Ex-Mayor in 'Jail-Sex' Row," 1992, p. 3).

Deviant misuse of the justice process refers to situations where offenders misuse the justice process in a way that gains them some sort of advantage. Filing unnecessary or unwarranted appeals, misuse of furloughs, and unnecessary participation in treatment programs are examples. Unnecessary participation in treatment programs is believed to be particularly problematic with white-collar offenders. While some believe that it is easier for white-collar offenders to be paroled than conventional offenders (e.g., one prosecutor said, "they present much better than a guy with scars and tattoos and a nickname like 'snake'" ["White-Collar Crime Rising," 2003]), others have said that the nature of programming at the federal level makes it more difficult for white-collar offenders to have time taken off their sentences.

In particular, offenders receive time off of their sentences if they participate in a certain number of hours of treatment programs. The problem that arises is that white-collar inmates are often not in need of the types of treatment programs that are available. To take advantage of the opportunity to have their sanctions reduced, some white-collar offenders have allegedly "faked" their way into treatment programs. In his presentence report, for example, Sam Waksal (the former ImClone Systems Inc. CEO caught up in Martha Stewart's scandal) told the probation officer that he was a social drinker and that he consumed about five glasses of wine a week. By the time his sentencing hearing came around—about 3 months later—Waksal's attorney told the judge that Waksal had "recently developed a dependence on alcohol and would benefit from treatment for his newly acquired addiction" (Falkenberg, 2008). Waksal is not alone in this category. Prison consultants report telling white-collar offenders how to get into the best treatment programs in order to be released earlier (Falkenberg, 2008). Of course, like Waksal, perhaps some of these offenders developed their drug abuse problems between their guilty conviction and the time they were sent to prison.

The phrase **jailstripe crimes** refers to criminal acts that offenders commit while incarcerated. In one case, for example, an offender who had been convicted of fraud and was serving his sentence in a minimum-security prison orchestrated an identity theft scheme from inside prison that netted him $250,000 ("Inmate Ran Identity Theft Ring," 2011). An investigation by the Department of Justice's Office of Inspector General found that inmates routinely used prison telephones to commit criminal acts. Their investigation found that U.S. attorneys had prosecuted 117 cases where offenders used prison phones to commit crime (U.S. Office of Inspector General, 1999). Of those 117, twenty-five were financial fraud cases. In one case uncovered in the investigation, an inmate used a prison telephone to run a "fraudulent employment match service" (p. 3). Consumers who contracted with the employment service would have been paying the inmate for services that he never provided. In another case, an inmate stole more than $100,000 from a trucking company (U.S. Office of Inspector General, 1999).

Doldrums

Another aspect of the white-collar inmates' experiences in prison can be characterized as "the doldrums." After becoming acquainted with the incarceration experience, white-collar inmates report being very bored with it. One former white-collar inmate told Benson and Cullen (1988): "It was kind of an unexperience. It was not nearly as frightening as I thought it would be" (p. 209). Perhaps that is because white-collar offenders expected the experience to be much worse than it actually was, and it turned out not to be as bad as feared, that boredom and monotony "have been cited as the worst part of the white-collar inmate's incarceration experiences" (Payne, 2003b, p. 105).

Adjusting to Prison Life

The above discussion is not meant to make it seem as if prison is too punitive for white-collar offenders or that white-collar offenders should be treated differently than conventional offenders. Instead, the intent was to call attention to the fact that the "incarceration experience" varies between conventional and white-collar offenders. One area where the experience is also different has to do with the tendency among members of the public to assume that white-collar offenders are not being "punished enough" during their prison stay. The moniker "Club Fed" is used to describe the supposed club-like atmosphere surrounding the prisons where white-collar inmates are often incarcerated. There are no bars, no fences, and no prison cells. Often, no structural barriers separate these prisons from the rest of society. Hence, it must not be that bad to be sentenced to Club Fed.

Club Fed is a myth. Being incarcerated can be a difficult process for any offender. Offenders have limited rights, they have no autonomy, they are away from their family members, there is nothing to do, and they have concerns about their safety. Describing the punitive nature of prisons for white-collar offenders, one author commented,

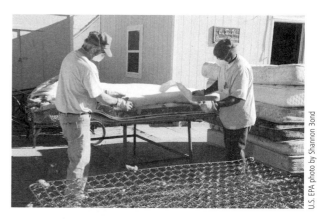

▲ **Photo 15.3**   White-collar inmates will look for ways to stay busy because incarceration can be an incredibly boring experience.

▲ **Photo 15.4**   Does this look like a club to you? Would you want to be stuck here for 6 months with 1,000 offenders and 200 staff members who have control over your every move?

But the grim reality of prison life for today's white-collar criminal—the utter absence of privacy, the body-cavity strip searches, standing in line 90 minutes, much of it outdoors in any weather, to get unspeakable food—is definitely worse than they or the public expect. (Colvin, 2004)

For white-collar offenders, the most significant part of the prison experience is their initial adjustment period. With this in mind, recall that judges justified shorter prison sentences (or no prison sentence) for white-collar offenders based on their "special sensitivity to incarceration" (Mann, Wheeler, & Sarat, 1980). Though it may be the case that the initial stages of incarceration are particularly difficult for white-collar offenders, some scholars have argued that white-collar offenders have the personalities, skills, and resources to adjust effectively to the stresses of prison life. Benson and Cullen (1988) interviewed 13 white-collar offenders incarcerated in four different correctional institutions. Their research showed that while offenders initially found incarceration to be quite stressful (probably the most stressful event they had ever faced), offenders were able to "eventually adjust to prison life" (p. 209). The authors note that some offenders found the experience "interesting in a sociological sense" (p. 209). They also found that many of the offenders denied their criminal status as a coping strategy. In addition, Benson and Cullen noted that white-collar inmates searched for ways to increase their social status (compared to fellow inmates) while incarcerated. In doing so, they "reject the prison subculture" (p. 213). A more recent study offered a similar conclusion, finding that white-collar inmates fare as well in prison as other inmates and have characteristics that "may mitigate the negative effects of imprisonment" (Stadler, Benson, & Cullen, 2011, p. 18).

Because of an increase in the number of white-collar offenders being sentenced to prison and convicted offenders' fears about their future incarceration experience, a new industry has evolved that can be coined the "white-collar prison consultant industry." In this field, experts (some of whom are former white-collar inmates themselves) provide future white-collar inmates advice on how to get used to prison. The consultants are hired to tell the future inmates "how to negotiate the perils of the U.S. penal system" (Kelly, 2009, p. 1). Said Kelly, "They teach you how to behave, they teach unwritten rules, most important, they teach how to survive" (p. 1). As noted above, they also teach white-collar inmates how to get into the "best" treatment programs to earn early release.

Steven Oberfest, CEO of Prison Coach, charges $200 an hour to prepare offenders for prison. He uses his past experience as an inmate as the source of his information (R. Schapiro, 2009). Oberfest, who calls himself an "inmate adaptation specialist," told another interviewer, "I can prepare you to go into hell" (K. Johnson, 2009, p. 1A). To capture this white-collar market (pun intended), one consultant even "changed his company name from American Prison Consultants to Wall Street Prison Consultants" (K. Johnson, 2009, p. 1A). Box 15.2, Careers in White-Collar Crime: Prison Consultant, provides additional details about prison consultants.

CAREERS RESPONDING TO WHITE-COLLAR CRIME

White-Collar Crime Convict Consultant

Some former white-collar defendants have embarked upon careers that can be referred to as prison consulting: they consult and advise future white-collar inmates how to adjust to the prison experience. Jim Tayoun, who was a Philadelphia city council member before being sentenced to forty months for a corruption conviction, may have been one of the earliest white-collar inmates turned prison consultant. He developed a 900 number for white-collar offenders on their way to prison. At the time, calls cost between five and eight dollars, and callers were given a general introduction to prison (Timko, 1995). The white-collar inmate prison consulting business has grown significantly since then and is now a competitive consulting area. *New York Times* reporter Matt Richtel (2012) identified three dozen prison consulting groups with names such as "Executive Prison Coaching," "The Real Prison Consultant," and "The Prison Doctor."

Source: Reprinted from Payne, B. K. (2015). Effects on white-collar defendants of criminal justice attention and sanctions. In S. Van Slyke, F. Cullen, & M. Benson (Eds.), *The Oxford Handbook of White-Collar Crime*. New York, NY: Oxford University Press.

● ● ● The Probation and Parole Experience for White-Collar Offenders

As shown above, many white-collar offenders are sentenced to probation, and some are placed on parole after their incarceration in states where parole still exists. These are **community-based sanctions**. Community-based alternatives are popular for all types of offenders—conventional and white-collar alike. There is a misperception that these sanctions are not punitive, when, in fact, offenders tend to define certain types of probation as especially punitive. While all types of offenders are subject to these sentencing alternatives, the way the sanctions are experienced varies between types of offenders.

One of the first studies on the probation experience of white-collar offenders was done by Michael Benson (1985b). He interviewed 22 federal probation officers and 30 white-collar probationers and found that for white-collar offenders, the probation experience could be characterized as "going through the motions" (p. 429). He also found that the types of interactions between probation officers and white-collar offenders often allowed the offenders to continue to deny their criminal status. The officers interviewed did not believe that white-collar probationers would get in trouble while on probation, and one agency viewed control as "unnecessary in the case of white-collar offenders" (p. 431). Said one probation officer, "They don't need supervision. Some of it is just chit chat" (p. 431). Other probation officers highlighted the need to help offenders get accustomed to the fact that they had been convicted and "to adjust psychologically to the stigmatization effects of conviction" (p. 432).

Focusing on their status, Benson (1985b) highlights one flaw that community supervision has for white-collar probationers. In particular, he notes that probation officers spend most of their time supervising offenders from a lower class than the officer's social class. In fact, one can argue that officers are trained both formally and informally how to supervise lower-class offenders. Conversely, officers are not always adequately prepared "to supervise their social equals or betters" (p. 435).

In a more recent study, Karen Mason (2007) interviewed 35 white-collar probationers to examine how shifts in penology have impacted their probation experiences. Her results highlighted the differences between white-collar offenders' probation experiences as compared to the experiences of other offenders. Among other things, she noted that the "workaday world of these offenders does not easily accommodate the demands of supervision, monitoring, and surveillance that are central to probation" (p. 28). The offenders described what they perceived as a bureaucratic model of probation that failed to offer offenders any sort of services or guidance. Referring to the loss of occupational status common among white-collar offenders, Mason noted that assisting white-collar offenders with reintegrative efforts "is no longer a priority in community supervision under the new penology" (p. 29).

Similar to Benson's research, Mason (2007) uncovered dynamics showing that white-collar offenders used aspects of the sanction to reject a criminal identity. In particular, she found that the probationers experienced the bureaucratic nature of probation (e.g., filling out forms in turning in records) in a way that allowed them to continue to deny their criminal status. They played by the rules in an effort to maintain "their own feelings of superiority and self-worth" (p. 30). Though maintaining a noncriminal identity, the white-collar probationers experienced a loss of autonomy, stigma, stress from the loss of autonomy, anxiety, shame for what they did to their families, and status degradation.

The notion of status degradation is particularly relevant with white-collar probationers. A power inversion occurs whereby probation officers gain a higher level of control over white-collar offenders (who are in an equal if not higher social status than probation officers). These aspects can be somewhat difficult to adjust to for white-collar offenders. Said one defense attorney about his client's probation sentence: "For someone who's not used to that, it's a real humiliation" (Sayre, 2011). Some have warned that community corrections officers might exert extra power over white-collar offenders in order to make up for the difference in social statuses between white-collar probationers and officers. Minkes (1990) wrote:

> There is a temptation to gloat at the discomfiture of the rich and leave them to their fate. After all, poor people are sent to prison every day for property offenses of far less value; how much more should the rich be punished. However, this argument must not be turned on its head. . . . Probation officers should be considering recommendations for probation, community service, compensation orders, and fines . . . and using formal and informal contacts with sentencers to press home the comparisons of seriousness. (p. 130)

In other words, probation officers have an important role in ensuring that white-collar offenders are punished fairly.

● ● ● Monetary Fines and White-Collar Offenders

White-collar offenders are punished through the use of different types of monetary penalties. **Monetary penalties** include criminal fines, restitution, civil settlements, and compensatory and punitive damages awarded in civil trials. **Criminal fines** are monetary penalties awarded by the judge after an offender has been convicted of a crime. The fine is collected by the state (or federal) government, and funds are allocated accordingly in the jurisdiction where the case was heard. Fines are not designed to go directly back to victims.

Some legal scholars have advocated that fines be the primary sanction given to white-collar offenders and that imprisonment is an inappropriate, ineffective, and costly alternative. Richard Posner (1979–1980) called for large fines to deter wrongdoing. He argued that a large fine would have deterrent power equal to imprisonment. He wrote,

> In a social cost benefit analysis of the choice between fining and imprisoning white-collar criminals, the cost side of the analysis favors fining because . . . the cost of collecting a fine from one who can pay it . . . is lower than the cost of imprisonment. (p. 410)

From his perspective, such a practice was not unfair or biased toward the poor because he viewed a large fine as just and to be as punitive as incarceration.

Research shows that judges do not see fines as having a significant impact on offending (Mann et al., 1980). In the judges' views, by the time offenders were convicted, many were either already bankrupt or too affluent to actually feel the effects of fines. Providing judges guidance on when to issue fines, the federal guidelines state "that a court must impose a fine in all cases, except where the defendant establishes that he is unable to pay and is not likely to become able to pay any fine" (Schanzenbach & Yaeger, 2006, p. 764). The amount of the fine is tied to the nature of the offense and the recommendations in the guidelines. In fraud cases, consideration is given to the economic harm experienced by the victim and the gain experienced by the offender, while in antitrust cases—where it may be virtually impossible to identify economic costs and offender gains—consideration is given to the impact that the offending had on the economy (Ryan-Boyle et al., 1991).

A theoretical perspective known as optimal penalty theory predicts that fines will be used "to the maximum extent possible before they are supplemented with imprisonment" (Waldfogel, 1995, p. 107). The basis for the assumption is that fines are "costless" and prison is costly. A study by Waldfogel (an economist) examined penalties given to 7,502 fraud offenders convicted at the federal level in 1984. He found that prison sentences were tied to harm from offenses and fines were tied to the offender's ability to pay the penalty. In line with optimal penalty theory, his research found that those who were given higher fines were sentenced to prison for shorter periods of time. A study of 22,508 federal white-collar offenders sentenced under the sentencing guidelines between 1991 and 2001 found similar results: Paying fines reduced the amount of prison time for white-collar offenders (Schanzenbach & Yaeger, 2006). Such a finding is potentially problematic because it means that lower-class individuals are being awarded longer prison sentences because of their inability to pay a fine.

Restitution is a monetary penalty that orders an offender to pay victims back for their suffering. In terms of white-collar crime, victims could be those individuals directly harmed by white-collar misconduct, the employer victimized by the offense, or a government agency that was either victimized or had to devote a great deal of resources to address the wrongdoing. The aim of restitution is to make victims "whole" through payments (Ryan-Boyle et al., 1991). Not surprisingly, those who receive restitution as a penalty are not as likely to be sent to prison (Van Slyke & Bales, 2012). One expert has called for "voluntary retribution" as a punitive strategy that would allow victims to be paid back and offenders to be held accountable (Faichney, 2014). The same expert believes that restitution would "mean more" if the offender chose to give it rather than being ordered to give it. Here is how he described his proposal:

> Voluntary restitution may remedy the harm caused by white-collar crime at the place where its effects have been most directly felt. In addition to improving victims' economic well-being, voluntary restitution may also be morally significant. An affirmative compensatory act by the offender may demonstrate acceptance of responsibility and restore social trust and goodwill, especially if the offender must work arduously to provide it. While a court may (and in many circumstances, must) order restitution, it can only do so after an adjudication of guilt. Ordering restitution at sentencing does not require the offender to accept any responsibility for his crime and does not discourage financial gamesmanship by offenders. (Faichney, 2014, p. 429)

Civil courts can order defendants found liable to pay several different types of monetary penalties. Monetary penalties awarded in civil court are called "damages." Compensatory damages and punitive damages are particularly relevant to white-collar crime cases. **Compensatory damages** are awards made to plaintiffs (victims) that the defendants are ordered to pay in order to compensate victims for their victimization experience. **Punitive damages** are "awarded when the defendant's conduct is determined to have been so 'willful, malicious, or fraudulent' that it exceeds the legal criteria for mere or gross negligence" (Cohen, 2005, p. 1). Awarded by juries, in theory punitive damages are designed to punish and deter (T. H. Cohen, 2005; Stevens & Payne, 1999).

Figure 15.2 shows the median amount of compensatory and punitive damages awarded to plaintiffs in different types of citizen-initiated civil trials held in state courts in 2005. Note that the amount of damages tends to be higher in white-collar crime cases (asbestos, medical malpractice, and employment discrimination) than in other types of cases (automobile accidents, seller plaintiff—which refers to credit collections and mortgage foreclosures).

Table 15.2 shows how the amount of damages awarded as a result of civil jury trials in specific types of white-collar crime cases changed between 1992 and 2005 in 75 of the most populated counties in the United States (Langton & Cohen, 2008). Note that between 1992 and 2005, and controlling for inflation, the amount of awards for all types of cases decreased by 40.3 percent, but the amount of awards given in medical malpractice and product liability cases increased by 143.6 percent and 386.9 percent, respectively. Damage awards in fraud trials increased by 6.2 percent.

Punitive damages are only rarely sought and applied in citizen-initiated civil cases. Langton and Cohen's (2008) reviews of civil jury trials in 2005 found that punitive damages were awarded to plaintiffs in about one out of 20 general civil jury trials. The same year, 8 percent of contract trials heard in state courts of general jurisdiction resulted in punitive damages (Farole, 2009), and just over 9 percent of tort trials involved punitive damages (Cohen, 2009).

Farole's (2009) review of state court civil trials found that the amount of punitive damages awarded exceeded compensatory damages nearly two thirds of the time when damages were awarded. Tables 15.3 and 15.4 show additional patterns surrounding punitive damages in white-collar crime cases adjudicated in civil proceedings in state courts. As shown in Table 15.3, the size of punitive damages can be quite large. Table 15.4 shows the amount of compensatory and punitive damages awarded in 2001 in large U.S. counties. Again, the size of some of the awards is striking, and for some types of white-collar crimes (e.g., failure to provide services and employment discrimination), the median amount of punitive awards exceeded compensatory awards.

Note that these estimates do not include monetary penalties arising out of civil settlements between the offender and the government or in civil trials initiated by a government or corporation. Recall from the discussion about the U.S. Environmental Protection Agency (EPA) that such settlements can be enormous and provide a method for recovering costs and using settlement monies to help fund regulatory and criminal justice efforts.

A number of issues arise regarding the use of punitive damages. For example, large punitive damage awards against a company may inadvertently punish innocent workers who lose their jobs or consumers who pay higher prices as the punished business continues to seek profits. Also, the question of whether large damages can be seen as cruel and unusual punishment has surfaced, with the U.S. Supreme Court deciding that such damages are not violations of the Eighth Amendment. However, it is expected that the damages "bear a reasonable relationship to the actual harm they are intended to punish" (Stevens & Payne, 1999, p. 198).

One can question the practice of justifying punitive damages on deterrent ideals. The sanction of punitive damages does not meet the tenets of classical deterrence theory, which suggests that sanctions must be swift, certain, and severe enough to outweigh offender gain without being too severe. The penalties are not applied quickly, especially given the lengthy judicial process and the fact that many defendants will tie the case up in a drawn-out appeals process. The size of the damages is random and uncertain, with little evidence that any sort of constant factors contribute to jury awards. Also, the size of some punitive damages often far exceeds what might be called for from a classical deterrence theory perspective (Stevens & Payne, 1999). Note that judges have the authority to reduce punitive damage penalties and that many judges exercise this right in cases involving large punitive damages.

Sometimes these financial penalties are negotiated as a way for white-collar and corporate offenders to avoid admitting guilt. These situations do not always meet the ideals of retribution. Here is an example from one criminologist illustrating this theme:

Figure 15.2   Median Compensatory and Punitive Final Awards for Plaintiff Winners in Select Trial Cases

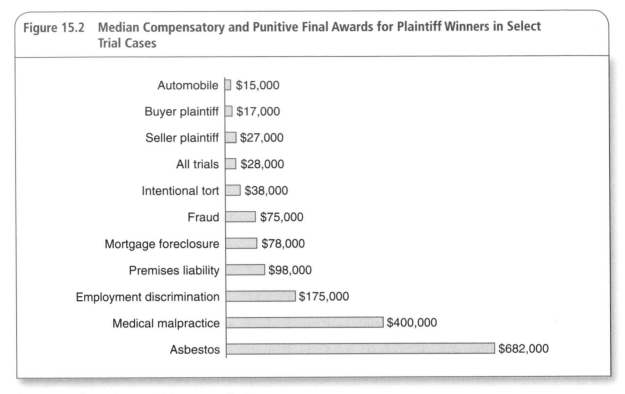

Source: Bureau of Justice Statistics, U.S. Department of Justice

In April 2013, news sources reported an agreement among federal agencies and some of the largest banks in the United States designed to compensate the millions of Americans who *"allegedly"* were targeted in wrongful foreclosures during the housing crisis. *I use the term allegedly because these types of settlements typically place no guilt on the offending parties and no admission of criminal conduct.* Bank of America, JPMorgan, Chase, Wells Fargo, and Citigroup, for example, agreed to pay $9.3 billion in cash and in reductions of mortgage balances. A total of $3.6 billion will go directly to borrowers who lost their homes or faced foreclosure. The 4.2 million victims will receive payments ranging from $300 to $125,000 as compensation. (Dodge 2013, p. 28) (italics added)

● ● ●   Alternative Sanctions and White-Collar Offenders

Several types of alternative sanctions, both formal and informal, are used to punish offenders. The way these sanctions are used for white-collar offenders is at least partly distinct from how the sanctions are used for conventional offenders. In this context, alternative sanctions include (1) house arrest, (2) community service, (3) shaming, and (4) loss of a job.

House Arrest and White-Collar Offenders

Under **house arrest**, offenders are told that they must be at home either all of the time or when they are not at work, the doctor's office, or a religious service. Probation and parole officers use various strategies to make sure that offenders are at

Table 15.2 Jury Trial Awards in State Courts in the Nation's 75 Most Populous Counties, by Selected Case Types, 1992, 1996, 2001, and 2005

Case Type	Median Jury Award Amounts Adjusted for Inflation				Percentage Change in Median Award Amounts	
	1992	1996	2001	2005	1992–2005	2001–2005
All cases	$72,000	$44,000	$41,000	$43,000	−40.3%	4.9%
Product liability	154,000	409,000	597,000	749,000	386.9	25.5
Medical malpractice	280,000	315,000	474,000	682,000	143.6	43.9
Fraud	98,000	98,000	90,000	92,000	6.2	10.4
Buyer plaintiff	61,000	61,000	69,000	61,000	0.0	−11.6
Employment	196,000	256,000	140,000	114,000	−41.8	−18.6

Source: Bureau of Justice Statistics, U.S. Department of Justice

Table 15.3 Plaintiff Winners Who Sought and Were Awarded Punitive Damages in Civil Trials, by Selected Case Types, 2005

Tort Trials	Number of Plaintiffs Who Sought Punitive Damages	Number Awarded Punitive Damages	Median Amount	Number of Cases With Punitive Damages Over $250,000	Number of Cases With Punitive Damages Over $1,000,000
Fraud	259	151	$100,000	67	7
Failure to provide services	372	138	53,000	20	3
Employment discrimination	84	10	115,000	1	1
Other employment disputes	93	86	10,000	12	10
Interfering with contractual relationship	42	18	6,888,000	12	11
Medical malpractice	56	6	2,835,000	5	5

Source: Bureau of Justice Statistics, U.S. Department of Justice

home. House arrest is used as (1) a pretrial strategy to keep offenders out of jail before trial, (2) a sanction imposed as part of the offender's probation experience, or (3) as a condition of release after an offender has been incarcerated in jail or prison.

Table 15.4	Comparing Compensatory to Punitive Damage Awards in Civil Trials Related to White-Collar Crimes With Plaintiff Winners in State Courts in the Nation's 75 Largest Counties, 2001

Case Types	Number of Trials With Punitive Damages	Median Damage Award Amounts		Amount of Punitive Damages Awarded: Maximum Amount	Number of Trials With Punitive Damages		Number of Punitive Damage Trials With Punitive Awards	
		Compensatory	Punitive		$1 Million or More	$10 Million or More	Greater Than Compensatory Damage Awards	More Than Four Times the Compensatory Damage Awards
All civil trials	356	$80,000	$50,000	$364,500,000	41	9	138	50
Product liability	3	16,562,000	433,000	500,000	–	–	–	–
Asbestos	2	20,000,000	500,000	500,000	–	–	–	–
Other	1	2,000,000	150,000	150,000	–	–	–	–
Medical malpractice	15	757,000	187,000	75,000,000	2	2	4	1
Professional malpractice	7	40,000	1,000	40,000	–	–	–	–
Fraud	60	119,000	63,000	275,000,000	5	2	16	2
Failure to provide services	16	160,000	275,000	5,000,000	3	–	13	3
Employment discrimination	13	493,000	606,000	3,500,000	5	–	6	–
Other employment dispute	16	150,000	151,000	1,500,000	1	–	10	–
Tortious interference	9	889,000	83,000	364,500,000	1	1	3	3

Source: Bureau of Justice Statistics, U.S. Department of Justice

With regard to white-collar crime, a perception exists that suggests it is better to be on house arrest in a white-collar offender's home than it is to be on house arrest in a conventional offender's home. Before Madoff was sentenced, he was placed on house arrest. Comments such as "Madoff has been under house arrest in his $7 million Manhattan penthouse" demonstrate the frustration that people seem to have with putting affluent individuals on house arrest (Neumeister & Hays, 2009). It is important to bear in mind that Madoff, at that point, had not yet been sentenced, and that punishment is a relative experience (Payne & Gainey, 1998). What one offender "feels" as punitive will be different from what another offender might "feel" as punitive. Where the punishment (or controlling actions of the justice system) occurs may actually have very little to do with the punitivenesss of house arrest. Having said that, I'll go ahead and contradict myself—if I were to be placed on house arrest, I'd prefer to be in a penthouse than one of my old college apartments. Either way, though, the experience of house arrest would be controlling and punitive for me.

House arrest has been lauded as an appropriate sanction for some types of white-collar offenders for four reasons (Rackmill, 1992). First, it is a cost-effective sanction in that there are no incarceration costs. Second, the sanction allows offenders to find (or maintain) employment, which will help the offender pay the victim back. Third, given that most white-collar offenders are nonviolent, there is little risk that they would physically harm anyone while on house arrest. Fourth, the house arrest sanction minimizes the trauma that the family might endure from the criminal justice process. To be sure, a number of different types of offenders—conventional and white-collar alike—are good candidates for house arrest sanctions.

House arrest with electronic monitoring is a variation of the house arrest alternative. In these situations, offenders wear an ankle monitor, and the probation or parole officer monitors the offender's whereabouts through the use of satellite technology. Many will recall how Martha Stewart was placed on house arrest with electronic monitoring after her brief stay in prison. As with house arrest in general, some assume that even the addition of electronic monitoring results in the sanction being lenient as compared to other sanctions. It is interesting to note, however, that studies show that certain types of individuals with exposure to the justice process actually prefer prison to electronic monitoring (May & Wood, 2005; Payne & Gainey, 1998). Offenders cite the degree of control that community corrections officers have over their lives as being particularly problematic for them. In other words, house arrest with electronic monitoring is a punitive experience (again, whether one lives in a penthouse or the trailer where I once lived).

Randy Gainey and I, in 1998, interviewed offenders on house arrest with electronic monitoring to shed some light on this punitive experience. We were able to identify how the sanction might apply similarly and differently to white-collar and conventional offenders. In particular, using Gresham Sykes' (1958) pains of imprisonment as a guide, we highlighted how offenders on electronic monitoring experienced the types of "pains" that offenders in prison experienced and how they experienced additional pains that are unique to the electronic monitoring experience (see Table 15.5).

As an illustration of how the electronic-monitoring experience can be punitive for white-collar offenders, consider the following deprivations experienced by incarcerated and electronically monitored offenders:

- *Deprivation of autonomy:* Just as inmates lose control over their lives, so white-collar offenders on house arrest with electronic monitoring are forced to give up their freedom and abide by controls and restrictions that are placed on them by the court and reviewed by probation officers. White-collar offenders are virtually always used to being in control of their lives and the lives of others. Having someone else control them, especially someone from a lower social status, could be difficult for some offenders.
- *Deprivation of goods and services:* Just as inmates have reduced access to goods and services, so white-collar offenders on house arrest with electronic monitoring will have limited access to the kinds of goods and services they are accustomed to. This could represent a major shift in an offender's lifestyle, which would be experienced as punitive.
- *Deprivation of liberty:* Convicted felons lose many rights (e.g., in various states—the right to own a gun, to vote). For white-collar offenders involved in the political process, losing the right to participate in that process can be especially difficult.
- *Deprivation of heterosexual relations:* Whereas inmates do not have the same kinds of heterosexual relationships while they are incarcerated, monitored offenders also have their intimate relationships disrupted while on house arrest with electronic monitoring. In a very real sense, the nonmonitored family members have more social power than monitored offenders because they are able to maintain a social lifestyle. For white-collar offenders accustomed to an active social life, the fact that their social lives are put on hold while family members continue engaging in social activities can be problematic.
- *Monetary costs:* These affect all offenders because they are required to pay for the costs of the monitoring experience. For white-collar offenders, however, paying for the electronic monitoring sanction may be less difficult.
- *Family effects:* Families of white-collar offenders can face a reduced quality of life, a lower social status, and a reduction in the types of materials and goods they are used to. With electronic monitoring, the stigma of wearing the ankle bracelet may also affect the family. In addition, these effects are experienced by white-collar offenders when the family loses its lifestyle, status, or other material goods as a result of the conviction. Also, the monitored offender will rarely have time alone in his or her own residence.

Table 15.5   **The Pains of Electronic Monitoring for White-Collar Offenders**

Pain	What It Means	White-Collar Offender Experience
Deprivation of autonomy	Electronically monitored offenders lose their freedom and have very little control over decisions about movement.	White-collar offenders would be permitted to leave home only for work, medical reasons, probation officer visits, and so on.
Deprivation of goods/services	Electronically monitored offenders are not permitted to engage in activities outside of the home that others take for granted.	White-collar offenders would lose their social activity and would not be permitted to shop, eat out, or do other things without approval.
Deprivation of liberty	Electronically monitored offenders lose many of their rights, with some losing their right to vote.	White-collar offenders would experience these same losses.
Deprivation of heterosexual relations	Electronically monitored offenders do not lose their ability to have relations with others, but these relations are certainly influenced by the sanction.	Because of the loss of status experienced by the offender, partners may also lose status, thereby potentially influencing the relationship.
Monetary costs	Electronically monitored offenders usually have to pay to be on the sanction.	White-collar offenders would experience the same losses as conventional offenders here, though relatively speaking this may be more of a cost for conventional offenders.
Family effects	The family members of electronically monitored offenders must change their actions when someone in their home is monitored.	The loss of status would be experienced by the entire family, and some may actually lose their home as well as other taken-for-granted comforts.
Watching-others effects	Electronically monitored offenders see others engaging in activities that they would like to be doing.	White-collar offenders would experience the same losses.
Bracelet effects	Electronically monitored offenders often complain about having to wear the bracelet.	Offenders who are working would find the most discomfort with the bracelet, especially if it was noticeable.

Source: Payne, B. (2003). *Incarcerating white-collar offenders: The prison experience and beyond.* Springfield, IL: Charles C Thomas.

- *Watching-others effects:* Monitored offenders have to watch others do things they are unable to participate in because of the restrictive probation conditions.
- *Bracelet effects:* This refers to instances when the monitor is felt as an invasive or stigmatizing tool attached to the body as a reminder of one's misdeeds. This can be particularly difficult for women in the workplace if they are unable to conceal the monitor (Payne, 2003b).

It is important to note that the *pains of electronic monitoring* typology was developed by focusing on all types of offenders, most of which are conventional offenders. Additional research on the experience of white-collar offenders on house arrest with electronic monitoring is needed.

Community Service

Community service involves situations where offenders are told to perform a certain number of hours or days of community service. In some cases, judges will order white-collar offenders to complete a specific type of community service, while in others, the offender might be ordered simply to perform some general service activities. Given the skills that white-collar offenders have, many are in positions to offer their specific skills for the good of the community. Consider the following examples:

- A judge ordered a pain management doctor, who pleaded guilty to knowing that her patients diverted controlled substances on four occasions, to perform 100 hours of community service, with half of the hours performed in a community clinic and half in her own office (D. E. Hoffman, 2008).
- A dentist was ordered to perform 1,000 hours of community service at a local clinic after being convicted of Medicaid fraud (Lehr, 2010).
- A bookkeeper convicted for embezzling performed community service for a nonprofit agency serving low-income women searching for jobs (Ellis, 2011).
- A defendant convicted in an offshore fraud cause was sentenced to perform community service by assisting "an inner-city Chicago high school in supervising, teaching, and mentoring the students and staff in developing a curriculum that addresses careers in business" (Hoelter, 2015).
- A judge ordered a public official convicted of corruption to provide four public appearances a month for three years and discuss her offense in these appearances. The judge told the woman: "You will speak to schools. You will speak to civic groups. In these presentations, you will discuss your life, the service you have provided to the state, the crimes you have committed, the effect those crimes had on you personally and the broader effect that they have had on the community as a whole" (Reed & Miller, 2015).

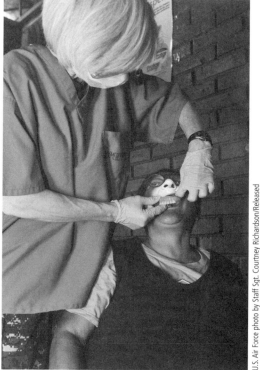

▲ **Photo 15.5** Sentencing white-collar inmates with community service makes great sense when their skills are used to serve the public. Sentencing a dentist to give free dental work would be an example of an appropriate use of the community service sanction.

U.S. Air Force photo by Staff Sgt. Courtney Richardson/Released

Community service has numerous advantages. The sanction holds offenders accountable for their misdeeds, helps reintegrate offenders back into the community, and benefits the community through the offenders' contributions. Despite these advantages, the sanction appears to be rarely applied. A study of home health care providers convicted of white-collar offending, for example, found that less than a third were sentenced to community service (Payne & Gray, 2001).

Shaming

Shaming is another alternative sanction strategy used to punish white-collar offenders. Shaming strategies are used for all types of offenders, but they may be particularly effective for white-collar offenders given the higher amount of stigma and shame that accompany the conviction of white-collar offenders (Benson, 1990). As examples of shaming strategies used against white-collar offenders, consider the following sanctions:

- A Cincinnati judge made a white-collar offender send community members apologies and purchase newspaper ad space to advertise his company's environmental offenses (Ivancevich, Konopaske, & Gilbert, 2008).
- A Maryland judge made an insurance agent "clean out the stalls of the city's mounted police unit" after the agent was convicted of defrauding Maryland horse trainers (Ivancevich et al., 2008, p. 403).

- A former senior vice president of Bristol Myers-Squibb was ordered to write a book about his conviction for lying to the Federal Trade Commission about a pharmaceutical deal that had gotten out of control (McCarthy, 2011).
- A physician was ordered to write a letter to a medical journal describing her after-the-fact involvement in a drug diversion scheme and how physicians can experience negative consequences as a result of misconduct (Hoffman, 2008).

In a more recent case, a judge ordered a former state official convicted of corruption to write a letter of apology and have it published in at least six outlets. Just a few days after the sentence was imposed, the following letter was published across the state:

Dear New Mexicans,

I cannot begin to express how deeply sorry I am for my transgressions and the damage I caused to the public's trust in public officials. I only hope the people of the state of New Mexico will move forward and someday forgive my actions which were not borne out of greed but rather a result of very tragic personal circumstances which led to some very poor decisions on my part. I have not made excuses for my actions. I have simply tried to explain the circumstances which led to my transgressions. I only hope the people of this great state find it within themselves to forgive me. (Duran, 2015)

Shaming can also be used as a strategy to punish corporations for wrongdoing. In fact, many federal and state agencies announce their sanctions and maintain a public database of offenders and do so out of shaming ideals. As well, judges may order companies to engage in behavior designed to shame the company. One company, for example, had to run the following advertisement:

We Apologize for Polluting

The Environment General Wood Preserving Company recently pled guilty in federal court to illegally disposing of hazardous waste in 1985 at its plant in Leland, North Carolina. As a result of that crime, General Wood Preserving was fined $150,000, and was ordered to publish the following advertisement:

We are sorry for what we did, and we hope that our experience will be a lesson to others that environmental laws must be respected.

Board of Directors General Wood Preserving Co., Inc. (Kostelnik, 2012, p. 150)

The idea of shaming white-collar offenders as a sanction has been gaining popularity over the years. Said one legal scholar, "Some of legal academia's brightest stars have jumped on the shame train, arguing that modern versions of the dunce cap, rather than shackles, best fit the 'white collar' criminal" (Owens, 2000, p. 1047). Shaming by itself can be counterproductive. Scholars have called for what is called **reintegrative shaming,** a process characterized by a shaming sanction followed by efforts to reengage offenders in the community.

John Braithwaite (1989a) and Michael Benson (1990) have been the leading criminologists calling for the use of reintegrative shaming for white-collar offenders. Braithwaite notes that overly punitive and stigmatizing responses to white-collar misconduct can be counterproductive and result in offenders becoming disengaged from the community. Building on Braithwaite's ideas, Benson notes that **disintegrative shaming** embarrasses offenders, causes anger, and potentially leads to additional harm. Alternatively, reintegrative shaming focuses on the bad act and communicates messages of disapproval, which are followed by efforts to reintegrate the offender back into the community.

One author team identified several reasons that reintegrative shaming strategies should be effective for white-collar offenders. These reasons included the following:

- White-collar offenders want to minimize the harm done to their family members, and reintegrative shaming strategies provide an opportunity to do this.
- Others possibly steer clear of white-collar misconduct because they do not want to be embarrassed.
- Those who have a higher attachment to their jobs, families, and society should be less likely to want to be shamed.
- Reintegration affirms individuals while disintegration breaks them down (Ivancevich et al., 2008).

For white-collar offenders, reintegrative shaming is effective inasmuch as offenders take responsibility for their actions. In other words, reintegrative shaming will be more powerful if offenders "respect the shamer" (Ivancevich et al., 2008). What this means is that if the offender has no respect for those doing the shaming, there is little likelihood that the shaming will have deterrent qualities. Or to put it more bluntly, if you don't care what someone thinks about you, their efforts to shame you will not keep you from behaving a certain way. Also, according to one author, "shaming sanctions are most viable when used in conjunction with alternative sanctions so that courts can impose sanction bundles of costs commensurate with the level of offense committed by an offender" (Kostelnik, 2012, p. 141).

Loss of Job

Loss of job is another sanction that can be imposed on white-collar offenders. For many individuals, this potential loss is likely enough to keep workers from engaging in misconduct. Once caught, not only do offenders lose their current jobs, but they are also often ordered out of their careers for various amounts of time. Martha Stewart, for example, was not able to serve as a CEO of a publicly traded company (including her own) from the time of her conviction until 2011. When Ivan Boesky was convicted of his securities crimes, he was barred from working in the securities industry for the remainder of his life (K. Adams, 2009). Boesky was not alone. A study of 2,206 individuals charged with financial misrepresentation in enforcement actions by the SEC and Department of Justice (DOJ) found that 93 percent of the individuals had lost their jobs by the time the enforcement action was completed (Karpoff, Lee, & Martin, 2008). When other professionals such as lawyers, doctors, educators, and so on are caught committing crime on the job, they too face the likelihood of losing their jobs.

At some point, white-collar offenders who lost their jobs and have completed their criminal justice sanction will seek new employment. A study by Kent Kerley and Heith Copes (2004) found that, for the most part, white-collar offenders "are better able to rebound following contact with the criminal justice system" (p. 65). In particular, they found that white-collar offenders were better able to find new jobs than conventional offenders were. The caveat they uncovered in their research was that white-collar offenders with more arrests and a later onset of offending found it just as difficult as conventional offenders to find a stable job.

● ● ● Punishing Corporations for White-Collar Crime

Corporations can be punished both formally and informally for misconduct. If they are convicted (in criminal court), found liable (in civil court), or determined responsible (in administrative or regulatory proceedings), various types of sentencing alternatives arise. Criminal penalties include fines, restitution, probation, and disbarment, and civil penalties, including compensatory and punitive damages, can be applied. In administrative proceedings, a corporate offender can be given civil fines and required to pay restitution. Corporations can also experience "marketplace sanctions," such as loss of investor confidence (M. A. Cohen, 1992). It is also important to note that when corporations are sanctioned, individuals leading the corporation are also sanctioned as individual offenders.

With regard to criminal sanctions, the *U.S. Sentencing Guidelines* includes an Organizational Guidelines section that provides judges guidance in determining how to sentence corporations. The guidelines specify three sanctions: probation, fines, and restitution. The Organizational Guidelines were implemented in November 1991 and included recommended sanctions that were stricter than the types of sanctions applied earlier. For example, fine amounts recommended in the Organizational Guidelines were 5 to 10 times higher in the guidelines than the fines that had traditionally been applied in corporate misconduct cases (M. A. Cohen, 1992). The guidelines have been critiqued for appearing to arbitrarily stipulate sanctions relative to organizational characteristics (e.g., size of the company, number of employees; see Rackmill, 1992). It is an interesting philosophical question: If two companies commit the exact same offense, should one of them be punished more severely because it is larger and wealthier? (A similar question can be asked about individual white-collar offenders.)

Fining Corporate Offenders

The use of fines to punish corporations has been a hotly debated issue among criminologists and economists. As suggested above, some economists apply concepts of cost-benefit analysis in determining the relevance of fines to control corporate misconduct. Some criminologists, on the other hand, view fines as less than useful, to put it nicely. Snider (1990) suggested that "fines for large organizations typically represent a fraction of the profits made in one hour of operation" (p. 380). Another scholar noted that fines are simply a "cost of doing business" and that ultimately fines hurt stockholders and corporations (Orland, 1980).

Cohen (1989) has considered how corporate fines compare to the harm committed by the corporation. Focusing on 288 non-antitrust corporate offenders prosecuted between 1984 and 1987, he found that monetary sanctions "seldom exceed—and often are much less than—total harm" (M. A. Cohen, 1989, p. 618). To quantify the difference, he suggested that "a firm convicted of causing $1.00 in harm might pay a criminal fine of $.76 in addition to any other sanctions such as criminal restitution or civil penalties" (p. 658).

While Cohen's study was done before the Organizational Guidelines were in effect, criminological studies since then also question the effectiveness of fines for corporations. A review of 405 cases where organizations were sentenced through 1996 found that organizational offenders were able to avoid paying fines "by convincing a U.S. District Court that they have no money" (Green & Bodapati, 1999, p. 556). The authors noted a particularly interesting irony: Organizations might commit crimes because of a lack of money. Then, they can argue that the "lack of money motive" can be used to avoid sanctioning the organization. They also call for organizational sales (where the business is sold) or forced dissolution (which is an organizational death penalty) in these cases. Judges are unwilling to make these decisions out of concern for workers, investors, and consumers (Orland, 1980).

More recently, Nicole Piquero and Jason Davis (2004) reviewed sanctions imposed on organizations after the guidelines were developed to see whether certain factors impacted the penalty given to corporations. They found that although legal factors consistent with the guidelines impacted sentencing to a degree, two extralegal variables influenced organizational sentencing: (1) economic solvency and (2) closely held organizations. These two factors influenced the amount of the fine, "but did not significantly impact the placement of the fine within the guideline range" (p. 652).

Probation and Corporate Offenders

Corporations can be sentenced to a term of probation. The first use of **organizational probation** occurred in 1971 in *U.S. v. Atlantic Richfield, Co.,* when Judge James B. Parsons, Jr., sentenced ARCO (the Atlantic Richfield Company) to probation and "ordered it to develop an oil response plan" (Lofquist, 1993, p. 160). Lofquist notes that by the eighties, one-fifth of all corporate offenders convicted at the federal level were given a probation sentence. The use of organizational probation was not formalized until the development of the Organizational Guidelines in 1991. The federal sentencing guidelines specify that corporations cannot be sentenced to more than 5 years of probation.

Corporations can be required to meet certain conditions while on probation. Probation conditions must be tied to the characteristic of the organization and the offense (Plimton & Walsh, 2010). Probation conditions are, as a result, tied to type of industry. For instance, judges have ordered bakeries convicted of wrongdoing to provide food for the underprivileged (Levin, 1984). One condition sometimes used is that companies are told to apologize publicly, in various media sources, for their misconduct (M. A. Cohen, 1992). Table 15.7 shows the factors that drive organizational probation decisions and the types of conditions that organizations can be ordered to abide by as part of their probation.

Issues Surrounding Corporate Sanctions

Two issues surface when considering how to sanction organizations. These include (1) determining appropriate sanctions to reduce recidivism and (2) avoiding harm to innocent parties. With regard to recidivism, one basis for punishing companies is to keep them from committing future acts of misconduct. Research shows that recidivism by corporations is tied more to the nature of the industry as opposed to the type of intervention (e.g., criminal justice, civil, or administrative) (Simpson & Koper, 1992). However, the authors found that for those corporations with past guilty verdicts, stiffer penalties (measured by changing from a misdemeanor to a felony) reduced subsequent recidivism. In terms of punishing innocent parties, some sentences (corporate manslaughter and penalties for violations of safety laws) are potentially too strict and harmful to innocent employees or shareholders (Stevens & Payne, 1999). As noted above, a desire to avoid harming individuals leads some judges to give relatively lenient sentences in some corporate misconduct cases.

● ● ● Reasons for Punishing White-Collar Offenders

Criminologists have described several reasons that society punishes criminals. These reasons include (1) retribution, (2) specific deterrence, (3) general deterrence, (4) rehabilitation, (5) just deserts, and (6) incapacitation, which refers to removing dangerous offenders from the street to protect society from harm. With the exception of the sixth reason, all of the reasons easily demonstrate reasons that white-collar criminals are punished.

Retribution and White-Collar Offenders

As a philosophy of punishment, **retribution** means that offenders should be punished to meet societal demands. Philosophers have long noted that formal punishment satisfies public demands. Another way to say it is that punishment of wrongdoers makes some people "happy." This may be especially the case for victims of white-collar crimes. When Bernie Madoff was being led away in handcuffs after being sentenced, one of his victims was heard saying, "What a sweet sight. What a sweet sight" (Healy & Mandell, 2009). Some members of the media could not help gloating over Madoff's plight. In a way that hinted at pleasure, one team of reporters said about Madoff the day after he was sentenced,

> the swanky East 64th Street duplex where Madoff spent the previous night must have felt like a distant memory as he looked around his Spartan cell. Instead of having his loving wife, Ruth, for company, Madoff is sharing a roof with . . . rapists, murderers, even thieves like him. (Zambito, Martinez, & Siemaszko, 2009)

Madoff is not the only white-collar offender members of society want punished. A survey of 1,512 respondents from across the United States found that more than three-fourths of the respondents supported longer prison sentences for white-collar offenders (Unnever, Benson, & Cullen, 2008, p. 177). Podgor (2007) wrote that "Wealth, education, and prestige are often cited as reasons for giving white-collar offenders a harsher punishment" (p. 750). As an illustration, one U.S. attorney commented that white-collar criminals "should be treated more harshly because you're talking about people who have gotten every opportunity that you can give them . . . the drug dealers have had no opportunities" (O'Donnell & Willing, 2003). It seems that some members of the public may be less forgiving of white-collar offenders.

Specific Deterrence and White-Collar Offenders

Specific deterrence ideals suggest that punishment should occur in order to stop the punished offender (in this context, either a white-collar offender or a corporation) from engaging in future wrongdoing. Deterrence theory has been addressed elsewhere in this text. At this point, it is sufficient to suggest that some believe that sanctions proportional to the harm committed by the offender will keep individuals and corporations from engaging in future misconduct (Spurgeon & Fagan, 1981). Note that some research has called into question the deterrent ability of imprisonment for individual offenders (Weisburd, Waring, & Chayet, 1995), while others have found that sanctions might deter corporations from future misconduct (Simpson & Koper, 1992).

Table 15.6	Dynamics Surrounding Corporate Probation	
The Court Shall Order a Term of Probation	**Mandatory Conditions of the Probation**	**Discretionary Conditions**
• If necessary to ensure satisfaction of other sanctions; • If an organization of fifty or more employees lacks an effective program to prevent and detect law violations; • If the organization or high-level personnel participating in the offense have been convicted of a similar offense in the past five years; • If necessary to ensure that changes are made within the organization to reduce the likelihood of future criminal conduct; • If the sentence does not include a fine; or • If necessary to accomplish one of the four purposes of sentencing.	• Commission of no further crimes • Payment of a fine or restitution, or performance of community service; and • Any other conditions reasonably related to the instant offense and imposing no unnecessary deprivations of liberty or property.	• Publicity paid for by the defendant in media specified by the court detailing the crime, conviction, sentence, and remedial steps taken; • Development by the defendant, with court approval, of an effective program to prevent and detect future law violations; • Notification of employees and shareholders of the offense and of the details of the compliance program; • Periodic reports to the court regarding progress in implementing the compliance program, occurrence of new offenses, or investigations involving the defendant; and • Periodic examinations of facilities and records, and interviews of employees by the court or a special probation officer to monitor compliance.

Source: Lofquist, W. (1993). Organizational probation and the U.S. sentencing commission. *Annals of the American Academy of Political and Social Science, 525,* 157–169.

General Deterrence and White-Collar Offenders

General deterrence ideals suggest that offenders should be punished in order to keep other potential offenders from engaging in misconduct. As noted earlier, judges often justify their stern responses to white-collar offenders on general deterrence ideals (Mann et al., 1980). There is a perception that fines and probation do not have general deterrent power for white-collar offenders. One government official with the Environmental Crime Division of the Department of Justice has been quoted saying, "incarceration is the cost of business that you can't pass on to the consumer" (Stuart, 1995, p. 255). The underlying assumption is that fines are passed on to consumers, and as a result, it will not keep offenders from engaging in white-collar misconduct.

In line with general deterrence ideals, educators have used incarcerated white-collar offenders to teach future white-collar professionals how to avoid white-collar offending. Castleberry (2007), a marketing professor, takes his students on prison field trips as part of his efforts to teach business ethics and to make sure that students understand the laws governing workplace behavior. He argues that the visits show students that laws apply to them, that there are consequences for bad workplace decisions, and that criminal workplace decisions sometimes result from "seemingly insignificant acts." He also argues that visits will help students understand what prison life is like for the white-collar offender and that from this, it is assumed that students would be less prone to engage in workplace misconduct.

Rehabilitation and White-Collar Offenders

Rehabilitation, as a philosophy of punishment, suggests that offenders are brought into the justice process so that the government can play a role in treating whatever issues offenders have that may have contributed to their wrongdoing. White-collar offenders might receive individual-level counseling from probation and parole officers to help them deal with their status degradation and to regain employment (Payne, 2003b). In general, though, treatment programs tend to be designed more for drug and violent offenders. If individuals with a white-collar status find themselves in a treatment program, it is more apt to result from a commission of a drug offense.

Just Deserts and White-Collar Offenders

Just deserts as a punishment orientation suggests that offenders should be punished for one primary reason: because they deserve it. Braithwaite (1982) highlights the difficulties that arise in applying this philosophy to white-collar offenders:

- How do you identify who is responsible?
- Do you punish the individual or the organization?
- If punishing both, how much punishment is appropriate, and how would it be divided?
- How do you keep individuals (consumers and workers) from being punished? (p. 525)

Braithwaite suggests that the negative consequences arising from overly strict responses to white-collar offending support the selective enforcement of white-collar crimes. He quotes the justice theorem: "Where desert is greatest, punishment will be the least" (p. 755).

Braithwaite draws attention to the debate about whether white-collar offenders should be punished more severely so that they are punished the same as conventional offenders. In doing so, he calls for a utilitarian approach to balance the scales of justice. His perspective is quite simple: Rather than punishing white-collar offenders more severely, why not punish conventional offenders less and white-collar offenders only slightly more so that both groups are punished similarly?

Experts recognize that effective punishments balance ideals of retribution, just deserts, deterrence, and rehabilitation. Benson (1985b) calls for short sentences of white-collar offenders that are split between a short prison sentence and a short probation sentence. Such an approach would have deterrent, retributive, and rehabilitative qualities. As well, it would be more cost-effective than other remedies.

SUMMARY

- White-collar offenders are subject to a wide range of sentencing alternatives, including prison, probation, restitution, fine, and various alternative sanctions. Organizations—as well as individuals—can be sanctioned in white-collar crime cases.
- Research on the sentencing of white-collar offenders has provided mixed messages about issues related to the disposition of white-collar offenders.
- Wheeler and his colleagues' (1982) interviews with judges found that the judges considered how the white-collar offender experienced the criminal justice process; some judges viewed participation in the process as a punishment in and of itself for white-collar offenders.
- The Sentencing Reform Act was passed in 1984 as part of the Comprehensive Crime Control Act. One aim of the act was "to remedy individualized disparity in federal criminal sentences and to equalize sentences for 'street criminals' and 'white-collar offenders'" (Ryan-Boyle et al., 1991, p. 739).
- Some have argued that the sentencing of white-collar offenders has gotten a little out of control, with some sentences seeming far too severe.
- Some have suggested that the apparently disparate sentencing resulting in long sentences for white-collar offenders might simply reflect the fact that the vast majority of white-collar offenders are kept out of the justice system in the first place.
- Very few studies have focused on the experience of white-collar offenders in prison. One can point to five dynamics of the white-collar prison experience: (1) depression, (2) danger, (3) deprivations, (4) deviance, (5) doldrums.
- For white-collar offenders, the sources of depression include (1) stressful changes coming from one's first exposure to prison life, (2) loss of job, (3) loss of status, (4) isolation, and (5) sentencing dynamics (Payne, 2003b).

- Four themes arise regarding danger and white-collar offenders: (1) celebrity bashing, (2) prison placement, (3) prison culture and socialization, and (4) exaggerated concerns.
- For white-collar inmates accustomed to certain lifestyles, the experience of deprivation might be particularly problematic.
- Three types of inmate violations are relevant with regard to white-collar inmates: rule violations, deviant use of the justice process, and jailstripe crimes (Payne, 2003b).
- After becoming acquainted with the incarceration experience, white-collar inmates report being very bored with prison.
- Benson (1985b) found that for white-collar offenders the probation experience could be characterized as "going through the motions" (p. 429).
- Monetary penalties include criminal fines, restitution, civil settlements, and the compensatory and punitive damages awarded in civil trials.
- Alternative sanctions given to white-collar offenders include (1) house arrest, (2) community service, (3) shaming, and (4) loss of a job.
- With regard to white-collar crime, a perception exists that it is better to be on house arrest in a white-collar offender's home than it is to be on house arrest in a conventional offender's home.
- Community service holds offenders accountable for their misdeeds and helps to reintegrate offenders back into the community, and the community benefits from the offenders' contributions.
- Shaming strategies are used for all types of offenders, but they may be particularly effective for white-collar offenders given the higher amount of stigma and shame that accompanies the conviction of white-collar offenders (Benson, 1990).
- A study of 2,206 individuals charged with financial misrepresentation in enforcement actions by the SEC and DOJ found that 93% of the individuals had lost their jobs by the time the enforcement action was completed (Karpoff et al., 2008).
- Corporations can be punished both formally and informally for misconduct. Depending on whether convicted (in criminal court), found liable (in civil court), or determined responsible (in administrative or regulatory proceedings), various types of sentencing alternatives are available.
- Two issues surface when considering how to sanction organizations: (1) determining appropriate sanctions to reduce recidivism and (2) avoiding harm to innocent parties.
- Reasons for punishing white-collar offenders include (1) retribution, (2) specific deterrence, (3) general deterrence, (4) rehabilitation, and (5) just deserts.

KEY TERMS

Celebrity bashing	General deterrence	Rehabilitation
Community-based sanctions	House arrest	Reintegrative shaming
Community service	Jailstripe crimes	Restitution
Compensatory damages	Just deserts	Retribution
Criminal fines	Monetary penalties	Shaming
Deviant misuse of the justice process	Organizational probation	Specific deterrence
Disintegrative shaming	Punitive damages	U.S. Sentencing Commission

DISCUSSION QUESTIONS

1. A blue-collar and a white-collar offender commit the same crime. The blue-collar offender is sentenced to prison for one year. Should the white-collar offender be given the same sentence?

2. A blue-collar and a white-collar offender both steal from their job. Each of them stole the same amount. The blue-collar offender is fined $500.00. Should the white-collar offender receive the same fine? Would it be unfair to punish the white-collar offender more because of the offender's higher income? Should the offender be given a lower prison sentence in exchange for the higher fine? Explain.

3. How is incarceration different for white-collar offenders as compared to conventional offenders?

4. What do you think of research that shows that white-collar offenders are more likely than conventional offenders to be sentenced to prison? What are some possible reasons for this finding?

5. Is probation an effective sanction for white-collar offenders? Explain.

6. How are fines appropriately and inappropriately used in white-collar crime cases?

7. Describe the different ways that organizations are punished. Do you think businesses should ever be forced to close as a result of misconduct? Explain.

8. Which types of alternative sanctions might be most appropriate for white-collar offenders? Explain.

9. Why do we punish white-collar offenders?

WEB RESOURCES

Correctional Alternatives, Inc.: http://www.correctionalalternatives.org/

Prison Activist Resource Center: http://www.prisonactivist.org/

White-Collar Prisoners: How not to get stuck in jail: http://www.economist.com/node/13528224

STUDENT RESOURCES

The open-access Student Study Site, available at study.sagepub.com/paynewccess2e, includes useful study materials including SAGE journal articles and multimedia resources.

Appendix

Executive Order— Improving Critical Infrastructure Cybersecurity

By the authority vested in me as President by the Constitution and the laws of the United States of America, it is hereby ordered as follows:

Section 1. Policy. Repeated cyber intrusions into critical infrastructure demonstrate the need for improved cybersecurity. The cyber threat to critical infrastructure continues to grow and represents one of the most serious national security challenges we must confront. The national and economic security of the United States depends on the reliable functioning of the Nation's critical infrastructure in the face of such threats. It is the policy of the United States to enhance the security and resilience of the Nation's critical infrastructure and to maintain a cyber environment that encourages efficiency, innovation, and economic prosperity while promoting safety, security, business confidentiality, privacy, and civil liberties. We can achieve these goals through a partnership with the owners and operators of critical infrastructure to improve cybersecurity information sharing and collaboratively develop and implement risk-based standards.

Sec. 2. Critical Infrastructure. As used in this order, the term critical infrastructure means systems and assets, whether physical or virtual, so vital to the United States that the incapacity or destruction of such systems and assets would have a debilitating impact on security, national economic security, national public health or safety, or any combination of those matters.

Sec. 3. Policy Coordination. Policy coordination, guidance, dispute resolution, and periodic in-progress reviews for the functions and programs described and assigned herein shall be provided through the interagency process established in Presidential Policy Directive-1 of February 13, 2009 (Organization of the National Security Council System), or any successor.

Sec. 4. Cybersecurity Information Sharing. (a) It is the policy of the United States Government to increase the volume, timeliness, and quality of cyber threat information shared with U.S. private sector entities so that these entities may better protect and defend themselves against cyber threats. Within 120 days of the date of this order, the Attorney General, the

Secretary of Homeland Security (the "Secretary"), and the Director of National Intelligence shall each issue instructions consistent with their authorities and with the requirements of section 12(c) of this order to ensure the timely production of unclassified reports of cyber threats to the U.S. homeland that identify a specific targeted entity. The instructions shall address the need to protect intelligence and law enforcement sources, methods, operations, and investigations.

(b) The Secretary and the Attorney General, in coordination with the Director of National Intelligence, shall establish a process that rapidly disseminates the reports produced pursuant to section 4(a) of this order to the targeted entity. Such process shall also, consistent with the need to protect national security information, include the dissemination of classified reports to critical infrastructure entities authorized to receive them. The Secretary and the Attorney General, in coordination with the Director of National Intelligence, shall establish a system for tracking the production, dissemination, and disposition of these reports.

(c) To assist the owners and operators of critical infrastructure in protecting their systems from unauthorized access, exploitation, or harm, the Secretary, consistent with 6 U.S.C. 143 and in collaboration with the Secretary of Defense, shall, within 120 days of the date of this order, establish procedures to expand the Enhanced Cybersecurity Services program to all critical infrastructure sectors. This voluntary information sharing program will provide classified cyber threat and technical information from the Government to eligible critical infrastructure companies or commercial service providers that offer security services to critical infrastructure.

(d) The Secretary, as the Executive Agent for the Classified National Security Information Program created under Executive Order 13549 of August 18, 2010 (Classified National Security Information Program for State, Local, Tribal, and Private Sector Entities), shall expedite the processing of security clearances to appropriate personnel employed by critical infrastructure owners and operators, prioritizing the critical infrastructure identified in section 9 of this order.

(e) In order to maximize the utility of cyber threat information sharing with the private sector, the Secretary shall expand the use of programs that bring private sector subject-matter experts into Federal service on a temporary basis. These subject matter experts should provide advice regarding the content, structure, and types of information most useful to critical infrastructure owners and operators in reducing and mitigating cyber risks.

Sec. 5. Privacy and Civil Liberties Protections. (a) Agencies shall coordinate their activities under this order with their senior agency officials for privacy and civil liberties and ensure that privacy and civil liberties protections are incorporated into such activities. Such protections shall be based upon the Fair Information Practice Principles and other privacy and civil liberties policies, principles, and frameworks as they apply to each agency's activities.

(b) The Chief Privacy Officer and the Officer for Civil Rights and Civil Liberties of the Department of Homeland Security (DHS) shall assess the privacy and civil liberties risks of the functions and programs undertaken by DHS as called for in this order and shall recommend to the Secretary ways to minimize or mitigate such risks, in a publicly available report, to be released within 1 year of the date of this order. Senior agency privacy and civil liberties officials for other agencies engaged in activities under this order shall conduct assessments of their agency activities and provide those assessments to DHS for consideration and inclusion in the report. The report shall be reviewed on an annual basis and revised as necessary. The report may contain a classified annex if necessary. Assessments shall include evaluation of activities against the Fair Information Practice Principles and other applicable privacy and civil liberties policies, principles, and frameworks. Agencies shall consider the assessments and recommendations of the report in implementing privacy and civil liberties protections for agency activities.

(c) In producing the report required under subsection (b) of this section, the Chief Privacy Officer and the Officer for Civil Rights and Civil Liberties of DHS shall consult with the Privacy and Civil Liberties Oversight Board and coordinate with the Office of Management and Budget (OMB).

(d) Information submitted voluntarily in accordance with 6 U.S.C. 133 by private entities under this order shall be protected from disclosure to the fullest extent permitted by law.

Sec. 6. Consultative Process. The Secretary shall establish a consultative process to coordinate improvements to the cybersecurity of critical infrastructure. As part of the consultative process, the Secretary shall engage and consider the advice, on matters set forth in this order, of the Critical Infrastructure Partnership Advisory Council; Sector Coordinating Councils; critical

infrastructure owners and operators; Sector-Specific Agencies; other relevant agencies; independent regulatory agencies; State, local, territorial, and tribal governments; universities; and outside experts.

Sec. 7. Baseline Framework to Reduce Cyber Risk to Critical Infrastructure. (a) The Secretary of Commerce shall direct the Director of the National Institute of Standards and Technology (the "Director") to lead the development of a framework to reduce cyber risks to critical infrastructure (the "Cybersecurity Framework"). The Cybersecurity Framework shall include a set of standards, methodologies, procedures, and processes that align policy, business, and technological approaches to address cyber risks. The Cybersecurity Framework shall incorporate voluntary consensus standards and industry best practices to the fullest extent possible. The Cybersecurity Framework shall be consistent with voluntary international standards when such international standards will advance the objectives of this order, and shall meet the requirements of the National Institute of Standards and Technology Act, as amended (15 U.S.C. 271 et seq.), the National Technology Transfer and Advancement Act of 1995 (Public Law 104-113), and OMB Circular A-119, as revised.

(b) The Cybersecurity Framework shall provide a prioritized, flexible, repeatable, performance-based, and cost-effective approach, including information security measures and controls, to help owners and operators of critical infrastructure identify, assess, and manage cyber risk. The Cybersecurity Framework shall focus on identifying cross-sector security standards and guidelines applicable to critical infrastructure. The Cybersecurity Framework will also identify areas for improvement that should be addressed through future collaboration with particular sectors and standards-developing organizations. To enable technical innovation and account for organizational differences, the Cybersecurity Framework will provide guidance that is technology neutral and that enables critical infrastructure sectors to benefit from a competitive market for products and services that meet the standards, methodologies, procedures, and processes developed to address cyber risks. The Cybersecurity Framework shall include guidance for measuring the performance of an entity in implementing the Cybersecurity Framework.

(c) The Cybersecurity Framework shall include methodologies to identify and mitigate impacts of the Cybersecurity Framework and associated information security measures or controls on business confidentiality, and to protect individual privacy and civil liberties.

(d) In developing the Cybersecurity Framework, the Director shall engage in an open public review and comment process. The Director shall also consult with the Secretary, the National Security Agency, Sector-Specific Agencies and other interested agencies including OMB, owners and operators of critical infrastructure, and other stakeholders through the consultative process established in section 6 of this order. The Secretary, the Director of National Intelligence, and the heads of other relevant agencies shall provide threat and vulnerability information and technical expertise to inform the development of the Cybersecurity Framework. The Secretary shall provide performance goals for the Cybersecurity Framework informed by work under section 9 of this order.

(e) Within 240 days of the date of this order, the Director shall publish a preliminary version of the Cybersecurity Framework (the "preliminary Framework"). Within 1 year of the date of this order, and after coordination with the Secretary to ensure suitability under section 8 of this order, the Director shall publish a final version of the Cybersecurity Framework (the "final Framework").

(f) Consistent with statutory responsibilities, the Director will ensure the Cybersecurity Framework and related guidance is reviewed and updated as necessary, taking into consideration technological changes, changes in cyber risks, operational feedback from owners and operators of critical infrastructure, experience from the implementation of section 8 of this order, and any other relevant factors.

Sec. 8. Voluntary Critical Infrastructure Cybersecurity Program. (a) The Secretary, in coordination with Sector-Specific Agencies, shall establish a voluntary program to support the adoption of the Cybersecurity Framework by owners and operators of critical infrastructure and any other interested entities (the "Program").

(b) Sector-Specific Agencies, in consultation with the Secretary and other interested agencies, shall coordinate with the Sector Coordinating Councils to review the Cybersecurity Framework and, if necessary, develop implementation guidance or supplemental materials to address sector-specific risks and operating environments.

(c) Sector-Specific Agencies shall report annually to the President, through the Secretary, on the extent to which owners and operators notified under section 9 of this order are participating in the Program.

(d) The Secretary shall coordinate establishment of a set of incentives designed to promote participation in the Program. Within 120 days of the date of this order, the Secretary and the Secretaries of the Treasury and Commerce each shall make recommendations separately to the President, through the Assistant to the President for Homeland Security and Counterterrorism and the Assistant to the President for Economic Affairs, that shall include analysis of the benefits and relative effectiveness of such incentives, and whether the incentives would require legislation or can be provided under existing law and authorities to participants in the Program.

(e) Within 120 days of the date of this order, the Secretary of Defense and the Administrator of General Services, in consultation with the Secretary and the Federal Acquisition Regulatory Council, shall make recommendations to the President, through the Assistant to the President for Homeland Security and Counterterrorism and the Assistant to the President for Economic Affairs, on the feasibility, security benefits, and relative merits of incorporating security standards into acquisition planning and contract administration. The report shall address what steps can be taken to harmonize and make consistent existing procurement requirements related to cybersecurity.

Sec. 9. Identification of Critical Infrastructure at Greatest Risk. (a) Within 150 days of the date of this order, the Secretary shall use a risk-based approach to identify critical infrastructure where a cybersecurity incident could reasonably result in catastrophic regional or national effects on public health or safety, economic security, or national security. In identifying critical infrastructure for this purpose, the Secretary shall use the consultative process established in section 6 of this order and draw upon the expertise of Sector-Specific Agencies. The Secretary shall apply consistent, objective criteria in identifying such critical infrastructure. The Secretary shall not identify any commercial information technology products or consumer information technology services under this section. The Secretary shall review and update the list of identified critical infrastructure under this section on an annual basis, and provide such list to the President, through the Assistant to the President for Homeland Security and Counterterrorism and the Assistant to the President for Economic Affairs.

(b) Heads of Sector-Specific Agencies and other relevant agencies shall provide the Secretary with information necessary to carry out the responsibilities under this section. The Secretary shall develop a process for other relevant stakeholders to submit information to assist in making the identifications required in subsection (a) of this section.

(c) The Secretary, in coordination with Sector-Specific Agencies, shall confidentially notify owners and operators of critical infrastructure identified under subsection (a) of this section that they have been so identified, and ensure identified owners and operators are provided the basis for the determination. The Secretary shall establish a process through which owners and operators of critical infrastructure may submit relevant information and request reconsideration of identifications under subsection (a) of this section.

Sec. 10. Adoption of Framework. (a) Agencies with responsibility for regulating the security of critical infrastructure shall engage in a consultative process with DHS, OMB, and the National Security Staff to review the preliminary Cybersecurity Framework and determine if current cybersecurity regulatory requirements are sufficient given current and projected risks. In making such determination, these agencies shall consider the identification of critical infrastructure required under section 9 of this order. Within 90 days of the publication of the preliminary Framework, these agencies shall submit a report to the President, through the Assistant to the President for Homeland Security and Counterterrorism, the Director of OMB, and the Assistant to the President for Economic Affairs, that states whether or not the agency has clear authority to establish requirements based upon the Cybersecurity Framework to sufficiently address current and projected cyber risks to critical infrastructure, the existing authorities identified, and any additional authority required.

(b) If current regulatory requirements are deemed to be insufficient, within 90 days of publication of the final Framework, agencies identified in subsection (a) of this section shall propose prioritized, risk-based, efficient, and coordinated actions, consistent with Executive Order 12866 of September 30, 1993 (Regulatory Planning and Review), Executive Order 13563 of January 18, 2011 (Improving Regulation and Regulatory Review), and Executive Order 13609 of May 1, 2012 (Promoting International Regulatory Cooperation), to mitigate cyber risk.

(c) Within 2 years after publication of the final Framework, consistent with Executive Order 13563 and Executive Order 13610 of May 10, 2012 (Identifying and Reducing Regulatory Burdens), agencies identified in subsection (a) of this section shall, in consultation with owners and operators of critical infrastructure, report to OMB on any critical infrastructure subject to ineffective, conflicting, or excessively burdensome cybersecurity requirements. This report shall describe efforts made by agencies, and make recommendations for further actions, to minimize or eliminate such requirements.

(d) The Secretary shall coordinate the provision of technical assistance to agencies identified in subsection (a) of this section on the development of their cybersecurity workforce and programs.

(e) Independent regulatory agencies with responsibility for regulating the security of critical infrastructure are encouraged to engage in a consultative process with the Secretary, relevant Sector-Specific Agencies, and other affected parties to consider prioritized actions to mitigate cyber risks for critical infrastructure consistent with their authorities.

Sec. 11. Definitions. (a) "Agency" means any authority of the United States that is an "agency" under 44 U.S.C. 3502(1), other than those considered to be independent regulatory agencies, as defined in 44 U.S.C. 3502(5).

(b) "Critical Infrastructure Partnership Advisory Council" means the council established by DHS under 6 U.S.C. 451 to facilitate effective interaction and coordination of critical infrastructure protection activities among the Federal Government; the private sector; and State, local, territorial, and tribal governments.

(c) "Fair Information Practice Principles" means the eight principles set forth in Appendix A of the National Strategy for Trusted Identities in Cyberspace.

(d) "Independent regulatory agency" has the meaning given the term in 44 U.S.C. 3502(5).

(e) "Sector Coordinating Council" means a private sector coordinating council composed of representatives of owners and operators within a particular sector of critical infrastructure established by the National Infrastructure Protection Plan or any successor.

(f) "Sector-Specific Agency" has the meaning given the term in Presidential Policy Directive-21 of February 12, 2013 (Critical Infrastructure Security and Resilience), or any successor.

Sec. 12. General Provisions. (a) This order shall be implemented consistent with applicable law and subject to the availability of appropriations. Nothing in this order shall be construed to provide an agency with authority for regulating the security of critical infrastructure in addition to or to a greater extent than the authority the agency has under existing law. Nothing in this order shall be construed to alter or limit any authority or responsibility of an agency under existing law.

(b) Nothing in this order shall be construed to impair or otherwise affect the functions of the Director of OMB relating to budgetary, administrative, or legislative proposals.

(c) All actions taken pursuant to this order shall be consistent with requirements and authorities to protect intelligence and law enforcement sources and methods. Nothing in this order shall be interpreted to supersede measures established under authority of law to protect the security and integrity of specific activities and associations that are in direct support of intelligence and law enforcement operations.

(d) This order shall be implemented consistent with U.S. international obligations.

(e) This order is not intended to, and does not, create any right or benefit, substantive or procedural, enforceable at law or in equity by any party against the United States, its departments, agencies, or entities, its officers, employees, or agents, or any other person.

Glossary

Academic dishonesty:intellectual theft

Academic incest: consensual "student-faculty relationships in which both participants are from the same department but not necessarily in a student-teacher relationship" (Skinner et al., 1995, p. 139)

Administrative proceedings:proceedings that are not designed to punish but are designed to control certain future actions

Advance-fee fraud:occurs when financial consultants or other individuals charge fees in advance of helping homeowners address their financial problems

Airbag fraud: when mechanics fraudulently repair airbags and charge customers for repair

Allocution:refers to the part of the trial process where individuals are permitted to address the court prior to sentencing

Alternative sanctions argument: suggests the use of less costly civil and administrative procedures to respond to misconduct

Annuities fraud:when insurance agents misrepresent the types of returns that their clients would get from investing in annuities

Antitrust laws:designed to promote and protect competition among businesses and corporations

Apolitical white-collar crime:situations where politicians get into trouble for doing things that are outside the scope of politics but are violations of the public trust

Appeal to higher loyalties: a neutralization where offenders justify their wrongdoing by suggesting that the misbehavior was done for the good of a larger group

Applied general systems theory:where society is considered to be composed of a number of different types of systems that operate independently and in conjunction with other systems

Appraisal fraud:occurs when appraisers misrepresent the actual value of a home

Archival research: studies that use some form of record (or archive) as a database in the study

Attorney-client privilege: a doctrine that protects confidential information shared by a defendant with attorney

Audits:conducted to identify fraud by financial-fraud or forensic accountants

Auto insurance fraud: when mechanics dupe the insurance company into paying for unnecessary or nonexistent repairs

Automotive sales fraud:a variety of actions, including turning an odometer back, selling unsafe cars, and selling stolen cars

Auto repair fraud: billing for services not provided, unnecessary repairs, airbag fraud, and insurance fraud

Awareness strategies: increasing awareness among employees about various issues related to employee theft

Bait and switch practices:instances when customers are lured into a store with the promise of a sale item that does not exist or is not available in an appropriate amount

Bid rigging: occurs when competitors conspire to set specific bids for goods or services they would supply in response to a request for bids; it is also known as collusion

Bid rotation:occurs when competitors take turns submitting the lowest bid on a series of bids

Bid suppression: refers to instances where competitors agree not to submit a bid for a particular job on the understanding that a specific competitor will likely be selected for that job

Billing for nonexistent prescriptions:when pharmacists bill for prescriptions that do not exist

Billing for services not provided:when auto mechanics bill customers for services not provided

Biological theory:explanations of crime that consider the physiological or genetic contributions toward crime

Boundary maintenance: individuals learn the rules of the workplace when some individuals are caught breaking those rules

Breach:term used to describe unauthorized access into computer programs or secure computer environments

Breadth of victimization:when one single corporate offense could harm thousands, perhaps millions, of individuals

Broker embezzlement:when brokers take money that is supposed to be in an investment account and use it for their own personal use

Broker fraud: when stockbrokers fail to meet their legal obligations to investors

Builder bailout scheme: occurs when builders offer buyers "excessive incentives" but hide those offers from the mortgage company to make it appear that the property is worth more than it is actually worth

Builder-initiated mortgage fraud: occurs when builders or developers engage in behaviors that are designed to defraud the lender or the buyer

Campaign finance laws:place restrictions on the way political campaigns are financed, with specific attention given to contributions and expenditures

Case records: official records that are housed in an agency that has formal social control duties

Case studies:entails researchers selecting a particular crime, criminal, event, or other phenomena and studying features surrounding the causes and consequences of those phenomena

Celebrity bashing:refers to instances where celebrity offenders are attacked by inmates seeking fame and notoriety

Censure: when officials may withdraw support or withhold information

Character witnesses: individuals who share information about the defendant that demonstrates that it is not like the defendant's character to engage in wrongdoing

Chunking:occurs when investors buy several properties without telling the bank about the properties other than the one the bank is financing

Churning: excessive selling of the same property for the purpose of generating fees and commissions

Civil justice system:the system of justice where individuals seek recourse for offenses by way of a civil lawsuit

Civil proceedings: occur when an individual or government representative, referred to as a plaintiff, files civil charges against an individual or business

Class action lawsuits: used to address corporate wrongdoing; it refers to situations in which a group of victims jointly sue a business or corporation for the harm caused by the corporation

Class bias: refers to bias implicit throughout the entire judicial processing of white-collar cases that includes the hiring of high powered defense attorneys, the complacency of criminal justice officials adjudicating the cases, the disparate treatment of corporations, and inadequate laws that all work to protect the powerful and weaken the minority

Client-oriented defense: occurs when the client is the one directing how the attorney is defending the case

Collective embezzlement: occurs when a crime is committed by the organization against the organization

Commodities: raw materials such as natural gas, oil, gold, agricultural products, and other tangible products sold in bulk form

Commodities fraud: the "fraudulent sale of commodities investments" (Federal Bureau of Investigation [FBI], 2009b)

Community-based sanctions: refer to instances where offenders are sentenced to probation or parole after their incarceration

Community integration: situation in which groups of individuals who otherwise would not have become acquainted with one another come together in their response to white-collar crime

Community service: refers to situations where offenders are told to perform a certain number of hours or days of service for the community

Compensatory damages: awards made to plaintiffs that the defendants are ordered to pay in order to compensate victims for their victimization experience

Complementary bidding: occurs when competitors submit bids with artificially high estimates or specific demands that cannot be met so that a specific competitor with a lower price or without the demands is awarded a contract

Compliance program: "organizational system aimed at comprehensively detecting and preventing corporate criminality" (Goldsmith & King, 1997, p. 9)

Comprehensive Environmental Response Compensation and Liability Act: also known as the Superfund Act, it was passed in 1980 to fund the cleanup of earlier environmental damage

Computer crime: a range of computer-related behaviors that are criminally illegal or otherwise harmful

Conceptual ambiguity: vaguely and loosely defined terms

Condemnation of condemners: a neutralization where offenders blame the criminal justice and social control systems for their misdeeds

Conflict theorists: focus on the way that those with power exert influence in order to use the law to their advantage as an instrument of power

Conspiracy appraisal fraud: occurs when appraisers work with other offenders as part of broader mortgage schemes

Contract lawsuits: refer to allegations between buyers and sellers and/or lenders and borrowers that involve fraud, employment discrimination, tortious interference, or allegations of unfulfilled agreements

Control theory: suggests that individuals' bonds to society keep them from engaging in criminal behavior

Cooperating witnesses: refers to witnesses who are cooperating with the prosecution as a result of some involvement they had in the case

Co-pay waivers: when providers waive the patient's co-pay but still bill the insurance company

Corporate crime: illegal behavior that is committed by employees of a corporation to benefit the corporation, company, or business

Corporate crime liability: occurs when a corporation is held liable and criminally prosecuted

Corporate system: businesses and corporations that carry out business activity as part of our capitalist society

Counterfeiting software crimes: when individuals make counterfeit copies of particular software programs

Coupon stuffing: when retail employees steal coupons and use them later

Crackers: individuals who crack into computer systems "with [the intent] to sabotage and cause chaos to [the] corporation" (Wiggins, 2002, p. 20)

Credits for nonexistent returns: when employees give credit for returns to collaborators

Crime: "an intentional act or omission committed in violation of criminal law without defense or justification and sanctioned by the state as a felony or misdemeanor" (Tappan, 1960, p. 10)

Crime Victims Rights Act: permits victims of all types of federal offenses to participate in the allocation process

Criminal fines: monetary penalty awarded by the judge after an offender has been convicted of a crime

Criminal justice system: the system of justice that handles violations of the criminal law

Criminaloid concept: engaging in harmful acts behind a mask of respectability

Criminal proceedings: occur when criminal charges are filed against the defendant; sanctions could include imprisonment, fines, probation, community service, and restitution

Critical infrastructure: refers to public services provided that society needs on a daily basis, including water, electricity, banking, and so on.

Culpable conduct: not quite intent but includes a history of misconduct, deliberate misconduct, concealing misconduct, tampering with monitoring equipment, and practicing business without a license

Damage control argument: orientation that emphasizes the importance restoring the public's confidence by means of public prosecutions

Deceptive sales: illicit sales practices that are driven by corporate policies and directives

Deferred prosecution agreement (DPA): refers to instances where the prosecutor agrees not to prosecute the corporation if the corporation agrees to certain conditions to be completed over a probationary period

Defiance: when officials block any efforts toward change

Definitions socially constructed by businesses: behaviors defined by a particular company or business as improper

Deflated appraisal fraud: occurs when appraisers underestimate the value of the home in order to force the seller to lower the home's price

Delivery of a controlled substance: when the pharmacist wrongfully provides a controlled substance to a customer

Denial of responsibility: refers to situations where offenders neutralize their behaviors by suggesting that they are not responsible for their misconduct

Denial of victim: refers to situations where offenders convince themselves that victims deserve the harm they experience

Determinism: behavior is caused or influenced by preceding events or factors

Deterrence theory: based on the assumption that punishment can stop individuals from offending if it is certain, swift, and severe

Deviant misuse of the justice process: refers to situations where offenders misuse the justice process in a way that gains them some sort of advantage

Differential association theory: assumes individuals learn to commit crime from their peers through a process in which they learn how to commit crimes, why to commit those crimes, and why laws restricting those crimes are inappropriate

Discovery-oriented defense: a particular defense strategy dictated by the characteristics of the charges, with no set formula used to respond to the cases

Disintegrative shaming: focuses on the bad act and embarrasses offenders, causes anger, and potentially leads to additional harm

Double billing: when two or more parties are billed for the same procedure or service

Dual settlement statements fraud: occurs when settlement agents send a settlement statement with a higher price to the bank and a different statement with the actual sales price to the seller

Due diligence defense: argues that the corporation did everything it could do, in good faith, to abide by the law

Economic system: the system that drives our economy

Educational system: where white-collar careers typically develop because this system provides opportunities to increase the understanding of white-collar crime

Elder abuse: "any criminal, physical, or emotional harm or unethical taking advantage that negatively affects the physical, financial, or general well being of an elderly person" (Payne, Berg, & Byars, 1999, p. 81)

Elder financial abuse: when workers steal money or property from older persons in their care

Elder neglect: when workers fail to provide the appropriate level of care required by the patient

Elder physical abuse: instances where workers hit, slap, kick, or otherwise physically harm an older person for whom they are being paid to provide care

Elder sexual abuse: when workers have inappropriate and harmful sexual contact with older persons in their care

Election law violations: situations where political officials violate rules guiding the way that elections are supposed to be conducted

Electronic and software piracy: the theft of copyright-protected electronic information, including software, electronic programs, and electronic files such as movies and music

Embezzlement: when employees steal money from an account to which they have access

Emotional consequences: experiences such as stress, violation of trust, and damage of public morale that victims of white-collar crime and all members of society are exposed to

Empirical ambiguity: refers to confusion regarding ways to measure white-collar crime in research studies.

Enemy civilian social system crimes: crimes against residents of countries in which the U.S. military is fighting

Entertainment service system: settings where customers consume or purchase various forms of services designed at least partially for entertainment or pleasure

Environmental Protection Agency (EPA): enforces criminal and civil laws as an agency aiming to protect public health and deter future misconduct as well as to facilitate fund generation and cost savings

Environmental racism: a term used to describe the heightened risk of victimization for minorities

Environmental state crime: refers to criminal or deviant behaviors by a governmental representative(s) that result in individuals and/or the environment being harmed by pollutants and chemicals

Equity fraud: occurs when the investor does not pay the equity loan or the mortgage, resulting in the homeowner losing his or her home to foreclosure; or it occurs when offenders steal the equity of a home by forging a homeowner's signature on equity loan forms and then directing the funds from the equity loan to the offenders' bank account

Equity skimming: occurs when investors persuade financially distressed homeowners to use their home equity to "hire" the investor to buy the home, or part of the home, from the homeowner and rent it back to the homeowner

Experimental group: the group that receives the independent variable (or the treatment)

Experiments: studies in which researchers examine how the presence of one variable produces an outcome

Expert witnesses: witnesses who share their professional insight and interpretation of the evidence used in a case

Exploitation: refers to situations where businesses take advantage of their workers

External audits: refers to audits conducted by consultants hired by the corporation

External whistleblowers: term for individuals who share damaging information regarding their employer with outside organizations such as law enforcement agencies or the media.

Extra-occupational crimes: crimes committed against the American civilian social system

Faculty double billing: when professors bill multiple sources for the same effort of work or reimbursement

Faculty embezzlement: when faculty members or college or university staffers steal funds from an account to which they have access

Failure to report: when workers in the health care field fail to report suspected cases of abuse

False advertising: occurs when businesses make inaccurate statements about their products or services in order to facilitate the sale of those items or services

False Claims Act and False Statements Act: govern against the submission of fraudulent claims or bills for services; these acts guard against situations where individuals try to defraud the government

Falsifying account information: when agents or brokers change account information without the client's knowledge

Falsifying records: when providers change medical forms in an effort to be reimbursed from the insurance provider

Fear mongering: when officials create fear to "overshadow" real issues

Federal Water Pollution Control Act: requires companies to self-disclose to the EPA instances when they have discharged potentially harmful substances into navigable waters

Field research: strategies where researchers enter a particular setting to gather data through their observations

Financial Crimes Section (FCS): the entity, or group, located in the FBI's Criminal Investigative Division that investigates cases of white-collar crime

Flipping: occurs when scammers buy and resell properties with inflated prices

Foreclosure rescue scams: various illicit activities that use impending foreclosures or a homeowner's financial distress as an element of the offense

Foreign exchange fraud: when brokers or other officials persuade "victims to invest in the foreign currency exchange market" (FBI, 2009b) through illegitimate and fraudulent practices

Foreign friendly civilian crimes: crimes committed against citizens of another country

Forensic accountants: review financial records and work schedules, read e-mail messages, interview workers and bosses, gather and review other available evidence, and develop a report detailing their conclusions about the presence of fraud in a business

Fraud: efforts to steal money from individuals through deceit.

Fraud audits: identify control mechanisms and weaknesses in a business that place the business at risk for fraud and identify those with access who have taken advantage of the weaknesses

Fraud-for-housing: occurs when borrowers lie about their qualifying information in order to secure a mortgage so they can purchase a home

Fraud-for-profit: occurs when offenders commit the fraud in order to reap a monetary benefit from the mortgage transaction

Fraudulent loan origination: scams where professionals help buyers qualify for loans for which the buyers are not actually qualified

Front running: when "a broker takes advantage of the special knowledge about a pending custom order and trades on his or her own account before executing that order" (Schlegel, 1993, p. 63)

Futures contracts: "agreement[s] to buy or sell a given unit of a commodity at some future date" (Schlegel, 1993, p. 60)

Futures trading fraud: fraud occurring in the trading of futures contracts and options on the futures trading market

Ganging: situations where providers bill for multiple family members, though they treat only one of them

Gender harassment: sexist remarks and behavior

General deterrence: suggests that offenders should be punished in order to keep other potential offenders from engaging in misconduct

General strain theory: a sociopsychological approach to explaining how crime is an adaptation to stress and frustration

Generic drug substitution: when pharmacists give the customer a generic drug but bill the insurance company for the more expensive brand-name drug

Ghostwriting: situations where professors or researchers have their work written by someone else, but only the professor's name appears on the work

Good faith defense: argues that the defendant lacked knowledge and intent and therefore did not know the crime was being committed

Government definitions: illegal acts characterized by deceit, concealment, or violation of trust that are not dependent on the application or threat of physical force or violence; individuals and organizations commit these acts to obtain money, property, or services or to secure personal or business advantage

Government witnesses: the category of witnesses that includes police officers, investigators, auditors, and other officials who developed a case as part of the investigation process

Grades for sex: where professors use the power of grading to solicit sexual favors from students

Group boycotts: situations where competitors agree not to do business with specific customers or clients

Harmful consumer products: goods that enter the marketplace that cause significant harm to consumers

Harmful treatment of consumers: refers to situations where businesses either intentionally or unintentionally put consumers who are using their services at risk of harm

Health Insurance Portability Act of 1996: made health care fraud a federal offense, with penalties ranging from 10 years to life in prison

Hedge fund fraud: fraudulent acts perpetrated in hedge fund systems

Hedge fund systems: "private investment partnership . . . [with] high net worth clients" (FBI, 2009b)

High-yield investment schemes: promise investors low risk or even no risk investment strategies when in fact the funds are not actually invested

Home health care: where the provision of health care services occurs at the patient's home

Home improvement scams: occur when agents or investors conceal problems with homes that should be disclosed to potential buyers

Home repair fraud: when contractors and repair persons rip off individuals for various types of repairs or repairs not made

Horizontal price fixing: involves instances where competing businesses conspire to charge prices at a similar level

House arrest: refers to instances where offenders are told that they must be at home either all of the time or when they are not at work, the doctor's office, or a religious service

Ignorance defense: refers to situations where the defendant argues that he or she did not know that the criminal acts were occurring

Illegal dumping: refers to situations where employees or businesses dump products they no longer need in sites that are not recognized as legal dump sites

Illegal emissions: refers to situations where companies or businesses illegally allow pollutants to enter the environment

Illegally buying prescriptions: when a pharmacist buys prescriptions from patients and then bills the insurance company without filling the prescription

Individual economic losses: the losses that individual victims or businesses experience due to white-collar crimes

Inflated appraisals: instances when there is an intentional overestimation of the value of a home in order to allow the home to be sold at an inflated price

Innovators: accept the goal of financial success but replace legitimate means with illegitimate means

Insider trading: when individuals share or steal information that is "material in nature" (Leap, 2007) for future investments

Institutional anomie: occurs because society promotes values related to financial success but fails to promote values that are consistent with using legitimate means to attain financial success

Internal audits: audits conducted by the organization's accounting department

Internal strategies: policies and practices performed within the retail setting in an effort to prevent employee theft

Internal whistleblowers: individuals who share information with officials within the organization where the employee works, often reporting the misconduct to the company's security program

International environmental crimes: environmental offenses that cross borders of at least two different countries or occur in internationally protected areas

Internet crimes: a range of offenses committed through the use of the Internet

Internet piracy: stealing software, music, videos, or other copyright protected material through the Internet.

Inter-occupational crimes: phrase Bryant (1979) uses to describe situations where members of the military criminally victimize the enemy

Intra-occupational crimes: phrase Bryant (1979) uses to describe instances where military officials commit criminal acts against the American military system

Investment fraud: when investments made by consumers are managed or influenced fraudulently by stockbrokers or other officials in the economic system

Iran-Contra affair: occurred in the mid-1980s when U.S. political officials authorized the sale of weapons to Iran as a part of covert efforts to trade arms for hostages

Isolated occurrence defense: argues that the misconduct was a rare event done by a single employee and not part of any systematic criminal activity

Jailstripe crimes: a term for criminal acts that offenders commit while incarcerated

Just deserts: a punishment orientation that suggests that offenders should be punished for one primary reason, because they deserve it

Kickbacks: when providers direct patients to other providers in exchange for pecuniary response from the other provider

Knowing endangerment: refers to situations where individuals or businesses intentionally mishandle hazardous wastes or pollutants that pose risks to their workers or to community members

Labeling theory: focuses on the way that individuals develop criminal labels; it suggests that the act of labeling individuals can result in behaviors consistent with those labels

Lack of fraudulent intent defense: argues that the defendant did not intend to commit a criminal act

Lay witnesses: individuals who have some relevant information to share about the white-collar crime case based on something they saw or experienced

Learning theory: body of theories that suggest that criminal behavior is learned

Liar loans: situations where investors lie about loans they have or are trying to get

Life course theory: uses a social psychological orientation to identify how events early in one's life course shape experiences later in one's life

Loss prevention strategies: efforts that businesses use to keep employees from stealing from the business

Mail fraud statutes: prohibit the use of the U.S. mail service to commit crimes

Market allocation: when competitors agree to divide markets according to territories, products, goods, or some other service

Market manipulation: situations where executives or other officials do things to artificially inflate trading volume and subsequently affect the price of the commodity or security

Media reports: news articles, press reports, and television depictions of white-collar crimes to help demonstrate what kind of information members of the public receive about white-collar crime and to uncover possible patterns guiding white-collar offenses that may not be studied through other means

Medicaid: a state-level health care program that serves the poor

Medical malpractice: situations where health care providers "accidentally" injure patients while delivering health care

Medical snowballing: when providers bill for several related services, though only one service was provided

Medicare: a federally funded program that serves the elderly population

Medication errors: when health care providers deliver or prescribe the wrong medications to patients

Meeting competition defense: argues that a business's price discriminations were done in good faith in order to stop undesirable actions of a competitor

Misdirection: when officials feign interest but change the subject

Mislabeling of drugs: when pharmacists label drugs incorrectly in an effort to hide that they did not provide the prescription drug to the patient

Misrepresentation: deliberately misinforming the customer about the coverage of an insurance policy

Monetary penalties: include criminal fines, restitution, civil settlements, and compensatory and punitive damages awarded in civil trials

Mortgage fraud: when a real estate or bank representative intentionally provides false information to a financial institution in order to secure a loan

Multiplicity of indictment defense: argues that the offender is being charged for one single offense on several different counts in the indictment

Natural law: behaviors or activities that are defined as wrong because they violate the ethical principles of a particular culture, subculture, or group

Neutralization theory: assumes juveniles understand right from wrong and that before delinquents commit delinquent acts, they neutralize or rationalize their behavior as appropriate

Non-prosecution agreement (NPA): refers to instances where the prosecutor indicates that the prosecution will not occur, based on the corporation's agreement to certain conditions

Objectivity: researchers must be value-free in doing their research

Occupational crime: phrase used by Clinard and Quinney (1973) to describe crimes committed in any type of legal occupation

Occupational system: the system where the bulk of professionals are found

Organizational advantage argument: the explanation for why prosecutors choose not to prosecute that suggests that "organizational structure may serve as a buffer between the white-collar offender and social control mechanisms" (Tillman et al., 1997, p. 55)

Organizational culture strategies: strategies for promoting a sense of organizational culture that inhibits theft

Organizational probation: refers to cases where corporations can be sentenced to a term of probation

Organizational misconduct: refers to instances where laws, rules, or administrative regulations are violated by an individual or group of individuals in an organization that, in its organizational role, acts or fails to act in ways that further the attainment of organizational goals

Overcharging: when employees charge customers more than they should

Over-ordering supplies: when employees order more supplies than are needed and keep the supplies that were not needed

Overtreatment: providing more auto repairs than are actually needed in order to charge more.

Pacification: a form of elder physical abuse where a worker overmedicates an elder

Parallel proceedings: instances where a specific white-collar crime is heard in more than one court simultaneously

Parsimony: researchers and scientists should keep their levels of explanation as simple as possible

Pecuniary-based offenses: misbehaviors that are ultimately done for the economic gain that comes along with the commission of the offenses

Phantom treatment: when providers bill Medicare, Medicaid, or other insurance agencies for services they never provided

Phishing: distribution of a large number of e-mails in an effort to scam someone

Physical harm: injuries victims experience that cause negative physical consequences

Pingponging: when patients are unnecessarily referred to other providers, or "bounced around" to various medical providers

Plausible deniability: when officials conceal actions to make behavior seem appropriate

Plea bargains: a stage of adjudication where the prosecutors decide whether to allow a defendant to plead guilty in exchange for a reduced sentence or some other incentive

Police corruption: when police officers violate the trust they have been given and abuse their law enforcement authority

Police sexual misconduct: "Any behavior by a police officer, whereby an officer takes advantage of his or her unique position in law enforcement to misuse his or her authority and power to commit a sexually violent act or to initiate or respond to some sexually motivated cure for the purpose of personal gratification" (Maher, 2003, p. 355)

Political extortion and bribery: political officials use their power to shape outcomes of various processes

Political system: defines laws and regulations describing all forms of crime

Ponzi schemes: those that scam investors by paying them from future investors' payments into the offender's scheme

Prearranged trading: when "brokers, or brokers and local brokers, first agree on a price and then act out the trade as a piece of fiction in the pit, thereby excluding other potential bidders from the offering" (Schlegel, 1993, p. 63)

Prescription fraud: schemes where pharmacists work with drug addicts to carry out an offense

Presentence reports: reports developed by probation officers that include a wealth of information about offenders, their life histories, their criminal careers, and the sentence they receive

Price discrimination: refers to practices where different prices are charged simply to restrict competition between competitors

Price fixing: occurs when competitors agree on a price at which goods or services should be sold

Price gouging: refers to situations where businesses conspire to set artificially high prices on goods and services

Proactive strategies: refer to situations where the police develop criminal cases in an active way

Process-oriented defense: this refers to instances when the attorneys process these cases the same way, independent of case or offender characteristics

Professional-disciplinary proceedings: proceedings that are administered through the state bar association where professional boards review allegations of wrongdoing

Promissory note fraud: when agents get clients to invest in promissory notes that are scams

Provision of unnecessary services: when health care providers perform and bill for tests or procedures that are not needed

Punitive damages: awarded when the defendant's conduct exceeds the legal criteria for mere or gross negligence

Qualifications fraud: refers to situations where professionals lie about a buyer's qualifications in order to secure a mortgage and allow the buyer to purchase the home

Quasi-experimental designs: studies that mimic experimental methods but lack certain elements of the classical experimental design

Questionable Doctors: a report and database published by the nonprofit group Public Citizen, which collects data on physicians involved in misconduct

Qui tam lawsuits: situations where an individual sues a corporation or company on behalf of the government

Racketeer Influenced and Corrupt Organizations (RICO) Act: found in Title IX of the Organized Crime Control Act; it targets criminal groups by legislating against extortion, violence, and fraud

Rational choice theory: considers the limits of human rationality while still considering humans as rational; it suggests that offenders will consider the benefits of offending and weigh those benefits against possible negative consequences that arise from misconduct

Reactive strategies: situations where the police respond to reports of criminal incidents

Real estate agent and/or investor fraud: a variety of scams committed by agents and investors, including home improvement scams, fraudulent loan origination, chunking, liar loans, and churning

Ransomware: type of virus that freezes a computer's operations and asks the owner to pay a ransom

Rebels: workers who reject the goals and means of society and replace the societal-prescribed goals and means with their own goals and means

Record reviews: occur when white-collar crime investigators review an assortment of records such as financial records, banking records, sales records, e-mail correspondence, phone records, property deeds, loan applications, and any other records that are relevant to the case under investigation

Recreational path: when pharmacists initially begin using illegal street drugs and then expand their drug use to include prescription drugs once they enter pharmacy training

Redirection: When officials feign interest but change the subject

Regulatory agencies: governmental agencies responsible for making sure that regulations are followed in industries and businesses across the United States; these exist to make sure that businesses and their workers are abiding by laws and regulations

Regulatory system: consists of local, state, and federal agencies charged with regulating various businesses

Rehabilitation: a philosophy of punishment that suggests that offenders are brought into the justice process so that the government can play a role in treating whatever issues the offenders have that may have contributed to their wrongdoing

Reintegrative shaming: focuses on the bad act and communicates messages of disapproval that are followed by efforts to reintegrate the offender back into the community

Relativism: where all things are related

Reliance on the advice of counsel defense: legal defense where defendants argue that their attorneys advised them to perform the action in question

Religious system deception: situations where church leaders lie to their congregants in an effort to promote an appearance of "holier than thou"

Relying on self-righteousness: when official minimize allegations

Resale fraud: refers to instances where used items are sold as new

Research definitions: when researchers define white-collar crime through studying and gathering data that allow them to reliably and validly measure the behavior

Research misconduct: a range of behaviors that center on researchers engaging in various forms of wrongdoing during the course of their research

Restitution: a monetary penalty that offenders are ordered to pay to victims for their suffering

Retail system: setting where consumers purchase various types of products

Retaliation: when corporate or business officials target advocates exposing the wrongdoing

Retreatist: a white-collar worker who accepts neither the goals of society nor the means to attain those goals

Retribution: a philosophy of punishment that suggests offenders should be punished to satisfy societal demands

Reverse mortgage fraud: situations where fraudulent activities occur as part of the reverse mortgage transaction

Ritualist: white-collar worker who does not accept the goals of society but goes through the motions of engaging in the means prescribed by society

Robinson-Patman Act: makes price discrimination illegal if it is done to lessen competition

Rogue employee defense: argues that corporate misconduct was the result of an individual employee and not the result of any corporate activities

Rolling over: persuading the customer to cancel an old insurance policy and replace it with a more expensive, "better" policy

Routine activities theory: assumes that crime occurs because of the presence of motivated offenders, the absence of capable guardians, and the availability of suitable targets that all exist at the same time and place

Sales-directed crimes: occur against consumers when agents or brokers steal from consumers by using fraudulent sales tactics

Sales/service system: businesses that sell basic goods and services to customers

Scapegoating: refers to excuses where offenders blame others for their wrongdoing

Seductive behavior: inappropriate sexual advance

Self-control theory: assumes all types of crime are caused by the presence of low self-control

Self-policing: refers to efforts by companies and businesses to develop their own policing responses to white-collar crime

Self-policing audits: refers to audits either done as part of routine procedures or that may be initiated out of concern that fraud is occurring in the organization

Sexual abuse: hands-on offenses where the offender inappropriately touches victims, hands-off offenses such as voyeurism and exhibitionism, and/or harmful genital practices where genital contact is made between the offender and the victim

Sexual bribery: offering rewards for sex

Sexual coercion: threatening punishment to get sex

Sexual contact with students: instances where professors have some form of direct contact of a sexual nature with students in their classes or under their supervision

Sexual harassment: a range of behaviors where employees perform sexually inappropriate actions against their colleagues or consumers

Sexualized behavior: goes beyond comments and includes actual activities of a sexual nature committed by the offending party

Sexualized comments: when individuals make comments to others that are of a sexual nature

Shaming: an alternative sanction strategy that promotes shaming and stigmatization

Sherman Antitrust Act: in general, an act that makes it illegal for competitors to engage in activities that restrict competition

Shortchanging: when employees do not give customers all of their change and pocket the difference

Short counting: when pharmacists dispense fewer pills than prescribed but bill the insurance company as if they had dispensed all of the pills

Short sale fraud: lending institutions allow homes to be sold for amounts that are lower than what the homeowner owed on the home's mortgage

Significant environmental harm: type of harm that includes actual environmental harm, threat of environmental harm, failure to report potentially environmentally harmful activities, and the possibility that the behavior will escalate if it is not handled criminally

Situational crime prevention: refers to strategies that alter features of a specific environment in an effort to prevent offending

Skepticism: the concept that social scientists must question and re-question their findings

Sliding: when agents include insurance coverage that was not requested by the customer

Slumlord: landlords who profit from renting rundown apartments that are not maintained by the property owner

Smoking gun: indisputable evidence that substantiates that a crime has been committed

Social change: occurs because those who survive white-collar crime victimization become stronger

Social disorganization theory: suggests that a neighborhood's crime rate is shaped by the ability of its members to agree on and work toward a common goal, such as crime control

Social harm: workplace behaviors that might not be illegal or deviant but might actually create forms of harm for various individuals

Social services system: the numerous agencies involved in providing services to members of the public

Social system: a setting where individuals have various needs fulfilled and learn how to do certain things, as well as why to do those things

Societal economic losses: the total amount of losses incurred by society from white-collar crime

Software crimes: situations that arise when computer software is central to the offense

Specific deterrence: suggests that punishment should occur in order to stop the punished offender from engaging in future wrongdoing

Stacking: persuading persons to buy more insurance policies than are needed

State crime: situations where governments, or their representatives, commit crime on behalf of the government

State-corporate crime: crimes and misconduct committed by employees of government agencies

Strain theory: traces the source of strain to interactions between the social and economic structures; it assumes strain is caused by the failure to achieve economically valued goals

Straw buyer fraud: individuals who do not plan on living in or even owning a house purchase it and then deed over the home to the person who will live there

Subcontracting: when competitors hire one another on subcontracts after the winning bid has been selected

Substitute providers: employees who perform medical services though they are not authorized to do so

Sweetheart deals: when employees give friends and family members unauthorized discounts

Switching: when a salesperson switches the customer's policy so that the coverage and the premiums are different from what the victim was told

System capacity argument: explanation for why prosecutors do not prosecute that points to the difficulties officials face in responding to these crimes

Systems theory: assumes all systems are interrelated and focuses on the interconnections between various societal systems and the way that various systems influence white-collar wrongdoing

Technological strategies: the use of various forms of technology to prevent employee theft in retail settings

Technological system: societal system that includes structures and agencies involved in developing and promoting technology

Textbook fraud: when faculty members sell complimentary textbooks that they received from publishers to book dealers who resell the books

Theft crimes against consumers: occur when workers or employers steal directly from clients or customers

Theft of credit card information: when employees steal a customer's credit card information

Theft of goods: when employees steal the items the retail setting is trying to sell

Theft of money from the cash register: when employees take money out of the register

Theft of production supplies and raw materials: when employees steal items used to produce goods for retail settings

Theft of software: when workers steal computer software that their company owns and use it for their own purposes

Tort lawsuit: refers to situations where someone claims loss, injury, or damage from the negligence or intent of another

Unauthorized access: when individuals break into various computer databases to which they do not have legitimate access

Unbundling: when providers bill separately for tests and procedures that are supposed to be billed as a single procedure

Undertreatment: providing fewer services than should be provided in auto repairs.

Unfair labor practices: corporate violations where workers are subjected to unethical treatment by their bosses and corporate leaders

Uniform Residential Landlord and Tenant Act (URLTA): a federal law stipulating that homes must be habitable, up to code, safe, and capable of providing the necessary utilities

Unnecessary auto repairs: when mechanics perform repairs that were not necessary and bill the customer for those services

U.S. Sentencing Commission: the entity responsible for developing strategies for promoting fairer sentencing at the federal level through the development of sentencing guidelines

Vertical price fixing: refers to situations where parties from different levels of the production and distribution chain agree to set prices

Viatical settlement fraud: when insurance agents conceal information on viatical settlement policies, allowing individuals to invest in other people's life insurance policies

Victimization surveys: surveys that sample residents and estimate the extent of victimization from the survey findings

Violations of criminal law: white-collar crimes defined as criminally illegal behaviors committed by upper-class individuals during the course of their occupation

Violations of regulatory law: workplace misdeeds that might not violate criminal or civil laws but that violate a particular occupation's laws

Violations of trust: when white-collar offenders use their positions of trust to promote misconduct

Virus: type of computer program or software that is designed to harm a computer system.

Warning light syndrome: outbreaks of white-collar crime that could potentially send a message to

individuals, businesses, or communities that something is wrong in a particular workplace system

Whistleblowers: individuals who notify authorities about wrongdoing in their organization

White-collar crime: any violations of criminal, civil, or regulatory law—or deviant, harmful, or unethical actions—committed during the course of employment in various occupational systems

White-collar crime victims: individuals, businesses, nongovernmental institutions, or the "government as a buyer, giver, and protector-gatekeeper" (Edelhertz, 1983, p. 117)

White-collar environmental crimes: situations where individuals or businesses illegally pollute or destroy the environment as part of an occupational activity

White-collar gangs: a gang is "a self-formed association of peers, bound together by mutual interests, with identifiable leadership, well-developed lines of authority, and other organizational features, who act in concert to achieve a specific purpose or purposes which generally include the conduct of illegal activity and control over a particular territory, facility, or type of enterprise" (Miller, 1975, p. 121); the phrase *white-collar gang* suggests that white-collar workers often commit their crimes in groups

White-collar undercover investigations: typically occur when white-collar crime investigators already have evidence of wrongdoing by the suspect or the corporation

Windshield appraisal fraud: occurs when appraisers fail to even go into the home to determine its value; the home's value is determined by appraisers looking through the windshield of their automobile

Withdrawal from conspiracy defense: used in antitrust offenses to argue that the defendant withdrew his or her involvement from the misconduct before the illegal actions occurred

Workplace deviance: broader definition of white-collar crime that includes all of those workplace acts that violate the norms or standards of the workplace, regardless of whether they are formally defined as illegal

Workplace interview: conducted in internal investigations to gather information about any wrongdoing

Workplace-disciplinary proceedings: allegations of wrongdoing reviewed through a company's equal opportunity office or human resources department

Worm: virus that spreads through computer networks

References

Abel, W. (2009). Agents, Trojans and tags: The next generation of investigators. *International Review of Law, Computers & Technology, 23*(1-2), 99–108.

Abramo, G., D'Angelo, C. A., & Murgia, G. (2013). Gender differences in research collaboration. *Journal of Infometrics, 3*, 811–822.

Accused dentist claims breast rubs appropriate. (2007, October 16). *MSNBC.com*. Retrieved July 30, 2011, from http://www.msnbc.msn.com/id/21325760/wid/11915773?GT1=10514

Ackerman, J. (2001, January 16). Massachusetts regulators take action against two securities dealers. *The Boston Globe*. Available from http://www.boston.com/news/special/archives/

Ackman, D. (2001). Tire trouble. *Forbes.com*. Retrieved July 30, 2011, from http://www.forbes.com/2001/06/20/tireindex.html

Adam, A. J. (2008, July 15). Fidelity investments life insurance—Fraud big time variable annuities—The gimmick—Targeting the seniors. *U.S. Securities and Exchange Commission*. Retrieved July 21, 2011, from http://www.sec.gov/comments/s7-14-08/s71408-306.htm

Adams, B., & Guyette, J. E. (2009, March). Dummy proof. *Automotive Body Repair News, 48*(3), p. 56.

Adams, K. (2009, July 2). Notorious white collar criminals: Where are they now? *Financial Edge*. Retrieved January 19, 2011, from http://financialedge.investopedia.com/financial-edge/0709/Notorious-White-Collar-Criminals-Where-Are-They-Now.aspx

Adams, M. (2010, May 8). Is Gulf oil rig disaster far worse than we're being told? *NaturalNews.com*. Retrieved August 10, 2010, from http://www.naturalnews.com/028749_Gulf_of_Mexico_oil_spill.html

Aeilts, T. (2005, January). Defending against cybercrime and terrorism: A new role for universities. *FBI Law Enforcement Bulletin. 74*(1), 14–20.

Agnew, R. (1985). A revised strain theory of delinquency. *Social Forces, 64*, 151–167.

Agnew, R. (1992). Foundation for a general strain theory of crime and delinquency. *Criminology, 30*, 47–88.

Alaimo, C. A. (2015, April 27). Longtime UA prof faces 10 felony charges. *Arizona Daily Star*. Retrieved December 27, 2015 from http://ssrn.com/abstract=2163644

Albanese, J. S. (1984). Corporate criminology: Explaining deviance of business and political organizations. *Journal of Criminal Justice, 12*, 11–19.

Albonetti, C. A. (1999). The avoidance of punishment: A legal-bureaucratic model of suspended sentencing in federal white-collar cases prior to federal sentencing guidelines. *Social Forces, 78*(1), 303–329.

Albrecht, W. S., & Searcy, D. J. (2001). Top 10 reasons why fraud is increasing in the U.S. *Strategic Finance, 82*, 58.

Albright, M. (2007, December 8). Retail thieves these days are often technically savvy and organized. *McClatchy-Tribune Business News*.

Allen, K. G. (2015, June). Retailers estimate shoplifting, incidents of fraud cost $44 billion in 2014. *National Retail Federation*. Retrieved October 28, 2015 from https://nrf.com/media/press-releases/retailers-estimate-shoplifting-incidents-of-fraud-cost-44-billion-2014

Allen, R. (2015, July 10). Cancer doc patients say 45 years in prison is not enough. *Detroit Free Press*. Retrieved January 4, 2016 from http://www.freep.com/story/news/local/michigan/oakland/2015/07/10/fata-sentence-handed-down/29952245/

Alschuler, A. W. (1972). Courtroom misconduct by prosecutors and trial judges. *Texas Law Review, 50*(4), 629–667.

Altschuler, M., Creekpaum, J. K., & Fang, J. (2008). Health care fraud. *American Criminal Law Review, 45*(2), 607–664.

Aluede, O., Omoregie, E. O., & Osa-Edoh, G. I. (2006). Academic dishonesty as a contemporary problem in higher education: How academic advisers can help. *Reading Improvement, 43*(2), 97–106.

Alvesalo, A. (2003). Economic crime investigators at work. *Policing and Society, 13*(2), 115–138.

Alvesalo, A., & Whyte, D. (2007). Eyes wide shut: The police investigation of safety crimes. *Crime, Law, and Social Change, 48*, 57–72.

Anderman, E. M., Cupp, P. K., & Lane, D. (2010). Impulsivity and academic cheating. *Journal of Experimental Education, 78*, 135–150.

Anderson, C. (2010, January 2). '09, the year of the Ponzi scam; schemes that collapsed quadrupled this year; investors lost $16.5 B., not counting Madoff case. *Newsday*, p. A27.

Anderson, G., Hussey, P., Frogner, B., & Waters, H. (2005). Health spending in the United States and the rest of the industrialized world. *Health Affairs, 24*, 903–914.

Anderson, J. (2015, December 21). Employee theft is popular but not inevitable. *Portland Tribune*. Retrieved January 1, 2016 from http://www.pamplinmedia.com/pt/239-business/286186-161176-employee-theft-is-popular-but-not-inevitable

Anderson, J. C. (2010, June 18). Arizona mortgage-fraud prosecutions. Retrieved June 21, 2010, from http://www.azcentral.com/12news/news/articles/2010/06/18/20100618arizona-mortgage-fraud-indictments.html

Anderson, K. (2010, September 10). More harsh criticism of EPA at D.C. forum. *Brownfield AG News for America*. Retrieved November 29, 2015 from http://brownfieldagnews.com/index.php?s=More+harsh+criticism+of+EPA+at+D.C.+forum

Anderson, K. B. (2013, April). *Consumer fraud in the United States: The third FTC survey*. Washington, DC: Government Printing Office. Retrieved October 28, 2015 from https://www.ftc.gov/sites/default/files/documents/reports/consumer-fraud-united-states-2011-third-ftc-survey/130419fraudsurvey_0.pdf

Anderson, T. (2007, October). Retail workers don't plan thefts. *Security Management, 51*(10), p. 38.

Andsager, J., Bailey, J. L., & Nagy, J. (1997). Sexual advances as manifestations of power in graduate programs. *Journalism & Mass Communication Educator, 52*(2), 33–42.

Angel, J., & McCabe, D. M. (2009). The ethics of speculation. *Journal of Business Ethics, 90*, 277–286.

Anonymous. (1991). Sexual harassment: A female counseling student's experience. *Journal of Counseling & Development, 69*(2), 502–506.

Appelbaum, B., Hilzenrath, D., & Paley, A. R. (2008, December 13). "All just one big lie"; Bernard Madoff was a Wall Street whiz with a golden reputation. Investors, including Jewish charities, entrusted him with billions. It's gone. *The Washington Post* (Suburban ed.), p. D01.

Appin, R., & O'Connor, C. M. (2003, May 5). Market rises as spectre of corporate fraud fades. *High Yield Report*. Retrieved July 30, 2011, from http://www.highbeam.com/doc/1G1-101171551.html

Argust, C. P., Litvack, D. E., & Martin, B. W. (2010). Racketeer influenced and corrupt organizations. *American Criminal Law Review, 47*(2), 961–1013.

Armstrong, T. A., & Boutwell, B. B. (2012). Low resting heart rate and rational choice: Integrating biological correlates of crime in criminological theories. *Journal of Criminal Justice, 40*, 31–39.

Armsworth, M. (1989). Therapy for incest survivors. *Child Abuse and Neglect, 13*, 549–562.

Arnold, B. L., & Hagan, J. (1992). Careers of misconduct: The structure of prosecuted professional deviance among lawyers. *American Sociological Review, 57*(6), 771–780.

Atkeson, L. R., Alvarez, R. M., Hall, T. E., & Sinclair, J. Q. (2014). Balancing fraud prevention and electoral participation: Attitudes toward voter identification. *Social Science Quarterly, 95*(5), 1381–1398.

Attorney General Holder announces civil lawsuit regarding Deepwater Horizon oil spill. (2010, December 15). *Justice News*. Retrieved July 29, 2011, from www.justice.gov/iso/opa/ag/speeches/2010/ag-speech-101215.html

Austin, Z., Simpson, S., & Reynen, E. (2005). "The fault lies not in our students, but in ourselves": Academic honesty and moral development in health professions education—Results of a pilot study in Canadian pharmacy. *Teaching in Higher Education, 10*(2), 143–156.

Aycock, E. B., & Hutton, M. F. (2010). Election law violators. *American Criminal Law Review, 47*, 363–400.

Ayers, K., & Frank, J. (1987). Deciding to prosecute white-collar crime: A national survey of state attorneys general. *Justice Quarterly, 4*(3), 425–439.

Baldston, K. (1979). Hooker Chemical's nightmarish pollution record. *Business and Society Review, 30*, 25.

Bancroft, K. X. (2013). Regulating information security in the government contracting industry: Will the rising tide lift all the boats? *American University Law Review, 62*, 1145–1202.

Banerjee, N., & Goodstein, L. (2006, November 5). Church board dismisses pastor for "sexually immoral conduct." *The New York Times*. Retrieved July 6, 2011, from http://www.nytimes.com/2006/11/05/us/05haggard.html?scp=1&sq=Church%20board%20dismisses%20pastor%20for%20%E2%80%98sexually%20immoral%20conduct&st=cse

Barboza, D., & Lohr, S. (2007, July 25). F.B.I. and Chinese seize $500 million of counterfeit software. *The New York Times*. Retrieved July 30, 2011, from http://www.nytimes.com/2007/07/25/business/worldbusiness/25soft.html

Barker, T. (2002). Ethical police behavior. In K. Lersch (Ed.), *Policing and misconduct* (pp. 1–25). Upper Saddle River, NJ: Prentice Hall.

Barker, T., & Roebuck, J. (1973). *Empirical typology of police corruption—A study in organizational deviance*. Springfield, IL: Charles C Thomas.

Barnard, J. W. (2001). Allocution for victims of economic crimes. *Notre Dame Law Review, 77*(1), 39–70.

Barnard, J. W. (2002). The SEC's suspension and bar powers in perspective. *Tulane Law Review(76)*, 1253–1273.

Barnard, R. (2009, July 2). Madoff case: Act gives fraud victims a voice. *Richmond Times-Dispatch*. Retrieved November 27, 2015 from http://www2.timesdispatch.com/search/?source=all&query=%22madoff+case%3A+act+gives+fraud+victims+a+voice%22

Barnes, W., & Kozar, J. M. (2008). The exploitation of pregnant workers in apparel production. *Journal of Fashion Marketing and Management, 12*, 285–293.

Barnett, C. (n. d.). The measurement of white-collar crime using uniform crime reporting (UCR) data. Federal Bureau of Investigation, U.S. Department of Justice. Retrieved from http://www.fbi.gov/about-us/cjis/ucr/nibrs/nibrs_wcc.pdf

Barnett, H. (1999). The land ethic and environmental crime. *Criminal Justice Policy Review, 10*(2), 161–191.

Barnett, H. C. (1981). Corporate capitalism, corporate crime. *Crime and Delinquency, 27*(1), 4–23.

Barnett, H. C. (1993). Crimes against the environment: Superfund enforcement at last. *Annals of the American Academy of Political and Social Science, 525*, 119–133.

Barrows, C. W., & Powers, T. (2009). *Introduction to management in the hospitality industry* (9th ed.). Hoboken, NJ: Wiley.

Bartels, J. (2015, July 17). *ASU professor Matthew Whitaker accused of plagiarism withdrawing from $268,000 contract with city*. Retrieved January 1, 2016, from http://www.abc15.com/news/region-phoenix-metro/central-phoenix/asu-professor-accused-of-plagiarism-withdrawing-from-268000-contract-with-city.

Batabyal, G., & Chowdhury, A. (2015). Curbing corruption, financial development and income inequality. *Progress in Development Studies, 15*(1), 49–72.

Bartolacci, M. R., LeBlanc, L. J., & Podhradsky, A. (2014). Personal denial of service (PDOS) attacks: A discussion and exploration of a new category of cyber crime. *Journal of Digital Forensics, Security and Law, 9*(1), 19–36.

Basken, P. (2009, September 10). Medical "ghostwriting" is still a common practice, study shows. *Chronicle of Higher Education*. Retrieved June 4, 2010, from http://chronicle.com/article/Medical-Ghostwriting-Is-a/48347/

Bassnett, S. (2006, September 29). Hands off my bottom, mister! *The Times Higher Education Supplement*. Retrieved June 7, 2010, from http://www.timeshighereducation.co.uk/story.asp?storyCode=205661&sectioncode=26

Beare, M. (2002). Organized corporate criminality: Tobacco smuggling between Canada and the US. *Crime, Law, and Social Change, 37*, 225–243.

Beaver, W. (2012). Fraud in for-profit higher education. *Social Science and Public Policy, 49*, 274–278.

Beccaria, C. (1764). *On crimes and punishment*. The Federalist Papers Project. Retrieved November 20, 2015 from http://www.thefederalistpapers.org/wp-content/uploads/2013/01/Cesare-Beccaria-On-Crimes-and-Punishment.pdf

Beck, D. G. (1981). The Federal Water Pollution Control Act's self-reporting requirement and the privilege against self incrimination: Civil or criminal proceeding and penalties? *United States v. Ward. Brigham Young University Law Review*, (Issue 4), 983–991.

Beck, E. (1979). The Love Canal tragedy. *EPA Journal*. Retrieved December 10, 2010, from http://www.epa.gov/aboutepa/history/topics/lovecanal/01.html

Beck, A., Kerschbamer, R., Qui, J., & Sutter, M. (2013). Car mechanics in the lab: Investigating the behavior of real experts on experimental markets for credence goods. *Working Papers in Economics and Statistics, 2014*(02).

Behrmann, N. (2005, September 19). Collapse of US fund exposes global debt scam: Bayou seen caught in fraudsters' trap while trying to recoup losses. *The Business Times Singapore*. Retrieved June 1, 2010, from http://www.aussiestockforums.com/forums/archive/index.php/t-1993.html

Belser, A. (2008, January 1). Be careful with thieving workers. *Pittsburgh Post-Gazette*. Retrieved March 2, 2010, from http://www.postgazette.com/pg/08021/850539-28.stm

Bennett, W. F. (2007). Real estate scam emerges. *North County Times*. Retrieved July 6, 2011, from http://www.nctimes.com/news/local/article_897f29dd-0903-53af-bbfc-7029267ac1d3.html

Bensinger, K., & Vartabedian, R. (2009, October 25). New details in crash that prompted Toyota recall. *Los Angeles Times*.

Benson, M. L. (1985a). Denying the guilty mind: Accounting for involvement in a white-collar crime. *Criminology, 23*(4), 583–607.

Benson, M. L. (1985b). White collar offenders under community supervision. *Justice Quarterly, 2*(3), 429–436.

Benson, M. L. (1989). The influence of class position on the formal and informal sanctioning of white-collar offenders. *Sociological Quarterly, 30*(3), 465–479.

Benson, M. L. (1990). Emotions and adjudication: Status degradation among white-collar criminals. *Justice Quarterly, 73*(3), 515–528.

Benson, M. L., & Cullen, F. T. (1988). The special sensitivity of white-collar offenders to prison: A critique and research agenda. *Journal of Criminal Justice, 16*, 207–215.

Benson, M. L., & Cullen, F. T. (1998). *Combating corporate crime: Local prosecutors at work*. Boston, MA: Northeastern University Press.

Benson, M. L., Cullen, F. T., & Maakestad, W. J. (1988). *Local prosecutors and white-collar crime: Final report.* Washington, DC: U.S. Department of Justice, National Institute of Justice.

Benson, M. L., Cullen, F. T., & Maakestad, W. J. (1990). Local prosecutors and corporate crime. *Crime and Delinquency, 36*(3), 356–372.

Benson, M. L., & Kerley, K. (2001). Life course theory and white-collar crime. In H. Pontell & D. Shichor (Eds.), *Contemporary issues in criminology and criminal justice: Essays in honor of Gilbert Geis* (pp. 121–136). Upper Saddle River, NJ: Prentice Hall.

Benson, M. L., & Moore, E. (1992). Are white-collar and common offenders the same? An empirical and theoretical critique of a recently proposed general theory of crime. *Journal of Research in Crime and Delinquency, 29,* 251–272.

Berg, B. L. (2009). *Qualitative research methods for the social sciences* (7th ed.). Boston: Allyn & Bacon.

Berkman, S., Boswell, N. Z., Bruner, F. H., Gough, M., McCormick, J. T., Egens, P., et al. (2008). The fight against corruption: International organizations at a crossroads. *Journal of Financial Crime, 15*(2), 124.

Bernard, T. S. (2010, July 19). Need a mortgage? Don't get pregnant. *The New York Times.* Retrieved November 20, 2015, from http://www.nytimes.com/2010/07/20/your-money/mortgages/20mortgage.html

Bernate, F. P., & Godlove, N. (2012). Understanding 21st century cybercrime for the 'common' victim: Frances P. Benat and Nicholas Godlove argue that it is time to extend the principles of universal justice to the typical types of cyber-offenses. *Criminal Justice Matters, 89*(1), 4–5.

Bertrand, D. (2003, August 14). Auto fixer in scam jam: 6 at shop busted in insure fraud. *New York Daily News,* (Suburban section), p. 1.

Bharara, P. (2007). Cry uncle and their employees cry foul: Rethinking prosecutorial pressure on corporate defendants. *American Criminal Law Review, 44*(1), 53–114.

Bierstedt, R. (1970). *The social order* (3rd ed.). Bombay, India: Tata McGraw-Hill.

Bilimoria, D. (1995). Corporate control, crime, and compensation: An empirical examination. *Human Relations, 48*(8), 891–908.

Bisson, D. (2015, September 1). The Ashley Madison hack-A timeline (updated: 9/10/15*). Tripwire Inc.* Retrieved January 5, 2016 from http://www.tripwire.com/state-of-security/security-data-protection/cyber-security/the-ashley-madison-hack-a-timeline/

Black, A. (2005, October 7). Unnecessary surgery exposed! Why 60% of all surgeries are medically unjustified and how surgeons exploit patients to generate profits. *Health.* Retrieved July 6, 2011, from http://www.naturalnews.com/012291.html

Block, A. A. (1996). American corruption and the decline of the Progressive ethos. *Journal of Law & Society, 23*(1), 18–35.

Bloomquist, L. (2006, December 21). Workers walk off jobs at Days Inn. *Knight Ridder/Tribune Business News,* p. 1.

Blumenstyk, G. (2012, May 29). Attorneys general urge congress to close military 'loophole' at for-profit colleges. *The Chronicle of Higher Education.* Retrieved January 3, 2016 from http://chronicle.com/article/Attorneys-General-Urge/132030/

Boesky, I. (n.d.). A golden opportunity, white-collar crime, Michael Milken, the junk bond king, the symbol of greed. *Law.com* Retrieved from http://law.jrank.org/pages/12165/Boesky-Ivan.html

Bohm, R. M., & Vogel, B. L. (2011). *A primer on crime and delinquency theory* (3rd ed.). Belmont, CA: Wadsworth.

Bolitho, J. (2009, November 2). Two CMU math faculty members violate integrity policy: University returns $619,489 in grant money. *Central Michigan Life.* Retrieved January 29, 2010, from http://www.cm-life.com/2009/11/02/two-cmu-math-faculty-members-violate-integrity-policy-university-returns-619489-in-grant-money/

Bolton, F. (2013). Cybersecurity and emergency management: Encryption and the inability to communicate. *Homeland Security and Emergency Management, 10* (1), 1–7.

Bossler, A. M., & Holt, T. J. (2013). Assessing officer perceptions and support for online community policing. *Security Journal, 26*(4), 349–366.

Botsko, C. A., & Wells, R. C. (1994). Government whistleblowers: Crime's hidden victims. *FBI Law Enforcement Bulletin, 63* (7), 17–21.

Bradley, D. (2008). Real estate fraud. *FBI Law Enforcement Bulletin, 77*(9), 1–4. Retrieved from December 2, 2015, from https://leb.fbi.gov/2008-pdfs/leb-september-2008

Brainard, J. (2008, August 29). Scientists who cheated had mentors who failed to supervise them. *Chronicle of Higher Education.* Retrieved June 4, 2010, from http://chronicle.com/article/Scientists-Who-Cheated-Had/1112

Braithwaite, J. (1982). Challenging just deserts: Punishing white-collar criminals. *Journal of Criminal Law and Criminology, 73*(2), 723–763.

Braithwaite, J. (1989a). *Crime, shame, and reintegration.* New York, NY: Cambridge University Press.

Braithwaite, J. (1991). Poverty, power, white-collar crime and the paradoxes of criminological theory. *Australian and New Zealand Journal of Criminology, 24*(1), 40–48.

Braithwaite, J. (1993). The nursing home industry. In M. H. Tonry & A. J. Reiss (Eds.), *Beyond the law: Crime in complex organizations* (pp. 11–54). Chicago, IL: University of Chicago Press.

Brasner, S. (2010, April 23). In brief: Florida agent hit with fraud charge. *Wall Street Journal Abstracts,* p. 3.

Brawley, O. (2009). Prostate cancer screening: Is this a teachable moment? *Journal of the National Cancer Institute, 101,* 19, 1295–1297.

Bredemeier, K. (2002, May 16). Memo warned of Enron's Calif. strategy: West Coast senators

complain about market manipulation during power crisis. *The Washington Post,* p. A04.

Brickey, K. F. (2006). In Enron's wake: Corporate executives on trial. *Journal of Criminal Law and Criminology, 96*(2), 397–433.

Brenner, S. W. (2006). Cybercrime jurisdiction. *Crime, Law and Social Change, 46,* 189–206.

Brenner, S. W. (2007). "At light speed": Attribution and response to cybercrime/terrorism/warfare. *The Journal of Criminal Law & Criminology, 97*(2), 379–475.

Brickner, D. B., Mahoney, L. S., & Moore, S. J. (2010). Providing an applied-learning exercise in teaching fraud detection: A case of academic partnering with IRS criminal investigation. *Issues in Accounting Education, 25*(4), 695–719.

Brinkley, J. (1994, January 23). The nation: The cover-up that worked: A look back. *The New York Times.* Retrieved July 29, 2011, from http://www.nytimes.com/1994/01/23/weekinreview/the-nation-the-cover-up-that-worked-a-look-back.html?scp=1&sq=The%20nation:%20The%20cover-up%20that%20worked:%20A%20look%20back&st=cse

Broggi, J. J. (2014). Building on executive order 13,363 to encourage information sharing for cybersecurity purposes. *Harvard Journal of Law & Public Policy, 37* (2), 653–676.

Brooks, G., Button, M., & Gee, J. (2012). The scale of health-care fraud: A global evaluation. *Security Journal, 25*(1), 76–87.

Brown, A. C. (2013). *Health effects of particles and black carbon.* Environmental Protection Agency. Retrieved November 6, 2015 from http://www2.epa.gov/sites/production/files/2014-05/documents/health-effects.pdf

Brown, E. (2004, December 12). Can for-profit schools pass an ethics test? *The New York Times.* Retrieved July 6, 2011, from http://query.nytimes.com/gst/fullpage.html?res=9907E3D81131F931A25751C1A9629C8B63&pagewanted=all

Brown, E. (2008, February 20). City throws slumlord in jail (for nine days). *New York Observer,* Retrieved June 29, 2010, from http://www.observer.com/2008/hpd-throws-apparent-slumlord-jail-9-days

Brown, W. (1995, December 9). It's getting tougher. *Thrifty Herald,* p. 21.

Brownlee, M. (2015, October 20). Audit finds more the $230,000 in misspent money in Neola. *The Daily Nonpareil.* Retrieved January 6, 2016 fromhttp://www.nonpareilonline.com/news/local/audit-finds-more-than-in-misspent-money-in-neola/article_0a006b5c-7739-11e5-bfc2-7355134f2cae.html

Bryant, C. (1979). *Khaki-collar crime.* New York, NY: Free Press.

Buckhoff, T., Higgins, L., & Sinclair, D. (2010). A fraud audit: Do you need one? *Journal of Applied Business Research, 26*(5), 29–34.

Bucy, P. H. (1989). Fraud by fright: White collar crime by health care providers. *North Carolina Law Review, 67*, 855–937.

Buell, M., Layman, E., McCampbell, S. W., & Smith, B. V. (2003). Addressing sexual misconduct in community corrections. *Perspectives, 27*(2), 26–37.

Buell, M., & McCampbell, S. W. (2003). Preventing staff misconduct in the community correction setting. *Corrections Today, 65*(1), 90–91.

Burdeau, C. (2010, December 2). Judge: Deal to fix homes with Chinese drywall going well. *Business Week*. Retrieved June 1, 2010, from http://www.businessweek.com/ap/financialnews/D9JS1TIG0.htm

Bureau of Justice Statistics. (2006). *Compendium of federal justice statistics, 2004*. Washington, DC: U.S. Department of Justice.

Bureau of Labor Statistics. (2010, November 9). *Nonfatal occupational injuries and illnesses requiring days away from work, 2009*. [News release, U.S. Department of Labor]. Retrieved February 1, 2011, from http://www.bls.gov/news.release/osh2.nr0.htm.

Bureau of Justice Statistics. (2011a). *State and federal prisoners and prison facilities*. Washington, DC: U.S. Department of Justice.

Bureau of Labor Statistics. (2011b). *2010 nonfatal occupational injuries and illnesses: Private industry, state government, and local government*. Washington, DC: U.S. Department of Labor. Retrieved October 31, 2015 from http://www.bls.gov/iif/oshwc/osh/case/osch0045.pdf

Bureau of Labor Statistics. (2012). *News release: Workplace injuries and illnesses, 2011*. Washington, DC: U.S. Department of Labor. Retrieved October 31, 2015, from http://www.bls.gov/news.release/archives/osh_10252012.pdf

Bureau of Labor Statistics. (2013). *Nonfatal occupational injuries and illnesses requiring days away from work, 2012*. Washington, DC: US Department of Labor. Retrieved October 30, 2015, from http://www.bls.gov/news.release/archives/osh2_11262013.pdf

Bureau of Labor Statistics. (2014). *Nonfatal occupational injuries and illnesses requiring days away from work, 2013*. Washington, DC: US Department of Labor. Retrieved October 30, 2015, from http://www.bls.gov/news.release/osh2.nr0.htm.

Bureau of Labor Statistics. (2015). *Nonfatal occupational injuries and illnesses requiring days away from work, 2014*. Washington, DC: U.S. Department of Labor. Retrieved January 5, 2016, from http://www.bls.gov/news.release/pdf/osh2.pdf

Burns, R. G., & Lynch, M. J. (2004). *Environmental crime: A sourcebook*. New York, NY: LFB Scholarly.

Burns, R. G., & Orrick, L. (2002). Assessing newspaper coverage of corporate violence: The dance hall fire in Goteborg, Sweden. *Critical Criminology, 11*, 137–150.

Burns, S. (2006, May 15). China rocked by "sandpaper" chip fraud. Retrieved July 30, 2011, from http://www.v3.co.uk/vnunet/news/2156106/china-shocked-chip-fraud

Burnstein, J. (2008a, November 19). Man arrested in Delray Beach on remodeling fraud charges; he's already awaiting trial in Broward: Awaiting trial in Broward, he's arrested in Delray Beach over 4 jobs never completed. *Sun Sentinel*, p. 6.

Burnstein, J. (2008b, November 18). Oakland Park man arrested on construction-related theft charges. *Sun Sentinel*, p. 7.

Burton, D., Erdman, E., Hamilton, G., & Muse, K. (1999). *Women in prison: Sexual misconduct by correctional staff* (GAO/GGD-99-104). Washington, DC: U.S. Government Accounting Office.

Byars, K., & Payne, B. K. (2000). Physicians' and medical students' attitudes about Medicaid. *Journal of Health and Human Services Administration, 15*(4), 242–250.

CBSNews.com. (2012, February 1). *Former Penn state professor accused of $3M dollar fraud*. Retrieved January 1, 2016, from http://www.cbsnews.com/news/former-penn-state-professor-accused-of-3m-fraud/

Calavita, K., & Pontell, H. N. (1991). Other people's money revisited: Collective embezzlement in the savings and loan and insurance industries. *Social Problems, 38*, 94–112.

Calavita, K., & Pontell, H. N. (1994). The state and white-collar crime: Saving the savings and loans. *Law & Society Review, 28*(2), 297–324.

Calavita, K., Pontell, H. N., & Tillman, R. H. (1997). *Big money crime: Fraud and politics in the savings and loan crisis*. Berkeley: University of California Press.

California Department of Real Estate. (2009). Advance fees for loan modifications now prohibited. *DRE California*. Retrieved December 1, 2011, from http://www.dre.ca.gov/cons_adv_fees_alert.html

Campbell, J. (2009). Mother of all swindles. *Sunday Herald Sun*, p. 70.

Canada, J., Kuhn, J. R., & Sutton, S. G. (2008). Accidentally in the public interest: The perfect storm that yielded the Sarbanes-Oxley Act. *Critical Perspectives in Accounting, 7*, 987–1003.

Candeub, A. (2013). Transparency in the administrative state. *Houston Law Review, 51*(2), 385–416.

Carden, A. (2008). Beliefs, bias, and regime uncertainty after Hurricane Katrina. *International Journal of Social Economics, 35*(7), 531–545.

Cardinal, C. (2010). Podium politics and the Olympics. *The Vancouver Observer*. Retrieved December 23, 2011, from http://www.vancouverobserver.com/olympics/2010/01/19/podium-politics-and-olympics.

Carlson, D. (2009). Guy who sued Facebook joins Facebook. *Gawker.com*. Retrieved July 6, 2011, from http://gawker.com/5053748/?tag=valleywag

Carlson, N. (2010, May 13). Well, these new Zuckerberg IMs won't help Facebook's privacy problems. Retrieved July 6, 2011, from http://www.businessinsider.com/well-these-new-zuckerberg-ims-wont-help-facebooks-privacy-problems-2010-5#ixzz0rswuPzMH

Carswell, A., Seay, M., & Polanowski, M. (2013). Reverse mortgage fraud against seniors: Recognition and education of a burgeoning problem. *Journal of Housing for the Elderly, 27*(1–2), 146–160.

Carter, D., L., & Katz, A., J. (1996). Computer crime: An emerging challenge for law enforcement. *FBI Law Enforcement Bulletin, 65*(12), 1.

Carter, T. S. (1999). Ascent of the corporate model in environmental-organized crime. *Crime, Law and Social Change, 31* (1), 1–30.

Carucci, D., Overhuls, D., & Soares, N. (2011). Computer crimes. *American Criminal Law Review, 48*, 375–419.

Casten, J. A., & Payne, B. K. (2008). The influence of perceptions of social disorder and victimization on business owners' decisions to use guardianship strategies. *Journal of Criminal Justice, 36*(5), 396–402.

Castillo, F. (2007). *Real estate closing fees kickback fraud*. Retrieved June 22, 2010, from http://ezinearticles.com/?Real-Estate-Closing-Fees-Kickback-Fraud&id=597525

Castleberry, S. B. (2007). Prison field trips: Can white-collar criminals positively affect the ethical and legal behavior of marketing and MBA students? *Journal of Marketing Research, 29*(5), 5–17.

Cauley, L. (2007, August 6). Rigas tells his side of the Adelphia story; on his way to prison, former cable mogul describes the scandal from his point of view. *USA Today*, p. 1B.

Cavender, G., & Miller, K. W. (2013). Corporate crime as trouble: Reporting on the corporate scandals of 2002. *Deviant Behavior, 36*, 916–931.

Centers for Disease Control (CDC). (2009). *Centers for disease Control and Prevention investigation update: Outbreak of* Salmonella typhimurium *infections*. Retrieved July 6, 2011, from http://www.cdc.gov/salmonella/typhimurium/update.html

Center for Disease Control. (2011). CDC Estimates of Foodborne Illness in the United States. Retrieved December 22, 2011, from http://www.cdc.gov/foodborneburden/2011-foodborne-estimates.html.

Center for Medicare and Medicaid Services. (2011). *National health expenditure fact sheet*. Retrieved July 30, 2011, from http://www.cms.gov/NationalHealthExpendData/25_NHE_Fact_Sheet.asp#TopOfPage

Chabinsky, S. (2013, November 5). Top five reasons to report computer intrusions to law enforcement. *Security*, 92. Retrieved December 26, 2015, from http://www.securitymagazine.com/articles/84898-top-5-reasons-to-report-computer-intrusions-to-law-enforcement

Chabinsky, S. (2015, April 1). The top 10 cybersecurity myths, part I. *Security*, 46. Retrieved December 26, 2015, from http://www.securitymagazine.com/articles/86207-the-top-10-cybersecurity-myths-part-1

Chabinsky, S. (2015, May 1). The top 10 cybersecurity myths, part II. *Security*, 26. Retrieved December

26, 2015, from http://www.securitymagazine .com/articles/86326-the-top-10-cybersecurity-myths-part-2

Chang, L. Y. C. (2013). Formal and informal modalities for policing cybercrime across the Taiwan Strait. *Policing & Society, 23*(2), 540–555.

Cheit, R. E., & Davis, Z. R. (2010). Magazine coverage of child sexual abuse. *Journal of Child Abuse, 19*(1), 99–117.

Chien, E., & Kleiner, B. H. (1999). Sex discrimination in hiring. *Equal Opportunities International, 18*(5/6), 32–36.

Chinese goods scare prods regulators. (2007). Oxford Analytica Daily Briefing Service. Retrieved July 6, 2011, from http://www.oxan.com/display.aspx? ItemID=DB137125

Chittum, M. (2003, December 20). USDA to investigate Natural Bridge Zoo bears. *Roanoke Times and World News.* Retrieved July 30, 2011, from http:// www.highbeam.com/doc/1P2-12671138.html

Chong, J. (2007, July 24). Study data at UCLA falsified. *Los Angeles Times.* Retrieved July 30, 2011, from http://articles.latimes.com/2007/jul/24/local/me-researcher24

Clarey, R. L. (1978). Prosecution of consumer fraud—New York's new approach. *Criminal Law Bulletin, 14*(3), 197–202.

Clarke, R. V., & Cornish, D. B. (1985). Modeling offenders' decisions. In M. Tonry & N. Morris (Eds.), *Crime and justice* (vol. 6, pp. 147–185). Chicago, IL: University of Chicago Press.

Clayton, C. (2010). Lincoln calls hearing on EPA impact on farmers. *Progressive Farmer.* Retrieved July 30, 2011, from http://www.dtnprogressive farmer. com/dtnag/view/ag/printablePage.do? ID=BLOG_PRINTABLE_PAGE&bypassCache=tr ue&pageLayout=v4&blogHandle=policy&blogEn tryId=8a82c0bc2a8c8730012b351b985a0825&art icleTitle=Lincoln+Calls+Hearing+on+EPA+Imp act+on+Farmers&editionName=DTNAgFreeSite Online

Clinard, M., & Quinney, R. (1973). *Criminal behavior systems: A typology* (2nd ed.). New York, NY: Holt, Rinehart & Winston.

Clinard, M. B., & Yeager, P. C. (1980). *Corporate crime.* New York, NY: Free Press.

Coburn, N. F. (2006). Corporate investigations. *Journal of Financial Crime, 13*(3), 348–368.

Coffee, J. C. (1980). Corporate crime and punishment: A non-Chicago view of the economics of criminal sanctions. *American Criminal Law Review, 17*(4), 419–476.

Coffey, L. T. (2000, January 23). Beware of door-to-door scams. *St. Petersburg Times,* p. 3H.

Cohen, L. E., & Felson, M. (1979). Social change and crime rate trends: A routine activities approach. *American Sociological Review, 44,* 588–608.

Cohen, M. A. (1989). Corporate crime and punishment: A study of social harm and sentencing practice in the federal courts, 1987–1987. *American Criminal Law Review, 26*(3), 605–660.

Cohen, M. A. (1992). Environmental crime and punishment: Legal/economic theory and empirical evidence on enforcement of federal environmental statutes. *Journal of Criminal Law and Criminology, 82*(4), 1054–1108.

Cohen, T. H. (2005, August). *Federal tort trials and verdicts, 2002–03* (Bureau of Justice Statistics). Washington, DC: Department of Justice.

Cohen, T. H. (2005). *Punitive damage awards in large counties, 2001.* Washington, DC: Bureau of Justice Statistics.

Cohen, T. H. (2009). *Tort bench and jury trials in state courts, 2005.* U.S. Department of Justice. Retrieved July 11, 2011, from http://bjs.ojp.usdoj .gov/content/pub/pdf/tbjtsc05.pdf

Cohen, T. H., & Hughes, K. A. (2007). *Bureau of Justice Statistics special report: Medical malpractice insurance claims in seven states, 2000–2004.* Retrieved July 6, 2011, from http://bjs.ojp.usdoj .gov/content/pub/pdf/mmicss04.pdf

Cole, C., Maroney, P., McCullough, K., & Powell, L. (2015). Automobile insurance vehicle repair practices: Politics, economics, and consumer interests. *Risk Management and Insurance Review, 18*(1), 101–128.

Coleman, J. (1982). *The asymmetric society.* Syracuse, NY: Syracuse University Press.

Coleman, J. (1994). *The criminal elite: The sociology of white-collar crime.* New York, NY: St. Martin's.

Coleman, J. W. (1987). Toward an integrated theory of white-collar crime. *American Journal of Sociology, 93*(2), 406–439.

Collin, B. C. (2001). *The future of cyberterrorism: Where the physical and virtual worlds converge.* 11th Annual International Symposium on Criminal Justice Issues. Retrieved July 29, 2011, from http://afgen.com/terrorism1.html

Collins, J. D., Saintano, V. A., & Khev, D. N. (2011). Organizational data breaches 2005–2010: Applying SCP to the healthcare and education sectors. *International Journal of Cyber Criminology, 5*(1), 794–810.

Collman, A. (2014, September 25). Sociology professor promised me an 'A' in exchange for sex, claims student. *Mailonline.* Retrieved January 1, 2016, from http://www.dailymail.co.uk/news/ article-2769569/We-just-cover-webcam-pull-blinds-University-Delaware-sociology-profes sor-promised-student-A-exchange-oral-sex .html

Colvin, G. (2004, July 26). White-collar crooks have no idea what they're in for. *Fortune Magazine.* Retrieved July 11, 2011, from http://money.cnn .com/magazines/fortune/fortune_archive/ 2004/07/26/377147/index.htm

Commission on Judicial Performance. (2015, December 1). *Judicial performance commission issues decision and order removing judge Valeriano Saucedo from office.* Retrieved January 2, 2016, from http://cjp.ca.gov/res/docs/press_releases/ Saucedo_PR_DO_12-01-15.pdf

Comte, F. (2006). Environmental crime and the police in Europe: A panorama and possible paths for future action. *European Environmental Law Review, 15*(7), 190–231.

Condon, S. (2010, May 3). How much does BP owe for Gulf oil spill? *Political hotsheet. Columbia Broadcasting System (CBS) News.* Retrieved July 6, 2011, from http://www.cbsnews.com/8301-503544_162-20004034-503544.html

Congressman resigns over affair with female aide; "I have sinned." (2010, May 10). *National Post.* Retrieved December 10, 2010, from http://www .nationalpost.com/news/world/story.html? id=3045823

Conley, J. (2007, October 18). Natural Bridge Zoo faces penalties. *Roanoke Times and World News.* Retrieved July 30, 2011, from http://www.roa noke.com/news/roanoke/wb/136282

Consumer Finance Protection Bureau. (n. d.). *About Us.* Available online at http://www.consumer finance.gov/the-bureau/.

Cooper, A. (2009, October 30). Obama rules over false US ads in the Wild West. *Campaign,* p. 19.

Cooper, J. A. (2012). Noble cause corruption as a consequence of role conflict in the police organization. *Policing & Society, 22*(2), 169–184.

Copes, H., & Vieraitis, L. M. (2009). Understanding identity theft: Offenders' accounts of their lives and crimes. *Criminal Justice Review, 33,* 329–349.

Corrado, K. (2015, December 22). Bristol apartment condemned, mayor calls homeowner 'slumlord.' *Fox61.* Retrieved January 3, 2016 from http:// fox61.com/2015/12/22/bristol-apartments-condemned-mayor-calls-homeowner-slumlord/

Cosgrove-Mather, B. (January 7, 2003). New era for white-collar criminals. *CBS News.* Retrieved November 18, 2015 from http://www.cbsnews .com/news/new-era-for-white-collar-criminals/

County of Los Angeles Department of Consumer Affairs. (2010). *False advertising.* Retrieved July 31, 2011, from http://dca.lacounty.gov/tsFalse Advertising.htm

Coutts, H. (2009). Enrollment abuse allegations plague University of Phoenix [Electronic version]. *The Nation.* Retrieved July 6, 2011, from http://www .thenation.com/article/enrollment-abuse-allega tions-plague-university-phoenix

Cox, L. (2010). The "July effect": Worst month for fatal errors, study says. *American Broadcasting Company (ABC) World News.Com.* Retrieved July 6, 2011, from http://abcnews.go.com/WN/Well nessNews/july-month-fatal-hospital-errors-study-finds/story?id=10819652

Coyle, P. (1995). Bench stress. *American Bar Association Journal, 81,* 60–63.

Cramm, P. D. (2009, May 26). The perils of prosecutorial misconduct. *FindLaw.* Retrieved July 6, 2011, from http://knowledgebase.findlaw.com/kb/2009/ May/1208577_1.html

Crawford, K. (June 21, 2005). For Kozlowski, future looks especially grim. *CNN Money.* Retrieved

November 18, 2015, from http://money.cnn.com/2005/06/21/news/newsmakers/prisons_state/

Cressey, D. R. (1953). *Other people's money: A study in the social psychology of embezzlement.* Glencoe, IL: Free Press.

Creswell, J. (2007, May 21). Mortgage fraud is up, but not in their backyards. *The New York Times.* Retrieved July 6, 2011, from http://www.nytimes.com/2007/05/21/business/21fraud.html?scp=1&sq=Mortgage%20fraud%20is%20up,%20but%20not%20in%20their%20backyards.%20&st=cse http://www.nytimes.com

Croall, H. (1989). Who is the white-collar criminal? *British Journal of Criminology, 29*(2), 157–174.

Croall, H. (1993). Business offenders in the criminal justice process. *Crime, Law and Social Change, 20*(4), 359–372.

Crofts, P. (2003). White collar punters: Stealing from the boss to gamble. *Current Issues in Criminal Justice, 15*(1), 40–52.

Crumb, D. J., & Jennings, K. (1998, February). Incidents of patient abuse in health care facilities are becoming more and more commonplace. *Dispute Resolution Journal,* pp. 37–43.

Cullen, F. T., Clark, G. A., Mathers, R. A., & Cullen, J. B. (1983). Public support for punishing white-collar crime: Blaming the victim revisited? *Journal of Criminal Justice, 11,* 481–493.

Cullen, F. T., Link, B. J., & Polanzi, C. W. (1982). The seriousness of crime revisited: Have attitudes toward white-collar crime changed? *Criminology, 20*(1), 83–102.

Cullen, F. T., Maakestad, W. J., & Cavender, G. (1987). *Corporate crime under attack: The Ford Pinto case and beyond.* Cincinnati, OH: Anderson.

Culpepper, D., & Block, W. (2008). Price gouging in the Katrina aftermath: Free markets at work. *International Journal of Social Economics, 35*(7), 512–520.

Curry, P. (2007). *Common forms of mortgage fraud.* Retrieved June 21, 2010, from http://www.bankrate.com/brm/news/real-estate/reminiguide07/mortgage-fraud-most-common-a1.asp

Dabney, D. (1995). Neutralization and deviance in the workplace: Theft of supplies and medicines by hospital nurses. *Deviant Behavior, 16,* 313–331.

Dabney, D. (2001). Onset of illegal use of mind-altering or potentially addictive prescription drugs among pharmacists. *Journal of American Pharmaceutical Association, 41,* 392–400.

Dabney, D., & Hollinger, R. C. (1999). Illicit prescription drug use among pharmacists: Evidence of a paradox of familiarity. *Work and Occupations, 26*(1), 77–106.

Dabney, D., & Hollinger, R. C. (2002). Drugged druggists: The convergence of two criminal career trajectories. *Justice Quarterly, 19*(1), 181–213.

Daly, K. (1989). Gender and varieties of white-collar crime. *Criminology, 27*(4), 769–794.

Danner, M. J. E. (1998). Three strikes and it's *women* who are out: The hidden consequences for women of criminal justice reforms. In S. L. Miller (Ed.), *Crime control and women: Feminist implications of criminal justice policy* (pp. 1–14). Thousand Oaks, CA: Sage.

Danner, P. (2009, July 14). BRIEF: Weston man charged with running $14M commodities fraud [Web log post]. *Fort Lauderdale Criminal Attorneys Blog.* Retrieved July 30, 2011, from http://www.fortlauderdalecriminalattorney_blog.com/2009/07/weston_man_charged_with_operat.html#more

Davies, K. R. (2003, December). Broken trust: Employee stealing. *Dealernews, 39*(12), p. 22.

Davila, M., Marquart, J. W., & Mullings, J. L. (2005). Beyond mother nature: Contractor fraud in the wake of natural disasters. *Deviant Behavior, 26*(3), 271–293.

Davis, J. B. (2003, August). Cybercrime fighters: Companies have more legal weapons to defend against attacks on their computer systems. *ABA Journal,* 37–42.

Debusmann, B., Jr. (2010, June 24). Madoff aide's arcade games, off-road vehicles up for auction. *Reuters.* Retrieved from http://www.reuters.com/article/2010/06/25/us-madoff-auction-idUSTRE65O0CJ20100625

DeJesus, N. (2007, November 13). Student workers caught stealing from campus bookstore. *The Mesa Press.* Retrieved November 20, 2015, from http://www.mesapress.com/news/2007/11/13/student-workers-caught-stealing-from-campus-bookstore/

Denzin, N. K. (1983). A note on emotionality, self, and interaction. *American Journal of Sociology, 89*(2), 402–409.

Dervan, L. (2011). Information warfare and civilian populations: How the law of war addresses a fear of the unknown. *Goettingen Journal of International Law, 3*(1), 373–396.

Devaney, E. (1994). *The exercise of investigative discretion.* Washington, DC: U.S. Environmental Protection Agency.

Dey, A. (2010). The chilling effect of Sarbanes-Oxley. *Journal of Accounting and Economics, 49,* 53–57.

Dey, I. (2009, June 28). The final curtain falls for Madoff: US prosecutors demand 150 years in jail for the $65Bn fraudster. *The Sunday Times* (1st ed.), p. 10.

Dhami, M. K. (2007). White-collar prisoners' perceptions of audience reaction. *Deviant Behavior, 28*(1), 57–77.

Dietrich Healthcare. (2015). *2015 medical malpractice payment analysis.* Retrieved October 31, 2015, from http://www.diederichhealthcare.com/wordpress_content/uploads/2015/03/infographic-800.jpg

DiGabriele, J. A. (2008). An empirical investigation of the relevant skills of forensic accountants. *Journal of Education for Business, 83*(6), 331–338.

Disability.gov. (2015, November 30). *Restaurant settles discrimination suit for firing employee with breast cancer.* Retrieved January 3, 2016, from https://www.disability.gov/restaurant-settles-discrimination-suit-for-firing-employee-with-breast-cancer/

Disaster in the Gulf: 107 days and counting. (2010, August 4). *FoxNews.com.* Retrieved July 29, 2011, from http://www.foxnews.com/politics/2010/05/28/disaster-gulf-days-counting

Dobovsek, B., & Slak, B. (2015). Old horizons on organised-white collar crime: Critical remarks about the current definition, development and perceptions of organized and white-collar crime. *Journal of Financial Crime, 22*(3), 305–317.

Doctor "threatened to withhold drugs from patient if she refused to have sex." (2009, August 24). *Telegraph.* Retrieved June 17, 2010, from www.telegraph.co.uk

Dodge, M. (2013). The importance of integrating victimology in white-collar crime: A targeted comment on Barak's analysis in theft of a nation. *Western Criminology Review, 14*(2), 27–30.

Dodge, M., Bosick, S. J., & Van Antwerp, V. (2013). Do men and women perceive white-collar crime and street crime differently? Exploring gender differences in the perception of motives, seriousness, and punishment. *Journal of Contemporary Criminal Justice, 29*(3), 399–415.

Donato, L. (2009). An introduction to how criminal profiling could be used as a support for computer hacking investigations. *Journal of Digital Forensic Practice, 2,* 183–195.

Donohue, K. (2004). *Statement of Kenneth Donohue, Inspector General Department of Housing and Urban Development. Statement before the House of Representatives Subcommittee on Housing and Community Opportunity Committee on Financial Services.* Retrieved July 30, 2011, from www.hud.gov/offices/oig/data/DonohueTestify10-7.doc

Donsanto, C. C., & Simmons, N. (2007). *Federal prosecutions of elected officials* (7th ed.). Washington, DC: U.S. Department of Justice.

doodlebug. (2009, August 4). Joel Tenenbaum fined $675,000 for illegally downloading music [Web log post]. *SodaHead Opinions.* Retrieved July 29, 2011, from http://www.sodahead.com/living/joel-tenenbaum-fined-675k-for-illegally-downloading-music-does-the-punishment-fit-the-crime/question-538253/

Dorn, N., Van Daele, S., & Vander Beken, T. (2007). Reducing vulnerabilities to crime of the European waste management industry: The research base and the prospects for policy. *European Journal of Crime, Criminal Law, and Criminal Justice, 15*(1), 23–36.

Doughman, A. (2010, May 21). Judge says UW can fire assistant research professor *The Seattle Times.* Retrieved July 30, 2011, from http://seattletimes.nwsource.com/html/localnews/2011924401_aprikyan22m.html

Doyle, C. (2014). Cybercrime: An overview of the federal computer fraud and abuse statute and related federal criminal laws. *Journal of Current Issues in Crime, Law and Law Enforcement, 5*(2), 69–162.

Dreese, J. J. (1998). Priest child molesters disgrace the Catholic priesthood. In B. Leone & B. Stalcup (Eds.), *Child sexual abuse* (pp. 68–73). San Diego, CA: Greenhaven Press.

Duke University. (2010). Southern Center on environmentally-driven disparities in birth outcomes. *Children's Environmental Health Initiative.* Retrieved July 30, 2011, from http://cehi.env .duke.edu/sceddbo/projecta.html

Duran, D. (2015, December 17). Hoping for forgiveness for transgressions. *Clovis News Journal.* Available online at http://www.cnjonline.com/ 2015/12/17/letter-to-the-editor-dec-18/.

Dyer, S. (2004, May 6). False transcripts add to Southern University grade-changing scandal. *Diverse Issues in Higher Education.* Retrieved February 1, 2011, from http://diverseeducation.com/article/3667/

Edelhertz, H. (1983). White-collar and professional crime: The challenge for the 1980s. *American Behavioral Scientist, 27,* 109–128.

Efrati, A. (2009, May 7). Madoff relatives got millions, court filing says; disgraced financier's long-time secretary says she believes he isn't cooperating with investigators in order to protect others. *Wall Street Journal,* p. B11.

Elis, L. A., & Simpson, S. S. (1995). Informal sanction threats and corporate crime: Additive versus multiplicative models. *Journal of Research in Crime & Delinquency, 32*(4), 399.

Ellis, S. (2011). Court-ordered community service. *Blue Avocado: A Magazine of Non-profits.* Available online at http://www.blueavocado.org/ content/court-ordered-community-service- volunteers-or-prison-labor.

Elofson, M. (2010, January 19). Troy criminal justice professor indicted. *Dothan Eagle.* Retrieved June 7, 2010, from http://www.gulfeast.com/dotha neagle/dea/news/crime_courts/article/criminal_ justice_professor_indicted/123781/

Epstein, J. (2011, February 10). Tom Delay lawyers seek a retrial. *Politico.* Retrieved February 23, 2011, from http://www.politico.com/news/stories/0211/ 49224.html

Equal Employment Opportunity Commission. (2010, January 6). *Job bias charges approach record high in fiscal year 2009, EEOC reports* [Press release]. Retrieved July 30, 2011, from http://www1.eeoc .gov/eeoc/newsroom/release/1-6-10.cfm? renderforprint=1

Ericson, R., & Doyle, A. (2006). The institutionalization of deceptive sales in life insurance. *British Journal of Criminology, 46,* 993–1010.

Ermann, M. D., & Lundman, R. (1978). *Corporate and governmental deviance: Problems of organizational behavior in contemporary society.* New York, NY: Oxford University Press.

Ermann, M. D., & Lundman, R. (2002). *Corporate and governmental deviance* (6th ed.). New York, NY: Oxford University Press.

Euben, D., & Lee, B. (2005, February 22). *Faculty misconduct and discipline.* Paper presented at the National Conference on Law and Higher Education, Stetson University College of Law. Retrieved June 15, 2010, from http://www.aaup.org/AAUP/programs/legal/ topics/misconduct–discp.htm

Evans, R. D., & Porche, D. A. (2005). The nature and frequency of Medicare/Medicaid fraud and neutralization techniques among speech, occupational, and physical therapists. *Deviant Behavior, 26,* 253–270.

Evans, S. S., & Scott, J. E. (1984). Effects of item order on the perceived seriousness of crime: A reexamination. *Journal of Research in Crime & Delinquency, 21,* 139–151.

Ex-mayor in "jail-sex" row. (1992, January 6). *Daily Telegraph,* p. 3.

Ex-pastor testifies in embezzlement trial. (2010, September 2). *Wolfe Bank News and Shoes (WBNS)-10TV.* Retrieved December 10, 2010, from http://www.10tv.com/live/content/local/ stories/2010/09/02/story-columbus-ex-pastor- testifies-embezzlement-trial.html?sid=102

Ex U.S. mortgage executive charged with huge fraud. (2010, June 16–17). *Reuters.* Retrieved July 30, 2011, from http://in.mobile.reuters.com/article/ businessNews/idUSN1614313320100616

Fabian, L. (2015, December 2). Former Macon bank attorney sentenced in theft of $263,700. *The Telegraph.* Retrieved December 29, 2015, from http://www.macon.com/news/local/crime/article 47600655.html

Faichney, D. (2014). Comments: Autocorrect? A proposal to encourage voluntary restitution through white-collar sentencing calculus. *The Journal of Law & Criminology, 104*(2), 389–430.

Falkenberg, K. (2008, December 22). Time off for bad behavior: White-collar offenders can get a year off their terms for doing rehab. *Forbes.* Retrieved July 11, 2011, from http://www.forbes.com/2008/12/20/ prison-crime-waksal-biz-beltway-cz_ kf_1222prison.html

Fannie Mae. (2007). *Mortgage fraud overview.* Retrieved July 30, 2011, from www.efanniemae. com/utility/legal/pdf/mtgfraudoverview.pdf

Faragher, J. (2007, December 4). Shut out. *Personnel Today,* 22–23.

Farole, D. J. (2009). *Contract bench and jury trials in state courts, 2005.* Washington, DC: Bureau of Justice Statistics. Retrieved November 13, 2015 from http://www.bjs.gov/content/pub/pdf/cbajtsc05 .pdf.

Fasanello, D., Umans, L., & White, T. (2011). Financial institutions fraud. *The American Criminal Law Review, 48*(2), 697–748.

Fatal crash spurs review of Toyota floor mats. (2009, September 15). *Associated Press.* Retrieved July 30, 2011, from at http://beta2.tbo.com/business/ breaking-news-business/2009/sep/15/fatal- crash-spurs-review-toyota-floor-mats-ar-74585/

FDA: Georgia plant knowingly sold peanut butter tainted with salmonella. *NYDailyNews.com.* (2009). Retrieved August 31, 2010, from http://articles.ny dailynews.com/2009-02-06/news/17916106_1_ private-lab-tests-peanut-butter-usda

Fearn, H. (2008, May 22). Sex and the university. *The Times Higher Education Supplement.* Retrieved from http://www.timeshighereducation.co.uk/ story.asp?sectioncode=26&storycode=40193 5&c=1

Federal Bureau of Investigation (FBI). (2005). *Mortgage fraud operation "quick flip."* [Press release]. Retrieved June 21, 2010, from http://www.fbi .gov/pressrel/pressrel05/quickflip121405.htm

Federal Bureau of Investigation (FBI). (2009b). *Financial crimes report to the public: Fiscal year 2008.* Retrieved July 29, 2011, from http://www .fbi.gov/stats-services/publications/fcs_ report2008

Federal Bureau of Investigation (FBI). (2009c). *2008 financial crimes report.* Retrieved from http:// www.fbi.gov/stats-services/publications/fcs_ report2008

Federal Bureau of Investigation (FBI). (2009d). *2008 mortgage fraud report.* Retrieved November 20, 2015, from https://www.fbi.gov/stats-services/ publications/mortgage-fraud 2008

Federal Bureau of Investigation (FBI). (2010a, January 11). *Hedge fund manager who bilked relatives out of $25 million sentenced to over 10 years in federal prison* [Press release]. Retrieved July 29, 2011, from http://www.fbi.gov/losangeles/press- releases/2010/la011110a.htm

Federal Bureau of Investigation (FBI). (2010b). *2009 financial crimes report.* Retrieved January 5, 2011, from http://www.fbi.gov/stats-services/ publications/financial-crimes-report-2009

Federal Bureau of Investigation (2010c). *Internet crime complaints on the rise.* Retrieved December 22, 2011, from http://www.fbi.gov/news/stories/2010/ march/ic3_031710

accomplishments, fiscal year 2009. Washington, DC: U.S. Department of Justice.

Federal Bureau of Investigation. (2011a). *Crime in the United States 2010.* Retrieved October 28, 2015, from https://www.fbi.gov/about-us/cjis/ucr/crime- in-the-u.s/2010/crime-in-the-u.s.-2010/ tables/10tbl29.xls.

Federal Bureau of Investigation (2011b). *2010 Internet Crime Report.* Fairmont, WV: National White Collar Crime Center. Retrieved October 30, 2015, from http://www.nw3c.org/docs/IC3-Annual- Reports/2010-ic3-internet-crime-report .pdf?sfvrsn=8.

Federal Bureau of Investigation (2012a). *Crime in the United States 2011.* Retrieved October 28, 2015, from https://www.fbi.gov/about-us/cjis/ucr/crime- in-the-u.s/2011/crime-in-the-u.s.-2011/tables/ table-29.

Federal Bureau of Investigation (2012b.). *2011 Internet Crime Report.* Fairmont, WV: National White Collar Crime Center. Retrieved October 30, 2015, http:// www.nw3c.org/docs/IC3-Annual-Reports/2011 ic3-internet-crime-report.pdf?sfvrsn=8.

Federal Bureau of Investigation. (2013). *Crime in the United States 2012.* Retrieved October 28, 2015, from https://www.fbi.gov/about-us/cjis/ucr/crime-in-the-u.s/2012/crime-in-the-u.s.-2012/tables/29tabledatadecpdf.

Federal Bureau of Investigation (2014). *Crime in the United States 2013.* Retrieved October 28, 2015, from https://www.fbi.gov/about-us/cjis/ucr/crime-in-the-u.s/2013/crime-in-the-u.s.-2013/tables/table-29/table_29_estimated_number_of_arrests_united_states_2013.xls.

Federal Bureau of Investigation. (2015a). *Crime in the United States 2014.* Retrieved October 28, 2015, from https://www.fbi.gov/about-us/cjis/ucr/crime-in-the-u.s/2014/crime-in-the-u.s.-2014/tables/table-29.

Federal Bureau of Investigation. (2015b). *Crime in the United States 2014: Offense analysis.* Retrieved from October 28, 2015, https://www.fbi.gov/about-us/cjis/ucr/crime-in-the-u.s/2014/crime-in-the-u.s.-2014/tables/table-23

Federal Bureau of Investigation. (2015, March 11). Canton couple sent to prison in $2.3 million student loan fraud scheme. Retrieved January 1, 2016, from https://www.fbi.gov/cleveland/press-releases/2015/canton-couple-sent-to-prison-in-2.3-million-student-loan-fraud-scheme

Federal Bureau of Investigation. (2015, July 6). *Pine Lawn mayor sentenced on extortion charges.* Retrieved January 4, 2015, from https://www.fbi.gov/stlouis/press-releases/2015/pine-lawn-mayor-sentenced-on-extortion-charges

Federal Bureau of Investigation. (2015, July 31). *Former employee of Atlantic County, New Jersey timeshare consulting firm sentenced to 30 months in prison for conspiring to defraud timeshare owners.* Retrieved January 4, 2016, from https://www.fbi.gov/newark/press-releases/2015/former-employee-of-atlantic-county-new-jersey-timeshare-consulting-firm-sentenced-to-30-months-in-prison-for-conspiring-to-defraud-timeshare-owners

Federal Bureau of Investigation (2015, August 11). *Nine people charged in largest known computer hacking and securities fraud scheme.* Available online at https://www.fbi.gov/newyork/press-releases/2015/nine-people-charged-in-largest-known-computer-hacking-and-securities-fraud-scheme.

Federal Bureau of Investigation. (2015, October 28). *Operator of multi-million-dollar Ponzi scheme sentenced to more than nine years in prison on securities fraud charges.* Retrieved January 1, 2016, from https://www.fbi.gov/charlotte/press-releases/2015/operator-of-multi-million-dollar-ponzi-scheme-sentenced-to-more-than-nine-years-in-prison-on-securities-fraud-charges

Federal Bureau of Investigation. (2015, October 29*). Financial fraud: Inside the investigation of a Las Vegas construction boss.* Retrieved January 6, 2016, from https://www.fbi.gov/news/stories/2015/october/financial-fraud/financial-fraud

Federal Bureau of Investigation (n. d.a). *2012 Internet Crime Report.* Fairmont, WV: National White Collar Crime Center. Retrieved October 30, 2015, from http://www.nw3c.org/docs/IC3-Annual-Reports/2012-ic3-internet-crime-report.pdf?sfvrsn=12

Federal Bureau of Investigation. (n. d.b). *2013 Internet Crime Report.* Fairmont, WV: National White Collar Crime Center. Retrieved October 30, 2015, from http://www.nw3c.org/docs/IC3-Annual-Reports/2013-ic3-internet-crime-report.pdf?sfvrsn=4

Federal Bureau of Investigation (n. d.c). *2014 Internet Crime Report.* Fairmont, WV: National White Collar Crime Center. Retrieved October 30, 2015, from https://www.fbi.gov/news/news_blog/2014-ic3-annual-report

Federal Bureau of Investigation (n. d.e). *Financial crimes reported to the public: Fiscal years 2009 (October 1, 2008-September 30, 2009).* Retrieved November 7, 2015, from https://www.fbi.gov/stats-services/publications/financial-crimes-report-2009

Federal Bureau of Investigation (n. d.f). *Financial crimes reported to the public: Fiscal years 2010-2011 (October 1, 2009-September 30, 2011).* Retrieved November 7, 2015, from https://www.fbi.gov/stats-services/publications/financial-crimes-report-2010-2011

Federal Deposit Insurance Corporation (FDIC). (2007). Staying alert to mortgage fraud. Retrieved July 29, 2011, from http://www.fdic.gov/regulations/examinations/supervisory/insights/sisum07/article02_staying-alert.html

Federal Trade Commission (FTC). (2001). *Advertising FAQs: A guide for small businesses.* Retrieved August 3, 2010, from http://business.ftc.gov/documents/bus35-advertising-faqs-guide-small-business.pdf

Federal Trade Commission (FTC). (2004). *KFCs claims that fried chicken is a way to eat better don't fly* [Press release]. Retrieved August 1, 2010, from http://www.ftc.gov/opa/2004/06/kfccorp.shtm

Federal Trade Commission (F TC). (2010). *Price discrimination among buyers: Robinson-Patman violations.* Retrieved June 30, 2010, from http://www.ftc.gov/bc/antitrust/price_discrimination.shtm

Federal Trade Commission (FTC). (2012, May). *Consumer information: Scholarship and financial aid scams.* Retrieved January 3, 2016, from https://www.consumer.ftc.gov/scholarshipscams

Federal Trade Commission (FTC). (2015, September 17). *FTC charges marketers of 'vision improvement' app with deceptive claims: Carrot neurotechnology & owners agree to stop making false claims that 'Ultimeyes' app improves users' vision; To pay $150,000 to settle FTC's allegations.* Retrieved January 3, 2016, from https://www.ftc.gov/news-events/press-releases/2015/09/ftc-charges-marketers-vision-improvement-app-deceptive-claims

Federal Trade Commission (FTC). (2015, October 1). *FTC returns money to customers who bought allegedly bogus weight-loss products.* Retrieved January 3, 2016, from https://www.ftc.gov/news-events/press-releases/2015/10/ftc-returns-money-consumers-who-bought-allegedly-bogus-weight

Federal Trade Commission (FTC). (2015, December 1). *Tommie Copper to pay $1.35 million to settle FTC deceptive advertising charges: Company made claims that its copper-infused clothing would relieve pain.* Retrieved January 3, 2016, from https://www.ftc.gov/news-events/press-releases/2015/12/tommie-copper-pay-135-million-settle-ftc-deceptive-advertising

Federal Trade Commission (FTC). (2015, December 9). *Nordstrom, Bed Bath & Beyond, Backcountry.com, and J. C. Penney to pay penalties totaling $1.3 million for falsely labeling rayon textiles as made of "bamboo."* Retrieved January 3, 2016, from, https://www.ftc.gov/news-events/press-releases/2015/12/nordstrom-bed-bath-beyond-backcountrycom-jc-penney-pay-penalties

Federal Trade Commission (FTC). (2015, December 17). *LifeLock to pay $100 million to consumers to settle FTC charges it violated 2010 order.* Retrieved January 3, 2016, from https://www.ftc.gov/news-events/press-releases/2015/12/lifelock-pay-100-million-consumers-settle-ftc-charges-it-violated

Federal Trade Commission (FTC). (n.d.). *Guide to antitrust laws.* Retrieved August 2, 2010, from http://www.ftc.gov/bc/antitrust/factsheets/antitrustlawsguide.pdf

Feldman, S. (2009, April 30). Dangerous liaisons. *The Times Higher Education Supplement.* Retrieved June 17, 2010, from http://www.timeshighereducation.co.uk/story.asp?storyCode=406375&sectioncode=26

Financial Crimes Enforcement Network (FinCEN). (2009). *Mortgage loan fraud connections with other financial crime.* Retrieved July 29, 2011, from http://www.fincen.gov/news_room/rp/files/mortgage_fraud.pdf

Financial Crimes Enforcement Network (FinCEN). (2010a, April 27). *FINCEN warns lenders to guard against home equity conversion mortgage fraud schemes.* Retrieved July 29, 2011, from http://www.fincen.gov/news_room/nr/pdf/20100427.pdf

Financial Crimes Enforcement Network (FinCEN). (2010b, May). *Mortgage loan fraud: Loan modification and foreclosure rescue scams.* http://www.fincen.gov/news_room/rp/files/MLFLoanMODForeclosure.pdf

Financial Crimes Enforcement Network (FinCEN). (2010c, October). *The SAR activity review: Trends, tips, and issues* (Issue 18). Washington, DC: U.S. Department of Treasury. Retrieved from http://www.fincen.gov/news_room/rp/files/sar_tti_18.pdf

Financial Crimes Enforcement Network (FinCEN). (2010d, December 14). *Mortgage fraud suspicious activity reports rise 7 percent.* Retrieved July 29, 2011, from http://www.fincen.gov/news_room/nr/pdf/20101214.pdf

Financial Crimes Enforcement Network (FinCEN). (n. d.). *FinCEN fraud SAR dataset.* Washington, DC: U. S. Department of the Treasury. Retrieved October 30, 2015, from https://www.fincen.gov/mlf_sar_data/

Finkel, E. (2014, July). Law firms' own employees are among the major cyberthreats to be protected against. *ABA Journal.* Retrieved December 26, 2015, from http://www.abajournal.com/magazine/article/law_firms_own_employees_are_among_the_major_cyberthreats_they_must_protect_

Fischer, A., & Sheppard, J. (2008). Financial institutions fraud. *American Criminal Law Review, 45,* 531–559.

Fisher, A. (2015, January 26). U.S. retail workers are no. 1 . . . in employee theft. *Fortune.* Retrieved December 31, 2015, from http://fortune.com/2015/01/26/us-retail-worker theft/

Fisher, L. M. (1992, June 23). Sears Auto Centers halt commissions after flap. *The New York Times.* Retrieved July 30, 2011, from http://www.nytimes.com/1992/06/23/business/sears-auto-centers-halt-commissions-after-flap.html

Fisse, B. (1991). Introduction: Corporate and white-collar crime. *Current Issues in Criminal Justice, 3*(1), 7–8.

Fitzgerald, J. D., & Cox, S. M. (1994). *Research methods in criminal justice.* Belmont, CA: Cengage.

Fitzgerald, L. F. (1990). Sexual harassment: The measurement of a construct. In M. Paludi (Ed.), *Ivory power: Sexual harassment on campus* (pp. 21–44). New York, NY: State University of New York Press.

Flaherty, C. (2015, November 4). Another harasser resigns. *Inside Higher Ed.* Retrieved January 1, 2016, from https://www.insidehighered.com/news/2015/11/04/northwestern-philosophy-professor-resigns-during-termination-hearing-over-sexual

Foo, L. J. (1994). The vulnerable and exploitable immigrant workforce and the need for strengthening worker protective legislation. *Yale Law Journal, 103*(8), 2179–2212.

Fox, M. F. (1994). Scientific misconduct and editorial and peer review processes. *Journal of Higher Education, 65*(3), 298–309.

Frank, N. (1984). Policing corporate crime: A typology of enforcement styles. *Justice Quarterly, 1*(2), 235–251.

Frank, N. (1993). Maiming and killing: Occupational health crimes. *Annals of Political and Social Science, 525,* 107–118.

Frank, N. K., & Lynch, M. J. (1992). *Corporate crime, corporate violence: A primer.* Albany, NY: Harrow and Heston.

Frankel, T. (2006). *Trust and honesty: America's business culture at a crossroad.* New York, NY: Oxford University Press.

Frean, A., & Lea, R. (2010, February 3). Toyota recall: Last words from a family killed as Lexus crashed. *The Times.* Retrieved on October 19, 2010, from http://www.timesonline.co.uk/tol/news/world/us_and_americas/article7012913.ece

Friedman, M. (2009, September 28). Retailers report "shrinkage" of inventory on the rise. *Arkansas Business, 26*(39), 17.

Friedrichs, D. (2004). Enron et al.: Paradigmatic white collar crime cases for the new century. *Critical Criminology, 12,* 113–132.

Friedrichs, D. O. (1997). The downsizing of America: A neglected dimension of the white collar crime problem. *Crime, Law and Social Change, 26,* 351–366.

Friedrichs, D. O. (2002). Occupational crime, occupational deviance, and workplace crime: Sorting out the difference. *Criminology and Criminal Justice, 2,* 243–256.

Frongillo, T. C., Simons, C. K., Essinger, J., & Knowles, M. (2014). The reinvigorated confrontation clause: A new basis to challenge the admission of evidence from nontestifying forensic experts in white collar prosecutions. *Defense Counsel Journal, 18*(1), 11–31.

Fugitive phony doctor nabbed. (October 12, 2004). *Reuters.* Retrieved July 30, 2011, from http://www.sysopt.com/forum/showthread.php?t=171184

Furnell, S. (2008). End-user security culture: A lesson that will never be learnt? *Computer Fraud & Security, 4,* 6–9.

Futty, J. (2010, July 16). Man sentenced for illegal tire dumping. *Columbus Dispatch.* Retrieved July 29, 2011, from http://www.dispatch.com/live/content/local_news/stories/2010/07/16/tire_dumping.html

Fyfe, J. J., & Kane, R. (2005). *Bad cops: A study of career ending misconduct among New York City police officers.* Rockville, MD: National Institute of Justice.

Galbraith, J. K. (2005). Introduction: Control fraud and economic criminology [Editorial]. *Journal of Socioeconomics, 34,* 731–733.

Garoupa, N. (2005). The economics of business crime: Theory and public policy. *Security Journal, 18*(1), 24–41.

Garrett, R. (2010, April). Digital defense begins at home: Protecting the Internet's digital borders begins with protecting local citizens from cyber harm. *Law Enforcement Technology,* 16–22.

Gathright, A. (2008, April 21). Bill to safeguard renters from slumlords' advances. *Rocky Mountain News.* Retrieved June 29, 2010, from http://blogs.rockymountainnews.com/live_from_the_colorado_legislature/archives/2008/04/post_34.html

Gauthier, D. K. (2001). Professional lapses: Occupational deviance and neutralization techniques in veterinary medical practice. *Deviant Behavior, 22*(6), 467–490.

Geis, G. (1975). Victims of crimes of violence and the criminal justice system. In D. Chappell & J. Monahan (Eds.), *Violence and criminal justice.* Lexington, MA: Lexington Books.

Geis, G. (1976). Defrauding the elderly. In J. Goldsmith & S. Goldsmith (Eds.), *Crime and the elderly* (pp. 7–19). Lexington, MA: D. C. Heath.

Geis, G. (1978). White-collar crime. *Crime and Delinquency, 24,* 89–90.

Geis, G. (2000). On the absence of self-control as the basis for a general theory of crime: A critique. *Theoretical Criminology, 4,* 35–53.

Geis, G., & Dimento, J. (1995). Should we prosecute corporations and/or individuals? In F. Pearce & L. Snider (Eds.), *Corporate crime: Contemporary debates* (pp. 72–90). Toronto, Ontario, Canada: University of Toronto Press.

Geis, G., Jesilow, P., Pontell, H., & O'Brien, M. (1985). Fraud and abuse of government medical programs by psychiatrists. *American Journal of Psychiatry, 142,* 231–234.

George, C. (2015, October 5). Ex-UH professors sentenced in research grant scam. *Houston Chronicle.* Retrieved January 2, 2016, from http://www.houstonchronicle.com/news/houston-texas/houston/article/Ex-UH-professors-sentenced-in-research-grant-6551959.php

Georgia State University. (2010). *Georgia State University Faculty Handbook.* Retrieved July 29, 2011, from http://www2.gsu.edu/~wwwfhb/fhb.html

Gerber, J. (1994). "Club Fed" in Japan? Incarceration experiences of Japanese embezzlers. *International Journal of Offender Therapy and Comparative Criminology, 38*(2), 163–174.

Gerber, J., Jensen, E. L., & Fritsch, E. J. (1996). Politics and white collar crime: Explaining government intervention in the savings and loan scandal. *Critical Criminology, 7*(2), 59–73.

Gershman, B. (1999). Judicial misconduct during jury deliberations. In L. Stolzenberg & S. J. D'Alessio (Eds.), *Criminal courts for the 21st century* (pp. 291–314). Upper Saddle River, NJ: Prentice Hall.

Gershman, B. L. (1982). Abscam, the judiciary, and the ethics of entrapment. *Yale Law Journal, 91*(8), 1565–1591.

Ghiselli, R., & Ismail, J. A. (1998). Employee theft and efficacy of certain control procedures in commercial food service operations. *Journal of Hospitality & Tourism Research, 22,* 174–187.

Gibbs, C. (2012). Corporate citizenship and corporate environmental performance. *Crime, Law and Social Change, 57,* 345–372.

Gibbs, C., Cassidy, M., & Rivers, L. (2013). A routine activities analysis of white-collar crime in carbon markets. *Law & Policy: University of Denver, 35*(4), 341–374.

Gibson Dunn (2015). *2014 year-end update on corporate non-prosecution agreements (NPAs) and deferred prosecution agreements (DPAs).* Retrieved November 19, 2015, from http://www.gibsondunn

.com/publications/Pages/2014-Year-End-Update-Corporate-Non-Prosecution-Agreements-and-Deferred-Prosecution-Agreements.aspx

Gibson, K. (2000). Excuses, excuses: Moral slippage in the workplace. *Business Horizons, 43*, 65–85.

Gilbert, D., & Kent, S. (2015, July 2). Spill claims: Settlement of all federal and state claims brings total costs to nearly $54 billion. *The Wall Street Journal.* Retrieved January 3, 2016, from http://www.wsj.com/articles/bp-agrees-to-pay-18-7-billion-to-settle-deepwater-horizon-oil-spill-claims 1435842739

Gill, M. (2011). Fraud and recessions: Views from fraudsters and fraud managers. *International Journal of Law, Crime and Justice, 39*, 204–214.

Ginsberg, B., & Shefter, M. (1995). Ethics probes as political weapons. *Journal of Law and Politics, 11*, 497–511.

Givens, A. D., & Busch, N. E. (2013). Investigating federal approaches to post-cyber incident mitigation. *Homeland Security & Emergency Management, 10*(1), 1–28.

Glasberg, D. S., & Skidmore, D. (1998a). The dialectics of white-collar crime: The anatomy of the savings and loan crisis and the case of Silverado Banking, Savings and Loan Association. *American Journal of Economics and Sociology, 57*(4), 423–449.

Glasberg, D. S., & Skidmore, D. L. (1998b). The role of the state in the criminogenesis of corporate crime: A case study of the savings and loan crisis. *Social Science Quarterly, 79*(1), 110–128.

Glazer, M. (1983, December). Ten whistleblowers and how they fared. *Hastings Center Report, 13*(6), 33–41.

Glen, D. (2010, May 17). Former U. of Louisiana dean is sentenced to more than 5 years. *Chronicle of Higher Education.* Retrieved July 30, 2011, from http://chronicle.com/article/Former-U-of-Louisville-Dean/65603/

Glink, I. (2009). *Mortgage fraud v. 2009.* Retrieved June 21, 2010, from http://moneywatch.bnet.com/saving-money/blog/home-equity/mortgage-fraud-v2009/715/

Glink, R. I., & Tamkin, S. J. (2008, April 5). The two types of mortgage fraud, plus a primer on tax sales. *The Washington Post.* Retrieved June 21, 2010, from http://www.washingtonpost.com/wp-dyn/content/article/2008/04/04/AR2008040401789.html

Glor, J. (2010, January 29). Toyota recall costing the automaker dearly. *Columbia Broadcasting System (CBS) News.* Retrieved October 19, 2010, from http://www.cbsnews.com/stories/2010/01/29/business/main6153710.shtml

Glovin, D. (2009a, March 17). Madoff property is subject to forfeiture, U.S. says. *The Globe and Mail,* p. B13.

Glovin, D. (2009b, April 4). Mum's the word; Madoff's secret say nothing about methods. *The Gazette,* p. C4.

Glovin D., & Hurtado, P. (2010, May 22). New Castle's Kurland gets 27 months in first Galleon sentence. *Bloomberg.* Retrieved July 30, 2011, from http://www.bloomberg.com/news/2010-05-21/new-castle-s-kurland-given-27-month-term-in-galleon-insider-trading-case.html

Goel, R. K., & Nelson, M. A. (2011). Government fragmentation versus fiscal decentralization ad corruption. *Public Choice, 148*, 471–490.

Gogolin, G. (2011). The chasm between law enforcement and digital crime. *Journal of Current Issues in Crime, Law and Law Enforcement, 4*(4), 469–478.

Goldman, B. M., Gutek, B. A., Stein, J. H., & Lewis, K. (2006). Employment discrimination in organizations: Antecedents and consequences. *Journal of Management, 32*, 786–830.

Goldsmith, M., & King, C. W. (1997). Policing corporate crime: The dilemma of internal compliance programs. *Vanderbilt Law Review, 50*(1), 1–47.

Goldstein, J. (2008, October 14). NIH suspends Emory grant amid questions over Pharma payments. *Wall Street Journal.* Retrieved July 30, 2011, from http://blogs.wsj.com/health/2008/10/14/nih-suspends-emory-psych-grant-amid-questions-over-pharma-payments/

Goodchild, J. (2008, December 1). Criminology professor Hollinger on forthcoming results from the National Retail Security Survey and trends in retail shrinkage. *CSO Online.* Retrieved June 30, 2011, from http://www.csoonline.com/article/461365/richard-hollinger-on-shoplifting-and-retail-shrink

Goodman, L. M. (2014, June 26). Nonsensical sentences for white collar criminals. *Newsweek.* Retrieved January 3, 2016, from http://www.newsweek.com/2014/07/04/nonsensical-sentences-white-collar-criminals-256104.html

Gordon, A. M. (2014). Rational choice and moral decision making in research. *Ethics & Behavior, 24*(3), 175–194.

Gordon, R. A., Michels, J. L., & Nelson, C. L. (1996). Majority group perceptions of criminal behavior: The accuracy of race-related crime stereotypes. *Journal of Applied Social Psychology, 26*, 148–159.

Gottfredson, M. R., & Hirschi, T. (1990). *A general theory of crime.* Stanford, CA: Stanford University Press.

Gottschalk, P. (2014a). *Financial crime and knowledge workers: An empirical study of defense lawyers and white-collar criminals.* New York, NY: Palgrave Macmillan.

Gottschalk, P. (2014b). White-collar crime defense knowledge: Predictors of lawyer fame. *Journal of Information & Knowledge Management, 13*(1), 1–9.

Gottschalk, P., & Glase, L. (2013). Corporate crime does pay! The relationship between financial crime and imprisonment in white-collar crime. *International Letters of Social and Humanistic Sciences, 5*, 63–78.

Grabosky, P., & Gant, F. (2000). *Improving environmental performance, preventing environmental crime.* Canberra, Australia: Australian Institute of Criminology.

Grady, T. (2003, December). Repairers balk at study citing 42 percent fraud rate. *Automotive Body Repair News, 42*(12), p. 1.

Graflage, S. (2015, July 9). *Attorney general sues Clay county auto-repair shop for alleged fraud.* Retrieved December 31, 2015 from http://fox4kc.com/2015/07/09/attorney-general-sues-clay-county-auto-repair-shop-for-alleged-fraud/

Grasmick, H. G., Tittle, C. R., Bursik, R. J., Jr., & Arneklev, B. J. (1993). Testing the core empirical implications of Gottfredson and Hirschi's general theory of crime. *Journal of Research in Crime & Delinquency, 30*, 5–29.

Gray, C. (2004). The line between legal error and judicial misconduct: Balancing judicial independence and accountability. *Hofstra Final, 32*, 1245–1269.

Gray, D., Citron, D. K., & Rinehart, L. C. (2013). Fighting cybercrime after United States v. Jones. *The Journal of Criminal Law & Criminology, 103*(3), 745–801.

Great White band manager faces relatives. (2006, May 9). *FoxNews.com.* Retrieved December 15, 2010, from http://www.foxnews.com/story/0,2933,194658,00.html

Green, G., & Bodapati, M. (1999). The "deterrence trap" in the federal fining of organizations: A research note. *Criminal Justice Policy Review, 10*(4), 547–559.

Green, G. S. (1990). *Occupational crime.* Chicago, IL: Nelson-Hall.

Green, G. S. (1993). White-collar crime and the study of embezzlement. *Annals of the American Academy of Political and Social Science, 525*, 95–106.

Green, S. (2007, December 11). Washing toilets for 12 cents an hour; Florida jail won't be Disney World. *Toronto Sun,* p. 4.

Greenblatt, M. (2012, November 24). Paul Frampton: Court in Argentina convicts UNC professor of drug smuggling. *ABC News.* Retrieved December 29, 2015, from http://abcnews.go.com/International/paul-frampton-court-argentina-convicts-unc-professor-drug/story?id=17799280.

Grisham, L. (2015, January 5). Timeline: North Korea and the Sony Pictures hack. *USA Today.* Retrieved January 5, 2016, from http://www.usatoday.com/story/news/nation-now/2014/12/18/sony-hack-timeline-interview-north-korea/20601645/.

Gunter, W. D. (2009). Internet scallywags: A comparative analysis of multiple forms and measurements of digital piracy. *Western Criminology Review, 10*(1), 15–28.

Hackett, E. J. (1993). A new perspective on scientific medicine. *Academic Medicine, 68*(9, Suppl.), S72–S76.

Hagan, J. (1982). The corporate advantage: A study of the involvement of corporate and individual victims in a criminal justice system. *Social Forces, 60*(4), 993–1022.

Hagan, J., Nagel, I., & Albonetti, C. (1980). The differential sentencing of white-collar offenders in ten federal district courts. *American Sociological Review, 48*, 802–820.

Hagan, J., & Palloni, A. (1986). Club Fed and the sentencing of white-collar offenders before and after Watergate. *Criminology, 24*(4), 603–621.

Hagan, J., & Parker, P. (1985). White-collar crime and punishment: The class structure and legal sanctioning of securities violations. *American Sociological Association, 50*(3), 302–316.

Haiken, M. (2011, May 18). Annuities may not be a good choice for your parents. *Your Guide to Better Living.* Retrieved July 29, 2011, from http://www.betterliving.com/finance/2011/05/beware-annuities-may-not-be-a-good-choice-for-your-aging-parents/

Haines, F. (2014, February). Corporate fraud as misplaced confidence: Exploring ambiguity in the accuracy of accounts and the materiality of money. *Theoretical Criminology, 18*, 20–37.

Hale, C. (2002). Cybercrime: Facts & figures concerning this global dilemma. *Crime and Justice International, 18*(65), 5–26.

Hall, J., & Brajer, V. (2008). *Benefits of meeting federal clean air standards in the South Coast and San Joaquin Valley Air Basins.* Fullerton: California State University. Retrieved July 30, 2011, from http://business.fullerton.edu/centers/iees/reports/Benefits%20of%20Meeting%20Clean%20Air%20Standards.pdf

Hall, P. (2015, November 20). Lehigh university professor and wife convicted of cheating NASA. *The Morning Call.* Retrieved January 2, 2016, from http://www.mcall.com/news/breaking/mc-lehigh-professor-nasa-fraud-verdict-20151120-story.html

Halsey, M. (1997). The wood for the paper. *Australian and New Zealand Journal of Criminology, 30*, 121–148.

Halsey, M. (2004). Against "green" criminology. *British Journal of Criminology, 44*(6), 833–853.

Halsey, M., & White, R. (1998). Crime, ecophilosophy, and environmental harm. *Theoretical Criminology, 2*(3), 345–371.

Halverson, R. (1992, July 6). Sears nixes commission pay in light of fraud charges. *Discount Store News.* Retrieved July 29, 2011, from http://findarticles.com/p/articles/mi_m3092/is_n13_v31/ai_12466021/

Hamermesh, D. (2009, November 6). Charity won't contain this secondary market. Retrieved July 30, 2011, from http://www.freakonomics.com/2009/11/06/charity-wont-contain-this-secondary-market/

Hamm, M. S. (2007). "High crimes and misdemeanors": George W. Bush and the sins of Abu Ghraib. *Crime, Media, & Culture, 3*(3), 259–284.

Hammett, T. M., & Epstein, J. (1993). *Local prosecution of environmental crime (Technical Report).* Washington D.C.: National Institute of Justice.

Hansard, S. (2007, June 18). Judges cracking down on securities fraud; states report more convictions, longer sentences. *Investment News.* Retrieved June 8, 2011, from http://www.investmentnews.com/article/20070618/FREE/70614017

Harkins, P. (2015, December 8). Former Tulsa police officer has paid more than $306,000 in embezzlement restitution, fines. *NewsOK.* Retrieved December 29, 2015, from http://newsok.com/article/5465610

Harknett, R. J., & Stever, J. A. (2009). The cybersecurity triad: Government, private sector partners, and the engaged cybersecurity citizen. *Journal of Homeland Security and Emergency Management, 6*(1), 1–14.

Harris, A. (1989, October 25). Jim Bakker gets 45-year sentence; Televangelist fined $500,000; Eligible for parole in 10 years. *The Washington Post.* Retrieved July 30, 2011, from http://www.highbeam.com/doc/1P2-1219165.html

Harris, D., & Benson, M. (1996). Nursing home theft: An overlooked form of elder abuse. In R. Cibik, R. Edwards, G. C. Graber, & F. H. Marsh (Eds.), *Advances in bioethics* (Vol. 1, pp. 171–188). Greenwich, CT: JAI Press.

Harris, D. K., & Benson, M. L. (1999). Theft in nursing homes: An overlooked form of elder abuse. *Journal of Elder Abuse & Neglect, 11*(3), 73–90.

Harris, G. (2008, October 3). Top psychiatrist didn't report drug makers' pay. *The New York Times.* Retrieved July 30, 2011, from http://www.nytimes.com/2008/10/04/health/policy/04drug.html

Harris, G. (2009, March 10). Doctors' pain studies were fabricated, hospital says. *The New York Times.* Retrieved June 4, 2010, from http://www.nytimes.com/2009/03/11/health/research/11pain.html?_r=2&adxnnl=1&ref=us&adxnnlx=1312053446-quDa4FtMaqjedJ592V8caA

Hasegawa, I. (2010). Film interview: Zac Efron and Claire Danes. *Buzzine.* Retrieved October 6, 2010, from http://www.buzzinefilm.com/interviews/film-zac-efron-claire-danes-01062010

Haugh, T. (2012). Can the CEO learn from the condemned? The application of capital mitigation strategies to white collar cases. *American University Law Review, 62*(1), 1–58.

Hay, K. (2010, October 19). Asbestos disposal draws fine: waste illegally put in Dumpster. *Albuquerque Journal.* Retrieved December 2, 2015, from http://www.abqjournal.com/biz/192154380471biz10-19-10.htm

Hays, K. (2006, May 16). Lay, Skilling, used 'hocus pocus' to hide fraud, prosecutor tells jury. *The New York Times.* Retrieved November 29, 2015, from https://news.google.com/newspapers?nid=1665&dat=20060516&id=tXU0AAAAIBAJ&sjid=YCUEAAAAIBAJ&pg=4395,3364258&hl=en

Hayman, G., & Brack, D. (2002). *International environmental crime: The nature and control of environmental black markets: Workshop report.* London, UK: Royal Institute of International Affairs, Sustainable Development Programme.

Hazard, G. (1991). The future of legal ethics. *Yale Law Journal, 100,* 1239–1250.

He made his own bed: Crooked investment banker gets 3 years in the pokey [Web log post]. (2006, May 16). *Wall Street Folly.* Retrieved July 30, 2011, from http://files.wallstreetfolly.com/wordpress/2006/05/he-made-his-own-bed-crooked-investment-banker-gets-3-years-in-the-pokey/

Healthcare Fraud and Abuse Program. (2015). *Annual report for FY 2014.* Retrieved January 6, 2016, from http://oig.hhs.gov/publications/docs/hcfac/FY2014-hcfac.pdf

Healy, B. (2009a, February 12). Madoff's wife pulled $15.5m from account withdrawals in weeks before husband's arrest. *The Boston Globe* (3rd ed.), p. A1.

Healy, B. (2009b, June, 23). Broker aided Madoff, US says; Jaffe's profits called fraudulent; SEC seeks return of investigator money. *The Boston Globe,* p. 1.

Healy, B., & Mandell, H. (2009, March 13). An apologetic Madoff goes to jail; admits to massive Ponzi scheme, awaits many-years sentence. *The Boston Globe,* p. A1.

Healy, B., & Syre, S. (2008, December 13). Boston donors bilked out of millions—Trader accused of $50 billion con game—One nonprofit closes; others may suffer. *The Boston Globe,* p. A1.

Heenan, P. T., Klarfeld, J. L., Roussis, M. A., & Walsh, J. K. (2010). Securities fraud. *American Criminal Law Review, 47*(2), 1015–1087.

Hemraj, M. B. (2002). The detection of financial irregularities in the US corporations. *Journal of Financial Crime, 10*(1), 85–90.

Henning, P. J. (2010, March 25). When legal bills become a cause for dispute. *The New York Times.* Retrieved July 29, 2011, from http://dealbook.blogs.nytimes.com/2010/02/01/when-legal-bills-become-an-item-of-dispute/

Herman, K., Sunshine, P., Fisher, M., Zwolenik, J., & Herz, J. (1994). Investigating misconduct in science. *Journal of Higher Education, 65,* 384–400.

Hernandez, J. C. (2010, April 2). U.S. urges homeowners to remove Chinese drywall. *The New York Times.* Retrieved July 30, 2011, from http://www.nytimes.com/2010/04/03/business/03drywall.html

Heslop, G. (2007). Fraud at the top. *Internal Auditor, 64*(2), 87–89.

Higgins, G. E. (2006). Gender differences in software piracy: The mediating roles of self-control theory and social learning theory. *Journal of Economic Crime, 4*(1), 1–22.

Higgins, G. E., Fell, B. D., & Wilson, A. L. (2006). Digital piracy: Assessing the contributions of an integrated self-control theory and social learning theory using structural equation modeling. *Criminal Justice Studies, 19*(1), 3–22.

Hill, T. J., & Lezell, S. B. (2010). Antitrust violations. *American Criminal Law Review, 47*(2), 245–285.

Hinduja, S. (2001). Correlates of Internet software piracy. *Journal of Contemporary Criminal Justice, 17,* 369–382.

Hinduja, S., & Kooi, B. (2013). Curtailing cyber and information security vulnerabilities through situational crime prevention. *Security Journal, 26*(4), 383–401.

Hinkes-Jones, L. (2015, December 15). *Patients, researchers demand further prosecution in Duke case.* Retrieved January 1, 2016 from http://www.bna.com/patients-researchers-demand-n57982065145/

Hippensteele, S. K., Adams, A. K., & Chesney, M. L. (1992). Sexual harassment in academia: Students' reactions to unprofessional behavior. *Journal of Criminal Justice Education, 3*(2), 315–330.

Hirschi, T. (1969). *Causes of delinquency.* Berkeley, CA: University of California Press.

Hirschi, T., & Gottfredson, M. (1987). Causes of white-collar crime. *Criminology, 25*(4), 949–972.

Hoelter, H. J. (2015, February). *Criminal defense update.* Baltimore, MD: National Center on Institutions and Alternatives (NCIA). Retrieved December 15, 2014, from http://www.ncianet.org/wp-content/uploads/2015/06/Why-Community-Service-Works-February-2015.pdf.

Hoffman, D. E. (2008). Treating pain versus reducing drug diversion and abuse. *St. Louis University Journal of Health Law and Policy, 1*, 233–311.

Hoffman, L. J., Burley, D., & Toregas, C. (2011, November 1). Thinking across stovepipes: Using a holistic development strategy to build the cyber security workforce. *The George Washington University Cyber Security Policy and Research Institute.* Report GW-CSPRI-2011-8. Retrieved January 5, 2016 from http://static1.squarespace.com/static/53b2efd7e4b0018990a073c4/t/553e79b7e4b0c962703678cc/1430157751568/stovepipes_gw_cspri_report_2011_8.pdf

Hohn, D. A., Muftic, L. R., & Wolf, K. (2006). Swashbuckling students: An exploratory study of Internet policy. *Security Journal, 19*, 110–127.

Hollinger, R. C., & Lanza-Kaduce, L. (1988). The process of criminalization: The case of computer crime laws. *Criminology, 26*(1), 101–126.

Hollinger, R. C., Slora, K. B., & Terris, W. (1992). Deviance in the fast-food restaurant: Correlates of employee theft, altruism, and counterproductivity. *Deviant Behavior, 13*(2), 155–184.

Holt, T. J., & Bossler, A. M. (2008). Examining the applicability of lifestyle-routine activities theory for cyber-crime victimization. *Deviant Behavior, 30*, 1–25.

Holt, T. J., & Bossler, A. M. (2012). Police perceptions of computer crimes in two southeastern cities: An examination from the viewpoint of patrol officers. *American Journal of Criminal Justice, 37*, 396–412.

Holt, T. J., & Bossler, A. M. (2013). Examining the relationship between routine activities and malware infection indicators. *Journal of Contemporary Criminal Justice, 29*(4), 420–436.

Holt, T. J., Bossler, A. M., & May, D. C. (2012). Low self-control, deviant peer associations, and juvenile cyberdeviance. *American Journal of Criminal Justice, 37*, 378–395.

Holt, T. J., & Lampke, E. (2010). Exploring stolen data markets online: Products and market force. *Criminal Justice Studies, 23*(1), 33–50.

Holtfreter, K. (2004). Fraud in US organisations: An examination of control mechanisms. *Journal of Financial Crime, 12*(1), 88–95.

Holtfreter, K. (2005). Is occupational fraud "typical" white collar crime? A comparison of individual and organizational characteristics. *Journal of Criminal Justice, 33*, 353–365.

Holtfreter, K., Reisig, M. D., & Pratt, T. C. (2008). Low self-control, routine activities, and fraud victimization. *Criminology, 46*(1), 189–220.

Holtfreter, K., Van Slyke, S., Bratton, J., & Gertz, M. (2008). Public perceptions of white-collar crime and punishment. *Journal of Criminal Justice, 36*, 50–60.

Holtz, D. (2009, March 21). Confections disappear, employee nabbed. *McClatchy-Tribune Business News.* Retrieved July 30, 2011, from ABI/INFORM Complete database (Document ID No. 1664682411).

Hood, M. V., & Gillespie, W. (2012). They just do not vote like the used to: A methodology to empirically assess election fraud. *Social Science Quarterly, 93*(1), 76–94.

Horn, B. (2015, September 30). State charges Dover doctor with felony health care fraud. *Delawareonline.com.* Retrieved January 6, 2016 from http://www.delawareonline.com/story/news/crime/2015/09/29/state-charges-dover-doctor-felony-health-care-fraud/73050736/

Hours before arrest, Barry gave anti-drug sermon. Mayor preached against drugs to teens just hours before arrest. (1990, January 20). *Baltimore Evening Sun.* Retrieved July 31, 2011 from http://articles.sun-sentinel.com/1990-01-20/news/9001200236_1_mayor-barry-cocaine-sting-fbi-agents-arrest

Howe, L. K. (1977). *Pink collar workers.* New York, NY: Avon.

Huber, N. (2010, August 6). Taking the risk out of hiring. *Caterer & Hotelkeeper, 200*, 40. Retrieved November 20, 2015 from https://www.thecaterer.com/articles/334609/staff-screening-taking-the-risk-out-of-hiring

Huey, L., & Rosenberg, R. S. (2004). Watching the web: Thoughts on expanding police surveillance opportunities under the cyber-crime convention. *Canadian Journal of Criminology and Criminal Justice, 46*(5), 597–606.

Huckabee, C. (2009, March 15). Professor whose article was retracted resigns from Harvard Medical School. *Chronicle of Higher Education.* Retrieved July 30, 2011, from http://chronicle.com/article/Professor-Whose-Article-Was/42521

Huff, R., Desilets, C., & Kane, J. (2010). *The national public survey on white collar crime.* Fairmont, WV: National White Collar Crime Center. Retrieved October 28, 2015 from http://www.fraudaid.com/library/2010-national-public-survey-on-white-collar-crime.pdf

Hundley, K. (2010, June 29). Whistle-blower case details allegations of massive fraud at WellCare. *Tampa Bay Times.* Retrieved July 30, 2011, from http://www.tampabay.com/news/business/whistle-blower-case-details-allegations-of-massive-fraud-at-wellcare/1105487

Hunter, R. D. (1999). Officer opinions on police misconduct. *Journal of Contemporary Criminal Justice, 15*, 155–170.

Illinois Environmental Protection Agency. (2010). Open dumps. Retrieved July 30, 2011, from http://www.epa.state.il.us/land/illegal-dumping/open-dumps.html

Inmate ran identity theft ring from inside prison: Judge sentences him to 14.5 more years behind bars. (2011, January 22). *Consumer Affairs.* Retrieved July 6, 2011, from http://www.consumeraffairs.com/news04/2011/01/inmate-ran-identity-theft-ring-from-inside-prison.html

Institute for College Access and Success. (2015, July 25). *Q&A on the for-profit college "90-10 rule."* Retrieved January 3, 2016 from http://ticas.org/sites/default/files/pub_files/90-10_qa_0.pdf

Insurance agent accused of scam. (2007, September 19). *St. Petersburg Times*, p. 1.

Insurers' recent success a milestone in a year of Chinese drywall litigation. (2010). *Insurance Journal.* Retrieved July 30, 2011, from http://www.insurancejournal.com/news/southcentral/2010/12/23/115924.htm

Interlandi, J. (2006, October 22). An unwelcome discovery. *New York Times.* Retrieved June 4, 2010, from http://www.nytimes.com/2006/10/22/magazine/22sciencefraud.html?pagewanted=1

Internal Revenue Service (IRS). (2010). *Examples of mortgage and real estate fraud investigations—fiscal year 2010.* Retrieved July 29, 2011, from http://www.irs.gov/compliance/enforcement/article/0,,id=230291,00.html

Internal Revenue Service (IRS). (2015). *Examples of mortgage and real estate fraud.* Retrieved December 26, 2015 from http://www.justice.gov/opa/pr/former-short-sale-specialist-convicted-mortgage-and-tax-fraud

Ionescu, L. (2013a). Perceptions of corrupt in emerging economics. *Economics, Management and Financial Markets, 8*(1), 365–395.

Ionescu, L. (2013b). The role of technology in combating corruption. *Economics, Management and Financial Markets, 8*(3), 126–131.

Iqbal, F., Binalleeh, H., Fung, B. C. M., & Debbabi, M. (2010). Mining writeprints from anonymous e-mails for forensic investigation. *Digital Investigation, 7*, 56–64.

Is Martha Stewart truly a changed woman? (2005, March 7). *MSNBC.com.* Retrieved January 19, 2011, from http://www.msnbc.msn.com/id/7112803/ns/business-us_business

Isely, P. J., Isely, P., Freiburger, J., & McMackin, R. (2008). In their own voices: A qualitative study of men abused as children by Catholic clergy. *Journal of Child Sexual Abuse, 17*(3/4), 201–215.

Ivancevich, J., Konopaske, R., & Gilbert, J. (2008). Formally shaming white-collar criminals. *Business Horizons, 51,* 401–410.

Iyer, R., & Eastman, J. K. (2006). Academic dishonesty: Are business students different from other college students? *Journal of Education for Business, 82*(2), 101–110.

Jacobsen, R. A., Jr., Seat, K. L., Shugarman, K. D., & Gildea, A. J. (1991). *International Financial Law Review: Supplement, 57* (United States). Retrieved July 30, 2011, from ABI/INFORM Global database (Document ID No. 1385266).

Jacobson, S. (2009, September 7). Ex-pastor delivers apology: Haggard, omits details of sex scandal in tour of churches with wife. *Dallas Morning News.* Retrieved July 30, 2011, from http://nl.newsbank.com/nl-search/we/Archives?p_product=DM&p_theme=dm&p_action=search&p_maxdocs=200&s_hidethis=no&s_dispstring=ex-pastor%20and%20haggard&p_field_advanced-0=&p_text_advanced-0=(ex-pastor%20and%20haggard)&xcal_numdocs=20&p_perpage=10&p_sort=YMD_date:D&xcal_useweights=no

Jarcho, N., & Shechter, N. (2012). Public corruption. *Criminal Law Review, 49,* 1107–1156.

Jarrell, M. L. (2007). *Environmental crime and the media: News coverage of petroleum refining industry violations.* New York, NY: LFB Scholarly.

Jayasuriya, D., & Sharp, C. (2006). Auditors in a changing regulatory environment. *Journal of Financial Crime, 13*(1), 51–55.

Jefferson, J. (1997, October). Deleting cyberbooks. *ABA Journal,* 68–74.

Jenkins, A., & Braithwaite, J. (1993). Profits, pressure and corporate lawbreaking. *Crime, Law and Social Change, 20,* 221–232.

Jenkins, C. (2008, October 6). State kicks off task force to protect seniors from fraud. *Tampa Bay Times.* Retrieved January 4, 2016 from http://www.tampabay.com/news/politics/state/state-kicks-off-task-force-to-protect-seniors-from-fraud/841696

Jennings, M. (2008). *Business ethics* (6th Ed.). Mason, OH: Southwestern Cengage.

Jesilow, P. (2012). Is Sweden doomed to repeat U.S. errors? Fraud in Sweden's health care system. *International Criminal Justice Review, 22*(1), 24–42.

Jesilow, P., Geis, G., & O'Brien, M. J. (1985). "Is my battery any good?" A field test of fraud in the auto repair business. *Journal of Crime and Justice, 8,* 1–20.

Jesilow, P., Geis, G., & O'Brien, M. J. (1986). Experimental evidence that publicity has no effect in suppressing auto repair fraud. *Sociology and Social Research, 70*(3), 222–223.

Jesilow, P., Pontell, H. N., & Geis, G. (1985). Medical criminals: Physicians and white-collar offenses. *Justice Quarterly, 2,* 149–166.

Jesilow, P., Pontell, H. N., & Geis, G. (1986). Physician immunity from prosecution and punishment for medical program fraud. In G. Newman &

W. B. Groves (Eds.), *Punishment and privilege* (pp. 7–22). Albany, NY: Harrow and Heston.

Jetha, K. (2013). Cybercrime and punishment: An analysis of the deontological and utilitarian functions of punishments in the information age. *ASFSL Conference on Digital Forensics, Security and Law,* 15–20.

John Jay College of Criminal Justice. (n. d.). *The nature and scope of the problem of sexual abuse of minors by Catholic priests and deacons in the United States: A research study conducted by the John Jay College of Criminal Justice.* Retrieved January 4, 2016, from http://www.nccbuscc.org/nrb/johnjaystudy/

Johnson, C. (2005, July 14). Ebbers gets 25 year sentence for role in WorldCom fraud. *The Washington Post.* Retrieved November 29, 2015 from http://www.washingtonpost.com/wp-dyn/content/article/2005/07/13/AR2005071300516.html

Johnson, C. (2006, May 26). Enron trial update. *The Washington Post.* Retrieved November 29, 2015, from http://www.washingtonpost.com/wp-dyn/content/discussion/2006/05/24/DI2006052400684.html

Johnson, H. (2010, May 31). And off to jail they go: Disney duo nabbed by SEC. *Investment News,* p. 50.

Johnson, K. (2009, July 15). White-collar cons ask the pros: The tab for prison prep: Up to $20K. *USA Today,* p. 1A.

Johnstone, P. (1999). Serious white collar fraud: Historical and contemporary perspectives. *Crime, Law and Social Change, 30,* 107–130.

Jones, A. (2008, April 4). Ex-tech professors put a family member on payroll. *Atlanta Journal Constitution.* Retrieved July 31, 2011, from http://www.ajc.com/metro/content/metro/stories/2008/04/23/tech0423.html?cxntlid=inform_artr.

Jordan, S. R. (2014). Research integrity, image, manipulation, and anonymizing photographs in visual social science research. *International Journal of Social Research Methodology, 17*(4), 441–458.

Judge not: Fall from honor. How Sol Watchler went from esteemed chief judge of New York to shamed prison inmate. (1997, July 1). *Psychology Today,* p. 30. Retrieved November 27, 2015, from https://www.psychologytoday.com/articles/199707/judge-not

Judicial Conduct Commission. (2011). Types of Judicial Misconduct. Retrieved December 22, 2011, from http://courts.ky.gov/NR/rdonlyres/DA400052-42DB-4129-89EF-8BE5554928B9/0/P12JudicialConductCommission Brochure711.pdf.

KHOU. (2015, September 17). *Houston mayor declares war on apartment slumlord.* Retrieved January 3, 2016, from http://www.khou.com/story/news/local/2015/09/18/houston-mayor-declares-war-apartment-slumlord/72380460/

KY3.com. (2015, July 22). *Springfield restaurant owner and son plead guilty in multi-million dollar fraud scheme.* Retrieved January 4, 2015, from http://www.ky3.com/news/local/springfield-restaurant-owner-son-plead-guilty-in-multimillion-dollar-fraud-scheme/21048998_34299122

Kane, J., & Wall, A. D. (2006). *The 2005 National Public Survey on White Collar Crime.* Fairmont, WV: National White Collar Crime Center.

Kane, P., & Cillizza, C. (2009, June 17). Sen. Ensign acknowledges an extramarital affair. *The Washington Post.* Retrieved July 30, 2011, from http://www.washingtonpost.com/wp-dyn/content/article/2009/06/16/AR2009061602746.html

Kane, R. J. (2002). Social ecology of police misconduct. *Criminology, 40*(4), 867–896.

Karpoff, J. M., Lee, D. S., & Martin, J. S. (2008). The consequences to managers for financial misrepresentation. *Journal of Financial Economics, 88*(2), 193–215.

Kass, J. (2009, August 21). From Quinn on down, all were on her side. *Chicago Tribune.* Retrieved July 30, 2011, from http://articles.chicagotribune.com/2009-08-21/news/0908200904_1_towns-home-politicians-deacon

Katz, I. (2007, March 13). South Florida a hot spot for commodities fraud. *McClatchy-Tribune Business News,* p. 1.

Kaufman, J. (1988, March 7). The fall of Jimmy Swaggart [Electronic version]. *People, 29*(9). Retrieved February 22, 2011, from http://www.people.com/people/archive/article/0,,20098413,00.html

Kawalec, A. (2013, April 15). As cited in J. Griffin: *Keeping up with the hackers.* Retrieved January 6, 2016 from http://www.securityinfowatch.com/blog/10915705/keeping-up-with-hackers

Kawalec, A. (2014, August). How do you steal $60 million in 60 seconds. BVEX. Retreved from http://businessvalueexchange.com/blog/2014/04/07/steal-60-million-60-seconds/

Keane, A. G., & Kitamura, M. (2009, November 25). Toyota's recalls test promise to make "better cars" (update 1). *Bloomberg News.* Retrieved July 1, 2010, from http://www.bloomberg.com/apps/news?pid=news archive&sid=ayG_dQWAhAp0

Keenan, C. E., Brown, G. C., Pontell, H. N., & Geis, G. (1985). Medical students' attitudes on physician fraud and abuse in the Medicare and Medicaid programs. *Academic Medicine, 60*(3), 167–173.

Kelly, C. (2009, August 29). Going to the big house? Let us plan your stay: A growing U.S. industry coaches criminals on how to prepare for, and survive, life behind bars. *Toronto Star,* p. IN01.

Kelley, F. (2005). The sweating system. *American Journal of Public Health, 95,* 49–52.

Kelley, M. L., & Parsons, B. (2000). Sexual harassment in the 1990s: A university-wide survey of female faculty, administration, staff, and students. *Journal of Higher Education, 71*(5), 548–568.

Kerbs, J. J., & Jolley, J. M. (2007). The joy of violence: What about violence is fun in middle-school? *American Journal of Criminal Justice, 32*(1), 12–29.

Kerley, K. R., & Copes, H. (2004). The effects of criminal justice contact on employment stability for white-collar and street-level offenders. *International Journal of Offender Therapy and Comparative Criminology, 48,* 65–84.

Kimball, P. (2005). *Syndi-Court justice: Judge Judy and exploitation of arbitration.* Retrieved June 24, 2010, from http://www.americanbar.org/content/dam/aba/migrated/dispute/essay/syndicourtjustice.authcheckdam.pdf

"Kingpin of commodities fraud" gets 17 1/2 years: Florida telemarketer even offered clients high-interest loans to buy his non-existent products. (2006, June 23). *Edmonton Journal*, p. E2.

Kinnaird, B. A. (2007). Exploring liability profiles: A proximate cause analysis of police misconduct: Part II. *International Journal of Police Science and Management, 9*(3), 201–213.

Kintisch, E. (2006, June 28). Poehlman sentenced to 1 year of prison. *ScienceNow.* Retrieved June 4, 2010, from http://news.sciencenow.org/sciencenow/2006/06/28-01.html

Klenowski, P. M. (2012). "Learning the good with the bad": Are occupational white-collar offenders taught how to neutralize their crimes? *Criminal Justice Review, 37*(4), 461–477.

Klenowski, P. M., Copes, H., & Mullins, C. W. (2011). Gender, identity, and accounts: How white collar offenders do gender when making sense of their crimes. *Justice Quarterly, 28*(1), 46–69.

Kline, P. M., McMackin, R., & Lezotte, E. (2008). Impact of the clergy abuse scandal on parish communities. *Journal of Child Sexual Abuse, 17*(3/4), 290–300.

Knight, J. (1995, November 17). The misuse of mandatory counseling. *Chronicle of Higher Education*, p. B1.

Knopp, J., Jr. (1966). Branding and the Robinson-Patman Act. *Journal of Business, 39*(1), 24.

Knottnerus, J. D., Ulsperger, J. S., Cummins, S., & Osteen, E. (2006). Exposing Enron: Media representations of ritualized deviance in corporate culture. *Crime, Media & Culture, 2*, 177–195.

Knox, N. (1997, September 7). Broker fraud sanctions hit a record high. *Chicago Sun-Times*, p. 56.

Knox, N. (2000, June 2). Task force scours for note fraud: 4,600 investors fell victim to promissory note scam. *USA Today*, p. 1B.

Kolker, R. (2009, September). The Madoff exfiles. *New York Magazine*. New York, NY: New York Media LLC.

Konigsmark, A. R. (2006, October 24). Crooked builders hit storm victims. *USA Today*, p. 3A.

Kopel, J. (2008, June 13). New law requires rental units to be habitable. *The Colorado Statesman*. Retrieved July 29, 2011, from http://www.coloradostatesman.com/kopel/new-law-requires-rental-units-be-habitable

Kopperud, S. (2010, September 24). Senate ag panel spanks EPA. *Brownfield Ag News.* Retrieved July 29, 2011, from http://brownfieldagnews.com/2010/09/24/senate-ag-panel-spanks-epa/

Korolishin, J. (2003, September). Store employees remain largest source of shrink. *Stores, 85*(9), p. LP24.

Kostelnik, J. (2012). Sentencing white-collar criminals: When is shaming viable? *Global Crime, 13*(3), 141–159.

Kovaleski, S. F. (2002, January 12). Monitoring device sought for slumlord; D.C. wants to make sure man lives in his building. *The Washington Post*, p. B03.

Kramer, R. C. (1984). Is corporate crime serious crime? Criminal justice and corporate crime control. *Journal of Contemporary Criminal Justice, 2*, 7–10.

Kramer, R. C. (2013). Carbon in the atmosphere and power in America: Climate change as state-corporate crime. *Journal of Crime and Justice, 36* (2), 153–170.

Kramer, R. C., Michalowski, R. J., & Kauzlarich, D. (2002). The origins and development of the concept and theory of state corporate crime. *Crime and Delinquency, 48*(2), 263–282.

Kreps, D. (2010, January 8). Settlements near for victims of 2003 Great White night club fire. *Rolling Stone.* Retrieved July 30, 2011, from http://www.rollingstone.com/music/news/settlements-near-for-victims-of-2003-great-white-nightclub-fire-20100108

Kresevich, M. (2007, February). Using culture to cure theft. *Security Management, 51*(2), p. 46.

Kuehn, B. M. (2014). WHO: More than 7 million air pollution deaths each year. *Journal of the American Medical Association, 311*(15), 1486.

Kurkjian, S., Ebbert, S., Ebbert, T., & Farragher, T. (2003, June 9). Series of errors sealed crowd's fate. *The Boston Globe.* Retrieved November 29, 2015, from http://www.boston.com/news/packages/nightclub_fire/Series_of_errors_sealed_crowd_s_fate+.shtml

La, J. (2005, March 30). Altered grades lead to student's arrest: Campus computer experts say security measures detected unauthorized access. *Daily Nexus, 94*(85), p. 1.

Landlord Jailed for Inhuman Conditions in Bronx Building. (2008). *Observer: Real estate.* Retrieved January 5, 2016, from http://observer.com/2008/02/city-throws-slumlord-in-jail-for-nine-days-updated/

Landlord Rating Breakdown. (n.d.a). Abet management. *Purdue off-campus Housing.* Retrieved January 3, 2016 from https://www.housing.purdue.edu/OffCampus/Survey/LandlordRatingBreakdown?landlordID=1ff6ba29-8de6-472b-bd74-c7b7a41b1085

Landlord Rating Breakdown. (n.d.b). Milo properties: Anna. *Purdue off-campus Housing.* Retrieved January 3, 2016, from https://www.housing.purdue.edu/OffCampus/Survey/LandlordRatingBreakdown?landlordID=bba22198-70f2-41ea-8ff7-bda5711966d9

Langton, L., & Cohen, T. H. (2008). *Civil bench and jury trials in state courts, 2005. Bureau of Justice Statistics.* Washington, DC: U.S. Department of Justice, Office of Justice Programs. Retrieved from November 27, 2015, from http://www.bjs.gov/content/pub/pdf/cbjtsc05.pdf

Langton, L., & Piquero, N. L. (2007). Can general strain theory explain white-collar crime? A preliminary investigation of the relationship between strain and select white-collar offenses. *Journal of Criminal Justice, 35*(1), 1–15.

Lardo, A. E. (2006). Comment: The 2003 extradition treaty between the United States and United Kingdom: Towards a solution to transnational white-collar crime prosecution. *Emory International Crime Review, 20*, 867–903.

Larsson, P. (2006). International police co-operation: A Norwegian perspective. *Journal of Financial Crime, 13*(4), 456–466.

Lasley, J. R. (1988). Toward a control theory of white-collar offending. *Journal of Quantitative Criminology, 4*(4), 347–362.

Latimer, P. (2002). Reporting suspicions of money laundering and "whistleblowing": The legal and other implications for intermediaries and their advisers. *Journal of Financial Crime, 10*(1), 23–29.

Lauchs, M., Keast, R., & Yousefpour, N. (2011). Corrupt police networks: Uncovering hidden relationship patterns, functions and roles. *Policing & Society, 21*(1), 110–127.

Lavis, R. (2015, December 23, 2015). Sears worker chose $600 from register cops say. Retrieved December 29, 2015, from http://www.silive.com/news/index.ssf/2015/12/sears_worker_stole_600_from_re.html

Lawless, J. F. (1988). The white-collar defendant: High visibility, high stakes. *Trial, 24*(9), 42–48.

Layman, E., McCampbell, S., & Moss, A. (2000). Sexual misconduct in corrections. *American Jails, 14*(5), 23–35.

Layton, L. (2009, October 13). Under Obama, regulatory agencies step up enforcement. *The Washington Post.* Retrieved July 31, 2011, from http://www.washingtonpost.com/wp-dyn/content/article/2009/10/12/AR2009101202554.html

Leap, T. L. (2007). *Dishonest dollars: The dynamics of white-collar crime.* Ithaca, NY: Industrial and Labor Relations (ILR) Press.

LeClair, J., Abraham, S., & Shih, S. (2013). An interdisciplinary approach to educating an effective cyber security workforce. *InfoSecCD '13*, 71.

Lederman, D. (2009, September 11). The game of ghost writing. *Inside Higher Ed.* Retrieved July 29, 2011, from http://www.insidehighered.com/news/2009/09/11/ghostwrite

Lee, D. E. (2009). Cheating in the classroom: Beyond policing. *Clearing House, 82*(4), 171–174.

Lee, H., Lim, H., Moore, D. D., & Kim, J. (2013). How police organizational structure correlates with frontline officers' attitudes toward corruption: A multilevel model. *Police Practice and Research, 14*(5), 386–401.

Lee, J. (2010, November 12). *What were you thinking? Criminal justice students and their social networking sites.* Paper presented at a meeting of the Georgia Political Science Associations, Savannah, GA.

Lee, M. S. (1998). *United States v. Nippon Paper Industries Co.*: Extending the criminal provisions of the Sherman Act to foreign conduct producing a substantial intended effect in the United States. *Wake Forest Law Review, 33*(1), 189–217.

Lee, M. T., & Ermann, M. D. (1999). Pinto "madness" as a flawed landmark narrative. *Social Problems, 46*, 30–47.

Leegin Creative Leather Products, Inc. v. PSKS, Inc., 127 S.Ct. 2705 (2007).

Lehr, J. (2010, March 23). Joplin dentist granted probation in Medicaid fraud. *All Business*. Retrieved July 29, 2011, from http://www.allbusiness.com/govern ment/government-bodies-offices-regional/ 14166639-1.html

Leighton, P. (2013). Corporate crime and the corporate agenda for crime control: Disappearing aware- ness of corporate crime and increasing abuses of power. *Western Criminology Review, 14*(2), 38–51

Leonning, C. D. (2001, December 14). Slumlord gets 60 days—In his building: D.C. man who denied ten- ants heat, hot water agrees to unusual sentence. *The Washington Post*, p. B01.

Leto, J. L., Pogrebin, M. R., & Stretesky, P. B. (2007). Defending the indigent white-collar criminal: Federal public defender defense strategies for post-indictment representation. *Journal of Crime and Justice, 30*(2), 79–113.

Levi, M. (2006). Media construction of financial white- collar crimes. *British Journal of Criminology, 46*(6), 1037–1057.

Levi, S. D. (2014, February). Cybersecurity: Amid increasing attacks and government controversy, a framework to reduce risk emerges. *Financial Fraud Law Report. 6*(2), 165–171.

Levin, M. (1984). Corporate probation conditions. *Fordham Law Review, 52*, 637–662.

Levine, J. P. (1983). Using jury verdict forecasts in criminal defense strategy. *Judicature, 66*(10), 448.

Lewis, C. A. (1983). Judicial misconduct in California. *San Fernando Valley Law Review, 11*, 43–69.

Lim, H. A. (2002). Women doctors and crime: A review of California physician sanctioning data 1990–1994. *Justice Professional, 15*(2), 149–167.

Litton, R. (1998). Fraud and the insurance industry: Why don't they do something about it, then? *International Journal of Risk and Crime Prevention, 3*(3), 193–205.

Loane, S. (2000, December). White-collar criminals suf- fer a bad case of jailhouse blues. *Sydney Morning Herald*. Retrieved July 30, 2011, from http://www .sheilas.com.au/sheilas-articles/2000/12/11/ whitecollar-criminals-suffer-a-bad-case-of-jail house-blues/

Locker, J. P., & Godfrey, B. (2006). Ontological boundar- ies and temporal watersheds in the development of white-collar crime. *British Journal of Criminol- ogy, 46*, 976–992.

Lofquist, W. S. (1993). Organizational probation and the U.S. sentencing commission. *Annals of the American Academy of Political and Social Science, 525*, 157–169.

Lokken, F., & Mullins, C. (2014). *Trends in eLearning Tracking the impact of eLearning at community colleges*. Washington, DC: Instructional Technology Council.

Londoño, E. (2007, August 19). Gaithersburg man admits to equity-skimming scam. *The Washington Post*. Retrieved July 29, 2011, from http://www.washing tonpost.com/wp-dyn/content/article/2007/08/18/ AR2007081801136.html?nav=emailpage

Longshore, D., & Turner, S. (1998). Self-control and criminal opportunity: Cross-sectional test of the general theory of crime. *Criminal Justice and Behavior, 25*(1), 81–98.

Louisiana Department of Environmental Quality. (2015, February 9). *Zachary man pleads guilty to illegal dumping of gasoline and diesel fuel*. Retrieved January 3, 2016, from http://www.deq .louisiana.gov/portal/portals/0/news/pdf/Wallace plearelease.pdf

Lunder, S. (2015). Asbestos kills 12,000-15,000 people per year in the U. S. *Asbestos Action Fund*. Retrieved October 28, 2015, from http://www .asbestosnation.org/facts/asbestos-kills-12000- 15000-people-per-year-in-the-u-s/

Lusthaus, J. (2012, May). Trust in the world of cyber- crime. *Global Crime, 13*(2), 71–94.

Lyman, F. (2003a). Anger builds over EPA's 9/11 report. *Msnbc.com*. Retrieved July 30, 2011, http://www .msnbc.msn.com/id/3076626/ns/health-your_ environment/t/anger-builds-over-epas-report/

Lyman, F. (2003b). *Messages in the dust: What are the lessons of the environmental health response to the terrorist attacks of September 11?* National Environmental Health Association. Retrieved July 30, 2011, from http://www.neha.org/pdf/ messages_in_the_dust.pdf

Lynch, M. J. (2013). The extraordinary relevance of Barak's *Theft of a Nation. Western Criminology Review, 13*(2): 52–60.

Lynch, M. J., McGurrin, D., & Fenwick, M. (2004). Disappearing act: The representation of corporate crime research in criminology journals and text- books. *Journal of Criminal Justice, 32*, 389–398.

Lynch, M. J., Stretesky, P., & Hammond, P. (2000). Media coverage of chemical crimes, Hillsborough County, Florida, 1987–97. *British Journal of Criminology, 40*, 112–126.

Madden, S., Hartley, R. D., Walker, J. T., & Miller, J. M. (2012). Sympathy for the devil: An exploration of federal judicial discretion in the processing of white-collar offenders. *American Journal of Criminal Justice, 37*, 4–18.

Madden, S., Walker, K. T., & Miller, M. J. (2008). Does size really matter? A reexamination of Sheldon's somatypes and criminal behavior. *The Social Science Journal, 45*, 330–344.

Madoff's victims. (2009). *Wall Street Journal*. Retrieved July 29, 2011, from http://s.wsj.net/public/ resources/documents/st_madoff_victims_ 20081215.html

Maher, T. M. (2003). Police sexual misconduct: Officers' perceptions of its extent and causality. *Criminal Justice Review, 28*(2), 355–381.

Mail Foreign Service. (2010, February 3). "'There's no brakes . . . hold on and pray': Last words of man

before he and his family died in Toyota Lexus crash." Available online at http://www.dailymail .co.uk/news/article-1248177/Toyota-recall-Last- words-father-family-died-Lexus-crash.html.

Maimon, D., Alper, M., Sobesto, B., & Cukier, M. (2014). Restrictive deterrent effects of a warning system banner in an attacked computer system. *Criminology, 52*(1), 33–59.

Maimon, D., Kamerdze, A., Cukier, M., & Sobesto, B. (2013). Daily trends and origin of computer-focused crimes against a large university computer network. *British Journal of Criminology, 53*, 319–343.

Maine Home Repair Fraud, Maine Criminal code §§907–909.

Makkai, T., & Braithwaite, J. (1991). Criminological theories and regulatory compliance. *Criminology, 29*(2), 191–217.

Makkai, T., & Braithwaite, J. (1994). Reintegrative shaming and compliance with regulatory stan- dards. *Criminology, 32*(3), 361–385.

Malos, S. (2007). Appearance-based sex discrimination and stereotyping in the workplace: Whose con- duct should we regulate? *Employment Responses Rights, 19*, 95–111.

Mann, K. (1985). *Defending white-collar crime: A por- trait of attorneys at work*. New Haven, CT: Yale University Press.

Mann, K., Wheeler, S., & Sarat, A. (1980). Sentencing the white-collar offender. *American Criminal Law Review, 17*, 479–500.

Mannheim, H. (1949). Sutherland, Edwin, H.: White- collar crime. *Annals of the American Academy of Political and Social Science, 266*, 243–244.

Manos, J., & Chase, D. (Writers), & Coulter, A. (Director). (1999). College [Television series epi- sode]. In D. Chase (Producer), *The Sopranos*. New York, NY: Silvercup Studios.

Mansfield-Devine, S. (2009, March). Google hacking 101. *Network Security*, 4–6.

Marcotte, D. (2008). Role of social factors in the sexual misconduct of Roman Catholic clergy: A second look at the John Jay data. *Sexual Addiction & Compulsivity, 15*(1), 23–38.

Marcum, C. D., Higgins, G. E., & Tewksbury, R. (2012). Incarceration or community placement: Examining the sentences of cybercriminals. *Criminal Justice Studies, 25*(1), 33–40.

Margret, J. J., & Sreenivasan, S. (2013). Implementation of data mining in medical fraud detection. *International Journal of Computer Applications, 69*(5), 1–4.

Mariani, P. (2013). How damages recovery actions can improve the fight against corruption: The crisis of criminal law policies. *Crime, Law and Social Change, 60*(2), 209–226.

Marquet, C. (2014). *The 2013 Marquet report on embez- zlement*. New York, NY: Marquet International.

Mars, G. (1983). *Cheats at work: An anthropology of workplace crime*. London: Allen and Unwin.

Martha Stewart reads a statement outside Manhattan federal court Friday after she was sentenced to five months in prison. (2004, July 17). *Associated Press.* Retrieved June 6, 2010, from http://nl.newsbank.com/nl-search/we/Archives?p_product=APAB&p_theme=apab&p_action=search&p_maxdocs=200&s_dispstring=martha%20stewart%20statement&p_field_advanced-0=&p_text_advanced-0=%28%22martha%20stewart%20statement%22%29&xcal_numdocs=20&p_perpage=10&p_sort=YMD_date:D&xcal_useweights=no

Martin, N., & Rice, J. (2011). Cybercrime: Understanding and addressing the concerns of stakeholders. *Computers & Security, 30,* 803–814.

Martin, R., Mutchnick, R., & Austin, W. T. (1990). *Pioneers in criminological thought.* New York, NY: Macmillan.

Martin, S. (2007). A rule of reason for vertical price fixing. *The Metropolitan Corporate Counsel.* Retrieved July 29, 2011, from http://www.metrocorpcounsel.com/current.php?artType=view&artMonth=June&artYear=2011&EntryNo=7284

Martin, S. L., Coyne-Beasley, T., Hoehn, M., Mathew, M., Runyan, C. W., Orton, S., et al. (2009). Primary prevention of violence against women: Training needs of violence practitioners. *Violence Against Women, 15*(1), 44–56.

Martin, V. (2004). Detection and prevention of mortgage loan fraud. *Risk Management Association (RMA) Journal.* Retrieved July 29, 2011, from http://findarticles.com/p/articles/mi_m0ITW/is_1_87/ai_n14897572/

Martinelli, T. J. (2007). Minimizing risk by defining off-duty police misconduct. *Police Chief, 74*(6), 40–45.

Marx, G. T. (1982). Who really gets stung? Some issues raised by the new police undercover work. *Crime & Delinquency, 28*(2), 165–200.

Maryland contractor fined $1.2 million for asbestos violations. (2010, June 7). *Mesothelioma News.* Retrieved July 29, 2011, from http://www.mesotheliomanews.com/2010/06/07/maryland-contractor-fined/

Mason, K. A. (2007). Punishment and paperwork: White-collar offenders under community supervision. *American Journal of Criminal Justice, 31*(2), 23–36.

Mason, K. A., & Benson, M. L. (1996). The effect of social support on fraud victims' reporting behavior: A research note. *Justice Quarterly, 13*(3), 511–524.

Mass, A. (1986). U.S. prosecution of state and local officials for political corruption: Is the bureaucracy out of control in a high-stakes operation involving the constitutional system? *Publius: Journal of Federalism, 17*(3), 195–230.

Masters, B. A. (2005, July 15). Are executives' sentences too harsh? Debate is rising about deterrence of corporate crime. *Houston Chronicle,* T2. Retrieved November 29, 2015, from http://www.chron.com/business/article/Are-executives-sentences-too-harsh-1926161.php

Matza, D. (1964). *Delinquency and drift.* New York, NY: Wiley.

May, D. C., & Wood, P. B. (2005). What influences offenders' willingness to serve alternative sanctions? *Prison Journal, 85*(2), 145.

Mazur, T. (2001, April 16). Culture beats internal theft. *DSN Retailing Today, 40*(8), p. 14.

McAllister, L. (2008). On environmental enforcement and compliance: A reply to Professor Crawford's review of *Making Law Matter: Environmental Protection and Legal Institutions in Brazil. George Washington International Law Review, 40*(3), 649–685.

McArdle, J., & Nelson, G. (2010, December 16). Environmental justice activist urges EPA chief to "roll up your sleeves" at tense W.H. forum. *The New York Times.* Retrieved July 29, 2011, from http://www.nytimes.com/gwire/2010/12/16/16greenwire-environmental-justice-activist-urges-epa-chief-24157.html

McBarnet, D. (1991). Whiter than white-collar crime. *British Journal of Sociology, 42,* 323–344.

McCarthy, B. (2011, January 12). *Crime and punishment: Judge orders book written as community service.* Retrieved November 27, 2015, from http://www.dailyfinance.com/2011/01/12/judge-orders-book-as-community-service/

McCarthy, B. J. (1981). *Exploratory study of corruption in corrections.* Unpublished doctoral dissertation, Florida State University.

McConnaughey, J., & Kunzelman, M. (2015, December 2). Manslaughter charges dropped for BP supervisors in oil spill. *Providence Journal.* Retrieved January 3, 2016, from http://www.providencejournal.com/article/ZZ/20151202/NEWS/312029907

McCormack, A. (1985). The sexual harassment of students by teachers: The case of students in science. *Sex Roles, 13*(1 & 2), pp. 21–32.

McCoy, K. (2009a, June 30). Appeal of Madoff's 150-year sentence wouldn't matter. *USA Today.* Retrieved January 20, 2011, from http://abcnews.go.com/Business/story?id=7973772&page=1

McCoy, K. (2009b, June 30). Madoff gets 150-year sentence as victims applaud. *USA Today.* Retrieved November 29, 2015 from http://www.usatoday.com/money/industries/brokerage/2009-06-29-madoff-sentencing_N.htm

McCready, B., & Tinley, J. (2009, December 16). Alleged embezzler in FBI custody. *New Haven Register.* Retrieved July 30, 2011, from http://www.nhregister.com/articles/2009/12/16/news/milford/al—embezzle_1216.txt

McDade, R. J., & O'Donnell, K. (1992). Parallel civil and criminal proceedings. *American Criminal Law Review, 29*(2), 697–738.

McDowell, M. G. (2013). 'Becoming a waste land where nothing can survive': Resisting state-corporate environmental crime in a 'forgotten' place. *Contemporary Justice Review, 16*(4), 394–411.

McGettrick, A. (2013, August 30). Toward curricular guidelines for cybersecurity: Report of on a workshop on cybersecurity education and training. *Association for Computing Machinery.* Retrieved January 1, 2016, from https://www.acm.org/education/TowardCurricularGuidelinesCybersec.pdf

McGurrin, D., Jarrell, M., Jahn, A., & Cochrane, B. (2013). White collar crime representation in the criminological literature revisited, 2001–2010. *Western Criminology Review, 14*(2), 3–19.

McGurrin, D., & Kappeler, V. E. (2002). Media accounts of police sexual violence: Rotten apples or state supported violence? In K. M. Lersch (Ed.), *Policing and misconduct* (pp. 121–142). Upper Saddle River, NJ: Prentice Hall.

McKay, B. (2006, July 6). Coke employee faces charges in plot to sell secrets. *Wall Street Journal,* p. B6.

McKinney, L., Roberts, T., & Shefman, P. (2013). Perspectives and experiences of financial aid counselors on community college students who borrow. *Journal of Student Financial Aid, 43*(1), 3–17.

Mclaughlin, T. (2010, April 15). BRIEF: Destin man gets 5 years for fraud: Owen collected $2.2 million for Oasis futures business. *Northwest Florida Daily New,* p. B1.

McMahon, P. (2015, September 25). Prominent south Florida activist admits $3.4M tax fraud. *Sun Sentinel.* Retrieved December 29, 2015, from http://www.sun-sentinel.com/local/broward/fl-pamella-watson-guilty-plea-20150925-story.html

McMullan, J. L., & Perrier, D. C. (2007). Controlling cyber-crime and gambling: Problems and paradoxes in the mediation of law and criminal organization. *Police Practice & Research, 8*(5), 431–444.

McNamara, M. (2006, May 23). FTC head opposes anti-gouging law: Says regulation would be hard to enforce and could cause fuel shortages. *Columbia Broadcasting System (CBS) News.* Retrieved July 29, 2011, from http://www.cbsnews.com/stories/2006/05/22/business/main1639514.shtml

McNeill, B. (2010, May 28). UV fights inquiry by Cuccinelli. *Charlottesville Daily Progress.* Retrieved July 29, 2011, from http://www2.dailyprogress.com/cdp/news/local/education/article/uva_fights_inquiry_by_cuccinelli/56663/

McNerney, M., & Papadopoulos, E. (2013). Hacker's delight: Law firm risk and liability in the cyber age. *American University Law Review, 62,* 1243–1269.

McNulty, P. (n.d.). *Principles of federal prosecution of business organizations.* Washington, DC: U.S. Department of Justice, Office of Deputy Attorney General.

McShane, L. (2009, July 31). Hoboken mayor Peter Cammarano resigns after arrest in sweeping corruption probe. *NY Daily News.* Retrieved July 29, 2011, from http://www.nydailynews.com/news/ny_crime/2009/07/31/2009-07-31_hoboken_mayor_peter_cammarano_resigns_after_arrest_in_sweeping_corruption_probe.html

Meddling at EPA? Activists point to survey. (2008, April 23). *Wapedia, Mobile Encyclopedia.* Retrieved December 15, 2010, from http://wapedia.mobi/en/United_States_Environmental_Protection_Agency?t=9

Medicare.Gov. (2008). *Nursing homes: About nursing home inspections.* Retrieved July 29, 2011, from http://www.medicare.gov/nursing/about inspections.asp?PrinterFriendly=true

Meerts, C. (2013). Corporate security–Private justice? (Un)settling employer-employee troubles. *Security Journal, 26*(3), 264–279.

Meier, K. J., & Holbrook, T. M. (1992). "I seen my opportunities and I took 'em": Political corruption in the American states. *Journal of Politics, 54*(1), 135–155.

Meincke, P. (2009, June 12). Chicago owner loses home in mortgage scam. *WLS-TV.* Retrieved June 29, 2010, from http://abclocal.go.com/wls/story?section=news/local&id=6862674

Meisner, J. (2015, September 21). Bentley driving preacher convicted of fraud and lying to the FBI. *Chicago Tribune.* Retrieved January 1, 2016, fromhttp://www.chicagotribune.com/news/local/breaking/ct-preacher-fraud-guilty-met-20150923-story.html

Melenyzer, L. (1999). Double jeopardy protection from civil sanctions after *Hudson v. United States. Journal of Criminal Law and Criminology, 89*(3), 1007.

Mell, P., Kent, K., & Nusbaum, J. (2005, November). Guide to malware incident prevention and handling: Recommendations of the national institute of standards and technology. *National Institutes of Standards and Technology,* Special Publication 800-83. Retrieved December 27, 2015, from http://csrc.nist.gov/publications/nistpubs/800-83/SP800-83.pdf

Mendez, F. (2014). Can corruption foster regulatory compliance? *Public Choice, 158,* 189–207.

Mercado, C. C., Tallon, J. A., & Terry, K. J. (2008). Persistent sexual abusers in the Catholic Church: An examination of characteristics and offenses patterns. *Criminal Justice and Behavior, 35,* 629–642.

Merton, R. K. (1938). Social structure and anomie. *American Sociological Review, 3,* 672–682.

Messner, S., & Rosenfeld, R. (2007). *Crime and the American dream* (4th ed.). Belmont, CA: Wadsworth.

Meyer, C. (2015, June). High stakes games: Cybersecurity awareness training. *Security,* 35–36.

Meyer, P. (2011, January 11). Tom DeLay is sentenced to three years. *Los Angeles Times.* Retrieved from http://articles.latimes.com/2011/jan/11/nation/la-na-tom-delay-20110111

Mian, A., & Sufi, A. (2015). *House of debt: How they (and you) caused the great recession, and how we can prevent it from happening again.* Chicago, IL: University of Chicago Press.

Microsoft. (2010). *What is counterfeiting?* Retrieved July, 29, 2011, from http://www.microsoft.com/resources/howtotell/en/counterfeit.mspx

Middlemiss, A. D., & Gupta, N. (2007). US interagency law enforcement cooperation since September 11, 2001: Improvements and results. *Journal of Financial Crime, 14*(2), 138–149.

Miller, G. (1993). White-collar criminals share one trait—Greed. *Corrections Today, 55*(3), 22–24.

Miller, W. (1975). *Violence by youth gangs and youth groups as a crime problem in major American cities* (Final Report). Washington, DC: U.S. Department of Justice, Office of Justice Programs, Office of Juvenile Justice and Delinquency Prevention.

Millspaugh, P. E. (2001, Winter). Can corporations be incarcerated? *Business and Society Review, 72,* pp. 48–51.

Minkel, W. (2002). Sniffing out the cheaters. *School Library Journal, 48*(6), 25.

Minkes, J. (1990). Crimes of the rich. *Probation Journal, 37,* 127–130.

Minnaar, A. (2008). 'You've received a greeting e-card from . . .' The changing face of cybercrime e-mail spam scams. *Acta Criminologica CRIMSA Conference Special Edition 2,* 92–116.

Minnaar, A. (2013). Editorial: Information security, cybercrime, cyberterrorism and the exploration of cybersecurity vulnerabilities. *Southern African Journal of Criminology, 26*(2), 1–4.

Minor, W. W. (1981). Techniques of neutralization: A reconceptualization and empirical examination. *Journal of Research in Crime and Delinquency, 18*(2), 295–318.

Mishra, B. K., & Prasad, A. (2006). Minimizing retail shrinkage due to employee theft. *International Journal of Retail and Distribution Management, 34*(11), p. 817.

Mohr, H., Pritchard, J., & Lush, T. (2010, June 9). BP spill response plans flawed. *MSNBC.com.* Retrieved October 20, 2010, from http://www.msnbc.msn.com/id/37599810/

Mokhiber, R. (n. d.). Top 100 corporate criminals of the decade. *Corporate Crime Reporter.* Retrieved July 29, 2011, from http://www.corporatecrimereporter.com/top100.html

Mon, W. (2002). Causal factors of corporate crime in Taiwan: Qualitative and quantitative findings. *International Journal of Offender Therapy and Comparative Criminology, 46*(2), 183–205.

Montano, E. (2001, June 21–22). *Technologies of electronic crime.* Paper presented at the 4th National Outlook Symposium on Crime, Canberra, Australia.

Montell, G. (2009). President of University of Texas-Pan American, accused of plagiarism, will retire. *Chronicle of Higher Education.* Retrieved June 10, 2010, from http://chronicle.com/blogs/onhiring/president-of-u-of-texas-pan-american-accused-of-plagiarism-will-retire/826

Montgomery, W. D., Baron, R. A., & Weisskopf, M. K. (2007). Potential effects of proposed price gouging legislation on the cost and severity of gasoline supply interruptions. *Journal of Competition Law & Economics, 3*(3), 357–397.

Moore, E., & Mills, M. (1990). The neglected victims and unexamined costs of white-collar crime. *Crime and Delinquency, 36,* 408–418.

Morgan, T. (1995). Sanctions and remedies for attorney misconduct. *Southern Illinois University Law Journal, 19,* 343–370.

Morris, J. (1999). Big hairy pile of whoa! Heroin, Pinochet, ABBA—Oh my! Retrieved July 29, 2011, from http://www.gettingit.com/article/261

Morris, J. (2010). America's asbestos age. *The Center for Public Integrity.* Retrieved July 29, 2011, from http://www.publicintegrity.org/investigations/asbestos/articles/entry/2184/

Morris, R. G., & Blackburn, A. G. (2009). Cracking the code: An empirical exploration of social learning theory and computer crime. *Journal of Crime and Justice, 32*(1), 1–34.

Morris, R. G., & El Sayed, S. (2013). The development of self-reported white-collar offending. *Journal of Contemporary Criminal Justice, 29*(3), 369–384.

Morrison, J., & Morrison, T. (2001). Psychiatrist disciplined by state medical board. *American Journal of Psychiatry, 158*(3), 474–478.

Mortgage Asset Research Institute. (2010). *12th periodic mortgage fraud case report.* Retrieved July 29, 2011, from http://www.lexisnexis.com/risk/downloads/literature/MortgageFraudReport 12thEdition.pdf

Motivans, M. (2015). *Federal justice statistics, 2012-statistical tables.* Washington, DC: U.S. Department of Justice. Retrieved November 8, 2015 from http://www.bjs.gov/index.cfm?ty=pbdetail&iid=5217.

Mortgage Bankers Association (MBA). (2007). *Mortgage fraud: Strengthening federal and state mortgage fraud prevention efforts.* Retrieved July 31, 2011, from http://www.mbaa.org/files/News/InternalResource/57274_Study.pdf

Moyer, L. (2009a, March 12). Bernie behind bars. *Forbes.com.* Retrieved July 30, 2011, from http://www.forbes.com/2009/03/12/madoff-white-collar-crime-fraud-business-wall-street-prisons.html

Moyer, L. (2009b, June 29). A history of long prison sentences. *Forbes.com.* Retrieved January 19, 2011, from http://www.cbc.ca/money/story/2009/06/25/f-forbes-madoff-prison-sentences.html

Moyer, W. (2010, December 18). Love Canal—A city built on a toxic dump. *Ezine Articles.* Retrieved July 29, 2011, from http://ezinearticles.com/?Love-Canal—A-City-Built-On-A-Toxic-Dump&id=5578148

Mueller, G. (1996). An essay on environmental criminality. In S. Edwards, T. Edwards, & C. Fields (Eds.), *Environmental crime and criminality* (pp. 1–34). New York, NY: Garland.

Mullen, F. (1999, January 25). Six steps to stopping internal theft. *Discount Store News, 38*(2), p. 12.

Mullins, C., & Rothe, D. (2007). The forgotten ones. *Critical Criminology, 15,* 135–158.

Mundy, L. (2008, October 5). When Michelle met Barack. *The Washington Post.* Retrieved July 29, 2011, from http://www.washingtonpost.com/wp-dyn/content/story/2008/10/03/ST2008100302144.html

Munroe, T. (1992, July 22). Senate panel hears about fraud, deception in auto-repair industry. *Washington Times,* p. C3.

Murphy, S. P. (2015, April 2). *Two ex-Chelsea housing officials guilty of corruption*. Retrieved January 4, 2016, from https://www.bostonglobe.com/metro/2015/04/02/two-chelsea-housing-agency-found-guilty-corruption-trial/TyOydubjfgOn17nQihLWhM/story.html

Murray, A. (2009a, June 25). Lax enforcement keeps slumlords from cleaning up act. *LA Progressive*. Retrieved June 29, 2010, from http://www.laprogressive.com/rankism/social-justice/lax-enforcement-keeps-slumlords-from-cleaning-up-act/

Murray, A. (2009b, December 17). Slumlord pays tenants $3.3 million to settle inner city law center lawsuit. *Tenants Together: California's Statewide Organization for Renters' Rights*. Retrieved June 29, 2010, from http://www.tenantstogether.org/article.php?id=1156

Nader, R. (2013, March 22). Getting tough on devastating corporate crime. *Huff Post Business*. Retrieved January 4, 2016, from http://www.huffingtonpost.com/ralph-nader/corporate-crime_b_2934600.html

Nahra, K. J. (1999, October). Handling the double-edged sword: Insurers and the fight against health care fraud. *Health Law, 12*, 12–17.

Nakayama, G. (2007, September 34). *Transmittal of final OECA parallel proceedings policy*. Washington, DC: Office of Enforcement and Compliance Assurance, Environmental Protection Agency. Retrieved December 2, 2015, from http://www2.epa.gov/sites/production/files/documents/parallel-proceedings-policy-09-24-07.pdf

Nammour, M. (2009, November 1). Two former hotel guards jailed for stealing guests' belongings. *McClatchy-Tribune Business News*. Retrieved July 30, 2011, from ABI/INFORM Complete database (Document ID No. 1890524941).

Nardo, M. (2004). Mapping the trails of financial crime. *Journal of Financial Crime, 12*(2), 139–143.

Nath, L., & Lovaglia, M. (2008). Cheating on multiple-choice exams: Monitoring, assessment, and an optional assignment. *College Teaching, 57*(1), 3–8.

National Association of Medicaid Fraud Control Units. (1991, March). *Medicaid fraud report March 1991*.

National Association of Medicaid Fraud Control Units. (1994, March). *Medicaid fraud report March 1994*.

National Association of Medicaid Fraud Control Units. (1995, September). *Medicaid fraud report September 1995*.

National Association of Medicaid Fraud Control Units. (1996, March). *Medicaid fraud report March 1996*.

National Association of Medicaid Fraud Control Units. (1998, September). *Medicaid fraud report September 1998*.

National Association of Medicaid Fraud Control Units. (2006, November). *Medicaid fraud report November 2006*. Retrieved November 30, 2015, from http://www.namfcu.net/resources/medicaid-fraud-reports-newsletters/2006-pulications/06%20Nov.pdf

National Association of Medicaid Fraud Control Units. (2009, May/June). *Medicaid fraud report May/June 2009*. Retrieved November 30, 2015, from http://www.namfcu.net/resources/medicaid-fraud-National Association of Medicaid Fraud Control Units. reports-newsletters/2009-publications/09MayJune.pdf

National Association of Medicaid Fraud Control Units. (2013, March/April). *Medicaid fraud report March/April*. Retrieved January 4, 2016, from http://www.namfcu.net/resources/medicaid-fraud-reports-newsletters/2013-publications/13MarApr.pdf

National Association of Medicaid Fraud Control Units. (2013, May/June). *Medicaid fraud report May/June*. Retrieved January 4, 2016, from http://www.namfcu.net/resources/medicaid-fraud-reports-newsletters/2013-publications/13MayJune.pdf

National Association of Medicaid Fraud Control Units. (2013, September/October). *Medicaid fraud report September/October*. Retrieved January 4, 2016, from http://www.namfcu.net/resources/medicaid-fraud-reports-newsletters/2013-publications/13SeptOct.pdf

National Association of Medicaid Fraud Control Units. (2013, November/December). *Medicaid fraud report November/December*. Retrieved January 4, 2016, from http://www.namfcu.net/resources/medicaid-fraud-reports-newsletters/2013-publications/13NovDec.pdf

National Association of Medicaid Fraud Control Units. (2014, November/December). *Medicaid fraud report November/December*. Retrieved January 4, 2016, from http://www.namfcu.net/resources/medicaid-fraud-reports-newsletters/2014-publications/14NovDec.pdf

National Association of Medicaid Fraud Control. (2015, January/February). *Medicaid fraud report January/February*. Retrieved January 4, 2016, from http://www.namfcu.net/resources/medicaid-fraud-reports-newsletters/2015-publications/15JanFeb.pdf

National Association of Attorneys General. (2009). *Top 10 complaints made to state attorneys general*.

National Center on Elder Abuse. (2008). *Major types of elder abuse*. Retrieved July 30, 2011, from http://www.ncea.aoa.gov/NCEAroot/Main_Site/FAQ/Basics/Types_Of_Abuse.aspx

National Commission on Urban Problems. (1972). *Building the American city*. Washington, DC: Government Printing Office.

National Health Care Anti-Fraud Association (2010). *The problem of health care fraud*. Retrieved November 27, 2015, from http://www.nhcaa.org/resources/health-care-anti-fraud-resources/the-challenge-of-health-care-fraud.aspx

National Highway Traffic Safety Administration. (2002, April). Preliminary report: The incidence rate of odometer fraud. *U. S. Department of Transportation*. Retrieved January 1, 2016, from http://www.nhtsa.gov/cars/rules/regrev/evaluate/809441.html

National Highway Traffic Safety Administration. (2010, February). Information about odometer fraud. *U. S. Department of Transportation*. Retrieved January 1, 2016, from file:///Users/stapp1/Downloads/811284.pdf

National Oceanic and Atmospheric Administration. (2010). *New federal rule allows NOAA to deny port entry to illegal fishing vessels* [Press release]. Retrieved July 30, 2011, from http://www.noaanews.noaa.gov/stories2010/20101013_fishing.html

National Practitioner Data Bank. (n. d.). *NPDB research statistics*. Washington, DC: U.S. Department of Health and Human Services. Retrieved October 31, 2015, from http://www.npdb.hrsa.gov/resources/npdbstats/npdbStatistics.jsp

National Science Foundation (NSF). (2015). *Women, minorities and people with disabilities in science and engineering*. Retrieved January 1, 2016, from http://www.nsf.gov/statistics/2015/nsf15311/

National White Collar Crime Center. (NW3C). (2009). *Welcome*. Retrieved July 30, 2011, from http://www.nw3c.org/

Near, J. P., & Miceli, M. P. (2008). Wrongdoing, whistle-blowing, and retaliation in the U.S. government: What have researchers learned from the merit systems protection board (MSPB) results? *Review of Public Personnel Administration, 28*(3), 263–281.

Neil, M. (2009, September 2). Pfizer whistle-blower's $51.5M payday could spark more qui tam suits. *American Bar Association Journal*. Retrieved July 31, 2011, from http://www.abajournal.com/news/article/pfizer_whistleblowers_51.5m_payday_could_spark_more_qui_tam_suits/

Nelson, J. (2010, February 5). Supervisor Blane spent $50,000 to hire white-collar criminal lawyer. *Daily Bulletin*. Retrieved July 31, 2011, from http://inlandpolitics.com/blog/2010/02/06/dailybulletin-supervisor-biane-spent-50000-to-hire-white-collar-criminal-lawyer/

Nestor, S. (2004). The impact of changing corporate governance norms on economic crime. *Journal of Financial Crime, 11*(4), 347–352.

Neumeister, L., & Hays, T. (2009). Madoff to plead guilty to eleven counts. *HuffingtonPost.com*. Retrieved July 29, 2011, from http://www.huffington post.com/2009/03/10/bernard-madoff-expected-t_n_173424.html

Nevel, J. (2015, November 6). Springfield woman accused of embezzling from auto repair business. *The State Journal Register*. Retrieved December 31, 2015, from http://www.sj-r.com/article/20151106/NEWS/151109713

Newbold, G., & Ivory, R. (1993). Policing serious fraud in New Zealand. *Crime, Law and Social Change, 20*, 233–248.

Newman, M. (2010, March 8). No misconduct by professor who used student's work in paper. *Times Higher Education* Retrieved June 1, 2010, from http://www.timeshigereducation.co.uk/story.asp?storycode= 410686

Nguyen, T. H., & Pontell, H. N. (2011). Fraud and inequality in the subprime mortgage crisis. In M. Deflem (ed.), *Economic crisis and crime: Sociology of crime, law and deviance* (vol. 16) (pp. tk–tk). Cambridge, MA: Emerald Group Publishing Limited.

Ninemsn staff. (2010, January 18). Doctor convicted over lemon juice antiseptic. *Ninemsn.* Retrieved July 29, 2011, from http://news.ninemsn.com.au/world/1001073/doctor-convicted-over-lemon-juice-antiseptic

Nolasco, C. A. R. I., Vaughn, M. S., & del Carmen, R. V. (2013). Revisiting the choice model of Ponzi and pyramid schemes: Analysis of case law. *Crime, Law and Social Change, 60,* 375–400.

O'Colmain, S. (2014, May/June). Skip class and collect cash: Student financial aid fraud schemes. *Fraud Magazine.* Retrieved January 1, 2016 from http://www.fraud-magazine.com/article.aspx?id=4294982419

O'Connor, T. (1991, November). *Workplace violence in the fast food domain.* Paper presented at the annual meetings of the American Society of Criminology, Baltimore, MD.

O'Donnell, J. (2004, March 18). State time or federal prison? *USA Today.* Retrieved January 19, 2011, from http://www.usatoday.com/money/companies/2004-03-18-statetime_x.htm

O'Donnell, J., & Willing, R. (2003, May 11). Prison time gets harder for white-collar crooks. *USA Today.* Retrieved January 19, 2011, from http://www.usatoday.com/money/companies/management/2003-05-11-bighouse_x.htm

O'Hear, M. M. (2004). Sentencing the green-collar offender: Punishment, culpability, and environmental crime. *Journal of Criminal Law and Criminology, 95*(1), 133–276.

O'Sullivan, S. (2011, February 3). Delaware crime: Wilmington pastor charged with embezzlement. *News Journal.* Retrieved March 10, 2011, from http://www.delawareonline.com/article/20110203/NEWS01/102030351/Delaware-crime-Wilmington-pastor-charged-embezzlement

Occupational Safety and Health Administration (OSHA). (2006). *All about OSHA.* Retrieved July 29, 2011, from http://www.osha.gov/Publications/3302-06N-2006-English.html

Occupational Safety and Health Administration (OSHA). (2010a). *OSHA frequently asked questions.* Retrieved December 17, 2010, from http://osha.gov/osha_faqs.html

Occupational Safety and Health Administration (OSHA). (2010b). *The whistleblower protection program.* Retrieved December 17, 2010, from http://www.whistleblowers.gov/index.html

Occupational Safety and Health Administration. (2011a). *About OSHA.* Retrieved December 23, 2011 from http://www.osha.gov/about.html

Occupational Safety and Health Administration. (2011b). *OSHA we can help.* Retrieved December 23, 2011 from http://www.osha.gov/workers.html

Occupational Safety and Health Administration (OSHA). (2014). *Occupational safety and health administration (OSHA) enforcement.* Retrieved January 3, 2016, from https://www.osha.gov/dep/2014_enforcement_summary.html

Occupational Safety and Health Administration. (2015b). *Worker fatalities reported to federal and state OSHA.* Washington, DC: US Department of Labor. Retrieved November 1, 2015, from https://www.osha.gov/dep/fatcat/dep_fatcat.html

Occupational Safety and Health Administration. (2016, January 5). *OSHA's 2015 top ten most frequently cited violations.* Washington, DC: U.S. Department of Labor. Retrieved from https://www.osha.gov/Top_Ten_Standards.html.

Occupational Safety and Health Administration. (n. d.a). *Young workers: You have rights.* Retrieved November 29, 2015, from https://www.osha.gov/youngworkers/

Occupational Safety and Health Administration. (n. d.b). *Teen workers: You have a right to a safe and healthy workplace and a responsibility to be safe.* Retrieved November 29, 2015, from https://www.osha.gov/Publications/teen_worker_brochure.html

Office of New York State Attorney General. (2010). Cuomo announces charges against former UB researcher for hiring actors to testify during misconduct hearing and attempting to siphon $4 million in taxpayer funds. *Office of the Attorney General Media Center.* Retrieved June 10, 2010, from http://www.ag.ny.gov/media_center/2010/feb/feb16a_10.html

Office of Research Integrity. (2010). *About ORI.* Rockville, MD: U.S. Dept. of Health & Human Services. Retrieved July 30, 2011, from http://ori.hhs.gov/about/

Office of Research Integrity. (2011). Case summary: Poehlman, Eric T. Retrieved November 29, 2015, from http://ori.hhs.gov/content/case-summary-poehlman-eric-t

Office of the Governor Rick Perry. (2010). *Statement by Gov. Rick Perry on EPA's efforts to take over Texas' air permitting program* [Press release]. Retrieved July 30, 2011, from http://governor.state.tx.us/news/press-release/14677/

Office of the Law Revision Counsel. (n. d.). *United States codes.* Washington, DC: U. S. House of Representatives. Retrieved December 2, 2015, from http://uscode.house.gov/

Olick, D. (2010, January 15). Big banks accused of short sale fraud. *Consumer News and Business Channel (CNBC).* Retrieved June 22, 2010, from http://www.cnbc.com/id/34877347/Big_Banks_Acussed_of_Short_Sale_Fraud

Oliphant, B. J., & Oliphant, G. C. (2001). Using a behavior-based method to identify and reduce employee theft. *International Journal of Retail and Distribution Management, 29*(10), 442–451.

Olivarez-Giles, N. (2010, January 26). Owner of 22 Midas auto shops settles fraud claims. *Los Angeles Times,* Business, Part B, p. 7.

Oppel, R., Jr. (2003, March 27). Panel finds manipulation by energy companies. *The New York Times,* p. A14.

Orland, L. (1980). Reflections on corporate crime: Law in search of theory and scholarship. *American Criminal Law Review, 17,* 501–520.

Owens, J. B. (2000, June). Have we no shame? Thoughts on shaming, "white-collar" criminals, and the Federal Sentencing Guidelines. *American University Law Review, 49,* 1047–1058.

Pacini, C., Qiu, L. H., & Sinason, D. (2007). Qui tam actions: Fighting fraud against the government. *Journal of Financial Crime, 14*(1), 64–78.

Page, R., Savage, A., Stitt, K., & Umhoffer, R. (1999). Environmental crimes. *American Criminal Law Review, 36*(3), 515–592.

Pao, T., Tzeng, L. Y., & Wang, K. C. (2014). "Typhoons and opportunistic fraud": Claim patterns of automobile theft insurance in Taiwan. *Journal of Risk and Insurance, 81*(1), 91–112.

Parker, W. (2009). *A gynecologist's second opinion.* New York, NY: Penguin.

Passas, N. (2001). False accounts: Why do company statements often offer a true and a fair view of virtual reality? *European Journal on Criminal Policy and Research, 9*(2), 117–135.

Passas, N. (2004). Law enforcement challenges in Hawala-related investigations. *Journal of Financial Crime, 12*(2), 112–119.

Passas, N. (2005). Lawful but awful: "Legal corporate crimes." *Journal of Socio-Economics, 34,* 771–786.

Patterson, L. A., & Koller, C. A. (2011). Diffusion of fraud through subprime lending: The perfect storm. In M. Deflem (ed.), *Economic crisis and crime: Sociology of crime, law and deviance,* (vol 16) (pp. tk–tk). Cambridge, MA: Emerald Publishing Group Limited

Paul, T. (2006). Five reverse home mortgage scams to watch out for. *Ezine Articles.* Retrieved July 29, 2011, from http://ezinearticles.com/?five-Home-Mortgage-Scams-to-Watch-Out-For&id=273604

Payne, B. K. (1995). Medicaid fraud. *Criminal Justice Policy Review, 7,* 61–74.

Payne, B. K. (2003a). *Crime in the home health care field.* Springfield, IL: Charles C Thomas.

Payne, B. K. (2003b). *Incarcerating white-collar offenders: The prison experience and beyond.* Springfield, IL: Charles C Thomas.

Payne, B. K. (2005). *Crime and elder abuse: An integrated perspective* (2nd ed.). Springfield, IL: Charles C Thomas.

Payne, B. K. (2006). Problems controlling fraud and abuse in the home health care field: Voices of fraud control unit directors. *Journal of Financial Crime, 13*(1), 77–92.

Payne, B. K. (2010). Understanding elder sexual abuse and criminal justice system's response: Comparisons to elder physical abuse. *Justice Quarterly, 27*(2), 206–224.

Payne, B. K. (2011). *Crime and elder abuse: An integrated perspective* (3rd ed). Springfield, IL: Charles C Thomas.

Payne, B. K. (2013). Elder physical abuse and failure to report cases: Similarities and differences in case type and the justice system's response. *Crime and Delinquency 59*(5), 697–717.

Payne, B. K. (2015). Expanding the boundaries of criminal justice: Emphasizing the "s" in the criminal justice sciences through interdisciplinary efforts. *Justice Quarterly, 33*(1), 1–20.

Payne, B. K., & Berg, B. L. (1997). Looking for fraud in all the wrong places. *The Police Journal: A Quarterly Review for the Police of the World, 70,* 220–230.

Payne, B. K., & Berg, B. L. (1999). Perceptions of nursing home workers, police chiefs, and college students regarding crime against the elderly. *American Journal of Criminal Justice, 24,* 139–149.

Payne, B. K., Berg, B. L., & Byars, K. (1999). A qualitative examination of the similarities and differences of elder abuse definitions among four groups: Nursing home directors, nursing home employees, police chiefs and students. *Journal of Elder Abuse & Neglect, 10*(3/4), 63–86.

Payne, B. K., & Burke-Fletcher, L. B. (2005). Elder abuse in nursing homes: Prevention and resolution strategies and barriers. *Journal of Criminal Justice, 33*(2), 119–125.

Payne, B. K., & Cikovic, R. (1995). An empirical examination of the characteristics, consequences, and causes of elder abuse in nursing homes. *Journal of Elder Abuse & Neglect, 7*(4), 61–74.

Payne, B. K., & Dabney, D. (1997). Prescription fraud: Characteristics, causes, and consequences. *Journal of Drug Issues, 27*(4), 807–820.

Payne, B. K., & Gainey, R. (1998). A qualitative assessment of the pains experienced on electronic monitoring. *International Journal of Offender Therapy and Comparative Criminology, 42,* 149–63.

Payne, B. K., & Gainey, R. (2004). Social and governmental altruism, deterrence theory, and nursing home regulatory violations: A state-level analysis. *Journal of Crime and Justice, 72*(2), 59–78.

Payne, B. K., & Gainey, R. (2006). The criminal justice response to elder abuse in nursing homes: A routine activities perspective. *Western Criminology Review, 7*(3), 67–81.

Payne, B. K., & Gainey, R. (2009). *Family violence and criminal justice.* Cincinnati, OH: Anderson.

Payne, B. K., & Gray, C. (2001). Fraud by home health care workers and the criminal justice response. *Criminal Justice Review, 26,* 209–232.

Payne, B. K., & Stevens, E. D. (1999). An examination of recent professional sanctions imposed on Alabama lawyers. *Justice Professional, 12,* 17–43.

Payne, B. K., & Strasser, S. M. (2012). Financial exploitation of older persons in adult care settings: Comparisons to physical abuse and the justice system's response. *Journal of Elder Abuse & Neglect, 24*(3), 231–250.

Payne, B. K., Time, V., & Raper, S. (2005). Regulating legal misconduct in the Commonwealth of Virginia: The gender influence. *Women and Criminal Justice, 15*(3), 81–95.

Pelofsky, J. (2010, June 17). Authorities reveal mortgage fraud crackdown, 485 arrests. *Reuters.* Retrieved July 31, 2011, from http://www.reuters.com/article/2010/06/17/us-mortgage-fraud-idUSTRE65F3E620100617

Pendlebury, R. (2010, June 18). Special investigation: Why is BP taking all the blame? *Daily Mail.* Retrieved September 12, 2010, from http://www.dailymail.co.uk/news/article-1287226/GULF-OIL-SPILL-Whys-BP-taking-blame.html

People v. Eubanks, 927 F.2d 310 (Cal. 1996).

Perri, F. S., & Brody, R. G. (2011). The dark triad: Organized crime, terror, and fraud. *Journal of Money Laundering Control, 14*(1), 44–59.

Peterson, B. K. (2004). Education as a new approach to fighting financial crime in USA. *Journal of Financial Crime, 11*(3), 262–267.

Petress, K. C. (2003). Academic dishonesty: A plague on our profession. *Education, 123*(3), 624–627.

Pfiefer, W. (2010, April 12). Bruce Karatz bring in star witness. *Los Angeles Times.* Retrieved July 31, 2011, from http://articles.latimes.com/2010/apr/02/business/la-fi-karatz2-2010apr02

Pfleeger, S. L., Sasse, M. A., & Furnham, A. (2014). From weakest link to security hero: Transforming staff security behavior. *Homeland Security & Emergency Management, 11*(4), 489–510.

Philippsohn, S. (2001). Trends in cybercrime—An overview of current financial crimes on the internet. *Computers & Security, 20*(1), 53–69.

Pillemer, K., & Moore, D. (1990). Highlights from a study of abuse of patients in nursing homes. *Journal of Elder Abuse & Neglect, 2,* 5–29.

Pimentel, D., Cooperstein, S., Randell, H., Filiberto, D., Sorrentino, S., Kaye, B., et al. (2007). Ecology of increasing diseases: Population growth and environmental degradation. *Human Ecology, 35*(6), 653–668.

Pino, N. W., & Smith, W. L. (2003). College students and academic dishonesty. *College Student Journal, 37*(4), 490–500.

Piquero, A. R., Piquero, N., Terry, K. J., Youstin, T., & Nobles, M. (2008). Uncollaring the criminal: Understanding criminal careers of criminal clerics. *Criminal Justice and Behavior, 35,* 583–599.

Piquero, N. L. (2012). The only thing we have to fear is fear itself: Investigating the relationship between fear of falling and white-collar crime. *Crime & Delinquency, 58*(3), 362–379.

Piquero, N. L., & Benson, M. L. (2004). White-collar crime and criminal careers: Specifying a trajectory of punctuated situational offending. *Journal of Contemporary Criminal Justice, 20*(2), 148–165.

Piquero, N. L., Carmichael, S., & Piquero, A. R. (2008). Research note: Assessing the perceived seriousness of white-collar and street crime. *Crime and Delinquency, 54,* 291–312.

Piquero, N. L., & Davis, J. (2004). Extralegal factors and the sentencing of organizational defendants: An examination of the federal sentencing guidelines. *Journal of Criminal Justice, 32*(6), 643–654.

Piquero, N. L., Exum, M. L., & Simpson, S. S. (2005). Integrating the desire-for-control and rational choice in a corporate crime context. *Justice Quarterly, 22*(2), 252–280.

Piquero, N. L., Schoepfer, A., & Langton, L. (2010). Completely out of control or the desire to be in complete control? How low self-control and the desire for control relate to corporate offending. *Crime & Delinquency, 56*(4), 627–647.

Piquero, N. L., Tibbetts, S. G., & Blankenship, M. B. (2005). Examining the role of differential association and techniques of neutralization in explaining corporate crime. *Deviant Behavior, 26,* 159–188.

Piquero, N. L., Vieraitis, L. M., Piquero, A. R., Tibbetts, S. G., & Blankenship, M. (2013). The interplay of gender and ethics in corporate offending decision-making. *Journal of Contemporary Criminal Justice, 29*(3), 385–398.

Pirrong, C. (2010). Energy market manipulation: Definition, diagnosis, and deterrence. *Energy Law Journal, 31*(1), 1–20.

Plimton, E. A., & Walsh, D. (2010). Corporate criminal liability. *American Criminal Law Review, 47,* 331–343.

Plushnick-Masti, R. (2010, December 30). Rick Perry, Texas continue to wage battle against EPA as fight over regulations grows fierce. *Huffington Post.* Retrieved July 31, 2011, from http://www.huffingtonpost.com/2010/12/30/rick-perry-texas-epa_n_802643.html

Podgor, E. S. (2007). The challenge of white collar sentencing. *Journal of Criminal Law and Criminology, 97*(3), 731–759.

Podgor, E. S. (2011). 100 years of white-collar crime in "Twitter." *The Review of Litigation, 30*(3), 535–558.

Policastro, C., & Payne, B. P. (2013). An examination of deviance and deviants in the durable medical equipment (DME) field: Characteristics, consequences, and responses to fraud. *Deviant Behavior, 34*(3), 191–207.

Pollack, H., & Smith, A. B. (1983). White-collar v. street crime sentencing disparity: How judges see the problem. *Judicature, 67*(4), 175–182.

Pollock, J. (2004). *Ethics in crime and justice* (4th ed.). Belmont, CA: Wadsworth.

Ponemon Institute. (2015, May). *2015 cost of data breach study: Global analysis.* Traverse City, MI: Ponemon Institute LLC.

Ponemon Institute. (2015, October). *2015 cost of cyber crime study: Global.* Traverse City, MI: Ponemon Institute LLC.

Pontell, H. N. (2005). White-collar crime or just risky business? The role of fraud in major financial debacles. *Crime, Law and Social Change, 42,* 309–324.

Pontell, H. N., Black, W. K., & Geis, G. (2014). Too big to fail powerful to jail? On the absence of criminal prosecutors after the 2008 financial meltdown. *Crime, Law and Social Change, 61,* 1–13.

Pontell, H. N., & Geis, G. (2014). The trajectory of white-collar crime following the great economic meltdown. *Journal of Contemporary Criminal Justice, 30*(1), 70–82.

Pontell, H. N., Jesilow, P., & Geis, G. (1982). Policing physicians: Practitioner fraud and abuse in a government medical program. *Social Problems, 30*(1), 117–125.

Pontell, H. N., Jesilow, P., & Geis, G. (1984). Practitioner fraud and abuse in medical benefit programs. *Law and Policy, 6,* 405–424.

A Ponzi nation. (2009, December 29). *New Zealand Herald.* Retrieved June 15, 2011, from http://www.nzinvestors.com/business-news/15831-ponzi-nation.html

Posner, R. (1979–1980). Optimal sentences for white-collar criminals. *American Criminal Law Review, 17,* 409–440.

Poveda, T. G. (1992). White-collar crime and the justice department: The institutionalization of a concept. *Crime, Law and Social Change, 17,* 235–252.

Powell, S. M. (2010, December 5). Perry taking his rebellion national: States' rights crusade will begin with EPA battle. *[Houston] Chron.com.* Retrieved July 30, 2011, from http://www.chron.com/disp/story.mpl/metropolitan/7324941

Power, L. G. (2009). University students' perceptions of plagiarism. *Journal of Higher Education, 80*(6), 643–662.

Pratt, M. K. (2001, November 23). Retailers take steps to combat employee-theft epidemic. *Boston Business Journal, 21*(42), 37.

Preiser, S. E., & Swisher, C. C., III. (1988). Representing the white collar defendant: How to avoid the trap. *Trial, 24*(10), 72–78.

Price Waterhouse v. Hopkins, 490 U.S. 228 (1989).

PriceWaterhouseCooper. (2015). *Global economic crime survey 2014.* Retrived December 29, 2015 from http://www.pwc.com/gx/en/services/advisory/consulting/forensics/economic-crime-survey.html

PR Newswire. (2007, August 9). *Profnet wire: Government & law: Safety of imported products.* Retrieved July 29, 2011, from http://www.smart brief.com/news/aaaa/industryPR-detail.jsp?id=24DF678E-43D9-453F-AD14-D0EFFF2F9015

Pulkkinen, L. (2010, May 25). State: UW doctor traded addict drugs for sex. *KATU-TV.* Retrieved June 17, 2010, from http://www.katu.com/news/94853414.html

Punch, M. (2000). Suite violence: Why managers murder and corporations kill. *Crime, Law and Social Change, 33,* 243–280.

Punch, M. (2008). The organization did it: Individuals, corporations, and crime. In J. Minkes & L. Minkes (Eds.), *Corporate and white-collar crime* (pp. 102–121). Thousand Oaks, CA: Sage.

Punch, M. (2009). *Police corruption: Deviance, accountability, and reform in policing.* Portland, OR: Willan.

Pusey, I. (2007). The role of the regulator in combating financial crimes: A Caribbean perspective. *Journal of Financial Crime, 14*(3), 299–319.

Queisser, S., Sutton, S., & Fultz, V. (2015, July). *Two loan disbursements + midterm grades = increase in student success.* Paper presented at the NASSAA national conference, New Orleans, LA.

Quinney, R. (1971). *The social reality of crime.* Boston, MA: Little, Brown.

R[X] for the "Ratlord": Live in your own slums. (1987, July 27). *Newsweek,* p. 54.

Rackmill, S. J. (1992). Understanding and sanctioning the white collar offender. *Federal Probation, 56*(2), 26–34.

Rader, N. (2008). *Criminal brain: Understanding biological theories of crime.* New York: NYU Press.

Raine, A., Laufer, W. S., Yang, Y., Narr, K. L., Thompson, P., & Toga, A. W. (2012). Increased executive functioning, attention, and cortical thickness in white-collar criminals. *Human Brain Mapping, 33,* 2,932–2,940.

Rakovski, C. C., & Levy, E. S. (2007). Academic dishonesty: Perceptions of business students. *College Student Journal, 41*(2), 466–481.

Rakowski, J. J. (2004). Does the consumer have an obligation to cooperate with price discrimination? *Business Ethics Quarterly, 14*(2), 263–274.

Raloff, J. (2010, June 2). July: When not to go to the hospital. *Science News.* Retrieved July 29, 2011, from http://www.sciencenews.org/view/generic/id/59865

Ramsey-Klawsnik, H. (1999, June). *Elder sexual abuse: Workshop handouts.* Presented at a workshop of the Virginia Coalition for the Prevention of Elder Abuse, June, Virginia Beach, Virginia.

Randall, D. (2010, May 9). Million gallons of oil a day gush into Gulf of Mexico. *The Independent.* Retrieved July 29, 2011, from http://www.independent.co.uk/news/world/americas/million-gallons-of-oil-a-day-gush-into-gulf-of-mexico.1969472.html

Rao, A., & Wang, E. (2015). *Demand for "healthy" products: False claims in advertising.* Available at http://ssrn.com/abstract=2559980

Rasmussen, D. G., & Leauanae, J. L. (2004). Expert witness qualifications and selection. *Journal of Financial Crime, 12*(2), 165–171.

Rataj, T. (2001). Cybercrime causes chaos. *Law and Order, 49*(5), 43–46.

Reardon, S. (2015, July 1). US vaccine researcher sentenced to prison for fraud. *International Weekly Research Journal of Science.* Retrieved January 2, 2016, from http://www.nature.com/news/us-vaccine-researcher-sentenced-to-prison-for-fraud-1.17660

Record number of shoplifters and dishonest employees apprehended by US retailers according to 20th Annual Theft Survey by Jack L. Hayes International. (2008, October 1). *Business Wire.* Retrieved July 31, 2011, from http://www.businesswire.com/news/home/20090901005013/en/Shoplifters-Dishonest-Employees-Apprehended-Record-Numbers-Retailers

Reed, G. E., & Yeager, P. C. (1996). Organizational offending and neoclassical criminology: Challenging the reach of a general theory of crime. *Criminology, 34*(3), 357–382.

Reed, M. A., & Scott, E. D. (2013, July/August). Five cybersecurity mistakes companies make that could result in their prosecution. *Financial Fraud Law Report,* 615–623.

Rege-Patwardhan, A. (2009). Cybercrimes against critical infrastructures: A study of online criminal organization techniques. *Criminal Justice Studies, 22*(3), 261–271.

Reilly, C. (2011, January 1). Raunchy videos starring *Enterprise* skipper come to light. *The Virginian-Pilot.* Retrieved February 22, 2011, from http://www.hamptonroads.com/2010/12/raunchy-videos-starring-enterprise-skipper-come-light

Reilly, M., Lott, B., & Gallogly, S. (1986). Sexual harassment of university students. *Sex Roles, 15,* 333–358.

Reiss, A. J., & Biderman, A. D. (1980). *Data sources on white-collar law-breaking.* Rockford, MD: National Institute of Justice.

Rejesus, R. M., Little, B. B., & Lovell, A. C. (2004). Using data mining to detect crop insurance fraud: Is there a role for social scientists? *Journal of Financial Crime, 12*(1), 24–32.

Restaurant closed briefly after dead deer found in kitchen. (2008, October 27). *USA Today.* Retrieved July 29, 2011, from www.usatoday.com/news/2008-10-27-2714710309_x.htm

Rhoten, D., & Pfirman, S. (2007). Women in interdisciplinary science: Exploring preferences and consequences. *Research Policy, 36,* 56–75.

Richardson, H. (2010). WVU tackles white-collar crime in forensic accounting program. *State Journal, 26*(27), 10.

Richburg, K. B. (2009, July 24). Rabbis, politicians snared in FBI sting: Corruption probe brings 44 arrests in N.J. and N.Y. *The Washington Post.* Retrieved March 19, 2011, from http://www.washingtonpost.com/wp-dyn/content/article/2009/07/23/AR2009072301449.html

Richter, M. (2010). *Reporting slumlords and landlords.* Retrieved June 29, 2010, from http://www.whow.com/way_5399687_reporting-slumlords.html

Riedel, G. (Producer), & Judge, M. (Director). (1999). *Office Space* [Motion picture]. USA: Twentieth Century Fox.

Riggs, A. (2007, August 20). Beware of post-storm home repair scams. *Knight Ridder/Tribune Business News.* Retrieved July 31, 2011, from ABI/INFORM Complete database (Document ID No. 1322672341).

Ritchie, D. (2014, July). Security talk: Why customized cybersecurity training is essential. *Security,* 50.

Roberts, C. (2007). Rarer than rabies: The legacy of Michael Nifong. *RenewAmerica.com.* Retrieved July 30, 2011, from http://www.renewamerica.com/columns/roberts/070725

Robie, C., Kidwell, R., & King, J. (2003). The ethics of professorial book selling. *Journal of Business Ethics, 47*, 61–76.

Robin, G. D. (1974). White-collar crime and employee theft. *Crime and Delinquency, 20*, 251–262.

Robinson, M. B. (2004). *Why crime? An integrated systems theory of antisocial behavior.* Upper Saddle River, NJ: Pearson/Prentice Hall.

Robinson, M., & Murphy, D. (2009). *Greed is good: Maximization and elite deviance in America.* Lanham, MD: Rowman & Littlefield.

Rogers, D. (2002). Eye of the storm: Cybercrime poses a threat to national security, but is the threat overblown or underestimated? *Law Enforcement Technology, 29*(11), 60–62, 64–65.

Rosenbaum, P. (2009, April). Loss prevention. *AFP Exchange, 29*(3), 40.

Rosenmerkel, S. P. (2001). Wrongfulness and harmfulness as components of seriousness of white-collar offenses. *Journal of Contemporary Criminal Justice, 17*, 308–327.

Rosoff, S. M. (1989). Physicians as criminal defendants. *Law and Human Behavior, 13*(2), 231–236.

Ross, E. A. (1907). *Sin and society: An analysis of latter-day iniquity.* Boston, MA: Houghton Mifflin.

Ross, J., & Rothe, D. (2008). Ironies of controlling state crime. *International Journal of Law, Crime, and Justice, 36*, 196–210.

Rossetti, S. J. (1995). Impact of child abuse on attitudes toward God and the Catholic Church. *Child Abuse & Neglect, 19*(12), 13.

Rothe, D. (2009). Beyond the law: The Reagan administration and Nicaragua. *Critical Criminology, 17*(1), 39–67.

Rothe, D., & Friedrichs, D. (2006). The state of the criminology of crimes by the state. *Social Justice, 33*, 147–161.

Rothe, D., Muzzatti, S., & Mullins, C. (2006). Crime on the high seas. *Critical Criminology, 14*, 159–180.

Rothe, D., & Ross, J. (2008). The marginalization of state crime in introductory textbooks on criminology. *Critical Sociology, 34*, 741–752.

Roustan, W. K. (2015, January 19). Accountant accused of embezzling $1 million from Fort Lauderdale company. *Sun Sentinel.* Retrieved January 6, 2016 from http://www.sun-sentinel.com/local/broward/fort-lauderdale/fl-lauderdale-accused-embezzlement-20150119-story.html

Rudra, A. (2010). What is title insurance & how you can use it to protect your home. *Daily Markets.* Retrieved June 22, 2010, from http://www.daily markets.com/contributor/2010/03/28/what-is-title-insurance-how-you-can-use-it-to-protect-your-home/

Ruggiero, V. (2007). It's the economy, stupid! Classifying power crimes. *International Journal of the Sociology of Law, 35*, 163–177.

Ruiz, M. (2010). Where is Bernie Madoff still a hero? *America Online (AOL) News.* Retrieved July 29, 2011, from http://www.aolnews.com/2010/06/06/where-is-bernie-madoff-still-a-hero-prison/

Rutledge, G. P. (2006). Disclosure and sharing of sensitive information: A US securities regulatory perspective. *Journal of Financial Crime, 13*(3), 339–347.

Ryan-Boyle, C., Simon, J., & Yebler, J. (1991). Sentencing of organizations. *American Criminal Law Review, 29*, 743–770.

Sambides, N., Jr. (2009, June 24). Police charge contractor with Lincoln paving scam. *McClatchy-Tribune Business News.* Retrieved July 31, 2011, from ABI/INFORM Complete database (Document ID No. 1758884291).

Sarna, S. F. (2012). Advertising on the Internet: An opportunity for abuse? *Journal of Civil Rights and Economic Development, 11*(3), 683–689.

Sayre, K. (2011, January 13). Developer who pleaded guilty to harboring stolen antiques gets 3 years probation. *Al.com.* Retrieved July 11, 2011, from http://blog.al.com/live/2011/01/matt_walker_sentenced_to_three.html

Scallan, E., Hoekstra, R. M., Angulo, F. J., Tauxe, R. V., Widdowson, M. A., & Roy, S. L. (2011). Foodborne illness acquired in the United States—Major pathogens. *Emerging Infectious Diseases, 17*, 7–15. Retrieved July 31, 2011, from http://www.cdc.gov/eid/content/17/1/7.htm

Scannell, K. (2007, May 7). Insider trading: It's back with a vengeance. *Wall Street Journal*, p. B1.

Schaefer, H. (2003, August 21). One theft charge remains in Whitetail Inn case. *Rhinelander Daily News*, p. A1.

Schanzenbach, M., & Yaeger, M. L. (2006). Prison time, fines, and federal white collar criminals: The anatomy of a racial disparity. *Journal of Criminal Law and Criminology, 96*(2), 757–793.

Schapiro, R. (2009, July 19). Shanks for the advice: White-collar crooks learn jail survival from ex-con. *New York Daily News.* Retrieved July 31, 2011, from http://www.nydailynews.com/news/money/shanks-advice-white-collar-crooks-learn-jail-survival-ex-con-article-1.400539

Schiff, M. B., & Kramer, L. C. (2004). Conducting internal investigations of employee theft and other misconduct. *The Brief, 33*(3), 62–64.

Schlegel, K. (1993). Crime in the pits. *Annals of the American Academy of Political and Social Science, 525*, 59–70.

Schmidt, P. (2003, September 19). Reports allege misconduct at UConn. *Chronicle of Higher Education, 50*(4), A26.

Schneider, C. (2004). *Dirty air, dirty power: Mortality and health damage due to air pollution from power plants.* Boston, MA: Clean Air Task Force.

Schneider, H. S. (2012). Agency problems and reputation in expert services: Evidence from auto repair. *The Journal of Industrial Economics, 60*(3), 406–433.

Schoenfeld, H. (2005). Violated trust: Conceptualizing prosecutorial misconduct. *Journal of Contemporary Criminal Justice, 21*(3), 250–271.

Schoepfer, A., Carmichael, S., & Piquero, N. L. (2007). Do perceptions of punishment vary between white-collar and street crime? *Journal of Criminal Justice, 35*, 151–163.

Schoepfer, A., & Piquero, N. L. (2006). Exploring white-collar crime and the American dream: A partial test of institutional anomie theory. *Journal of Criminal Justice, 34*(3), 227–235.

Schoepfer, A., Piquero, N. L., & Langton, L. (2014). Low self-control versus the desire-for-control: An empirical test of white-collar crime and conventional crime. *Deviant Behavior, 35*, 197–214.

Schrager, L. S., & Short, J. F. (1978). Toward a sociology of organizational crime. *Social Problems, 25*, 407–419.

Schram, S. (2013). Acupuncture, medical necessity, and automobile insurance fraud. *American Acupuncturist, 62*, 33–38.

Schudson, M. (2004). Notes on scandal and the Watergate legacy. *American Behavioral Scientist, 47*(9), 1231–1238.

Schwemberger, J., Mosby, J., Doa, M., Jacobs, D., Ahsley, P., Brody, D., et al. (2005). Blood lead levels: United States, 1999–2002. *Mortality Weekly Report, 54*(20), 513–516.

Sci Tech Blog. (2009, August 5). *Student arrested for "modding" Xbox consoles* [Web log post]. Retrieved January 4, 2016 from http://scitech.blogs.cnn.com/2009/08/05/student-arrested-for-modding-xbox-consoles/

Scott, M. B., & Lyman, S. (1968). Accounts. *American Sociological Review, 33*, 46–62.

Scullin, S. (2014, April). Big crime, big borders and the bitcoin. *Law Enforcement Technology*, 8–11.

Searcey, D. (2010, October 20). BP claims process moves forward, but not without grumbling. *Wall Street Journal.* Retrieved July 31, 2011, from http://blogs.wsj.com/law/2010/10/20/bp-claims-process-moves-forward-but-not-without-grum bling/

Searcey, D., & Efrati, A. (2011, March 18). Madoff beaten in prison: Ponzi schemer was assaulted by another inmate in December; officials deny incident. *Wall Street Journal.* Retrieved January 19, 2011, from http://online.wsj.com/article/SB1000 14240527487047434045751280311434249 28.html

Securities and Exchange Commission. (2009a). Ponzi schemes—Frequently asked questions [Press release]. Retrieved July 29, 2011, from http://www.sec.gov/answers/ponzi.htm#Ponzi VsPyramid

Securities and Exchange Commission. (2009b, April 30). SEC charges Wall Street investment banker and seven others in widespread insider trading scheme [Press release]. Retrieved July 29, 2011, from http://www.sec.gov/news/press/2009/2009-99.htm

Securities and Exchange Commission. (2009c, November 5). SEC charges Wall Street ring that made over $20 million serially trading on acquisition information tipped by attorney at international law firm [Press release]. Retrieved July 29, 2011, from http://www.sec.gov/litigation/litreleases/2009/lr21283.htm

Securities and Exchange Commission. (2010). *Investigation of the failure of the SEC to uncover Bernard Madoff's Ponzi scheme.* Washington, DC: SEC Office of Investigations. Retrieved July 31, 2011, from http://www.sec.gov/news/studies/2009/oig-509.pdf

Securities and Exchange Commission. (2015). *SEC charges: False tweets sent two stocks reeling in market manipulation.* Retrieved January 2, 2016 from http://www.sec.gov/news/pressrelease/2015-254.html

Securities and Exchange Commission, Division of Enforcement. (2015, June 15). Enforcement manual. Retrieved November 20, 2015 from http://www.sec.gov/divisions/enforce/enforcementmanual.pdf

Seibel, J. (2009, June 11). Warrant accuses auto repair shop of fraud. *Journal Sentinel, Inc.* Retrieved July 31, 2011, from http://www.jsonline.com/news/waukesha/47881922.html

Shapiro, S. (1985). The road not taken: The elusive path to criminal prosecution for white-collar offenders. *Law and Society Review, 12,* 179–218.

Shapiro, S. P. (1990). Collaring the crime, not the criminal: Reconsidering the concept of white-collar crime. *American Sociological Review, 55*(3), 346–365.

Shea, D. J. (2008). Effects of sexual abuse by Catholic priests on adults victimized as children. *Sexual Addiction and Compulsivity, 15*(3), 250–268.

Shelman, J. (2008a, April 22). U has questions on prof's e-mail claims. *Minneapolis StarTribune.* Retrieved June 17, 2010, from http://www.startribune.com/local/18028664.html

Shelman, J. (2008b, April 29). U profs' pay cut as probe continues. *Minneapolis StarTribune.* Retrieved June 17, 2010, from http://www.startribune.com/local/18340159.html

Sherman, N. I. (2005, January 12). Yale professor ousted for misconduct. *Harvard Crimson.* Retrieved June 17, 2010, from http://www.thecrimson.com/article/2005/1/12/yale-professor-ousted-for-misconduct-following/?print=1

Sheuya, S. (2008). Improving the health and lives of people living in slums. *Annals of the New York Academy of Sciences, 1136,* 298–306.

Shichor, D. (1989). Corporate deviance and corporate victimization: A review and some elaborations. *International Review of Victimology, 1*(1), 67–88.

Shover, N., Fox, G., & Mills, M. (1994). Long term consequences of victimization by white-collar crime. *Justice Quarterly, 11,* 75–98.

Shover, N., & Routhe, A. (2005). Environmental crime. *Crime and Justice, 32,* 321–371.

Shuler, D. (2010). Connie Francis and Dionne Warrick: Two divas in Vegas. Retrieved December 24, 2011 from http://www.examiner.com/arts-in-new-york/connie-francis-and-dionne-warwick-two-divas-las-vegas.

Simon, D. (2006). *Elite deviance* (8th ed.). New York, NY: Random House.

Simon, D. R. (2000). Corporate environmental crimes and social inequality: New directions for environmental justice research. *American Behavioral Scientist, 43*(4), 633–645.

Simon, D. R., & Swart, S. L. (1984). The Justice Department focuses on white-collar crime: Promises and pitfalls. *Crime and Delinquency, 30*(1), 107–119.

Simpson, S. S. (2013). White-collar crime: A review of recent developments and promising directions for future research. *Annual Review of Sociology, 39,* 309–331.

Simpson, S. S., & Koper, C. S. (1992). Deterring corporate crime. *Criminology, 30*(3), 347–375.

Simpson, S. S., & Koper, C. S. (1997). The changing of the guard: Top management characteristics, organizational strain, and antitrust offending. *Journal of Quantitative Criminology, 13*(4), 373–404.

Simpson, S. S., & Piquero, N. L. (2002). Low self-control, organizational theory, and corporate crime. *Law & Society Review, 36*(3), 509–547.

Simpson, S. S., Gibbs, C., Rorie, M., Slocum, L. A., Cohen, M. A., & Vandenbergh, M. (2013). An empirical assessment of corporate environmental crime-control strategies. *Journal of Criminal Law and Criminology, 103*(1), 231–278.

Simpson, S. S., & Yeager, P. C. (2015). *Building a comprehensive white-collar violations data system, final technical report.* Available online at https://www.ncjrs.gov/pdffiles1/bjs/grants/248667.pdf.

Sims, B. (2009, July 8). UAB animal transplant studies by two researchers found falsified. *Birmingham News.* Retrieved July 30, 2011, from http://blog.al.com/spotnews/2009/07/uab_animal_transplant_studies.html

Sims, R. L. (1993). The relationship between academic dishonesty and unethical business practices. *Journal of Education for Business, 68*(4), 207–211.

Singer, R. (1999). Slumlord legislation on the agenda. *The Inquirer: Philly.com.* Retrieved July 30, 2011, from http://articles.philly.com/1999-11-15/news/25495020_1_slumlords-blight-manufacturing-exemption

Singletary, M. (2000, June 7). Promissory scams leave many broke. *The Washington Post,* p. H01. Retrieved from http://articles.sun-sentinel.com/2000-06-12/news/0006090663_1_con-artists-promissory-notes-investors.

Sinrod, E. J., & Reilly, W. P. (2000). Cyber-crimes: A practical approach to the application of federal computer crime laws. *Santa Clara Computer and High Technology Law Journal, 16,* 177–196. [E-version, pp. 1–55: http://www.sinrodlaw.com/cybercrime.doc]

Sipes, D. D. (1988). Legal and ethical perspectives of selling complimentary copies of the college textbook. *Journal of Law and Education, 17*(3), 355–373.

Skinner, L., Giles, M. K., Griffith, S. E., Sonntag, M. E., Berry, K. K., & Beck, R. (1995). Academic sexual intimacy violations: Ethicality and occurrence reports from undergraduates. *Journal of Sex Research, 32*(2), 131–143.

Skinner, W. F., & Fream, A. M. (1997). A social learning theory analysis of computer crime among college students. *Journal of Research in Crime and Delinquency, 34*(4), 495–518.

Sky News. (2015, January 21). *Revealed: The top 25 most common passwords.* Retrieved January 1, 2016 from http://news.sky.com/story/1412124/revealed-the-top-25-most-common-passwords

Skylar, V. (2012). Cyber security of safety-critical infrastructure: A case study for nuclear facilities. *Information & Security: An International Journal, 28*(1), 98–107.

Slapper, G. (1993). Corporate manslaughter: An examination of the determinants of prosecutorial policy. *Social and Legal Studies, 2,* 423–443.

Smietana, B. (2005). New interfaith report focuses on pastors who steal from unsuspecting congregations. *Religion News Service.* Retrieved February 22, 2011, from http://www.adventistreview.org/2005-1508/story5.html

Smith, B. V., & Yarussi, J. M. (2007). *Breaking the code of silence: Correctional officers' handbook on identifying and addressing sexual misconduct with offenders.* Washington, DC: National Institute of Corrections.

Smith, C. (2011, February 16). Heiress to testify in Edwards inquiry. *Pittsburgh Tribune-Review.* Retrieved February 23, 2011, from http://www.pittsburghlive.com/x/pittsburghtrib/news/pittsburgh/s_723051.html

Smith, G. S. (2015). Management models for international cybercrime. *Journal of Financial Crime, 22*(1), 104–125.

Smith, M. L., Rengifo, A. F., & Vollman, B. K. (2008). Trajectories of abuse and disclosure: Child abuse by Catholic priests. *Criminal Justice and Behavior, 35*(5), 570–582.

Smith, R. (1997, December). Some used car dealers may be dishonest. *Credit Management,* p. 16.

Smith, R. (2006). Research misconduct: The poisoning of the well. *Royal Society of Medicine, 99,* 232–237.

Smith, T. R. (2004). Low self-control, staged opportunity, and subsequent fraudulent behavior. *Criminal Justice and Behavior, 31*(5), 542–563.

Snider, L. (1990). Cooperative models and corporate crime: Panacea or cop-out? *Crime and Delinquency, 36*(3), 373–390.

Snyder, E. A. (1989). New insights into the decline of antitrust enforcement. *Contemporary Policy Issues, 7*(4), 1–18.

Snyder, E. A. (1990). The effect of higher criminal penalties on antitrust enforcement. *Journal of Law and Economics, 33*(2), 439–462.

Solomon, C. M. (1992, July). Keeping hate out of the workplace. *Personnel Journal, 71*(7), 30–36.

Sorensen, P. T. (2009). The failure of *Sprint v. Mendelsohn* and what courts should do now. *Labor Law Journal, 60,* 185–195.

Sorkin, M. (2008). Watchdog group blasts agency over child safety. *St. Louis Post-Dispatch.* Retrieved July 29, 2011, from http://business.highbeam .com/435553/article-1G1-174735507/watchdog-group-blasts-agency-over-child-safety

Souryal, S. S. (2009). Deterring corruption by prison personnel: A principle-based perspective. *Prison Journal, 89*(1), 21–45.

Sowa, T. (2010, March 20). GU joins police to fight fraud: Accountant teams help solve small-scale crime. *Spokesman Review.* Retrieved July 31, 2011, from http://www.spokesman.com/stories/2010/mar/20/gu-joins-police-^=to-fight-fraud/

Spahr, L. L., & Alison, L. J. (2004). US savings and loan fraud: Implications for general and criminal culture theories of crime. *Crime, Law and Social Change, 41,* 95–106.

Spalek, B. (2001, October). White-collar crime victims and the issue of trust. *British Society of Criminology, Vol. 4* [Papers from the British Society of Criminology Conference, Leicester, July 2000]. Abstract retrieved July 31, 2011, from http://www.britsoccrim.org/volume4/003.pdf

Speaks, G. E. (1997). Documenting inadequate care in the nursing home: The story of an undercover agent. *Journal of Elder Abuse & Neglect, 8*(3), 37–45.

Speer, D. L. (2000). Redefining borders: The challenges of cybercrime. *Crime, Law and Social Change, 34*(3), 259–273.

Spivack, P., & Raman, S. (2008). Regulating the "new regulators": Current trends in deferred prosecution agreements. *American Criminal Law Review, 45*(2), 159–193.

Spurgeon, W. A., & Fagan, T. P. (1981). Criminal liability for life-endangering corporate conduct. *Journal of Criminal Law and Criminology, 72*(2), 400.

Sramcik, T. (2004, January 1). San Diego shop chain latest to be accused of fraud. *Automotive Body Repair News (ABRN),* p. 16. Retrieved July 29, 2011, from http://www.search-autoparts.com/searchautoparts/Industry+News/San-Diego-shop-chain-latest-to-be-accused-of-fraud/ArticleStandard/Article/detail/88775

St. Louis Police Department. (2006). *Home repair fraud.* Retrieved July 29, 2011, from http://ww5.stlouisco.com/police/PDFDIR/Brochures/Repair_Fraud.pdf

Stadler, W. A., & Benson, M. L. (2012). Revisiting the guilty mind: The neutralization of white-collar crime. *Criminal Justice Review, 37*(4), 494–511.

Stadler, W. A., Benson, M. L., & Cullen, F. T. (2011). Revisiting the special sensitivity hypothesis: The prison experience of white-collar inmates. *Justice Quarterly, 30*(6), 1–25.

Stanko, E. A. (1992). Intimidating education: Sexual harassment in criminology. *Journal of Criminal Justice Education, 3*(2), 331–340.

Stannard, C. I. (1973). Old folks and dirty work: The social conditions for patient abuse in a nursing home. *Social Problems, 20,* 329–342.

State of California Commission on Judicial Performance. (2010). *2009 Annual Report.* Retrieved July 31, 2011, from http://cjp.ca.gov/res/docs/Annual_Reports/2009_Annual_Report(1).pdf

State of California Commission on Judicial Performance. (2015). *2014 Annual Report.* Retrieved October 29, 2015 from http://cjp.ca.gov/res/docs/annual_reports/2014_Annual_Report.pdf

State of California Office of the Attorney General. (2015, December 3). *FAQs about Corinthian College (Heald, Everest, and Wyotech campuses).* Retrieved January 3, 2016 from https://oag.ca.gov/consumers/general/consumers_cii_faqs

Steen, R. G. (2010). Retractions in the scientific literature: Do authors deliberately commit research fraud? *Journal of Medical Ethics,* 1–5.

Steen, R. G. (2011). Misinformation in the medical literature: What role do error and fraud play? *Journal of Medical Ethics, 37,* 498–503.

Steffensmeier, D. J., Schwartz, J., & Roche, M. (2013). Gender and twenty-first-century corporate crime: Female involvement and the gender gap in Enron-era corporate frauds. *American Sociological Review, 78*(3), 448–476.

Stempel, J., & Plumb, C. (2008, December 13). Billions "gone to money heaven": Friends, high-profile firms among those who invested with alleged fraudster Bernie Madoff. *Toronto Star,* p. B04.

Stendahl, M. (2015, July 29). Ex-Wilson Sonsini employee gets 2 years for insider trading. *Law360.* Retrieved January 4, 2016 from http://www.law360.com/articles/684716/ex-wilson-sonsini-employee-gets-2-years-for-insider-trading

Stenzel, P. L. (2011). Resource Conservation and Recovery Act. In *Encyclopedia of Business* (2nd ed.). Retrieved November 29, 2015 from http://www.referenceforbusiness.com/encyclopedia/Res-Sec/Resource-Conservation-and-Recovery-Act.html

Stephenson-Burton, A. (1995). Public images of white collar crime. In D. Kidd-Hewitt & R. Osborne (Eds.), *Crime and the media: The post-modern spectacle.* London: Pluto.

Stern, S., & Lemmens, T. (2011). Legal remedies for medical ghostwriting: Imposing fraud liability on guest authors of ghostwritten articles. *Policy Forum, 8*(1), 1–5.

Stevens, E., & Payne, B. K. (1999). Applying deterrence theory in the context of corporate wrongdoing: Limitations on punitive damages. *Journal of Criminal Justice, 27*(3), 195–207.

Stewart, M. (2004, June 15). Letter to judge Cedarbaum. Retrieved December 2, 2015 from http://www.thesmokinggun.com/file/stewarts-letter-judge

Stinson, P. M. (2009). *Police crime: A newsmaking criminology study of sworn law enforcement officers arrested, 2005–2007.* Unpublished doctoral dissertation, Indiana University of Pennsylvania.

Stinson, P. M. (2015). Police crime: The criminal behavior of sworn law enforcement officers. *Sociology Compass, 9*(1), 1–13.

Stinson, P. M., Liederbach, J., & Freiburger, T. L. (2012). Off-duty and under arrest: A study of crimes perpetuated by off-duty police. *Criminal Justice Policy Review, 23*(2), 139–163.

Stroebe, W., Postmes, T., & Spears, R. (2012). Scientific misconduct and the myth of self-correction in science. *Perspectives on Psychological Science, 7*(6), 670–688.

Strom, P., & Strom, R. (2007). Cheating in middle school and high school. *Educational Forum, 71*(2), 104–116.

Stuart, D. (1995). Punishing corporate criminals with restraint. *Criminal Law Forum, 6*(2), 219–256.

Summerford, R. Q. (2002, July–August). Expert witnessing. *The White Paper: Topical Issues on White-Collar Crime (A bimonthly publication from the Association of Certified Fraud Examiners).* Retrieved July 30, 2011, from http://www.forensicstrategic.com/Articles/Expert%20Witnessing%20The%20Changing%20Landscape.pdf

Sutherland, E. (1949). *White collar crime.* Austin, TX: Holt, Rinehart & Winston.

Sutherland, E. H. (1934). *Principles of criminology* (2nd ed.). Philadelphia, PA: J. B. Lippincott.

Sutherland, E. H. (1939). *Principles of criminology* (3rd ed.). Philadelphia, PA: J. B. Lippincott.

Sutherland, E. H. (1940). White-collar criminality. *American Sociological Review, 5,* 1–12.

Sutherland, E. H. (1941). Crime and business. *Annals of the American Academy of Political and Social Science, 217,* 112–118.

Sutter, J. D. (2010, August 9). Gulf oil spill is stopped, but true story of damage will be long in coming, scientists say. *Cleveland.com.* Retrieved July 31, 2011, from http://www.cleveland.com/science/index.ssf/2010/08/gulf_oil_spill_is_stopped_but.html

Sweetman, C. (2015, December 21). *Contractor charged with bank fraud for destroyed home.* Retrieved December 31, 2015 from http://www.wcyb.com/news/contractor-charged-with-fraud-blamed-for-destroyed-home/37072680

Sykes, G. (1958). *A society of captives.* Princeton, NJ: Princeton University Press.

Sykes, G., & Matza, D. (1957). Techniques of neutralization. *American Sociological Review, 22,* 664–670.

Tappan, P. (1960). *Crime, justice, and correction.* New York, NY: McGraw-Hill.

Tappan, P. D. (1947). Who is the criminal? *American Sociological Review, 12,* 96–102.

Taub, S. (2006, December 20). Four former Enterasys execs convicted. *CFO.com.* Retrieved July 31, 2011, from http://www.cfo.com/article.cfm/8466560/c_8465548?f=todayinfinance_next

Taylor, M. (2001). Fraud control central. *Modern Healthcare, 31*(19), 22–23.

Tergesen, A. (2009, August 27). Mortgage fraud: A classic crime's latest twist: As "reverse" loans grow more popular, scams put older adults at risk. *Wall Street Journal Online*. Retrieved July 31, 2011, from http://online.wsj.com/article/SB100014240 5297020404420457436264133819 7748.html

Terry, J. (2015, December 23). *Odometer fraud on the rise in used car sales*. Retrieved December 31, 2015, from http://www.tmj4.com/news/i-team/odomoter-fraud-on-the-rise-in-used-car-sales

Terry, K. J., & Ackerman, A. (2008). Child sexual abuse in the Catholic Church: How situational crime prevention strategies can help create safe environments. *Criminal Justice and Behavior, 35*(5), 643–657.

Thomas, M. (2005, July/August). A victory over the slumlords. *ShelterforceOnline* (Issue 142). Retrieved June 29, 2010, from http://www.nhi.org/online/issues/142/organize.html

Thomas, O. (2010, May 19). Facebook CEO's latest woe: Accusations of securities fraud. *VentureBeat*. Retrieved July 31, 2011, from http://venture beat.com/2010/05/19/facebook-connectu-securities-fraud/

Thomsen, L. C. (2006). Testimony concerning insider trading before the Senate Judiciary Committee, December 5. Washington, DC: U.S. Securities and Exchange Commission. Retrieved July 29, 2011, from http://www.sec.gov/news/testimony/2006/ts120506lct.pdf

Thompson, B., & Yong, A. (2012). Corporate criminal liability. *American Criminal Law Review, 49,* 489–522.

Thrall, R., III. (2003). "Study" a fraud. *Automotive Body Repair News, 42*(12), 6.

Tillman, R. (2013). Too big to jail. *Western Criminology Review, 14*(2), 31–37.

Tillman, R., Calavita, K., & Pontell, H. (1997). Criminalizing white-collar misconduct: Determinants of prosecution in savings and loan fraud cases. *Crime Law and Social Change, 26*(1), 53–76.

Tillman, R., & Pontell, H. (1992). Is justice "collar blind"? Punishing Medicaid provider fraud. *Criminology, 30*(4), 547–574.

Tillman, R., & Pontell, H. (1995). Organizations and fraud in the savings and loan industry. *Social Forces, 73*(4), 1439–1463.

Tomasic, R. (2011). The financial crisis and the haphazard pursuit of financial crime. *Journal of Financial Crime, 18*(1), 7–31.

Tombs, S. (2008). Corporations and health safety. In J. Minkes & L. Minkes (Eds.), *Corporate and white-collar crime* (pp. 18–38). Thousand Oaks, CA: Sage.

Toyoda, A. (n. d.). *Remarks to the House Committee on Oversight and Reform*. Washington, DC: House Committee on oversight and reform.

Toyota president Akio Toyoda's statement to Congress (2010, February 24). *The Guardian*. Retrieved January 5, 2016 from http://www.theguardian.com/business/2010/feb/24/akio-toyoda-statement-to-congress

Trac Reports (2015). *Justice department data reveals 29 percent drop in criminal prosecutions of corporations. Retrieved November 7, 2015 from http://trac.syr.edu/tracreports/crim/406/*

Trahan, A., Marquart, J. W., & Mullings, J. (2005). Fraud and the American dream: Toward an understanding of fraud victimization. *Deviant Behavior, 26*(6), 601–620.

Traub, S. H. (1996). Battling employee crime: A review of corporate strategies and programs. *Crime and Delinquency, 42*(2), 244–256.

Triplett, R. (1993). The conflict perspective, symbolic interactionism and the status characteristics hypothesis. *Justice Quarterly, 10,* 541–558.

Trischitta, L. (2001, March 8). Three south Florida restaurants briefly closed by state inspectors. *Sun Sentinel*. Retrieved July 29, 2011, from http://articles.sun-sentinel.com/keyword/inspector/recent/2

Troy criminal justice professor indicted on rape charge involving 21-year-old student. (2010, January 20). *Press-Register*. Retrieved June 7, 2010, from http://blog.al.com/live/2010/01/troy_criminal_justice_professo.html

Trumka, R. (2008). Employment-related crimes. *American Criminal Law Review, 45*(2), 341–380.

Tu, Y. (2014). *Toy-related deaths and injuries calendar year 2013*. Bethesda, MD: U. S. Consumer Product Safety Commission. Retrieved November 1, 2015 from http://www.cpsc.gov/Global/Research-and-Statistics/Injury-Statistics/Toys/ToyReport2013.pdf

Two Miami doctors convicted of Medicare, Medicaid fraud. (2009). Federal Bureau of Investigation [Press release]. Retrieved July 29, 2011, from http://www.fbi.gov/miami/press-releases/2009/mm081709b.htm

Ugrin, J. C., & Odom, M. D. (2010). Exploring Sarbanes-Oxley's effect on attitude: Perceptions of norms, and intentions to commit financial statement fraud from a general deterrence perspective. *Journal of Accounting and Public Policy, 29*(5), 439–458.

Ulrich, L. (2000). Music on the Internet: Is there an upside to downloading? Hearing before the Committee on the Judiciary, United States Senate, July 11, 2000. Retrieved July 29, 2011, from http://www.gpo.gov/fdsys/pkg/CHRG-106shrg74728/html/CHRG-106shrg74728.htm

Union of Concerned Scientists (UCS). (2008, April). *Interference at the EPA: Science and politics at the U.S. Environmental Protection Agency*. Retrieved November 29, 2015 from ty/interference-at-the-epa.pdf

University of Colorado Investigative Committee Report. (2006). *Report of the Investigative Committee on the standing committee on research misconduct at the University of Colorado at Boulder concerning allegations of academic misconduct against Professor Ward Churchill*. Retrieved July 29, 2011, from http://www.colorado.edu/news/reports/churchill/down load/WardChurchillReport.pdf

University of Phoenix parent guilty of fraud. (2008, January 16). Associated Press. Retrieved July 29, 2011, from http://www.azcentral.com/business/articles/0116biz-apollogroupsuit16-ON.html

Unnever, J. D., Benson, M. L., & Cullen, F. T. (2008). Public support for getting tough on corporate crime: Racial and political divides. *Journal of Research in Crime and Delinquency, 45*(2), 163–190.

U. S. Attorneys. (n. d.). *2012 United States Attorneys Annual Statistical Report*. Retrieved November 11, 2015 from http://www.justice.gov/sites/default/files/usao/legacy/2013/10/28/12statrpt.pdf.

U. S. Conference of Catholic Bishops. (2004). *The nature and scope of the problem of sexual abuse of minors by Catholic priests and deacons in the United States 1950–2002: A research study conducted by the John Jay College of Criminal Justice*. Washington, DC: Author Retrieved from http://www.usccb.org/issues-and-action/child-and-youth-protection/upload/The-Nature-and-Scope-of-Sexual-Abuse-of-Minors-by-Catholic-Priests-and-Deacons-in-the-United-States-1950-2002.pdf

U.S. Consumer Product Safety Commission (USCPSC). (2010a). *Imported drywall and health: A guide for health care professionals*. Retrieved November 29, 2015 from http://www.atsdr.cdc.gov/drywall/docs/Drywall_for_Healthcare_Providers.pdf

U.S. Consumer Product Safety Commission (USCPSC). (2010b). *Investigation of imported drywall: Status update, September 2010*. Retrieved July 31, 2011, from http://www.cpsc.gov/info/drywall/sep2010status.pdf

U.S. Consumer Product Safety Commission (USCPSC). (2010c). *2010 performance and accountability report*. Retrieved November 29, 2015 from http://www.sec.gov/about/secpar2010.shtml

U. S. Consumer Product Safety Commission (USCPSC). (2013). *2013 annual report to the president and Congress*. Retrieved October 28, 2015 from http://www.cpsc.gov//Global/About-CPSC/Reports/Annual-Reports/FY13AnnualReport.pdf

U. S. Consumer Product Safety Commission (USCSPC). (2015, September 10). *Phil&teds USA agrees to pay $3.5 million civil penalty, implement internal compliance programs for failure to report defective clip-on high chairs*. Retrieved January 3, 2016 from http://www.cpsc.gov/en/Newsroom/News-Releases/2015/phil-and-teds-Agrees-to-Pay-3-Point-5-Million-Dollar-Civil-Penalty-for-Failure-to-Report-Defective-Clip-On-High-Chairs/

U. S. Department of Education. (2014). *Semiannual report to Congress, no. 68: October 1, 2013-March 31, 2014*. Retrieved January 1, 2016 https://www2.ed.gov/about/offices/list/oig/semiann/sar68.pdf

U. S. Department of Education. (2014, April 9). Cleveland man charged with fraudulently receiving $55,000 in student aid. *United States Attorney's Office: Northern District of Ohio*. Retrieved January 4, 2016 from http://www2.ed.gov/about/offices/list/oig/invtreports/oh042014.html

U. S. Department of Education. (2014, November 14). *Federal Student Aid Annual report FY 2014*.

Retrieved January 1, 2016 from https://www2
.ed.gov/about/reports/annual/2014report/fsa-
report.pdf

U.S. Department of Education. (2014, November). *FY
2015 Management Challenges*. Available online at
http://www2.ed.gov/about/offices/list/oig/misc/
mgmtchall2015.pdf).

U. S. Department of Education. (2014, December 10).
Chelsea man pleads guilty to student financial
aid. *United States Attorney's Office: District of
Massachusetts*. Retrieved January 4, 2016 from
http://www2.ed.gov/about/offices/list/oig/invtre
ports/ma122014.html

U. S. Department of Education. (2015, August 3).
Atwater woman sentenced for student aid fraud
and identity theft. *United State's Attorney's Office:
Eastern District of California*. Retrieved January
4, 2016 from http://www2.ed.gov/about/offices/
list/oig/invtreports/ca080315.html

U. S. Department of Education. (2015, November 30).
*FastTrain owner and admissions representative
convicted of federal student aid scheme*. Retrieved
January 4, 2016 from http://www2.ed.gov/about/
offices/list/oig/invtreports/fl112015.html

U.S. Department of Health and Human Services.
(2010). *Office of Inspector General semiannual
report to Congress*. Washington, DC: Health and
Human Services.

U. S. Department of Health and Human Services.
(2015, May 1). Findings of research misconduct,
24936 [2015–10203]. *Federal Register, 80*(84),
24936.

U.S. Department of Housing and Urban Development.
(2010, November 10). *HUD to Investigate mortgage lenders who discriminate* [Press release].
Retrieved November 20, 2015 from http://portal.
hud.gov/hudportal/HUD?src=/press/press_
releases_media_advisories/2010/HUDNo.10-158

U.S. Department of Justice (USDOJ). (1994). *Environmental justice strategy*. Washington, DC: U.S.
Department of Justice.

U.S. Department of Justice (USDOJ). (2010). *Report to
Congress on the activities and operations of the
Public Integrity Section for 2009*. Retrieved July
29, 2011, from http://www.justice.gov/criminal/
pin/docs/arpt-2009.pdf

U.S. Department of Justice (USDOJ). (2010, May 14).
*Arlington security guard, who hacked into hospi-
tal's computer system, pleads guilty to federal
charges* [Press release]. Retrieved July 30, 2011,
from http://www.justice.gov/usao/txn/PressRel
10/mcgraw_ple_pr.html

U. S. Department of Justice (USDOJ). (2014). *Report to
congress on the activities and operations of the
public integrity section for 2013*. Available online at
http://www.justice.gov/sites/default/files/crimi-
nal/legacy/2014/09/09/2013-Annual-Report.pdf

U. S. Department of Justice (USDOJ). (2014, September
15a). *Former congressman Richard G. Renzi convicted of extortion and bribery in illegal federal
land swap*. Retrieved January 1, 2016 from http://

www.justice.gov/opa/pr/former-congressman-
richard-g-renzi-convicted-extortion-and-bribery-
illegal-federal-land-swap

U. S. Department of Justice (USDOJ). (2014, September
15b). *Three Georgia men charged in alleged widespread corruption schemes at local military base*.
Retrieved January 1, 2016 from http://www
.justice.gov/opa/pr/three-georgia-men-charged-
alleged-widespread-corruption-schemes-local-
military-base

U. S. Department of Justice (USDOJ). (2014, September
15c). *Former Puerto Rico police officers charged
with extorting a commonwealth defendant for
$50,000*. Retrieved January 1, 2016 from http://
www.justice.gov/opa/pr/former-puerto-rico-
police-officers-charged-extorting-common
wealth-defendant-50000

U. S. Department of Justice (USDOJ). (2015, April 23).
*Deutsche Bank's London subsidiary agrees to plead
guilty in connection with long-running manipulation
of LIBOR*. Retrieved January 3, 2016 from http://
www.justice.gov/opa/pr/deutsche-banks-london-
subsidiary-agrees-plead-guilty-connection-long-
running-manipulation

U. S. Department of Justice (USDOJ). (2015, June 26).
*Former executive of Qualcomm sentenced to 18
months and fined for insider trading and money
laundering*. Available online at http://www.jus
tice.gov/opa/pr/former-senior-executive-qual
comm-sentenced-18-months-and-fined-
500000-insider-trading-and

U. S. Department of Justice (USDOJ). (2015, August
19). *Former U. S. government employee charged in
computer hacking and cyber stalking scheme*.
Retrieved January 1, 2016 from https://www.fbi
.gov/atlanta/press-releases/2015/former-u.s.-
government-employee-charged-in-computer-
hacking-and-cyber-stalking-scheme

U.S. Department of Justice (USDOJ). (2015, October
15). *Navy civilian engineer sentenced to 11 years
for attempted espionage*. Available online at
https://www.fbi.gov/norfolk/press-releases/2015/
navy-civilian-engineer-sentenced-to-11-years-
for-attempted-espionage

U. S. Department of Justice (USDOJ). (2015, October 29).
*Warner Chilcott agrees to plead guilty to felony
health care fraud scheme and pay $125 million to
resolve criminal liability and false claims act allegations*. Retrieved January 3, 2016 from http://www
.justice.gov/opa/pr/warner-chilcott-agrees-plead-
guilty-felony-health-care-fraud-scheme-and-pay-
125-million

U. S. Department of Justice (USDOJ). (2015, November
16). *For-profit college company to pay $95.5 mil-
lion to settle claims of illegal recruiting, consumer
fraud and other violations*. Retrieved January 3,
2016, from http://www.justice.gov/opa/pr/profit-
college-company-pay-955-million-settle-claims-
illegal-recruiting-consumer-fraud-and

U.S. Department of Justice (USDOJ). (n.d.a). *Anti-
Trust Enforcement and the Consumer*. Retrieved

November 27, 2015, from http://www.justice.gov/
sites/default/files/atr/legacy/2015/03/06/anti
trust-enfor-consumer.pdf

U.S. Department of Justice (USDOJ). (n.d.b). *Price fixing, bid rigging, and market allocation schemes:
What they are and what to look for*. Available
online at http://www.justice.gov/atr/price-fixing-
bid-rigging-and-market-allocation-schemes.

U.S. Department of Justice, Environment and Natural
Resources Division. (2010). *Summary of litigation*

U.S. Environmental Protection Agency (EPA). (1992).
The guardian: Origins of the EPA. Retrieved
online from http://epa.gov/aboutepa/history/
publications/print/origins.html.

U.S. Environmental Protection Agency (EPA). (1980, May
21). *EPA, New York State announce temporary relocation of love canal residents*. Retrieved December 1,
2015, from http://www2.epa.gov/aboutepa/epa-
new-york-state-announce-temporary-relocation-
love-canal-residents

U.S. Environmental Protection Agency (EPA). (1998).
*Illegal dumping prevention guidebook: U.S. EPA
Region 5, Waste, Pesticides, and Toxics Division*.
Chicago, IL: Region.

U.S. Environmental Protection Agency (EPA). (2010a).
About the Office of Research and Development.
Retrieved July 30, 2011, from http://www.epa
.gov/aboutepa/ord.html

U.S. Environmental Protection Agency (EPA). (2010b,
December 2). *Beazer Homes USA, Inc. settlement*
[Press release]. Retrieved July 30, 2011, from
http://www.epa.gov/compliance/resources/cases/
civil/cwa/beazer.html

U.S. Environmental Protection Agency (EPA). (2010c,
October 8). *Doe Run Resources Corporation settlement* [Press release]. Retrieved November 14,
2010, from http://www.epa.gov/compliance/
resources/cases/civil/mm/doerun.html

U.S. Environmental Protection Agency (EPA). (2010d).
Environmental justice. Retrieved December 17,
2010, from http://www.epa.gov/compliance/
environmentaljustice/basics/index.html

U.S. Environmental Protection Agency (EPA). (2010e).
Laws that we administer. Retrieved on December
17, 2010, from http://www.epa.gov/lawsregs/
laws/index.html

U.S. Environmental Protection Agency (EPA). (2010f).
What is an environmental crime? Retrieved on
December 17, 2010, from http://www.epa.gov/
compliance/criminal/investigations/environmen
talcrime.html

U.S. Environmental Protection Agency (EPA). (2010g).
*Fiscal year 2010 enforcement and compliance
annual results*. Available online at http://www
.epa.gov/compliance/resources/reports/endo
fyear/eoy2010/fy2010results.pdf.

U. S. Environmental Protection Agency (EPA). (2011a).
Enforcement and compliance numbers at a glance.
Retrieved November 6, 2015 from http://archive
.epa.gov/enforcement/annual-results/web/pdf/
eoy2010.pdf

U. S. Environmental Protection Agency (EPA). (2011b). *Benefits and costs of the Clean Air Act 1990-2020, the second prospective study.* Retrieved November 7, 2015 from http://www2.epa.gov/clean-air-act-overview/benefits-and-costs-clean-air-act-1990-2020-second-prospective-study

U. S. Environmental Protection Agency (EPA). (2012). *Enforcement annual results analysis and trends for fiscal year (FY) 2011.* Retrieved November 6, 2015 from http://archive.epa.gov/enforcement/annual-results/web/pdf/eoy2011.pdf

U. S. Environmental Protection Agency (EPA). (2013). *Enforcement annual results analysis and trends for fiscal year (FY) 2012.* Retrieved November 6, 2015 from http://archive.epa.gov/enforcement/annual-results/web/pdf/eoy2012.pdf

U. S. Environmental Protection Agency (EPA). (2014). *Enforcement annual results analysis and trends for fiscal year (FY) 2013.* Retrieved November 6, 2015 from http://archive.epa.gov/enforcement/annual-results/web/pdf/eoy2013.pdf

U. S. Environmental Protection Agency (EPA). (2014, May). *Environmental crimes case bulletin.* Retrieved January 3, 2016 from http://www.epa.gov/sites/production/files/2014-06/documents/may_2014_enviromental_crimes_case_bulletin.pdf

U.S. Environmental Protection Agency (EPA). (2014, May 22). *Contractor sentenced to prison for environmental crime.* Available online at http://yosemite.epa.gov/opa/admpress.nsf/d0cf6618525a9efb85257359003fb69d/1c89567e549656e185257ce0006ea14a!OpenDocument

U. S. Environmental Protection Agency (EPA). (2015). *Enforcement annual results numbers at a glance for fiscal year (FY) 2014.* Retrieved November 6, 2015 from http://www2.epa.gov/enforcement/enforcement-annual-results-analysis-and-trends fiscal-year-fy-2014

U. S. Environmental Protection Agency (EPA). (2015, September 10). *Duke energy corruption clean air act (CAA) settlement.* Retrieved January 5, 2016 from http://www.epa.gov/enforcement/duke-energy-corporation-clean-air-act-caa-settlement

U. S. Environmental Protection Agency (EPA). (2015, December 16a). *Enforcement annual results for fiscal year (FY) 2015.* Retrieved January 3, 2016 from http://www.epa.gov/enforcement/enforcement-annual-results-fiscal-year-fy-2015

U. S. Environmental Protection Agency (EPA). (2015, December 16b). *2015 major criminal cases.* Retrieved January 3, 2016 from http://www.epa.gov/enforcement/2015-major-criminal-cases

U.S. Equal Employment Opportunity Commission. (n.d.). *Charge statistics FY 1997 through FY 2014.* Retrieved November 29, 2015 from http://www.eeoc.gov/eeoc/statistics/enforcement/charges.cfm

U.S. Government Accountability Office (USGAO). (2003). *Medicaid: A program highly vulnerable to fraud.* Washington, DC: Government Printing Office.

U.S. Government Accountability Office (USGAO). (2005). *Mutual fund trading abuses: Lessons can be learned.* Washington, DC: U. S. Government Printing Office.

U.S. Government Accountability Office (USGAO). (2009). *Corporate crime: DOJ has taken steps to better track its use of deferred and non-prosecution agreements, but should evaluate effectiveness.* Washington DC: Government Printing Office.

U.S. Government Accountability Office (USGAO). (2010). *For-profit colleges: Undercover testing finds colleges encouraged fraud and engaged in deceptive and questionable marketing practices.* Retrieved November 29, 2015 from http://www.gao.gov/products/GAO-10-948T

U.S. Office of Inspector General (USOIG). (1999). *Criminal calls: A review of the Bureau of Prisons' management of inmate telephone privileges* [Report]. Retrieved July 29, 2011, from http://www.justice.gov/oig/special/9908/index.htm

U.S. Office of Inspector General (USOIG). (2008). *An investigation of allegations of politicized hiring and other improper personnel actions in the Civil Rights Division.* Washington, DC: U.S. Department of Justice.

U. S. Office of Personal Management. (1972, June). *Position classification standard for consumer safety series, GS-0696.* Retrieved from https://www.opm.gov/policy-data-oversight/classification-qualifications/classifying-general-schedule-positions/standards/0600/gs0696.pdf

U.S. Sentencing Commission. (1996). *Adequacy of federal sentencing guideline penalties for computer fraud and vandalism offenses: Report to the Congress.* Washington, DC: U.S. Sentencing Commission.

U. S. v. Ward 448 U.S. 242 (Supreme Court, 1980).

Vakkur, N., McAfee, R., & Kipperman, F. (2010). The unintended effects of the Sarbanes-Oxley Act of 2002. *Research in Accounting Regulation, 22,* 18–20.

Valeri, L. (1998). The information warriors. *Journal of Financial Crime, 6*(1), 52–53.

Van Cleef, C. R., Silets, H. M., & Motz, P. (2004). Does the punishment fit the crime? *Journal of Financial Crime, 12*(1), 56–65.

Van den Berg, E. A. I. M., & Eshuis, R. J. (1996). *Major investigations of environmental crimes.* Arnheim, Netherlands: Gouda Quint.

van der Wagen, W., & Pieters, W. (2015). From cybercrime to cyborg crime: Botnets as hybrid criminal actor-networks. *British Journal Criminology, 55,* 578–595.

Van Gigch, J. P. (1978). *Applied general systems theory 2nd edition.* New York, NY: Harpercollins.

van Rijnsoever, F. J., & Hessels, L. K. (2011). Factors associated with disciplinary and interdisciplinary research collaboration. *Research Policy, 40*(3), 551–562.

Van Slyke, S., & Bales, W. D. (2012). A contemporary study of the decision to incarcerate white-collar and street property offenders. *Punishment & Society, 14*(2), 217–246.

Van Slyke, S., & Bales, W. D. (2013). Gender dynamics in the sentencing of white-collar offenders. *Criminal Justice Studies, 26*(2), 168–196.

Van Wyk, J. A., Benson, M. L., & Harris, D. K. (2000). A test of strain and self-control theories: Occupational crime in nursing homes. *Journal of Crime and Justice, 23*(2), 27–44.

Varian, B. (2000, February 3). Former insurance agent guilty of fraud. *St. Petersburg Times,* p. 1.

Vaughan, D. (1992). The macro-micro connection in white-collar crime theory. In K. Schlegel & D. Weisburd (Eds.), *White-collar crime reconsidered* (pp. 124–145). Boston, MA: Northeastern University Press.

Vaughan, D. (2001). Sensational cases, flawed theories. In H. N. Pontell & D. Shichor (Eds.), *Contemporary issues in crime and criminal justice: Essays in honor of Gilbert Geis* (pp. 45–66). Upper Saddle River, NJ: Prentice Hall.

Vaughan, D., & Carlo, G. (1975). The appliance repairman: A study of victim responsiveness and fraud. *Journal of Research in Crime and Delinquency, 12,* 153–161.

Velez, M. B., Lyons, C. R., & Boursaw, B. (2012). Neighborhood housing investments and violent crime in Seattle, 1981–2007. *Criminology, 50*(4), 1025–1056.

Verstein, E. (2014). The law as violence: Essay: Violent white-collar crime. *Wake Forest Law Review, 49,* 873–887

Viano, E. C. (2006). Cybercrime: A new frontier for criminology. *International Annals of Criminology, 44*(1/2), 11–22.

Vickers, M. (2007). Are you at risk for mortgage fraud? *Fortune.* Retrieved June 21, 2010, from http://www.moneycnn.com/popups/2006/fortune/fraud/index.html

Vieraitis, L. M., Piquero, N. L., Piquero, A. R., Tibbetts, S. G., & Blankenship, M. (2012). Do women and men differ in their neutralizations of corporate crime? *Criminal Justice Review, 37*(4), 478–493.

Vinten, G. (1994). Asset protection through whistle-blowing. *Journal of Asset Protection and Financial Crime, 2*(2), 121–131.

Vito, G. F., Wolfe, S., Higgins, G. E., & Walsh, W. F. (2011). Police integrity: Rankings of scenarios on the Klockars scale by "management cops." *Criminal Justice Review, 36*(2), 152–164.

Volunteer Lawyers Program community legal services. (2009). *Arizona tenants' rights and responsibilities handbook.* Phoenix, AZ: LSC Legal Services Corporation.

Vukelic, G. (2015, September 27). UA professor receives tenure after plagiarizing student's work. *The Daily Wildcat.* Retrieved January 1, 2016 from http://www.wildcat.arizona.edu/article/2015/09/ua-professor-receives-tenure-after-plagiarizing-students-work

WFMJ.com. (2015, December 29). Man convicted of stealing form church fired by city of Niles.

Retrieved December 30, 2015 from http://www .wfmj.com/story/30847461/man-convicted-of- stealing-from-church-fired-by-city-of-niles

WLWT.com (2015, July 21). *Cincinnati man sentenced for role in oil investment scheme in Kentucky.* Retrieved January 4, 2016 from http://www.wlwt .com/news/cincinnati-man-sentenced-for-role- in-oil-investment-scheme-in-kentucky/34287962

Wahl, A. (2009, November 23). Toy safety still a crap- shoot. *Canadian Business, 82*(20), 16.

Waldfogel, J. (1995). Are fines and prison terms used efficiently? Evidence on federal fraud offenders. *Journal of Law and Economics, 38*(1), 107–139.

Walker, J. (2010, May 19). Academics fight Cuccinelli's call for climate-change records. *The Virginian-Pilot.* Retrieved from http://hamptonroads.com/2010/ academics-fight-cuccinellis-call-climatechange- records

Walker, S., & Alpert, G. P. (2002). Early warning systems as risk management for police. In K. M. Lersch (Ed.), *Policing and misconduct* (pp. 219–230). Upper Saddle River, NJ: Prentice Hall.

Wall, D. S. (2007). Policing cybercrimes: Situating the public police in networks of security within cyberspace. *Police Practice and Research, 8*(2), 183–205.

Wall, D. S. (2008). Cybercrime, media and insecurity: The shaping of public perceptions of cybercrime. *International Review of Law Computers & Technology, 22*(1–2), 45–63.

Wall, D. S. (2013). Policing identity crimes. *Policing and Society: An International Journal of Research and Policy, 23*(4), 437–460.

Wallack, T. (2013, March 18). Attorneys generals to Congress: Don't let for-profit colleges use federal grants and loans for advertising: States seek lim- its on US funds. *boston.com.* Retrieved January 3, 2016 from http://www.boston.com/business/ news/2013/03/17/attorney-generals-congress- don-let-for-profit-colleges-use-federal-grants- and-loans-for-advertising/lMzPoQYWO jKHlCepMMffOL/story.html

Waller, M. (2007, December 29). Even in prison Martha Stewart could not resist breaking the rules. *The Times* (London). Retrieved July 31, 2011, from http://business.timesonline.co.uk/tol/ business/columnists/article3105406.ece

Walsh, A. (2002). *Biosocial criminology: Introduction and integration.* Cincinnati, OH: Anderson.

Walters, R. (2007). Food crime, regulation, and the biotech harvest. *European Journal of Criminology, 4*(2), 217–235.

Washington, E. (2006). The impact of banking and fringe banking regulation on the number of unbanked Americans. *Journal of Human Resources, 41*(1), 106–137.

Watt, R. (2012). University students' propensity towards white-collar versus street crime. *Studies by Undergraduate Researchers at Guelph, 5*(2), 5–12.

Wear, D., Aultman, J. M., & Borges, N. J. (2007). Retheorizing sexual harassment in medical edu-

cation: Women students' perceptions at five U.S. medical schools. *Teaching and Learning in Medicine,* 19(1), 20–29.

Webb, T., & Pilkington, E. (2010, June 20). Gulf oil spill: BP accused of lying to Congress. *The Guardian.* Retrieved October 20, 2010, from http://www.guardian.co.uk/environment/2010/ jun/20/gulf-oil-spill-bp-lying

Weber, J., Kurke, L. B., & Pentico, D. W. (2003). Why do employees steal? Assessing differences in ethical and unethical employee behavior using ethical work climates. *Business & Society, 42,* 359–380.

Weisburd, D., Chayet, E. F., & Waring, E. (1990). White-collar crime and criminal careers: Some preliminary findings. *Crime and Delinquency, 36,* 342–355.

Weisburd, D., Waring, E., & Chayet, E. (1995). Specific deterrence in a sample of offenders convicted of white-collar crimes. *Criminology, 33,* 587–607.

Weisburd, D., Waring, E., & Wheeler, S. (1990). Class, status, and the punishment of white-collar crimi- nals. *Law and Social Inquiry, 15*(2), 223–243.

Weisburd, D., Wheeler, S., Waring, E., & Bode, N. (1991). *Crimes of the middle class: White-collar offenders in the federal courts.* New Haven, CT: Yale University Press.

Welch, H. (2008, February 5). Avoiding scams: 20,700 Americans fall for these investment schemes every year. *Jacksonville.Com,* Retrieved July 21, 2011 from http://jacksonville.com/tu-online/ stories/020508/bus_ 243662551.shtml

Welch, M. (2009). Fragmented power and state-corporate killings: A critique of Blackwater in Iraq. *Crime, Law and Social Change, 51,* 351–364.

Wells, C. (2014, April 2). Morgan state university pro- fessor convicted of fraud scheme. *The Baltimore Sun.* Retrieved January 1, 2016 from http://arti cles.baltimoresun.com/2014-04-02/news/bs-md- morgan-professor-convicted-20140402_1_mor gan-state-university-infrastructure-engineering- research-manoj-kumar-jha

Wells, J. T. (2003a). Follow the greenback road. *Journal of Accountancy, 196*(5), 84–87.

Wells, J. T. (2003b). The fraud examiners. *Journal of Accountancy, 196*(4), 76–79.

Wells, J. T. (2010). Ponzis and pyramids. *CPA Journal, 80*(2), 6–10.

Wheeler, S., Mann, K., & Sarat, A. (1988). *Sitting in judgment: The sentencing of white-collar crimi- nals.* New Haven, CT: Yale University Press.

Wheeler, S., Weisburd, D., & Bode, N. (1982). Sentencing the white collar offender: Rhetoric and reality. *American Sociological Review, 47*(5), 641–659.

Wheeler, S., Weisburd, D., & Bode, N. (1988). *Nature and sanctioning of white collar crime, 1976–1978.* Rockville, MD: National Institute of Justice.

Wheeler, S., Weisburd, D., & Bode, N. (2000). *Nature and sanctioning of white collar crime, 1976– 1978: Federal judicial districts.* Ann Arbor, MI: Inter-university Consortium of Political and social Research.

Wheeler, S., Weisburd, D., Waring, E., & Bode, N. (1987–1988). White-collar crimes and criminals. *American Criminal Law Review, 25,* 331–358.

Whetten, B. (2015, December 15).Former city employee convicted of forgery. *Douglas Dispatch.* Retrieved December 29, 2015 from http://www .douglasdispatch.com/news/former-city-employ ee-convicted-of-forgery/article_1a896728-a342- 11e5-a82b-5323648f1cdc.html

White, G., & Schneider, C. (2008, October 14). Depression expert at Emory pulls out of research projects. *Atlanta Journal Constitution,* p. A1.

White, J. B., Power, S., & Aeppel, T. (2001, June 20). Agency to comment on Ford tire safety, while inquiry into Explorer is considered. *Wall Street Journal,* p. A.3.

White, M. D., & Kane, R. J. (2013). Pathways to career- ending police misconduct: An examination of patterns, timing, and organizational responses to officer malfeasance in the NYPD. *Criminal Justice and Behavior, 40*(11), 1301–1325.

White, M. D., & Terry, K. J. (2008). Child sexual abuse in the Catholic Church: Revisiting the rotten apples explanation. *Criminal Justice and Behavior, 35*(5), 658–678.

White, R. (2008). Depleted uranium, state crime, and the politics of knowing. *Theoretical Criminology, 12*(1), 31–54.

White-collar crime rising. (2003, December 23). *Desert News.* Retrieved January 19, 2011, from http:// findarticles.com/p/articles/mi_qn4188/ is_20031223/ai_n11419131/?tag=rbxcra.2.a.11

Wiggins, L. M. (2002). Corporate computer crime: Collaborative power in numbers. *Federal Probation, 66*(3), 19–29.

Wiggins, O. (2009, June 12). Insurance agent accused of defrauding seniors of $280,000. *The Washington Post,* p. B02.

Wilkins, L. (1965). *Social deviance.* Englewood Cliffs, NJ: Prentice Hall.

Williams, F. P., & McShane, M. D. (2008). *Criminological theory* (5th ed.). Upper Saddle River, NJ: Prentice Hall.

Williams, J. W. (2005). Governability matters: The pri- vate policing of economic crime and the chal- lenge of democratic governance. *Policing and Society: An International Journal of Research and Policy, 15*(2), 187–211.

Williams, J. W. (2008). Out of place and out of line: Positioning the police in the regulation of finan- cial markets. *Law and Policy, 30*(3), 306–355.

Wilson, J. Q., & Kelling, G. L. (1982). Broken windows: The police and neighborhood safety. *Atlantic Monthly, 249,* 29–38.

Wilson, P. R., Lincoln, R., Chappell, D., & Fraser, S. (1986). Physician fraud and abuse in Canada: A preliminary examination. *Criminology, 28,* 129–143.

Wislar, J., Flanagin, A., Fontanarosa, P., & DeAngelis, C. D. (2010). Prevalence of honorary and ghost authorship in six general medical journals. *Peer*

Review Congress 2009. Retrieved July 29, 2011, from http://www.ama-assn.org/public/peer/abstracts-0910.pdf

Wolfe, S. M., Kahn, R., & Resnevic, K. (2010, April 5). *Ranking of state medical boards' serious disciplinary actions: 2007–2009*. Washington, DC: Public Citizen. Retrieved July 29, 2011, from http://www.citizen.org/page.aspx?pid=3168

Wolfe, S. E., & Piquero, A. R. (2011). Organizational justice and police misconduct. *Criminal Justice and Behavior, 38*(4), 332–353.

Wolfe, S. M., Williams, C., & Zaslow, A. (2012, May). *Public Citizen's Health Research Group Ranking of the Rate of State Medical Boards' Serious Disciplinary Actions, 2009–2011*. Washington, D. C.: Government Printing Office.

Worcester, B. A. (1998, July 6). Summer staffs open to scrutiny. *Hotel and Motel Management, 213*(12), 7.

World Health Organization (WHO). (2015). *7 million premature deaths annually linked to air pollution*. Retrieved November 6, 2015 from http://www.who.int/mediacentre/news/releases/2014/air-pollution/en/

WorldWatch Institute (2015). *Air pollution now threatening health worldwide*. Retrieved November 5, 2015 from http://www.worldwatch.org/air-pollution-now-threatening-health-worldwide

Wright, D. E, Titus, S. L., & Cornelison, J. B. (2008). Mentoring and research misconduct: An analysis of research mentoring in closed ORI cases. *Science and Engineering Ethics, 14*(3), 323–336.

Wright, J. P., Tibbetts, S. G., & Daigle, L. E. (2008). *Criminals in the making: Criminality across the life course*. Thousand Oaks, CA: Sage.

Wright, R. (2006). Why (some) fraud prosecutions fail. *Journal of Financial Crime, 13*(2), 177–182.

Yakovlev, P., & Sobel, R. (2010). Occupational safety and profit maximization: Friends or foes. *Journal of Socio-Economics, 39*, 429–435.

Yaniv, O., & Moore, T. (2008, February 21). Surrender deadline today for Bronx slumlord. *Daily News*, p. 18.

Yar, M. (2006). *Cybercrime and society*. Thousand Oaks, CA: Sage.

Yeager, P. (1986). Analyzing corporate offenses. In J. E. Post (Ed.), *Research on corporate social performance and policy*. Greenwich, CT: JAI Press.

Yohay, S. C., & Dodge, G. E. (1987). Criminal prosecutions for occupational injuries: An issue of growing concern. *Employee Relations Law Journal, 13*(2), 197–223.

Yoskowitz, A. (2007, April 5). 2/3 of students don't care about illegal downloading says survey. Oulu, Finland: AfterDawn.com. Retrieved July 31, 2011, from http://www.afterdawn.com/news/article.cfm/2007/04/06/2_3_of_students_don_t_care_about_illegal_downloading_says_survey

Young, J. R. (2008). Judge rules plagiarism-detection tool falls under "fair use." *Chronicle of Higher Education, 54*(30), A13.

Yu, O., & Zhang, L. (2006). Does acceptance of corporate wrongdoing begin on the "training ground" of professional managers? *Journal of Criminal Justice, 34*, 185–194.

Zambito, T., Martinez, J., & Siemaszko, C. (2009, June 29). Bye, bye Bernie: Ponzi king Madoff sentenced to 150 years. *New York Daily News*. Retrieved July 11, 2011, from http://articles.nydailynews.com/2009-06-29/news/17924560_1_ruth-madoff-ira-sorkin-bernie-madoff

Zane, P. C. (2003). The price fixer's dilemma: Applying game theory to the decision of whether to plead guilty to antitrust crimes. *Antitrust Bulletin, 48*(1), 1–31.

Zeman, N., & Howard, L. (1992, June 22). Trading places. *Newsweek*, p. 8.

Zernike, K. (2003, September 20). Students shall not download. Yeah, sure. *The New York Times*. Retrieved July 31, 2011, from http://www.nytimes.com/2003/09/20/technology/20COLL.html

Zhang, Z. (2011). Cyberwarfare implications for critical infrastructure sectors. *The Homeland Security Review, 5*(3), 281–295.

Zuckoff, M. (2005). *Ponzi's scheme*. New York, NY: Random House.

Zwolinski, M (2008). The ethics of price gouging. *Business Ethics Quarterly, 18*(3), 347–378.

Index

Abscam, 99
Abu Ghraib abuses, 103, 104 (photo)
Abuse:
    elder, 75–77
    financial, 8 (table), 76
    fraud versus, 64–65
    physical, 8 (table), 75
    of power, 278 (table)
    See also Sexual abuse
Abusers, serial, 301
Academic dishonesty, 134–136, 325
Academic sexual relationships, 128
Academy of Experimental Criminology, 9
Access, unauthorized, 169–171, 171 (photo)
Accidents, 238–239, 295
Accountants and accounting, forensic, 321, 322 (table),
    341–342
Account information, falsifying, 57
Accounts, 294–296
Achievement, as American value, 287, 287 (table)
ACM Transportation, 353
Active elder neglect, 76
Acute workplace injuries, 234
Adam, A., 57
Adams, B., 54
Adelphia Communications, 156 (table), 295
ADM. *See* Archer Daniels Midland
Administrative law judges, 354
Administrative proceedings, 354–355
Adrian Project, 337
Ads, celebrity, 226–227
Advance-fee fraud, 148, 169, 173, 204
Advertising, 225–227, 230
Age Discrimination Act, 231
Agencies involved in responding to white-collar crime, 317–323,
    317 (figure), 318–319 (table)
    See also Federal Bureau of Investigation; *specific agencies*
Agnew, Robert, 288–289
Airbag fraud, 54

AirNow, 268
Air pollution, 38
    See also Environmental crime
Alabama, attorney misconduct in,
    88, 89, 90 (figure)
Albanese, J. S., 312
Albonetti, C. A., 389
Albrecht, W. S., 285
Alienation, public, 37–38
Alison, L. J., 290
Allocution, 377
All the President's Men (movie), 329 (table)
Alper, M., 191
Alschuler, A. W., 94
Alternative sanctions, 404–411
    community service, 408–409, 409 (photo)
    house arrest, 404–408, 408 (table)
    job loss, 411
    shaming, 409–411
Alternative sanctions argument, 360
Alvesalo, A., 334
Ambiguity:
    conceptual, 24–25, 382
    empirical, 25
    legal, 25
    methodological, 25
    policy, 25
Americans with Disabilities Act, 218, 231
American values, 287–288, 287 (table)
Amerigroup Corporation, 63–64
Anderson, G., 70
Anderson, K. B., 33
Anderson, Mark, 75
Anderson, Robert, Jr., 320
Angel, J., 223
Animals, harmful treatment of, 261–262
Animal Welfare Act, 261–262
Annuities fraud, 57
Anonymous hotlines, 339

Antitrust laws, 220
Antitrust offenses, 220–225
    about, 220–221, 221 (table)
    bid rigging, 222
    dynamics surrounding, 224–225, 225 (table)
    group boycotts, 224
    market allocation, 223
    price discrimination, 222
    price fixing, 221–222
    price gouging, 223
Antivirus software, 167
Anza, Santo, Jr., 274
Apolitical white-collar crime, 101
Appeal to accidents, 295
Appeal to defeasibility, 295
Appeal to higher loyalties, 292, 293–294
Appliances, word-burning, 271
Applied general systems theory, 15–16, 17 (figure)
Appraisal fraud, 199–200
Archer Daniels Midland (ADM), 225 (table), 329 (table)
Archival research, 6–8, 8 (table)
ARCO. *See* Atlantic Richfield Company
Argust, C. P., 363
Arizona, slumlords in, 213
Arneklev, B., 298
Arroyo-Cruz, Abimael, 85
Arsenic, 270 (table)
Arson, 203–204
Asbestos, 38, 243, 245, 257, 259
Ashley Madison (dating site), 164
Assault, sexual, 75
Asset Forfeiture/Money Laundering Unit (FBI Financial Crimes Section), 319
Association of Certified Fraud Examiners, 4
Atlantic Richfield Company (ARCO), 412
Attachment, 296
Attorney-client privilege, 372
Attorney misconduct, 7, 88–89, 90 (figure)
Attorneys, defense, 368, 370–372
Audits, 48, 326, 340
Austin, W. T., 290
Australia, nursing home violations in, 283
Authority, corruption of, 86
Authority excuses, 295, 296
Authorship, honorary, 123, 125 (figure)
Auto insurance fraud, 54–55
Automatic brutality theory, 103
Automobiles, harmful, 241–242, 243
Automotive sales fraud, 46, 55
Autonomy, deprivation of, 407, 408 (table)
Auto repair fraud, 54–55, 56
Avol, Milton, 214
Awareness, denial of, 294
Awareness strategies, 49

Backcountry.com, 226
Backdoor, 167
Back to School (movie), 143
Bad apple explanations, 58–59, 87, 103, 108–109
Baisden, David, 387
Bait and switch practices, 226
Bakker, Jim, 105–106
Bales, W. D., 394
Ballard, Douglas, 146
Banker's Trust, 225 (table)
Bank fraud laws, 363
Bank insider trading, 146
Bankruptcy filings, unauthorized, 204
BankScan initiative, 322 (table)
Bank Secrecy Act, 318 (table)
Barker, T., 85–86
Barnes, W., 231
Barnett, H., 255, 256
Baron, R. A., 223
Barron, Clarence, 149
Barry, Marion, 101, 398
BASF Aktiengesellschaft, 224, 225 (table)
Bauer v. Sampson, 134 (table)
Beare, M., 363
Beato, Cristina V., 132
Beccaria, Cesare, 284–285
Becerril-Ramos, Josue, 85
Beck, E., 259
Beck, R., 128
Bed Bath & Beyond Inc., 226
Behaviors, sexualized, 128
Belief, in control theory, 296
Benson, Michael:
    accounts, 295
    corporate crime, prosecutors' response to, 365–366
    defense attorneys, 371
    doldrums, 398–399
    elder abuse by health care workers, 76
    just deserts, 415
    labeling theory, 309
    life course theory, 306–307
    networking, 380
    objectivity, 11
    offender characteristics, 42
    prison experience, 395, 396, 397, 399–400
    probation experience, 401
    reintegrative shaming, 410
    self-control theory, 298
    sentencing practices, 388
Bernard, Tara, 345
Berry, K. K., 128
Beverly Hills Hotel Corp., 155 (table)
BFI. *See* Browning Ferris Industries
Bharara, Preet, 145

Bidding, complementary, 222
Biden, Joe, 85, 173
Bid rigging, 222
Bid rotation, 222
Bid suppression, 222
Biechele, Dan, 248
Bierstedt, Robert, 11
Big-game operators, 262
Billing for nonexistent prescriptions, 72
Billing for services not provided, 54
Biological theories, 309–310, 310 (photo)
Birth outcomes, disparities in, 265
Black, A., 70
Black, W. K., 361
Blackwater, 102–103
Blagojevich, Rod, 294
Blakely, Robert, 363
Blankenship, M. B., 290
Blended attack, 167
Block, Alan, 101
Block, W., 223
Blum, Barbara, 260
Bode, N., 6–7, 42–43, 284, 289, 388, 389
Boesky, Ivan, 153, 155 (table), 411
Bonnell v. Lorenzo, 134 (table)
Booker v. Washington, 389
Boot sector virus, 167
Borrowing, 295
Boston, slumlords in, 214
Botnets, 174
Botsko, C. A., 329
Boundary maintenance, 39
Boycotts, group, 224
BP oil spill, 253–254, 255 (photo), 256 (photo), 276, 295, 366
Bracelet effects, 408, 408 (table)
Bradley, Daniel, 325, 335
Brainard, J., 121
Braithwaite, John, 284, 285, 311, 348, 410, 415, 441
Brawley, Otis, 69
Breadth of victimization, 249
Brean Murray, Carret & Co., 154
Brenner, Susan, 181
Bribery, 100–101, 128
Brickey, K. F., 360, 373
Bristol Myers-Squibb, 410
Britain, sexual harassment in educational system, 129
Broken windows theory, 212
Broker embezzlement, 144
Broker fraud, 144
Browning Ferris Industries (BFI), 262
Bryant, Clifford, 101–102
Bucketing, 147
Builder bailout schemes, 204
Builder-initiated fraud, 204–205

Bureau of Justice Statistics, 360
Burley, D., 182, 183
Burns, R. G., 250
Bursik, R. J., Jr., 298
Bush, George W., 276, 277 (photo)
Businesses, definitions socially constructed by, 28
Business fraud, 34–35
Business students, 135, 285, 290, 293
Butler, Daniel, 47

Cadmium, 270 (table)
Calavita, Kitty, 10, 286, 358, 360
California:
    auto repair/sales fraud, 54, 55
    deceptive sales, 227, 229 (table)
    energy industry, market manipulation in, 143
    foreclosure rescue scams, 204
    judicial misconduct, 91–92, 94, 95 (figure)
    Medicaid fraud offenders, sentencing of, 388
    pollution, economic costs of, 264
    Proposition 190, 91
    prosecutors' response to corporate crime, 366
California Attorney General, 218
California Commission on Judicial Performance, 91–92, 94, 95 (figure)
California Department of Consumer Affairs, 54, 227
California State University, Fullerton, 136
Cameras, video, 49, 301, 330
Cammarano, Peter, 100
Campaign finance laws, 100
Camps, Frank, 242
Canales, Suzie, 266
Cancer, 12, 69
Capable guardians, 299, 301, 302
Carbon monoxide, 270 (table)
Careers responding to white-collar crime:
    about, 18
    administrative law judges, 354
    consumer safety officers, 343
    environmental protection specialists, 258
    FDIC investigations specialists, 158
    general safety and health inspectors, 300
    human resource specialists, 40
    industrial security specialists, 48
    information security specialists, 188
    investigative analysts, 66
    investigative scientists, 119
    motor carrier safety specialists, 243
    prison consultants, 400
    U.S. Air Force criminal investigators, 103
    U.S. Air Force housing management specialists, 214
    U.S. Department of Agriculture investigators, 19
Caregivers, stressed out, 301
Carey, Hugh, 260
Carlos, John, 287

Carter, Jimmy, 260
Carter, T. S., 262
Casa Madrona Hotel, 146
Case descriptions, 7, 8 (table)
Case records, 6
Cases, fixing, 86
Case studies, 10
Cash register money, theft of, 47
Castleberry, S. B., 414
Category I loss prevention strategies, 338
Category II loss prevention strategies, 338–339
Category III loss prevention strategies, 339
Catholic Church sexual abuse scandal, 106–111, 107 (figure), 108 (figure)
Causes of Delinquency (Hirschi), 296
Cavender, G., 10, 250–251
Cease and desist orders, 354
Cedarbaum, Marian, 375, 376
Celebrity ads, 226–227
Celebrity bashing, 396
Cendant, 155 (table)
Censure, 105
Center for Medicare and Medicaid Services (CMS), 318 (table), 344–345
Center for Public Integrity, 95
Central Intelligence Agency (CIA), 103
CFTC. *See* Commodity Futures Trading Commission
Change:
    in priorities, 278 (table)
    social, 39
    stressful, 395
    structural, 179
    technological, 312
Character witnesses, 374
Charges, deciding, 361–364
Chatman Thomsen, Linda, 145
Chavez-Beltran, Raul, 267, 268 (figure)
Chayet, E., 309
Cheating by students, 135, 136
Check cashing businesses, 223
Chelsea Housing Authority, 386
Chen, Peter, 124
Chien, E., 231
Chin, Denny, 150, 154, 352, 354 (photo)
China:
    cybercrime, 181
    drywall, 245, 247
    recalled goods from, 247, 247 (photo)
    research misconduct, 121
Chronic workplace injuries, 234
Chunking, 206
Churchill, Ward, 119
Churning, 58, 206
CIA. *See* Central Intelligence Agency
Cikovic, R., 75

Citigroup, 140
Citizens for Environmental Justice, 266
Civil Justice Survey of State Courts, 378, 378 (table), 379 (table)
Civil justice system, 16
Civil lawsuits, 377–380, 378 (table), 379 (table)
Civil law violations, 27–28
Civil proceedings, 354
Civil settlements, 365, 403
Clark, G. A., 41
Class action lawsuits, 380
Class bias, 380–381
Classical strain theory, 286–287
Class status, 333, 333 (table), 388–389, 401
Clayton Act, 221 (table)
Clean Air Act, 255, 257
Clean energy, 271
Clean Water Act, 254–255, 257, 269
Client-oriented defense, 371
Clinard, Marshall, 26, 218, 220, 231
Clinton, Bill, 329 (table)
Clocking, 46, 55
Club Fed, 399, 399 (photo)
CMS. *See* Center for Medicare and Medicaid Services
Coakley, Martha, 274
Coburn, N. F., 339 340
Coca-Cola, 327
Coercion, sexual, 128
Cohen, L. E., 299
Cohen, M. A., 358, 412
Cole, Robert, 85
Coleman, James, 283, 304
Collaboration, 181, 334–335
Collective embezzlement, 249, 286
College faculty and researchers. *See* Professors and researchers in educational system
College of William and Mary, 116
Colleges:
    cybercrime and, 183–186, 184 (figure), 186 (photo)
    for-profit, 217, 218, 227–228, 229 (table), 230
College students. *See* Students
Collie, Melissa, 46
Collin, Barry C., 172
Collusion, 222
Colman, Jeannette, 120
Colorado, slumlords in, 211, 213
Columbia Savings and Loan Association (Beverly Hills), 10
Columbus, OH, 261
Colvin, G., 399
Combating Corporate Crime (Benson & Cullen), 365–366
Comey, James B., 79, 362
Comments, sexualized, 128
Commitment, in control theory, 296
Commodities, 141
Commodities fraud, 141

Commodity Futures Trading Commission (CFTC), 141, 147, 318 (table)
Community-based sanctions, 400–401
Community integration, 39
Community service, 408–409, 409 (photo)
Compensation programs, loss prevention, 49
Compensatory damages, 403, 404 (figure), 406 (table)
Competition, culture of, 283–284
Compiled viruses, 167
Complacency, 381
Complementary bidding, 222
Complexity, in white-collar crime investigation, 334–335, 335 (photo)
Complexity of intent, 249
Compliance programs, 340
Comprehensive Environmental Response Compensation and Liability Act, 272
Comptroller of the Currency, Office of the, 319 (table)
Computer crime. *See* Cybercrime
Computer Fraud and Abuse Act, 189
Conceptual ambiguity, 24–25, 382
Condemnation of condemners, 292
Conflict explanations, 70
Conflicts of interest, 127
Conflict theory, 302–303
Conformists, 286, 287
ConnectU, 139–140
Connolly, Hope, 301
Consensual sex, 96
Consequences of white-collar crime, 36–40
  emotional consequences, 37–38, 212, 213 (figure)
  individual economic losses, 36–37
  physical harm, 38–39, 39 (photo)
  positive consequences, 39–40, 41 (photo)
  societal economic losses, 37
Conspiracy appraisal fraud, 200
Conspirator straw buyers, 197, 198
Construction material, harmful, 243, 245, 247
Consumer Finance Protection Bureau, 344, 346 (figure)
Consumer fraud, 33–34, 36 (figure)
Consumer products, harmful. *See* Harmful consumer products
Consumers:
  complaints by, 52
  harmful treatment of, 247–248
  sales-directed crimes against, 57–58
  theft crimes against, 57
Consumer safety officers, 343
Contract lawsuits, 378, 378 (table), 379 (table)
Contractors, private, 102–103
Control center viruses, 192
Control groups, 9
Controlled substance, delivery of, 72
Control theory, 296–297
Cookies, 167

Cooper, J. A., 87
Cooperating witnesses, 374
Cooperation strategies, 345, 347
Co-pay waivers, 65
Copes, Heith, 411
Copper, 270 (table)
Copyright violations, 173
Corinthian Colleges, 218
Corporate crime, 217–251
  about, 217–218
  antitrust offenses, 220–225, 221 (table), 225 (table)
  benefits, 249
  conceptualizing, 26, 27 (table), 218–220, 219 (figure), 382
  consumer products, harmful, 240–247, 241 (photo), 241 (table), 245 (photo), 247 (photo)
  consumers, harmful treatment of, 247–248
  criminologists' coverage of, 250 (figure), 251
  cycle of, 304–305, 305 (figure)
  deceptive sales, 227–228, 229 (table), 230
  dynamic organizational explanations for, 305–306
  dynamics, 248–249
  explaining, 304–306, 305 (figure)
  false advertising, 225–227
  labor practices, unfair, 230–231, 232 (table), 233
  media coverage, 250–251
  organizational processes and, 304–305, 305 (figure)
  organizational structure and, 304
  problems responding to, 249
  public concern about, 250–251, 250 (figure)
  unsafe work environments, 233 (figure), 234–235, 236–237 (table), 238–240, 238 (table)
Corporate crime liability, 278 (table), 366
Corporate Crime Reporter, 224, 225 (table)
Corporate probation, 412, 414 (table)
Corporate system, 16
Corporate violence. *See* Unsafe work environments
Corporations:
  charging, 364–367, 367 (table)
  defined, 218, 219 (figure), 304
  disparate treatment of, 381
  punishing for white-collar crime, 411–413, 414 (table)
  recidivism by, 413
  See also Corporate crime
Correctional officer misconduct, 96–97
Correctional sexual misconduct, 96–97
Corrections subsystem, 385–416
  about, 385–387
  alternative sanctions, 404–411, 408 (table)
  monetary penalties, 401–404, 404 (figure), 405 (table), 406 (table)
  prison experience, 395–400, 396 (photo), 399 (photo)
  probation and parole experience, 400–401
  punishing corporations for white-collar crime, 411–413, 414 (table)

punishment, reasons for, 413
    sentencing dynamics, 388–394, 391–393 (table),
        394 (figure)
Corruption, 85–88, 86 (photo), 100–101
Cosentino, Michael, 10
Cost savings entity, EPA as, 272–273 (table), 274–275
Counterfeiting, 31 (table), 32
Counterfeiting software crimes, 172–173
Coupon stuffing, 47
Cox, L., 71
Cox, S. M., 11
Crackers, 169–170, 171–172
Craig, Larry, 101
Cramm, P. D., 95
Credit card information, theft of, 47
Credit enhancements, faulty, 204–205
Credits for nonexistent returns, 47
Cressey, Donald, 289, 310
Crime, defined, 26
    See also specific crimes
Crime and the American Dream (Messner & Rosenfeld), 287–288,
        287 (table)
Crime in the Home Health Care Field (Payne), 78
Crimes by the corporate system. *See* Corporate crime
Crimes in the military, 101–103, 104 (photo)
Crime Victims Rights Act, 377
Criminal Behavior Systems (Clinard & Quinney), 26, 218
Criminal fines, 401–402
Criminality, in self-control theory, 297
Criminal justice journals, 250 (figure), 251
Criminal justice officials, surveys of, 4
Criminal justice professors, sexual harassment by, 129, 130
Criminal justice system, 16, 312
Criminal justice system crimes, 85–98
    attorney misconduct, 88–89, 90 (figure)
    correctional officer misconduct, 96–97
    judicial misconduct, 89–92, 91 (photo), 95 (figure)
    police corruption, 85–88, 86 (photo)
    prosecutorial misconduct, 92–96
Criminal law violations, 26–27
Criminaloid concept, 24, 27 (table)
Criminal proceedings, 354
Crippen, Michel, 136
Critical infrastructure, 176–178, 178 (photo)
Croall, Hazel, 9, 49–50, 342
Crofts, P., 6
Crum, Eugene, 387
Cuccinnelli, Ken, 122
Cukier, M., 191
Cullen, Frank, 10, 41, 365–366, 380, 395, 399–400
Cullen, J. B., 41
Culpable conduct, 358
Culpepper, D., 223
Cultural factors, 66, 180

Cultural theories, 283–284, 283 (photo)
Culture of competition, 283–284
Cunningham, Martha, 58
Cunningham, Randy "Duke," 396
Curry, P., 197
Cutillo, Arthur J., 145
Cybercrime, 163–192
    about, 163–164
    collaboration issues, 181–182
    colleges and, 183–186, 184 (figure), 186 (photo)
    conceptualizing, 165, 165 (photo), 166 (figure)
    costs, 176–178, 178 (photo)
    cybercriminal characteristics, 173–176
    defined, 165
    explaining, 178–180
    Federal Bureau of Investigation, 173, 174 (table), 177, 320
    jurisdictional issues, 181
    misconceptions, 180–181
    preventing, 189–192
    responding to, 180–183, 186–189
    students and, 185–186
    terminology, 167–168
    types, 166–173, 174 (table)
Cybergangs, 174–175
Cyber mercenaries, 174
Cyber system, 15
    See also Cybercrime
Cyberterrorism, 172
Cyborg crime, 179

Dabney, Dean, 5, 72–73, 73–74, 293
Daiwa Bank Ltd., 225 (table)
Daly, Kathleen, 308
Damage control argument, 360
Damages:
    compensatory, 403, 404 (figure), 406 (table)
    punitive, 403, 404 (figure), 405 (table), 406 (table)
Danger, in prison, 396–397
Danner, Mona, 308
Darkode, 177
Davies, Kent, 49
Davis, Jason, 412
DB Group Services (UK) Limited, 218
DE. *See* U.S. Department of Education
Death, 39
Deception, in religious system, 106
Deceptive sales, 227–228, 229 (table), 230
Decision making, rational, 13
Declination rates, 359–360
DeCoster, Austin "Jack," 246
DeCoster, Peter, 246
Decriminalization, 278 (table)
"Deep Throat," 329 (table)
Defeasibility, appeal to, 295

Defendants, in judicial proceedings, 375–376
Defending White-Collar Crime (Mann), 368
Defense attorneys, 368, 370–372, 380
Defense of entitlement, 295
Deferred prosecution agreements (DPAs), 368, 369–370 (table)
Defiance, 105
Definitions socially constructed by businesses, 28
Deflated appraisals, 199
Dehumanization, 211
DeLay, Tom, 100, 397
Delivery of controlled substance, 72
De minimis OSHA violations, 238 (table)
Demoralization costs, 3
Denial:
    of awareness, 294
    of crime, 294
    of fact, 294
    of guilt, 294–295
    of injury, 291, 293, 294 (table)
    of law, 295
    of responsibility, 292, 294, 294 (table)
    of victim, 291
    of wrongfulness, 295
Denial-of-service attacks, 172
Denials, 294–296
DeNino, Walter F., 131, 132
Deny by default configuration, 167
Depression, 395–396
Deprivation:
    of autonomy, 407, 408 (table)
    of goods/services, 407, 408 (table)
    of heterosexual relations, 407, 408 (table)
    of liberty, 407, 408 (table)
    in prison, 397–398
Derderian, Jeffery, 248
Derderian, Michael, 248
Deregulation, 311
Determinism, 13
Deterrence theory, 284–285, 403, 413
Deterrent, EPA as, 269–271
Devaney, Earl, 358
Deviance:
    elite, 27 (table)
    organizational, 27 (table)
    police, 86
    prison, 398
    workplace, 28
Deviant misuse of the justice process, 398
Differential association theory, 289–290, 291
Digital Millennium Copyright Act, 173
Digital piracy, 136, 173, 185–186, 186 (photo)
Dimento, J., 366
Dipascali, Frank, Jr., 150
Dirty Harry character, 347–348
Discovery-oriented defense, 370

Discrimination, 231, 232 (table), 233, 345
Dishonesty, academic, 134–136, 325
Disinfecting, 167
Disintegrative shaming, 410
Disney, 145
Disposal of hazardous wastes, illegal, 259–260, 265
Distribution networks, 175–176
District of Columbia:
    fraud by doctors, 63–64
    group boycotts, 224
    slumlords, 214
Doctors:
    fraud by, 8 (table), 63–69, 67 (figure), 68 (figure)
    general offending by, 71–72
Dodd-Frank Wall Street Reform and Consumer Protection Act, 343–344
Dodge, M., 404
Doe Run Resources Corporation, 269, 270 (table)
Doldrums, 398–399, 399 (photo)
Door-to-door home repair scams, 52
Dose-response assessment, 269
Double billing, 72, 126–127
Douglas, William O., 212
Doyle, A., 58–59
DPAs. *See* Deferred prosecution agreements
Drug-induced relationships, 75
Drugs, 8 (table), 72, 73–74
Drywall, Chinese, 245, 247
Dual settlement statements fraud, 203
Due diligence defense, 366
Duke Energy Corporation, 254–255, 269–271
Duke University Lacrosse players, 95–96
Dumping, illegal, 261, 274
Dumps, 176
Dunkin' Donuts, 218
Durable medical equipment fraud, 78, 80
Duran, D., 410
Durkheim, Emile, 14, 39
Dynamic organizational theories, 305–306

Eastman, J. K., 135
Ebbers, Bernard, 155 (table)
Economic Crime Unit (FBI Financial Crimes Section), 317
Economic losses, 36–37
Economic policies, 311
Economic power, 333, 333 (table)
Economic system, 16, 141
Economic system crimes, 139–161
    about, 139–141, 141 (photo)
    advance-fee fraud, 148, 204
    broker fraud and embezzlement, 144
    foreign exchange fraud, 147
    futures trading fraud, 147
    hedge fund fraud, 144

high-yield investment schemes, 147
insider trading, 145–147, 147 (photo)
investment fraud, 141–157
market manipulation, 143
patterns surrounding, 151, 153–154,
    155–156 (table), 157
pyramid schemes, 148, 148 (table)
student loan fraud, 140–141, 157–160, 159 (figure),
    228, 229 (table)
See also Ponzi schemes
Edelhertz, H., 25, 321
Educational system, 15
Educational system crimes, 116–137
about, 116–117, 117 (photo)
disciplining professors, 131–133, 133–134 (table)
embezzlement, 125
faculty double billing, 126–127
ghostwriting, 123, 125, 125 (figure)
outside work, unapproved, 127–128
pecuniary-oriented offenses, 125–128
by professionals, 117–134
research misconduct, 118–123, 122 (photo), 123 (figure),
    132–133
sexual harassment, 128–131, 130 (photo)
by students, 134–136
textbook fraud, 125–126
Education Management Corporation, 230
Edwards, John, 100
Edwards v. California Univ. of Pennsylvania, 133 (table)
EEOC. *See* Equal Employment Opportunity Commission
Eggs, tainted, 246
Ego seeking by workers, 284
Egress filtering, 167
Elder abuse by health care workers, 75–77
Elder financial abuse, 76
Elderly persons:
    as insurance crime victims, 58
    as vulnerable targets, 301–302
Elder neglect, 76
Elder physical abuse, 75
Elder sexual abuse, 76–77
Election law violations, 99–100
Electric vehicle charging infrastructure, 271
Electronic and software piracy, 136, 173, 185–186,
    186 (photo)
Electronic monitoring, house arrest with, 407–408,
    408 (table)
Electronic Subpoena Production initiative, 322 (table)
Elis, L. A., 285
Elite deviance, 27 (table)
El Sayed, S., 307
Email messages, 326
Embezzlement:
    arrests reported in *Uniform Crime Reports,* 31 (table), 32
    broker, 144

causes, 310
collective, 249, 286
in educational system, 125
general strain theory and, 105–106 289
in insurance system, 57
in religious system, 105–106
in retail system, 47
Emissions, illegal, 258–259
Emory University, 127
Emotional consequences, of white-collar crime, 37–38, 212,
    213 (figure)
Empirical ambiguity, 25
Empirical issues, 277–279
Employee-based strategies for preventing cybercrime, 190,
    190 (photo)
Employee theft, 46–49, 47 (photo)
Employer-based strategies for preventing cybercrime, 189
Employment discrimination, 231, 232 (table), 233
Encryption, 190
Endangerment, knowing, 262
Enemy civilian social system crimes, 102
Energy efficiency, 271
Energy Independence and Security Act, 143
Energy industry, 143
Enforcement, inadequate, 278 (table)
Engelmayer, Paul, 386
Enron, 143, 155 (table), 156 (table), 329 (table), 373
Enron (movie), 329 (table)
Ensign, John, 101
Enterprise (ship), 102
Entertainment services system, 49–51
Entitlement, defense of, 295
Environmental crime, 253–280
about, 253–255, 255 (photo)
conceptualizing, 255–257, 256 (photo)
consequences, 264–266, 265 (photo)
dumping, illegal, 261, 274
emissions, illegal, 258–259
empirical issues and, 277–279
environmental state crime, 263
environmental threats, 262–263
evidentiary issues and, 276–277, 277 (photo), 278 (table)
hazardous waste disposal, illegal, 259–260, 265
international, 263–264
laws, 255–256
media portrayals, 276, 277 (photo)
problems addressing, 276–279, 277 (photo), 278 (table)
property/wildlife, harmful destruction of, 261–262,
    261 (photo)
prosecutorial decision making and, 358
varieties, 257–264, 261 (photo)
See also Environmental Protection Agency
Environmental harm, significant, 358
Environmental justice, 265–266
Environmental Justice Initiative, 265

Environmental Protection Agency (EPA), 266–276
  about, 266, 318 (table)
  criticisms, 275–276
  declination rate, 359
  as deterrent, 269–271
  as enforcer of criminal and civil laws, 257, 266–267, 267 (figure), 268 (figure)
  environmental justice, 265
  as fund generator and cost savings entity, 272–273 (table), 274–275
  Love Canal tragedy, 259, 260
  Office of Criminal Enforcement, 266, 358
  Office of Environmental Justice, 265
  Office of Inspector General, 275
  Office of Research and Development, 268–269
  penalties assessed by, 272–273 (table), 403
  as public health protector, 267–269, 269 (table), 270 (table)
Environmental protection specialists, 258
Environmental racism, 265–266
Environmental risk assessment research, 269
Environmental state crime, 263
Environmental threats, 262–263
EPA. *See* Environmental Protection Agency
Equal Employment Opportunity Commission (EEOC), 218, 231, 232 (table), 318 (table)
Equal Pay Act, 231
Equity fraud, 201
Equity skimming, 201, 209 (figure)
Ericson, R., 58–59
Ermann, M. D., 219, 249, 304
Ethical violations, 26
Evans, R. D., 292, 294 (table)
"Everyone does it" (neutralization), 292, 293, 294 (table)
Evidence gathering strategies, 325–330
  audits, 326
  record reviews, 326
  technological devices, 330
  undercover investigations, 315–316, 326–328, 328 (table)
  whistleblowers, 328–330, 329 (table)
Evidentiary issues, 276–277, 277 (photo), 278 (table)
Excuses, 295–296
Experimental groups, 9
Experiments, 9–10
Expert witnesses, 374–375, 374 (figure)
Explaining white-collar crime, 281–313
  about, 281–283
  conflict theory, 302–303
  control theory, 296–297
  corporate crime, explaining, 304–306, 305 (figure)
  cultural theories, 283–284, 283 (photo)
  deterrence theory/rational choice theory, 284–285
  institutional anomie theory, 287–288, 287 (table)
  integrated efforts at, 310–311
  learning theory, 289–290

  neutralizing and justifying white-collar crime, 291–296, 293 (photo), 294 (table)
  routine activities theory, 299–302
  self-control theory, 297–299
  strain theory, 285–289, 287 (table)
  systems theory, 311–312
  theories ignored in white-collar crime literature, 306–310, 307 (photo), 309 (photo), 310 (photo)
Exploitation, 230–231
Exposure assessment, 269
External audits, 341
External whistleblowers, 328
Extra-occupational crimes, 102
Extrusion, 170
Exum, M. L., 285
Exxon Corporation, 225 (table)
Exxon Shipping, 225 (table)
Exxon Valdez grounding, 28, 37 (photo), 253, 258

F. Hoffmann-LaRoche, 224, 225 (table)
Facebook, 139–140, 339
Face-to-face interviews, 5 (table)
Fact, denial of, 294
FACTS. *See* Forensic Accountant Core Training Session
Faculty. *See* Professors and researchers in educational system
Faculty double billing, 126–127
Faculty embezzlement, 125
Faichney, D., 402
Failing, fear of, 289
Failure to abate OSHA violations, 238 (table)
Failure to report suspected elder abuse, 77
Falana, Ricardo, 50
False advertising, 225–227
False Claims Act, 363
False negative, 167
False positive, 167
False Statements Act, 363
Falsifying account information, 57
Falsifying records, 65
Familiarity, paradox of, 74
Family effects, of electronic monitoring, 407, 408 (table)
Family groups, 230
Farkas, Lee, 207
Farole, D. J., 403
Fastow, Andrew, 155 (table)
FastTrain, 158
Fata, Farid, 385–386
Faulty credit enhancements, 204–205
FBI. *See* Federal Bureau of Investigation
FCS. *See* Financial Crimes Section
FDA. *See* Food and Drug Administration
FDIC. *See* Federal Deposit Insurance Corporation
Fear mongering, 105
Fearn, H., 129

"Fear of failing," 289
Federal Bureau of Investigation (FBI):
about, 318 (table)
Abscam, 99
Archer Daniels Midland investigation, 329 (table)
BankScan initiative, 322 (table)
Coca-Cola investigation, 327
Criminal Investigation Division, 322 (table)
cybercrime, 173, 174 (table), 177, 320
economic costs of white-collar crime, 2
Electronic Subpoena Production initiative, 322 (table)
Financial Crimes Section, 317, 319, 322 (table), 324
Forensic Accountant Core Training Session (FACTS),
    322 (table)
Forensic Accounting Program, 321, 322 (table)
Health Care Fraud Initiative, 319
insider trading, 146
Internet Crime Complaint Center, 173, 174 (table)
mortgage fraud, 196, 198
political extortion and bribery, 100
Uniform Crime Reports, 31 (table), 32
white-collar crime, 317, 319–322, 323 (figure)
white-collar crime definition, 29
Federal Deposit Insurance Corporation (FDIC), 146, 158,
    205, 318 (table)
Federal facilities, misuse of, 262
Federal Trade Commission (FTC):
about, 318 (table)
antitrust offenses, 223, 224, 225
corporate crime, 217–218
false advertising, 226
National Consumer Protection Week, 34
research survey, 33–34, 36 (figure)
student loan fraud, 160
Federal Trade Commission Act, 221 (table), 225
Federal Water Pollution Control Act, 258–259
Fédération Internationale de Football Association (FIFA), 362
Feldman, S., 129
Felson, M., 299
Felt, W. Mark ("Deep Throat"), 329 (table)
Fenwick, M., 250 (figure), 251
Field research, 8–9
FIFA. *See* Fédération Internationale de Football Association
Fifth Amendment, 242, 258–259, 366
File infector viruses, 167
Financial abuse, 8 (table), 76
Financial aid fraud, 140–141, 157–160, 159 (figure),
    228, 229 (table)
Financial Crimes Enforcement Network (FinCEN),
    197, 202 (figure), 318 (table)
Financial Crimes Section (FCS), 317, 319, 322 (table), 324
Financial Fraud Enforcement Task Force, 209
Financial Industry Regulatory Authority, 318 (table)
Financial offenses, in religious system, 105–106

FinCEN. *See* Financial Crimes Enforcement Network
Fines, 401–404, 404 (figure), 405 (table), 412
Firestone, 242
Fishing, illegal, 261
Fitzgerald, J. D., 11
Fitzgerald, L. F., 128
Fixing cases, 86
Flipping, 205
Florida:
commodities fraud, 141
cybercrime, 165
deceptive sales, 229 (table)
insurance crimes, 58
Fly dumping, 261, 274
Fonville, Tamira, 50
Foo, L. J., 230–231
Food, harmful, 242–243, 245 (photo), 246
Food and Drug Administration (FDA):
about, 318 (table)
food safety, 242, 247 (photo)
physical harm, 38
workers, 3 (photo), 33 (photo)
Food contamination, 242
Food poisoning, 243
Forbes, Walter, 155 (table)
Ford Explorer, 242
Ford Motor Company, 10
Ford Pinto case, 10, 242, 249
Foreclosure rescue scams, 203–204
Foreclosures, wrongful, 404
Foreign exchange fraud, 147
Foreign friendly civilian crimes, 102
Forensic Accountant Core Training Session (FACTS),
    322 (table)
Forensic accountants and accounting, 321, 322 (table), 341–342
Forensic Accounting Program, 321, 322 (table)
Forensic Accounting Unit (FBI Financial Crimes Section), 319,
    322 (table)
Forgery, 31 (table), 32, 57, 72
For-profit colleges, 217, 218, 227–228, 229 (table), 230
Foster, Joseph Todd, 146
Fox, G., 154, 156
Fox, M. F., 121
Francis, Connie, 248
Frank, Nancy, 219, 234, 347
Frankel, T., 37
Fraud:
abuse versus, 64–65
arrests reported in *Uniform Crime Reports,* 31 (table), 32
during closing/settlement, 203
defined, 64
by doctors, 8 (table), 63–69, 67 (figure), 68 (figure)
by pharmacists, 8 (table), 72–73, 73 (photo)
See also specific types of fraud

Fraud Accounting and Fraud Investigator program (University of West Virginia), 337
Fraud audits, 341
Fraud-for-housing, 197
Fraud-for-profit, 197
Fraudulent loan origination, 206
Free, J. Robin, 353
"Free agent" policing style, 347–348
Free will, 13
Freiburger, T. L., 88
Friedrichs, David, 24–25, 153, 154, 312
Frogner, B., 70
Frois, James, 207
Front running, 147
FTC. *See* Federal Trade Commission
Fund generator, EPA as, 272–273 (table), 274–275
Futures contracts, 147
Futures trading fraud, 147

Gainey, Randy, 301–302, 407, 408 (table)
Galbraith, J. K., 28
Ganging, 65, 67 (figure)
Gangs, 154
Garbage heads, 74
Gauthier, D. K., 293
Geffin, Daniel, 247 (photo)
Geis, Gilbert:
    auto repair/sales fraud, 55
    corporate crime liability, 366
    defendants, 375
    doctors, fraud by, 64
    prosecution of white-collar crime, 359, 361
    self-control theory, 299
    surgery, unnecessary, 70
    victims, in judicial proceedings, 377
Gender harassment, 128
Gender theories, 308
General deterrence, 414
General offending by doctors, 71–72
General safety and health inspectors, 300
General strain theory, 288–289
General Theory of Crime, A (Gottfredson & Hirschi), 297
General Wood Preserving Company, 410
Generic drug substitution, 72
Georgia, voter fraud in, 99
Georgia State University, 126
Gerber, J., 390
Gershman, B. L., 99
Ghiselli, R., 51, 51 (photo)
"Ghost Exodus" (defendant), 164
Ghostwriting, 123, 125, 125 (figure)
Gibbs, Carole, 278
Gibson, Fred W., Jr., 146
Gibson, K., 295, 296

Giles, M. K., 128
Ginsberg, B., 101
Giuliano, Mark F., 146, 177
Glasberg, D. S., 311
GlaxoSmithKline, 127
Global issues, 224, 247, 263–264, 348–349
Godfrey, B., 14
Goffer, Zvi, 145
Going-out-of-business sales, 226
Goldfarb, Jason, 145
Goldsmith, M., 372
Gonzaga University Justice for Fraud Victims project, 337
Good faith defense, 371
Goods, 47, 407, 408 (table)
Gordon, R. A., 373
Gottfredson, Michael, 284, 297, 298, 299
Government definitions, 29
Government witnesses, 374
Grades for sex, 129
Grasmick, H. G., 298
Gratuities, illegal, 100
Gray, C., 92, 311
Great White (band), 248, 249
Greed, 153, 283–284, 283 (photo)
Green, Gary, 30–31, 310
Greenhouse gas permits, 275
Griffith, S. E., 128
Grifo, Francesca, 276
Gripka, Mark, 93
Group boycotts, 224
Guardians, capable, 299, 301, 302
"Guardians of Peace" (hackers), 163–164
Guilt, denial of, 294–295
Gulf Wars, 263
Gunderson, Steve, 230
Guyette, J. E., 54

Haarman & Reimer Corp., 225 (table)
Hackers, 169
Hackett, E. J., 118
Hactivism, 169
Hagan, John, 381, 388
Haggard, Ted, 106
Hair scam, 50
Hall v. Board of Trustees of State Institutions of Higher Learning, 133 (table)
Halsey, M., 256
Hamm, M. S., 103
Hanson, Edward, 58
Harm:
    physical, 38–39, 38 (photo)
    social, 28–29
Harmful consumer products, 240–247

automobiles, 241–242, 243
   China, recalled goods from, 247, 247 (photo)
   construction material, 243, 245, 247
   food, 242–243, 245 (photo), 246
   toys, harmful, 241, 241 (photo), 241 (table), 247
Harmful destruction of property/wildlife, 261–262,
      261 (photo)
Harmful treatment of consumers, 247–248
Harris, Diane, 76
Harwell, R. Bryan, 255
Haugh, T., 372
Hayward, Tony, 254
Hazard identification, 269
Hazardous waste disposal, illegal, 259–260, 265
Health Care Fraud and Abuse Program, 321
Health Care Fraud Initiative, 319
Health care fraud laws, 363–364
Health Care Fraud Unit (FBI Financial Crimes Section), 317, 319
Health Care Prevention and Enforcement Action
      Team, 321
Health care system crimes, 61–82
   about, 61–63, 63 (photo)
   doctors, fraud by, 8 (table), 63–69, 67 (figure), 68 (figure)
   doctors, general offending by, 71–72
   durable medical equipment fraud, 78, 80
   elder abuse by health care workers, 75–77
   home health care fraud, 78
   medical malpractice, 80–81
   medication errors, 71
   pharmacists, drug use by, 73–74
   pharmacists, fraud by, 8 (table), 72–73, 73 (photo)
   sexual abuse, 74–75
   surgery, unnecessary, 38, 67 (figure), 69–70, 69 (photo)
Health Insurance Portability and Accountability Act,
      66, 321
Hedge fund fraud, 144
Hedge fund systems, 144
Hellein, Sean, 330
Heslop, G., 341
Heterosexual relations, deprivation of, 407, 408 (table)
HHS. See U.S. Department of Health and Human Services
Hierarchy of needs, Maslow's, 212, 213 (figure)
Higher loyalties, appeal to, 292, 293–294
High-yield investment schemes, 147
Hirschi, Travis, 284, 296–297, 298, 299
Hoffman, L. J., 182, 183
Hollinger, Richard, 47, 73–74, 165
Holt, T. J., 176
Holtfreter, K., 298
Home health care fraud, 8 (table), 78, 311
Home improvement scams, 206
Home repair fraud, 52–54, 53 (photo)
Home shops, 230
Honey nets, 190

Honorary authorship, 123, 125 (figure)
Hooker Chemical Company, 259, 260
Horizontal price fixing, 221
Host-based intrusion prevention system, 167
Hotel industry, 51
Hotlines, anonymous, 339
House arrest, 404–408, 408 (table)
Housing system crimes, 194–196, 196 (photo)
      See also Mortgage fraud; Slumlords
Houston, TX, 194
Howard Johnson's, 248
Howe, L. K., 308
Hoxie, Bonnie, 145
Huber, N., 338
HUD. See U.S. Department of Housing
      and Urban Development
Human factors, 179
Human resource specialists, 40
Hunter, R. D., 86, 87
Hurricane Katrina, 53, 223, 245, 276, 277 (photo)
Hurricane Rita, 223, 245
Hussey, P., 70
Hygiene offenses by restaurants, 49
Hyman-Pillot, Veronica F., 146
Hyundai-Kia, 254

Identity theft, 29, 169, 173
Ignorance defense, 371
Illegal activities, protection of, 86
Illegal disposal of hazardous wastes, 259–260, 265
Illegal dumping, 261, 274
Illegal emissions, 258–259
Illegal gratuities, 100
Illegally buying prescriptions, 72–73
Illinois, mortgage fraud in, 197–199
Illnesses and injuries, workplace, 233 (figure), 234–235,
      236–237 (table), 238–240, 238 (table)
Image manipulation, 120
ImClone, 145, 156 (table)
"Impact Team, The" (hackers), 164
Importation strategies, 48
"Improving Critical Infrastructure Cybersecurity"
      (executive order), 182
Incapacitation, 413
Indication, 167
Individual economic losses, 36–37
Individualism, 287 (table), 288
Industrial security specialists, 48
Industry insider fraud, 197
"Inflate and crash" fraud, 206
Inflated appraisals, 199
Informant, The (movie), 329 (table)
Information security specialists, 188
Infrastructure, critical, 176–178, 178 (photo)

Ingress filtering, 167
Injury:
    as consequence, 38
    denial of, 291, 293, 294 (table)
    workplace, 233 (figure), 234–235, 236–237 (table), 238–240,
        238 (table)
Innocence Project, 95
Innovators, 286, 287
Insider trading, 145–147, 147 (photo)
Inside shops, 230
Inspections, random, 48
Institutional anomie theory, 287–288, 287 (table)
Institutional excuses, 295, 296
Insurance crimes, 56–59
    consequences, 58
    patterns, 58–59, 58 (photo)
    types, 56–57
Integrity Bank, 146
Intellectual property, theft of, 169
Intent, complexity of, 249
Internal audits, 341
Internal control policies, 48
Internal payoffs, 86
Internal Revenue Service (IRS), 146, 318 (table), 322 (table), 337
Internal strategies, 48
Internal whistleblowers, 328
International Institute for Corporate Governance, 127
International issues, 224, 247, 263–264, 348–349
Internet crimes, 173, 174 (table)
Internet piracy, 136, 173, 185–186, 186 (photo)
Inter-occupational crimes, 102
Interpreted virus, 167
Interview, The (movie), 163–164
Interviews, 5 (table), 339
Intra-occupational crimes, 101
Investigation stages, 324–325
Investigative analysts, 66
Investigative scientists, 119
Investigators, U.S. Department of Agriculture, 19, 246
Investment-focused crimes, 56–57
Investment fraud, 141–157
    advance-fee fraud, 148, 204
    broker fraud and embezzlement, 144
    foreign exchange fraud, 147
    futures trading fraud, 147
    hedge fund fraud, 144
    high-yield investment schemes, 147
    insider trading, 145–147, 147 (photo)
    market manipulation, 143
    patterns surrounding, 151, 153–154, 155–156 (table), 157
    pyramid schemes, 148, 148 (table)
    See also Ponzi schemes
Investment schemes, high-yield, 147
Involvement, in control theory, 296
Iowa State University, 117, 131

Iran-Contra affair, 99
IRS. *See* Internal Revenue Service
Ismail, J. A., 51, 51 (photo)
Isolated occurrence defense, 371
Isolation, 396
Iyer, R., 135

Jackson, Michael, 61–62, 63 (photo), 71
Jailstripe crimes, 398
JC Penney, 226
Jenkins, A., 441
Jerry Maguire (movie), 337
Jesilow, Paul, 55, 64, 66, 70, 359, 375
Job loss, 395–396, 411
Jobs, Steve, 191 (photo)
John Jay College of Criminal Justice, 106–110, 107 (figure),
    108 (figure), 125
Johnson, J. Britt, 198
Jordan, S. R., 120
Journal of Experimental Criminology, 9–10
Journal of the American Medical Association, 123
Journal of Vibration and Control, 124
Journals:
    criminal justice, 250 (figure), 251
    medical, 123, 125 (figure)
Judge Judy (television show), 90
Judges, 356–357, 357 (photo)
    See also specific judges
Judicial misconduct, 89–92, 91 (photo), 93, 95 (figure)
Judicial networking, 380
Judicial proceedings, 352–383
    about, 352–354, 354 (photo)
    civil lawsuits, 377–380, 378 (table), 379 (table)
    defendants in, 375–376
    defense attorneys in, 368, 370–372
    issues in, 380–382, 382 (table)
    judges in, 356–357, 357 (photo)
    jurors in, 373
    prosecutors in, 358–368, 361 (figure), 367 (table), 369–370 (table)
    types, 354–355, 356 (figure)
    victims in, 377
    witnesses in, 374–375, 374 (figure)
"July effect" (medication errors), 71
Jurisdictional issues, 181, 321
Jurors, 373
Jury deliberation, judicial misconduct during, 90–91
Just deserts, 415
Justice:
    environmental, 265–266
    organizational, 87
Justice for Fraud Victims project (Gonzaga University), 337
Justifications, 295

Kane, J., 37
Kass, Douglas, 150

Katrina, Hurricane, 53, 223, 245, 276, 277 (photo)
Kauzlarich, D., 303
Kelley, Florence, 230
Kelly, C., 400
Kentucky, judicial misconduct in, 91
Kentucky Fried Chicken, 226
Kerley, Kent, 306–307, 411
Keystroke logger, 167
Khaki-collar crime, 101–102
Khan, Hamid, 214
Kickbacks, 65, 86
Kids in Danger, 241
Killian, James Michael, 85
King, C. W., 372
Kirby, David V., 132
Kleiner, B. H., 231
Klenowski, Paul, 292, 293–294
Kline, P. M., 110
Klinge v. Ithaca College, 134 (table)
Knauf Plasterboard Tianjin Co., 247
Knowing endangerment, 262
Koller, C. A., 209–210
Kopchinski, John, 380
Koper, C. S., 285, 305
Kornak, Paul H., 12
Kostelnik, J., 410
Koster, Chris, 46
Kozar, J. M., 231
Kozlowski, Dennis, 155 (table)
Kramer, Ronald, 104, 303

Labeling theory, 308–309, 309 (photo)
Labor practices, unfair, 230–231, 232 (table), 233
Lack of fraudulent intent defense, 371–372
Lafferty, Jim, 387
Lampke, E., 176
Land ethic, 256
Langton, L., 286, 289, 298
Lanza-Kuduce, L., 165
Larry the Cable Guy (movie), 347
Larsson, P., 349
Lasley, J. R., 296–297
Laufer, W. S., 310
Law enforcement strategies, 323–336
    about, 323–324
    evidence gathering strategies, 325–330, 328 (table),
        329 (table)
    improving, 336 (figure), 337–338
    investigation stages, 324–325
    problems with, 331–336, 332 (table), 333 (table),
        336 (photo)
Laws:
    antitrust, 220
    bank fraud, 363
    campaign finance, 100

denial of, 295
environmental protection, 255–256
EPA as enforcer of, 257, 266–267, 267 (figure), 268 (figure)
health care fraud, 363–364
home repair fraud, 53–54
inadequate, 381
natural, 26
regulatory, 28
securities and commodities fraud, 364
voter identification, 100
    See also specific laws
Lawsuits, 377–380, 378 (table), 379 (table)
    See also specific cases
Lay, Kenneth, 155 (table), 329 (table)
Lay witnesses, 374
Lead, 270 (table)
LeanSpa, 226
Learning theory, 289–290
"Least culpable" participants, 325
Ledger, metaphor of the, 295
Lee, D. E., 136
Lee, M. T., 249
Leegin Creative Leather Products, Inc. v. PSKS, Inc., 222
Legal ambiguity, 25
"Legalistic" policing style, 347
Leno, Jay, 40
Leopold, Aldo, 256
Leto, Jessica, 370, 371
Levi, Michael, 7
Lewinsky, Monica, 329 (table)
Lexus, 241–242
Lezotte, E., 110
Liability:
    corporate crime, 278 (table), 366
    status, 67, 111
    strict, 278 (table)
    vicarious, 278 (table)
Liar loans, 206
Liberty, deprivation of, 407, 408 (table)
LIBOR. *See* London Interbank Offered Rate
Liederbach, J., 88
Life course theory, 306–307
LifeLock, 217–218
Lim, H. A., 71
Limas, Abel, 93
Lincoln, Blanche, 275
Link, B. J., 41
Litigotiation, 331
Litvack, D. E., 363
Locker, J. P., 14
Lofquist, W. S., 412
Lokken, F., 160
Loles, Gregory, 144
London Interbank Offered Rate (LIBOR), 218
Los Angeles Traffic Surveillance Center, 178

Loss prevention strategies, 47–49, 338–340
Louisiana Department of Environmental Quality, 353
Love Canal tragedy, 259–260
Loyalties, appeal to higher, 292, 293–294
Lundman, R., 219, 249, 304
Lush, T., 254
Lyman, S., 295
Lynch, Loretta E., 79, 362
Lynch, Michael, 38, 219, 234, 250 (figure), 251

Maakestad, W. J., 10, 366, 380
Macro virus, 167
Madoff, Bernie:
    celebrity bashing and, 396
    effects of crime on others, 3
    excuse offered by, 295
    house arrest, 406
    neutralization offered by, 292
    Ponzi scheme, 149–151, 151 (photo), 152 (figure), 154,
        155 (table)
    prison experience, 396
    retribution and, 413
    sentencing, 352–353, 354 (photo), 377
Mafia, 262–263
Magnolia Capital Advisors, 142–143
Magnum, Crystal Gail, 95–96
Maher, T. M., 86
Mail fraud statutes, 363
Mail surveys, 5 (table)
Maimon, David, 191
Maine home repair fraud law, 53
Majoras, Deborah Platt, 223
Makkai, T., 311, 348
Malware, 167
Manifest system, 259
Mann, Kenneth, 356, 357, 368, 371
Mann, Michael, 122
Marcotte, D., 109–110
Market allocation, 223
Market manipulation, 143
Markey, Edward, 242
Marquart, J. W., 288
Martin, B. W., 363
Martin, Randy, 290
Martinez, J., 413
Marx, Gary, 327
Maryland Department of Environment, 259
Maslow's hierarchy of needs, 212, 213 (figure)
Mason, Karen, 401
Massachusetts Department of Environmental
        Protection, 274
Mass mailing worms, 167
Materialism, 287 (table), 288
Mathers, R. A., 41
Mattson Terminals, Inc., 255

Matza, David, 291–292, 293, 296
Maxwell, Robert, 37
Mazur, T., 49
MBA. *See* Mortgage Bankers Association
McBarnet, D., 96
McCabe, D. M., 223
McCarthy, Bernard, 96
McClellan v. Board of Regents of the State Univ., 134 (table)
McCollum, Bill, 62
McCoy, Alfred, 103
McDowell, M. G., 265
McGurrin, D., 250 (figure), 251
McKelvey, Andrew, 141
McKinney, L., 157
McMackin, R., 110
McNulty, P., 365
Media:
    corporate crime coverage, 250–251
    environmental crime portrayal, 276, 277 (photo)
    investment fraud, attention to, 151, 153, 155–156 (table)
    regulatory investigations stemming from, 345
    See also Social media
Media reports, 7
Medicaid, 64
    See also Medicare/Medicaid fraud
Medicaid Fraud Control Units, 7, 325
Medicaid Fraud Report, 7, 8 (table)
Medicalized socialization, 70
Medical journals, 123, 125 (figure)
Medical malpractice, 80–81
Medical snowballing, 65
Medical students, 290
Medicare, 64
    See also Medicare/Medicaid fraud
Medicare Fraud Strike Force, 79, 321
Medicare/Medicaid fraud:
    cameras for detecting, 301
    doctors, 64, 65, 66, 67 (figure), 68 (figure)
    durable medical equipment fraud, 80
    health care system crimes, 62, 79
    home health care workers, 78
    investigations, 330
    medical student attitudes toward, 290
    neutralizations in, 292, 294 (table)
    policing, 321, 325
    qui tam lawsuits, 380
    sentencing of offenders, 388
Medication errors, 71
Meeting competition defense, 371
Memory resident, 168
Mental health controlling relationships, 74–75
Mentors and research misconduct, 121–122
Mercado, C. C., 109
Merrifield, Michael, 211
Merton, Robert, 286

Message, sending, 153–154

Messner, Steve, 287–288, 287 (table)

Metallica, 185, 186 (photo)

Metaphor of the ledger, 295

Methodological ambiguity, 25

Michalowski, R. J., 303

Michels, J. L., 373

Microsoft, 172–173

Midnight dumping, 261, 274

Military, crimes in the, 101–103, 104 (photo)

Military students, 228

Milken, Michael, 156 (table)

Miller, G., 283–284

Miller, K. W., 250–251

Mills, M., 38, 154, 156

Mingo County, WV, 387

Minimization excuses, 295, 296

Minkes, J., 401

Minorities, as STEM majors, 183

Misconduct:

    attorney, 7, 88–89, 90 (figure)

    correctional officer, 96–97

    judicial, 89–92, 91 (photo), 93, 95 (figure)

    organizational, 219–220

    police, 7, 86

    prosecutorial, 92–96

    sexual, 86, 96–97

    See also Research misconduct; *specific crimes*

Misdirection, 105

Mislabeling of drugs, 72

Misrepresentation, 58

Misrepresenting services, 65

Mississippi, home repair fraud in, 53

Misuse of federal facilities and public lands, 262

Mitchell, Guy, 146

Mizer, Benjamin C., 353

Mob, 262–263

Mobile code, 168

Model Code of Judicial Conduct, 90–91

Mohr, H., 254

Monetary costs, of electronic monitoring, 407, 408 (table)

Monetary penalties, 401–404, 404 (figure), 405 (table),
    406 (table)

Money from cash register, theft of, 47

Moneypak virus, 172

Monster Nationwide Inc., 141

Montgomery, W. D., 223

Moore, D., 75

Moore, E., 11, 38, 42, 298

Moral or ethical violations, 26

Morgan, T., 88–89

Morris, R. G., 307

Mortgage Bankers Association (MBA), 209

Mortgage-for-housing, 197

Mortgage-for-profit, 197

Mortgage fraud, 196–210

    about, 196–197, 202 (figure)

    appraisal fraud, 199–200

    builder-initiated fraud, 204–205

    consequences, 206–207, 210 (photo)

    defined, 196

    equity skimming/equity fraud, 201, 209 (figure)

    flipping, 205

    foreclosure rescue scams, 203–204

    fraud during closing/settlement, 203

    patterns surrounding, 207–210, 208 (table), 210 (photo)

    qualifications fraud, 206

    real estate agent/investor fraud, 206

    reverse mortgage fraud, 201, 203, 203 (photo)

    short sale fraud, 199

    straw buyer fraud, 197–199

    types, 197–206

Mortgages, denial to pregnant women/new mothers, 345

Mosiman, Mary, 316

Motor carrier safety specialists, 243

Movies about whistleblowers, 329 (table)

Mueller, Gerhard, 276–277, 278 (table)

Mullings, J., 288

Mullins, C., 160

Multipartite viruses, 168

Multiplicity of indictment defense, 371

Murphy, D., 297

Murray, Adam, 210

Murray, Conrad, 61–62, 71

Mutchnick, R., 290

Nader, Ralph, 34 (photo), 39

Nadler, Jerrold, 275

Napster, 185

Nardo, M., 338

Narenda, Divya, 139–140

Narr, K. L., 310

National Broadcasting Company (NBC), 40, 41 (photo)

National Center on Elder Abuse, 76

National Commission on Urban Problems, 211

National Consumer Protection Week, 34

National Federation of Independent Businesses, 47

National Health Care Anti-Fraud Association, 64

National Heritage Life Insurance, 390

National Highway Traffic Safety Administration (NHTSA), 242,
    318 (table)

National Incident Based Reporting System (NIBRS), 32

National Institute of Corrections, 97

National Institute of Standards and Technology, 189

National Institutes of Health, 132, 133

National Labor Relations Board, 318 (table)

National Mortgage Fraud Team (FBI Financial Crimes Section),
    319, 324

National Park Service, 271

National Pingtung University of Education, 124

National Retail Security Survey, 46
National Science Foundation, 182, 183, 253
National White-Collar Crime Center (NW3C), 29, 33, 35 (table), 39, 41
Natural energy industry, 143
Natural law, 26
Nayfeh, Ali H., 124
NBC. *See* National Broadcasting Company
Necessity, defense of, 293
Needs, Maslow's hierarchy of, 212, 213 (figure)
Neglect, elder, 76
Nelson, C. L., 373
Nemeroff, Charles, 127
Nestor, S., 340, 341
Network-based intrusion prevention system, 168
Networking, 380
Network service worms, 168
Neutralization theory, 291–296
    accounts, 294–296
    neutralizations, 291–294, 293 (photo), 294 (table)
    purposes of rationalization/accounts, 296
Newman v. Burgin, 133 (table)
New York City, slumlords in, 214
New York Police Department (NYPD), 87, 329 (table)
New York Times, 345
Nguyen, T. H., 210
NHTSA. *See* National Highway Traffic Safety Administration
NIBRS. *See* National Incident Based Reporting System
Nifong, Mike, 95–96
90/10 rule, 228
Nitrogen oxides, 270 (table)
Nixon, Richard, 98, 266
Noble cause corruption, 87
Nobles, M., 108
Non-prosecution agreements (NPAs), 368, 369–370 (table)
Nordstrom, Inc., 226
Norman, Sean, 50
North Central Medical Plaza (Dallas), 164
North Korea, cybercrime in, 163
Noyes, Thomas L., II, 198
NPAs. *See* Non-prosecution agreements
Nurses, 8 (table), 293
Nursing homes:
    Australia, violations in, 283
    general strain theory and, 289
    inspections, 344–345
    institutional neglect in, 248
    patient abuse in, 301–302
    regulation of, 28
    undercover investigations, 315–316
NW3C. *See* National White-Collar Crime Center
NYPD. *See* New York Police Department

Obama, Barack, 130 (photo), 182, 276
Obama, Michelle, 130 (photo)

Oberfest, Steven, 400
Objectivity, 11–13
O'Brien, Conan, 40, 41 (photo)
O'Brien, M. J., 55
Occupational crime, 26, 27 (table), 29–31, 218
Occupational Safety and Health Act, 235, 238
Occupational Safety and Health Administration (OSHA), 234–235, 238, 238 (table), 239–240, 318 (table)
Occupational system, 16, 31–32
Occupational therapists, 292, 294 (table)
Odometer fraud, 46, 55
Offenders:
    characteristics, 42–43
    motivated, 299, 301–302
    police officers and, 333, 333 (table)
    punishing, reasons for, 413
    repeat, 262
    students as, 18
    surveys, 5–6
    victims and, 332
    witnesses and, 332–333
    See also specific crimes
Office of Research Integrity (ORI), 118, 132, 318 (table)
Office of the Comptroller of the Currency, 319 (table)
Office of Thrift Supervision, 319 (table)
Officer-offender relationship, 333, 333 (table)
Office Space (movie), 281–283
Official government definitions, 29
O'Hear, M. M., 264
OHM Concessions Group, LLC, 218
Oil Pollution Act, 254
Oil spill, BP, 253–254, 255 (photo), 256 (photo), 276, 295, 366
Old Colony Foreign Exchange Company, 156 (table)
Olympic athletes, 287
On-access scanning, 168
On Crimes and Punishments (Beccaria), 284–285
On-demand scanning, 168
On-site survey administration, 5 (table)
Operation Bid Rig, 100
Operation Shrouded Horizon, 177
Opportunistic theft, 86
Opportunity explanations, 135, 179
Optimal penalty theory, 402
Organizational advantage argument, 360
Organizational crime, 27 (table)
Organizational culture strategies, 49
Organizational deviance, 27 (table)
Organizational Guidelines, 357, 411–412
Organizational justice, 87
Organizational misconduct, 219–220
Organizational probation, 412, 414 (table)
Organizational processes and corporate crime, 304–305, 305 (figure)
Organizational structure and corporate crime, 304
Organized crime, 175, 262–263
ORI. *See* Office of Research Integrity

Orland, Leonard, 357, 382
Orrick, L., 250
OSHA. *See* Occupational Safety and
    Health Administration
Ostrich excuses, 295, 296
Other-than-serious OSHA violations, 238 (table)
Outside shops, 230
Outside work, unapproved, 127–128
Overcharging, 47, 47 (photo), 56, 65
Over-ordering supplies, 47
Overpayment fraud, 173
Overtreatment, 56

Pacification, 75
Pains of electronic monitoring, 407–408, 408 (table)
Panetta, Leon, 178
Paradox of familiarity, 74
Parallel proceedings, 381–382, 382 (table)
Parker, Gwendolyn, 71
Parker, P., 388
Parole, 400–401
Parsimony, 13
Particulate matter, 270 (table)
Partners, collaborations with, 334–335
Passas, N., 28–29, 282
Passive elder neglect, 76
Passwords, popular, 170
Pathological tormentors, 301, 302
Patients, 8 (table), 65, 301–302
Patterson, L. A., 209–210
Pay exploitation, 230
Payload, 168
Payne, Brian K.:
    doctors, fraud by, 65
    durable medical equipment fraud, 80
    elder abuse by health care workers, 75, 76–77
    home health care fraud, 78
    pains of electronic monitoring, 407–408, 408 (table)
    pharmacists, fraud by, 72–73
    routine activities theory, 301–302
    systems theory, 311
Payoffs, internal, 86
Peanut Butter Corporation of America, 242
    Pecuniary-based offenses, 125–128
    embezzlement, 125
    faculty double billing, 126–127
    outside work, unapproved, 127–128
    textbook fraud, 125–126
Peer association explanations, 179
Penalization, problem of, 278 (table)
Penn State University, 122
Pennsylvania, deceptive sales in, 229 (table)
People v. Eubanks, 377
PepsiCo, 327
Permanent denial-of-service attacks, 172

Permenter, Grant, 246
Perry, Rick, 275
Persistent cookies, 168
Personal denial-of-service attacks, 172
Persuasion strategies, 345, 347
Peterson, B. K., 337–338
Pfizer Inc., 380
Phantom treatment, 65
Pharmacists, 8 (table), 72–74, 73 (photo)
Phillips, David, 71
Philpot, Jeffrey, 85
phil&teds USA, 218
Phishing, 168, 169
Phlashing, 172
Photo-fiction, 120
Physical abuse, 8 (table), 75
Physical disorder, 212
Physical harm, 38–39, 38 (photo)
Physical therapists, 292, 294 (table)
Pillemer, K., 75
Pine Lawn, MO, 386
Pingponging, 65, 67 (figure)
Piquero, Alex, 108, 111
Piquero, Nicole:
    Catholic Church sexual abuse scandal, 108, 111
    classical strain theory, 286
    differential association theory, 290
    dynamic organizational explanations for corporate crime, 305–306
    fining corporate offenders, 412
    general strain theory, 289
    institutional anomie theory, 288
    life course theory, 307
    organizational processes and corporate crime, 304
    rational choice theory, 285
    self-control theory, 298
Piracy, Internet, 136, 173, 185–186, 186 (photo)
Plagiarism, 119–120, 136
Plaintiffs, 354
Plausible deniability, 105
Plea bargains, 364, 364 (photo)
Podgor, Ellen, 42, 390, 413
Poehlman, Eric T., 131, 132–133
Pogrebin, M. R., 370, 371
Polanzi, C. W., 41
Policastro, C., 80
Police corruption, 85–88, 86 (photo)
Police deviance, 86
Police misconduct, 7, 86
Police officer-offender relationship, 333, 333 (table)
Police officers, regulatory officials as, 344–345, 347 (photo)
Police sexual misconduct, 86
Policing white-collar crime, 315–350
    about, 315–316
    agencies involved in, 317–323, 317 (figure), 318–319 (table),
        321 (photo), 323 (figure)

evidence gathering strategies, 325–330, 328 (table), 329 (table)

global police, 348–349

investigation stages, 324–325

law enforcement response, improving, 336 (figure), 337–338

law enforcement response, problems with, 331–336, 332 (table), 333 (table), 336 (photo)

law enforcement strategies, 323–336

public perceptions of, 336, 336 (photo)

regulatory policing, 342–348, 346 (figure), 347 (photo)

self-policing, 338–342

Policy ambiguity, 25

Policymakers, students as future, 18

Political corruption, 100–101

Political extortion/bribery, 100–101

Political power, 333, 333 (table)

Political system, 15, 311

Political system crimes, 97–105

about, 97–98 (table), 98–99, 98 (photo), 109–113 (figure)

apolitical white-collar crime, 101

campaign finance violations, 100

crimes in the military, 101–103, 104 (photo)

election law violations, 99–100

political extortion/bribery, 100–101

state-corporate crime, 104–105

Politicizing:

of environmental disasters, 276, 277 (photo)

of science process, 275–276

Pollock, Jocelyn, 93–94

Pollution, 38, 256, 257 (photo), 258, 264

See also Environmental crime

Poly-drug users, 74

Ponemon Institute, 178

Pontell, Henry:

classical strain theory, 286

corporate crime, explaining, 304

defendants, 375

doctors, fraud by, 64

mortgage fraud, 210

prosecution of white-collar crime, 358, 359, 360, 361

savings and loan crisis, 10

sentencing practices, 388

surgery, unnecessary, 70

systems theory, 311

Ponzi, Charles, 149, 156 (table)

Ponzi schemes:

defined, 148

history, 149

Madoff's, 149–151, 151 (photo), 152 (figure), 154, 155 (table)

pyramid schemes versus, 148, 148 (table)

victims of, 288

warning signs, 151

Porche, D. A., 292, 294 (table)

Positive consequences, of white-collar crime, 39–40, 41 (photo)

Posk, Peter, 316

Posner, Richard, 402

Potts, Mitchell, 85

Poveda, T. G., 322

Poverty, 284

Power, 278 (table), 333, 333 (table)

Power and prestige relationships, 74

Pratt, T. C., 298

Prearranged trading, 147

Precursors, 168

Pregerson, Dean D., 200

Pregnant women, 231, 345

Premeditated short sale fraud, 199

Premium diversion theft, 57, 58

Prescription fraud, 72–73, 73 (photo)

Presentence reports, 6–7

Prevention strategies, 47–49

Price discrimination, 222

Price fixing, 221–222

Price gouging, 223

PricewaterhouseCoopers Global Economic Crime Survey, 34–35

Price Waterhouse v. Hopkins, 231

Primary victims of corporate crime, 249

Priorities, changing, 278 (table)

Prison Coach, 400

Prison consultant industry, white-collar, 400

Prison culture and socialization, 397

Prison deviance, 398

Prisoners of war, military treatment of, 103, 104 (photo)

Prison experience, 395–400

adjusting to prison life, 399–400

danger, 396–397

depression, 395–396

deprivations, 397–398

doldrums, 398–399, 399 (photo)

prison deviance, 398

Prison life, adjusting to, 399–400

Prison placement, 396–397

Pritchard, J., 254

Private contractors, 102–103

Proactive strategies, 323

Probation, 400–401, 412, 414 (table)

Proceedings, parallel, 381–382, 382 (table)

Process-oriented defense, 370

Production supplies, theft of, 47

Professional-disciplinary proceedings, 355

Professors and researchers in educational system:

academic dishonesty, role in promoting/preventing, 136

crime, examples of, 116–117

criminal justice, 129, 130

disciplining, 131–133, 133–134 (table)

embezzlement, 125

faculty double billing, 126–127

ghostwriting, 123, 125, 125 (figure)

outside work, unapproved, 127–128

pecuniary-oriented offenses, 125–128
 research misconduct, 118–123, 122 (photo), 123 (figure), 132–133
 sexual harassment, 128–131, 130 (photo)
 textbook fraud, 125–126
Promissory note fraud, 57
Proof, 278 (table), 335–336
Property values, decreased, 212
Property/wildlife, harmful destruction of, 261–262, 261 (photo)
Proposition 190 (California), 91
Prosecution:
 deciding about, 358–361, 361 (figure)
 deferring, 367–368, 369–370 (table)
Prosecutorial misconduct, 92–96
Prosecutors, role of, 358–368
 about, 358, 358 (photo)
 charges, 361–364
 corporations, charging, 364–367, 367 (table)
 plea bargains, 364, 364 (photo)
 prosecution, 358–361, 359 (table), 361 (figure)
 prosecution, deferring, 367–368, 369–370 (table)
Prostate cancer treatment, 69
Protection of illegal activities, 86
Providers, substitute, 65, 67 (figure)
Provision of unnecessary services, 65
Proxies, 168
Psychiatrists, 65, 68 (figure)
Psychologists, 65, 68–69, 68 (figure)
PTL Television Network, 106
Public alienation, 37–38
Public Citizen, 71–72
Public Company Accounting Oversight Board, 319 (table)
Public health protector, EPA as, 267–269, 269 (table), 270 (table)
Public Health Service, 132
Public lands, misuse of, 262
Public opinion:
 about corporate crime, 250–251, 250 (figure)
 about white-collar crime, 40–42, 42 (table)
 about white-collar crime police work, 336, 336 (photo)
 surveys, 4
Pump and dump, 143
Pump-and-pay schemes, 204
Punch, Maurice, 239, 249, 304
Punishing corporations for white-collar crime, 411–413
 corporate sanctions, issues surrounding, 413
 fines, 412
 probation, 412, 414 (table)
Punishment, reasons for, 413–415
Punishment strategies, 347
Punitive damages, 403, 404 (figure), 405 (table), 406 (table)
Punitiveness, for investment fraud, 153–154
Pyramid schemes, 148, 148 (table)

Qualcomm, 353
Qualification, problem of, 278 (table)
Qualifications fraud, 206

Quality Egg, 246
Quantification, problem of, 278 (table)
Quarantining, 168
Quasi-experimental designs, 9
Questionable Doctors, 71
Quinney, Richard, 26, 104, 218, 302–303
Qui tam lawsuits, 379–380

Racism, environmental, 265–266
Racketeer Influenced and Corrupt Organization (RICO) Act, 262, 361, 363
Raine, Adrian, 310
Rakowski, J. J., 222
Random inspections, 48
Ransomware, 172
Rape, 129
Rational choice theory, 285
Rational decision making, 13
Raw materials, theft of, 47
Reactive strategies, 323
Real estate agent/investor fraud, 206
Reason, rule of, 222
Rebels, 286, 287
Recidivism by corporations, 413
Records:
 case, 6
 falsifying, 65
 review of, 326, 345
 searches, complex, 334, 335 (photo)
Recreational path to drug use by pharmacists, 74
Redirection, 105
Regulatory agencies, 342
 See also Regulatory policing
Regulatory laws, 28
Regulatory policing, 342–348
 about, 342
 conceptualizing, 342–344, 346 (figure)
 criticisms, 348
 regulatory officials as police officers, 344–345, 347 (photo)
 styles, 345, 347–348
Regulatory system, 16
Rehabilitation, 414–415
Reilly, W. P., 170
Reintegrative shaming, 410–411
Reisig, M. D., 298
Relationship dynamics in white-collar crime investigations, 332–334, 333 (table)
Relativism, 14–16, 17 (figure)
Reliance on the advice of counsel defense, 371
Religious system, 15
Religious system crimes, 105–111
 Catholic Church sexual abuse scandal, 106–111, 107 (figure), 108 (figure)
 deception, 106
 financial offenses, 105–106

Religious system deception, 106
Remote administration tools, 168
Rengifo, A. F., 107
Renzi, Richard G., 85
Repeated OSHA violations, 238 (table)
Repeat offenders, 262
Reporting trends for household victimization, 33, 35 (table)
Resale fraud, 226
Research-based conflicts of interest, 127
Research definitions, 29
Researchers. *See* Professors and researchers in educational system
Researchers, students as future, 19
Researching white-collar crime, 4–10
    archival research, 6–8, 8 (table)
    case studies, 10
    experiments, 9–10
    field research, 8–9
    survey research, 4–6, 5 (table)
Research misconduct:
    about, 122 (photo)
    consequences, 120–121, 122–123, 123 (figure), 124
    federal oversight of, 118, 132–133
    mentors and, 121–122
    patterns, 121
    plagiarism, 119–120
    prevalence, 119
    reasons for, 121
    types, 118
Research subjects, students as, 18–19
Resistance, 105
Resource Conservation and Recovery Act, 257, 259, 260
Resource problems, in white-collar crime investigation, 331, 332 (table)
Responsibility, denial of, 292, 294, 294 (table)
Restaurant industry, 49–51, 51 (photo), 344
Restitution, 402–403
Retail system, employee theft in, 46–49, 47 (photo)
Retaliation, 105
Retraction, 122–123, 123 (figure), 124
Retreatists, 286, 287
Retribution, 413
Retributive strategies, 189, 347
Returns, retail, 47, 48
Reverse mortgage fraud, 201, 203, 203 (photo)
Rich, Jessica, 34, 226
Richtel, Matt, 400
RICO Act. *See* Racketeer Influenced and Corrupt Organization Act
Rigas, John, 156 (table), 295
Riordan, Richard, 374
Rippers, 176
Rita, Hurricane, 223, 245
Ritualists, 286, 287
Roberts, C., 95
Roberts, T., 157

Robin, G. D., 24, 29–30
Robin Hood defense, 375
Robinson, M., 297
Robinson-Patman Act, 222
Roche, M., 308
Roebuck, J., 85–86
Rogue employee defense, 366
Rokke, Doug, 263
Rolling over, 58
Rootkits, 168
Ropes & Gray LLP, 145
Rosenfeld, Richard, 287–288, 287 (table)
Rosoff, S. M., 67, 111
Ross, E. A., 24
Ross, Jeffrey, 105
Rothe, Dawn, 105
Rotten apple explanations, 58–59, 87, 103, 108–109
Routine activities theory, 299–302
Ruggiero, V., 11
Rule of reason, 222
Rule violations, 398
Rural areas, overregulation of, 275
Rush, David P., 386
Rusling, Michael, 75

SAGE, 124
Sales, deceptive, 227–228, 229 (table), 230
Sales-directed crimes, 57–58
Sales-related occupations, 45–60
    about, 45–46
    entertainment services system crimes, 49–51
    insurance crimes, 56–59, 58 (photo)
    retail system, employee theft in, 46–49
    sales/service system fraud, 52–56, 53 (photo), 56 (photo)
Sales/service system fraud, 52–56, 53 (photo), 56 (photo)
Salmonella, 242, 246
Sanctions:
    alternative, 404–411, 408 (table)
    for attorney misconduct, 88–89, 90 (figure)
    community-based, 400–401
    corporate, 413
Sandlin, James, 85
Sanford, Mark, 101
Sarat, Austin, 356, 357
Sarbanes-Oxley Act (SOX), 341, 389
SARs. *See* Suspicious Activity Reports
Saturday Night Live (television show), 329 (table)
Savings and loan industry, 10, 311
Saylor, Mark, 241–242
Scams:
    door-to-door home repair, 52
    foreclosure rescue, 203–204
    hair, 50

home improvement, 206
    scholarship, 160
Scannell, Kara, 145
Scapegoating, 105, 295
Schlegel, K., 147
Schlozman, Bradley S., 233
Schneider, C., 264
Schoenfeld, H., 95
Schoepfer, A., 288, 298
Scholarship scams, 160
Schottenfeld Group, LLC, 145
Schwartz, J., 308
Science process, politicizing of, 275–276
Scott, M. B., 295
Searcy, D. J., 285
Sears Auto Centers, 227
Sears Bankruptcy Recovery Management Services, 225 (table)
Sebbag, Yonni, 145
SEC. *See* Securities and Exchange Commission
Secondary short sale fraud, 199
Secondary victims of corporate crime, 249
Securities and commodities fraud laws, 364
Securities and Exchange Commission (SEC):
    about, 319 (table)
    administrative proceedings, 355
    insider trading, 140, 145
    Ponzi schemes, 148, 148 (figure), 149, 150–151
    resource allocation, 331, 332 (table)
    securities fraud, 142–143
Securities Exchange Act, 364
Securities fraud, 141, 142–143
Security, in loss prevention strategies, 338
Security banners, 191
Seductive behavior, 128
Self-control, 135, 297–299
Self-fulfilling prophecy, 308
Self-initiated Google hacking, 191
Self-medicators, therapeutic, 74
Self-policing, 338–342
    audits, 340
    compliance strategies, 340
    forensic accounting, 341–342
    loss prevention strategies, 338–340
Self-policing audits, 340
Self-righteousness, relying on, 105
Semel Institute for Neuroscience and Human Behavior, 121
Sentencing:
    about, 388
    depression and, 396
    judges and, 356–357
    patterns surrounding, 389–390, 391–393 (table), 394, 394 (figure)
    policies, 389
    practices, 388–389
Sentencing Reform Act, 389

September 11, 2001, terror attacks, 275
Serial abusers, 301
Serious OSHA violations, 238 (table)
Serpico (movie), 329 (table)
Serpico, Frank, 329 (table)
Services:
    deprivation of, 407, 408 (table)
    misrepresenting, 65
    not provided, billing for, 54
    provision of unnecessary, 65
"Service style" of regulatory policing, 347
Session cookies, 168
Sex, grades for, 129
Sexual abuse:
    Catholic Church, 106–111, 107 (figure), 108 (figure)
    elder, 76–77
    in health care system, 74–75
Sexual assault, 75
Sexual bribery, 128
Sexual coercion, 128
Sexual contact with students, 128–129
Sexual harassment, 128–131, 130 (photo)
Sexualized behaviors, 128
Sexualized comments, 128
Sexual misconduct, 86, 96–97
Sexual relationships, academic, 128
SGL Carbon Aktiengesellschaft, 225 (table)
Shakedowns, 86
Shaming, 409–411
Shapiro, Susan, 25, 29, 348
Shefman, P., 157
Shefter, M., 101
Sheindlin, Judy, 90
Sherman, N. I., 127
Sherman Antitrust Act, 220, 221 (table), 224
Shortchanging, 47
Short counting, 72
Short measuring, 49–50
Short sale fraud, 199
Short sales, 199
Short weighting, 49–50
Shover, N., 154, 156
Shrouded Horizon, Operation, 177
Siemaszko, C., 413
Signature, 168
Significant environmental harm, 358
Silkwood (movie), 329 (table)
Silkwood, Karen, 329 (table)
Silvestre, Reinaldo, 38
Simon, D. R., 279, 322
Simon, Jonathan, 390
Simpson, Sally, 32–33, 271, 285, 304, 305–306, 394
Sims, R. L., 135
Sin and Society (Ross), 24
Singletary, M., 57

Sinrod, E. J., 170
Sin tax, 259
Sitting in Judgment (Wheeler, Mann, & Sarat), 356
Situational crime prevention, 190–191
Skepticism, 14, 326
Skidmore, D., 311
Skilling, Jeffrey, 156 (table)
Skinner, L., 128
Sliding, 58
Sloman, Jeffrey H., 62
Slumlords:
    about, 194–195, 196, 210–211
    consequences of behavior of, 211–213, 213 (figure)
    defined, 210
    responding to, 214
Smith, G. S., 174–175
Smith, M. L., 107
Smith, R., 118
Smith, Tommie, 287
Smoking gun, 336 (figure), 337
Snider, E. A., 348, 412
Sobesto, B., 191
Soccer investigation, 362
Social change, 39
Social control systems, 84–85
        See also Criminal justice system; Political system; Religious
            system
Social disorder, 212
Social disorganization theory, 307–308, 307 (photo)
Social harm, 28–29
Socialization, 69, 70, 397
Social media, 41–42, 42 (table)
Social networking sites, 338–339
Social Reality of Crime, The (Quinney), 302–303
Social services system, 16
"Social Structure and Anomie" (Merton), 286
Social system, 15–16
Societal economic losses, 37
Software, theft of, 172
Software crime, 172–173
Sonntag, M. E., 128
Sony, 163–164
Sopranos, The (television show), 262–263
Sorkin, Ira, 352
Souder, Mark, 101
Southern Center on Environmentally Driven Disparities in Birth
        Outcomes, 265
Southern Illinois University system, 120
Southland Industrial Banking Commission, 154
SOX. *See* Sarbanes-Oxley Act
Spahr, L. L., 290
Spalek, Robert Maxwell, 37
Spam filters, 190
Sparks, Michael, 387

Speaks, Garrett, 315–316
Specific deterrence, 413
Speech therapists, 292, 294 (table)
Spitzer, Eliot, 101, 365
SplashData, 170
Spyware, 168
Spyware detection and removal utilities, 168
St. Barbara's Greek Orthodox Church (Easton, CT), 144
Stacking, 58
Stannard, C. I., 8–9
State-corporate crime, 104–105
State crime, 104–105
Station, The (nightclub), 248
Status degradation, 396, 397, 401
Status liability, 67, 111
Steen, R. G., 122
Steffensmeier, Darrell, 308
STEM majors, 183
Stewart, Martha:
    charges/conviction, 145, 156 (table), 336
    job loss, 411
    prison deviance, 398
    sentencing, 375, 376
Stimulus frauds, 204
Stinson, Philip, 7, 86, 88
Strain theory, 285–289
    classical strain theory, 286–287
    general strain theory, 288–289
    institutional anomie theory, 287–288, 287 (table)
Strasser, S. M., 76
Stratton VA Medical Center, 12
Straw buyer fraud, 197–199
Stressed out caregivers, 301
Stress from victimization, 37
Stressful changes, 395
Stress-induced illnesses, 234
Stretesky, P. B., 370, 371
Strict liability, 278 (table)
Structural changes, 179
Student loan fraud, 140–141, 157–160, 159 (figure), 228,
        229 (table)
Students:
    business, 135, 285, 290, 293
    cheating by, 135, 136
    cybercrime and, 185–186
    educational system crimes by, 134–136
    Internet/digital piracy by, 136, 185–186
    medical, 290
    military, 228
    offenses committed on job, 134
    sexual contact with, 128–129
    white-collar crime, role in, 17–19, 20 (photo)
Subcontracting, 222
"Subject matter" test for attorney-client privilege, 372

Substitute providers, 65, 67 (figure)
Sudden Impact (movie), 348
Sulfur dioxide, 270 (table)
Superfund Act, 272
Supplies, over-ordering, 47
Surgery, unnecessary, 38, 67 (figure), 69–70, 69 (photo)
Surveys:
    about, 4–6, 5 (table)
    Civil Justice Survey of State Courts, 378, 378 (table),
        379 (table)
    victimization, 33–35, 35 (table), 36 (table)
Suspicious Activity Reports (SARs), 196, 197, 202 (figure),
        208 (table)
Sutherland, Edwin:
    archival research, 8
    consequences of white-collar crime, 36–37, 37–38
    corporations, charging, 364
    differential association theory, 289–290, 291
    educational/work background, 19
    explaining white-collar crime, 282
    fraud by doctors, 64
    religious background, 15
    survey research, 5
    white-collar crime definition/conceptualization, 2, 24–26
Suuberg, Martin, 274
Swaggart, Jimmy, 106
Swart, S. L., 322
Sweatshops, 230–231
Sweden, fraud by doctors in, 66
Sweetheart deals, 47
Switching, 58
Sykes, Gresham, 291–292, 293, 296, 407
Systematic approach, lack of, 335
System capacity argument, 360
Systems theory, 311–312

Taiwan, cybercrime in, 181
Tallon, J. A., 109
Tampa Tribune, 276
Targets, in routine activities theory, 299
Tax 325/327 studies, 12
Taylor, Bean, and Whitaker Mortgage Corporation, 207
Tayoun, Jim, 400
Teaching and service-based conflicts of interest, 127
Team Mingo, 387
Technological changes, 312
Technological devices, 330
Technological strategies, 49
Technological system, 15
Technological system crimes. *See* Cybercrime
Technology and political corruption, 100–101
Telephone interviews, 5 (table)
TennCare, 62
Tennessee Bureau of Investigation, 62, 68–69

Terry, Karen, 108–109
Tertiary victims of corporate crime, 249
Texas:
    campaign finance laws, 100
    deceptive sales, 229 (table)
    EPA (U.S.) and, 275
Textbook fraud, 125–126
Textile industry, 231
Theft:
    of credit card information, 47
    as cybercrime, 169
    employee, 46–49, 47 (photo)
    of goods, 47
    identity, 29, 169, 173
    of intellectual property, 169
    of money from cash register, 47
    opportunistic, 86
    premium diversion, 57, 58
    of production supplies/raw materials, 47
    of software, 172
Theft crimes against consumers, 57
Therapeutic self-medicators, 74
Thies, Tamara, 275
Thompson, P., 310
Thomsen, Linda Chatman, 145
Thornsbury, Michael, 387
Thrift industry, 10, 311
Thrift Supervision, Office of, 319 (table)
Tibbetts, S. G., 290
Tillman, Robert, 10, 286, 304, 360, 365, 388
Time, as problem in white-collar crime investigation, 334
Time-based conflicts of interest, 127
Tires, illegal dumping of, 261
Title VII, 231
Titrating, 74
Tittle, C. R., 298
Toga, A. W., 310
Tommie Copper Inc., 226
Toregas, C., 182, 183
Tormentors, pathological, 301, 302
Tort lawsuits, 377–378, 378 (table), 379 (table)
Torture by military, 103, 104 (photo)
Towns, Lessie, 197–199
Toyoda, Akio, 244–245
Toyota Motor Corporation, 241–242, 244–245
Toys, harmful, 241, 241 (photo), 241 (table), 247
Tracking cookies, 168
Trading, prearranged, 147
Trahan, Adam, 288
Trasviña, John, 345
Traub, S. H., 338
Treatment programs, unnecessary participation in, 398
Triggers, 168
Triplett, Ruth, 308–309

Tripp, Linda, 329 (table)
Trojan horse, 168
Truck stop electrification, 271
Trust, 29, 37–38, 64, 69–70
Tucker, Richard T., 274
Turnitin, 136
Twitter, 42, 42 (table)
Tyco, 155 (table), 373

UCAR International, Inc., 225 (table)
UCLA's Semel Institute for Neuroscience and Human
    Behavior, 121
UCR. See Uniform Crime Reports
Ulrich, Lars, 185, 186 (photo)
Ultimeyes app, 226
Unauthorized access, 169–171, 171 (photo)
Unbundling, 65
Undercover investigations, 315–316, 326–328, 328 (table)
Undertreatment, 56
Under water mortgages, 205
Unfair labor practices, 230–231, 232 (table), 233
Uniform Crime Reports (UCR), 31 (table), 32
Uniform Residential Landlord and Tenant Act, 210
Union of Concerned Scientists, 275–276
Universalism, 287–288, 287 (table)
Universities. *See* Colleges
University faculty and researchers. *See* Professors and researchers
    in educational system
University of Akron, 164
University of Colorado at Boulder, 119
University of Houston, 117
University of Louisville School of Education, 125
University of Maryland, 133
University of Minnesota, 353
University of Texas–Pan American, 120
University of Vermont, 131, 132, 133
University of Virginia, 122
University of Washington, 120–121
University of West Virginia, College of Business and
    Economics, 337
University students. *See* Students
Unnecessary auto repairs, 54
Unnecessary services, provision of, 65
Unreported white-collar crimes, 7–8, 32
Unsafe work environments, 233 (figure), 234–235,
    236–237 (table), 238–240, 238 (table)
Upcoding/upgrading, 65, 67 (figure)
Uranium, depleted, 263
U.S. Air Force criminal investigators, 103
U.S. Air Force housing management specialists, 214
U.S. Army Corps of Engineers, 319 (table)
U.S. Consumer Product Safety Commission, 38, 218, 245,
    247, 318 (table)
U.S. Department of Agriculture, 19, 133, 246, 261–262, 319 (table)

U.S. Department of Education (DE), 140–141, 158,
    227–228, 319 (table)
U.S. Department of Health and Human Services (HHS):
    Health Care Fraud and Abuse Program, 321
    Office of Inspector General, 319 (table), 321, 326
    Office of Research Integrity, 118, 132, 318 (table)
U.S. Department of Homeland Security, 136
U.S. Department of Housing and Urban Development
    (HUD), 345
U.S. Department of Justice (DOJ):
    Antitrust Division, 220
    BP oil spill lawsuit, 254
    Criminal Division, 368, 369–370 (table)
    Criminal Division Fraud Section, 322 (table)
    cybercriminals, 174
    Health Care Prevention and Enforcement Action Team, 321
    Office of Inspector General, 319 (table), 398
    Poehlman case, 132–133
    white-collar crime definition, 321–322
U.S. Department of Labor, Wage and Hour Division, 319 (table)
U.S. Department of the Interior, Office of Inspector General,
    319 (table)
U.S. Fish and Wildlife Service, 319 (table)
U.S. Forest Service, 271
U.S. General Accounting Office, 96
U.S. Government Accountability Office (USGAO), 33, 217, 229
    (table), 230–231, 339, 368
U.S. Navy, 102
U.S. Office of Inspector General, 233
U.S. Office of Professional Responsibility, 233
U.S. Postal Inspection Service, 198, 319 (table)
U.S. Sentencing Commission, 357, 389
U.S. Sentencing Guidelines, 340, 411–412
U.S. v. Atlantic Richfield, Co., 412
U.S. v. Ward, 258–259
USA Federal Critical Infrastructure Protection Policy,
    176–177
USGAO. *See* U.S. Government Accountability Office
USS *Enterprise,* 102

Vacation Ownership Group LLC, The, 386
Value fraud, 199
Values, American, 287–288, 287 (table)
Van Gigch, John, 15
Van Slyke, S., 394
Vaughan, Diane, 249, 306
Vecchiarelli, Nancy A., 164
Vehicles, electric, 271
Vertical price fixing, 221–222
Veterinary practices, 293, 293 (photo)
Viano, E. C., 191
Viatical settlement fraud, 56
Vicarious liability, 278 (table)
Vickers, M., 196

Victim blaming explanations, 59
Victimization:
    breadth of, 249
    stress from, 37
    surveys, 33–35, 35 (table), 36 (table)
Victims:
    denial of, 292
    in judicial proceedings, 377
    offenders and, 332
    primary, 249
    secondary, 249
    students as, 18
    surveys, 4–5
    tertiary, 249
    See also specific crimes
Victim straw buyers, 197–199
Video cameras, 49, 301, 330
Villalobos, Armando, 93
Violations:
    campaign finance, 100
    civil law, 27–28
    copyright, 173
    criminal law, 26–27
    election law, 99–100
    moral/ethical, 26
    in occupational systems, 31–32
    OSHA, 234–235, 238, 238 (table)
    of regulatory laws, 28
    rule, 398
    of trust, 29
    See also specific crimes
Virginia, attorney misconduct in, 89, 90 (figure)
Viruses, 168
Virus introduction, 171–172
Vitamin producers, 224
Volatile organic compounds, 270 (table)
Vollman, B. K., 107
Voluntary restitution, 402
Voter identification laws, 100

Wachtler, Sol, 397–398
Wage and Hour Division of Department of Labor, 319 (table)
Waksal, Samuel, 156 (table), 398
Waldfogel, J., 402
Wall, A. D., 37
Wall Street (movie), 153
Walters, R., 242
Waring, E., 284, 309, 388–389
Warner Chilcott U.S. Sales LLC, 353
Warning light syndrome, 39
Washington, D.C.:
    fraud by doctors, 63–64
    group boycotts, 224
    slumlords, 214

Washington state, slumlords in, 212–213
Watching-others effects, 408, 408 (table)
"Watchman" policing style, 347
Watergate scandal, 98–99, 329 (table)
Waters, H., 70
Watkins, Sherron, 329 (table)
Web browser plug-in, 168
Web bug, 168
Weisburd, David, 6–7, 42–43, 284, 289, 309, 388–389
Weiskopf, M. K., 223
Weiss, Shalmon, 390
Welch, M., 103
WellCare, 330
Wells, J. T., 151, 337
Wells, R. C., 329
Wheeler, Stanton, 6–7, 42–43, 284, 289, 356, 357, 388–389
Whistleblower lawsuits, 379–380
Whistleblowers, 328–330, 329 (table)
Whitacre, Mark, 329 (table)
White, Michael, 108–109
White, R., 263
White-collar crime:
    conceptualization of, evolving, 2, 24–26, 27 (table)
    conceptualization of, modern, 26–32, 30 (figure)
    consequences, 36–40, 37 (photo)
    defined, 31
    effects, 3–4
    extent, 31 (table), 32–35, 35 (table), 36 (figure),
        36 (table)
    functions, 39
    researching, 4–10, 5 (table), 8 (table)
    student role in, 17–19, 20 (photo)
    studying, from scientific perspective, 10–17, 17 (figure)
    studying, reasons for, 2–3
    traditional crime versus, 2
    unreported, 7–8, 32
    See also Explaining white-collar crime; Policing white-collar
        crime; *specific topics*
White Collar Crime (Sutherland), 2, 15
White-collar environmental crimes, 257
    See also Environmental crime
White-collar gangs, 154
White-collar prison consultant industry, 400
White House Forum on Environmental Justice, 266
Wildcat dumping, 261, 274
Wildlife, harmful destruction of, 261–262, 261 (photo)
Willful OSHA violations, 238 (table)
Williams, J. W., 331, 342
Williams v. Texas Tech University Health Sciences Center,
    133 (table)
Wilson Sonsini Goodrich & Rosati PC, 386
Windshield appraisal fraud, 199–200
Winklevoss, Cameron, 139–140
Winklevoss, Tyler, 139–140

Wirsing v. Board of Regents of Univ. of Colorado, 133 (table)
Withdrawal from conspiracy defense, 371
Witnesses, 332–333, 374–375, 374 (figure)
Women:
    neutralizations, 294
    pregnant, 231, 345
    STEM majors, 183
Wood-burning appliances, 271
Worcester, B. A., 51
Worcester, MA, 178
Work environments, unsafe, 233 (figure), 234–235, 236–237 (table), 238–240, 238 (table)
Workers' compensation, 238
Workplace deviance, 28
Workplace-disciplinary proceedings, 355
Workplace injuries and illnesses, 233 (figure), 234–235, 236–237 (table), 238–240, 238 (table)
Workplace interviews, 339
WorldCom, 155 (table)

Worms, 168
Wrongfulness, denial of, 295

Xie, 102–103

Yale's International Institute for Corporate Governance, 127
Yang, Y., 310
Yates, Sally Quillian, 146, 198
Yeager, P. C., 32–33, 220, 231
Yeshiva University, 149–150
"Young Workers" (Occupational Safety and Health Administration), 239–240
Youstin, T., 108

Zambito, T., 413
Zinc, 270 (table)
Zombies, 168
Zoos, 261–262, 261 (photo)
Zuckerberg, Mark, 139–140, 141 (photo)

About the Author

Brian K. Payne is vice provost for academic affairs at Old Dominion University. His research interests include family violence and criminal justice, elder abuse, electronic monitoring, and white-collar crime. He has published seven books, including *Introduction to Criminal Justice: A Balanced Approach* (with Will Oliver and Nancy Marion), *Incarcerating White-Collar Offenders: The Prison Experience and Beyond* (2003), and, with R. Gainey, *Family Violence and Criminal Justice* (3rd ed., 2009). Payne is the former president of the Academy of Criminal Justice Sciences and the Southern Criminal Justice Association.